C000285831

STREET

Carmarthenshire
Pembrokeshire
Swansea

ATLAS STRYDOEDD
Abertawe, Sir Benfro, Sir Gaerfyrddin

First published in 2005 by

Philip's, a division of
Octopus Publishing Group Ltd
2-4 Heron Quays, London E14 4JP

First edition 2005
Third impression 2010
CPSAB

ISBN   978-1-84907-078-2

© Philip's 2007

 Ordnance Survey®

This product includes mapping data licensed
from Ordnance Survey® with the permission of
the Controller of Her Majesty's Stationery Office.
© Crown copyright 2007. All rights reserved.
Licence number 100011710.

Printed by Toppan, China

Contents

III	**Administrative and Postcode boundaries**
IV	**Key to map pages**
VI	**Route planning**
X	**Key to map symbols**
2	**Street maps** at 1¾ inches to 1 mile
118	**Street maps** at 3½ inches to 1 mile
174	**Street map of Swansea city centre** at 7 inches to 1 mile
175	**Index** of towns and villages
178	**Index** of streets, hospitals, industrial estates, railway stations, schools, shopping centres, universities and places of interest

Digital Data

The exceptionally high-quality mapping found in this atlas is available as digital data in TIFF format, which is easily convertible to other bitmapped (raster) image formats.

The index is also available in digital form as a standard database table. It contains all the details found in the printed index together with the National Grid reference for the map square in which each entry is named.

For further information and to discuss your requirements, please contact
victoria.dawbarn@philips-maps.co.uk

PHILIP'S

STREET ATLAS
Carmarthenshire
Pembrokeshire
Swansea

ATLAS STRYDOEDD
Abertawe, Sir Benfro, Sir Gaerfyrddin

Contents

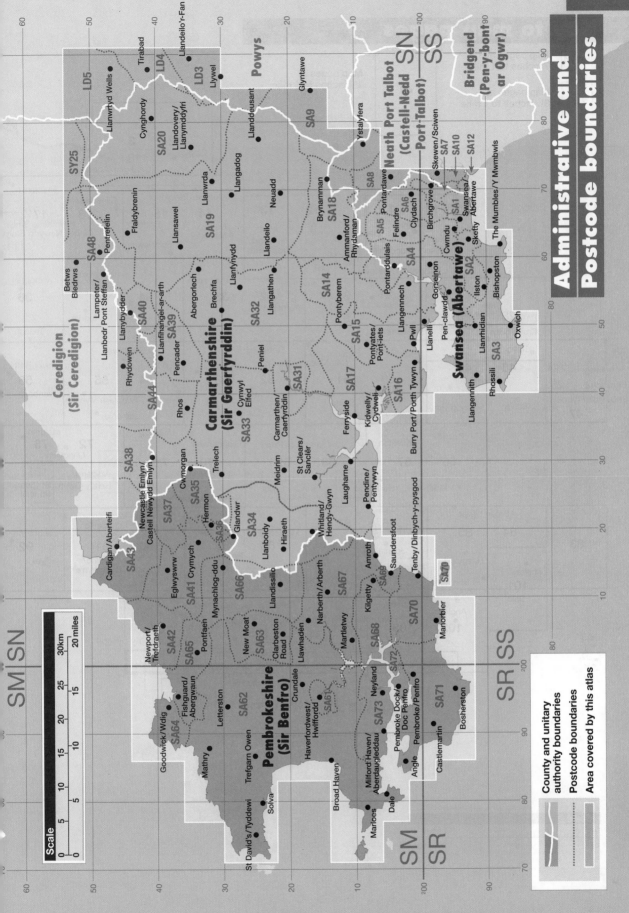

Administrative and Postcode boundaries

Scale

0 5 10 15 20 25 30km
0 5 10 15 20 miles

Powys

Ceredigion (Sir Ceredigion)

Carmarthenshire (Sir Gaerfyrddin)

Pembrokeshire (Sir Benfro)

Swansea (Abertawe)

Neath Port Talbot (Castell-Nedd Port-Talbot)

Bridgend (Pen-y-bont ar Ogwr)

County and unitary authority boundaries

Postcode boundaries

Area covered by this atlas

IV

Key to map pages

174 Map pages at 7 inches to 1 mile

139 Map pages at 3½ inches to 1 mile

41 Map pages at 1¾ inches to 1 mile

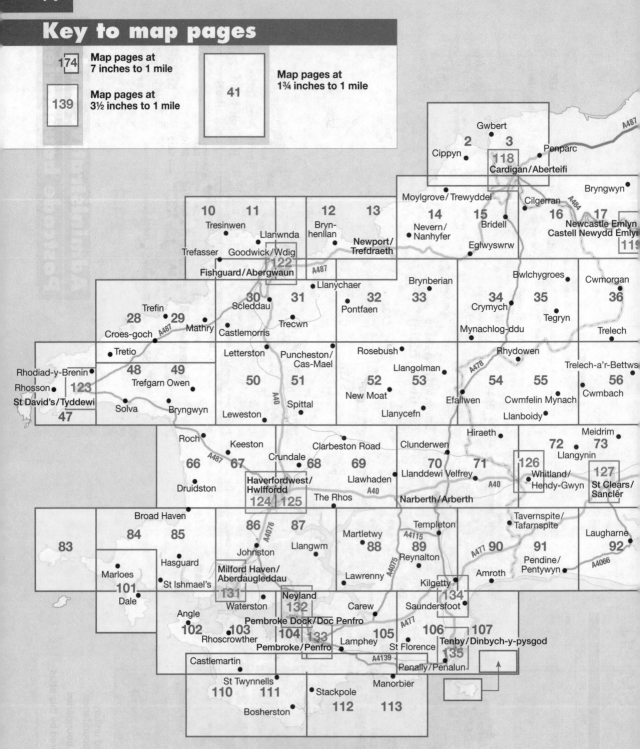

Scale

0 5 10 15 km

0 5 10 miles

New Quay/
Ceinewydd

Aberarth
Aberaeron

**Ceredigion &
South Gwynedd
STREET ATLAS**

Betws
Bledrws **4**
Llanfair
Clydogau **5**
120
Lampeter/
Llanbedr Pont Steffan
Pentrefelin

6   **7**

8   **9**
Llanwrtyd Wells

Ystradffin

Coed-y-bryn
18   **19**
Rhydowen
20   **21**
Llanybydder
Ffaldybrenin
22   **23**
Pumsaint
24   **25**
Rhandirmwyn
26   **27**
Cefn-gorwydd

Tirabad

Llandysul
Henllan
Llanfihangel-ar-arth
Rhydcymerau
Caio
Cilycwm
Cynghordy

37
Rhos
38   **39**
Pencader
Alltwalis
40   **41**
Gwernogle
Abergorlech
42   **43**
Llansawel
Talley/
Talyllychau
Llanwrda
121
Llandovery/
Llanymddyfri
Pentrebach
44   **45**
Myddfai
46
Llandeilo'r-Fan

Llywel

Hermon
Cwmduad

57
Cynwyl
Elfed
58   **59**
Pontarsais
Peniel
Horeb
60   **61**
Llanfynydd
Salem
62   **63**
Cwmifor
Llangadog
64   **65**
Talsarn
Llanddeusant

Sennybridge/
Pont Senni

Talog
Abernant
Bronwydd
Arms
Felingwmisaf
Llangathen
Capel Gwynfe

128 **129**
Carmarthen/
Caerfyrddin
Nantgaredig
76   **77**
Dryslwyn
78   **79**
Ffairfach
130
Llandeilo
Neuadd
80   **81**
Rhosaman
82
Glyntawe

**Powys
STREET ATLAS**

Bancyfelin
74   **75**
Llangynog   Llangain
Nantycaws
Llangyndeyrn
Porthyrhyd
Carmel
Llandybie
Brynamman

Llansteffan
93
Ferryside
Llandyfaelog
94   **95**
Bancffosfelen
Pontyberem
96   **97**
Saron
Tycroes
Ammanford/
Rhydaman
98   **99**
Tairgwaith
Garnswllt
Cwmgors
Godre'r-graig
138
100
Cwm-twrch Isaf
Ystalyfera
139

Glyn-Neath/Glynedd

Kidwelly/
Cydweli
136
Pontyates/
Pont-iets
Llannon

Trimsaran
140 **141**
Felinfoel
142 **143**
Pontarddulais
144 **145**
Felindre
Pontardawe
146 **147**
Craig-cefn-parc
Clydach
**Cardiff, Swansea
and the Valleys
STREET ATLAS**

Pinged
108
137   **109**
Burry Port/Porth Tywyn
Pwll
Horeb

Llanelli
148   **149**
Bynea
Llangennech
150   **151**
Gorseinon
Pontlliw
152   **153**
Penllergaer
154   **155**
Birchgrove
Neath/Castell-Nedd
Skewen/Sciwen
Tynewydd

114   **115**
Langennith   Llanrhidian
Reynoldston
Rallt
156   **157**
Pen-clawdd
158   **159**
Gowerton/
Tre-gwyr
160   **161**
Cwmdu
Trallwn
162
Llandarcy
Port Tennant
Baglan
Cymer
Blaengarw
Pontycymer

Swansea/Abertawe
174
168   **169**
Maesteg

163   **164**   **165**
Ilston
166   **167**
Black Pill
Port Talbot

Rhossili
Bishopston
Manselfield
170   **171**   **172**   **173**
Southgate
The Mumbles/Y Mwmbwls

Margam

116   **117**
Overton   Port Eynon
Oxwich

Pyle

Bridgend/
Pen-y-bont ar Ogwr

Porthcawl

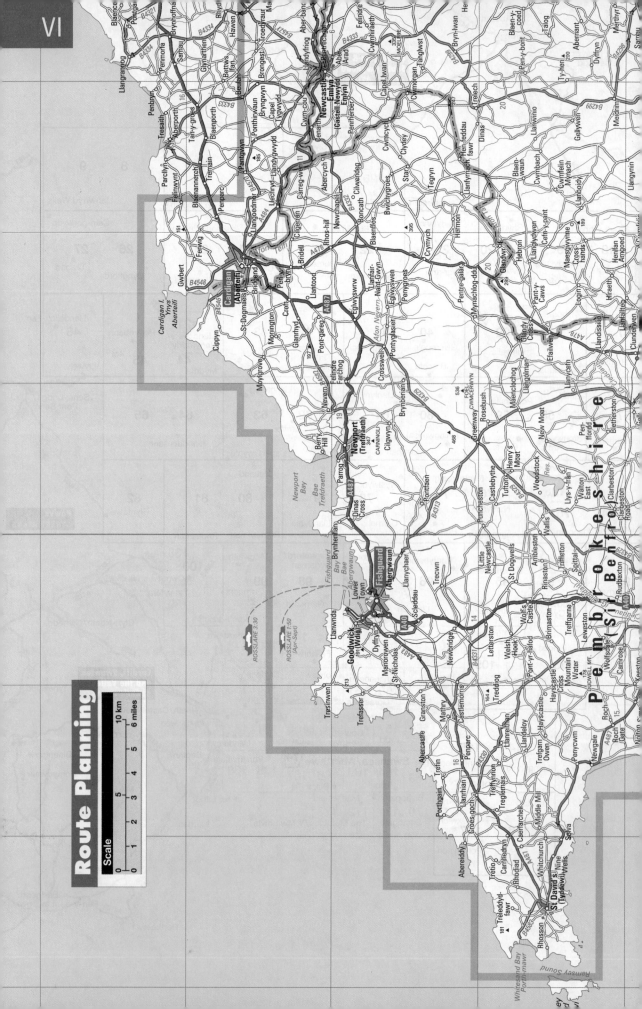

Route Planning

Scale

0	1	2	3	4	5		10 km
0		1	2	3	4	5	6 miles

Allwedd i symbolau'r map

	Traffordd gyda rhif y gyffordd
	Prif dramwyfeydd – ffordd ddeuol/un lôn
	Ffordd A – ffordd ddeuol/un lôn
	Ffordd B – ffordd ddeuol/un lôn
	Ffyrdd bychan – ffordd ddeuol/un lôn
	Ffyrdd bychan eraill – ffordd ddeuol/un lôn
	Ffordd yn cael ei hadeiladu
	Twnnel, ffordd dan orchudd
	Trac gwledig, ffordd breifat, neu ffordd mewn ardal ddinesig
	Llidiart neu rhwystr i draffig (gall fod cyfyngiadau ddim yn ddilys ar gyfer bob amser neu i bob drafnidiaeth)
	Llwybr, llwybr march, cilffordd yn agored i bob trafnidiaeth, ffordd a ddefnyddir yn lwybr cyhoeddus
	Mân cerddwyr
DY7	Ffiniau codau-post
	Ffiniau Sir ac awdurdod unedol
	Rheilffordd, twnnel, rheilffordd yn cael ei hadeiladu
	Tramffordd, tramffordd yn cael ei hadeiladu
	Rheilffordd ar raddfa fychan
Walsall	Gorsaf rheilffordd
	Gorsaf rheilffordd breifat
South Shields	Gorsaf metro
	Atalfa tram, atalfa tram yn cael ei hadeiladu
	Gorsaf fysiau

	Gorsaf ambiwlans
	Gorsaf gwylwyr y glannau
	Gorsaf Dân
	Swyddfa'r heddlu
	Mynedfa damwain ac argyfwng i'r ysbyty
H	Ysbyty
	Lle o addoliad
i	Canolfan gwybodaeth (a'r agor drwy'r flwyddyn)
	Canolfan siopa
P P&R	Parcio, Parcio a chludo
PO	Swyddfa'r post
	Safle gwersylla, Safle carafan
	Cwrs golff
	Safle picnic
Prim Sch	Adeiladau pwysig, ysgolion, colegau, prifysgolion ac ysbytai
	Ardal adeiledig
	Coed
River Ouse	Dŵr llanw, Enw dŵr
	Dim dŵr llanw – llyn, afon, camlas neu nant
	Loc, cored, twnnel
Church	Hynafiaeth anrhufeinig
ROMAN FORT	Hynafiaeth rhufeinig
87 228	Arwyddion dalennau cyfagos a bandiau gorymylon Y mae lliw y saeth â'r band yn dynodi gradd y ddalen gyfagos â'r ddalen gorymyl (gwelwch y graddau islaw)

Mapio wedi ei fwyhau yn unig

	Rheilffordd neu gorsaf bws adeilad
	Man o ddiddordeb
	Parcdir

Acad	Academi	Inst	Institiwt	PH	Tŷ tafarn
Allot Gdns	Gerddi ar osod	Ct	Llys cyfraith	Recn Gd	Maes chwaraeon
Cemy	Mynwent	L Ctr	Canolfan hamdden	Resr	Cronfa ddŵr
C Ctr	Canolfan ddinesig			Ret Pk	Parc adwerthu
CH	Tŷ Clwb	LC	Croesfan wastad	Sch	Ysgol
Coll	Coleg	Liby	Llyfrgell	Sh Ctr	Canolfan Siopa
Crem	Amlosgfa	Mkt	Marchnad	TH	Neuadd y dref
Ent	Menter	Meml	Coffa	Trad Est	Ystad Fasnachol
Ex H	Neuadd Arddangos	Mon	Cofgolofn	Univ	Prifysgol
Ind Est	Ystad ddiwydiannol	Mus	Amgueddfa	W Twr	Tŵrdŵr
IRB Sta	Gorsaf bad achub y glannau	Obsy	Arsyllfa	Wks	Gwaith
		Pal	Palas brenhinol	YH	Hostel ieuenctid

■ Y mae'r rhifau bach o gwmpas ochrau'r mapiau yn dynodi llinelli grid cenedlaethol 1 cilomedr

■ Mae'r ffin llwyd tywyll ar ochr fewn rhai tudalennau yn dynodi nad yw'r mapio yn canlyn ymlaen i'r tudalen gyffiniol

Graddfa	Scale bar
Gradd y mapiau ar y dalennau gyda rhifau glas yw 5.52 cm i 1 km • 3½ modfedd i 1 filltir • 1: 18103	0 ¼ ½ ¾ 1 milltir / 0 250m 500m 750m 1 km
Gradd y mapiau ar y dalennau gyda rhifau gwyrdd yw 2.76 cm i 1 km • 1¾ modfedd i 1 filltir • 1: 36206	0 ¼ ½ ¾ 1 milltir / 0 250m 500m 750m 1 km
Gradd y mapiau ar y dalennau gyda rhifau coch yw 11.04 cm i 1 km • 7 modfedd i 1 filltir • 1: 9051	0 220 llathenni 440 llathenni 660 llathenni ½ milltir / 0 125m 250m 375m ½ km

(22a)	**Motorway** with junction number
	Primary route – dual/single carriageway
	A road – dual/single carriageway
	B road – dual/single carriageway
	Minor road – dual/single carriageway
	Other minor road – dual/single carriageway
	Road under construction
	Tunnel, covered road
	Rural track, private road or narrow road in urban area
	Gate or obstruction to traffic (restrictions may not apply at all times or to all vehicles)
	Path, bridleway, byway open to all traffic, road used as a public path
	Pedestrianised area
DY7	**Postcode boundaries**
	County and unitary authority boundaries
	Railway, tunnel, railway under construction
	Tramway, tramway under construction
	Miniature railway
Walsall	**Railway station**
	Private railway station
South Shields	**Metro station**
	Tram stop, tram stop under construction
	Bus, coach station

Acad	**Academy**	Inst	**Institute**	Recn Gd	**Recreation Ground**
Allot Gdns	**Allotments**	Ct	**Law Court**		
Cemy	**Cemetery**	L Ctr	**Leisure Centre**	Resr	**Reservoir**
C Ctr	**Civic Centre**	LC	**Level Crossing**	Ret Pk	**Retail Park**
CH	**Club House**	Liby	**Library**	Sch	**School**
Coll	**College**	Mkt	**Market**	Sh Ctr	**Shopping Centre**
Crem	**Crematorium**	Meml	**Memorial**	TH	**Town Hall/House**
Ent	**Enterprise**	Mon	**Monument**	Trad Est	**Trading Estate**
Ex H	**Exhibition Hall**	Mus	**Museum**	Univ	**University**
Ind Est	**Industrial Estate**	Obsy	**Observatory**	W Twr	**Water Tower**
IRB Sta	**Inshore Rescue Boat Station**	Pal	**Royal Palace**	Wks	**Works**
		PH	**Public House**	YH	**Youth Hostel**

■ The small numbers around the edges of the maps identify the 1 kilometre National Grid lines
■ The dark grey border on the inside edge of some pages indicates that the mapping does not continue onto the adjacent page

◆	**Ambulance station**
◆	**Coastguard station**
◆	**Fire station**
◆	**Police station**
+	**Accident and Emergency entrance to hospital**
H	**Hospital**
+	**Place of worship**
i	**Information Centre** (open all year)
	Shopping Centre
P P&R	**Parking, Park and Ride**
PO	**Post Office**
⚊	**Camping site, caravan site**
⚑	**Golf course**
☒	**Picnic site**
Prim Sch	**Important buildings, schools, colleges, universities and hospitals**
	Built up area
	Woods
River Ouse	**Tidal water, water name**
	Non-tidal water – lake, river, canal or stream
	Lock, weir, tunnel
Church	**Non-Roman antiquity**
ROMAN FORT	**Roman antiquity**
87	**Adjoining page indicators and overlap bands** The colour of the arrow and the band indicates the scale of the adjoining or overlapping page (see scales below)
228	

Enlarged mapping only

	Railway or bus station building
	Place of interest
	Parkland

The scale of the maps on the pages numbered in blue is 5.52 cm to 1 km • 3½ inches to 1 mile • 1: 18103

| 0 | ¼ | ½ | ¾ | 1 mile |

| 0 | 250m | 500m | 750m | 1 kilometre |

The scale of the maps on pages numbered in green is 2.76 cm to 1 km • 1¾ inches to 1 mile • 1: 36206

| 0 | ¼ | ½ | ¾ | 1 mile |

| 0 | 250m | 500m | 750m | 1kilometre |

The scale of the maps on pages numbered in red is 11.04 cm to 1 km • 7 inches to 1 mile • 1: 9051

| 0 | 220 yards | 440 yards | 660 yards | ½ mile |

| 0 | 125m | 250m | 375m | ½ kilometre |

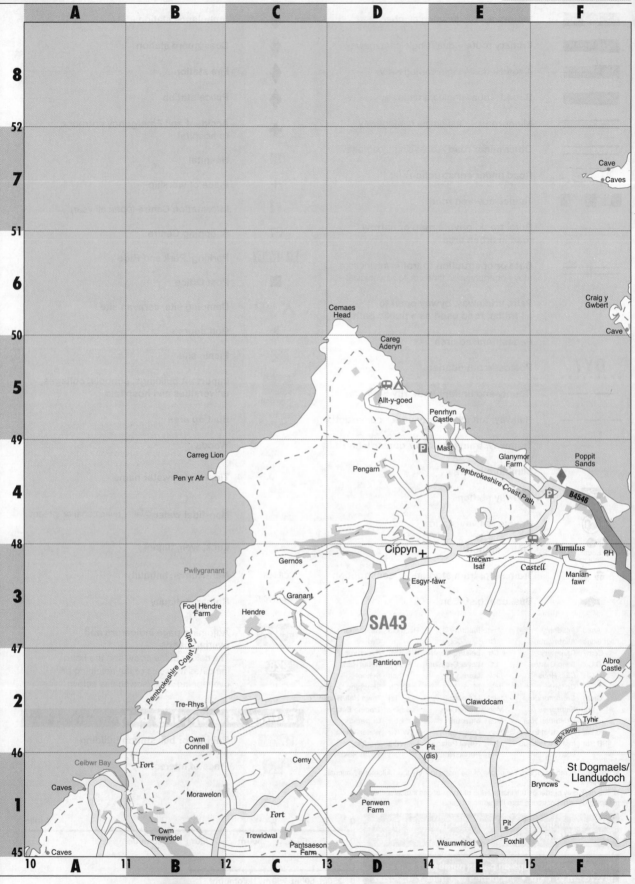

A   B   C   D   E   F

8

52

7

Cave
Caves

51

6

Craig y
Gwbert

50

Cemaes
Head

Cave

5

Careg
Aderyn

Allt-y-goed

Penrhyn
Castle

49

Carreg Lion

Pengarn

P   Mast

Glanymor
Farm

Poppit
Sands

Pen yr Afr

Pembrokeshire Coast Path

P   B4546

4

48

Cippyn +

Trecwn-
Isaf

Tumulus

PH

Gernos

Castell

Manian-
fawr

Pwllygranant

Esgyr-fawr

3

Granant

Foel Hendre
Farm

Hendre

SA43

Pembrokeshire Coast Path

47

Pantirion

Albro
Castle

2

Tre-Rhys

Clawddcam

Tyhir

PEN-Y-RHIW

Cwm
Connell

Pit
(dis)

46

Ceibwr Bay

Cerny

St Dogmaels/
Llandudoch

Fort

Bryncws

Caves

Morawelon

Penwern
Farm

1

Fort

Pit

Cwm
Trewyddel

Trewidwal

Foxhill

Waunwhiod

45

Caves

Pantsaeson
Farm

10   A   11   B   12   C   13   D   14   E   15   F

14   15

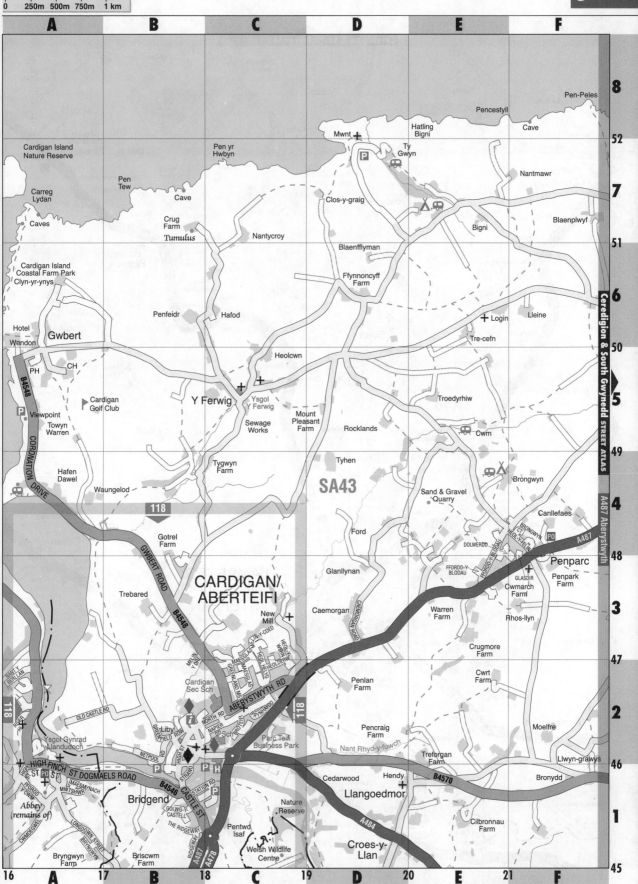

Scale: 1¾ inches to 1 mile

0   ¼   ½ mile
0   250m 500m 750m 1 km

Ceredigion & South Gwynedd STREET ATLAS

A   B   C   D   E   F

8
52
7
51
6
50
5
49
4
48
3
47
2
46
1
45

Pen-Peles
Pencestyll
Cave
Hatling Bigni
Nantmawr
Mwnt
Ty Gwyn
Clos-y-graig
Bigni
Blaenplwyf
Pen yr Hwbyn
Cardigan Island Nature Reserve
Pen Tew
Cave
Crug Farm
Tumulus
Nantycroy
Blaenfflyman
Ffynnoncyff Farm
Login
Lleine
Carreg Lydan
Caves
Penfeidr
Hafod
Tre-cefn
Cardigan Island Coastal Farm Park
Clyn-yr-ynys
Hotel Wendon
Gwbert
Heolcwn
Troedyrhiw
PH
CH
Y Ferwig
Ysgol Y Ferwig
Mount Pleasant Farm
Cwm
B4548
Viewpoint
Cardigan Golf Club
Sewage Works
Rocklands
Troedyrhiw
CORONATION DRIVE
Towyn Warren
Tyhen
Brongwyn
Hafen Dawel
Waungelod
Tygwyn Farm
SA43
Sand & Gravel Quarry
Brongwyn
118
Gotrel Farm
Ford
Canllefaes
GWBERT ROAD
CT HEOL-Y-FELIN
PO
A487 Aberystwyth
Glanllynan
DOLWERDD
A487
Penparc
CARDIGAN/ABERTEIFI
Caemorgan
FFORDD-Y-BLODAU
Penpark Farm
GLASDIR
Trebared
B4548
Warren Farm
Cwmarch Farm
Rhos-llyn
New Mill
CAEMORGAN ROAD
Crugmore Farm
HEOL-Y-COED
MAESGLAS
LLYN-Y-COED
HEOL WEN
HEOL DERW
Moelfre
Cardigan Sec Sch
MAESYRHAF
GREENLAND MS
Penlan Farm
Cwrt Farm
OLD CASTLE RD
NORTH RD
Liby
GREENFIELD ROW
NAPIER GD
SCHOOL ST
MAESYCWM
Pencraig Farm
Llwyn-grawys
NANT Y BERLLAN
ABERYSTWYTH RD
Parc Teifi Business Park
Nant Rhyd-y-fuwch
Treforgan Farm
Ysgol Gynrad Llandudoch
NETPOOL
HIGH ST
STRAND
118
Cedarwood
Hendy
B4570
Bronydd
HIGH ST
HIGH FINCH ST
DOGMAELS ROAD
CASTLE ST
Llangoedmor
Cilbronnau Farm
PO
MAESMYNACH
B4546
STATION RD
Croes-y-Llan
MWTSNWR
Bridgend
GOLWG-Y-CASTELL
Nature Reserve
A484
Abbey (remains of)
LONGDOWN STREET
BRYNGWYN
THE RIDGEWAY
RIDGEWAY
Pentwd Isaf
Welsh Wildlife Centre
A478
A487
Bryngwyn Farm
Briscwm Farm

16   A   17   B   18   C   19   D   20   E   21   F   45

118   15   16
For full street detail of the highlighted area see page 118.

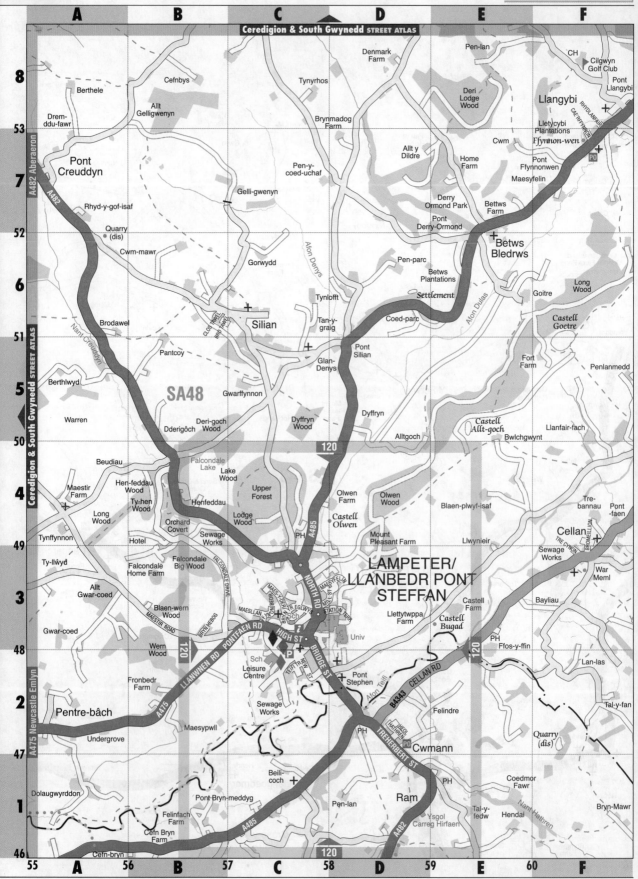

Scale: 1¾ inches to 1 mile

LAMPETER/
LLANBEDR PONT
STEFFAN

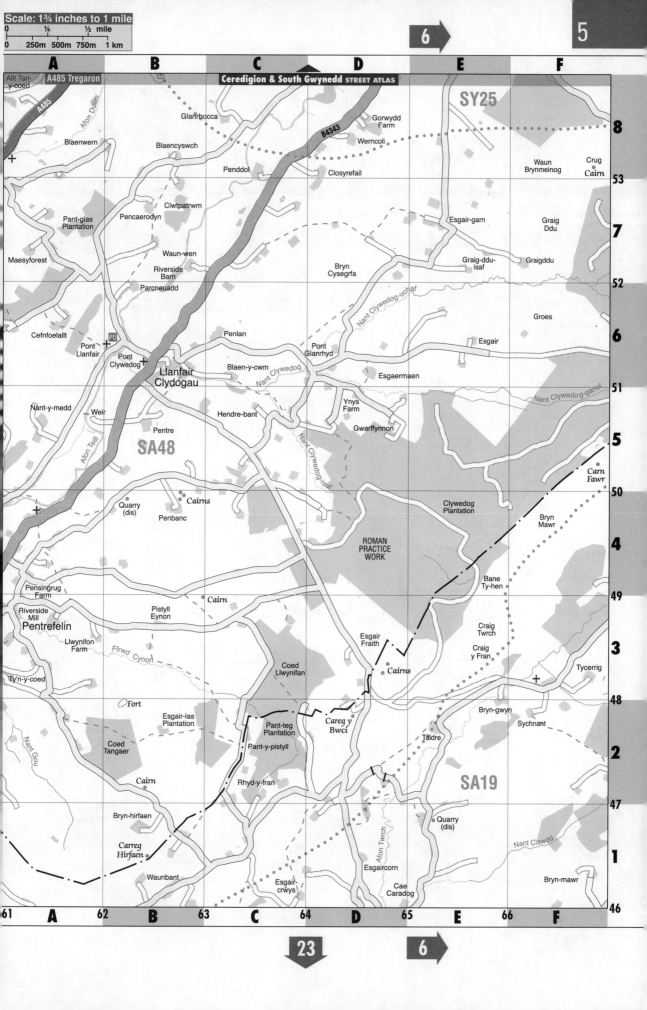

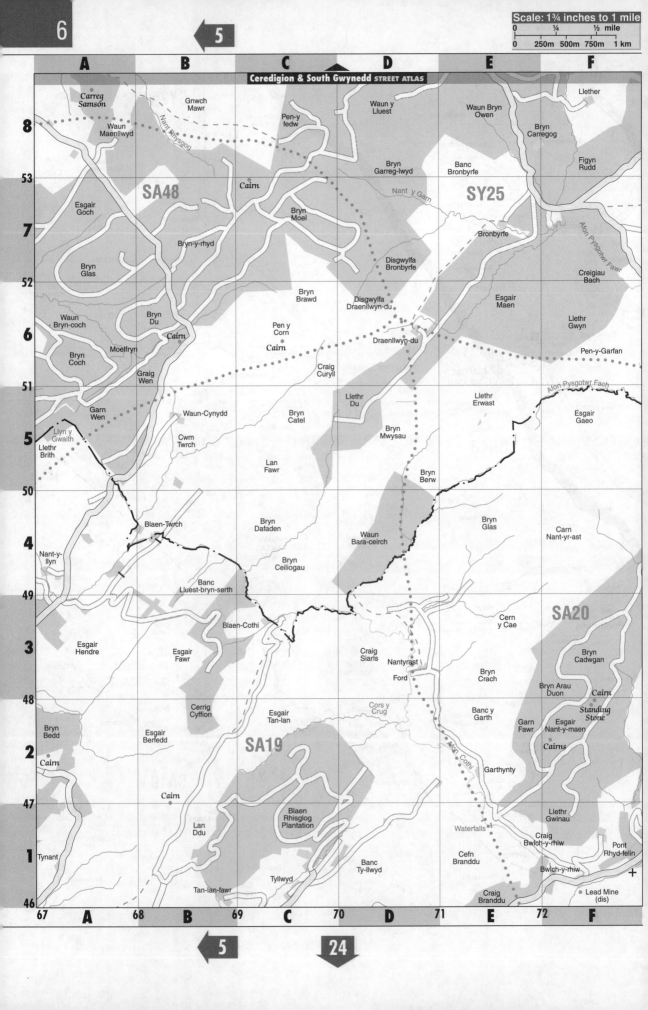

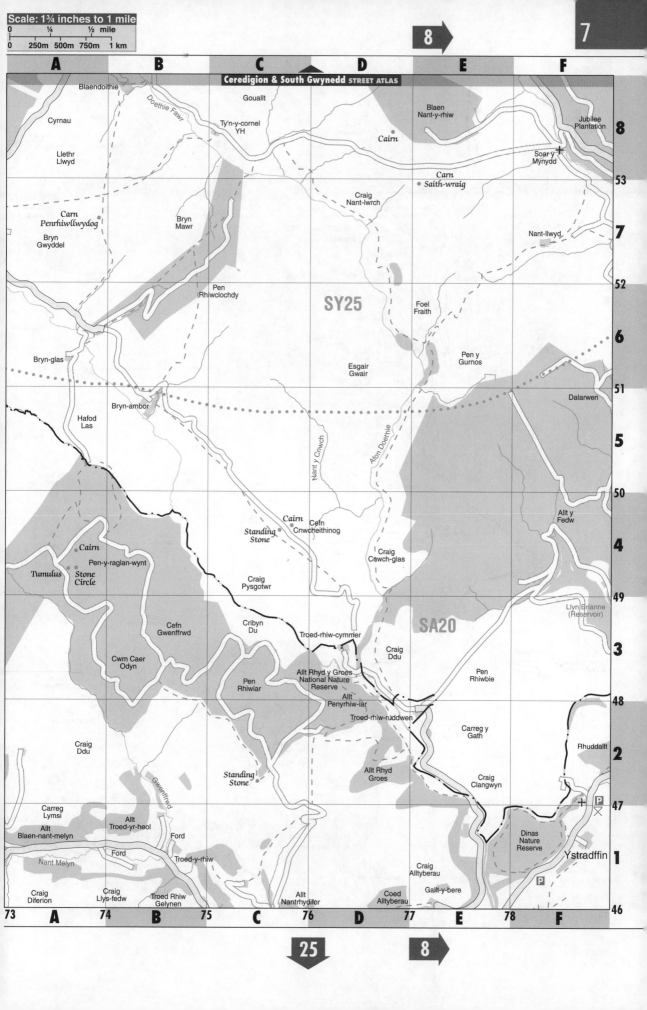

A   B   C   D   E   F

Ceredigion & South Gwynedd STREET ATLAS

Blaendoithie

Cyrnau

Llethr
Llwyd

Carn
Penrhiwllwydog

Bryn
Gwyddel

Goualtt

Ty'n-y-cornel
YH

Bryn
Mawr

Pen
Rhiwclochdy

Blaen
Nant-y-rhiw

Cairn

Carn
Saith-wraig

Craig
Nant-lwrch

Jubilee
Plantation

Soar y
Mynydd

Nant-llwyd

SY25

Foel
Fraith

Pen y
Gurnos

Dalarwen

Bryn-glas

Bryn-ambor

Hafod
Las

Esgair
Gwair

Nant y Cnwch

Afon Doethie

Cairn

Standing
Stone

Cefn
Cnwcheithinog

Allt y
Fedw

Tumulus

Cairn

Pen-y-raglan-wynt

Stone
Circle

Craig
Pysgotwr

Craig
Cnwch-glas

SA20

Llyn Brianne
(Reservoir)

Cefn
Gwenffrwd

Cribyn
Du

Troed-rhiw-cymrrier

Craig
Ddu

Pen
Rhiwbie

Cwm Caer
Odyn

Pen
Rhiwiar

Allt Rhyd y Groes
National Nature
Reserve

Allt
Penyrhiw-iar

Troed-rhiw-ruddwen

Carreg y
Gath

Rhuddallt

Craig
Ddu

Standing
Stone

Allt Rhyd
Groes

Craig
Clangwyn

Carreg
Lymsi

Allt
Blaen-nant-melyn

Allt
Troed-yr-heol

Ford

Dinas
Nature
Reserve

Ystradffin

Nant Melyn

Ford

Troed-y-rhiw

Craig
Diferion

Craig
Llys-fedw

Troed Rhiw
Gelynen

Allt
Nantrhydifor

Coed
Alltyberau

Craig
Alltyberau

Gallt-y-bere

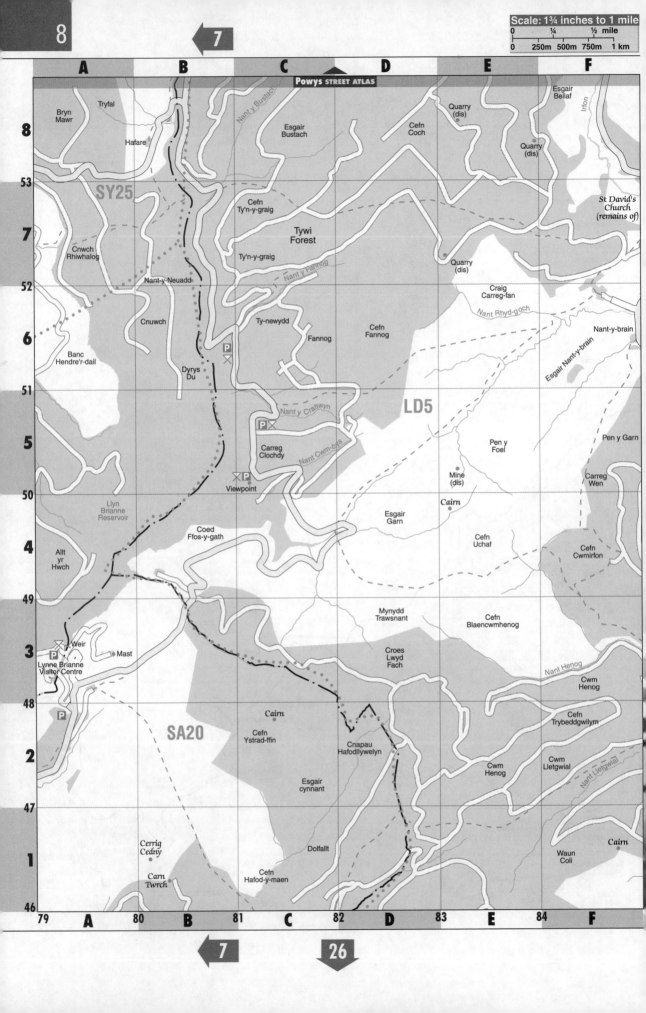

Scale: 1¾ inches to 1 mile

0   ¼   ½ mile
0   250m 500m 750m 1 km

Powys STREET ATLAS

A   B   C   D   E   F

Esgair
Bellaf

Irfon

8

Bryn
Mawr

Tryfal

Quarry
(dis)

Cefn
Coch

Quarry
(dis)

Esgair
Bustach

Hafare

53

SY25

St David's
Church
(remains of)

Cefn
Ty'n-y-graig

Tywi
Forest

7

Cnwch
Rhiwhalog

Ty'n-y-graig

Quarry
(dis)

Nant-y-brain

52

Nant-y-Neuadd

Nant y Fannog

Craig
Carreg-fan

Nant Rhyd-goch

Esgair Nant-y-brain

Cnuwch

Ty-newydd

Fannog

Cefn
Fannog

6

Banc
Hendre'r-dail

P

Dyrys
Du

LD5

Nant-y-brain

51

Nant y Crallwyn

Pen y Garn

5

P

Carreg
Clochdy

Nant Cwm-bys

Pen y
Foel

Carreg
Wen

50

Llyn
Brianne
Reservoir

Viewpoint

P

Esgair
Garn

Mine
(dis)

Cairn

4

Allt
yr
Hwch

Coed
Ffos-y-gath

Cefn
Uchaf

Cefn
Cwmirfon

49

Mynydd
Trawsnant

Cefn
Blaencwmhenog

3

Weir

Mast

Croes
Lwyd
Fach

Nant Henog

Cwm
Henog

P
Lynne Brianne
Visitor Centre

48

P

SA20

Cairn

Cefn
Ystrad-ffin

Cnapau
Hafodllywelyn

Cefn
Trybeddgwilym

2

Cwm
Henog

Cwm
Lletgwial

Nant Lletgwial

Esgair
cynnant

47

Dolfallt

1

Cerrig
Cedny

Waun
Coli

Cairn

Carn
Twrch

Cefn
Hafod-y-maen

46

79   A   80   B   81   C   82   D   83   E   84   F

Scale: 1¾ inches to 1 mile

0 ¼ ½ mile
0 250m 500m 750m 1 km

Powys STREET ATLAS

A483 Builth Wells **Powys** STREET ATLAS

Bryn Clun
Quarry (dis)
Glangwesyn
Bryn Mawr
Cefn-cendu-isaf
Llan Uchaf
Shaft
Quarry (dis)
Ty-mawr
Llethr Melyn
Llofft-y-bardd
Cairn
Garn Wen
Cefn-cendu-uchaf
Pentwyn Farm
Carn Rhys-Rowland
Banc Paderau
Bryn
Graig y Cwm
Abergwesyn
Llethr Dal-iar
Cairn
Esgair-las
Allt-y-gest
Llwyn Madoc
Cynfiad
Cefn Waun-lwyd
Cribyn Bedw
Coed y Felin
Ffynnon Ffos-yr-haidd (Spring)
Cae-gwyn
Llyn Cwmamell
Cairn
Crug Farm
Cefn Crug
Crugwydd
Cwm Siâms
Cefn Cynllaith
Nant yr Annell
Cwm Annell
Cefn Pen-y-pont
Cwm Cerdin
Esgair Fraith
Cefn Blaeneinon
Nant Einon
Irfon Forest
Craig Disgwylfa
Pen Disgwylfa
LD5
Bwlchmawr
Tir-gorw
Pwllbo
Craig Dinas Fach
Nant-y-cerdin
Esgair Foel
Llwynmeurig Farm
Brynarth
Llethr Penygarreg
Penybont Uchaf
Pen Beddowen
Carcwm
A483
Waterfall
Pen y Garn-goch
Penfedw
Mine (dis)
Standing Stone
Waterfall
Coed Alltwinau
Mynydd Gwyn
Pistyllgwyn
Troedrhiw-goch
Cwmirfon Farm
Cefn Alltwinau
Ffosyrhyddod
Coed Llawes-heli
Cwm Irfon
Waterfall
Craig Cwmirfon
Craig Cwm-bach
Alltwineu
Pen-y-banc
Llawes-heli
Irfon
Craig Cwmhenog
Garn Dwad
Gilfach
Ty-gwyn
Tynypant
Cwm-Henog
Nant-Gwyn
Y Foel
Pen y Ddinas
Cairns
Geufron
Penhenwernfach
LD4
Kilsby
Cemy
Pont Newydd
Pont Maes-y-gwaelod
Bronffynnon
Llanwrtyd
Quarry (dis)
Cambrian Mill Heritage Centre
Standing Stone
Dinas Mill
Tweedside
Cemy
LLANWRTYD WELLS
Victoria Wells
Banc y Ddinas
Ysgol Dolafon
Ffos Farm
Banc Blyngyrnant
Hen Fron Farm
Maesdre Ind Est
Sewage Works
Penmaenllwyd
Hotel
Llanwrtyd
Irfon
Nant Cynant
Abernant Lake
A483 IRFON CRESCENT
BEULAH RD
FFOSS RD
STATION RD
DOLCOED RD
VICTORIA RD
ZION ST

27

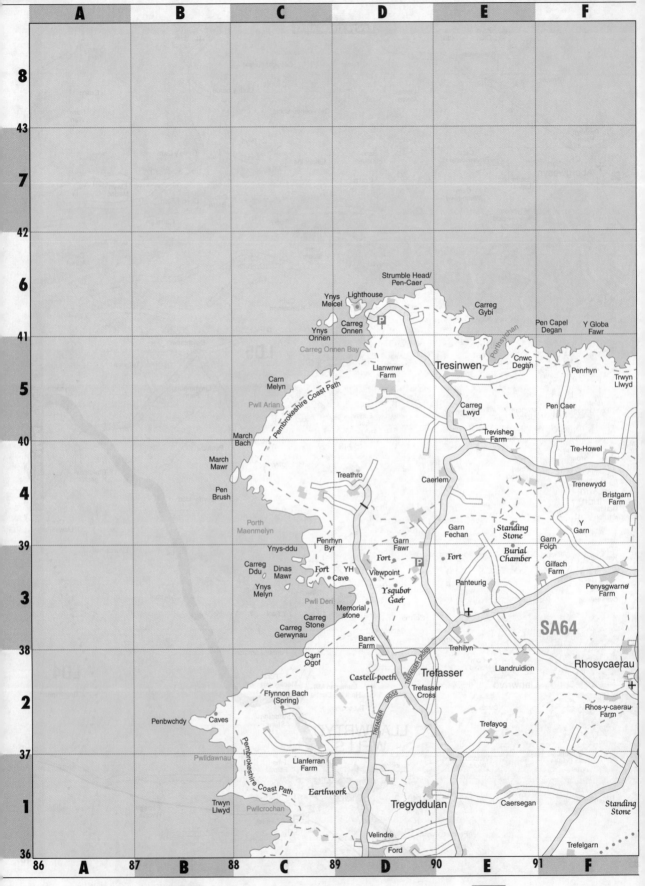

A   B   C   D   E   F

8
43
7
42
6

Strumble Head/
Pen-Caer

Ynys
Meicel   Lighthouse

Carreg
Gybi

Pen Capel
Degan   Y Globa
Fawr

Ynys
Onnen   Carreg
Onnen

Cnwc
Degan

41

Carreg Onnen Bay

Porthsychan

Tresinwen

Penrhyn   Trwyn
Llwyd

5

Carn
Melyn

Pwll Arian

Pembrokeshire Coast Path

Llanwnwr
Farm

Carreg
Lwyd

Pen Caer

Trevisheg
Farm

40

March
Bach

Tre-Howel

March
Mawr

Treathro

Caerlem

Trenewydd   Bristgarn
Farm

4

Pen
Brush

Porth
Maenmelyn

Garn
Fechan

Standing
Stone

Y
Garn

Garn
Folch

Penrhyn
Byr

Garn
Fawr

39

Ynys-ddu

Burial
Chamber

Gilfach
Farm

Carreg
Ddu   Dinas
Mawr

Fort   YH
Cave

Fort

Fort

Panteurig

Penysgwarne
Farm

3

Ynys
Melyn

Pwll Deri

Ysgubor
Gaer

SA64

Memorial
stone

Carreg
Stone

Bank
Farm

Trehilyn

38

Carreg
Gerwynau

Carn
Ogof

Rhosycaerau

Castell-poeth

Trefasser

Llandruidion

TREFASSER CROSS

2

Ffynnon Bach
(Spring)

Trefasser
Cross

Rhos-y-caerau
Farm

Penbwchdy   Caves

Trefayog

37

Pwlldawnau

Pembrokeshire Coast Path

Llanferran
Farm

1

Trwyn
Llwyd   Pwllcrochan

Earthwork

Tregyddulan

Caersegan

Standing
Stone

Velindre
Ford

Trefelgarn

36
86   A   87   B   88   C   89   D   90   E   91   F

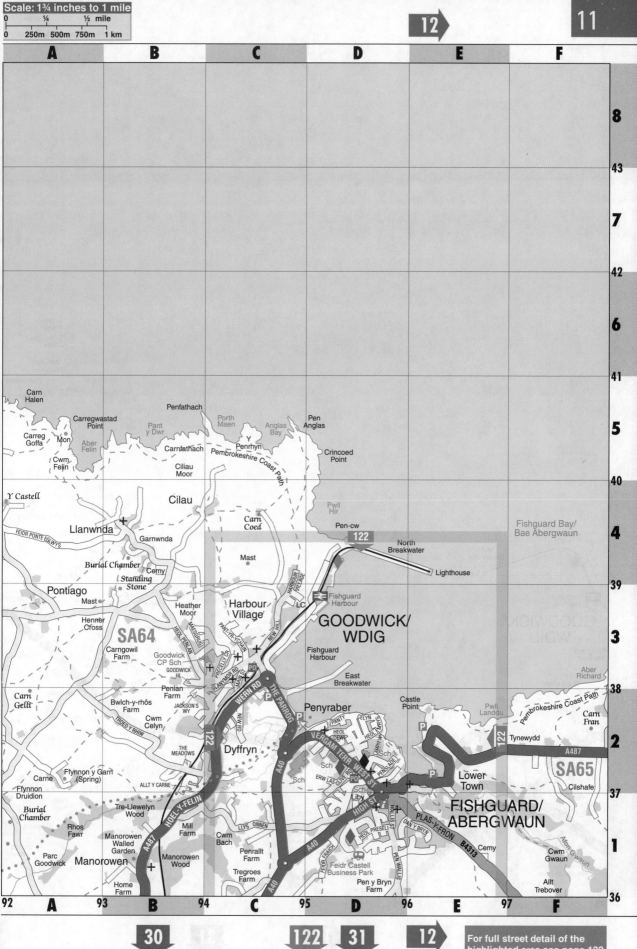

11

A B C D E F

8

43

7

42

6

Dinas Head
Caves
Aber Pen-clawdd
Viewpoint Pen y Fan
41
Cafnau
Pen-clawdd
Aber Pensidan
Cave
Dinas Island
Aber Careg-y-Fran
5
Careg-y-Fran
Pen Castell

Crincoed Point
40
Pwllgwaelod
PH
Pwll Hir
Pwll Cwm
Bryn-henllan
4
Pen-cw
Fishguard Bay/ Bae Abergwaun
122
Cwm Gwylog
Llwyn Hendy
North Breakwater
Pwll Gwylog
SA42
Lighthouse
Cerrig Duon
39
Aber Bach
Dinas Or Sqh
Fishguard Harbour
Carreg Pen-las
Dinas Cross
Y DDERWEN MAES
LC
Penrhyn Erw-goch
Pont y Meddyg
GOODWICK/ WDIG
Penrhyn Ychen
Penrhyn Mawr
3
Aber Grugog
Viewpoint
Fishguard Harbour
Penrhyn
Pen y Foel
FEIDR CEFN
East Breakwater
Aber Richard
Trewrach Farm
Glendower
Bwlch-mawr
38
Castle Point
Castell Farm
Rhos Isaf
Penyraber
Pwll Landdu
Pembrokeshire Coast Path
Carn Fran
Cwm Mawr
P
Carn Gelli
VERGAM TERR
2
HEOL DEWP
122
Tynewydd
A487
HEOL MWR Y
SCH
PENBLADE
SA65
Bryn-Awelon
ERW LAS
Cilshafe
Carn Slani
Mynydd Dinas
P
Lower Town
37
Liby
Sch
HIGH ST
Crug Cilshafe
Garn Fawr
FISHGUARD/ ABERGWAUN
Pen-y-mynydd
PLAS-Y-FRON
HEOL PRESELI
PEN WALLIS
Brigwarn
B4313
Cemy
Afon Gwaun
1
A40
Cwm Gwaun
Cwm Gwyn
Trenewydd
Myndd Llanllawer
Feidr Castell Business Park
Allt Trebover
Cilshafe Wood
Trellan Farm
Pen y Bryn Farm
36

95 A 96 B 97 C 98 D 99 E 00 F

For full street detail of the highlighted area see page 122.

122

11

31

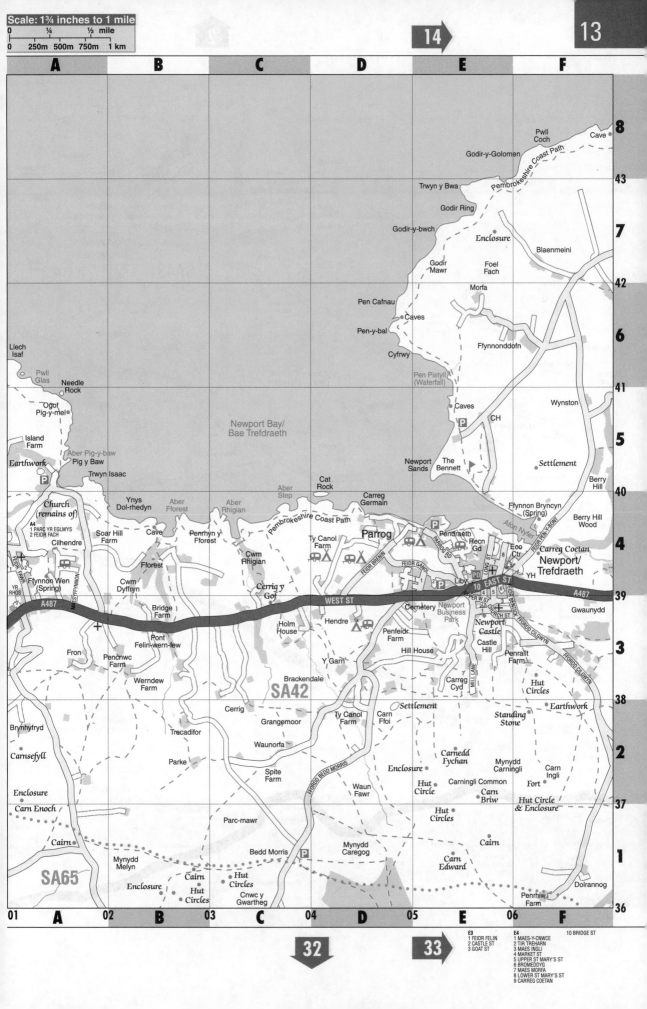

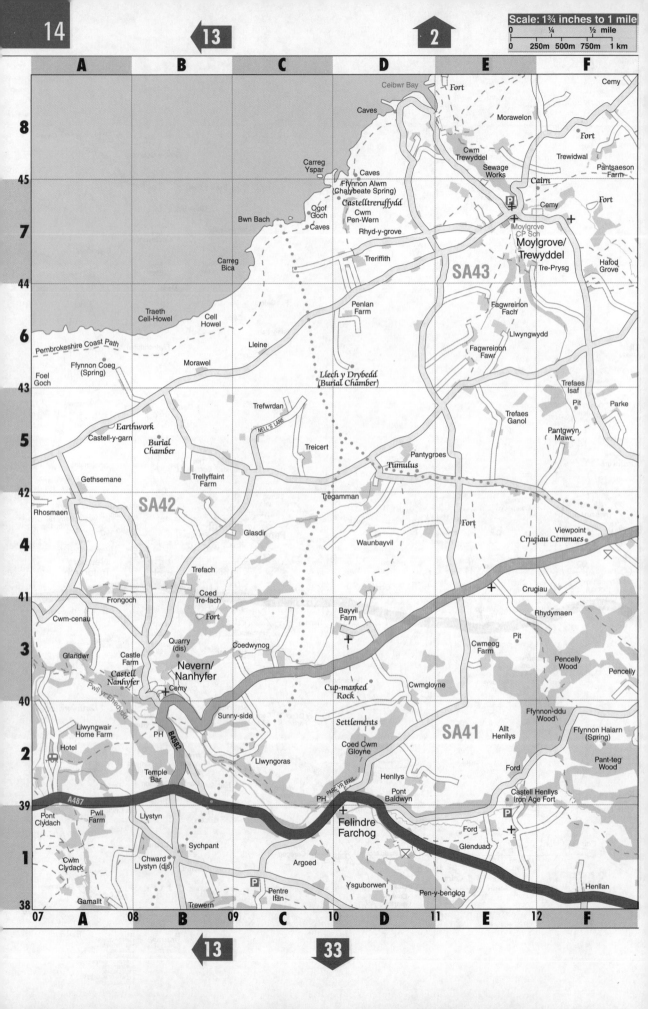

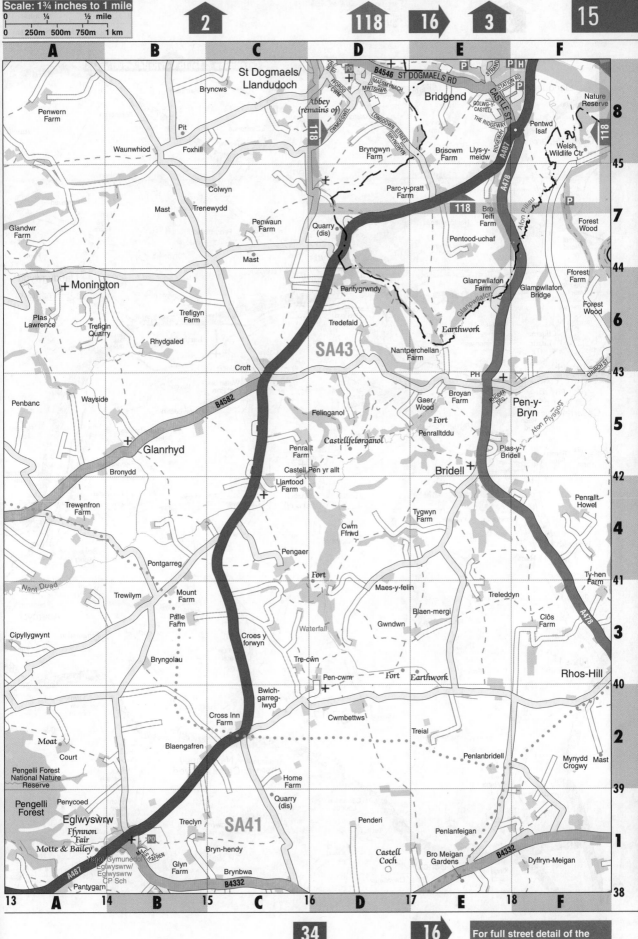

A   B   C   D   E   F

8
45
7
44
6
43
5
42
4
41
3
40
2
39
1
38

Penwern Farm
Bryncws
St Dogmaels/
Llandudoch
Abbey (remains of)
PO
MWTSHWR
MAESMYNACH
B4546 ST DOGMAELS RD
Bridgend
P
STRAND
P H
STATION RD
Nature Reserve
118

Waunwhiod
Foxhill
Pit
Mast
Colwyn
Trenewydd
CWMDEGWEL
FFORDD CWM
LONGDOWN STREET
BRYNGWYN
GOLWG-Y-CASTELL
THE RIDGEWAY
CASTLE ST
RIDGEWAY
Pentwd Isaf
Welsh Wildlife Ctr
118

Glandwr Farm
Penwaun Farm
Mast
Bryngwyn Farm
Briscwm Farm
Llys-y-meidw
A487
A478
Afon Piliau
P
Forest Wood

Monington
Trefigyn Farm
Rhydgaled
Mast
Quarry (dis)
Parc-y-pratt Farm
118
Bro Teifi Farm
Pentood-uchaf
Fforest Farm
Forest Wood

Plas Lawrence
Trefigin Quarry
Pantygrwndy
Glanpwllafon Farm
Glampwllafon Bridge
Earthwork
Tredefaid
SA43
Nantperchellan Farm

Croft
Penbanc
Wayside
B4582
Glanrhyd
Bronydd
Felinganol
Gaer Wood
Broyan Farm
PH
Pen-y-Bryn
CHURCH ST
RHODFA DEG
A
Fort
Penralltddu
Plas-y-Bridell
Bridell

Trewenfron Farm
Penrallt Farm
Castellfelorganol
Castell Pen yr allt
Llantood Farm
Tygwyn Farm
Penrallt Howel

Cipyllygwynt
Pontgarreg
Trewilym
Mount Farm
Pengaer
Cwm Ffrwd
Maes-y-felin
Treleddyn
Clôs Farm
Ty-hen Farm
A478

Nant Duad
Palle Farm
Bryngolau
Croes y forwyn
Fort
Waterfall
Gwndwn
Blaen-mergi

Moat
Court
Bryn-hendy
Cross Inn Farm
Blaengafren
Bwlch-garreg-lwyd
Tre-cwn
Pen-cwm
Fort
Earthwork
Penlanbridell
Rhos-Hill

Pengelli Forest National Nature Reserve
Pengelli Forest
Penycoed
Eglwyswrw
Ffynnon Fair
Motte & Bailey
Ysgol Gymunedol Eglwyswrw/ Eglwyswrw CP Sch
PO
MAES CAFREN
A487
Treclyn
Glyn Farm
SA41
Bryn-hendy
Brynbwa
Home Farm
Quarry (dis)
Cwmbettws
Treial
Penderi
Penlanfeigan
Bro Meigan Gardens
Castell Coch
B4332
Mynydd Crogwy
Mast
Dyffryn-Meigan
Pantygarn
B4332

For full street detail of the highlighted area see page 118.

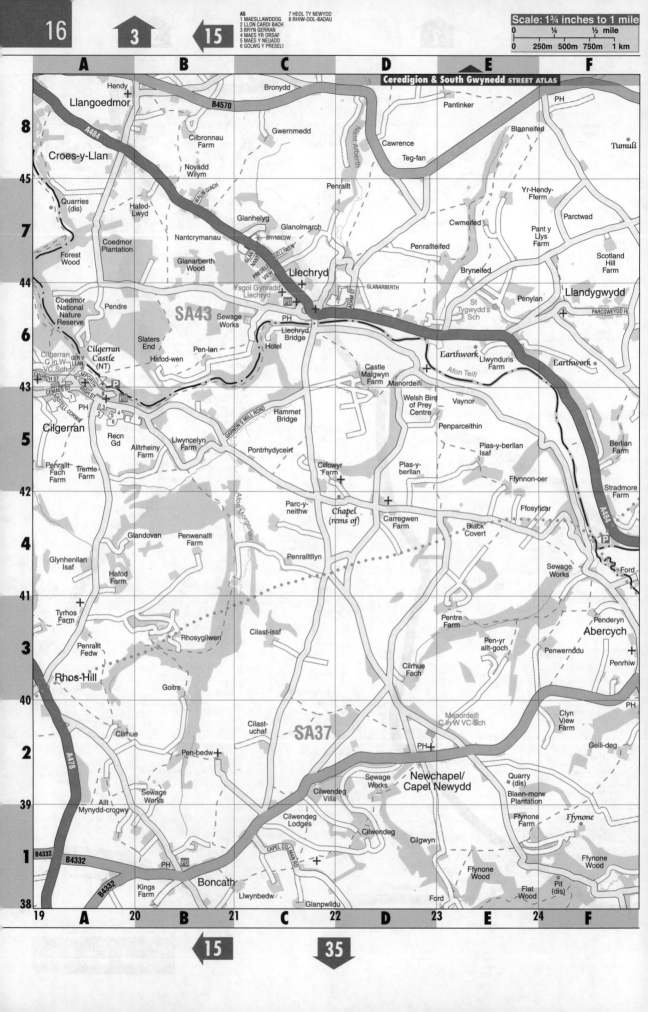

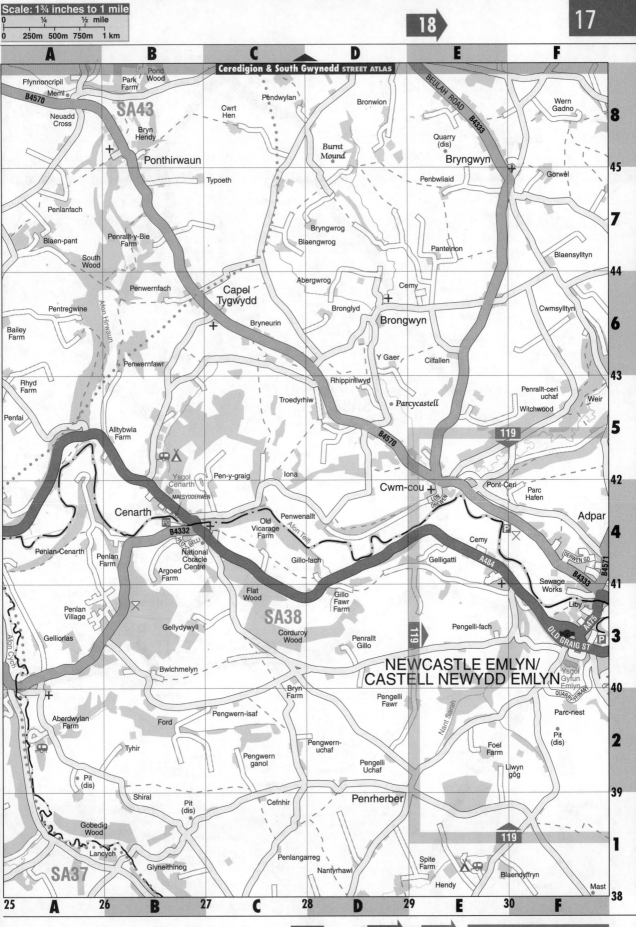

Ceredigion & South Gwynedd STREET ATLAS

A   B   C   D   E   F

Ffynnoncripil
Meml
B4570
Neuadd Cross
Park Farm
Pond Wood
SA43
Bryn Hendy
Cwrt Hen
Pendwylan
Bronwion
Burnt Mound
Wern Gadno
Quarry (dis)
Bryngwyn
Gorwel
45

Ponthirwaun
Typoeth
Penbwliaid
Penlanfach
Bryngwrog
Blaengwrog
Panteinon
Blaensylltyn
7
Blaen-pant
Penrallt-y-Bie Farm
South Wood
Penwernfach
Capel Tygwydd
Abergwrog
Cemy
Cwmsylltyn
44
Pentregwine
Bronglyd
Brongwyn
6
Bailey Farm
Bryneurin
Penwernfawr
Y Gaer
Cilfallen
Rhyd Farm
Rhippinllwyd
Penrallt-ceri uchaf
Witchwood
Weir
43
Penfai
Troedyrhiw
Parcycastell
B4570
119
5
Alltybwla Farm
Pen-y-graig
Iona
Cwm-cou
Pont-Ceri
Parc Hafen
Adpar
42
Ysgol Cenarth
MAESYDDERWEN
Penwenallt
Afon Teifi
Cemy
B4571
4
Cenarth
PO
Old Vicarage Farm
Gelligatti
A484
B4333
B4332
HEOL GELLI
National Coracle Centre
Gillo-fach
DERWEN GD
Sewage Works
Liby
41
Penlan-Cenarth
Penlan Farm
Argoed Farm
Flat Wood
Gillo Fawr Farm
A475
SA38
Corduroy Wood
Penrallt Gillo
Pengelli-fach
OLD GRAIG ST
P
3
Penlan Village
Gellydywyll
119
NEWCASTLE EMLYN/
CASTELL NEWYDD EMLYN
Ysgol Gyfun Emlyn
Gelliorlas
Bwlchmelyn
Bryn Farm
Pengelli Fawr
QUARRY TERRACE
Parc-nest
Aberdwylan Farm
Ford
Pengwern-isaf
Pengwern-uchaf
Pengelli Uchaf
Foel Farm
Pit (dis)
2
Tyhir
Pengwern ganol
Nant Sarah
Llwyn gôg
Shiral
Pit (dis)
Cefnhir
Penrherber
39
Gobedig Wood
Lancych
Glyneithinog
Penlangarreg
Nantyrhawl
Spite Farm
Hendy
Blaendyffryn
Mast
SA37
38

25   A   26   B   27   C   28   D   29   E   30   F   38

36   18   119   For full street detail of the highlighted area see page 119.

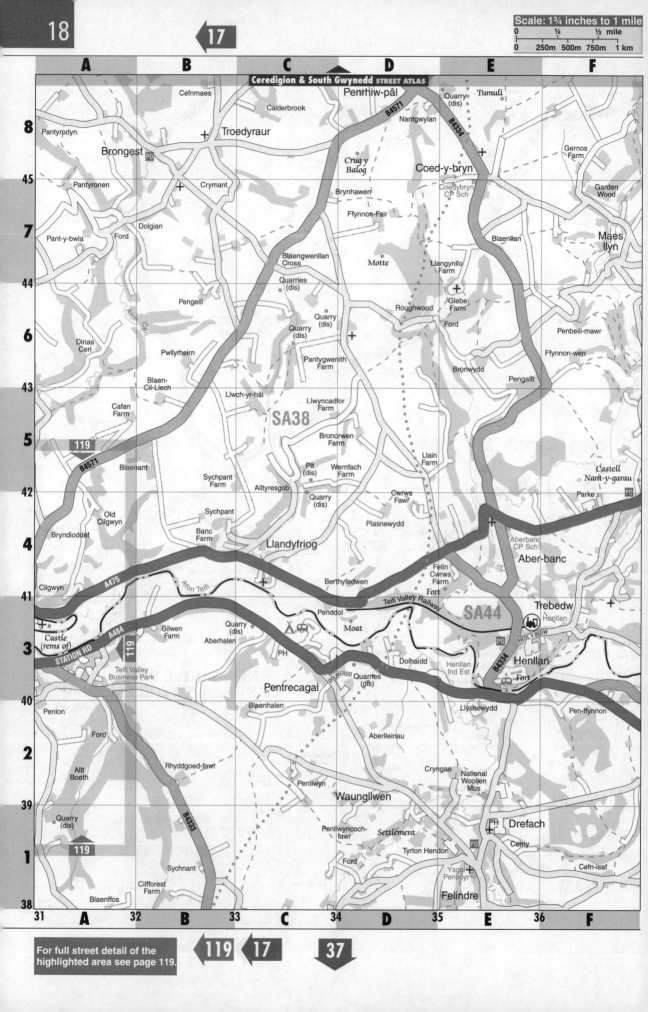

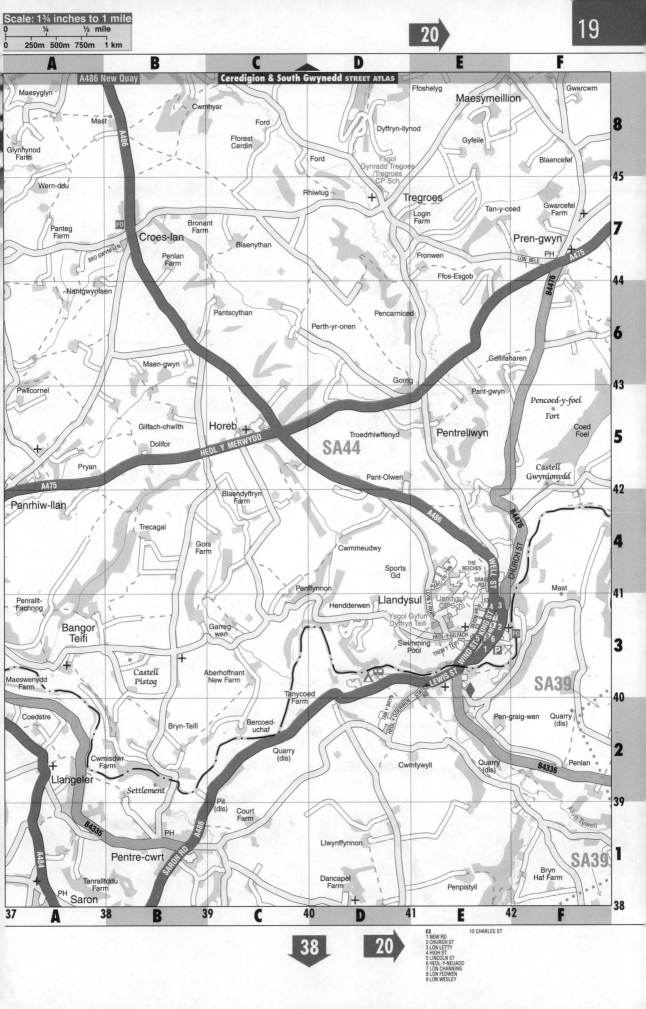

A486 New Quay

Ceredigion & South Gwynedd STREET ATLAS

Maesyglyn
Mast
Cwmhyar
Ford
Ffoshelyg
Maesymeillion
Gwarcwm

Glynhynod Farm
Fforest Cerdin
Dyffryn-llynod
Gyfeile
Blaencefel

Wern-ddu
Rhiwlug
Ysgol Gynradd Tregoes /Tregroes CP Sch
Tregroes
Tan-y-coed
Gwarcefel Farm

Panteg Farm
Bronant Farm
Login Farm
Pren-gwyn
PH
A475

Croes-lan
Penlan Farm
Blaenythan
Fronwen
LON BELE
B4476

Nantgwynfaen
Pantscythan
Ffos-Esgob

Maen-gwyn
Perth-yr-onen
Pencarniced
Gellifaharen

Pwllcornel
Gorrig
Pant-gwyn
Pencoed-y-foel Fort

Gilfach-chwith
Horeb
Troedrhiwffenyd
Pentrellwyn
Coed Foel

Dolifor
HEOL Y MERWYDD
SA44
Castell Gwynionydd

Pryan
Pant-Olwen
B4476

A475
Penrhiw-llan
Blaendyffryn Farm
Pant-Olwen
A486

Trecagal
Cwmmeudwy
THE BEECHES
Mast

Gors Farm
Sports Gd
PARC-YR-YNN
GRAIG RD
WELL ST
CHURCH ST

Penralt-Fachnog
Penffynnon
Hendderwen
Llandysul
Llandysul CP Sch
LLYN Y FRAN

Bangor Teifi
Garreg-wen
Ysgol Gyfun Dyffryn Teifi
HEOL-Y-GILFACH
SEION HILL
KING ST
PO
P

Maeswenydd Farm
Castell Pistog
Aberhoffnant New Farm
Swimming Pool
TREM Y TEIFI
WIND ST
LEWIS ST
SA39

Coedstre
Bryn-Teifi
Tanycoed Farm
Bercoed-uchaf
TAN Y BRYN
HEOL TODERWEN
STATION RD
Pen-graig-wen
Quarry (dis)

Cwmisdwr Farm
Quarry (dis)
Cwmtywyll
Quarry (dis)
B4336
Penlan

Llangeler
Settlement
Pit (dis)
Court Farm
Llwynffynnon
Afon Tywell

Cwmsiwr
PH
SARON RD
Dancapel Farm
Penpistyll
Bryn Haf Farm
SA39

A484
B4335
A486
Pentre-cwrt
Saron
PH
Tanralltddu Farm

E3
1 NEW RD
2 CHURCH ST
3 LON LETTY
4 HIGH ST
5 LINCOLN ST
6 HEOL-Y-NEUADD
7 LON CHANNING
8 LON FEDWEN
9 LON WESLEY

10 CHARLES ST

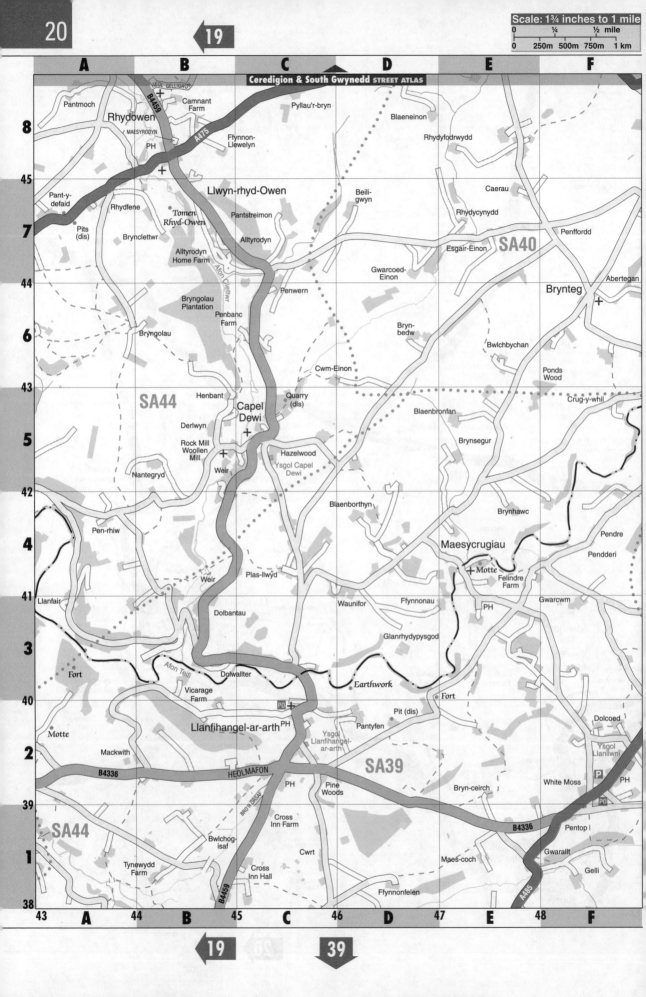

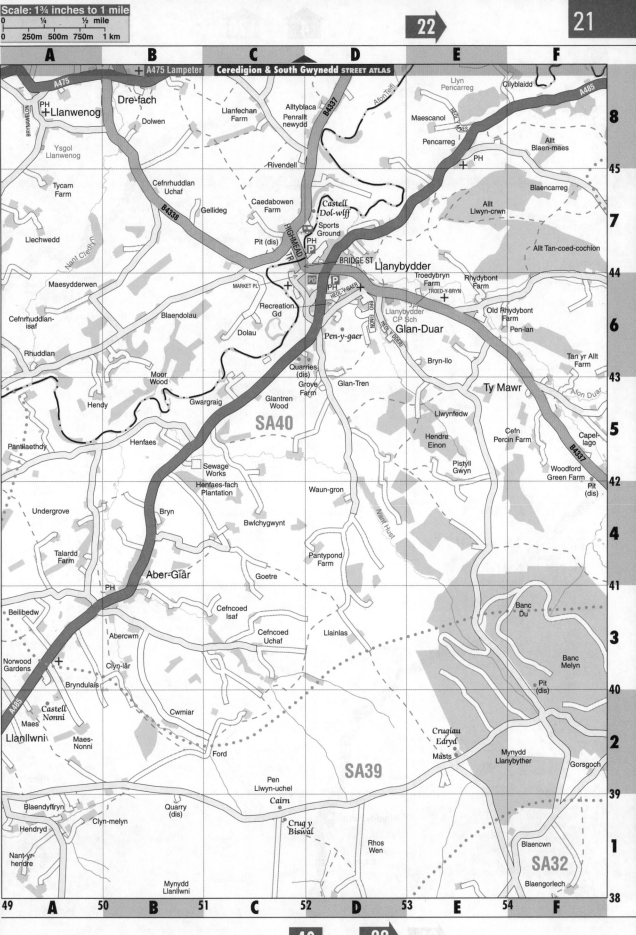

Scale: 1¾ inches to 1 mile

0   ¼   ½   mile
0   250m   500m   750m   1 km

A   B   C   D   E   F

A475 Lampeter

Ceredigion & South Gwynedd STREET ATLAS

A475
Llanwenog
PH
BRYNAWELON
Dre-fach
Dolwen
Ysgol Llanwenog
Llanfechan Farm
Alltyblaca
Penrallt newydd
Afon Teifi
B4337
Llyn Pencarreg
Ollyblaidd
A485
HEOL-Y-FAES
Maescanol
Pencarreg
PH

Tycam Farm
Cefnrhuddlan Uchaf
B4338
Gellideg
Caedabowen Farm
Rivendell
Castell Dol-wlff
Sports Ground
Allt Blaen-maes
Blaencarreg
Allt Llwyn-crwn
Allt Tan-coed-cochion

Llechwedd
Pit (dis)
HIGHMEAD
TR
PH
P
Llanybydder
Troedybryn Farm
TROED-Y-BRYN
Rhydybont Farm

Maesyderwen
MARKET PL
BRIDGE ST
PO
PH
P
HEOL-Y-GAER
Llanybydder CP Sch
Old Rhydybont Farm

Cefnrhuddlan-isaf
Blaendolau
Recreation Gd
Dolau
BRO EINON
HEOL-Y-DDERI
Glan-Duar
Pen-lan

Rhuddlan
Pen-y-gaer
Bryn-llo
Tan yr Allt Farm
Afon Duar

Moor Wood
Quarries (dis)
Grove Farm
Glan-Tren
Llwynfedw
Ty Mawr

Hendy
Gwargraig
Glantren Wood
SA40
Hendre Einon
Cefn Percin Farm
Capel-lago
B4337

Pantlaethdy
Henfaes
Sewage Works
Pistyll Gwyn
Woodford Green Farm
Pit (dis)

Henfaes-fach Plantation
Waun-gron

Undergrove
Bryn
Bwlchygwynt
Pantypond Farm
Banc Du

Talardd Farm
Aber-Giâr
Goetre
Llainlas
Banc Melyn

PH
Cefncoed Isaf
Pit (dis)

Beilibedw
Abercwm
Cefncoed Uchaf
Crugiau Edryd
Masts
Mynydd Llanybyther
Gorsgoch

Norwood Gardens
Clyn-lâr
Bryndulais
Cwmiar

A485
Castell Nonni
Maes
Maes-Nonni
Ford
SA39

Llanllwni
Pen Llwyn-uchel
Cairn
Blaencwn
SA32

Blaendyffryn
Clyn-melyn
Quarry (dis)
Crug y Biswal
Rhos Wen
Blaengorlech

Hendryd
Nant-yr-hendre
Mynydd Llanllwni

45
7
44
6
43
5
42
4
41
3
40
2
39
1
38

8

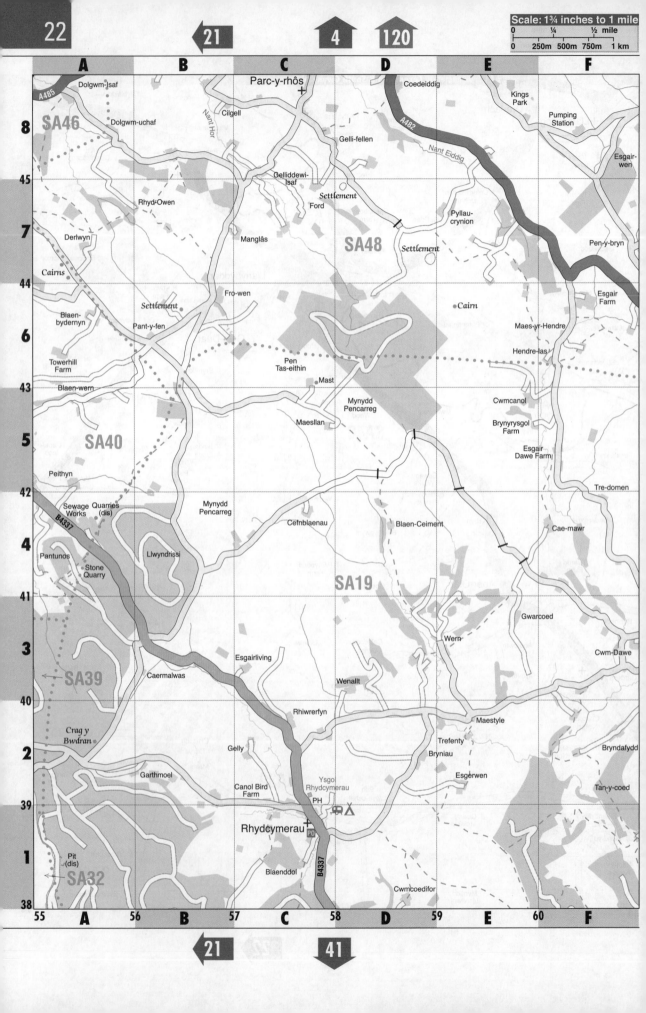

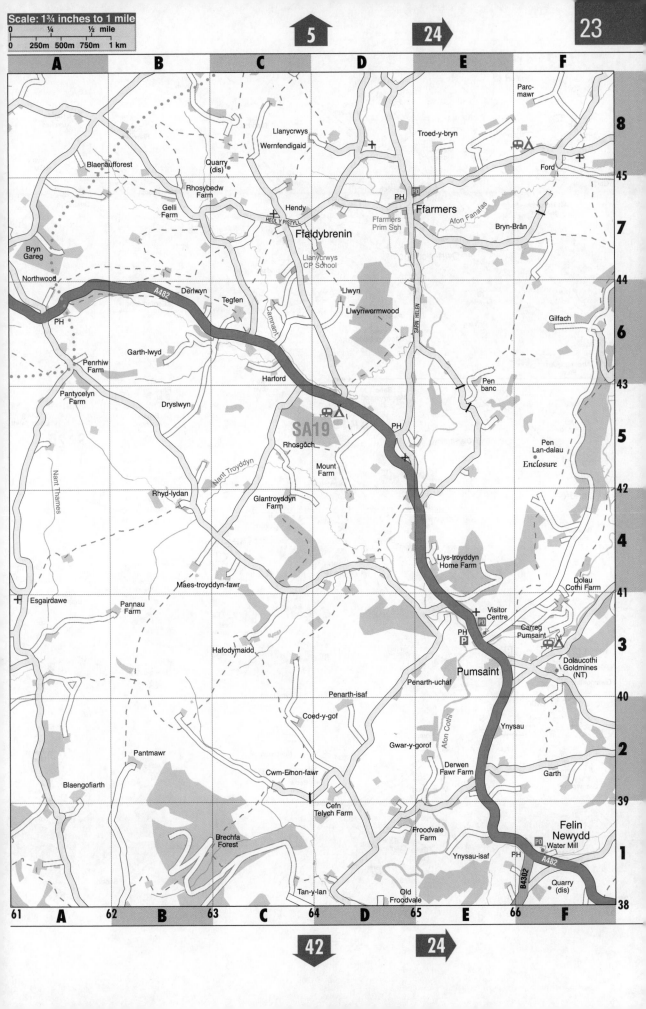

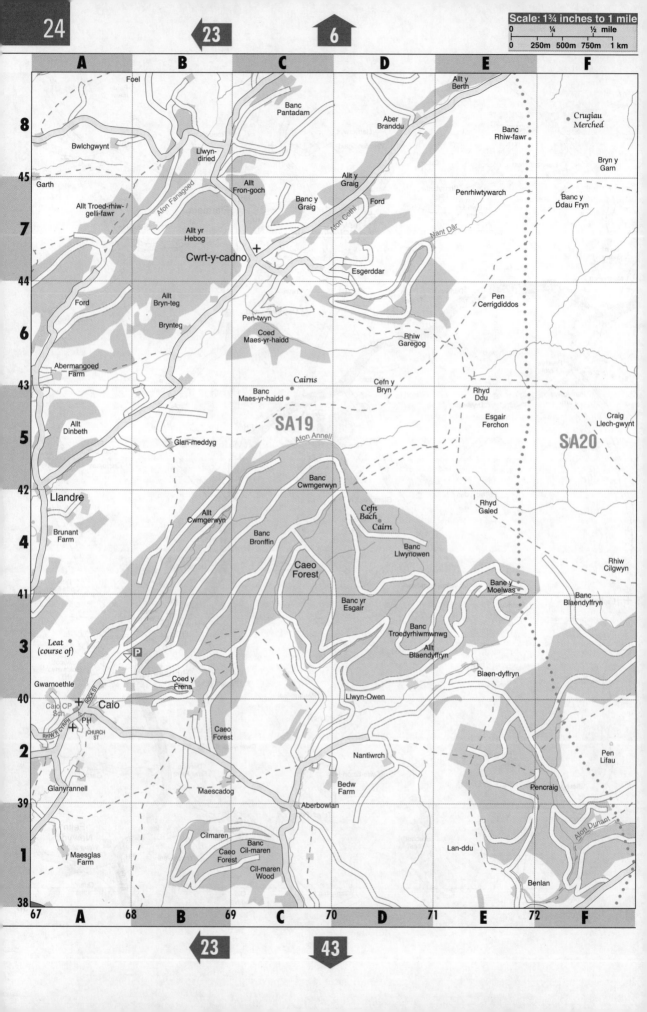

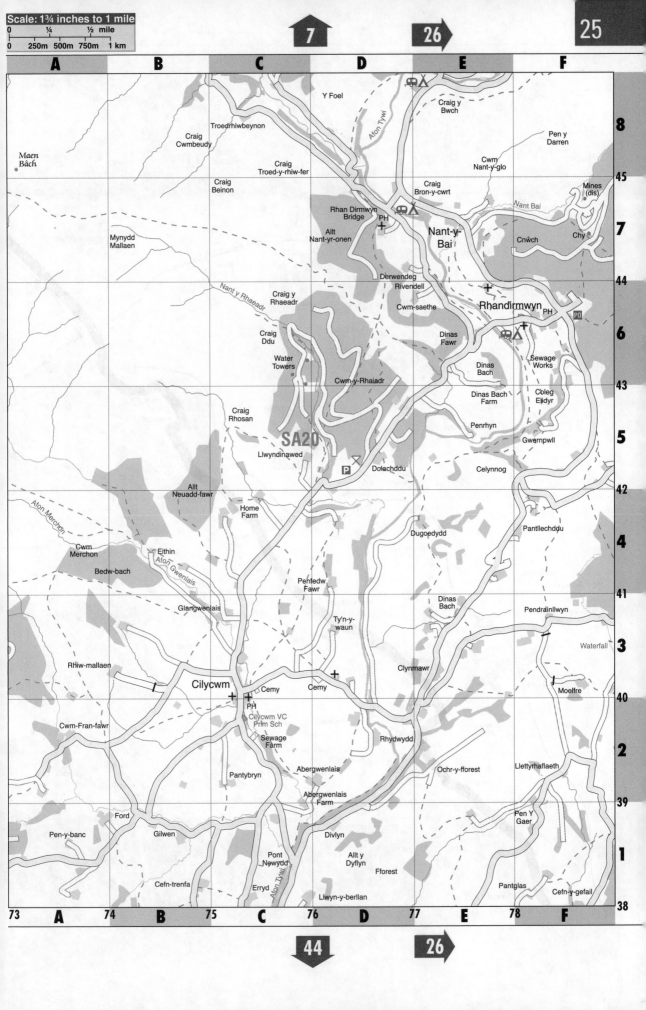

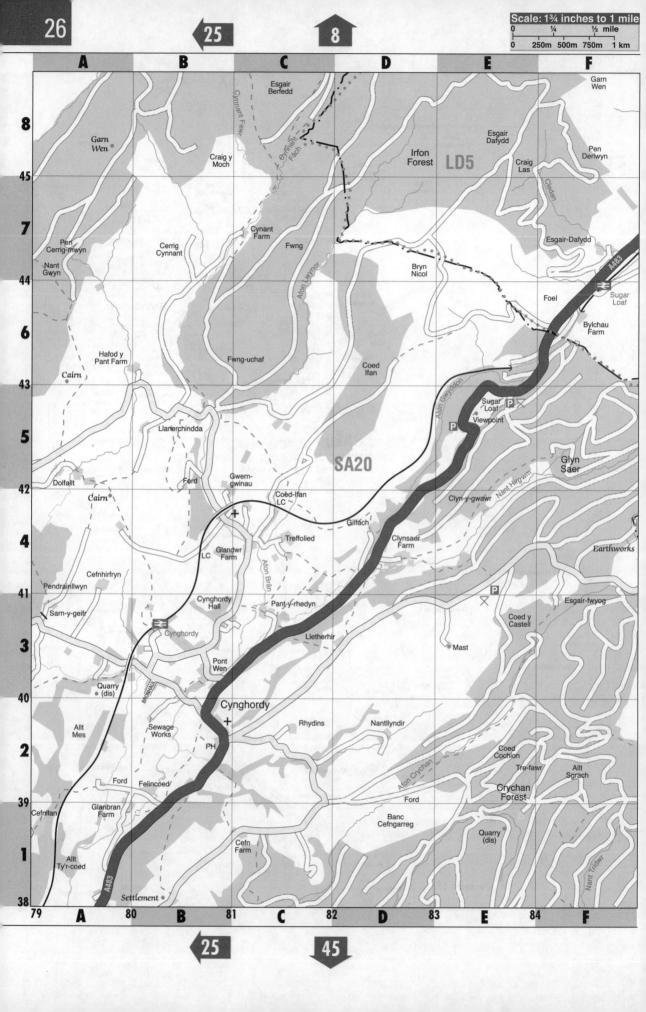

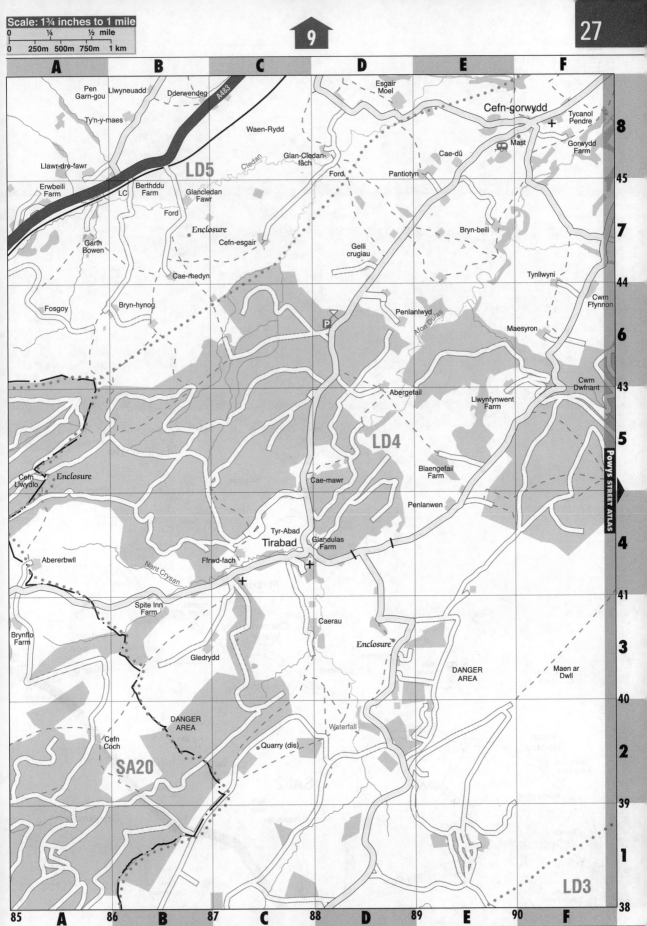

A B C D E F

8
45
7
44
6
43
5
4
41
3
40
2
39
1
38

Pen Garn-gou
Llwyneuadd
Dderwendeg
Esgair Moel
Cefn-gorwydd
Tycanol Pendre
Ty'n-y-maes
Waen-Rydd
Cae-dû
Mast
Gonwydd Farm
Llawr-dre-fawr
Glan-Cledan-fâch
Pantiotyn
Erwbeili Farm
LD5
Cleddan
Ford
LC
Berthddu Farm
Glancledan Fawr
Ford
Bryn-beili
Garth Bowen
Enclosure
Cefn-esgair
Gelli crugiau
Tynllwyni
Cae-rhedyn
Cwm Ffynnon
Fosgoy
Bryn-hynog
Penlanlwyd
Afon Dulas
Maesyron
P
Cwm Dwfnant
Abergefail
Llwynfynwent Farm
LD4
Cefn Llwydlo
Enclosure
Cae-mawr
Blaengefail Farm
Penlanwen
Tyr-Abad
Tirabad
Glandulas Farm
Abererbwll
Nant Crysan
Ffrwd-fach
Brynffo Farm
Spite Inn Farm
Caerau
Enclosure
DANGER AREA
Maen ar Dwll
Gledrydd
DANGER AREA
Cefn Coch
Waterfall
Quarry (dis)
SA20
LD3

85 A 86 B 87 C 88 D 89 E 90 F

Scale: 1¾ inches to 1 mile

0   ¼   ½ mile
0 250m 500m 750m 1 km

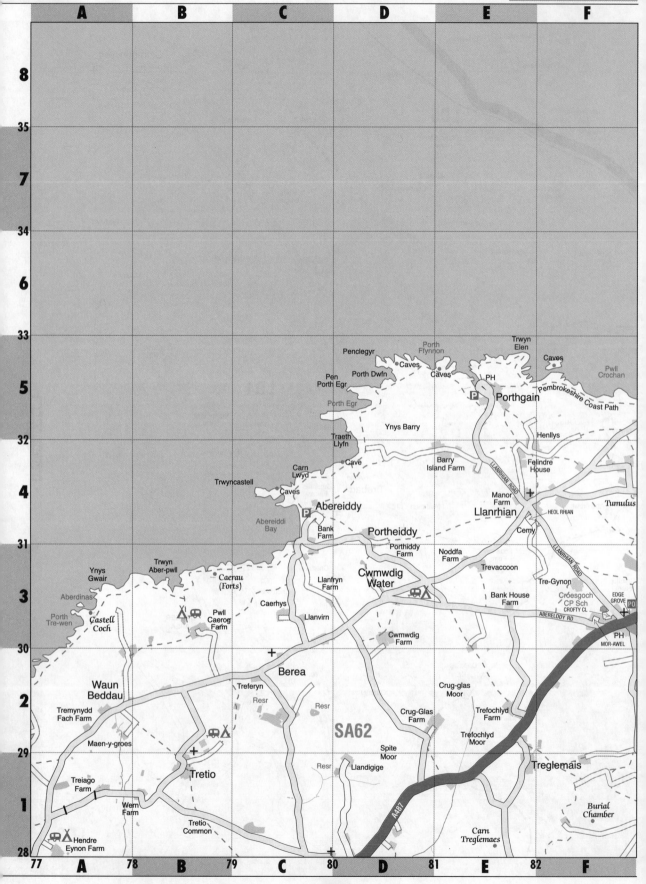

A   B   C   D   E   F

8

35

7

34

6

33

5   Penclegyr   Porth Fynnon   Trwyn Elen   Caves
     Caves   Porth Dwfn   Caves   PH   Pwll Crochan
     Pen Porth Egr   Porth Egr   Porthgain   Pembrokeshire Coast Path

32   Traeth Llyfn   Ynys Barry   Henllys
      Carn Lwyd   Cave   Barry Island Farm   Felindre House
      Trwyncastell   Caves   LLANRHIAN ROAD   Manor Farm   Tumulus

4   Abereiddy   Llanrhian   Heol Rhian
     Abereiddi Bay   Bank Farm   Portheiddy   Cemy
                     Porthiddy Farm   Noddfa Farm   LLANRHIAN ROAD   EDGE GROVE

31   Ynys Gwair   Trwyn Aber-pwll   Caerau (Forts)   Cwmwdig Water   Trevaccoon   Tre-Gynon   Cröesgoch CP Sch   CROFTY CL   PO
      Aberdinas   Caerhys   Llanfryn Farm   Bank House Farm   ABEREIDDY RD

3   Porth Tre-wen   Castell Coch   Pwll Caerog Farm   Llanvirn   Cwmwdig Farm   PH MOR-AWEL

30   Waun Beddau   Berea   Treferyn   Crug-glas Moor   Trefochlyd Farm   Treglemais
      Tremynydd Fach Farm   Resr   Resr   Crug-Glas Farm   Trefochlyd Moor

2   Maen-y-groes   SA62   Spite Moor

29   Treiago Farm   Tretio   Resr   Llandigige   Burial Chamber
      Wern Farm

1   Tretio Common   A487   Carn Treglemaes

28   Hendre Eynon Farm

77   A   78   B   79   C   80   D   81   E   82   F

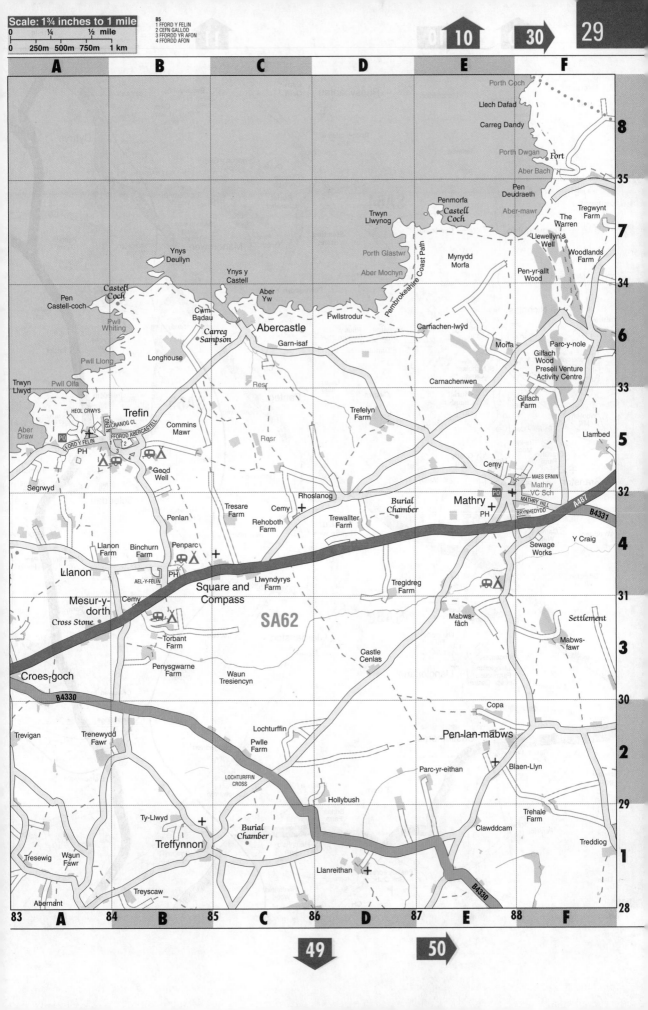

Scale: 1¾ inches to 1 mile

0   ¼   ½ mile
0 250m 500m 750m 1 km

B5
1 FFORD Y FELIN
2 CEFN GALLOD
3 FFORDD YR AFON
4 FFORDD AFON

0 10 30

A   B   C   D   E   F

Porth Coch
Llech Dafad
Carreg Dandy

8

Porth Dwgan
Aber Bach
Fort

35

Pen
Deudraeth

Penmorfa
Castell
Coch

Trwyn
Llwynog

Aber-mawr

Tregwynt
Farm

The
Warren

7

Ynys
Deullyn

Porth Glastwr

Aber Mochyn

Mynydd
Morfa

Llewellyn's
Well

Woodlands
Farm

Ynys y
Castell

Aber
Yw

Pen-yr-allt
Wood

34

Pen
Castell-coch

Castell
Coch

Pwll
Whiting

Cwm
Badau

Carreg
Sampson

Abercastle

Pwllstrodur

Carnachen-lwyd

Morfa

Parc-y-nole

6

Longhouse

Garn-isaf

Gilfach
Wood

Preseli Venture
Activity Centre

Pwll Llong

Resr

Carnachenwen

33

Trwyn
Llwyd

Pwll Olfa

Gilfach
Farm

Aber
Draw

HEOL CRWYS

Trefin

Commins
Mawr

Trefelyn
Farm

Llambed

5

PO

Cemy

MAES ERNIN
Mathry
VC Sch

FFORD Y FELIN

PH

Geod
Well

Tresare
Farm

Cemy

Rhoslanog

Burial
Chamber

Mathry

A487

32

Segrwyd

Rehoboth
Farm

Trewallter
Farm

PH

MATHRY HILL
BRYNHEDYDD

B4331

Penlan

Y Craig

Llanon
Farm

Binchurn
Farm

Penparc

Sewage
Works

4

Llanon

PH

AEL-Y-FELIN

Llwyndyrys
Farm

Tregidreg
Farm

Mesur-y-
dorth

Cemy

Square and
Compass

31

Cross Stone

SA62

Mabws-
fâch

Settlement

Torbant
Farm

Castle
Cenlas

Mabws-
fawr

3

Penysgwarne
Farm

Waun
Tresiencyn

Croes-goch

Copa

B4330

30

Trevigan

Trenewydd
Fawr

Lochturffin

Pen-lan-mabws

2

Pwlle
Farm

Parc-yr-eithan

Blaen-Llyn

LOCHTURFFIN
CROSS

Hollybush

Trehale
Farm

29

Ty-Llwyd

Burial
Chamber

Clawddcam

Treddiog

Treffynnon

Llanreithan

1

Tresewig

Waun
Fawr

B4330

Treyscaw

Abernant

28

83 A 84 B 85 C 86 D 87 E 88 F

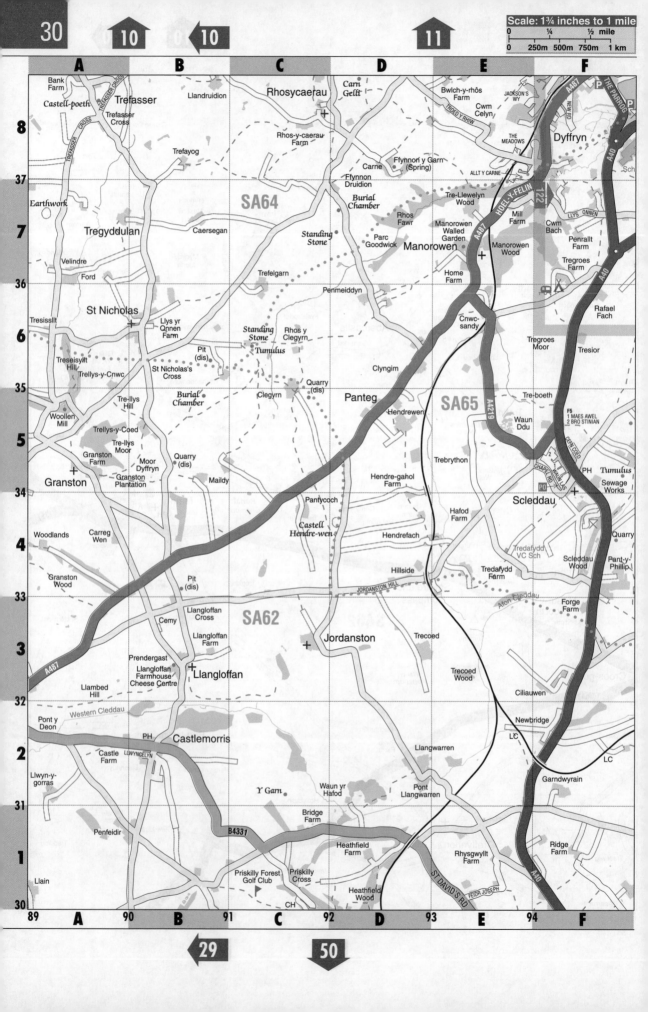

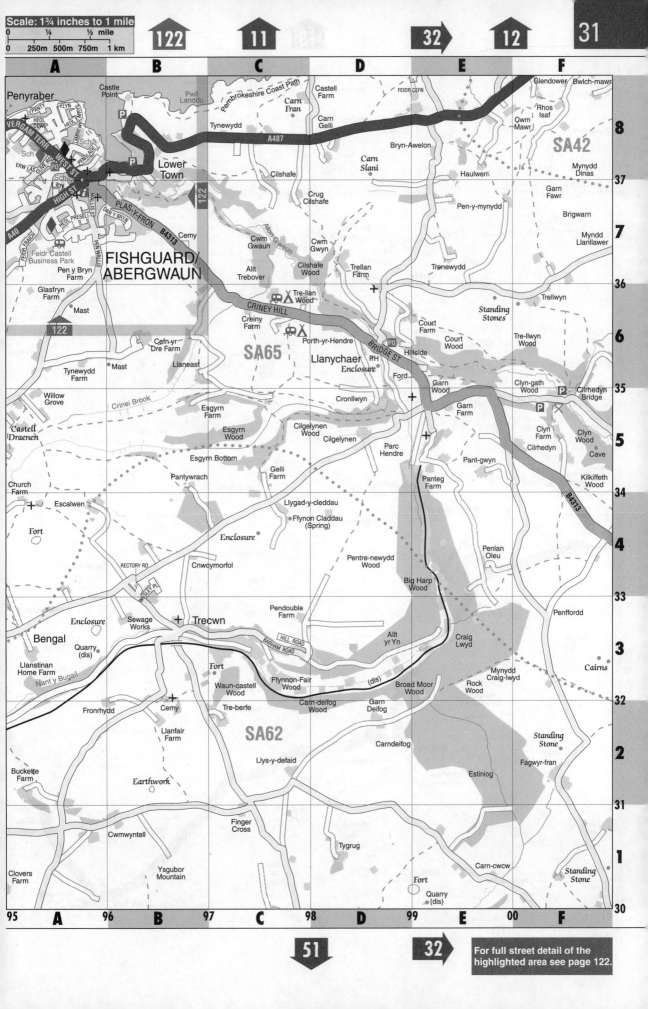

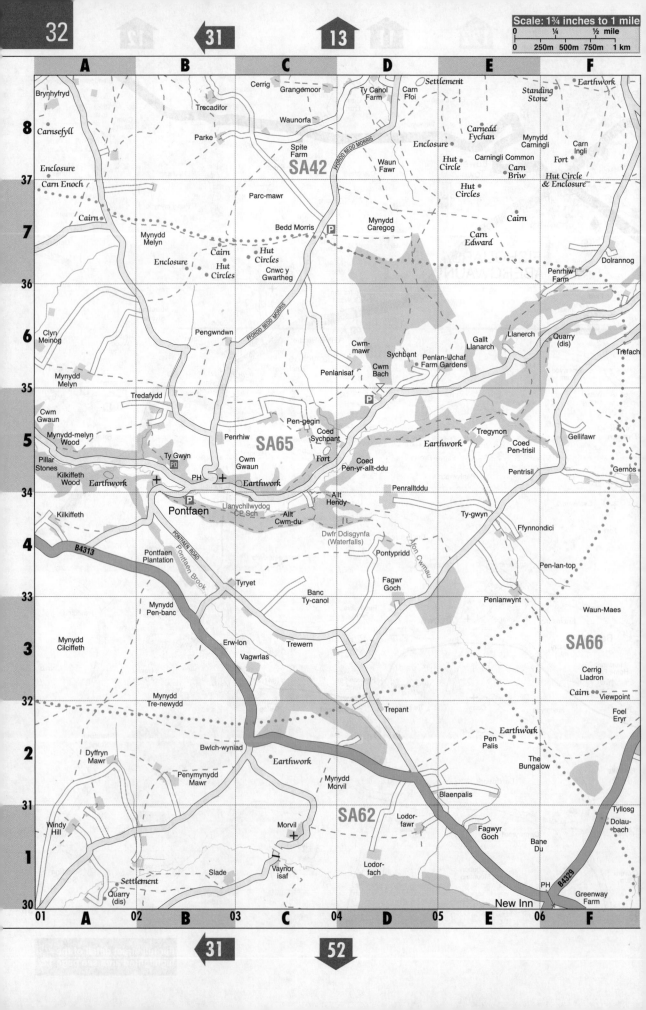

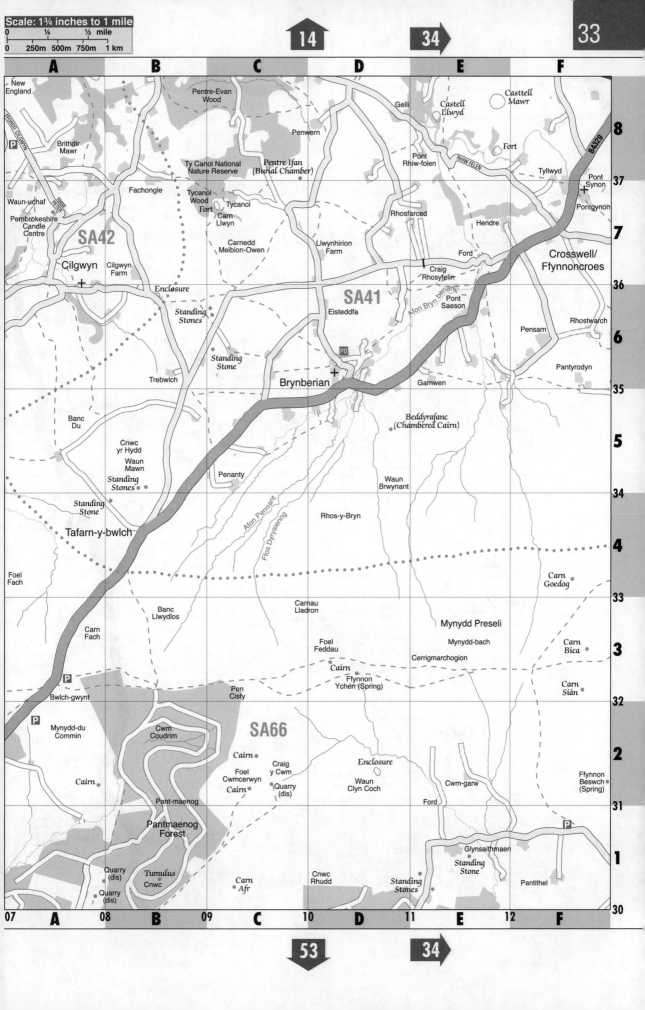

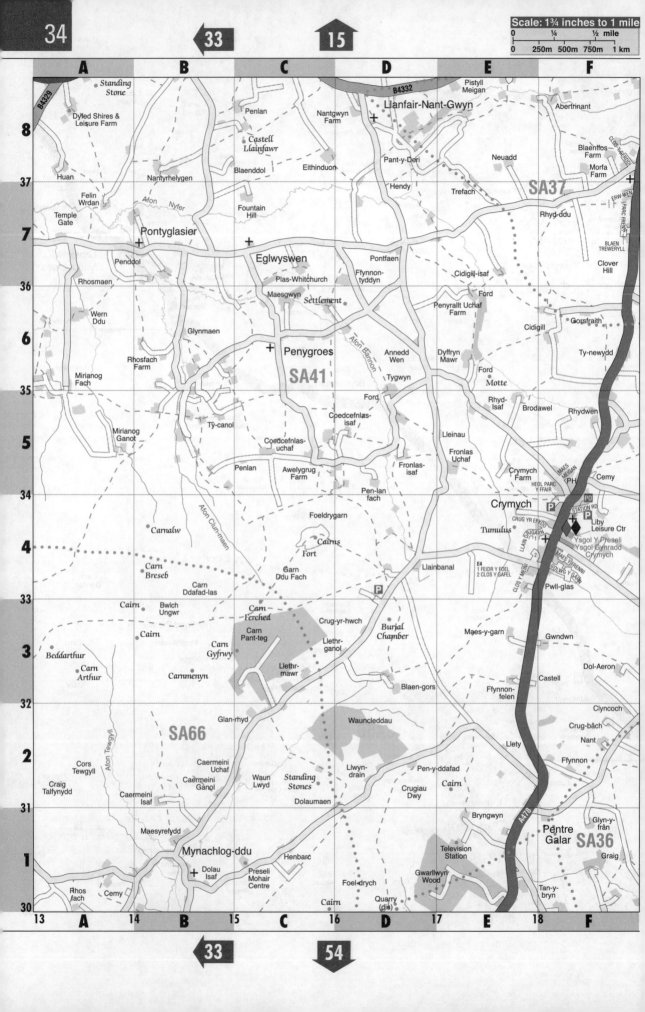

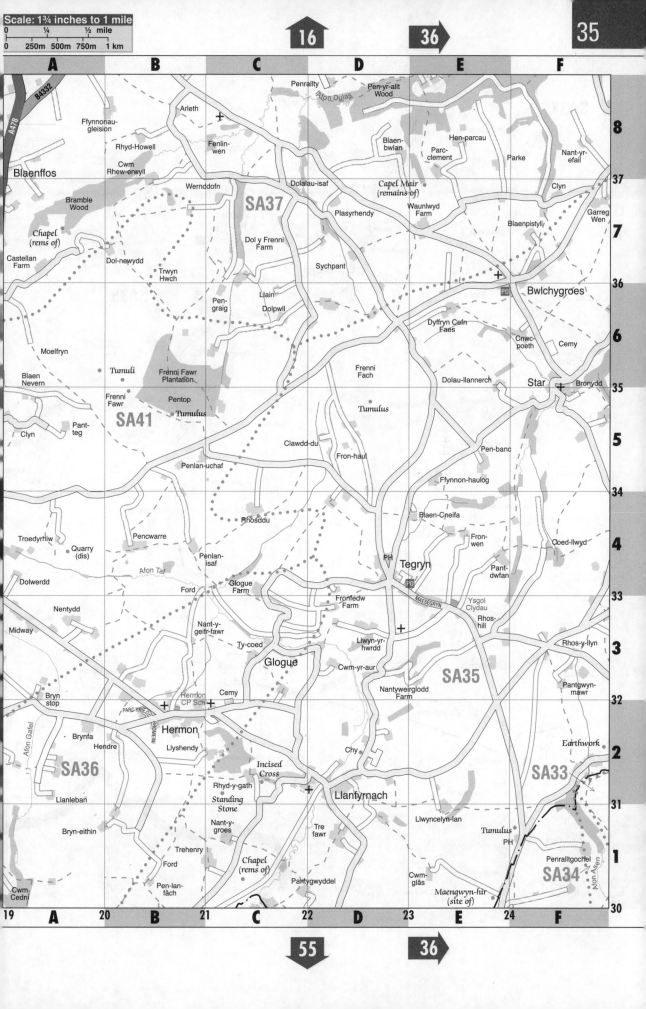

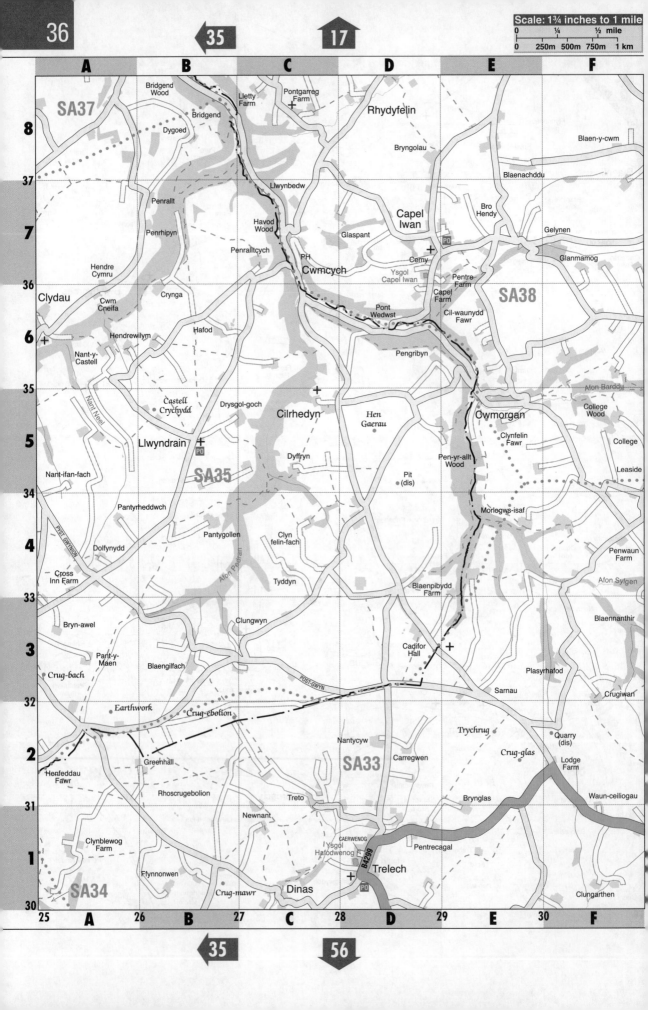

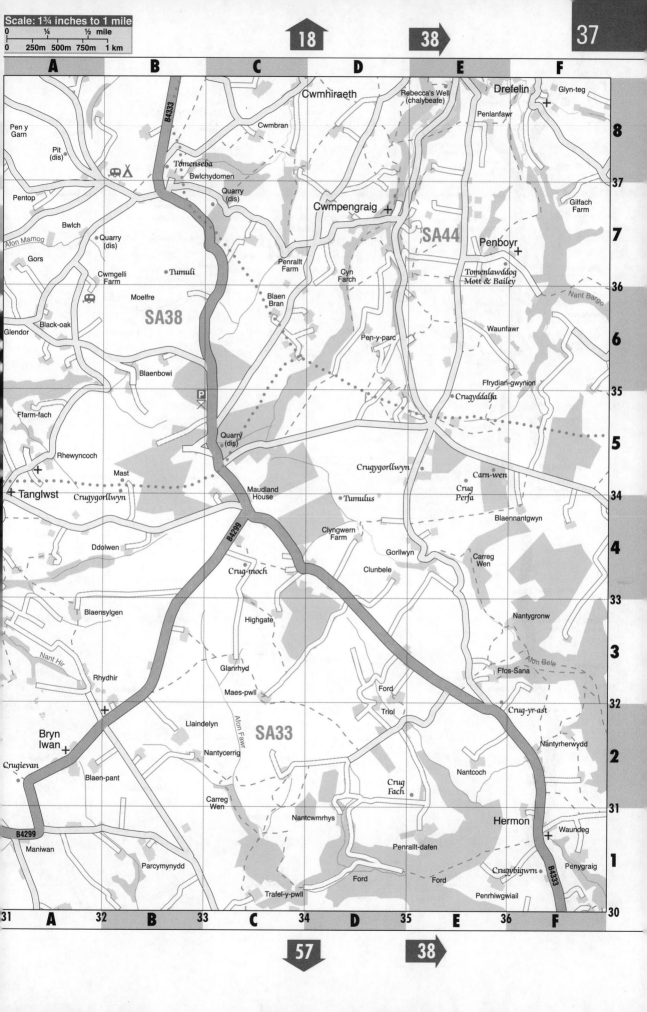

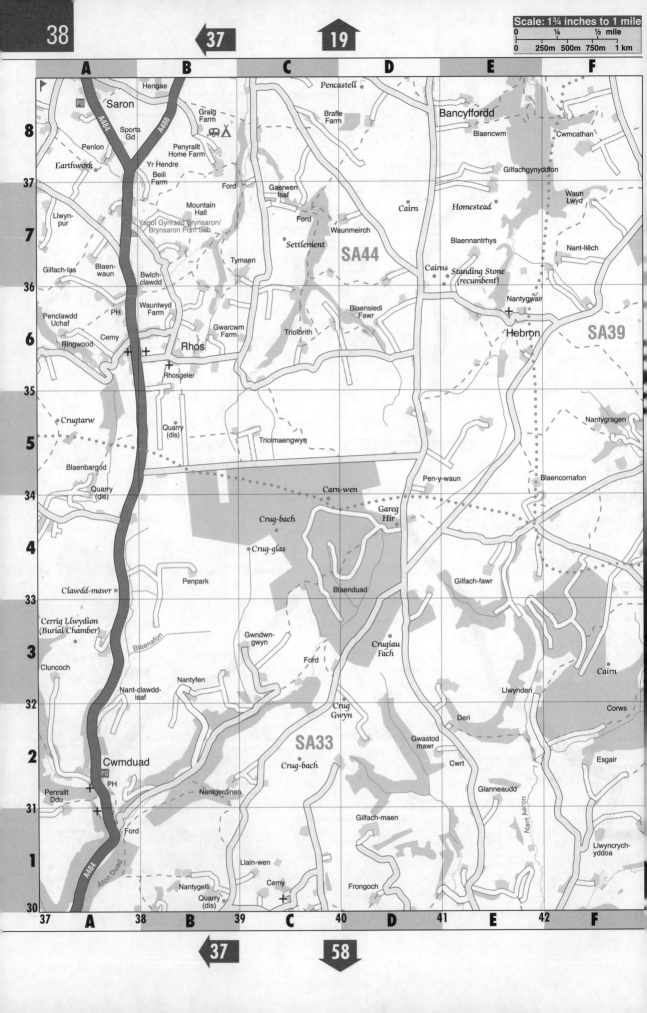

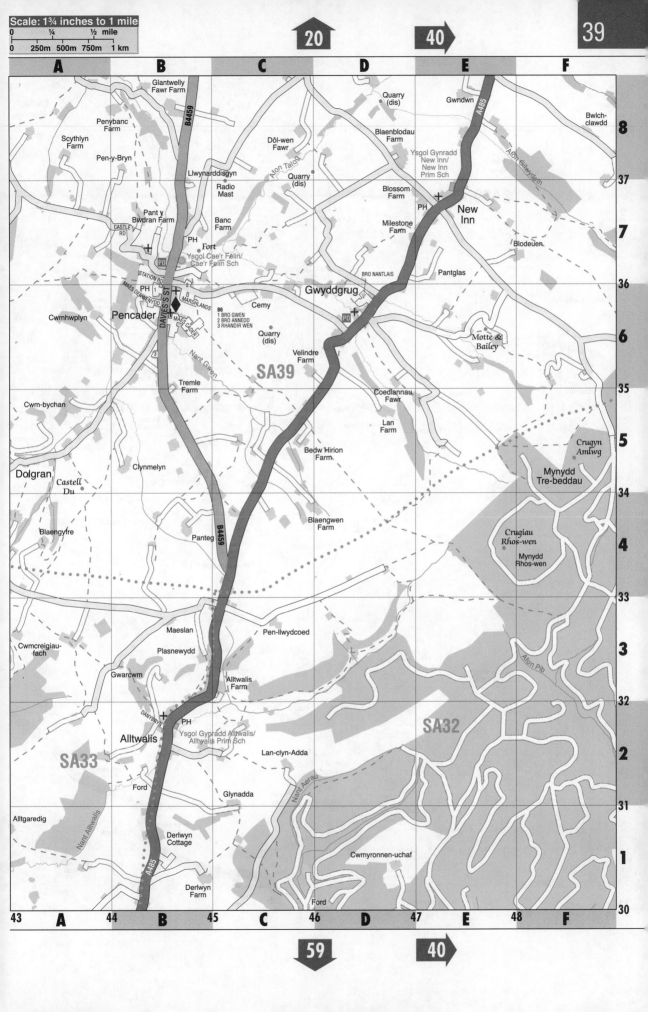

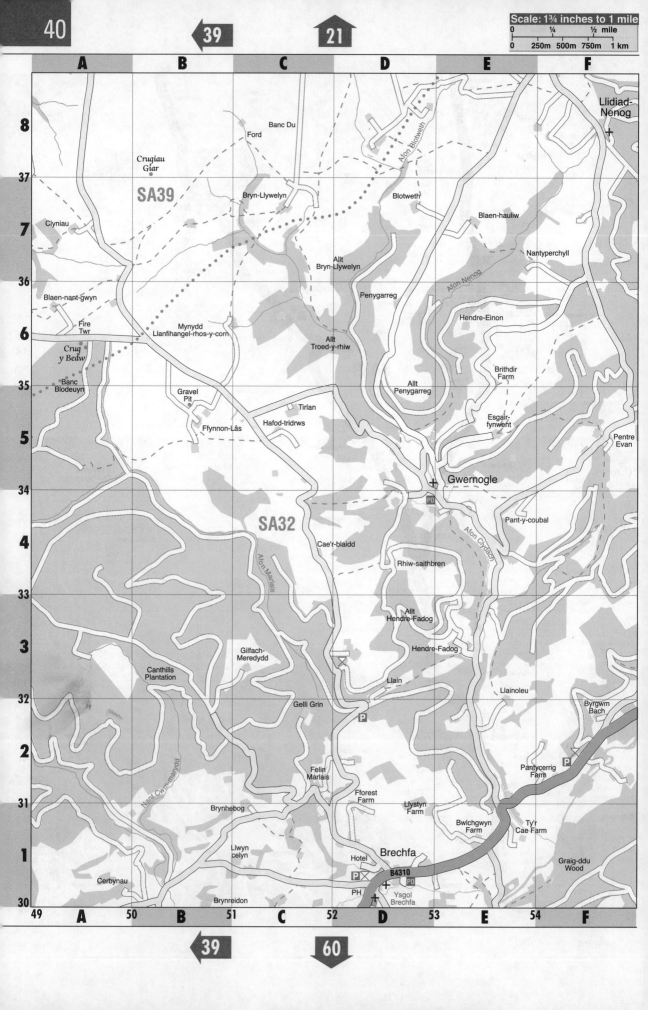

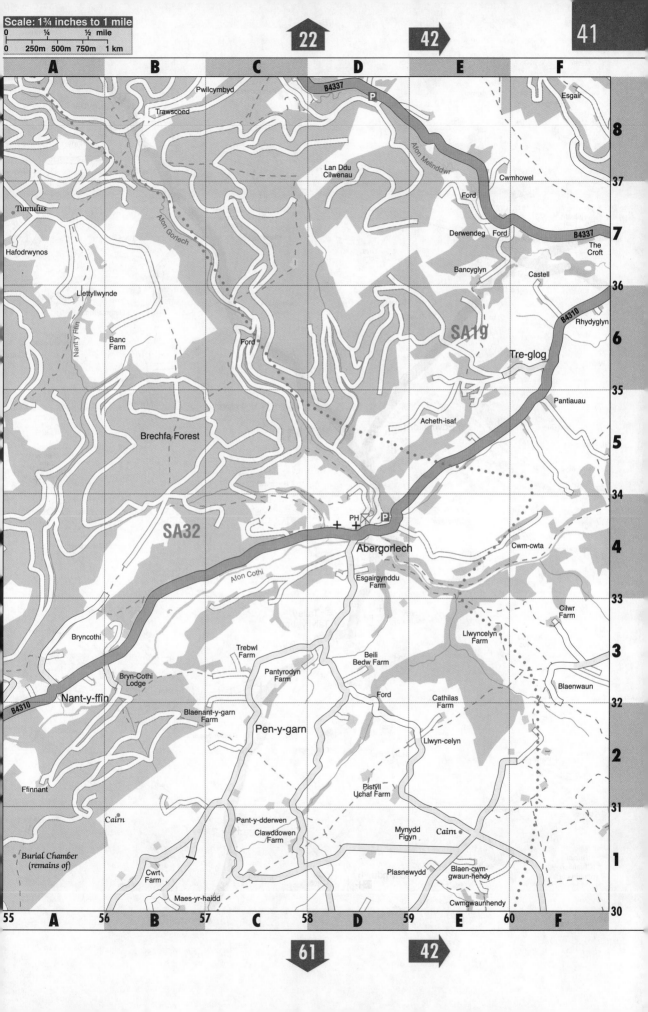

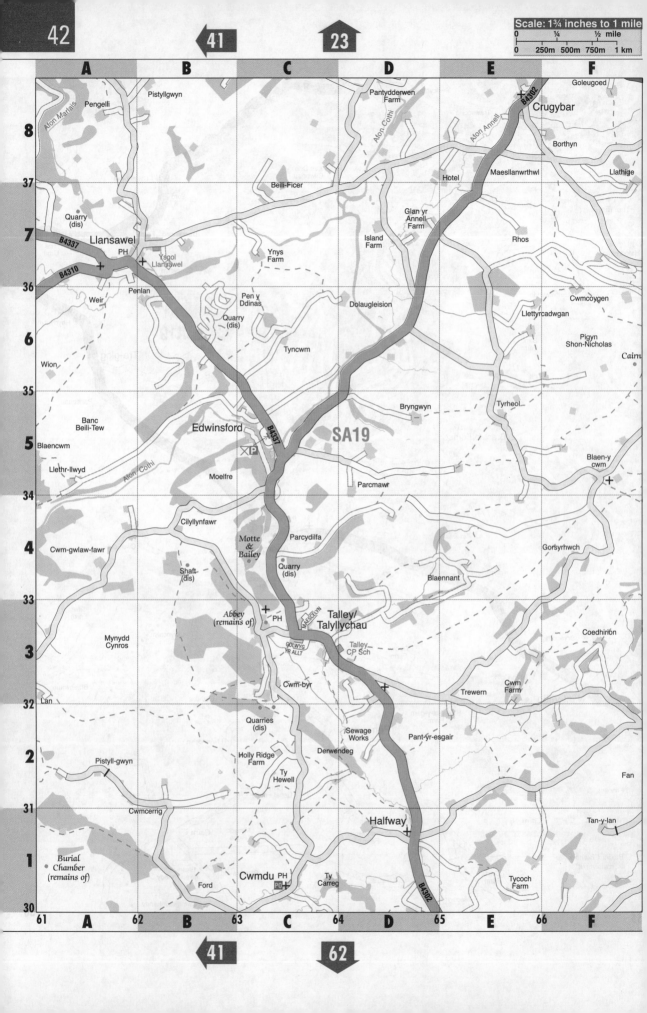

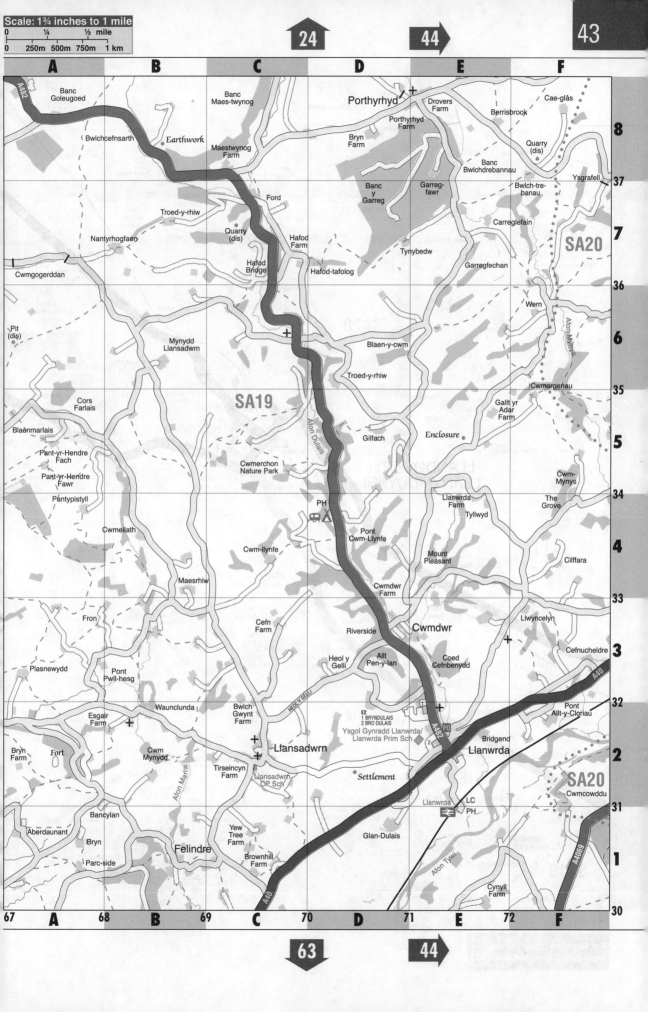

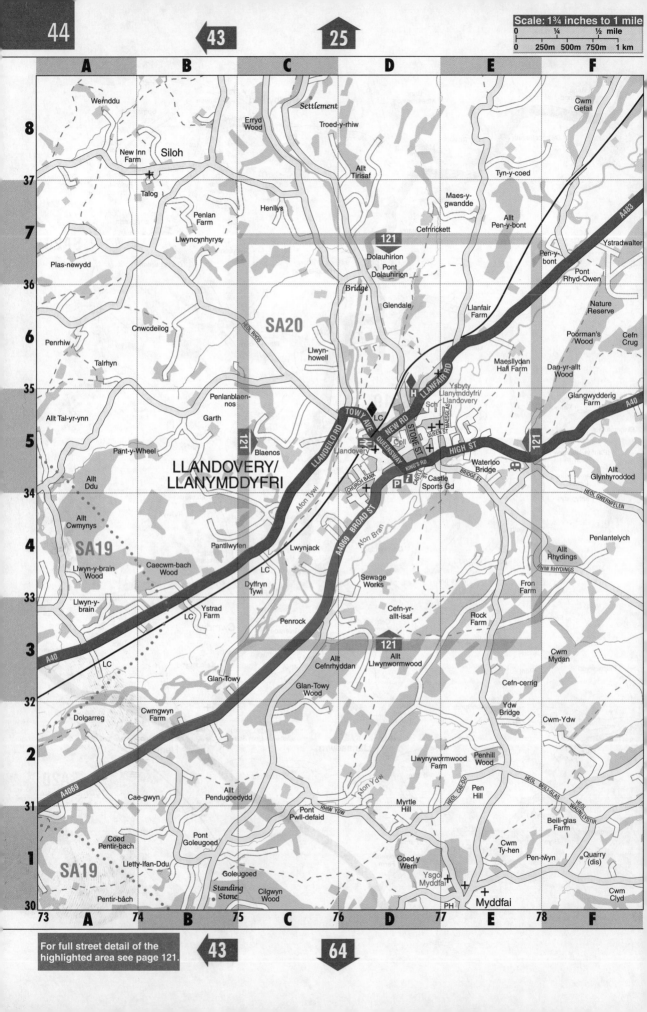

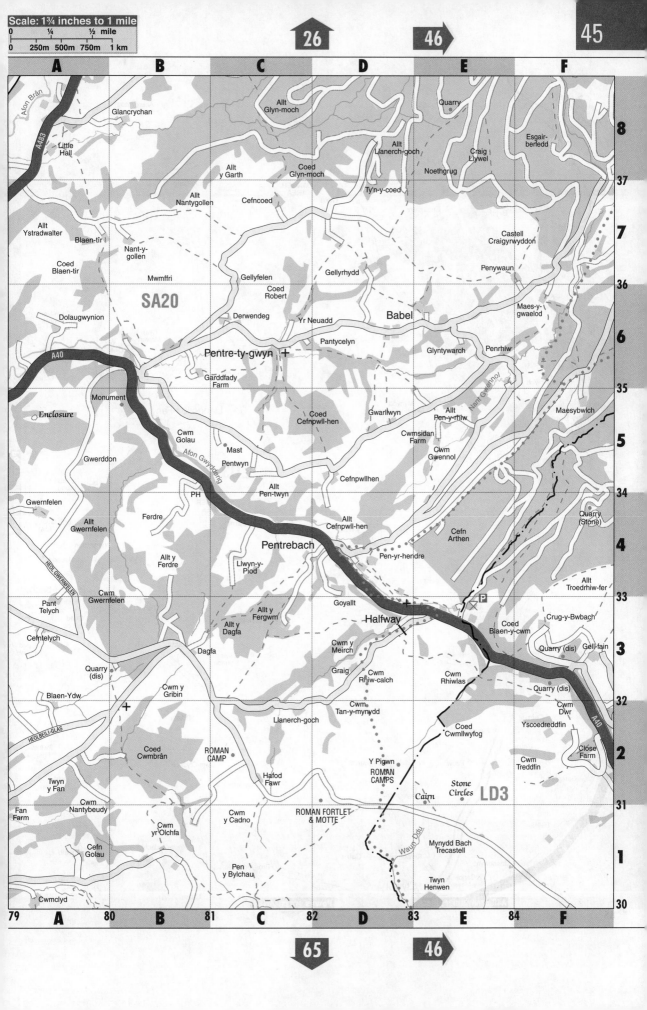

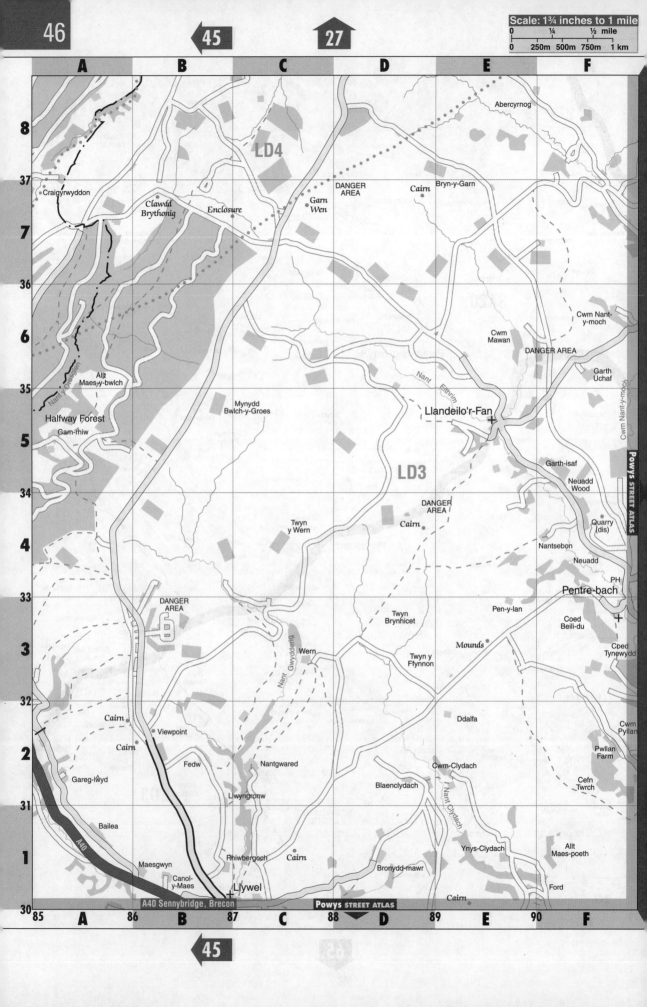

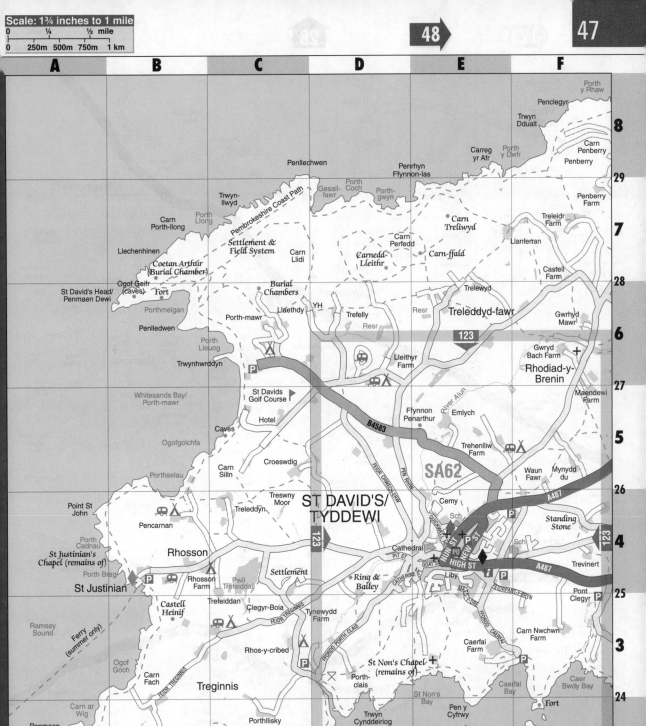

St David's Head/Penmaen Dewi

Ogof Geifr (caves)

Fort

Coetan Arthur (Burial Chamber)

Llechenhinen

Carn Porth-llong

Carn Porth-llong

Porthmelgan

Penlledwen

Trwynhwrddyn

Whitesands Bay/Porth-mawr

Ogofgolchfa

Porthselau

Porth Lleuog

Porth-mawr

Settlement & Field System

Pembrokeshire Coast Path

Trwyn-llwyd

Porth Llong

Penllechwen

Burial Chambers

Carn Llidi

Llaethdy

YH

Carn Perfedd

Carnedd Lleithr

Trefelly

Carn Treliwyd

Carn-ffald

Resr

Resr

Trelewyd

Treleddyd-fawr

Penrhyn Ffynnon-las

Porth Coch

Porth-gwyn

Gesail-fawr

Porth y Dwfr

Carreg yr Afr

Penclegyr

Trwyn Dduault

Porth y Rhaw

Carn Penberry

Penberry

Penberry Farm

Treleidr Farm

Llanferran

Castell Farm

Gwrhyd Mawr

Gwryd Bach Farm

Rhodiad-y-Brenin

Maendewi Farm

St Davids Golf Course

Hotel

Caves

Croeswdig

Carn Silln

Caves

Treswny Moor

Treleddyn

Lleithyr Farm

Ffynnon Penarthur

Emlych

River Alun

Trehenlliw Farm

Waun Fawr

Mynydd du

B4583

PEN RHIW

FEIDR CAMSGWRN

SA62

Standing Stone

A487

123

Point St John

Porth Cadnau

Pencarnan

Rhosson

St Justinian's Chapel (remains of)

St Justinian

Porth Brag

Rhosson Farm

Castell Heinif

Trefeiddan

Settlement

Clegyr-Boia

Pwll Trefeiddan

Tynewydd Farm

Ring & Bailey

Cemy

Sch

Cathedral

PIT ST

GOAT ST

CATHERINE ST

CAUCKWELL H'L

NUN ST

HIGH ST

NEW ST

PO

Liby

ST DAVID'S/TYDDEWI

Sch

Trevinert

Pont Clegyr

MAES-y-EGLWYS

FFORDD CAERFAI

FEIDR PANT-y-BRYN

A487

Carn Nwchwn Farm

Ramsey Sound

Ferry (summer only)

Ogof Goch

Carn Fach

FEIDR TREGINNIS

Trefeiddan

FEIDR TREGINNIS

Rhos-y-cribed

Treginnis

Carn ar Wig

Penmaen melyn

Pen Dal-aderyn

Porthtaflod

Porth Henllys

Maen Llwydwyn

Ogof Mrs Morgan

Carreg yr Esgob

Carreg Frân

Porthllisky

Cave

Ogor Lle-sugn

Llech Cyllyll

Trwyn Cynddeiriog

St Non's Chapel (remains of)

Porth-clais

FFORDD PORTH CLAIS

St Non's Bay

Pen y Cyfrwy

Penpleidiau

Caerfai Farm

Caerfai Bay

Caer Bwdy Bay

Fort

123

123

123

Pembrokeshire Coast Path

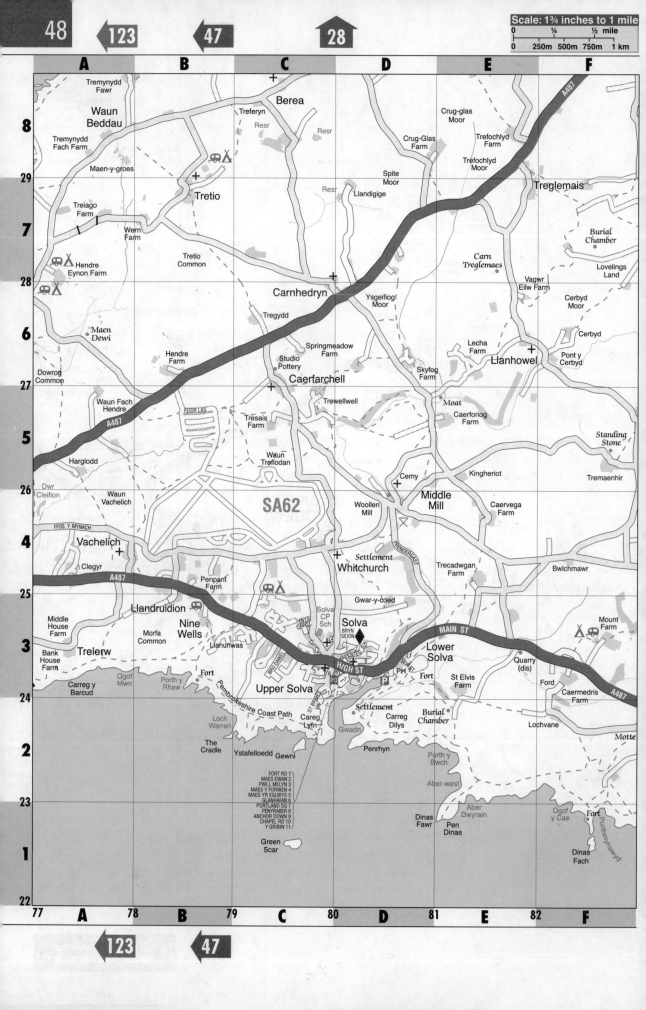

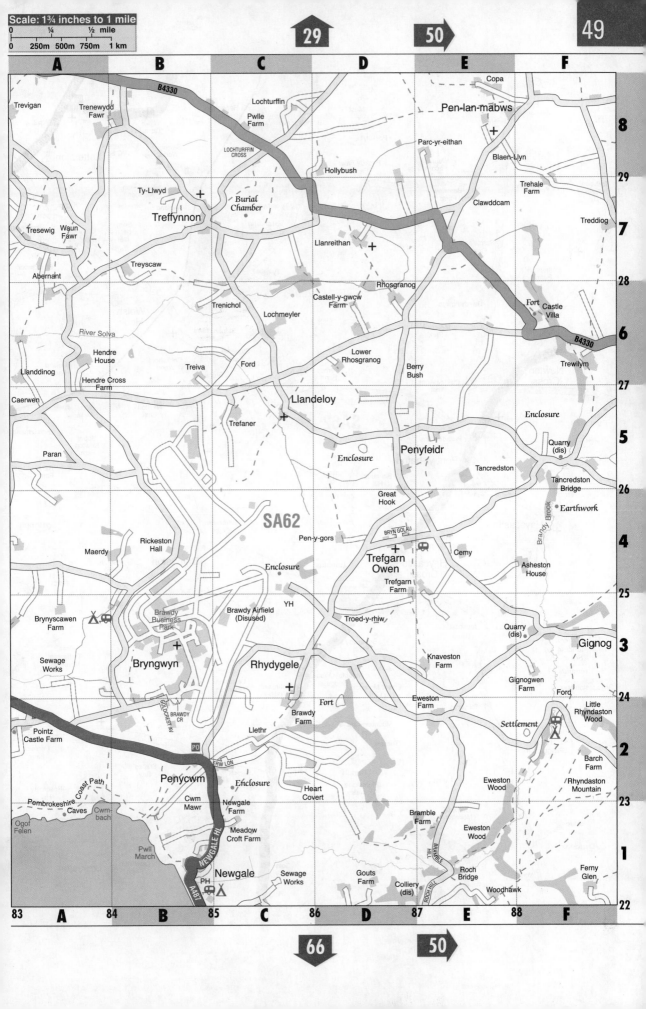

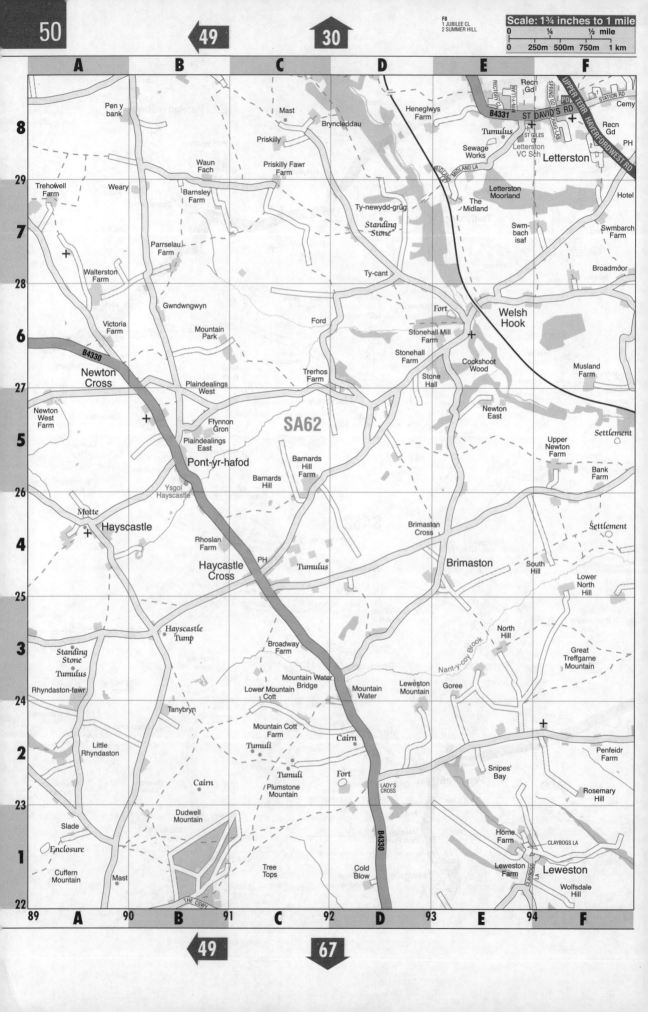

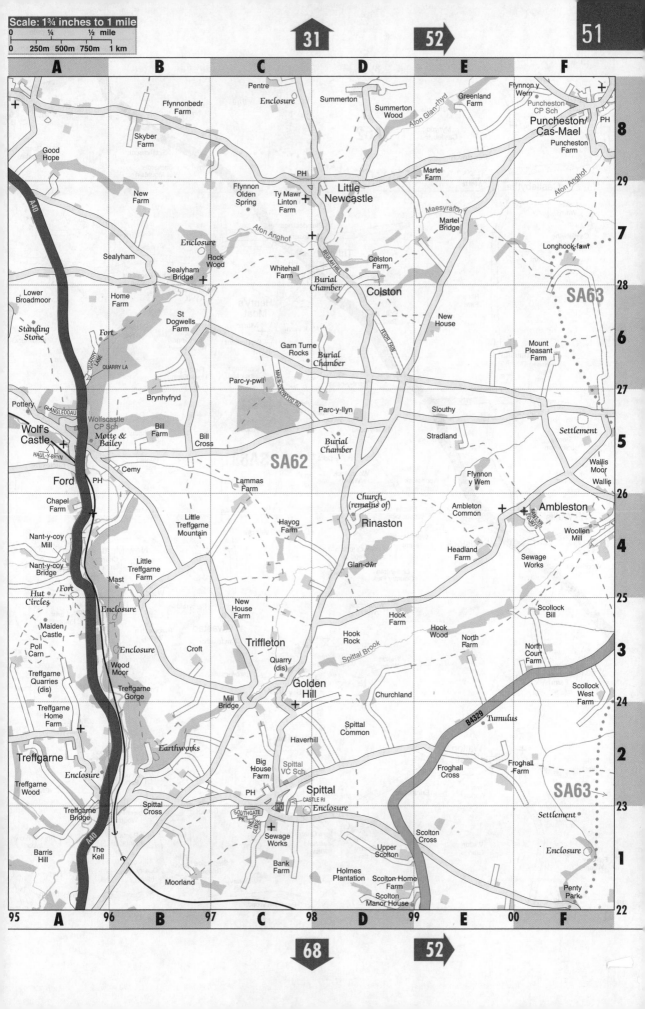

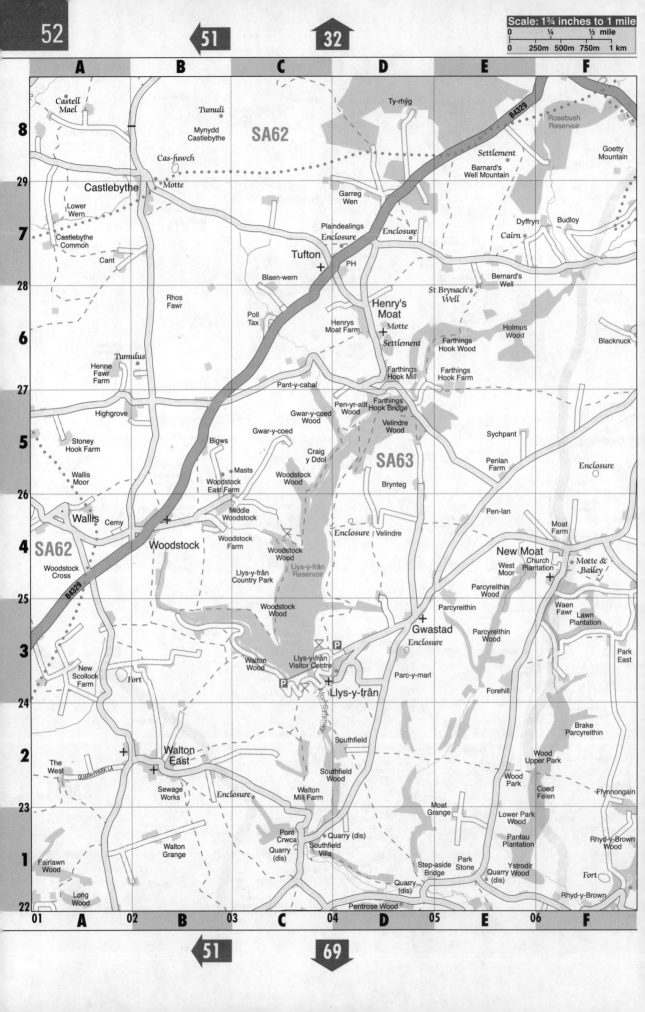

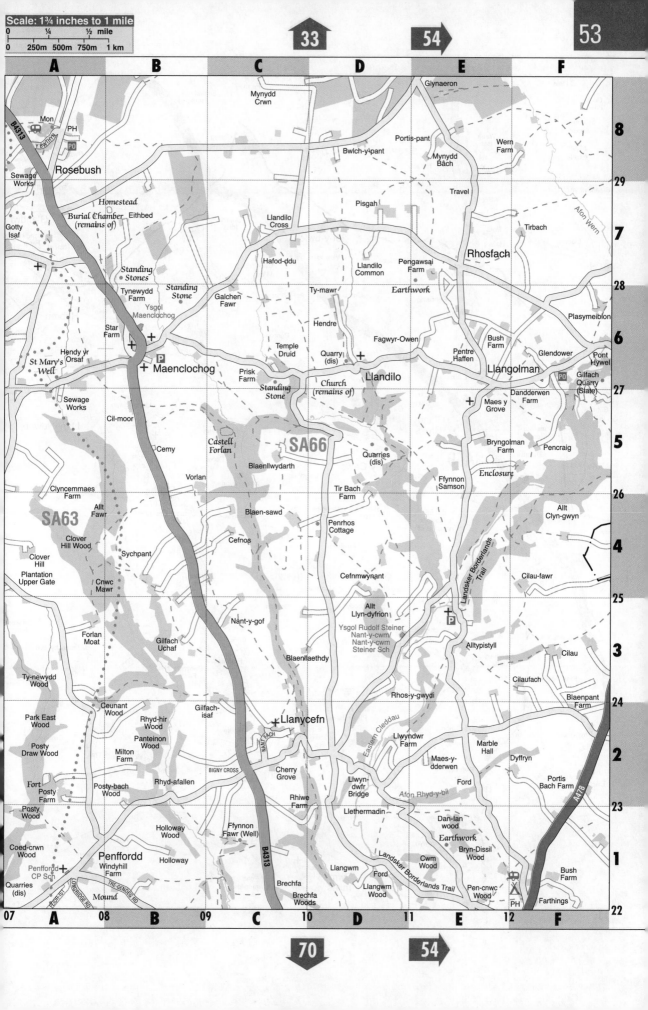

A   B   C   D   E   F

8

29

7

28

6

27

5

26

4

25

3

24

2

23

1

22

Mynydd Crwn

Glynaeron

B4313
Mon
PH
PO
Y Bwthyn
Rosebush

Sewage Works

Gotty Isaf

Homestead
Burial Chamber (remains of)
Eithbed

Standing Stones

Tynewydd Farm

Standing Stone

Ysgol Maenclochog

Star Farm

St Mary's Well

Hendy yr Orsaf

P
Maenclochog

Sewage Works

Cil-moor

Cemy

Castell Forlan

Clyncemmaes Farm

SA63

Allt Fawr

Clover Hill Wood

Clover Hill

Plantation Upper Gate

Cnwc Mawr

Ty-newydd Wood

Park East Wood

Ceunant Wood

Posty Draw Wood

Milton Farm

Panteinon Wood

Rhyd-hir Wood

Gilfach-isaf

Fort Posty Farm

Posty Wood

Posty-bach Wood

Rhyd-afallen

Coed-crwn Wood

Penffordd CP Sch

Penffordd

Windyhill Farm

Holloway Wood

Holloway

Quarries (dis)

Mound

Ffynnon Fawr (Well)

B4313

Brechfa

Brechfa Woods

Bwlch-y-pant

Portis-pant

Mynydd Bâch

Wern Farm

Travel

Pisgah

Afon Wern

Llandilo Cross

Tirbach

Rhosfach

Hafod-ddu

Llandilo Common

Pengawsai Farm

Earthwork

Plasymeibion

Galchen Fawr

Ty-mawr

Hendre

Fagwyr-Owen

Pentre Haffen

Bush Farm

Glendower

Pont Hywel

Gilfach Quarry (Slate)

PO

Llangolman

Temple Druid

Quarry (dis)

Llandilo

Prisk Farm

Standing Stone

Church (remains of)

Dandderwen Farm

Maes y Grove

Bryngolman Farm

Pencraig

Enclosure

Allt Clyn-gwyn

SA66

Vorlan

Blaenllwydarth

Quarries (dis)

Ffynnon Samson

Cefnos

Blaen-sawd

Tir Bach Farm

Penrhos Cottage

Cilau-fawr

Sychpant

Cefnmwynant

Cilau

Nant-y-gof

Allt Llyn-dyfrion

Ysgol Rudolf Steiner
Nant-y-cwm/
Nant-y-cwm
Steiner Sch

P

Alltypistyll

Cilaufach

Forlan Moat

Gilfach Uchaf

Blaenllaethdy

Rhos-y-gwydi

Blaenpant Farm

Landsker Borderlands Trail

Llanycefn

NANT FACH

Cherry Grove

Eastern Cleddau

Llwyndwr Farm

Maes-y-dderwen

Marble Hall

Dyffryn

Portis Bach Farm

A478

BIGNY CROSS

Rhiwe Farm

Llwyn-dwfr Bridge

Afon Rhyd-y-bil

Ford

Llethermadin

Dan-lan wood

Earthwork

Bryn-Dissil Wood

Holloway

Llangwm

Ford

Llangwm Wood

Landsker Borderlands Trail

Cwm Wood

Pen-cnwc Wood

PH

Bush Farm

Farthings

Farthings

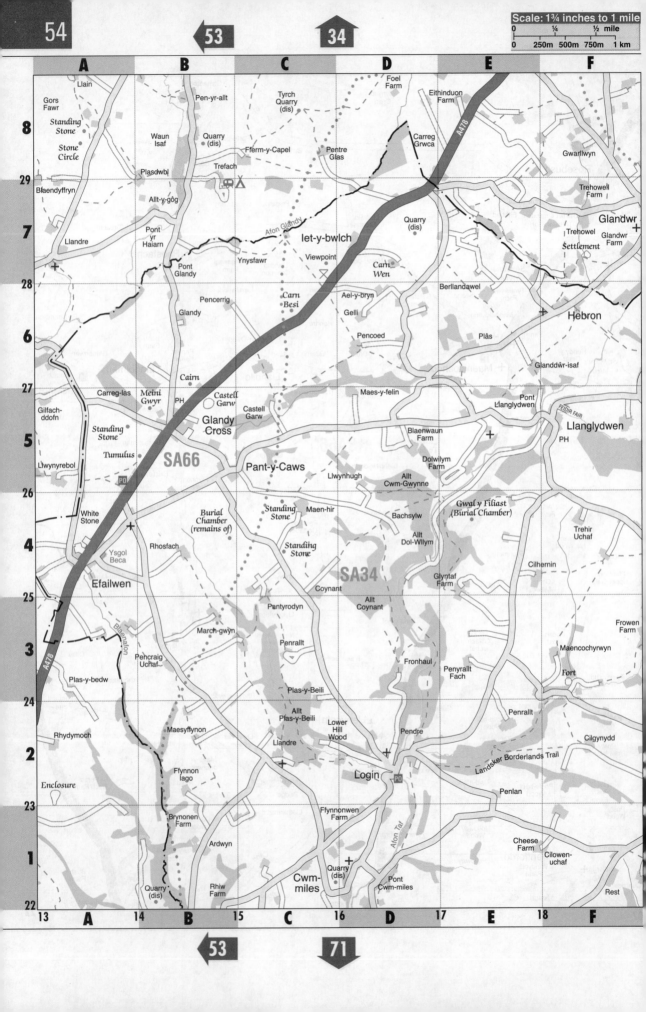

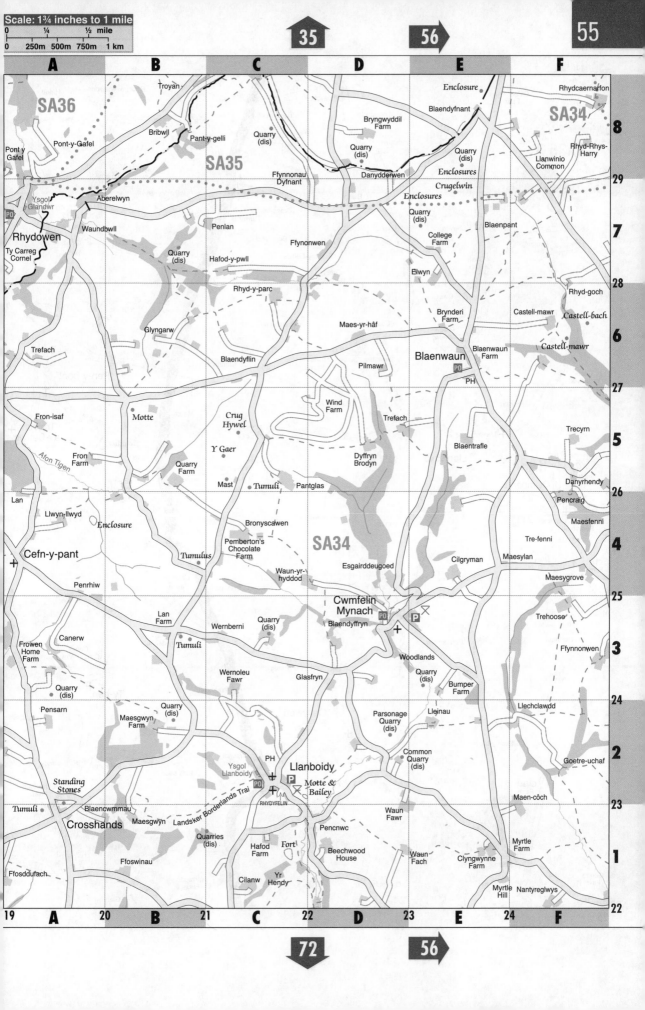

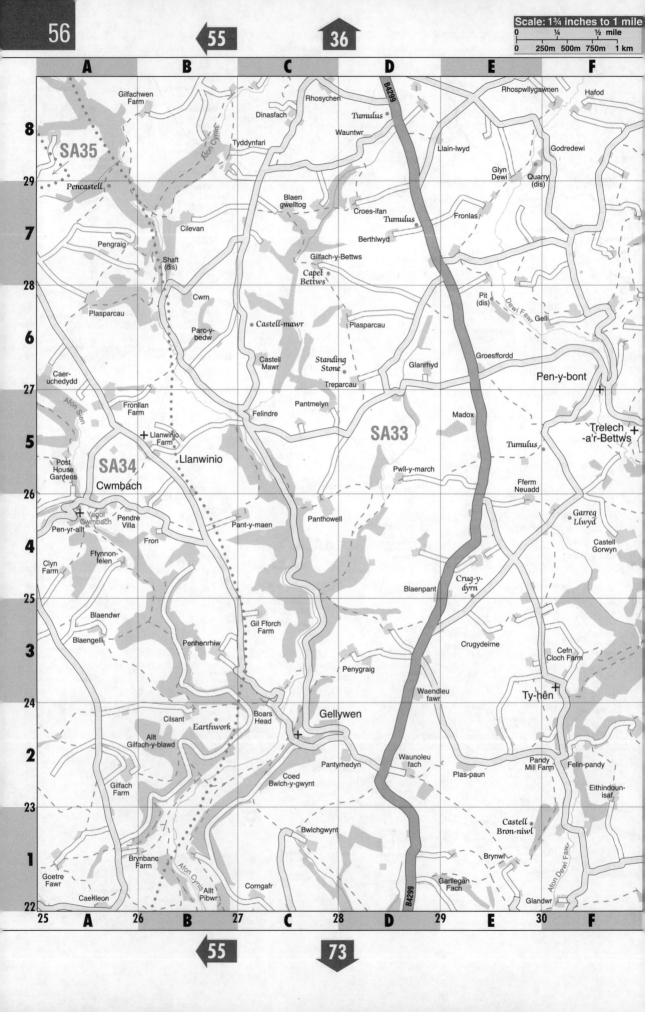

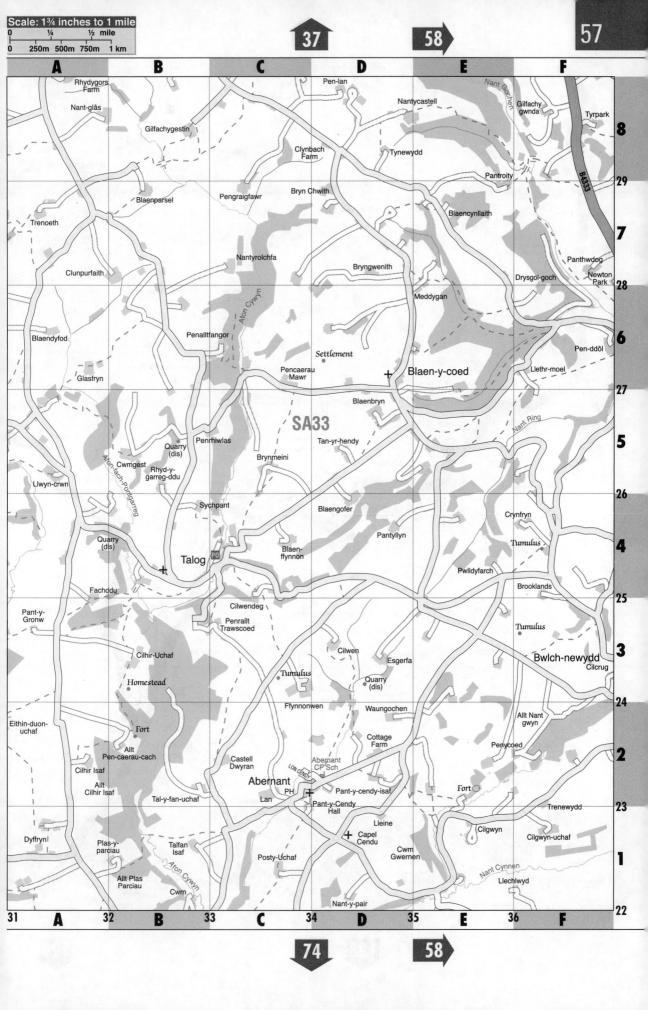

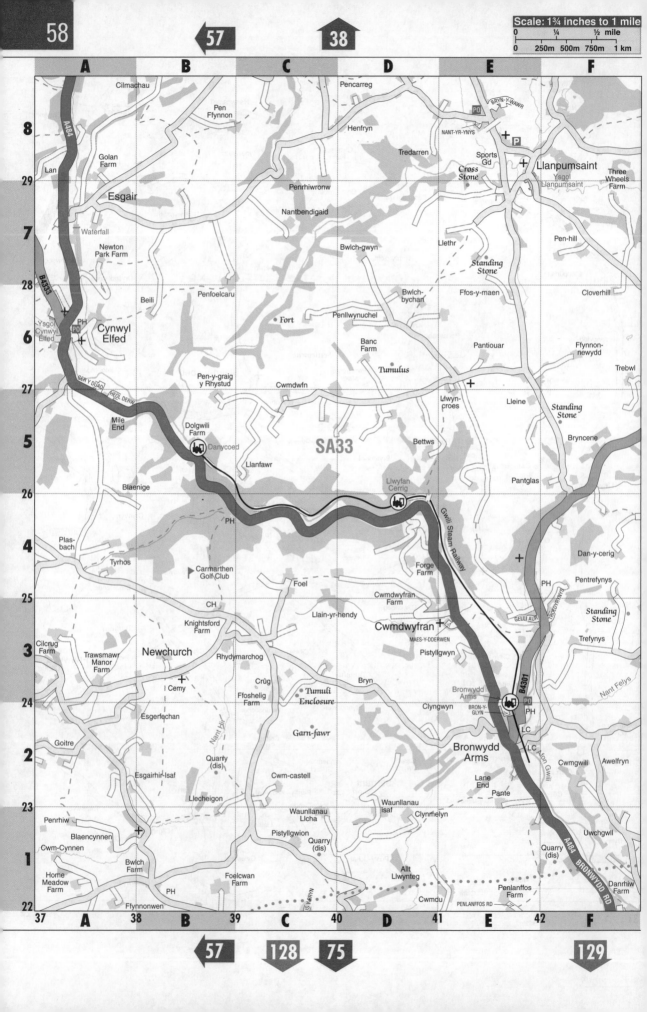

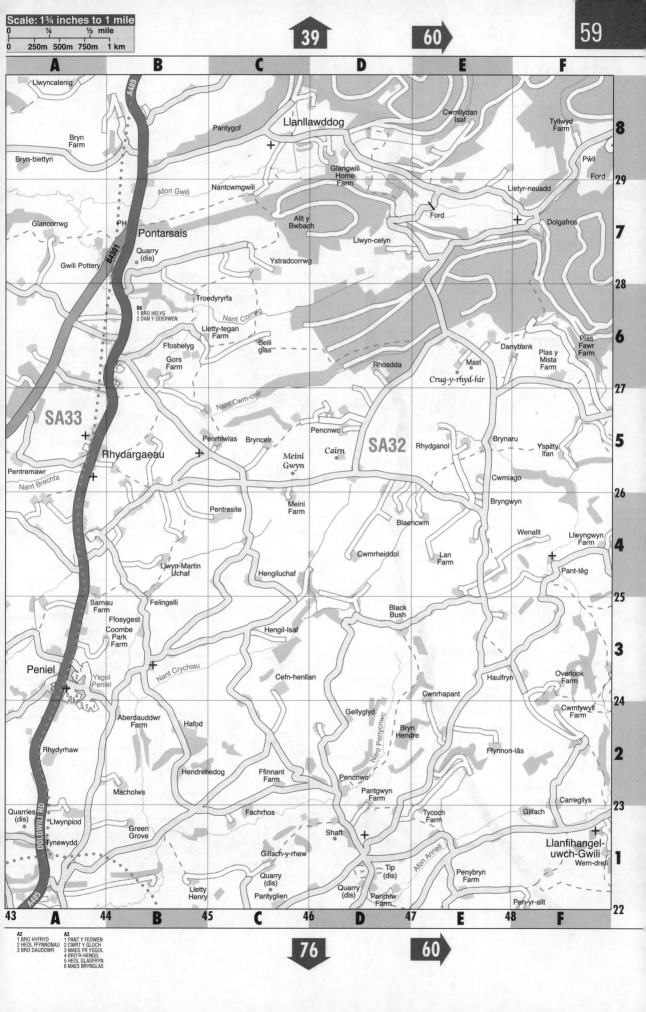

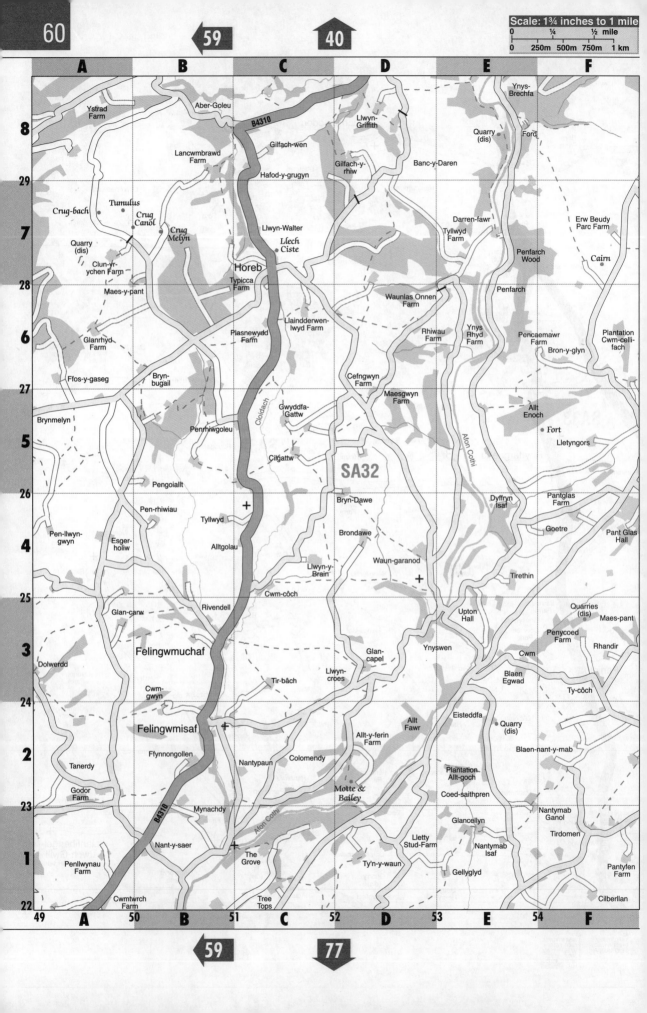

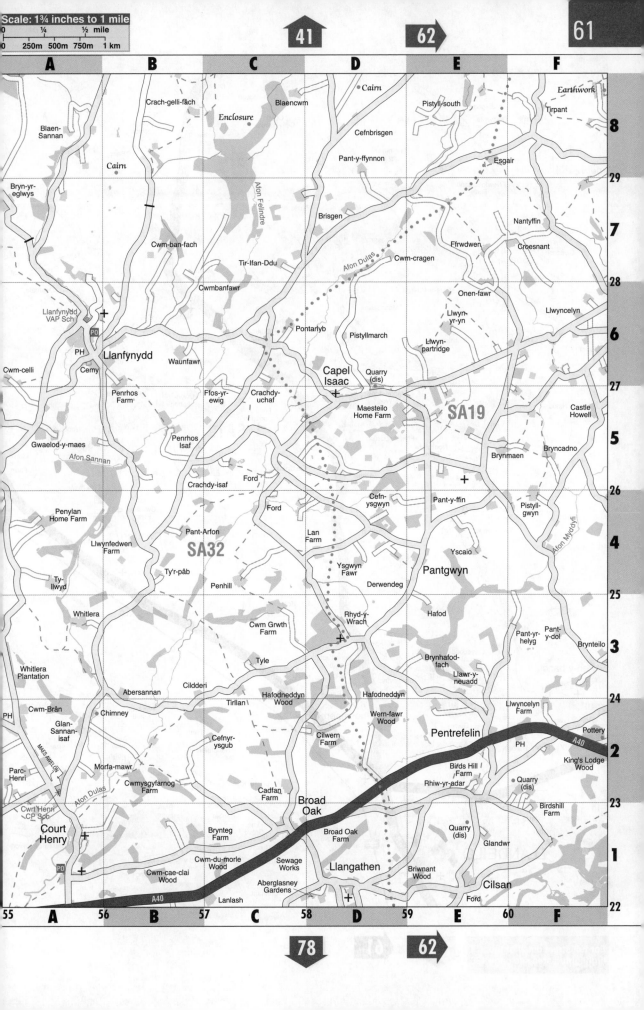

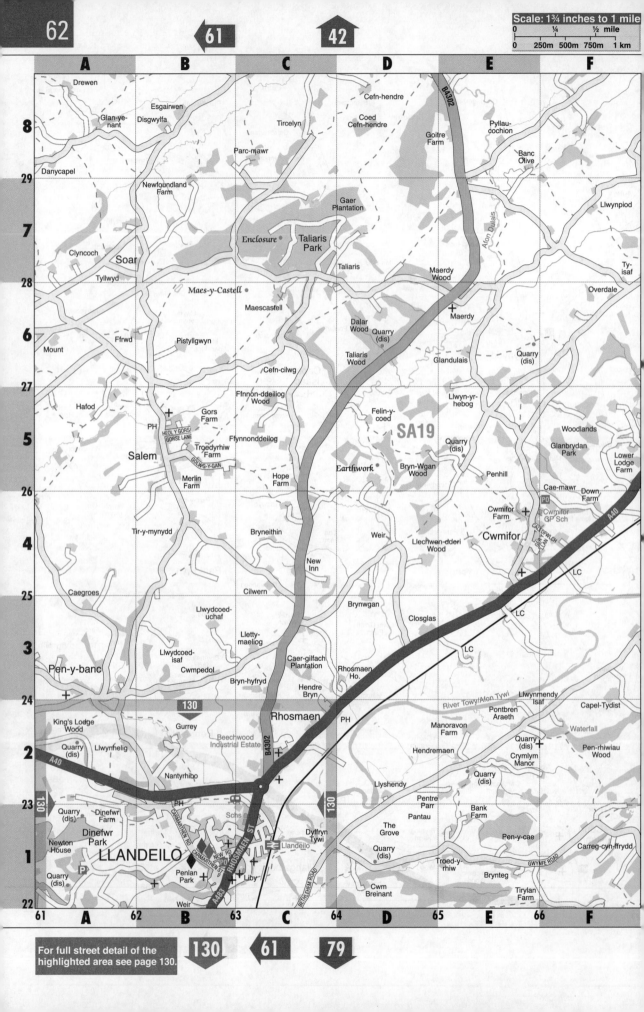

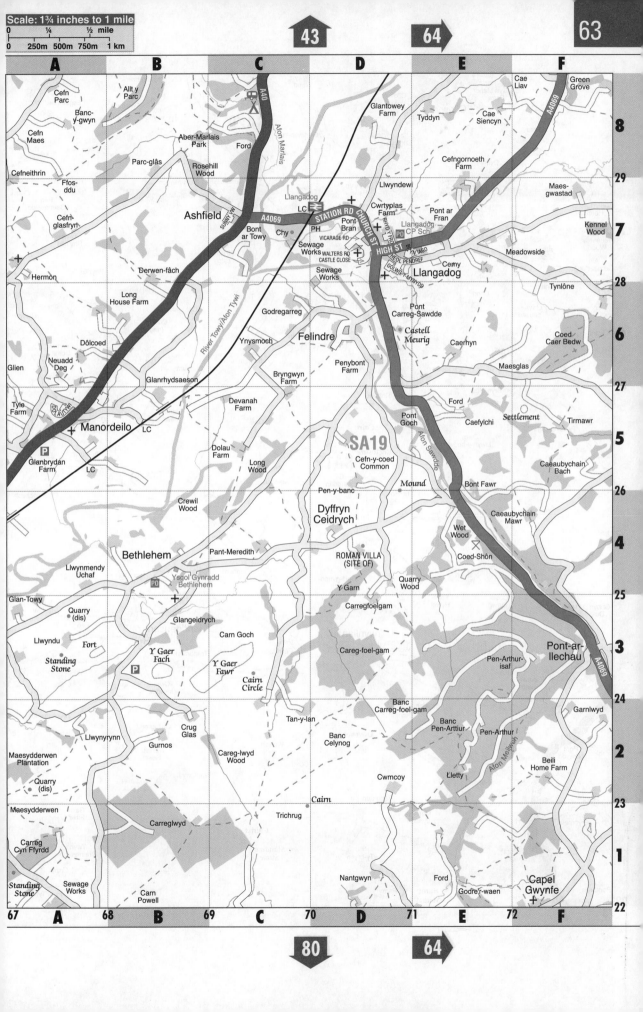

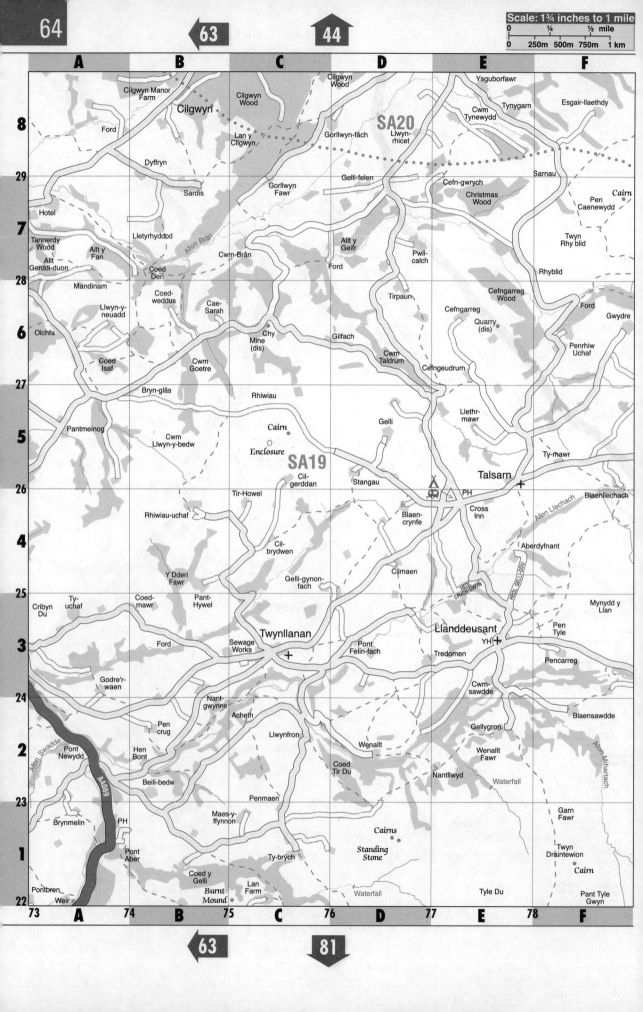

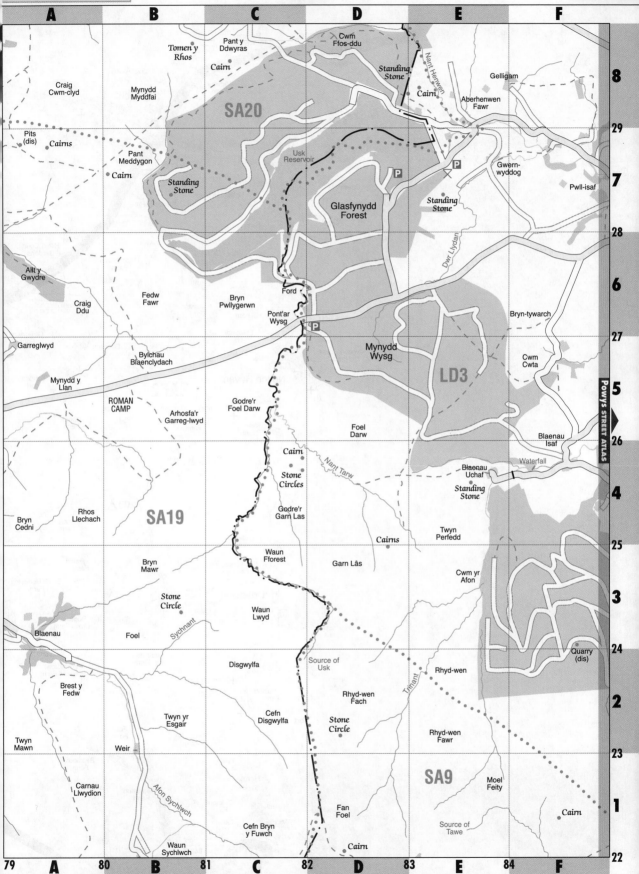

Scale: 1¾ inches to 1 mile

0   ¼   ½   mile
0   250m 500m 750m 1 km

A   B   C   D   E   F

Craig
Cwm-clyd

Tomen y
Rhos

Pant y
Ddwyras

Cwm
Ffos-ddu

Cairn

Standing
Stone

Gelligam

8

Mynydd
Myddfai

SA20

Cairn

Nant Henwen

Cairn

Aberhenwen
Fawr

Pits
(dis)

Cairns

Pant
Meddygon

Usk
Reservoir

P

P

Gwern-
wyddog

29

Cairn

Standing
Stone

Glasfynydd
Forest

Standing
Stone

Pwll-isaf

7

Allt y
Gwydre

Fedw
Fawr

Bryn
Pwllygerwn

Ford

Dwr Llydan

Bryn-tywarch

28

Craig
Ddu

Pont'ar
Wysg

P

Mynydd
Wysg

Cwm
Cwta

6

Garreglwyd

Bylchau
Blaenclydach

LD3

27

Mynydd y
Llan

ROMAN
CAMP

Arhosfa'r
Garreg-lwyd

Godre'r
Foel Darw

Blaenau
Isaf

Powys STREET ATLAS ▶

5

Bryn
Cedni

Rhos
Llechach

SA19

Cairn

Stone
Circles

Godre'r
Garn Las

Foel
Darw

Nant Tarw

Cairns

Blaenau
Uchaf

Standing
Stone

Waterfall

26

Bryn
Mawr

Waun
Fforest

Garn Lâs

Twyn
Perfedd

Cwm yr
Afon

25

Stone
Circle

Waun
Lwyd

Sychnant

Quarry
(dis)

3

Blaenau

Foel

Disgwylfa

Source of
Usk

Rhyd-wen

24

Brest y
Fedw

Twyn yr
Esgair

Cefn
Disgwylfa

Rhyd-wen
Fach

Trinant

Rhyd-wen
Fawr

2

Twyn
Mawn

Weir

Afon Sychlwch

Stone
Circle

SA9

Moel
Feity

Cairn

23

Carnau
Llwydion

Cefn Bryn
y Fuwch

Fan
Foel

Cairn

Source of
Tawe

1

Waun
Sychlwch

79   A   80   B   81   C   82   D   83   E   84   F   22

Scale: 1¾ inches to 1 mile

0   ¼   ½   mile

0   250m   500m   750m   1 km

A   B   C   D   E   F

8   Wood

Porter's Well

WOOD HILL

Hill Side

A487

Southwood

Roch CP Sch

GRASS HOLM CL

Newgale Sands

Midway Farm

PH

Roch

Castle

21   Sibbernock Point

ST BRID ST CW

Church Hill

PILGRIMS WY

PO

CASTLE CL

Chapel Farm

Bathesland Water

Bathesland Wood

CHURCH RD

Motel

7   Caves

Folkeston Moor

Maidenhall Point

Rainbolts Hill Farm

Little Hilton

Hilton Court Gardens

20   Trefrane Farm

FOLKESTON ROAD

Hilton Home Farm

A487

6   WELSH ROAD

Folly

Folkeston Hill Farm

Folkeston Farm

SUMMERHILL CL 1
KEEP HILL END 2

19   Shaft (dis)

Black Cliff

FOLKESTON LN

Folkeston Hill

Simpson

Greenacre Farm

Rickets Head

Nolton Haven Farm

Simpson Hill

5   Nolton Haven

SA62

Trapps Farm

Nolton Haven

Nolton Haven

Nolton

East Nolton Farm

Cemy

North Nolton Farm

WEST LANE

18   Madoc's Haven

Pembrokeshire Coast Path

Longlands Farm

South Nolton Farm

Hill Side

4   Druidston Haven

Marlsborough Farm

Quarry (dis)

17   Shortlands Farm

Rogeston Farm

South Rogeston Farm

Hotel

LEYS LANE

3   Druidston

New House Farm

Rogeston Cross Farm

16   Haroldston Chins

Haroldston Hall Farm

Quarry

Haroldston Tonges Farm

Settling Nose

Haroldston Farm

Haroldston West

2   Black Point

Fort

Timber Hill Farm

Folly Farm

Broomsgrove Farm

Bellmoor Farm

15   HAROLDSTON HILL

Timber Hill

LONG LANE

Harold Stone

Williamston Farm

1   Sleek Stone

Headlands

Belmont Farm

TASKERS LANE

Millmoor

Quarry (dis)

B4341

MILLMOOR WY

B4341

14

83   A   84   B   85   C   86   D   87   E   88   F

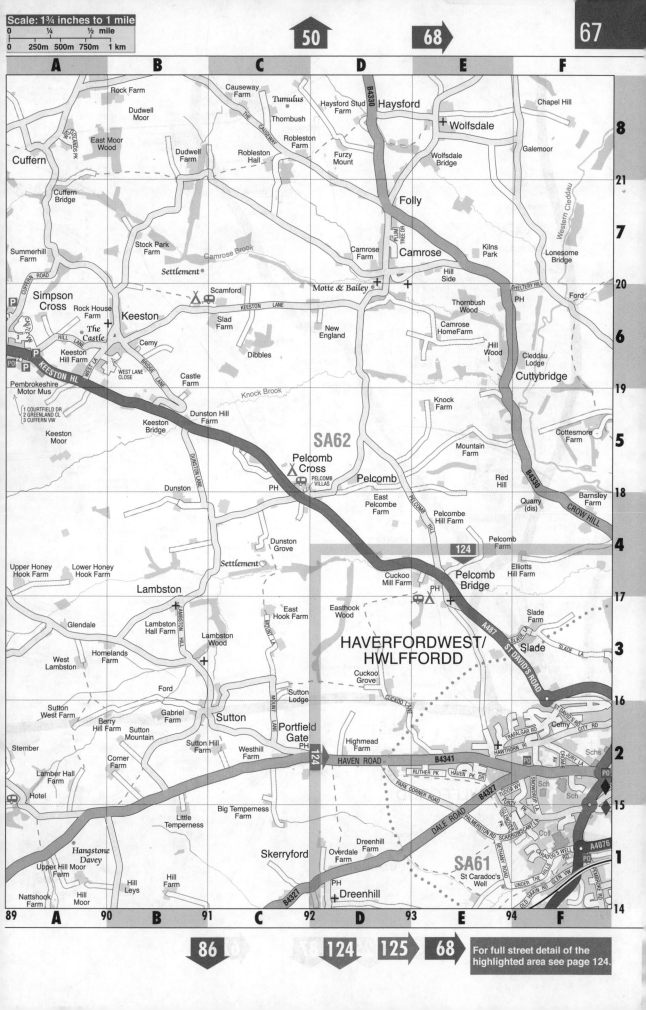

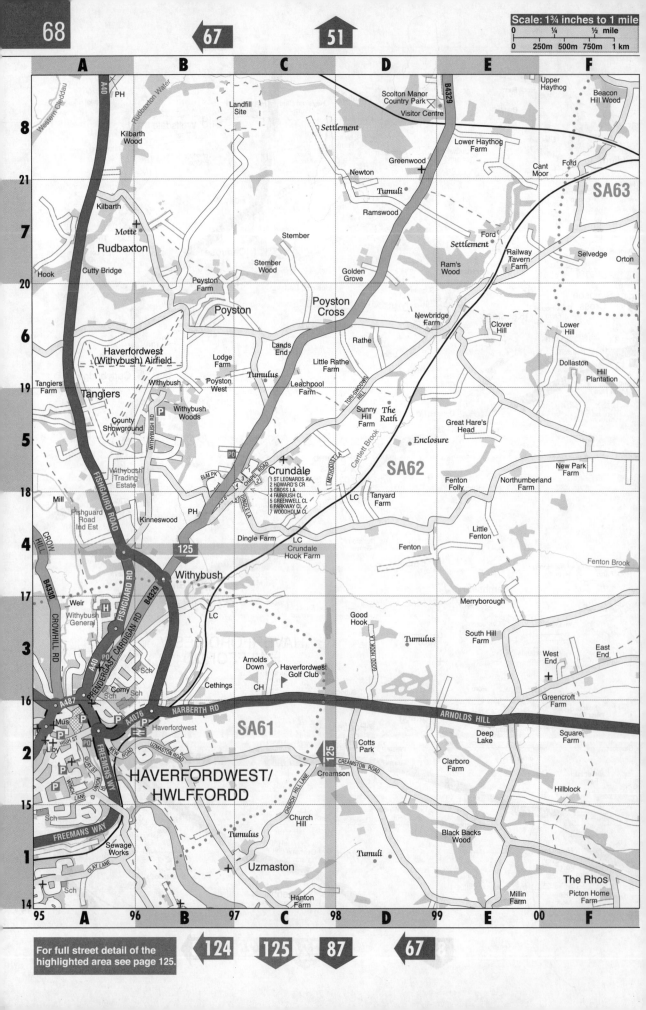

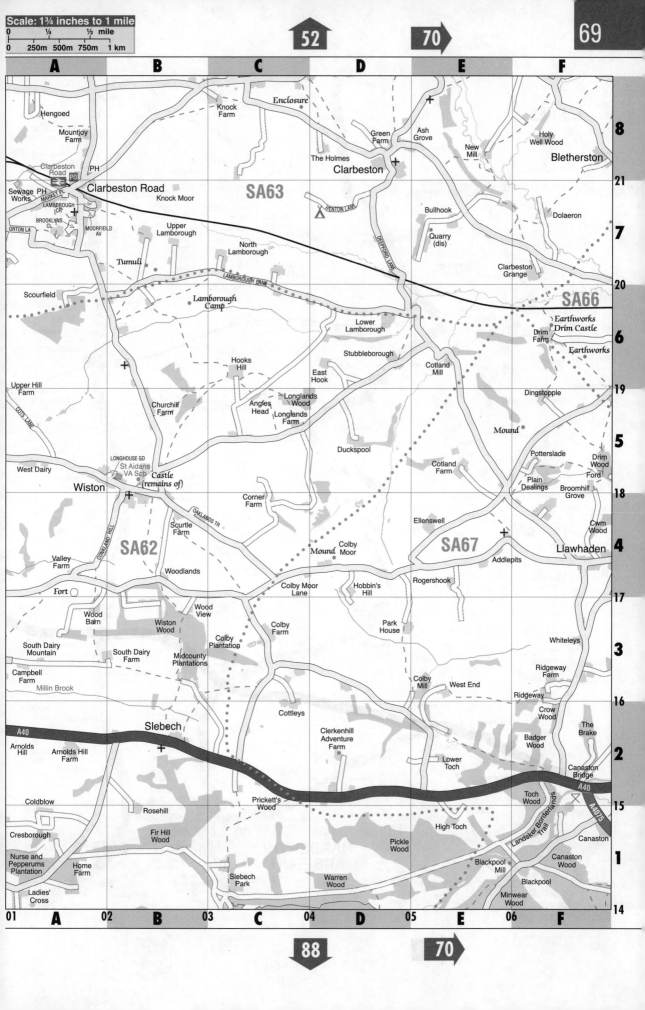

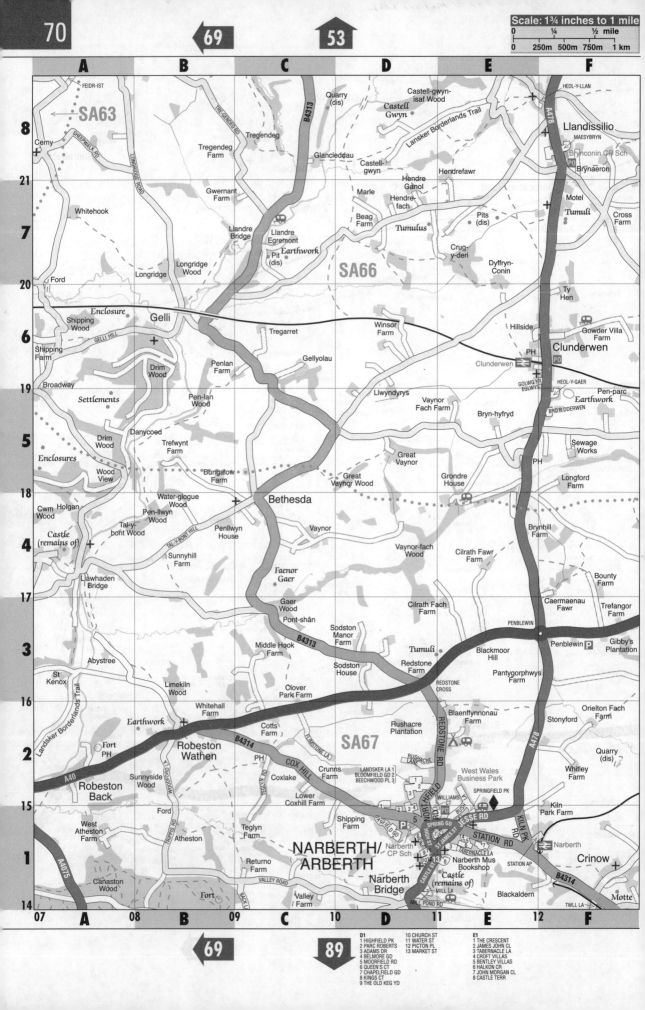

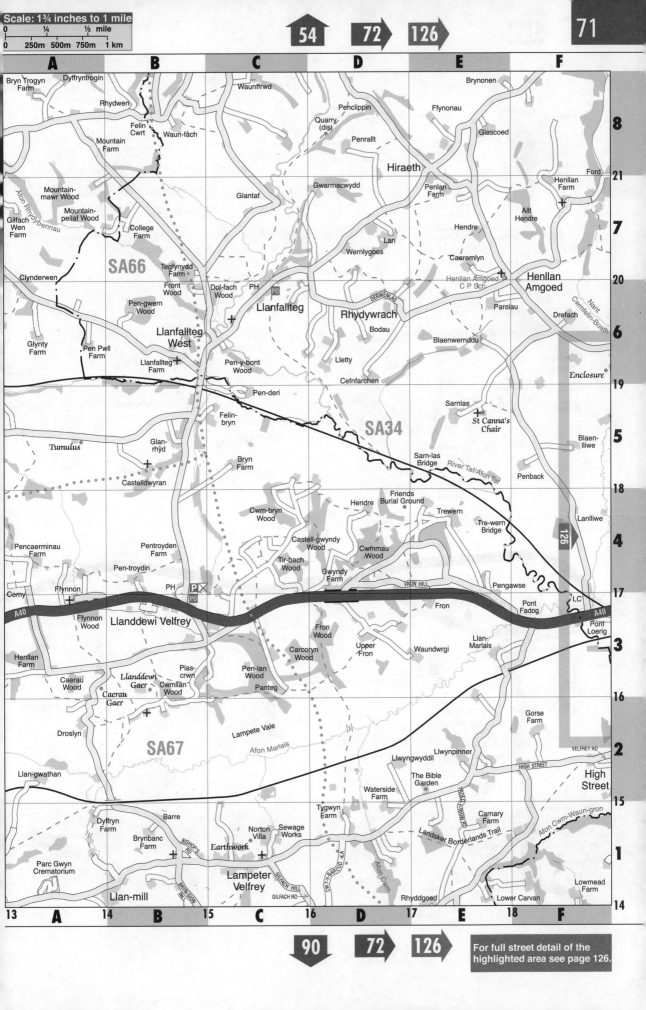

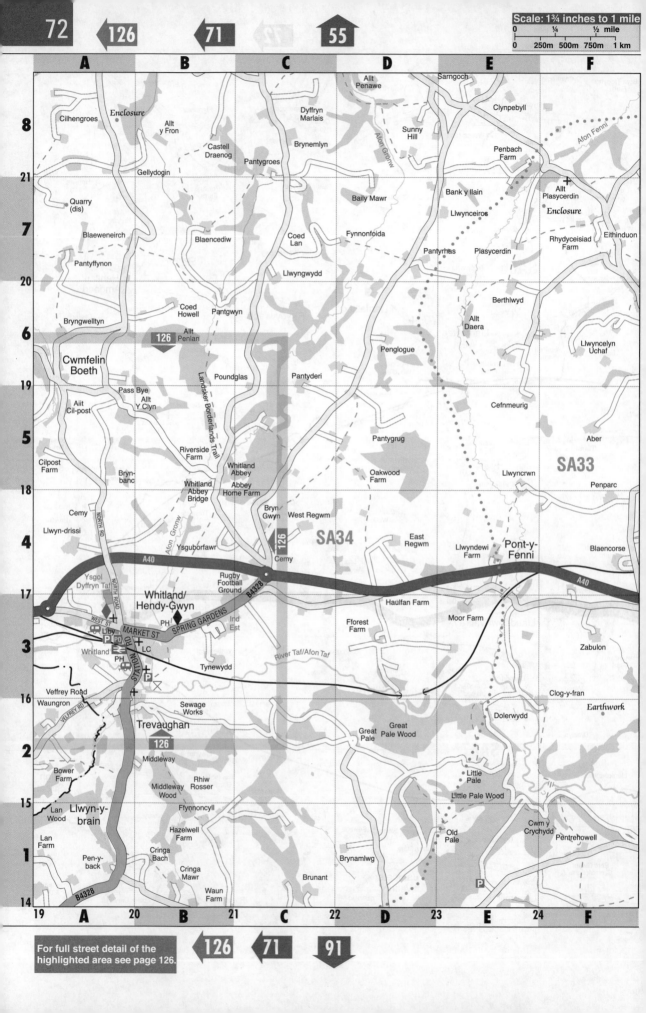

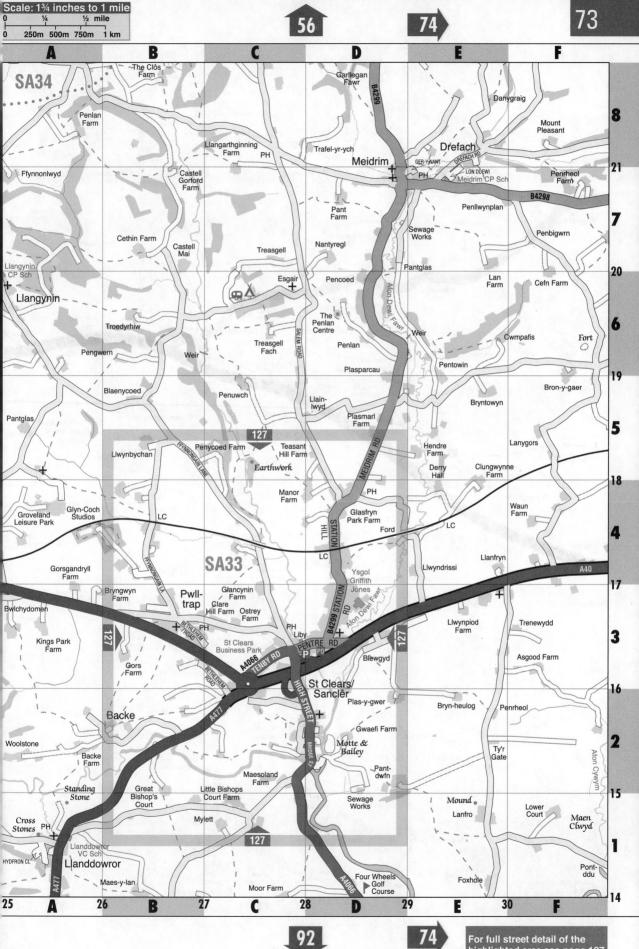

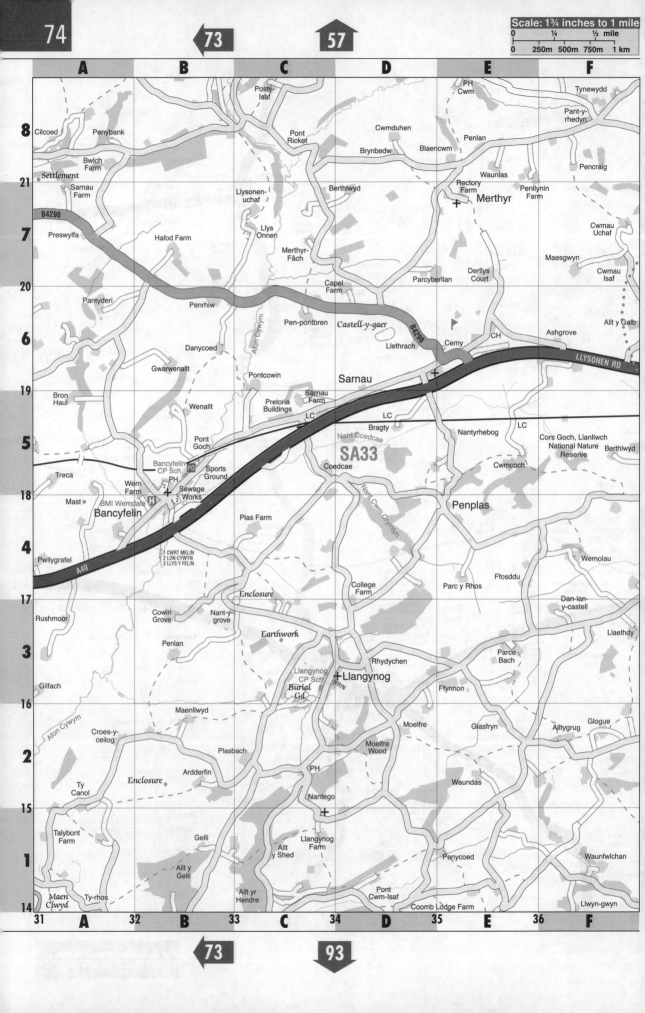

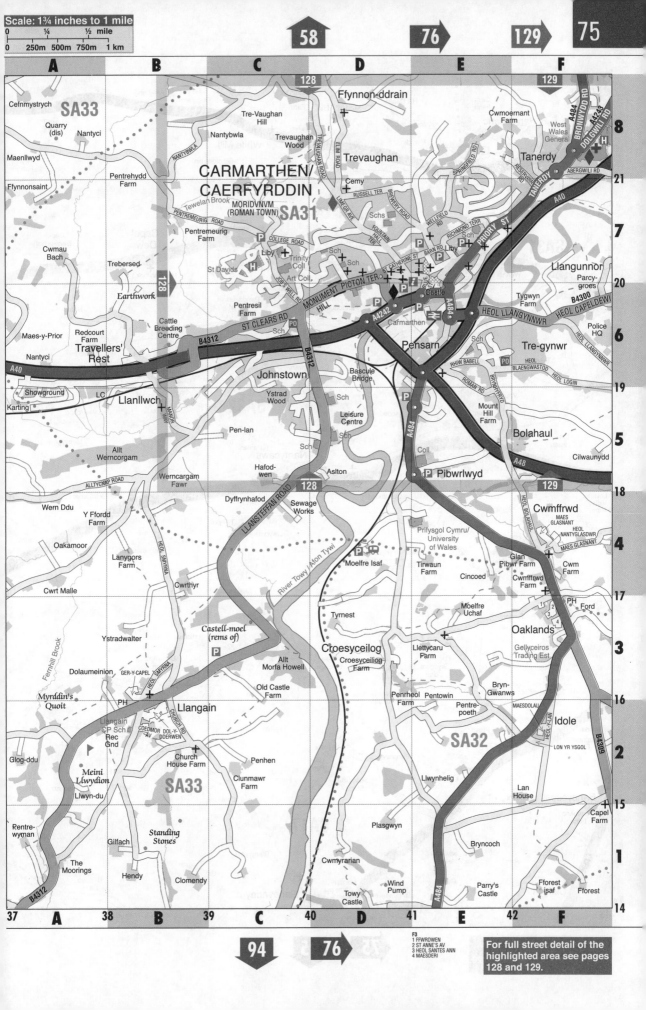

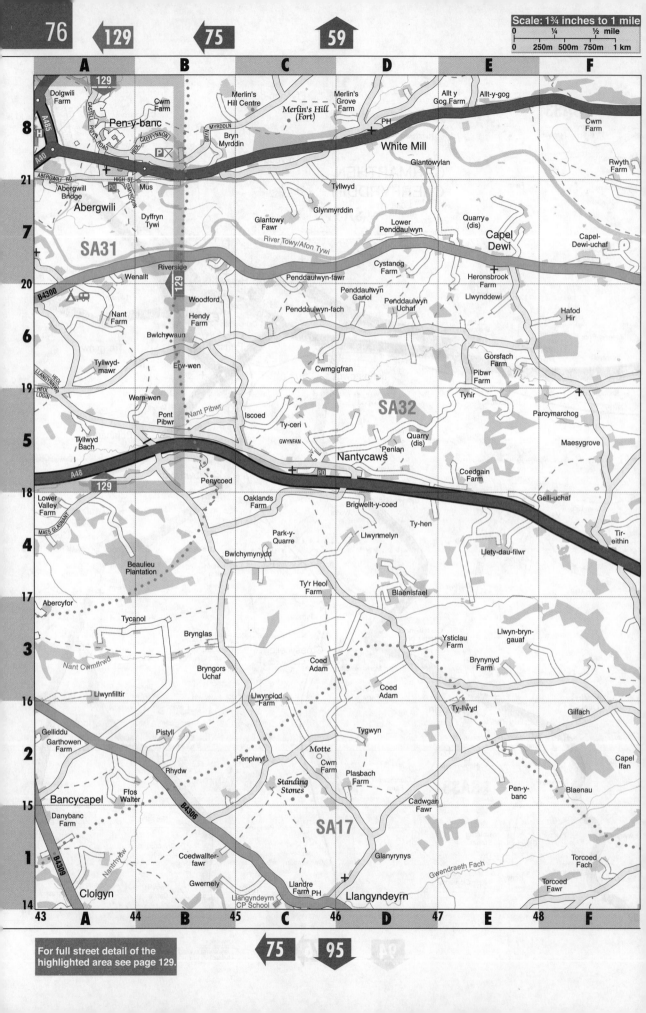

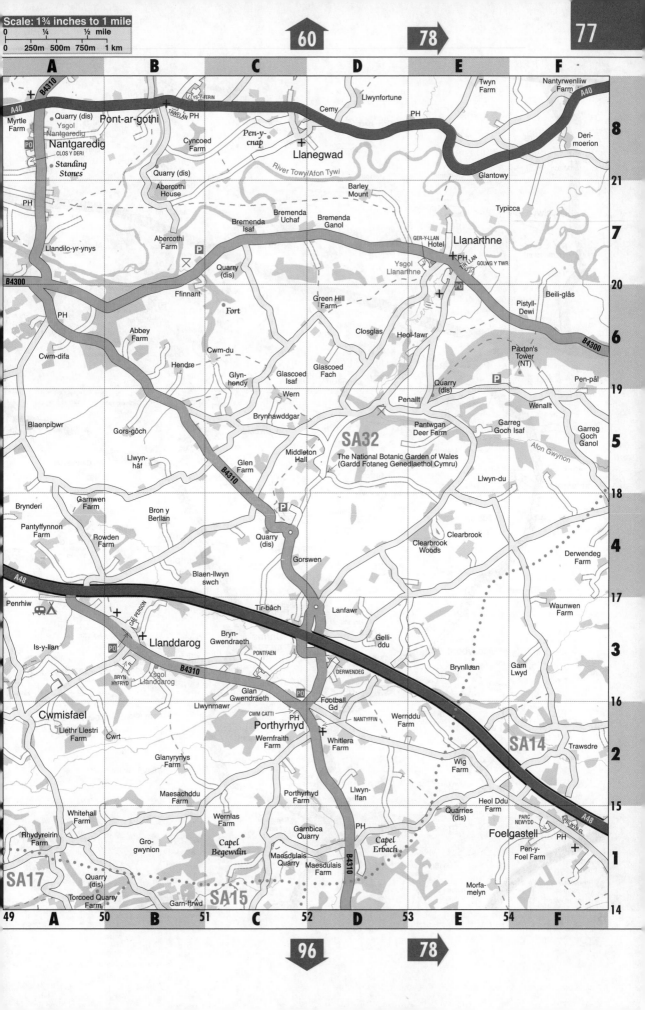

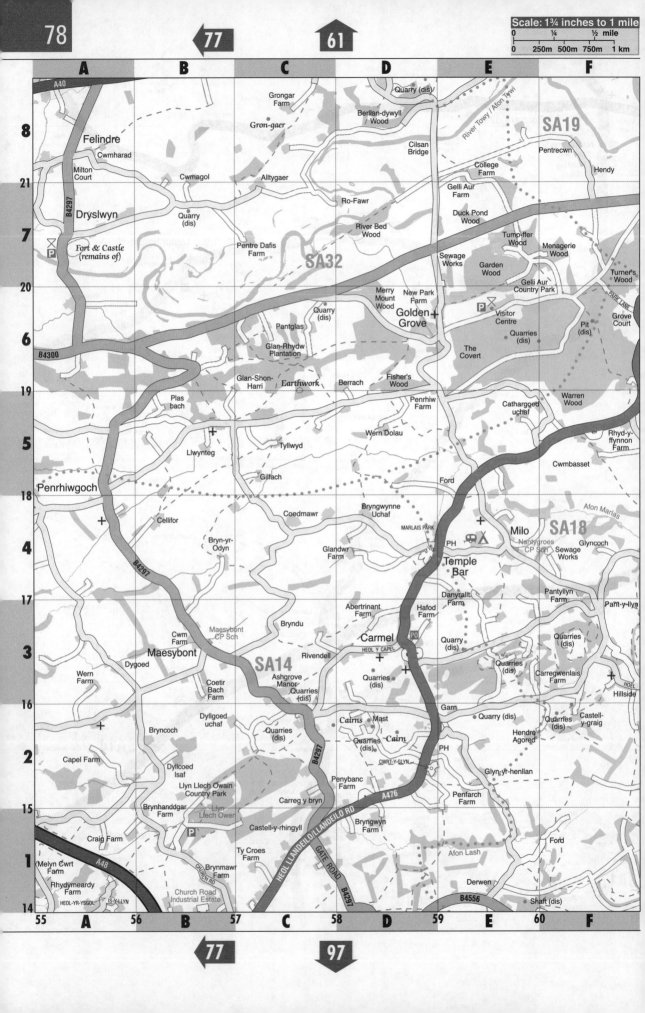

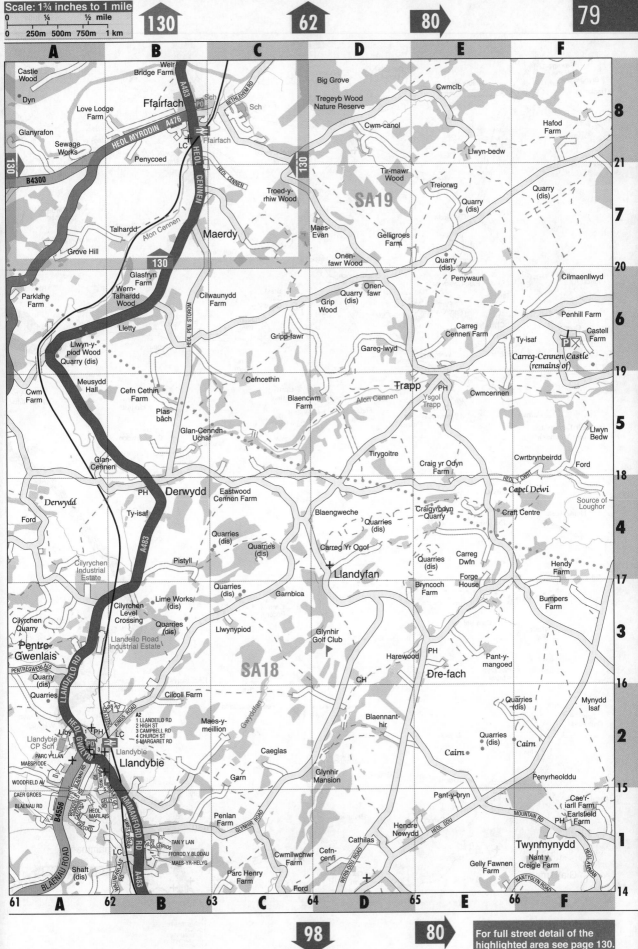

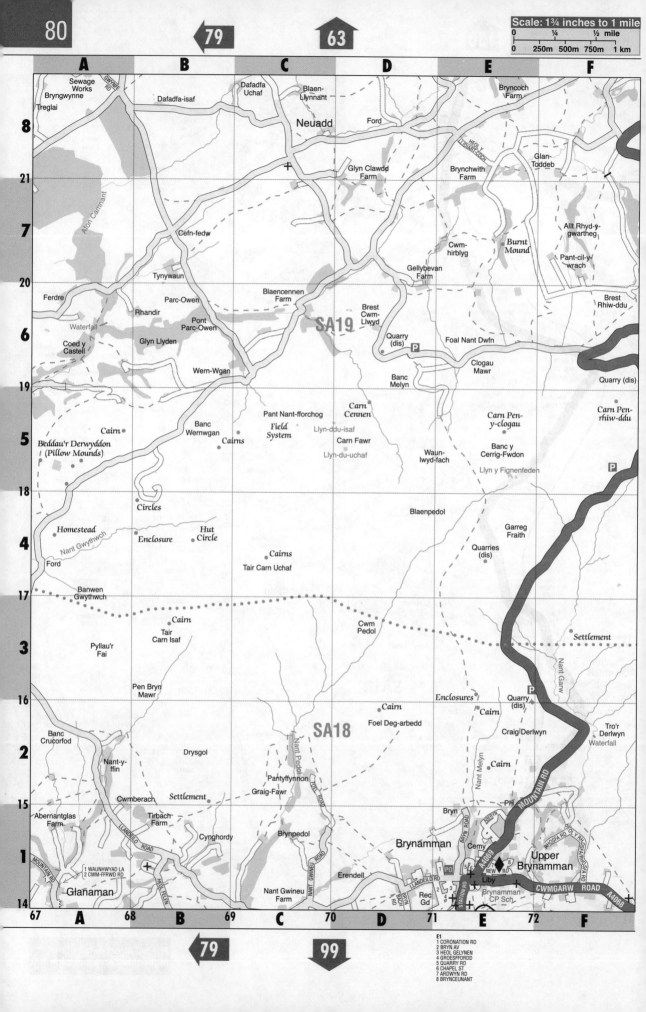

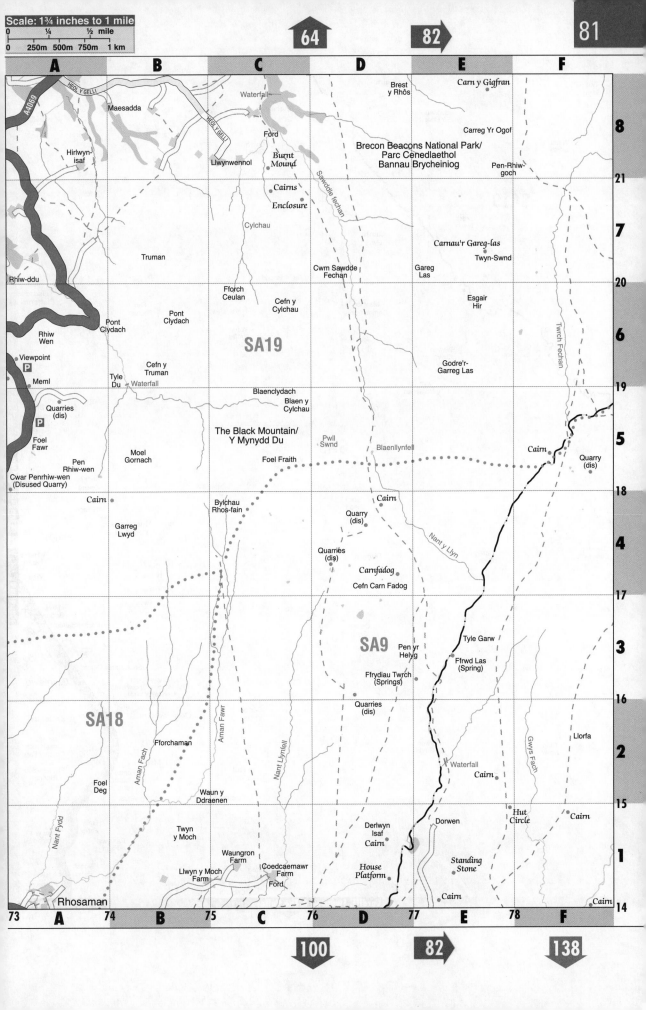

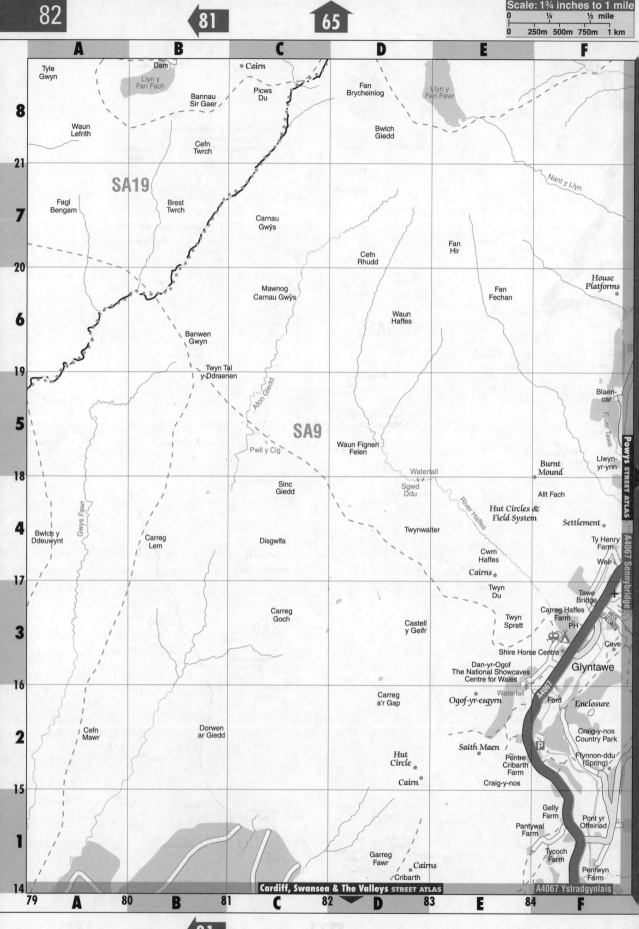

Scale: 1¾ inches to 1 mile

0   ¼   ½   mile
0   250m 500m 750m 1 km

A   **B**   **C**   **D**   **E**   **F**

8

Tyle
Gwyn   Dam   Cairn

Llyn y
Fan Fach   Bannau   Picws   Fan
Sir Gaer   Du   Brycheiniog   Llyn y
Fan Fawr

Waun   Bwlch
Lefrith   Cefn   Giedd
Twrch
21

SA19   Nant y Llyn

7
Fagl   Brest   Carnau
Bengam   Twrch   Gwŷs   Fan
Hir

Cefn   House
20   Rhudd   Platforms

Mawnog   Fan
6   Carnau Gwŷs   Waun   Fechan
Banwen   Haffes
Gwyn

Twyn Tal   Blaen-
y Ddraenen   car

5   Waun Fignen
Pwll y Cig   Felen   Burnt   Llwyn-
SA9   Mound   yr-ynn

Waterfall

18   Sinc   Sgwd   Allt Fach
Giedd   Ddu
Hut Circles &
Gwys Fawr   Field System   Settlement

4   Bwlch y   Twynwalter
Ddeuwynt   Carreg   Ty Henry
Lem   Disgwlfa   Farm

Cwm   Weir
Haffes
17   Cairns
Twyn
Du   Twyn   Tawe
Carreg   Spratt   Bridge
3   Goch   Castell
y Geifr   Carreg Haffes
Shire Horse Centre   Farm PH

Dan-yr-Ogof   Cave
16   The National Showcaves
Carreg   Centre for Wales   Glyntawe
a'r Gap   Ogof-yr-esgyrn Waterfall   Ford   Enclosure

2   Cefn   Dorwen   Craig-y-nos
Mawr   ar Giedd   Hut   Saith Maen   Pentre   Country Park
Circle   Cribarth   Ffynnon-ddu
Cairn   Craig-y-nos   Farm   (Spring)

15
Gelly
Farm   Pont yr
Pantywal   Offeiriad
Garreg   Cairns   Farm
1   Fawr   Tycoch
Cribarth   Farm   Pentwyn
Farm

14
Cardiff, Swansea & The Valleys STREET ATLAS   A4067 Ystradgynlais

79   **A**   **80**   **B**   **81**   **C**   **82**   **D**   **83**   **E**   **84**   **F**

Powys STREET ATLAS   A4067 Sennybridge

Scale: 1¾ inches to 1 mile

0   ¼   ½ mile

0   250m   500m   750m   1 km

A   **B**   **C**   **D**   **E**   **F**

8

13

7

12

6

St Brides Bay

11

5

Garland
Stone

Skomer Marine
Nature Reserve

10

Bull Hole

Waybench

Settlement

The
Table

Settlement

Ferry P
(summer only)

Tusker
Rock

Wooltack
Point

Haven
Point

High
Point

4

Skomer Island
National Nature
Reserve

Settlement

North
Haven

Exhibition
Centre

09

Pigstone
Bay

End Wall
Ridge

The Neck

Midland
Isle

Jack
Sound

Pig
Stone

Settlement

Gorse
Hill

Fort

SA62

Skomer
Head

Settlement

South
Haven

Thorn
Rock

The
Anvil

Renny Slip

3

The Basin

The Wick

Shag
Rock

Skomer Marine
Nature Reserve

Deadman's
Bay

Mew
Stone

The
Bench

Fort

08

Rainy
Rock

2

Broad Sound

07

1

06

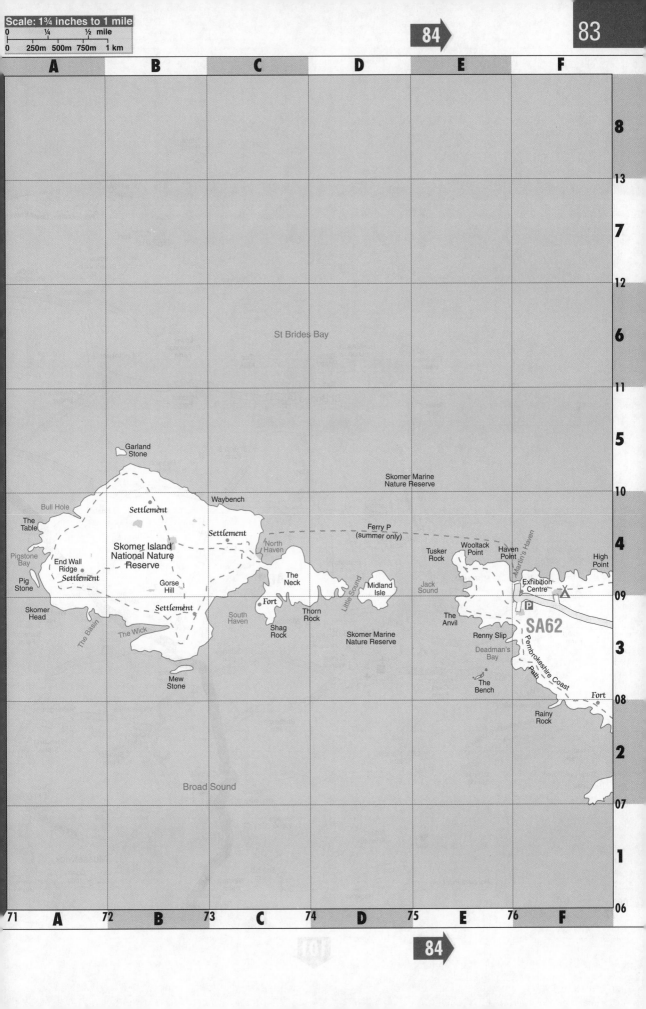

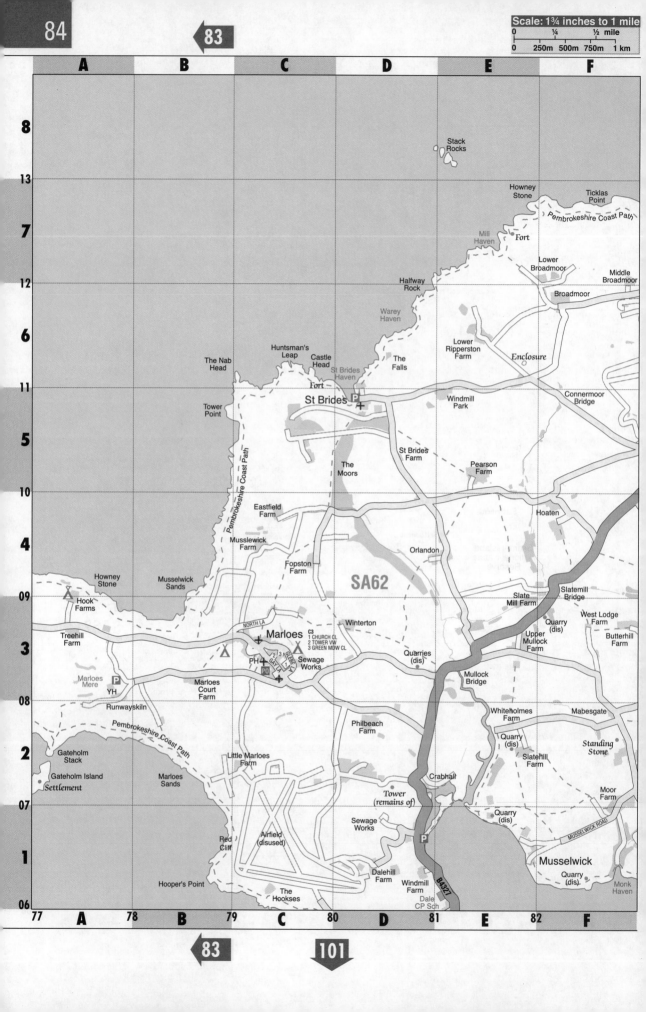

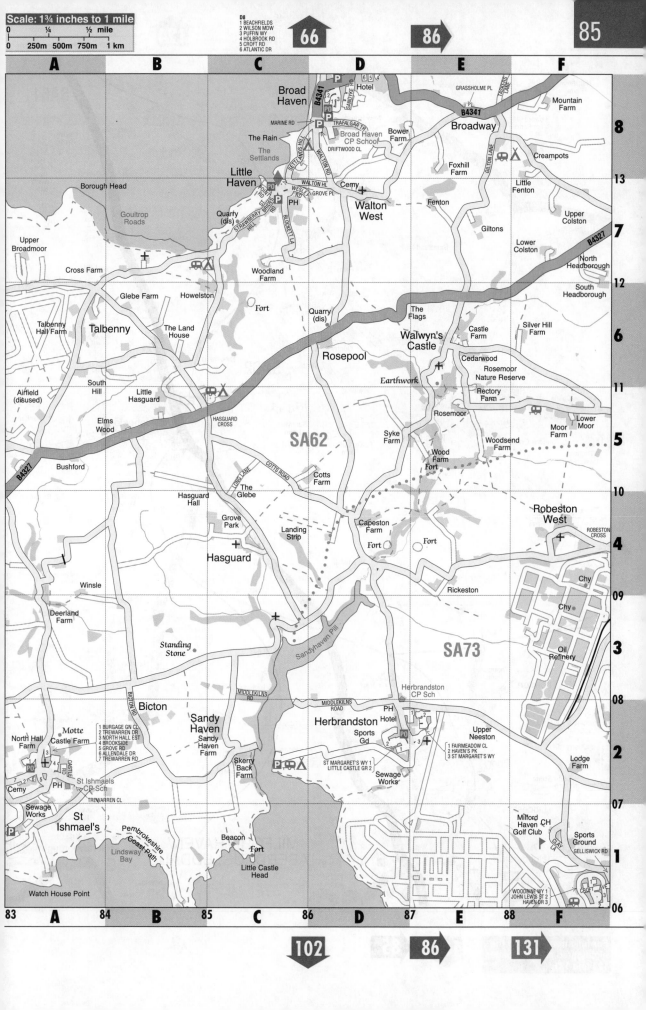

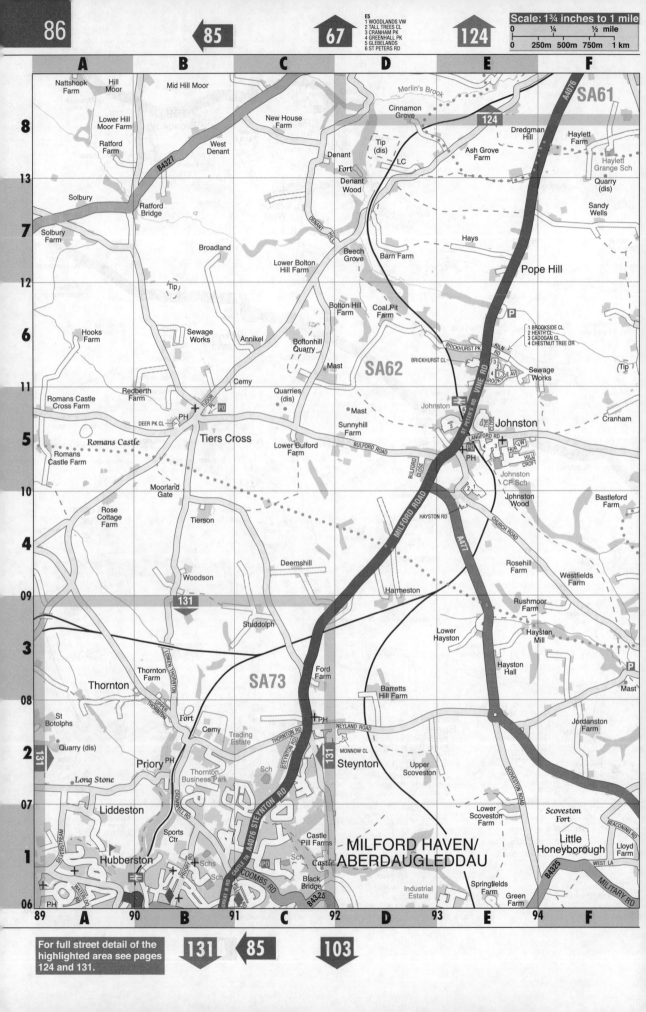

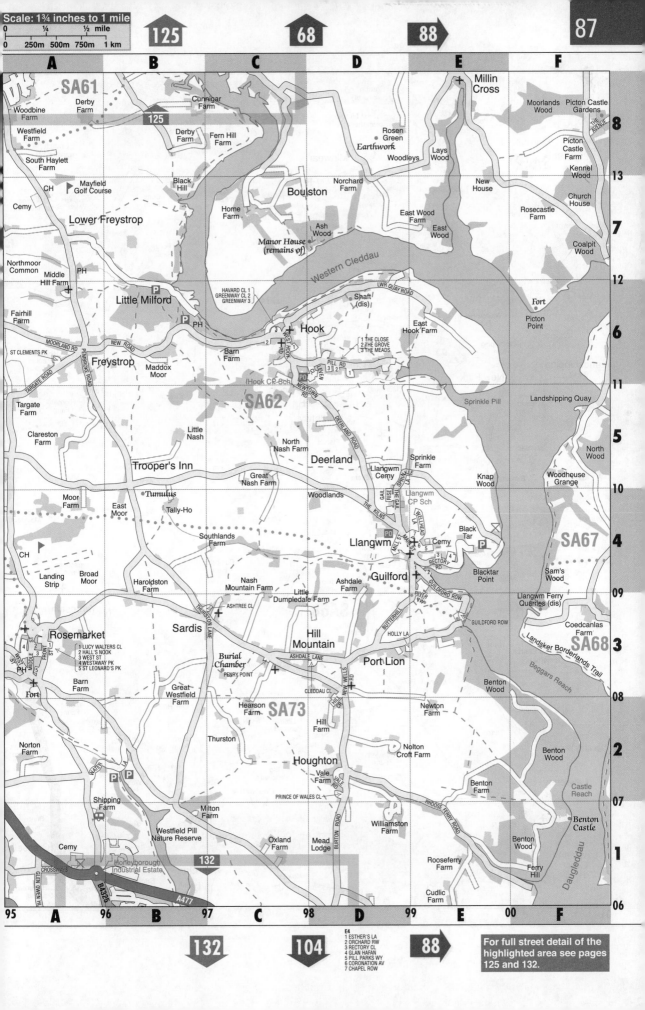

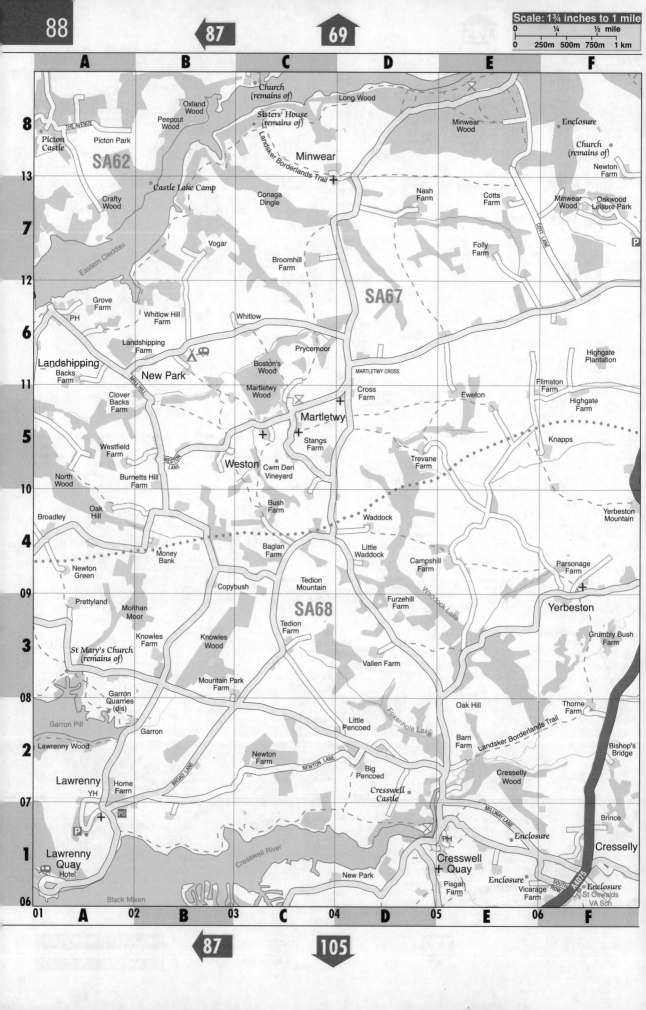

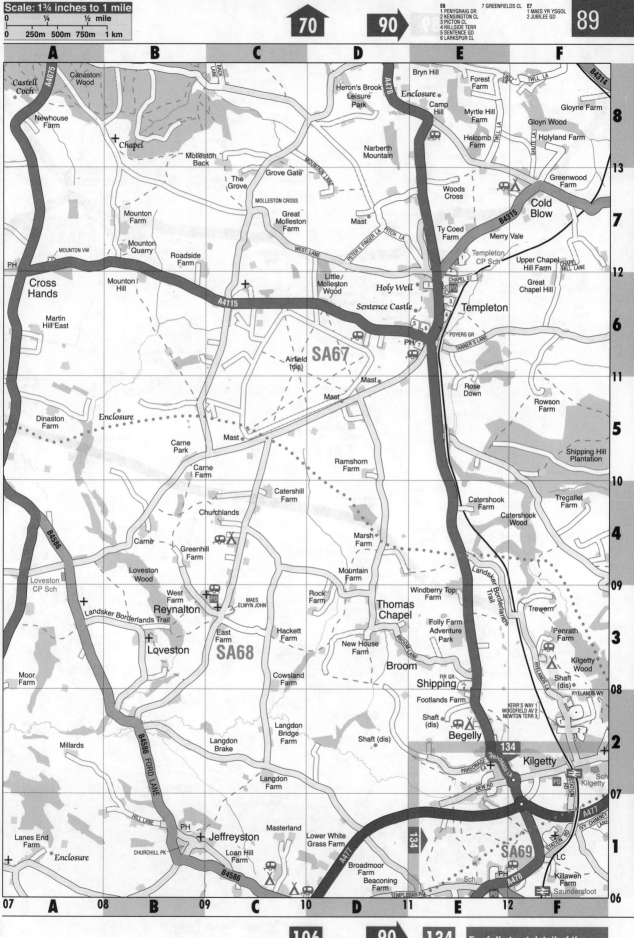

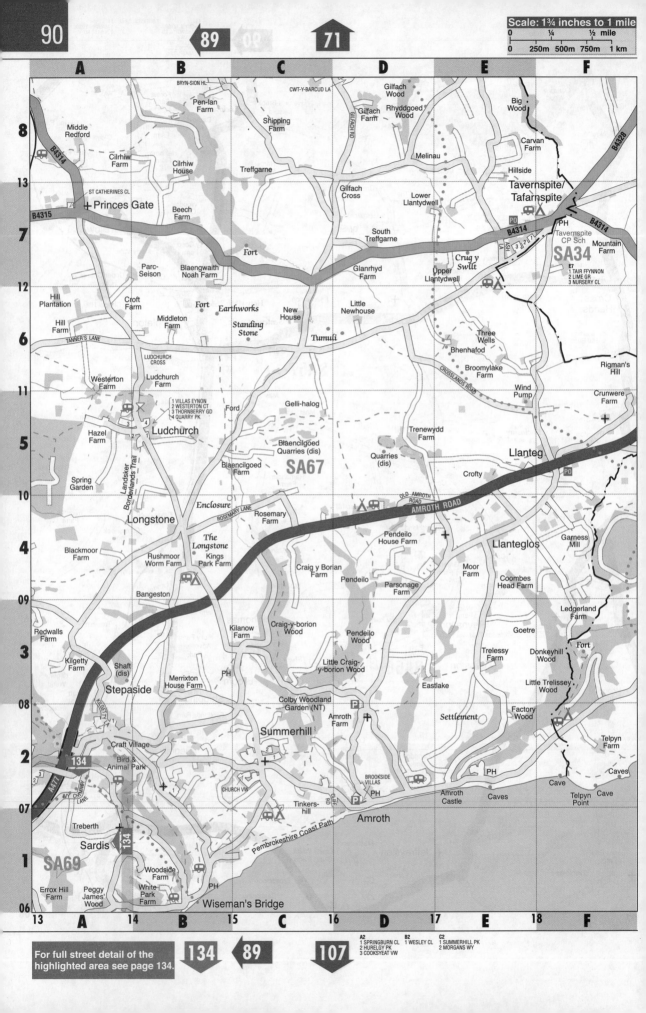

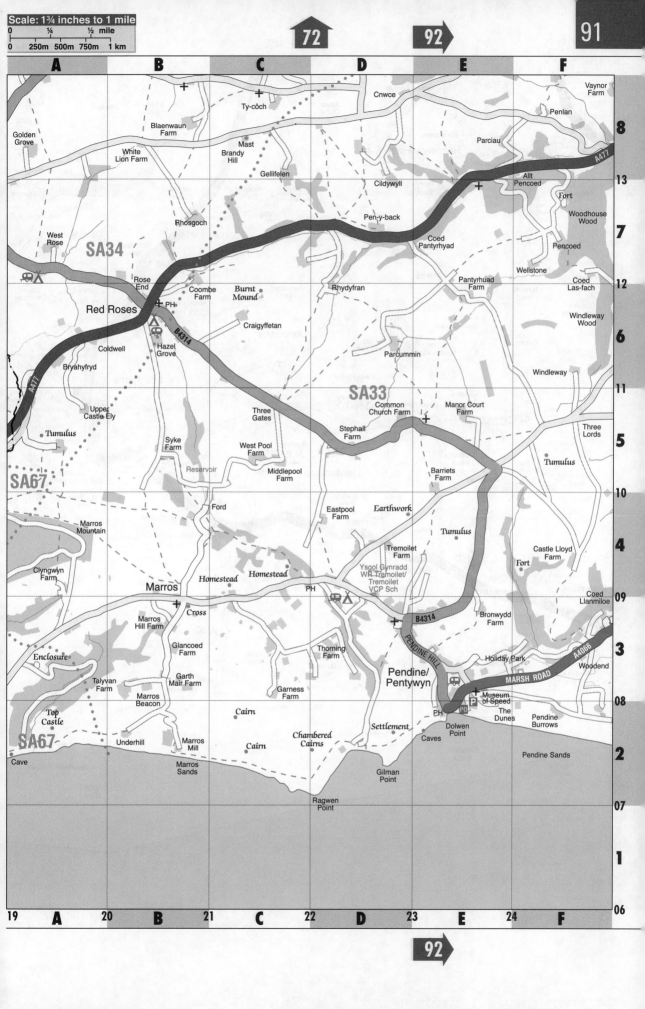

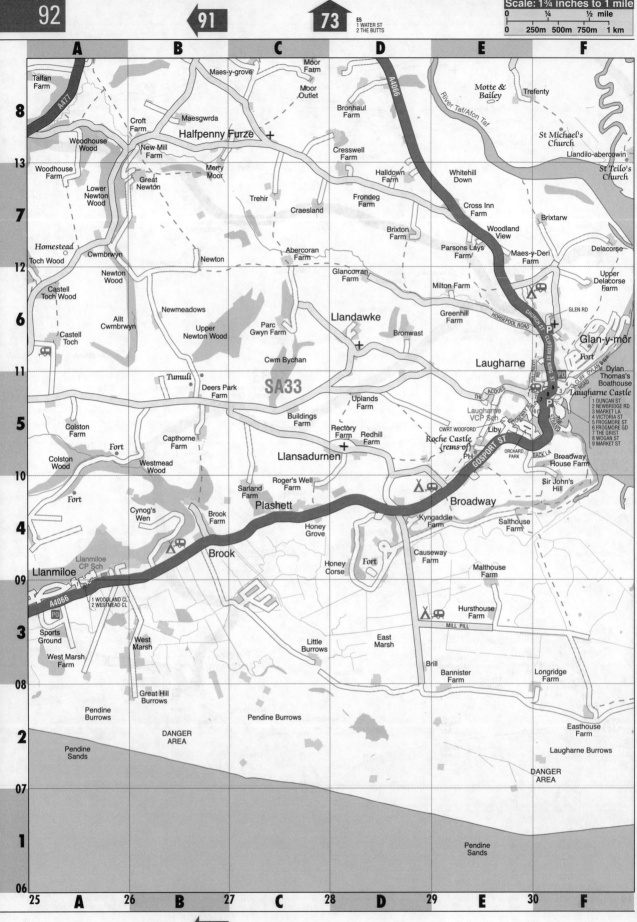

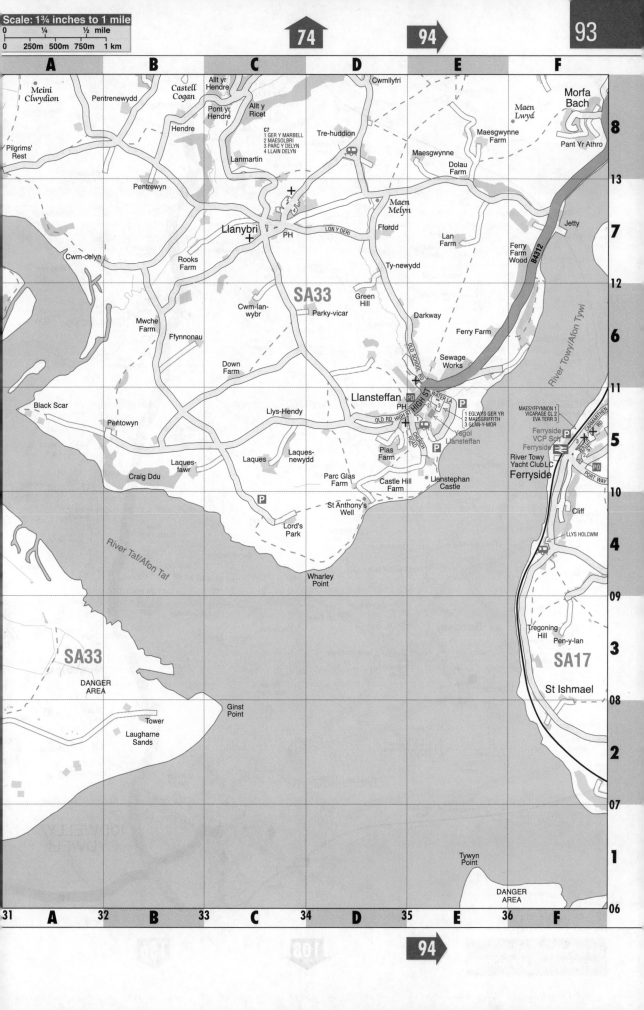

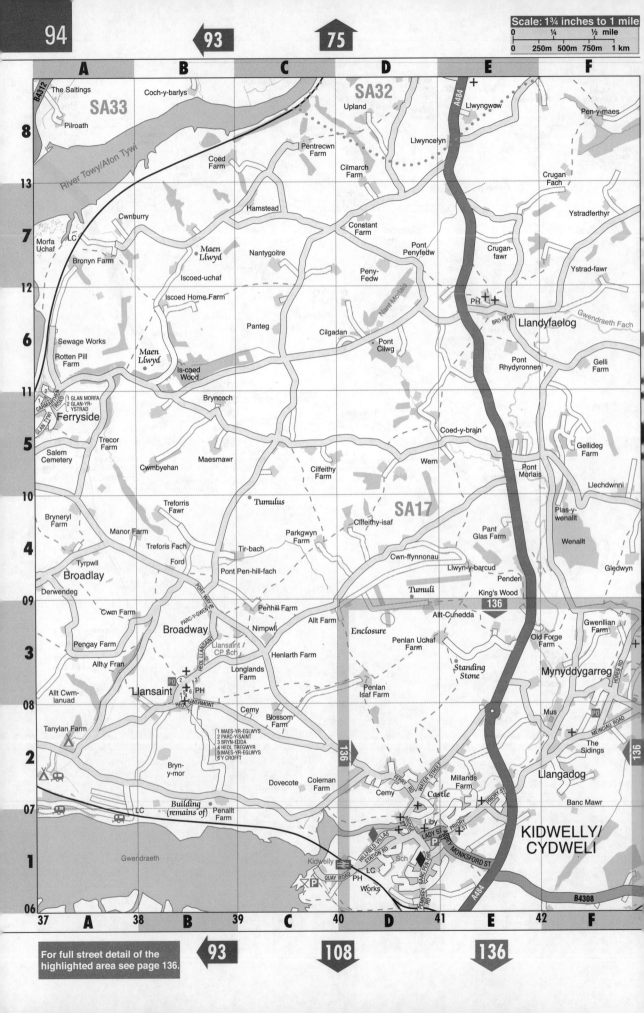

A   B   C   D   E   F

8
B4312   The Saltings
SA33   Coch-y-barlys
Pilroath
SA32
Upland
Llwyngwow
Pen-y-maes
A484

13
River Towy/Afon Tywi
Coed Farm
Pentrecwn Farm
Cilmarch Farm
Llwyncelyn
Crugan Fach
Ystradferthyr

7
Morfa Uchaf
LC
Cwnburry
Hamstead
Constant Farm
Pont Penyfedw
Crugan-fawr
Ystrad-fawr
Bronyn Farm
Maen Llwyd
Nantygoitre
Peny-Fedw

12
Iscoed-uchaf
Iscoed Home Farm
PH
Bro-Pedr
Llandyfaelog
Gwendraeth Fach

6
Sewage Works
Rotten Pill Farm
Maen Llwyd
Panteg
Cilgadan
Pont Cilwg
Nant Morlais
Pont Rhydyronnen
Gelli Farm

11
1 GLAN MORFA
2 GLAN-YR-YSTRAD
Is-coed Wood
Bryncoch
Coed-y-brain
Pont Morlais
CARMARTHEN ROAD
GLAN TYW
Ferryside

5
Salem Cemetery
Trecor Farm
Wern
Gellideg Farm
Cwmbyehan
Maesmawr
Cilfeithy Farm
Llechdwnni

10
Bryneryl Farm
Treforris Fawr
Tumulus
Cilfeithy-isaf
SA17
Plas-y-wenallt
Pant Glas Farm
Wenallt

4
Tyrpwll
Manor Farm
Treforis Fach
Ford
Tir-bach
Parkgwyn Farm
Cwn-ffynnonau
Llwyn-y-barcud
Penderi
Gledwyn
Broadlay
Derwendeg
Pont Pen-hill-fach
Tumuli
King's Wood

09
Cwm Farm
Penhill Farm
Allt Farm
Allt-Cunedda
Old Forge Farm
Gwenllian Farm
136

3
Pengay Farm
Broadway
Nimpwll
Enclosure
Penlan Uchaf Farm
Standing Stone
Mynyddygarreg
Allt y Fran
Llansaint CP Sch
Llanarth Farm
HEOL LLANSAINT
PARC-Y-GWENYN
HOREB RD

Allt Cwm-lanuad
PO
Llansaint
PH
Longlands Farm
Penlan Isaf Farm
Mus
PO
MEINCIAU ROAD

8
HEOL GWERMONT
Cemy
Blossom Farm
The Sidings

Tanylan Farm
1 MAES-YR-EGLWYS
2 PARC-Y-SAINT
3 BRYN-EDDA
4 HEOL TREGWYR
5 MAES-YR-EGLWYS
6 Y CROFFT
Llangadog
136

2
Bryn-y-mor
Dovecote
Coleman Farm
Cemy
FERRY RD
WATER STREET
Millands Farm
Banc Mawr
136

07
LC
Building (remains of)
Penallt Farm
Castle
Liby
PRIORY ST
KIDWELLY/CYDWELI
HILLFIELD VILLAS
STATION RD
BRIDGE ST
LADY ST
PRIORY ST
MONKSFORD ST

1
Gwendraeth
Kidwelly
LC
PH
Works
QUAY ROAD
P
Sch
BANC PEN-DRE
A484
B4308
PEMBREY RD

06
37   A   38   B   39   C   40   D   41   E   42   F

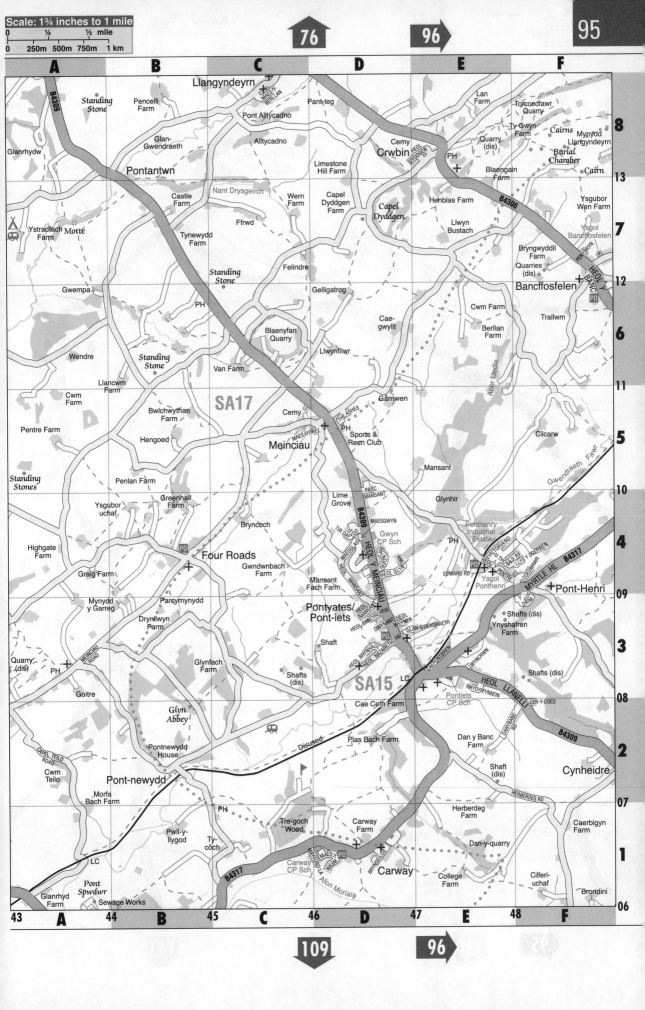

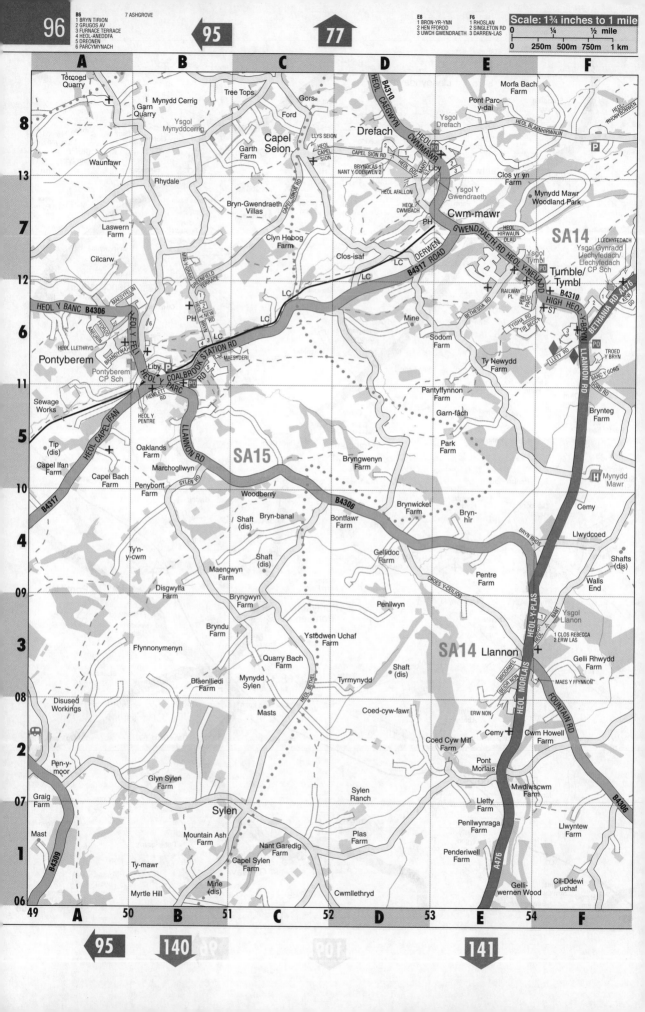

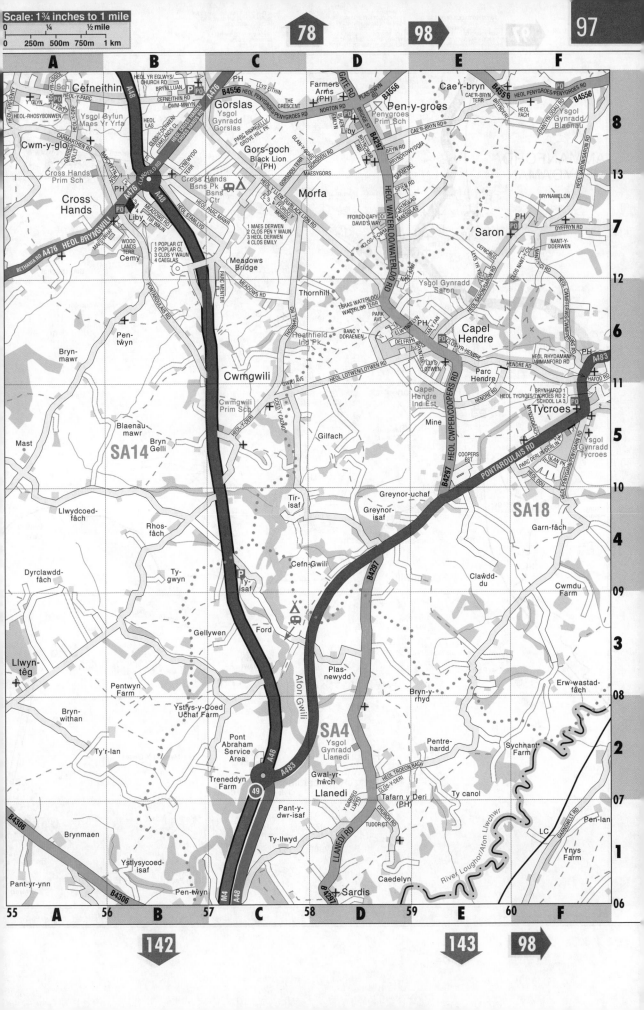

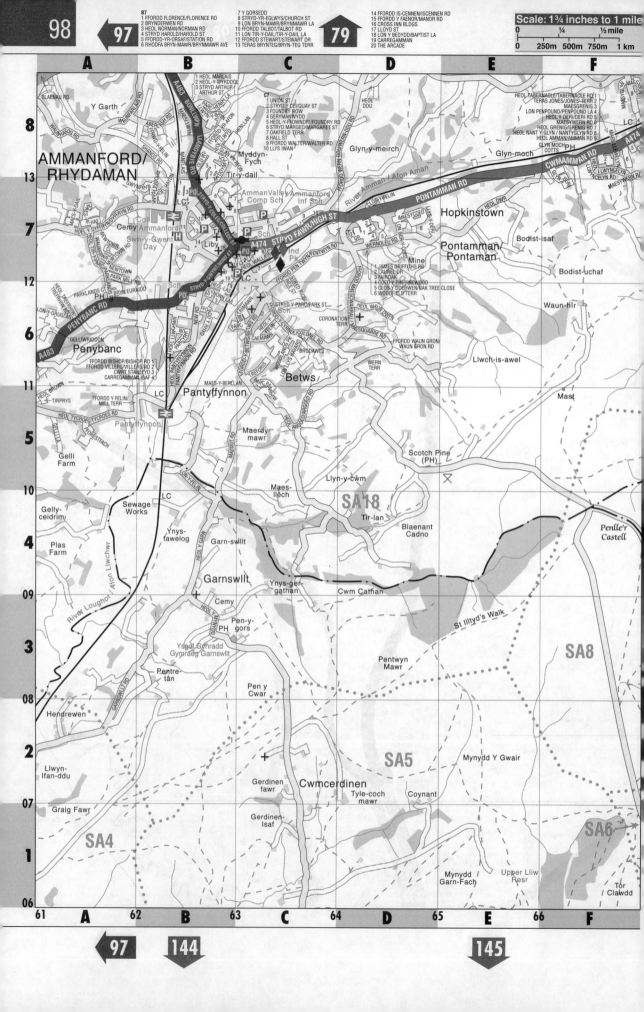

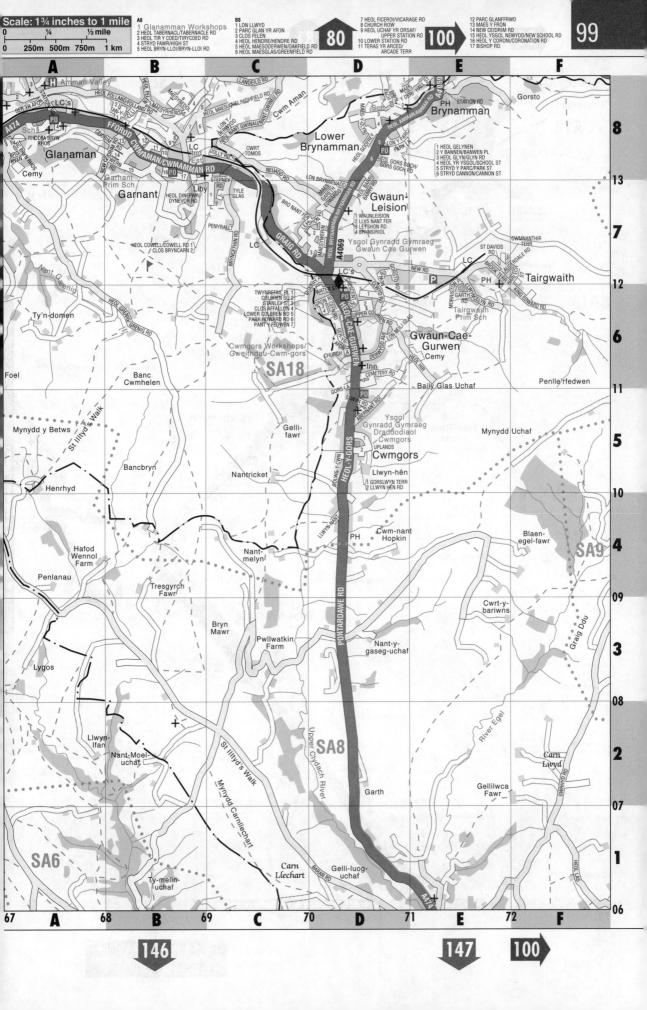

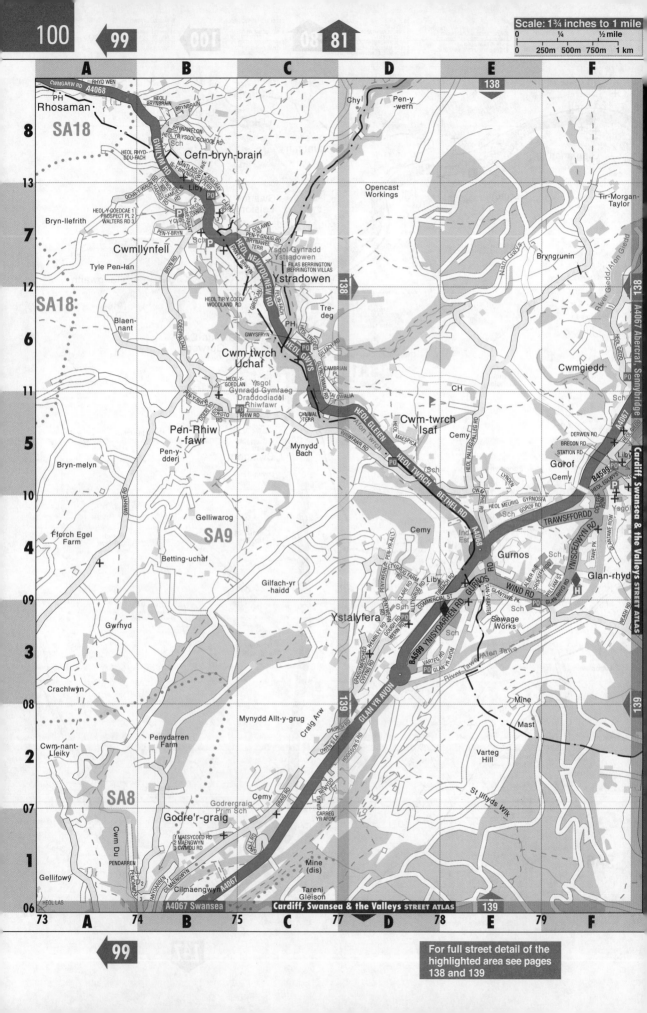

Scale: 1¾ inches to 1 mile
0   ¼   ½ mile
0   250m 500m 750m 1 km

A
Howney Stone
Hook Farms
Treehill Farm
Marloes Mere
YH
P
Runwayskiln
Pembrokeshire Coast Path
Gateholm Stack
Gateholm Island
Settlement
Hooper's Point

B
Pembrokeshire Coast Path
Musselwick Sands
Marloes Court Farm
Little Marloes Farm
Marloes Sands
Red Cliff
The Hookses

C
Eastfield Farm
Musselwick Farm
Fopston Farm
North La
Glebe La
Marloes
PH
PO
Sewage Works
Airfield (disused)

C7
1 CHURCH CL
2 TOWER VW
3 GREEN MDW CL

D
The Moors
Orlandon
Winterton
Quarries (dis)
Philbeach Farm
Tower (remains of)
Sewage Works
SA62
Dalehill Farm
Windmill Farm
Dale CP Sch

E
Hoaten
Slate Mill Farm
Slatemill Bridge
Quarry (dis)
West Lodge Farm
Butterhill Farm
Upper Mullock Farm
Mullock Bridge
Whiteholmes Farm
Mabesgate
Standing Stone
Quarry (dis)
Slatehill Farm
Moor Farm
Quarry (dis)
Musselwick Road
Musselwick
Quarry (dis)
Monk Haven

F

B4327

Crabhall Farm
P

Westdale Bay
Fort
Great Castle Head
Iron Point
Hayguard Hay Farm
Hayguard Hay Wood
Broomhill Farm
Point Farm
Castlebeach Wood
Maryborough Farm
Long Point
Moorland Farm
Welshman's Bay
P
Kete
Little Castle Point
Fort
Frenchman's Bay
Brunt Farm
Pembrokeshire Coast Path
Radio Mast
Lighthouse
St Ann's Head

Dale Roads
Castle Way
Blue Anchor Way
Dale
South St
PO PH
Dale Fort Field Centre
Fort
Dale Point
Castlebeach Bay
Watwick Point
Watwick Bay
Beacon
West Blockhouse Point
Mill Bay

09 08 07 06 05 04 03 02 8 7 6 5 4 3 2 1

77 A 78 B 79 C 80 D 81 E 82 F

101
85

A B C D E F

8

05

7

04

6

03

5

02

4

01

3

00

2

99

1

98

Great Castle Head

Kilroom

South Hook Point

SA73

Gelliswick
Windmill
Headlands
FAIRSEA CL
Gelliswick
Bay

Jetty

Jetty

Milford Haven/
Aberdaugleddyf

Thorn
Island
Hotel

West Pill
Mast

West
Angle Bay

Chapel
Bay

North Hill

Sewage
Works

Angle

Angle VC Sch

Angle Point

Sawdern Point

East Brock House
(remains of)

Wimblewood

SHIRBURN CL

PH
PO
Cemy

Castle
(remains of)

Angle
Bay

Rat
Island

Masts

North Studdock

B4320

The
Hall
Swimming
Pool

Pembrokeshire Coast Path

Castles
Bay
Fort

South
Studdock Farm

SA71

Hubberton
Farm

Windmill

Bangeston
Farm

Hardings
Hill

Middlehill

Sheep
Island

Parsonsquarry
Bay

Guttle
Hole

Carters
Green Farm

West
Pickard Bay

Fort

East Pickard Bay

Black Cave

Gravel
Bay

B4319

The Devil's
Quoit
(Burial
Chamber)

Broomhill
Burrows

Freshwater
West

Gupton
Burrows

Little Furzenip

Mast

Great Furzenip

Frainslake
Sands

83 A 84 B 85 C 86 D 87 E 88 F

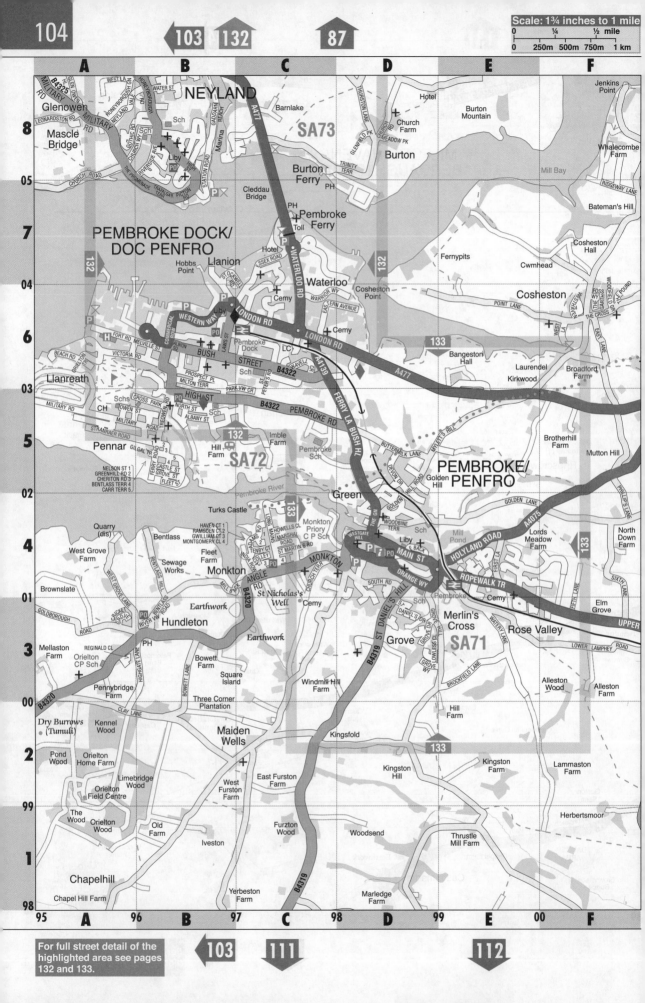

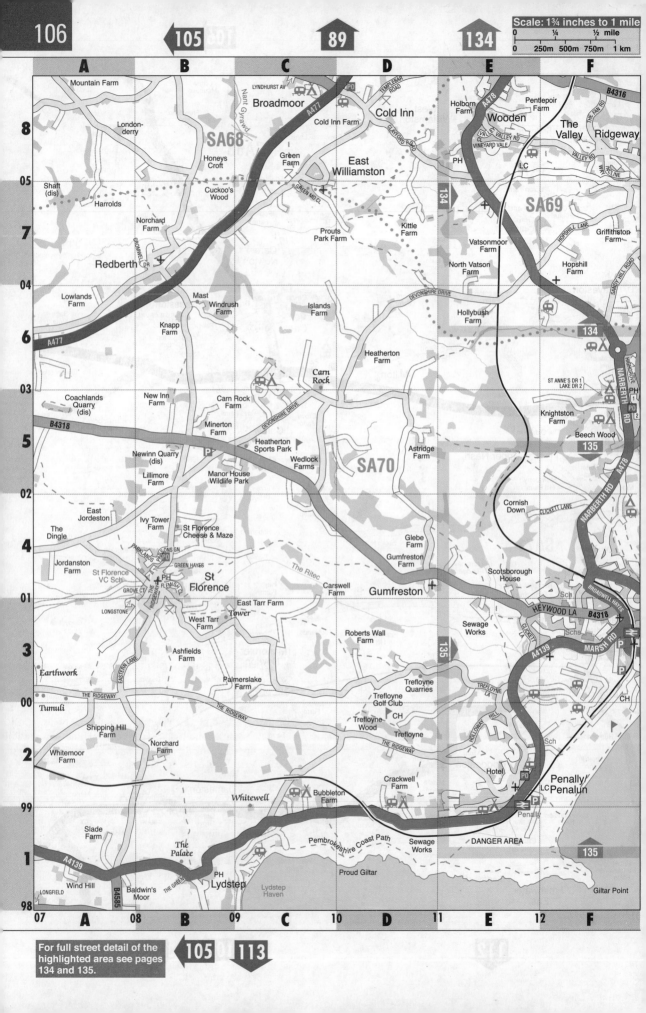

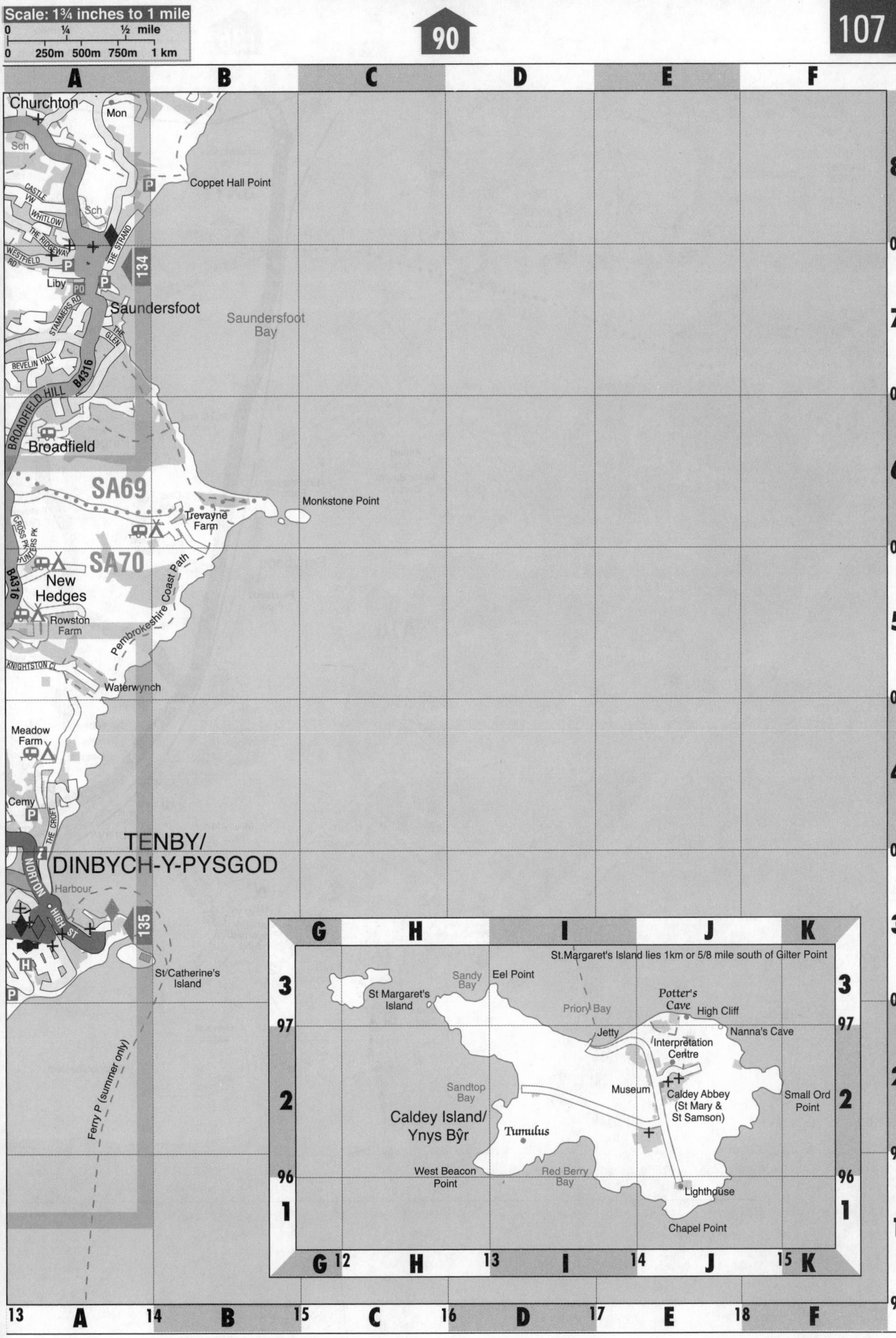

Scale: 1¾ inches to 1 mile
0 ¼ ½ mile
0 250m 500m 750m 1 km
90
A B C D E F
8 7 6 5 4 3 2 1
05 04 03 02 01 00 99 98
13 14 15 16 17 18
Churchton
Mon
Sch
Coppet Hall Point
CASTLE VW
WHITLOW
THE RIDGEWAY
WESTFIELD RD
THE STRAND
134
Liby
PO
STAMMERS RD
Saundersfoot
Saundersfoot Bay
THE GLEN
BEVELIN HALL
B4316
BROADFIELD HILL
Broadfield
SA69
Monkstone Point
Trevayne Farm
CROSS PK
HUNTERS PK
SA70
New Hedges
Pembrokeshire Coast Path
Rowston Farm
KNIGHTSTON CL
Waterwynch
Meadow Farm
Cemy
THE CROFT
TENBY/ DINBYCH-Y-PYSGOD
NORTON
Harbour
HIGH ST
135
St Catherine's Island
Ferry P (summer only)
G H I J K
12 13 14 15
96 97
St.Margaret's Island lies 1km or 5/8 mile south of Gilter Point
Sandy Bay
Eel Point
St Margaret's Island
Priory Bay
Potter's Cave
High Cliff
Nanna's Cave
Jetty
Interpretation Centre
Museum
Caldey Abbey (St Mary & St Samson)
Small Ord Point
Sandtop Bay
Caldey Island/ Ynys Bŷr
Tumulus
West Beacon Point
Red Berry Bay
Lighthouse
Chapel Point

Scale: 1¾ inches to 1 mile

0   ¼   ½   mile
0   250m 500m 750m   1 km

8

DANGER
AREA

DANGER
AREA

SA17

Muddlescwm

Commissioners'
Bridge

Gwendraeth Fawr

136

136

Morfa Mawr
Farm

Panteg
Farm

Ty Cornel
Farm

05

7

Poplar
Tree Farm

Morfa Isaf
Farm

PH   Pinged

04

Tygwyn
Farm

B4317

6

Airfield

Motor Sports
Centre

Brooklands
Farm

Clos
Farm

Fairview
Farm

Pembrey Forest

Tynawr
Farm

Ffrwd
Farm

Penybedd

Coed
Farm

03

LC

Penybedd
Farm

PENYBEDD ROAD

Renllwyn Isaf
Farm

5

SA16

Swan Pool Drain

PH   Fort

137

Cefn Sidan
Sands

Penybedd
Wood

DAN-Y-BRYN

GOLWGFOR

LANDO RD

GARREGLWYD

02

MAES-YR-AWEL
TRE-NEL

DANLAN RD   DANLAN PK

4

Meusydd
Farm

WAUN
SIDAN

P

Pembrey/
Pen-bre

PO

MAENOR HELYG

Pembrey
CP Sch

01

P

Pembrey Country Park

FACTORY RD

St Illtyd's Walk

ROTARY WY

Ashburnham
Golf Club

3

Miniature
Railway

Pembrey
Properties
Ind Est

P

Dry Ski
Slope

P

00

Visitor
Centre

P

Sewage
Works

Pembrey Burrows

2

99

1

98

37   38   39   40   41   42

For full street detail of the
highlighted area see pages
136 and 137.

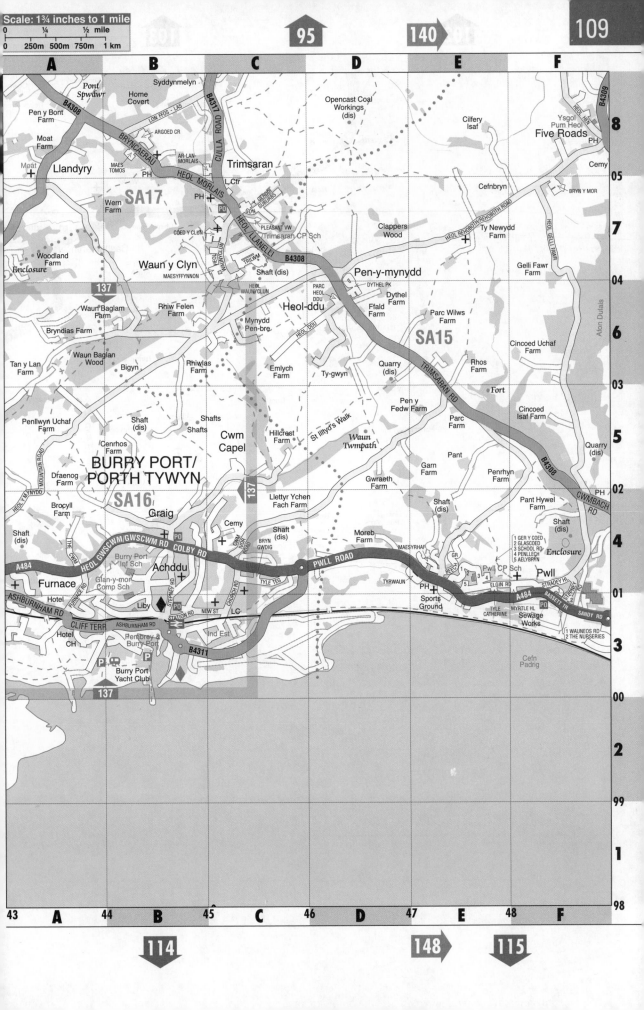

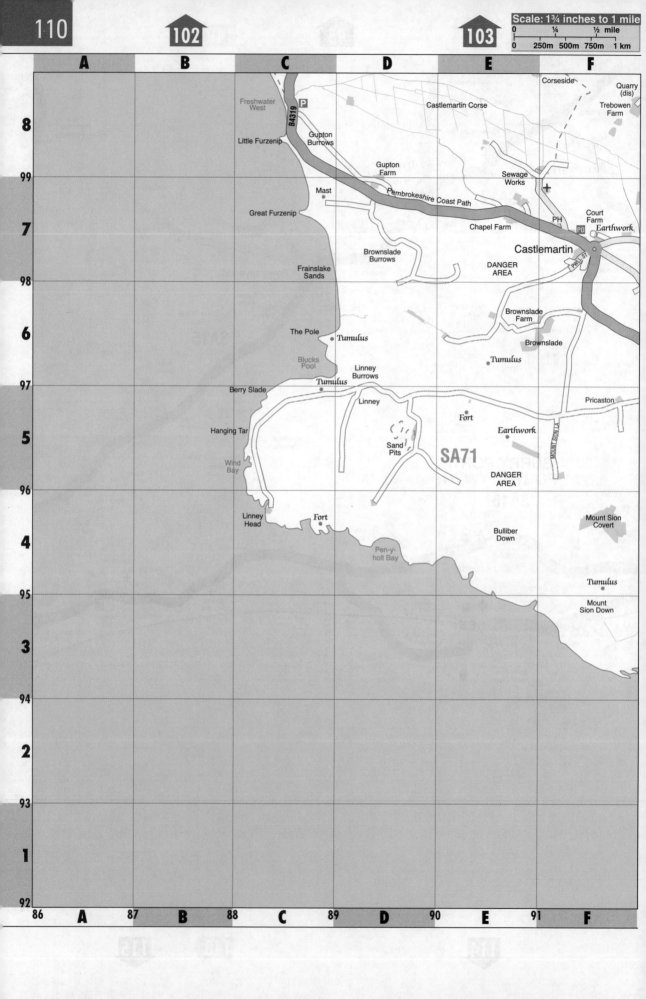

110

102

103

Scale: 1¾ inches to 1 mile
0   ¼   ½   mile
0   250m 500m 750m   1 km

A   B   C   D   E   F

8

99

7

98

6

97

5

96

4

3

94

2

93

1

92

Freshwater West

Little Furzenip

B4319

P

Gupton Burrows

Gupton Farm

Mast

Great Furzenip

Pembrokeshire Coast Path

Castlemartin Corse

Sewage Works

Court Farm

PH

PO

Earthwork

Chapel Farm

Castlemartin

Frainslake Sands

Brownslade Burrows

DANGER AREA

The Pole

Tumulus

Brownslade Farm

Brownslade

Blucks Pool

Linney Burrows

Tumulus

Tumulus

Berry Slade

Linney

PWLL ST

Pricaston

Hanging Tar

Fort

Earthwork

MOUNT SION LA

Sand Pits

SA71

Wind Bay

Linney Head

Fort

DANGER AREA

Mount Sion Covert

Pen-y-holt Bay

Bulliber Down

Tumulus

Mount Sion Down

Corseside

Quarry (dis)

Trebowen Farm

86   87   88   89   90   91

A   B   C   D   E   F

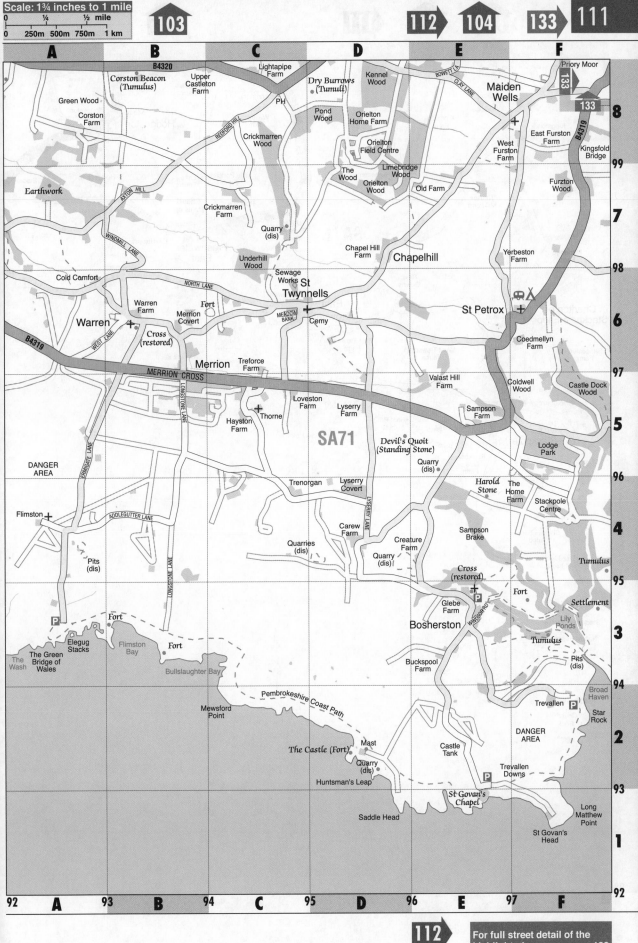

A   B   C   D   E   F

B4320

Corston Beacon
(Tumulus)

Green Wood

Corston
Farm

Upper
Castleton
Farm

Lightapipe
Farm

Dry Burrows
(Tumuli)

Kennel
Wood

Maiden
Wells

133

133

8

Earthwork

Crickmarren
Wood

PH

Pond
Wood

Orielton
Home Farm

Limebridge
Wood

West
Furston
Farm

East Furston
Farm

Kingsfold
Bridge

B4319

99

The
Wood

Orielton
Field Centre

Furzton
Wood

7

Crickmarren
Farm

Quarry
(dis)

Orielton
Wood

Old Farm

Yerbeston
Farm

98

Cold Comfort

NORTH LANE

Underhill
Wood

Sewage
Works St
Twynnells

Chapel Hill
Farm

Chapelhill

St Petrox

6

Warren
Farm

Fort

Merrion
Covert

MEADOW
BANK

Cemy

Coedmellyn
Farm

Warren

Cross
(restored)

97

B4319

MERRION CROSS

Merrion

Treforce
Farm

Valast Hill
Farm

Coldwell
Wood

Castle Dock
Wood

Loveston
Farm

Lyserry
Farm

Sampson
Farm

Hayston
Farm

Thorne

SA71

Devil's Quoit
(Standing Stone)

Lodge
Park

5

DANGER
AREA

Trenorgan

Lyserry
Covert

Quarry
(dis)

Harold
Stone

The
Home
Farm

Stackpole
Centre

96

Flimston

Pits
(dis)

ADDLEGUTTER LANE

LONGSTONE LANE

Quarries
(dis)

Carew
Farm

Quarry
(dis)

Creature
Farm

Sampson
Brake

Cross
(restored)

Fort

Tumulus

95

P

Fort

Glebe
Farm

Settlement

Elegug
Stacks

Fort

Bosherston

WINDSOR RD

Lily
Ponds

Tumulus

3

The
Wash

The Green
Bridge of
Wales

Flimston
Bay

Bullslaughter Bay

Buckspool
Farm

Pits
(dis)

94

Pembrokeshire Coast Path

Mewsford
Point

DANGER
AREA

Trevallen

Star
Rock

Broad
Haven

2

The Castle (Fort)

Mast

Quarry
(dis)

Castle
Tank

Trevallen
Downs

P

Huntsman's Leap

P

St Govan's
Chapel

Long
Matthew
Point

93

Saddle Head

St Govan's
Head

1

92   93   94   95   96   97   92

A   B   C   D   E   F

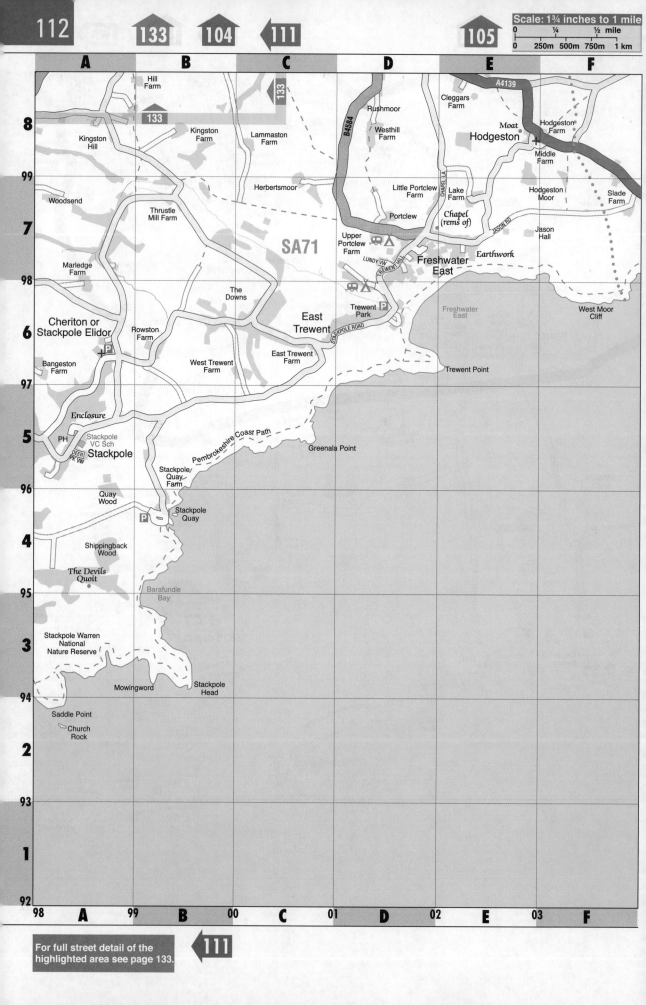

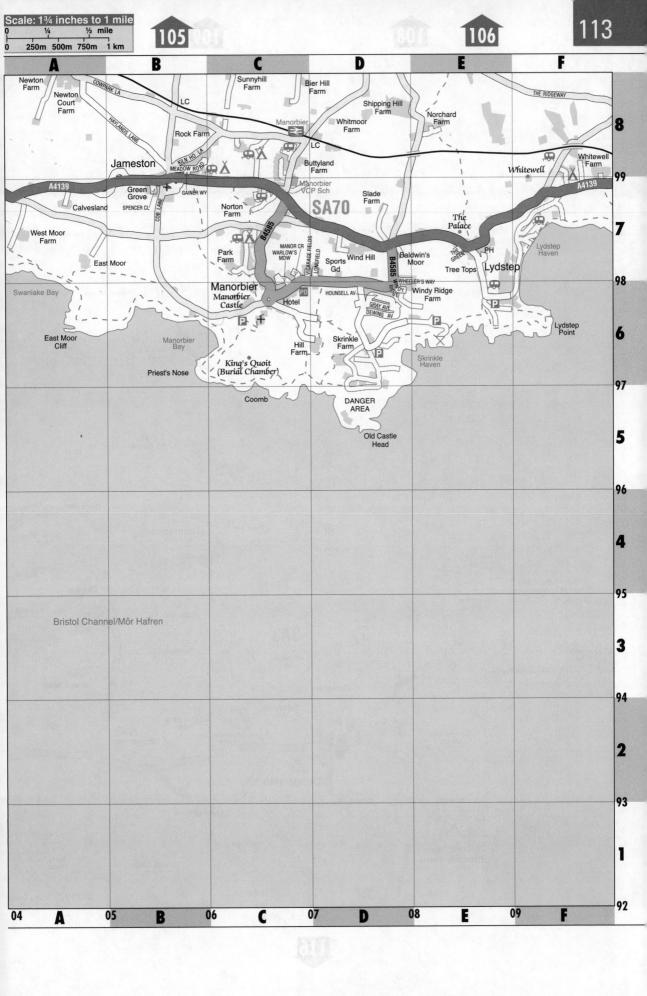

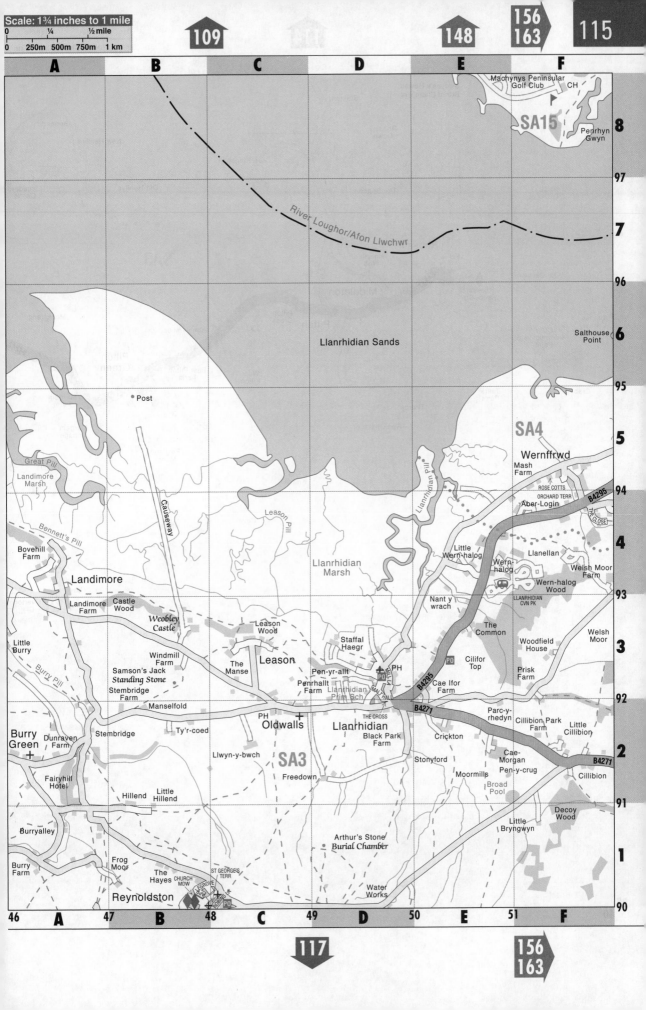

Scale: 1¾ inches to 1 mile

0 ¼ ½ mile
0 250m 500m 750m 1 km

A B C D E F

8

Sweyne's Howes
Burial Chambers

Sluxton

Rhossili
Down

Betlands

New Henllys

Kingshall

89

Rhossili
Bay

The Beacon

Old Henllys

Llanddewi
Castle

7

Rhossili

Talgarth's
Well

SA3

PH

Old Castle

88

B4247

Middleton

Rhossili
Visitor Ctr

BUNKER'S HILL

P

Pitton
Cross

Monksland

6

Kitchen
Corner

CCW
Information
Point

Pitton

Kimleymoor

Pilton
Green

B4247

Fall Bay

West
Pilton

East Pilton
Farm

Margam
Farm

87

Crabart

Tears
Point

Mewslade Bay

Margam
Cottage

Thurba

Paviland
Manor

Littlehills

5

Red Chamber

The
Knave

86

Foxhole
Slade

Paviland
Cave

Blackhole
Gut

Common
Cliff

4

Longhole
Cave

85

Overton
Cliff

3

84

2

83

1

82

40 A 41 B 42 C 43 D 44 E 45 F

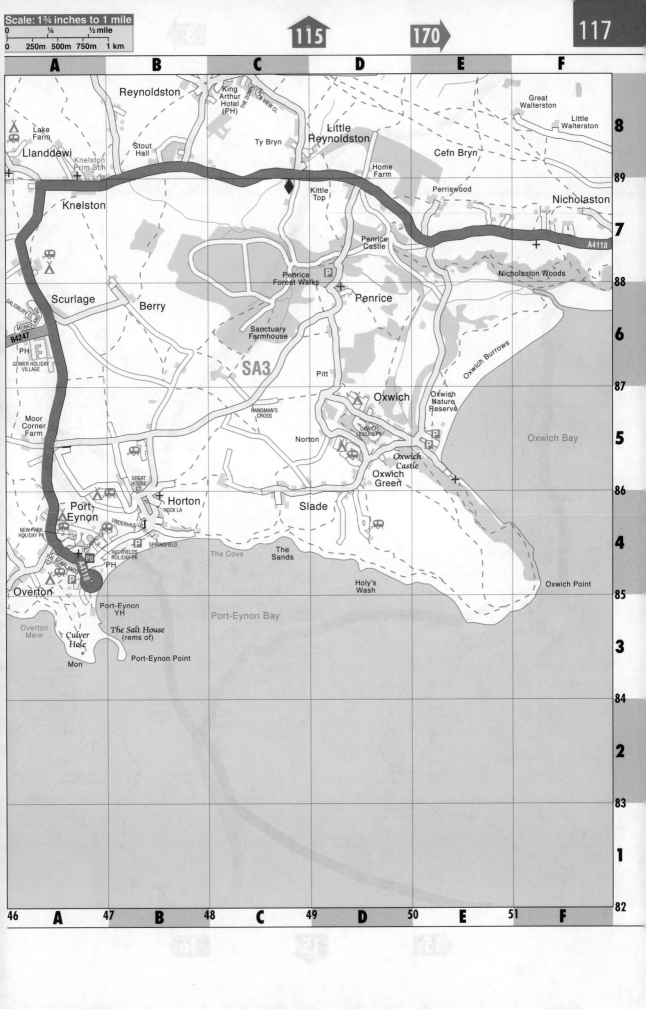

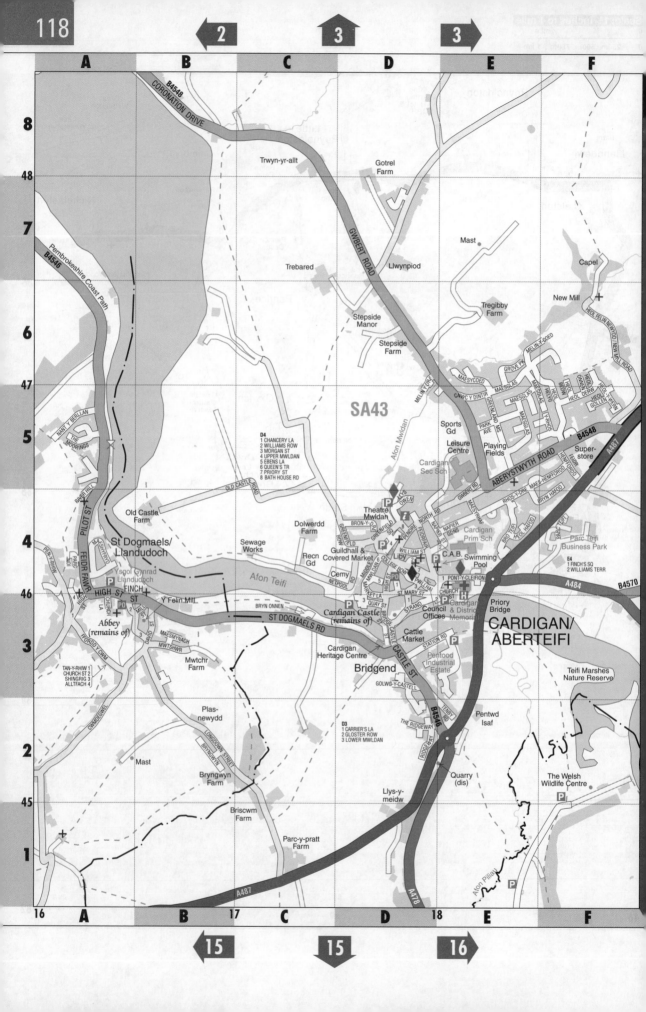

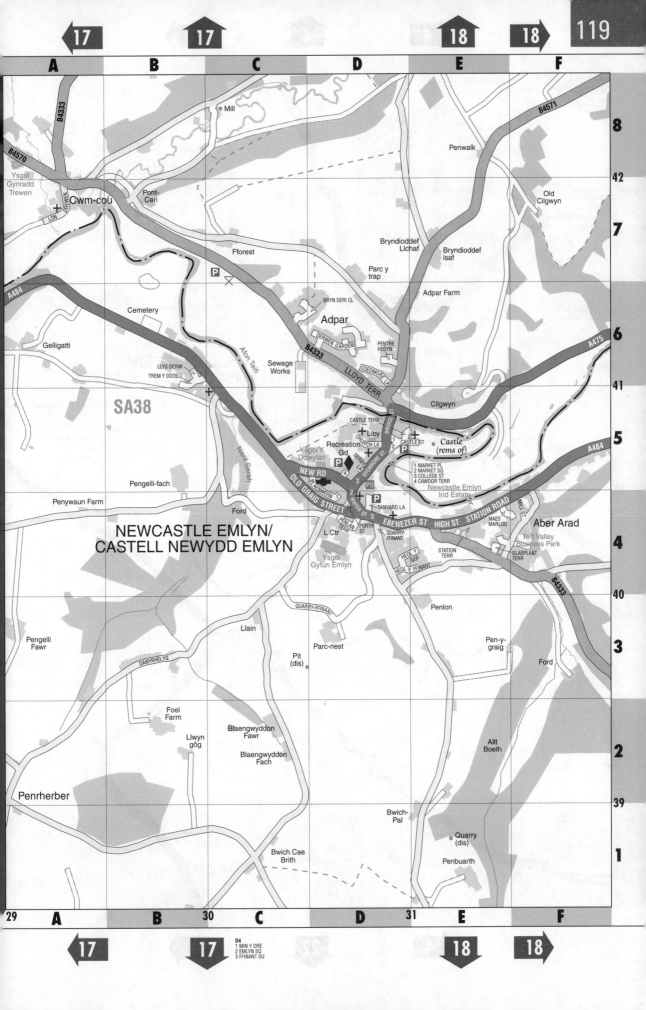

A   B   C   D   E   F

8
42
7
6
41
5
40
3
39
1

B4333

B4571

B4570

Mill

Penwalk

Old
Cilgwyn

Ysgol
Gynradd
Trewen

Pont-
Ceri

Cwm-cou

Fforest

Bryndioddef
Llchaf

Bryndioddef
isaf

A484

Parc y
trap

Adpar Farm

Cemetery

BRYN DERI CL

Adpar

Afon Teifi

DERWEN GARDENS

PENTRE
HEDYN

A475

Gelligatti

Sewage
Works

B4333

LLOYD TERR

COEDMORE LA

Cilgwyn

LLYS DERW
TREM Y DDOL

SA38

CASTLE TERR

BRIDGE ST

Castle
(rems of)

A484

Nant Sarah

Ysgol Y
Ddwylan

CH'CH LA

CASTLE ST

Liby

Recreation
Gd

1 MARKET PL
2 MARKET SQ
3 COLLEGE ST
4 CAWDOR TERR

Pengelli-fach

NEW RD

DERBY LA

SYCAMORE ST

P

Newcastle Emlyn
Ind Estate

Penywaun Farm

OLD GRAIG STREET

BLAENWERN

WATER ST

PO

EBENEZER ST

HIGH ST

STATION ROAD

Aber Arad

Ford

Teifi Valley
Business Park

NEWCASTLE EMLYN/
CASTELL NEWYDD EMLYN

PENLAN
TERR

PORTH
ST

TANYARD LA

QUARRY-
FFINANT

STATION
TERR

MAES
MARLOG

MILL ST

GLASPLANT
TERR

L Ctr

Ysgol
Gyfun Emlyn

HEOL Y
GOF

HEOL Y FFINANT

QUARRY-FFINANT

Penlon

B4333

Pen-y-
graig

Ford

Llain

Pengelli
Fawr

DANYRHELYG

Parc-nest

Pit
(dis)

Allt
Boeth

Foel
Farm

Llwyn
gôg

Blaengwyddon
Fawr

Blaengwyddon
Fach

Penrherber

Bwlch-
Pal

Quarry
(dis)

Penbuarth

Bwlch Cae
Brith

D4
1 MIN Y DRE
2 EMLYN SQ
3 FFINANT SQ

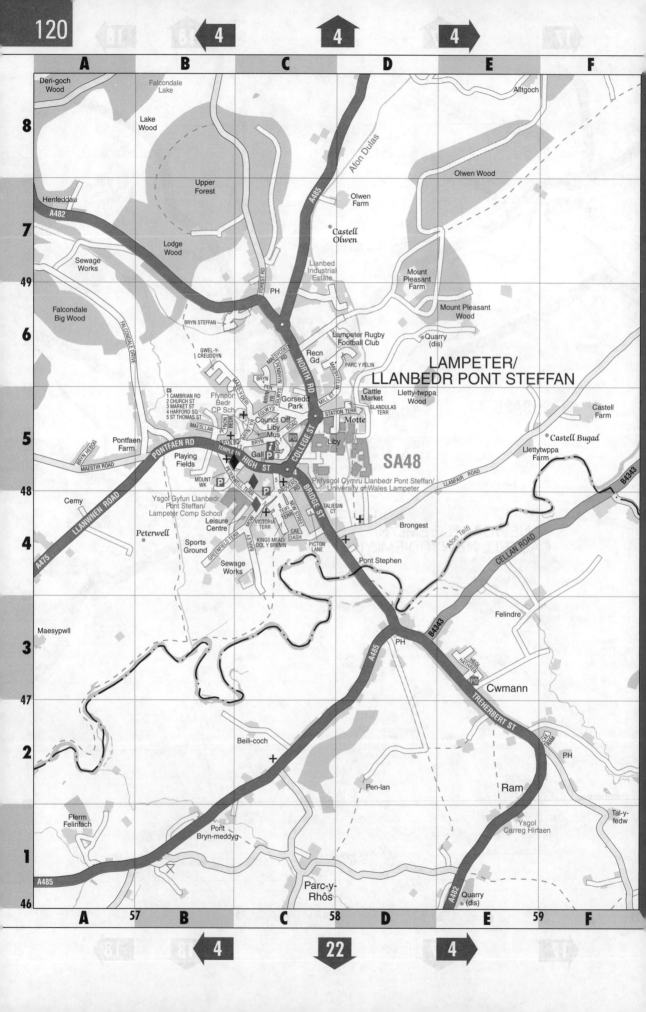

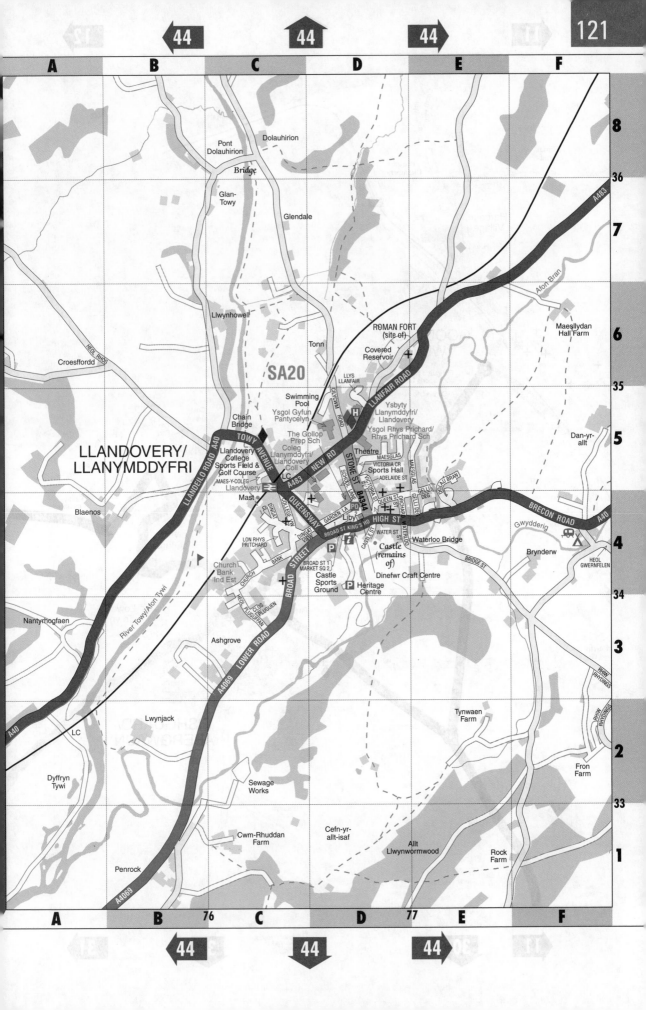

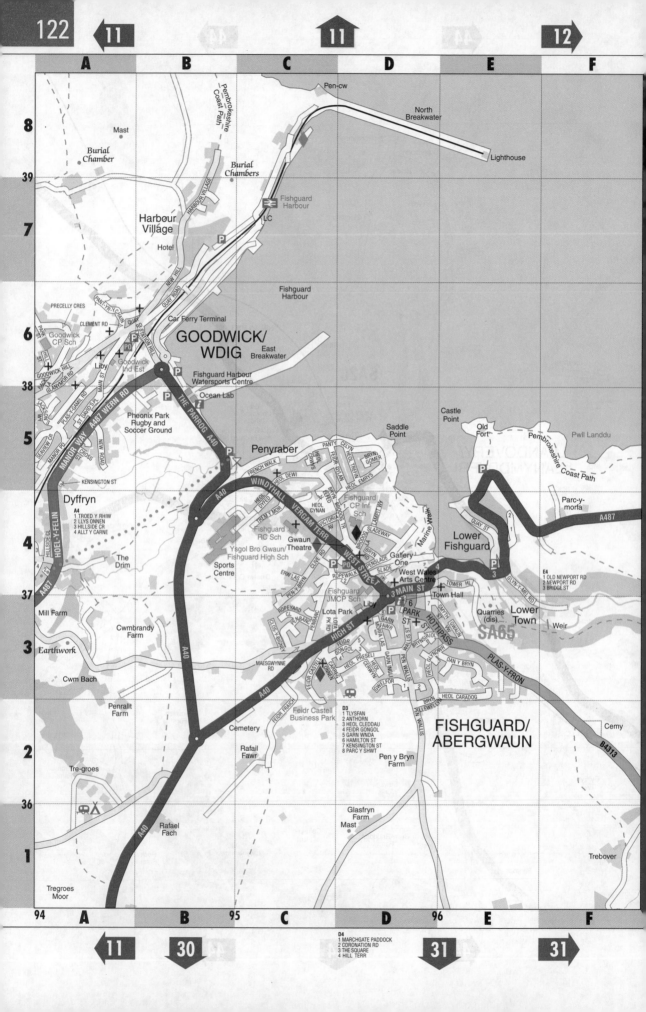

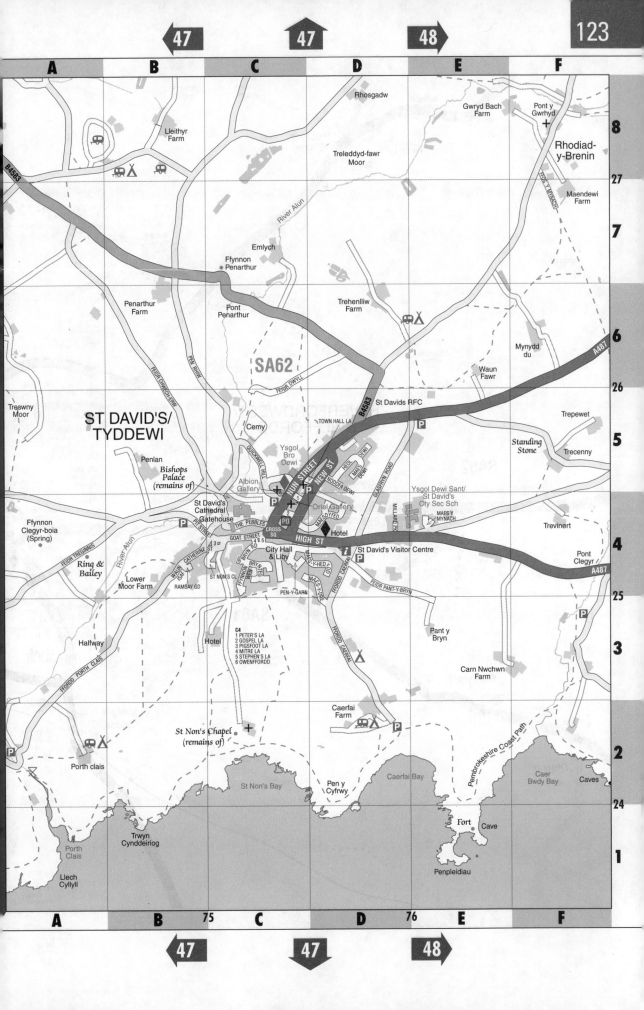

A   B   C   D   E   F

8
27
7
6
26
5
25
4
3
2
24
1

B4583

Lleithyr Farm

Rhosgadw

Gwryd Bach Farm

Pont y Gwrhyd

Rhodiad-y-Brenin

FFOS Y MYNACH

Maendewi Farm

River Alun

Treleddyd-fawr Moor

Emlych

Ffynnon Penarthur

Trehenlliw Farm

A487

Penarthur Farm

Pont Penarthur

SA62

Mynydd du

Waun Fawr

FEIDR CWMCOCHENI

PEN RHIW

FEIDR DWYLL

St Davids RFC

TOWN HALL LA

B4583

Standing Stone

Trepewet

Traeswny Moor

ST DAVID'S/ TYDDEWI

Cemy

Ysgol Bro Dewi

Trecenny

5

QUICKWELL HILL

Penlan

Bishops Palace (remains of)

Albion Gallery

St David's Cathedral Gatehouse

NUN STREET

NEW ST

HEOL DEWI

MAES DEWI

NODDFA DEWI

Oriel Gallery

Ysgol Dewi Sant/ St David's Cty Sec Sch

MAES Y MYNACH

GLASFRYN ROAD

MILLARD PK

Trevinert

Ffynnon Clegyr-boia (Spring)

FEIDR THEGINNIS

River Alun

PIT STREET

THE PEBBLES

GOAT STREET

CROSS SQ

PO

HIGH ST

Hotel

MAES-Y-DYFED

i

St David's Visitor Centre

Pont Clegyr

A487

Ring & Bailey

CATHERINE ST

City Hall & Liby

WAUN ISAF

RAMSAY GD

ST NON'S CL

FFYNNON WEN

BRYN RD

BRYN-Y-TEG

PEN-Y-GARN

MAES-Y-HED

MAES-Y-ORE

FFORDD CAERFAI

FEIDR PANT-Y-BRYN

Pant y Bryn

Lower Moor Farm

Halfway

Hotel

FFORDD PORTH CLAIS

C4
1 PETER'S LA
2 GOSPEL LA
3 PIGSFOOT LA
4 MITRE LA
5 STEPHEN'S LA
6 OWENFFORDD

Carn Nwchwn Farm

St Non's Chapel (remains of)

Caerfai Farm

Caerfai Bay

Pembrokeshire Coast Path

Caer Bwdy Bay

Caves

Porth clais

St Non's Bay

Pen y Cyfrwy

Fort

Cave

Trwyn Cynddeiriog

Porth Clais

Penpleidiau

Llech Cyllyll

A   75   B   C   76   D   E   F

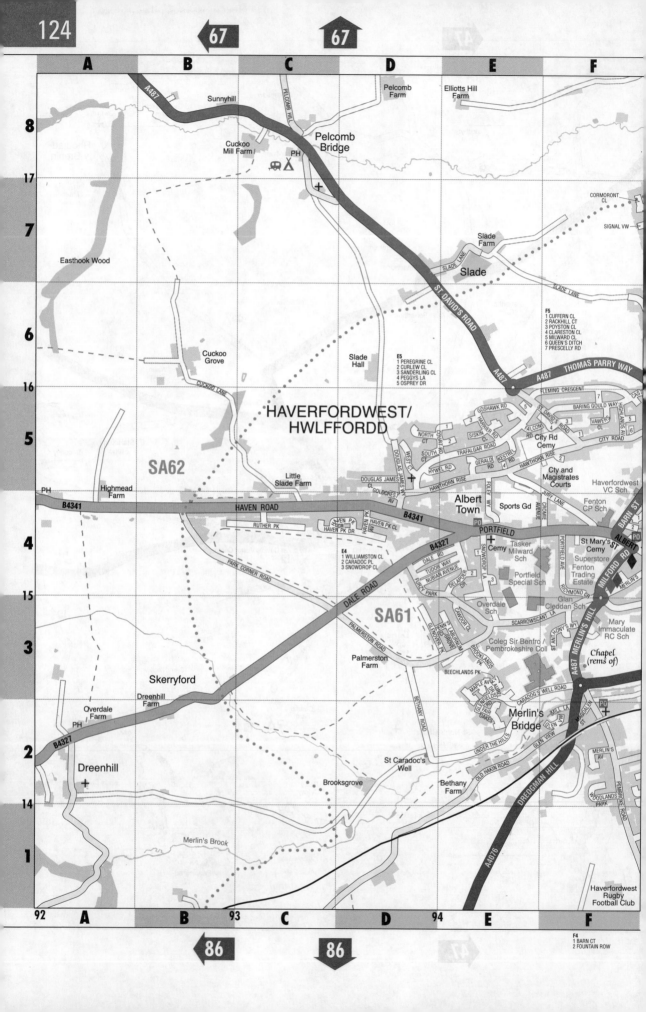

A   B   C   D   E   F

8

Sunnyhill

Pelcomb
Farm

Elliotts Hill
Farm

A487

17

Cuckoo
Mill Farm

Pelcomb
Bridge

PH

7

Slade
Farm

CORMORONT
CL

SIGNAL VW

Easthook Wood

SLADE LANE

Slade

ST DAVID'S ROAD

SLADE LANE

6

Cuckoo
Grove

Slade
Hall

A487

A487 THOMAS PARRY WAY

F5
1 CUFFERN CL
2 RACKHILL CT
3 POYSTON CL
4 CLARESTON CL
5 MILWARD CL
6 QUEEN'S DITCH
7 PRESCELLY RD

CUCKOO LANE

E5
1 PEREGRINE CL
2 CURLEW CL
3 SANDERLING CL
4 PEGGYS LA
5 OSPREY DR

FLEMING CRESCENT

16

HAVERFORDWEST/
HWLFFORDD

GOSHAWK RD

ST DAVID'S ROAD

BARING GOULD WAY

5

SA62

Little
Slade Farm

NORTH
CT

COFH RD

SOUTH
CT

HARRIER RD

SISKIN

FALCON

Trafalgar Road

City Rd Cemy

CITY ROAD

DOUGLAS JAMES CL

HYWEL RD

GERALD
RD

KESTREL

Hawthorn Rise

Cty and
Magistrates
Courts

Haverfordwest
VC Sch

Highmead
Farm

GOLDCREST
AV

Douglas James
CL

Hawthorn Rise

FOLEY RD

Sports Gd

CROME
AVENUE

Fenton
CP Sch

BARN ST

PH

B4341

HAVEN ROAD

B4341

Albert
Town

JURY LANE

4

RUTHER PK

HAVEN PK
DR

HAVEN PK CL

HAVEN PK
AV

HAVEN PK

PORTFIELD

PO

Cemy

Tasker
Milward
Sch

St Mary's
Cemy

ALBERT ST

Superstore

MILFORD RD

MERLIN'S

PO

E4
1 WILLIAMSTON CL
2 CARADOC PL
3 SNOWDROP CL

B4327

SNOWDROP LA

DALE RD

St Mary's
Cemy

PORTFIELD AVE

Fenton
Trading
Estate

PARK CORNER ROAD

TUDOR WAY

NUBIAN AVENUE

DELAPOER
DR

Portfield
Special Sch

RICHMOND CR

Glan
Cleddan Sch

Mary
Immaculate
RC Sch

15

DALE ROAD

FURZY PARK

Overdale
Sch

CAWDOR CL

SCARROWSCANT LA

SA61

PENN'S LA
GLENDOVEY PK

BRENIN LA

Coleg Sir Benfro /
Pembrokeshire Coll

A487 MERLIN'S HILL

ST ANT'ONY'S WY

Chapel
(rems of)

3

Palmerston
Farm

PALMERSTON ROAD

BROOKLANDS

BEECHLANDS PK

MAPLE AV

CARADOG'S WELL ROAD

Skerryford

BETHANY ROAD

GLENHEATH
FAIR
OAKES

MILL LA

Merlin's
Bridge

MAGDALEN ST

Merlin's
AV

Dreenhill
Farm

St Caradoc's
Well

UNDER THE HILLS

GLEN VIEW

WOODLANDS
PARK

Overdale
Farm

PH

OLD HAKIN ROAD

DREDGMAN HILL

2

B4327

Dreenhill

Brooksgrove

Bethany
Farm

PEMBROKE ROAD

14

Merlin's Brook

A4076

1

Haverfordwest
Rugby
Football Club

92   A   B   93   C   D   94   E   F

F4
1 BARN CT
2 FOUNTAIN ROW

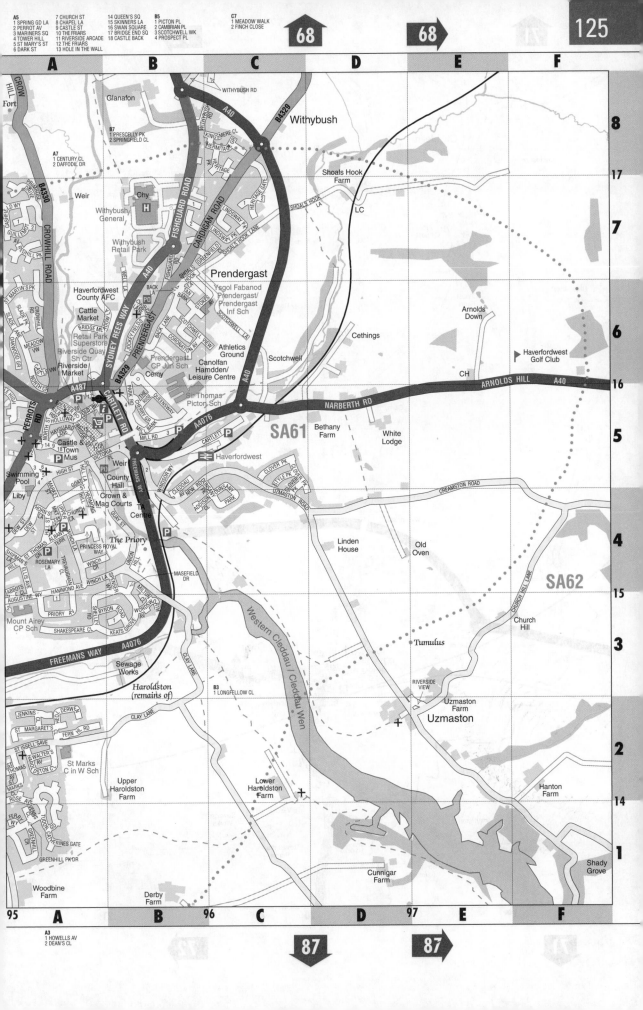

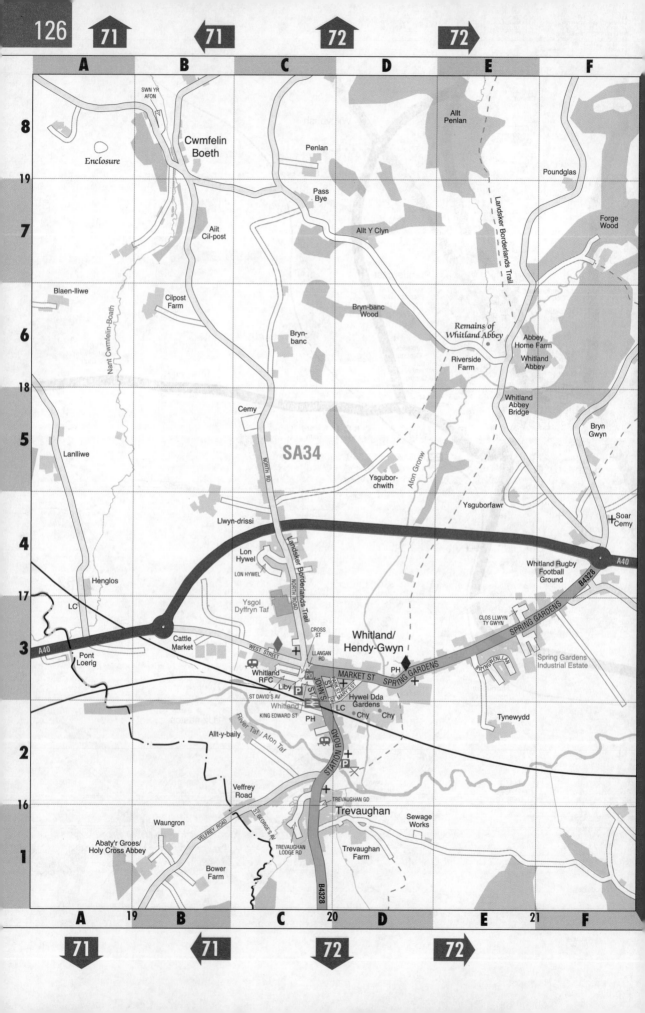

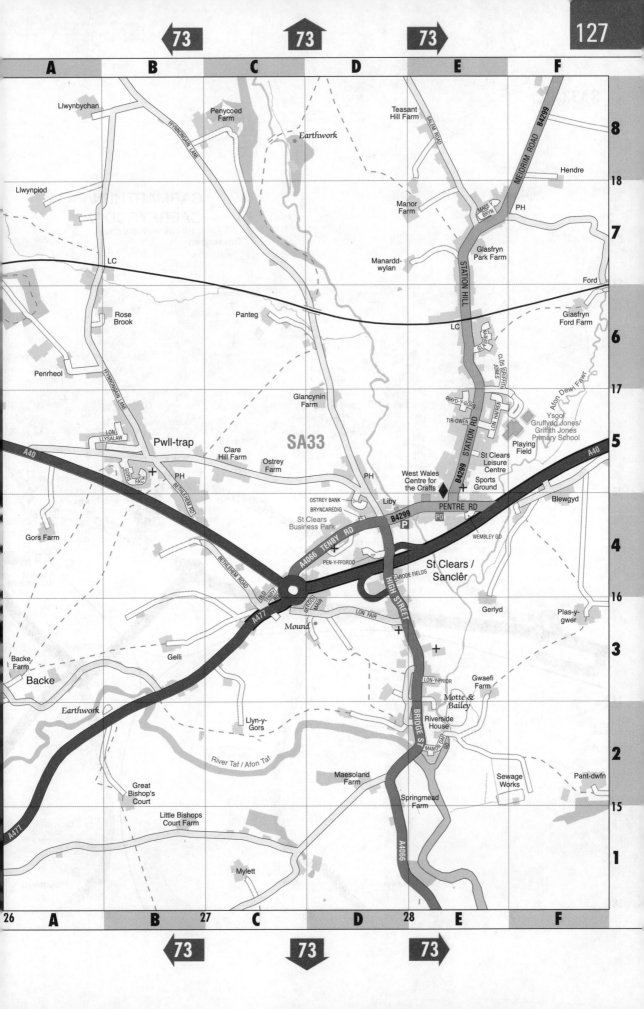

Llwynbychan
Penycoed Farm
Earthwork
Teasant Hill Farm
SALEM ROAD
MEIDRIM ROAD B4299
Hendre
Llwynpiod
Manor Farm
PH
MAES BRYN
Glasfryn Park Farm
FFYNNONGAIN LANE
Manardd-wylan
STATION HILL
LC
Ford
Rose Brook
Panteg
LC
Glasfryn Ford Farm
Penrheol
Glancynin Farm
CLOS GRIFFITH JONES
Aton Dewi Fawr
FFYNNONGAIN LANE
RHYD-Y-GORS
TIR-OWEN
Ysgol Gruffydd Jones/ Griffith Jones Primary School
LON LLYSALAW
Pwll-trap
Clare Hill Farm
SA33
STATION RD
LON HAFREN
Playing Field
A40
GORS FACH
PH
Ostrey Farm
PH
St Clears Leisure Centre
A40
5
West Wales Centre for the Crafts
B4299
Sports Ground
Blewgyd
OSTREY BANK
BRYNCAREDIG
Liby
PENTRE RD
Gors Farm
BETHLEHEM RD
St Clears Business Park
B4299
PO
P
WEMBLEY GD
A4066 TENBY RD
PEN-Y-FFORDD
St Clears / Sanclêr
Backe Farm
BETHLEHEM ROAD
A477
GERDDI MAIR
OLD TENBY RD
LON FAIR
GARODE FIELDS
Gerlyd
Plas-y-gwer
16
Backe
Mound
HIGH STREET
Gelli
+
+
Earthwork
LON-Y-PRIOR
Gwaefi Farm
Llyn-y-Gors
Motte & Bailey
River Taf / Afon Taf
BRIDGE ST
Riverside House
MANOR RD
Great Bishop's Court
Maesoland Farm
Sewage Works
Pant-dwfn
Little Bishops Court Farm
Springmead Farm
A477
A4066
Mylett

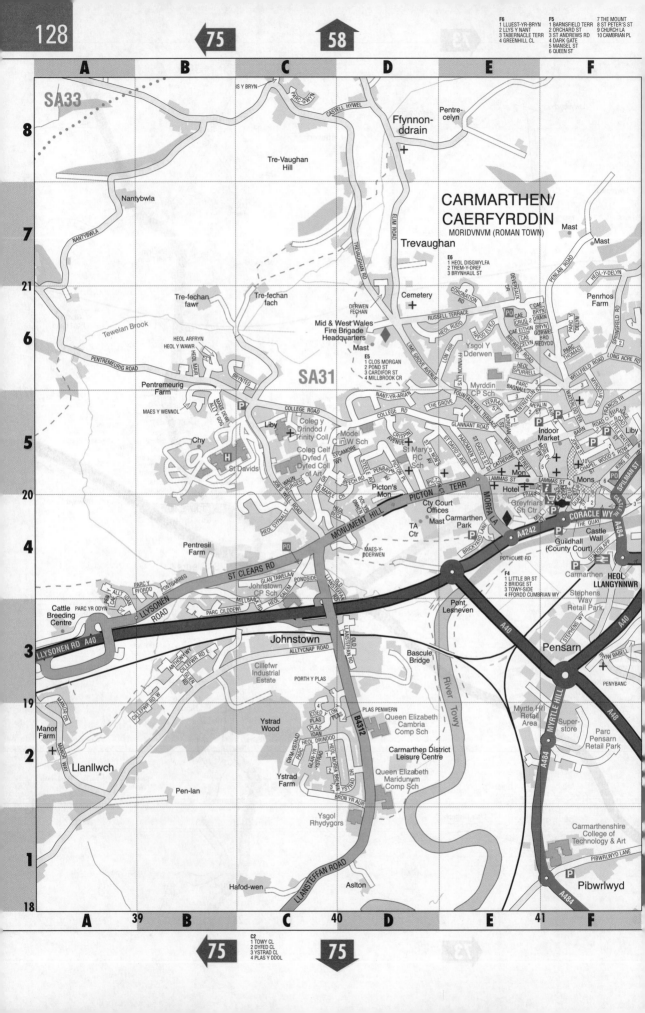

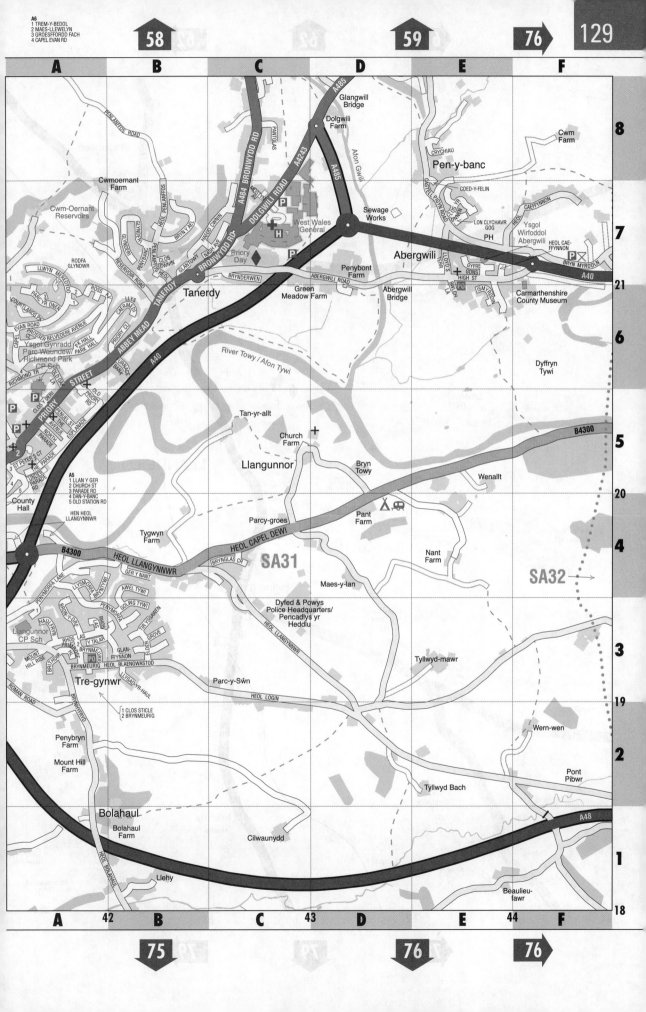

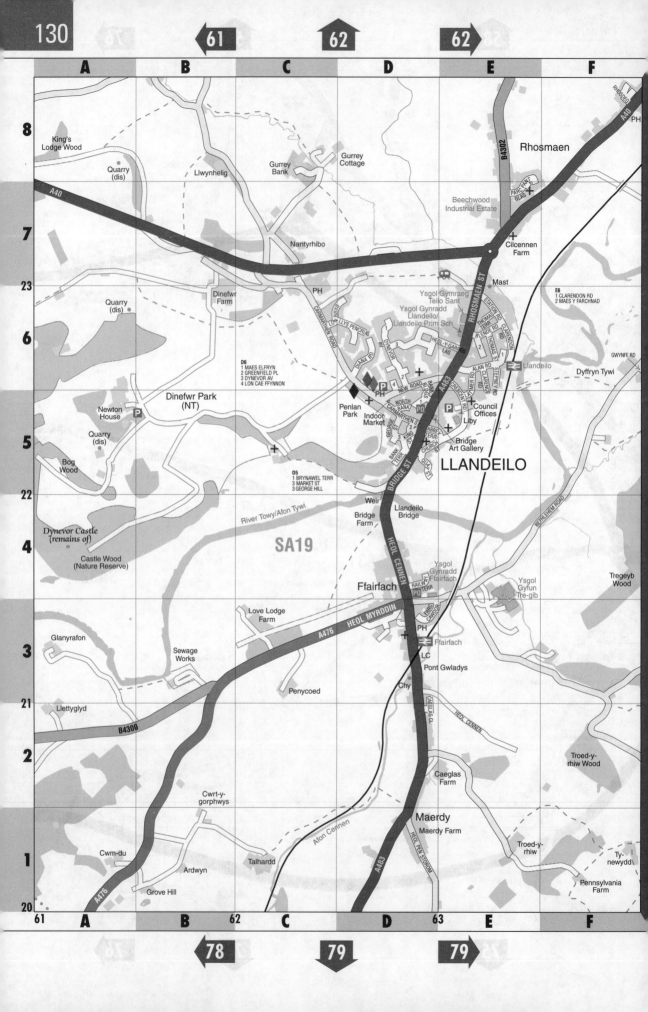

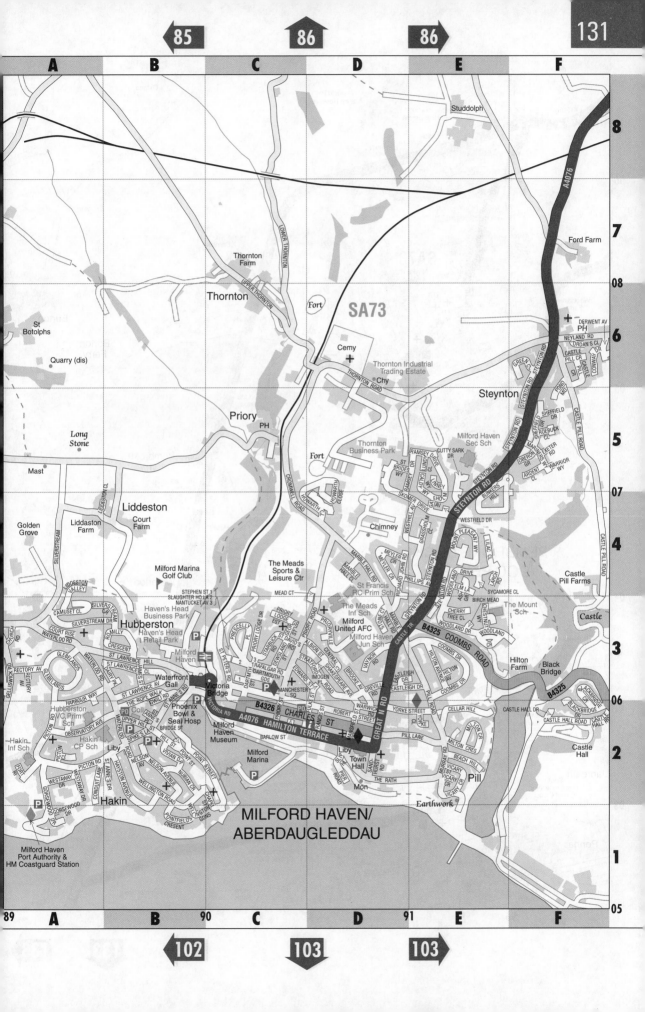

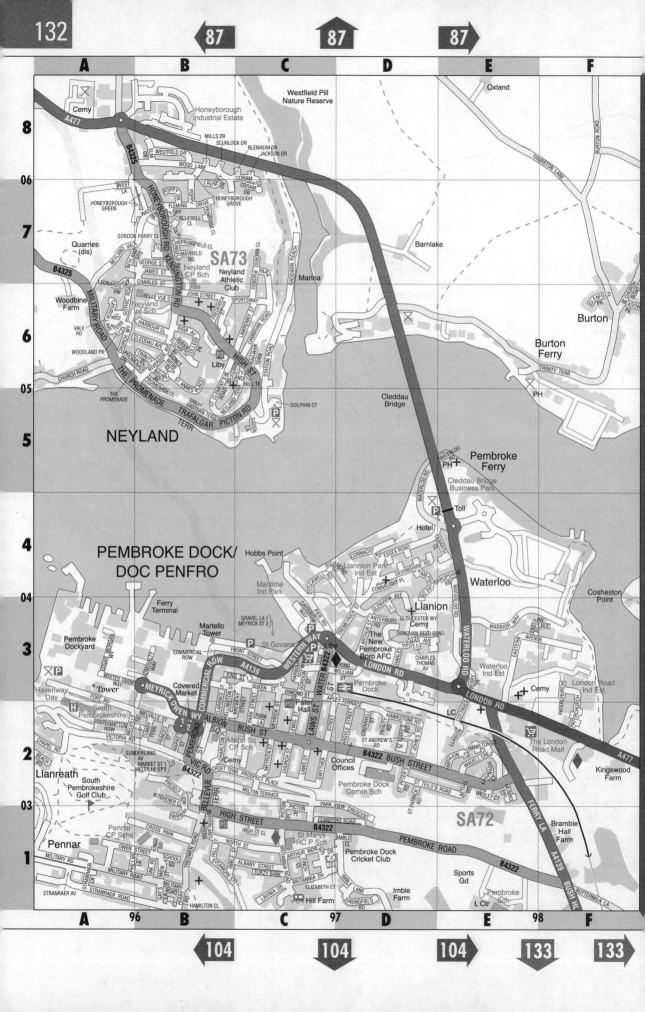

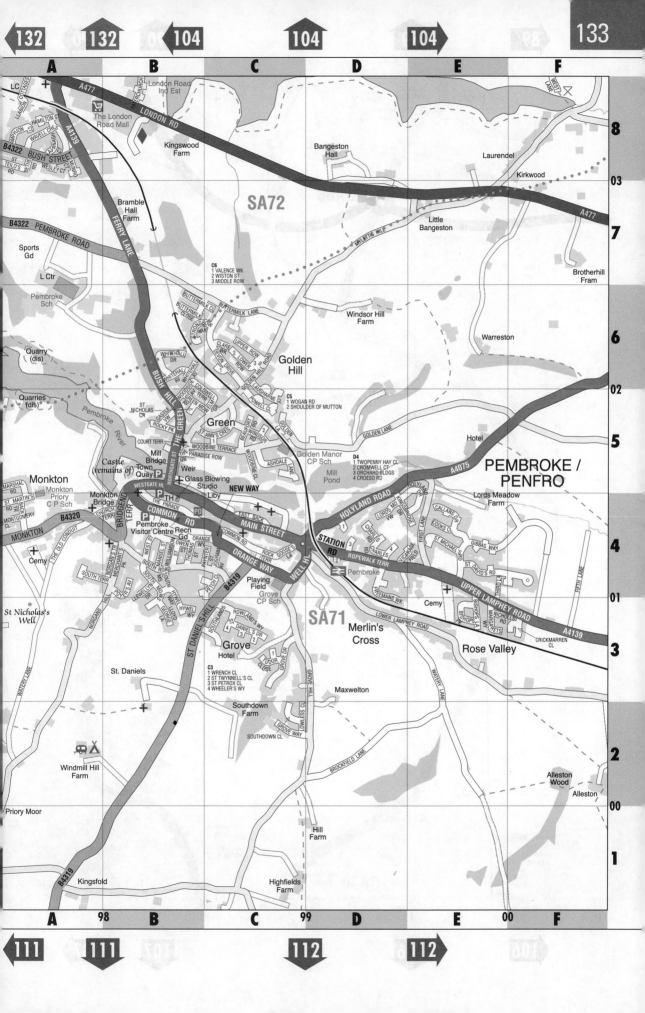

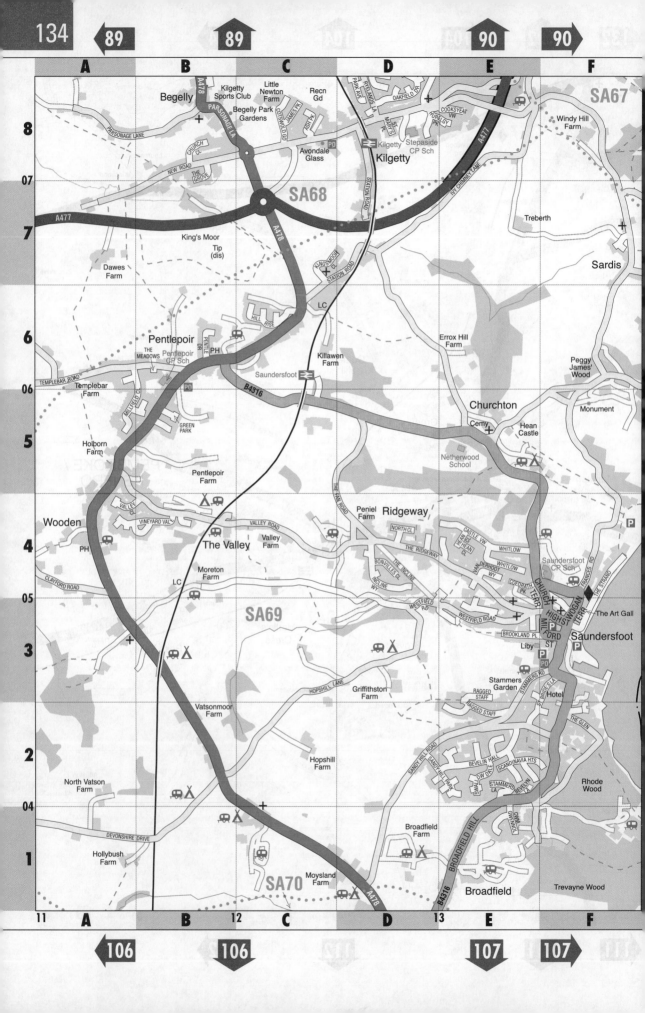

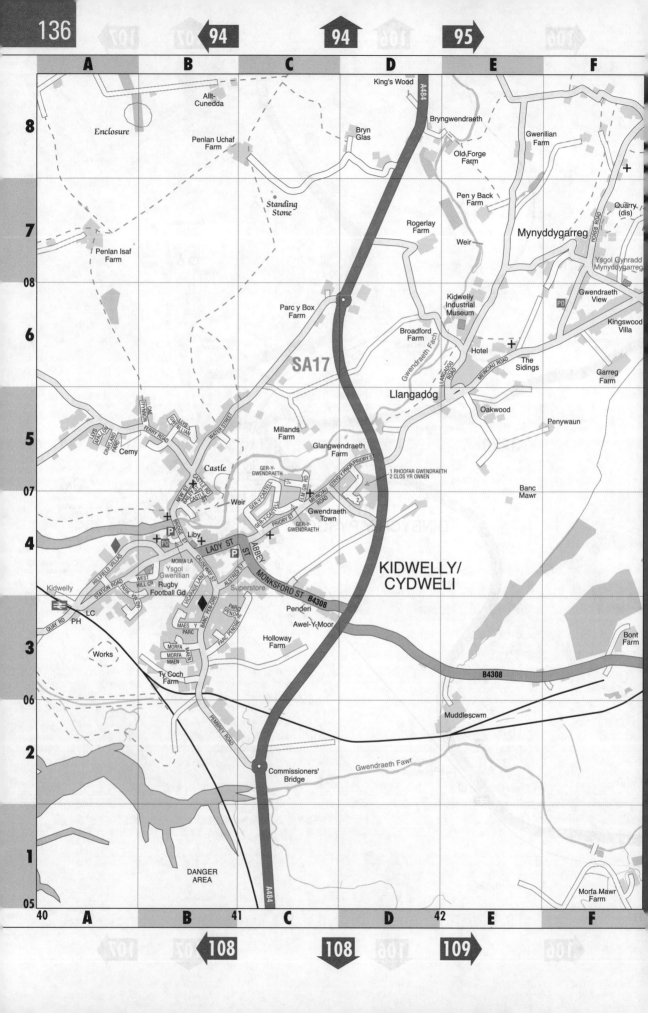

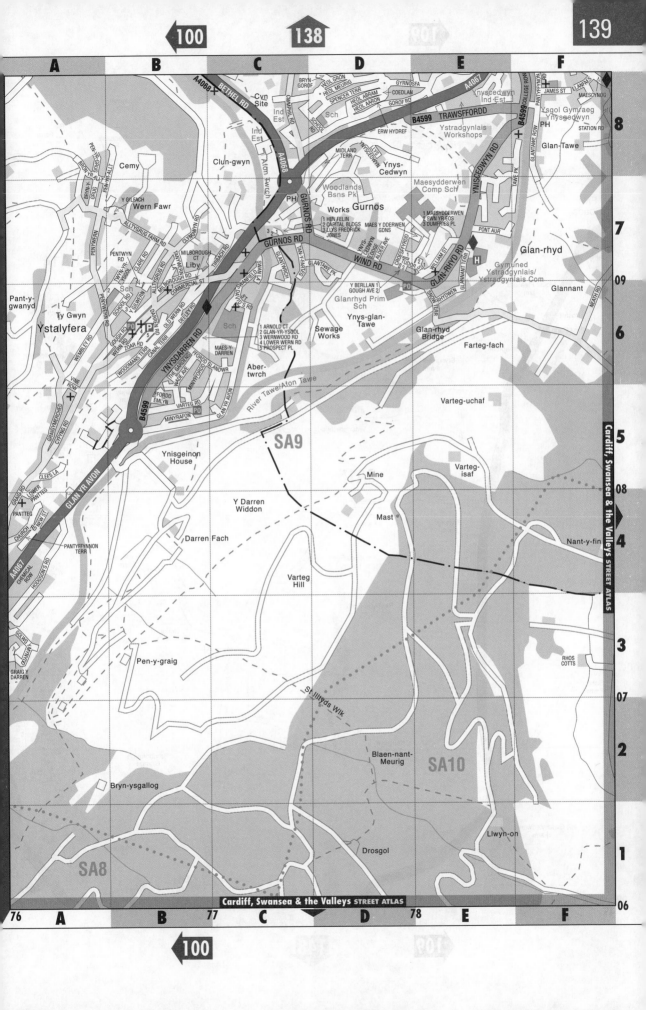

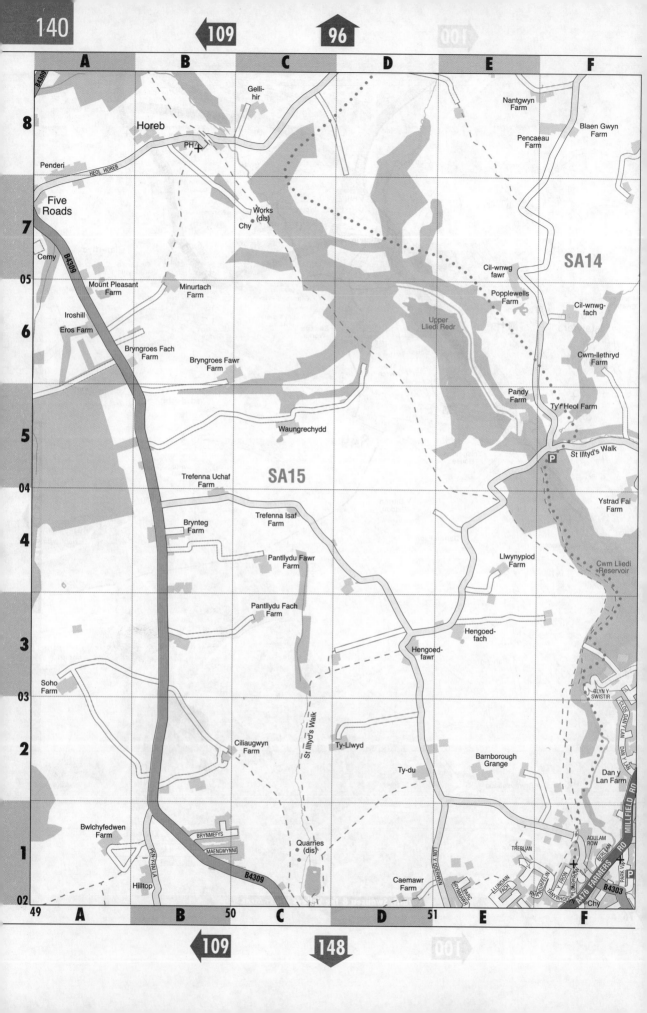

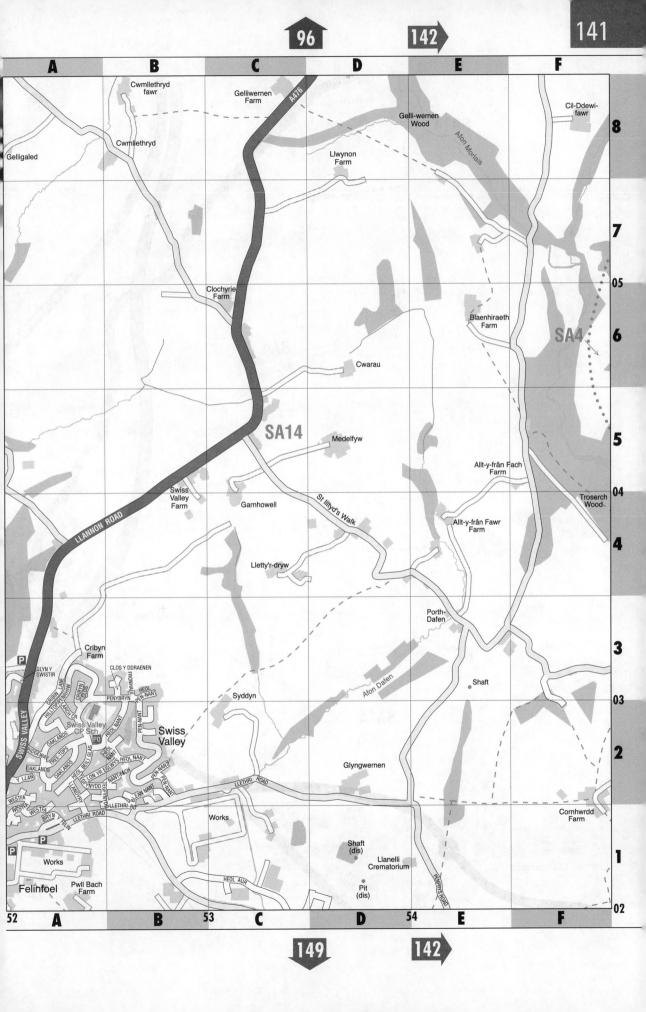

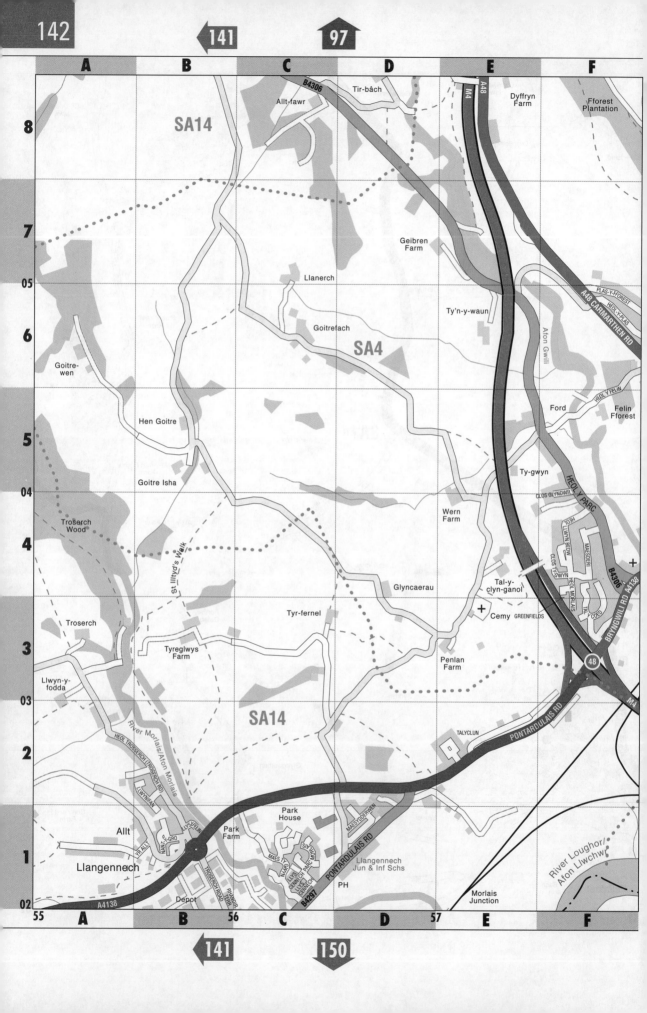

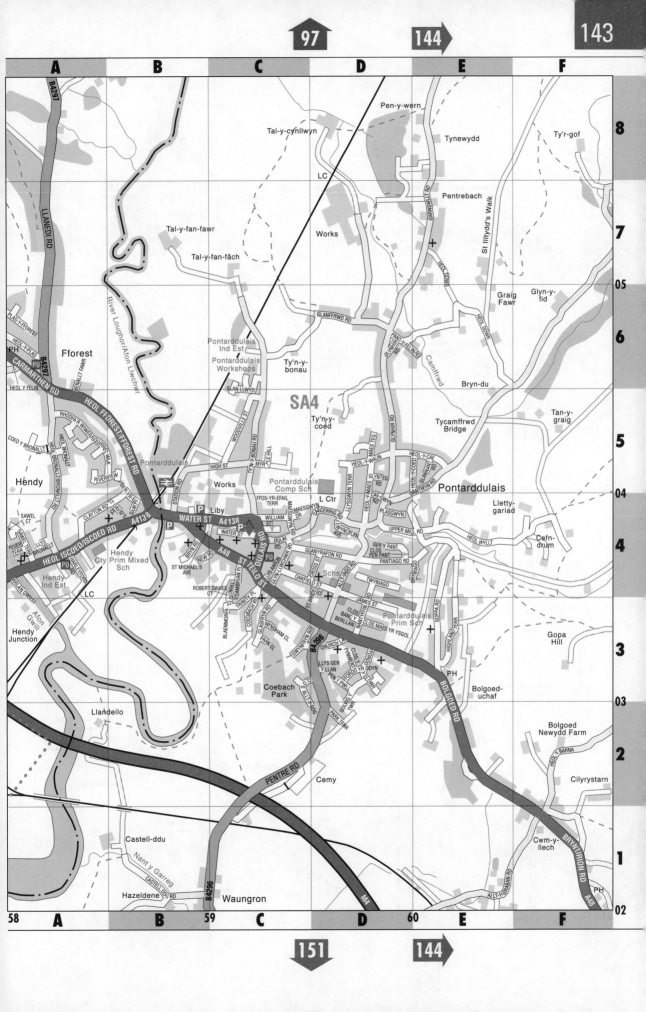

A B C D E F

8

Llandremor
ganol

Llandremor-
fawr

7

Camffrwd

05

Fir-
bâch

6

Twr
Maggie

Cefn
Drum

SA4

5

04

Dulais

4

Cwm
Dulais

3

03

Bryn-bach-
Common

Bryn-
Bâch

Pant-y-ffin

2

Brynawel

Tynrheol

Ty-llwyd

1

02

HEOL Y BARWR

BRYN BACH RD

Twyn
Tyle

Gelli-gwm
Rock

Gelli-gwm-
uchaf

Cwm Dulais

Hafod
las

Palé-bâch

Palé-mawr

Craig y Bedw

Tŵyn tyle

Gelli-gwm-
isaf

Cwm-
Dulais

Penlle'r
Bebyll

Mynydd
Pysgodlyn

Hen-
glawd

Ysgîach-
uchaf

Ysgîach

Cwrt-
mawr

Cwm Ysgîach

SA5

Sgiach Ganol

Ffynnon-
fedw

Tŵyn

Tyn-y-cwm

Crwca

Gelli-wern-
isaf

Gelli-wern-
fawr

Gelli-wern
ganol

Blaen-nant-
ddu

Ffynnon-
Sant

Nature
Reserve

Llwyngwenno

Careg-
lwyd

BWLCH Y GWYN

Sewage
Works

Ysgol Gynradd Gymraeg
Felindre

Felindre

PH

Cîl faen

HEOL GLYN-DÊL

HEOL MYDDFAI

61 A B 62 C D 63 E F

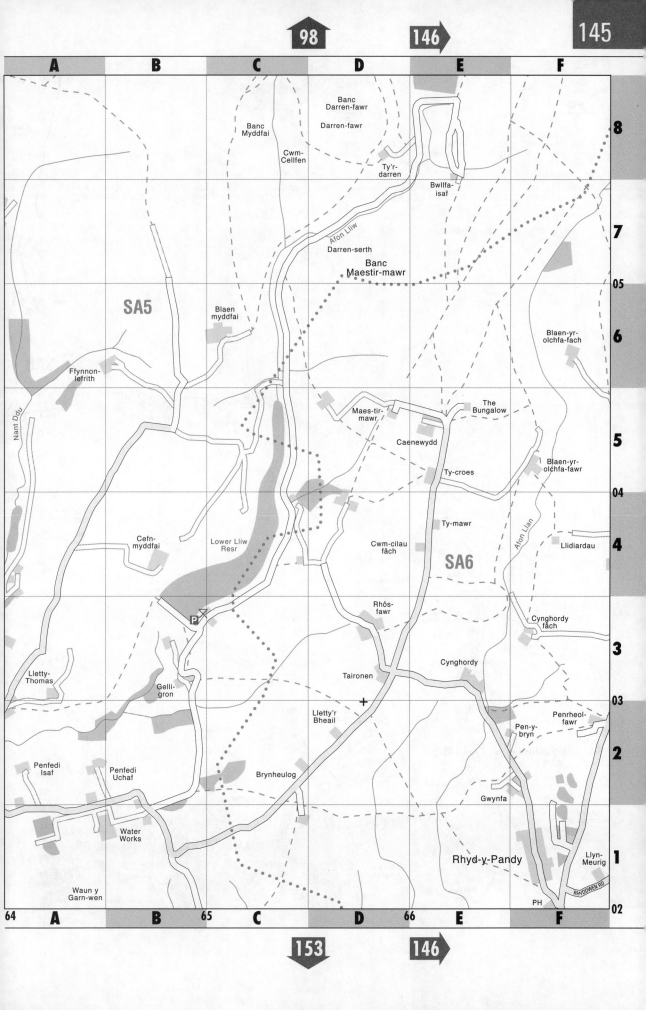

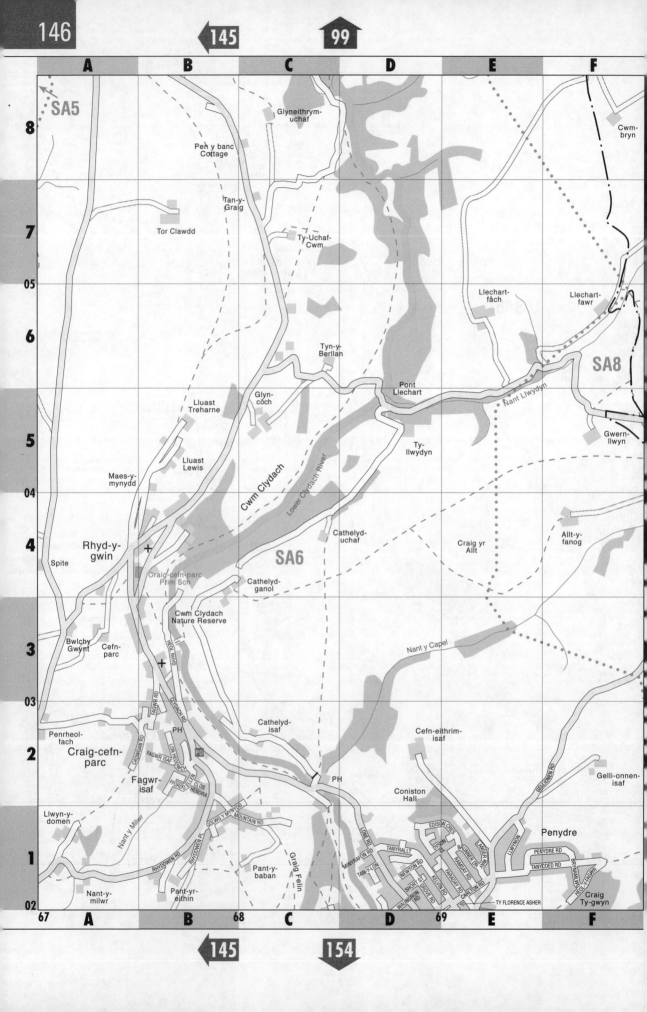

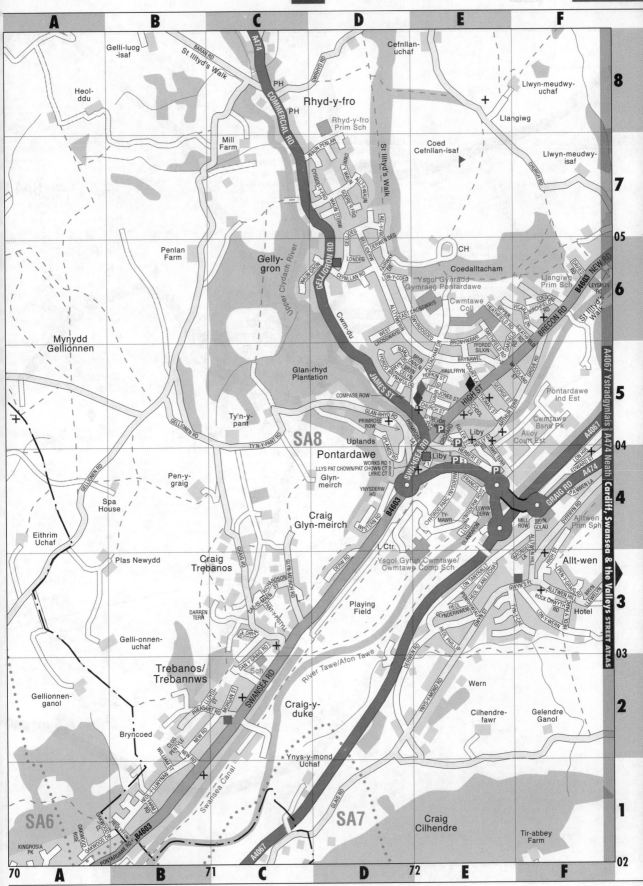

◀ 109

140 ⬡

115 ⬢

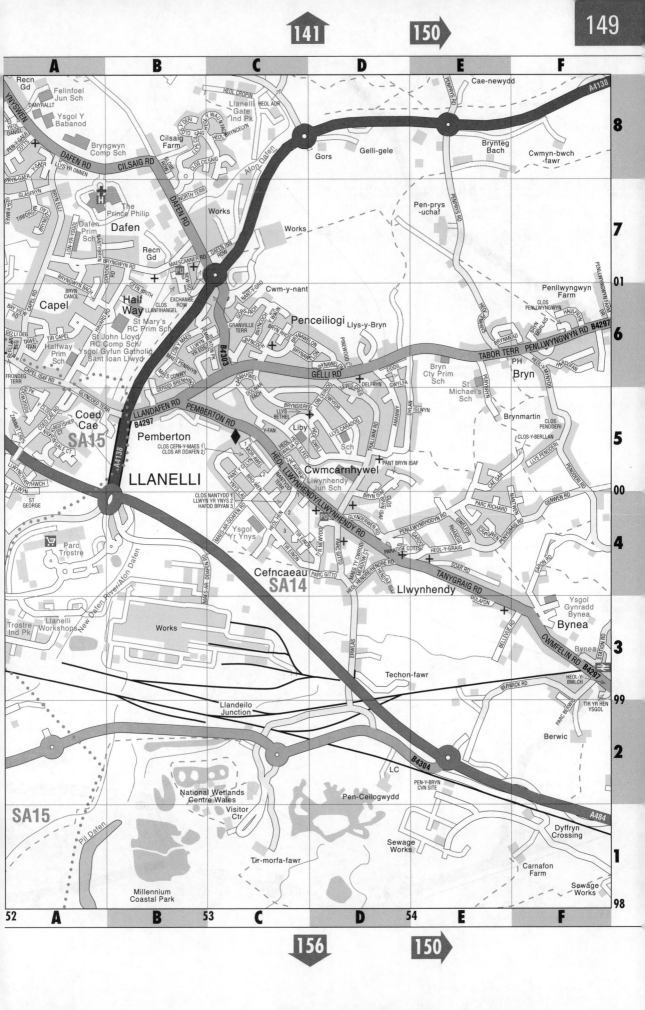

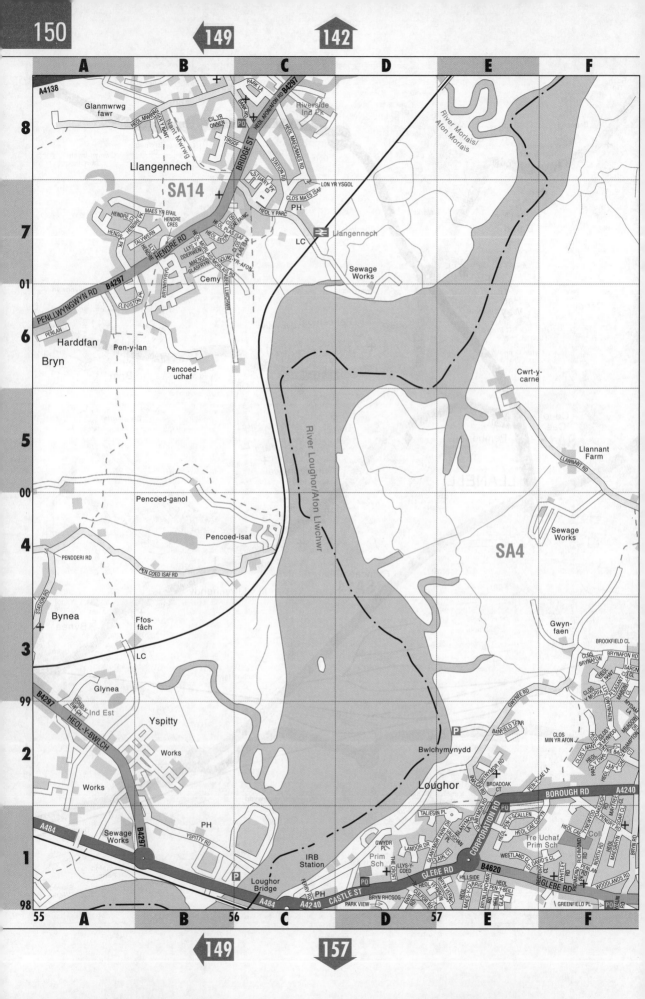

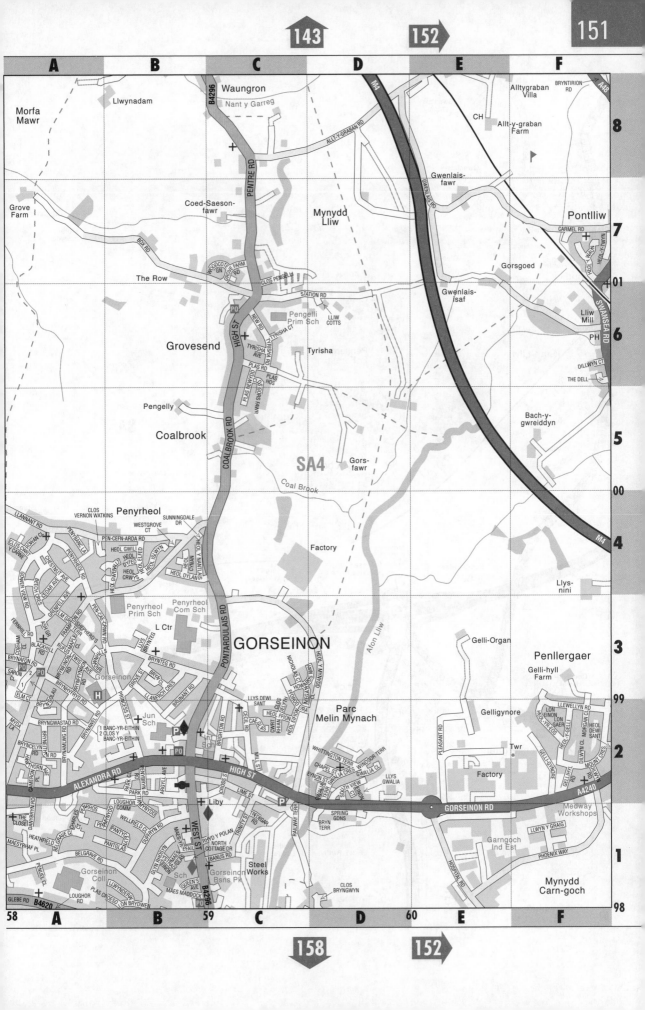

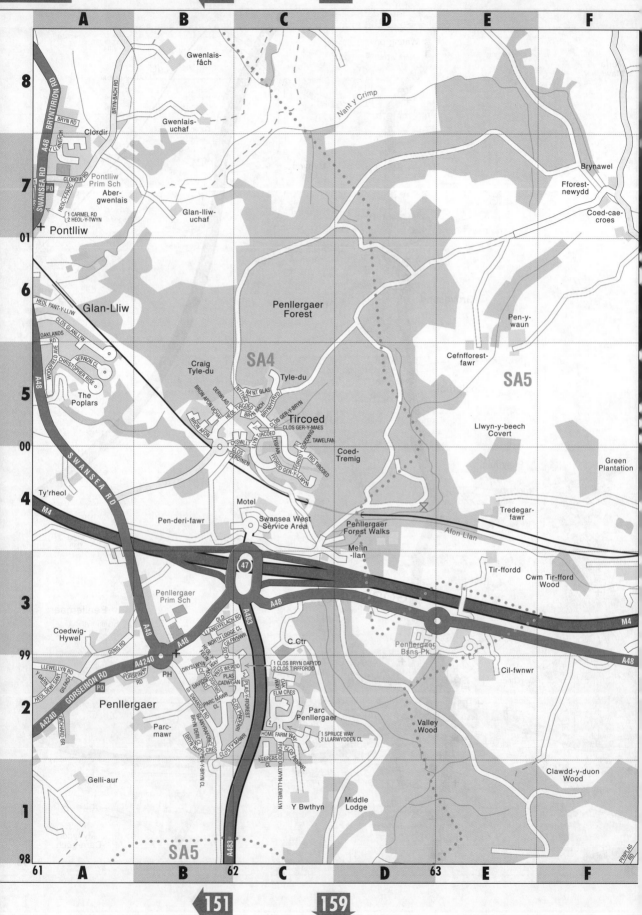

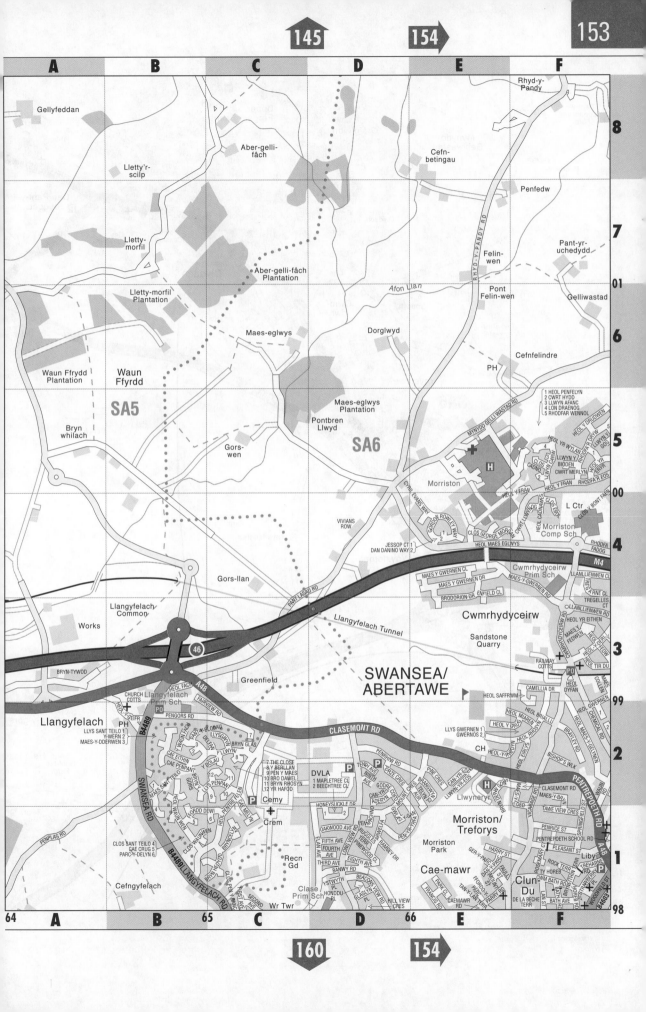

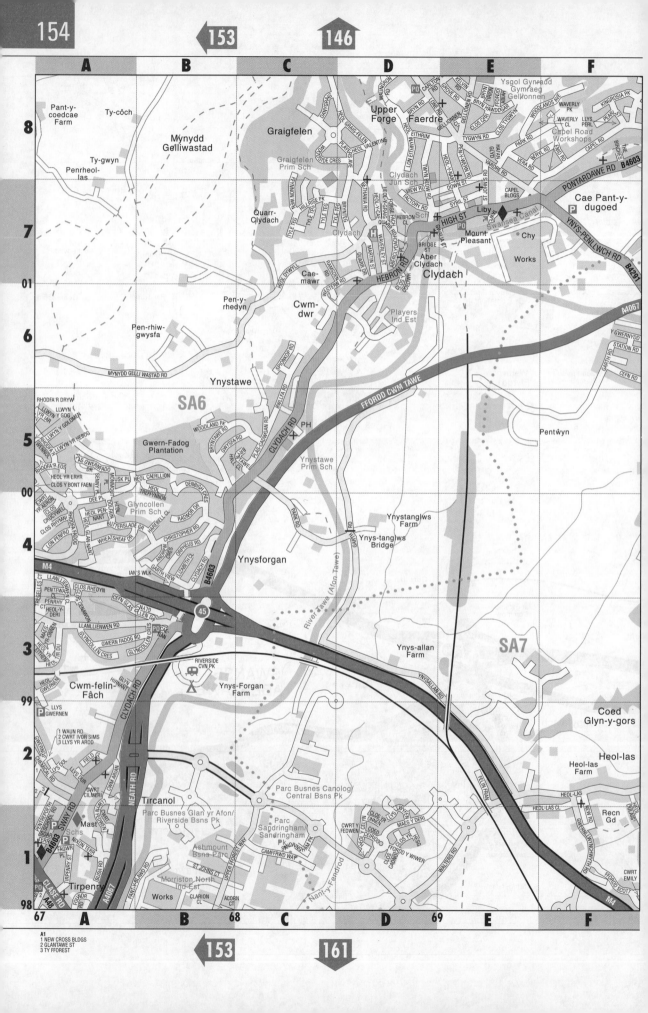

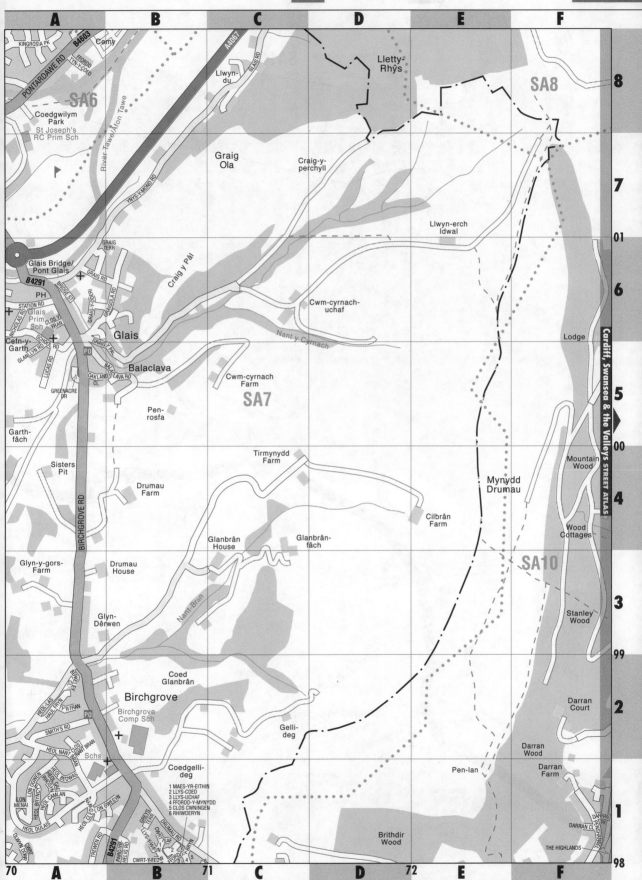

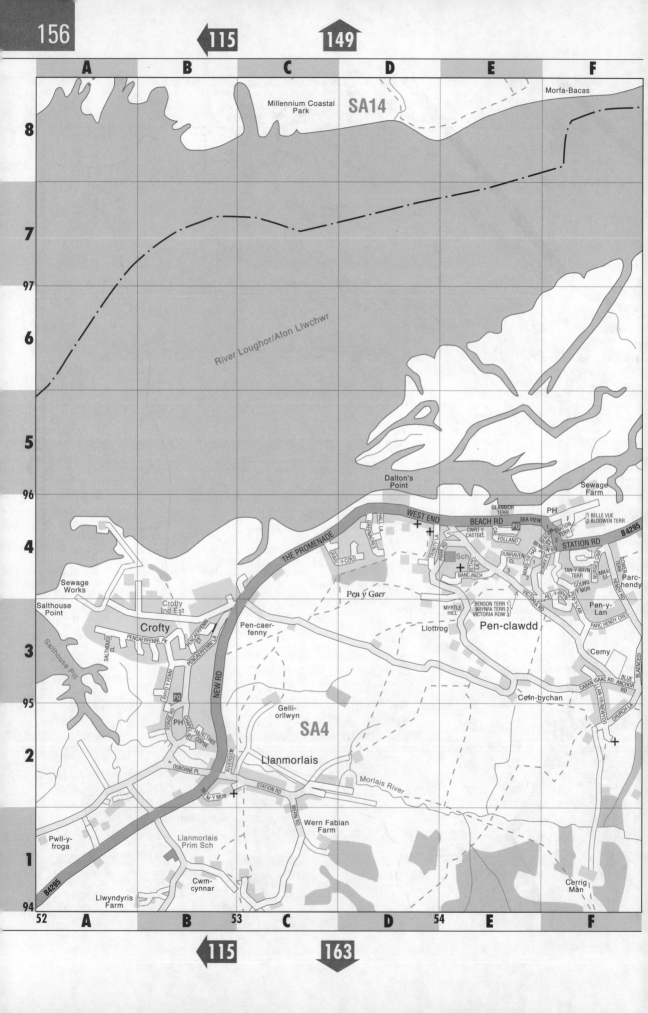

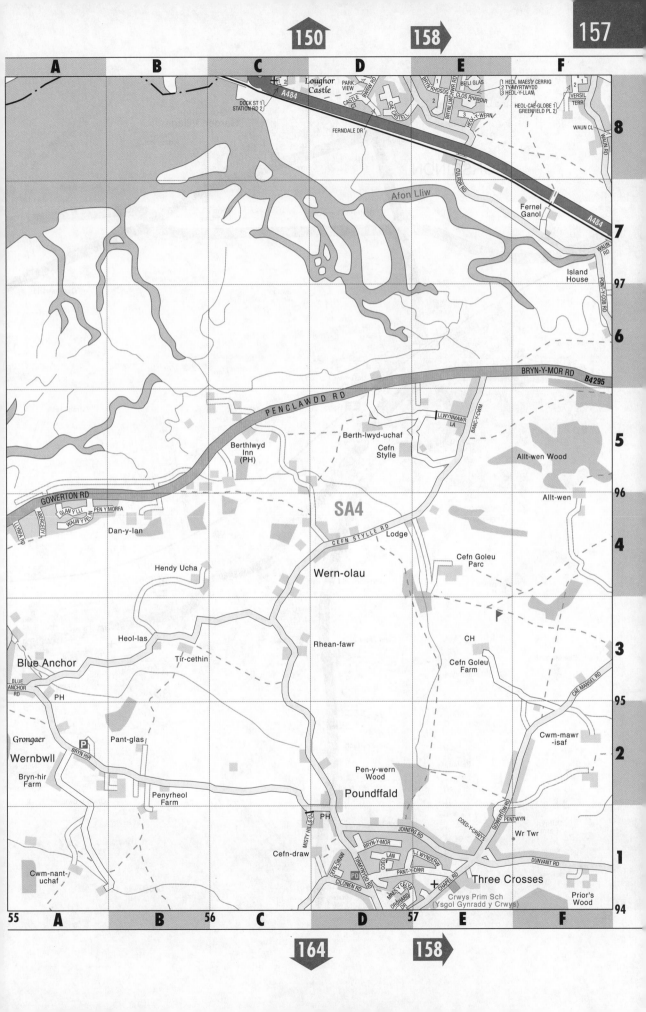

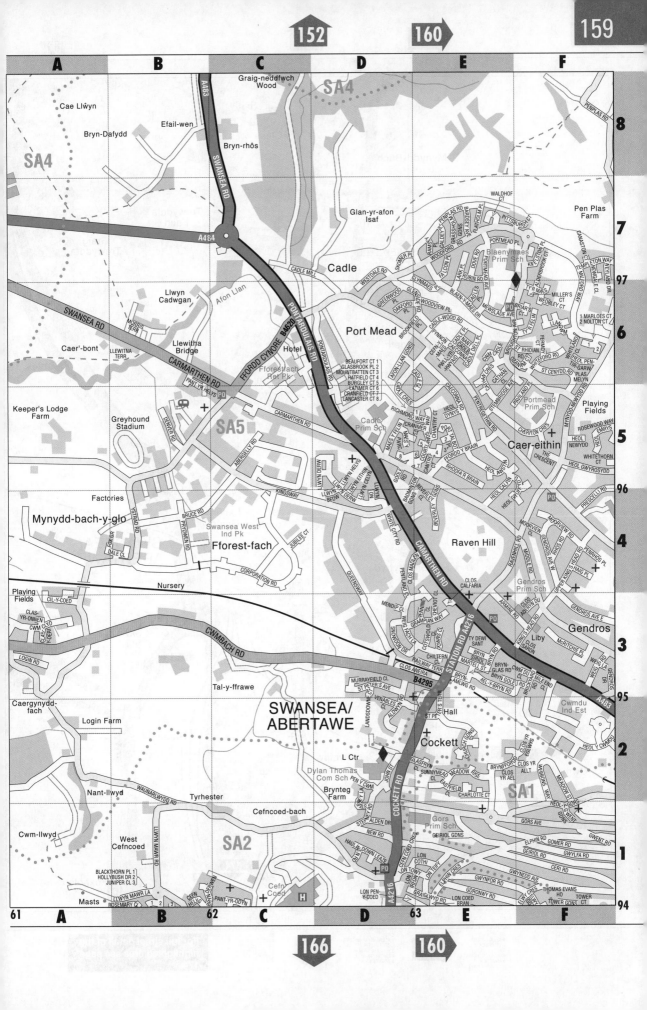

159 153

F8
1 LAN AVE
2 STAPLETON PL
3 BEDFORD HO
4 MARKET MEWS
5 MARKET ST
6 LOWER BANWELL ST

SA6
SA5
SA1
SWANSEA/ABERTAWE

Cefn Cadle Farm
Mynydd-Bâch
Daniel James Com Sch
Ty-côch
Clase
Clase Prim Sch
Bishop Vaughan RC Sch
Mynydd-Garn-Lwyd
Penybryn Senior Specl Sch
Trewyddfa Fach
Graig Trewyddfa
Pumplas-fâch
Mast
Tirdeunaw
Mynydd Cadle Common
Wr Twr
Llewelyn Park
Cwmgelli
Tre-boeth
Ysgol Gyfun Bryn Tawe
Waun-Gron
Cnap-Llwyd
Plasmarl
Plasmarl Prim Sch
Beaufort CT
Birmingham Mount
Plasmarl Ind Est
Playing Fields
1 PRIMROSE CT
2 BLUEBELL WAY
3 REDWOOD CT
4 FERN CT
Pen-lan
Gwyrosydd Jun & Inf Sch
Liby
Siemens Way
Llansamlet Ind Est
Lisbon
Penfilia
Landore/Glandwr
Superstore
Dry Ski Slope
Clwyd Com Prim Sch
Brynhyfryd
Morfa Sh Pk
Superstore
Liberty Stadium (Swansea City FC)
Tennis Ctr
Manselton
Manselton Prim Sch
1 DAVID ISSAC CL
2 WESTERN TERR
Wks
Vale Rd
Pentre
Pentre Mawr Rd
Penttrehafod Sch
Hafod
Hafod Prim Sch
Cwmdu
Superstore
Clos Burlais
Cwmbwrla
Cwmbwrla Prim Sch
John's Ho
Mayhill
Foxhole

CARMARTHEN RD
NEATH RD
PENTRECHWYTH RD
FFORDD CWM TAWE
River Tawe / Afon Tawe

159 167

C2
1 ALLAWAY CT
2 LYDBROOK CT
3 MILLWOOD CT
4 GORDON THOMAS CL
5 MARSDEN ST
6 JOSEPH DAVIES' CL

C4
1 PLEASANT VIEW TERR
2 CROFT TERR
3 PENFILIA TERR
4 BRYNHYFRYD SQ
5 WEAVERS MILL

D1
1 MONGER ST
2 GRANDISON ST
3 HARRINGTON PL
4 PONT-Y-GLASDWR

For full street detail of the highlighted area see page 174.

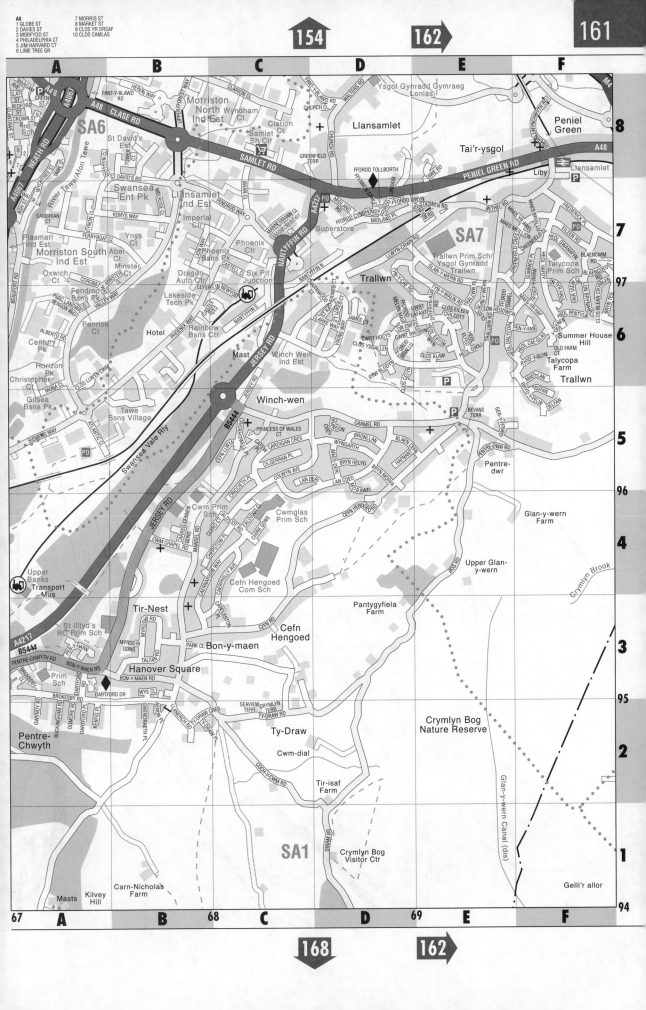

161
155

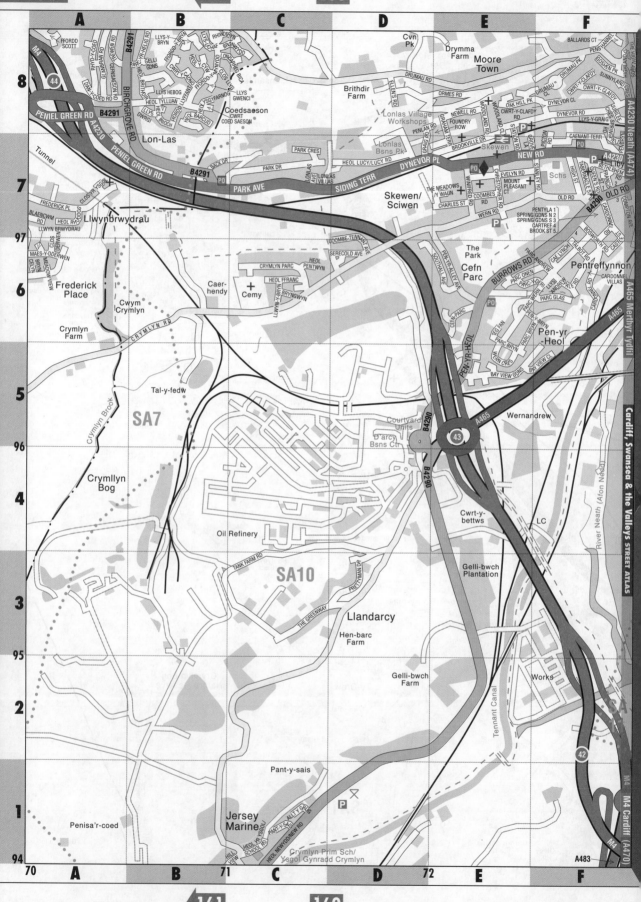

161
169

Cardiff, Swansea & the Valleys STREET ATLAS

115 156 164

A B C D E F

8

Rallt

Wern View

Penllwyn-Robert

The Farm

Highfield Farm

Ramblingay

Cil-onen

Gelli-groes

SA4

7

Bryn Farm

Bryn

Tircoch-isaf

Tircoch

Bryn-gwas

93

West Hills

6

Welsh Moor

Forest Common

Malthouse Farm

Windmill Wood

Roland's Wood

5

Little Hills

East Hills

Cillibion Plantation

92

SA3

Pengwern Common

SA2

4

Penrose Farm

B4271

3

Llethrid Bridge

Pengwern

Furzeland Farm

91

Llethrid Cwm

Furzehill Farm

2

Willoxton Farm

Lodge Cwm

Park Woods

Cathole Rock

1

90

52 A B 53 C D 54 E F

163
157

A **B** **C** **D** **E** **F**

8

Cilonnen-fach

Forgemill
Farm

Whitewalls
Farm

CHAPEL RD
THE GABLES
DUKEFIELD

Prior's
Meadow

SA4

Mynydd-Bach
-y-Cocs

Erw-fawr

Gelli-hîr

TIRMYNYDD RD

7

Fairwood

93

Wimblewood-
ganol

Caehendy
Wood

Wind Mill
Wood Farm

Gelli-hîr
Wood

6

Hafod Mill
Wood

Fairwood
Corner

B4271

A4118

5

Wimblewood-
isaf

SA2

92

Coed
Bryn-côch

Fairwood Common

4

Bryncoch
Farm

Swansea Airport

B4271

Cartersford
Bridge

P

BLACKHILLS LA

Blackhills

3

Blackhills Stream

91

Pen-y-banc

Werganrows
Farm

2

Bryn-afel

Moorlakes

Moorlakes
Wood

Ilston

1

Courthouse
Farm

SA3

Hams
Wood

Carey's
Wood

Canisland
Wood

CANNISLAND
PK

A4118

90

55 **A** **B** **56** **C** **D** **57** **E** **F**

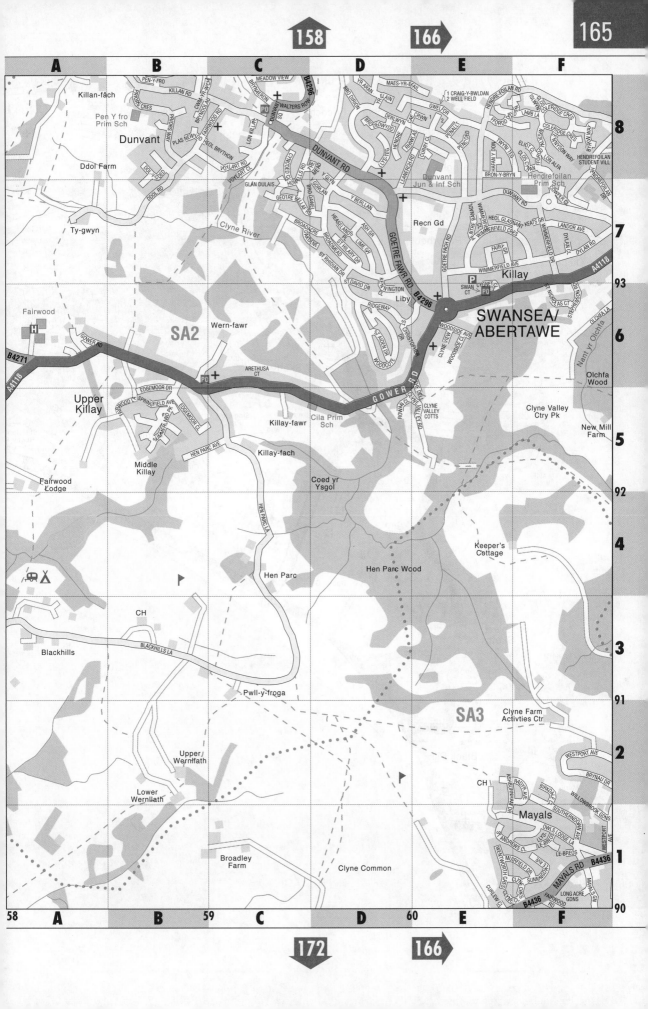

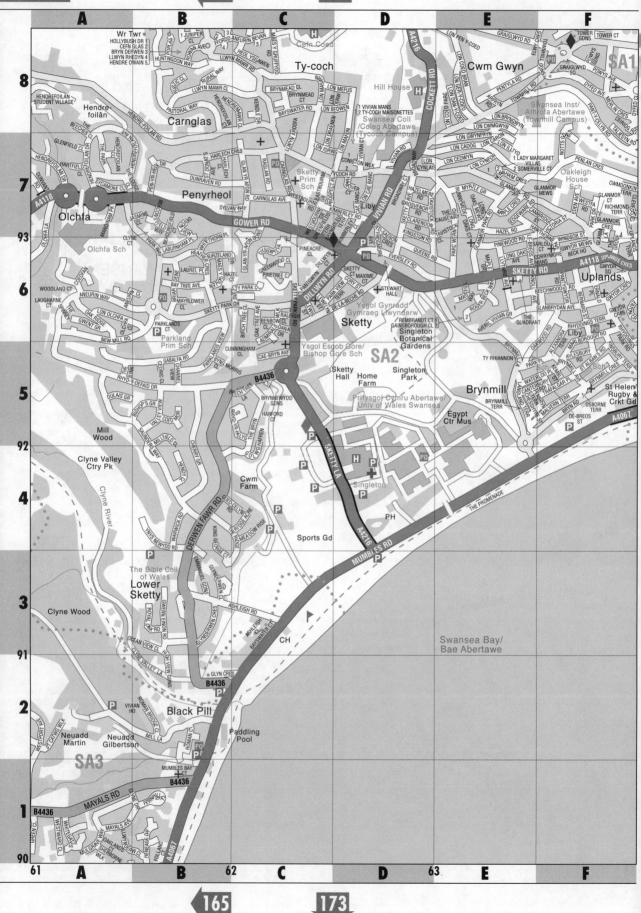

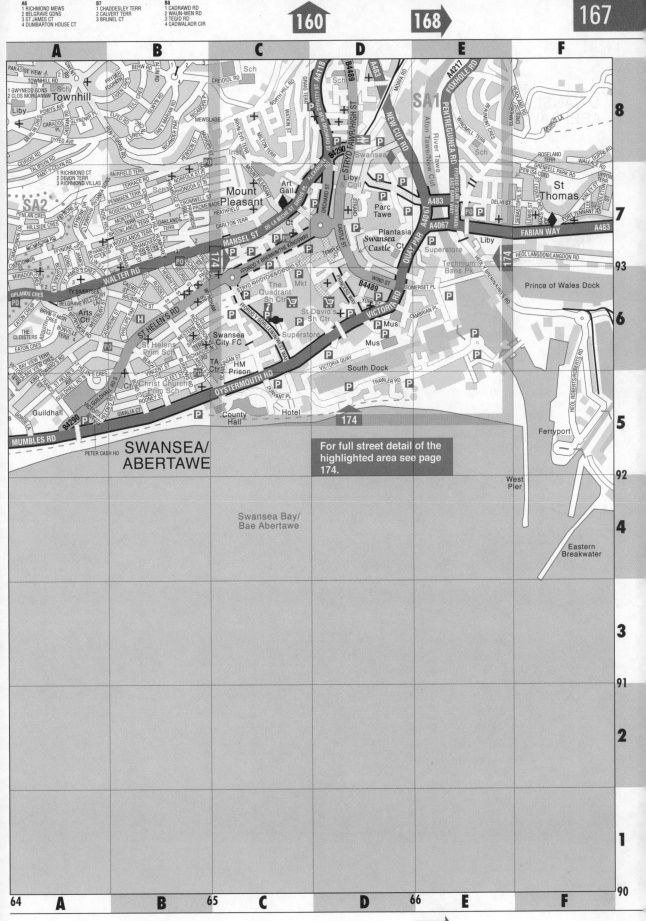

A6
1 RICHMOND MEWS
2 BELGRAVE GDNS
3 ST JAMES CT
4 DUMBARTON HOUSE CT

B7
1 CHADDESLEY TERR
2 CALVERT TERR
3 BRUNEL CT

B8
1 CADRAWD RD
2 WAUN-WEN RD
3 TEGID RD
4 CADWALADR CIR

For full street detail of the highlighted area see page 174.

SWANSEA/
ABERTAWE

Swansea Bay/
Bae Abertawe

A B C D E F

8

SWANSEA/
ABERTAWE

Windmill
(remains of)

Pen-y-graig

Port Tennant

GWYNNE TERR
HARBOUR VIEW
RD
ST ILLTYD'S CRES
Cemy
Dan-y-graig
TY
BEDDOE
ROBERT OWEN GDNS
DAVID WILLIAMS TERR
TIR JOHN NORTH RD
P

SA1

Tennant Canal (dis)

KINLEY
ST
MARGARET TERR
UPTON TERR
LONGFORD
CRES
OSTERLEY
ST
LINKINTON
TERR
ORMSBY
TERR
REGINALD ST
BAGLAN
ST
BAY ST
PORT TENNANT RD
DANYGRAIG RD
PANT ST
TYMAWR ST
GRAFOG ST
JERSEY TERR
GELLI ST
WILLIAM MORRIS
GDNS
CWM LA ST
KOOL ST
WERN TERR
WERN
FAWR RD

Works

7

A483
KSGOL ST
Danygraig
Prim Sch
P&R
VALE OF NEATH ST
FABIAN WAY

Works

93
HEOL LANGDON/LANGDON RD
BEVAN'S ROW
Works

BALDWIN'S CRES
BALDWIN'S CRES
Works

P
PQ
A483

LC's

6

King's Dock

LC

Jetties

5

Queen's Dock

Jetties

Jetties

Dry
Dock

Jetties

92

Jetty

4

3

91

2

1

90

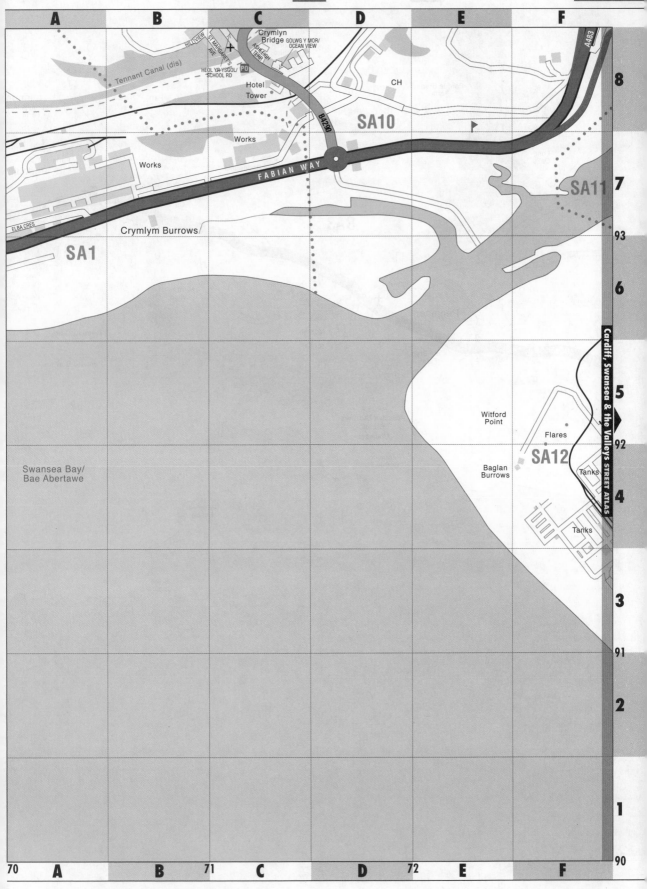

A B C D E F

8

7

93

6

5

92

4

3

91

2

1

90

Tennant Canal (dis)

Crymlyn
Bridge
GOLWG Y MOR/
OCEAN VIEW

HILLVIEW
ST MARGARET'S AVE
HEDL YR YSGOL/
SCHOOL RD
ASHLEIGH TERR
PO

Hotel
Tower

CH

B4290

SA10

Works

Works

FABIAN WAY

ELBA CRES

SA1

Crymlym Burrows

SA11

Swansea Bay/
Bae Abertawe

Witford
Point

Flares

Baglan
Burrows

SA12

Tanks

Tanks

A483

Cardiff, Swansea & the Valleys STREET ATLAS

◀ 117
163 ▲

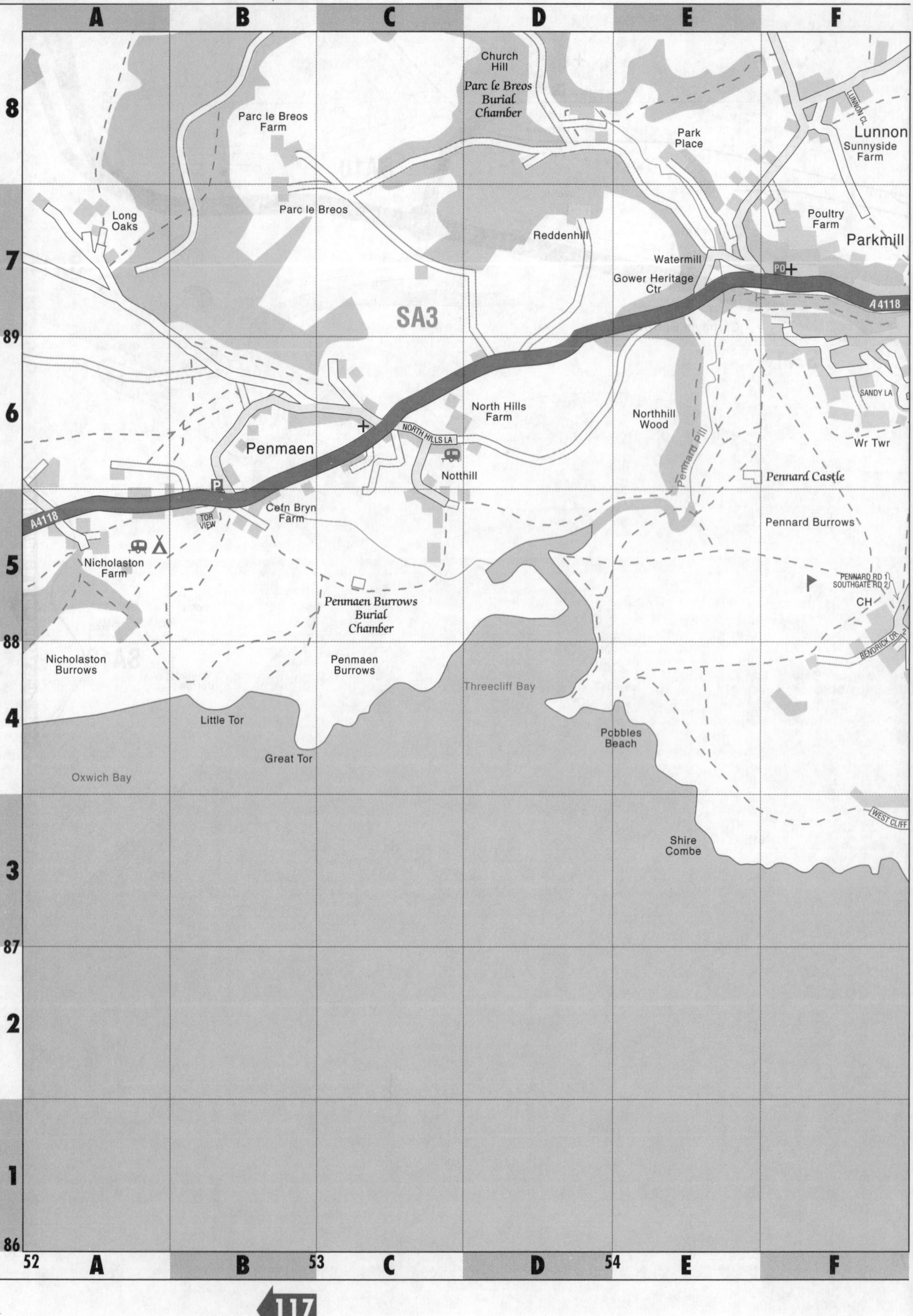

A B C D E F

8

Church Hill
Parc le Breos Burial Chamber

Parc le Breos Farm

Park Place

Lunnon

LUNNON CL

Sunnyside Farm

Long Oaks

Parc le Breos

Reddenhill

Poultry Farm

Parkmill

7

Watermill
Gower Heritage Ctr

PO ✚

A 4118

SA3

89

SANDY LA

North Hills Farm

Northhill Wood

Wr Twr

6

Penmaen

NORTH HILLS LA

Notthill

Pennard Castle

Pennard Pill

P

Cefn Bryn Farm

Pennard Burrows

A4118

TOR VIEW

PENNARD RD 1
SOUTHGATE RD 2

▶

5

Nicholaston Farm

CH

Penmaen Burrows Burial Chamber

BEVERICK DR

88

Nicholaston Burrows

SA

Penmaen Burrows

Threecliff Bay

WEST CLIFF

4

Little Tor

Great Tor

Pobbles Beach

Oxwich Bay

Shire Combe

3

87

2

1

86

52 A B 53 C D 54 E F

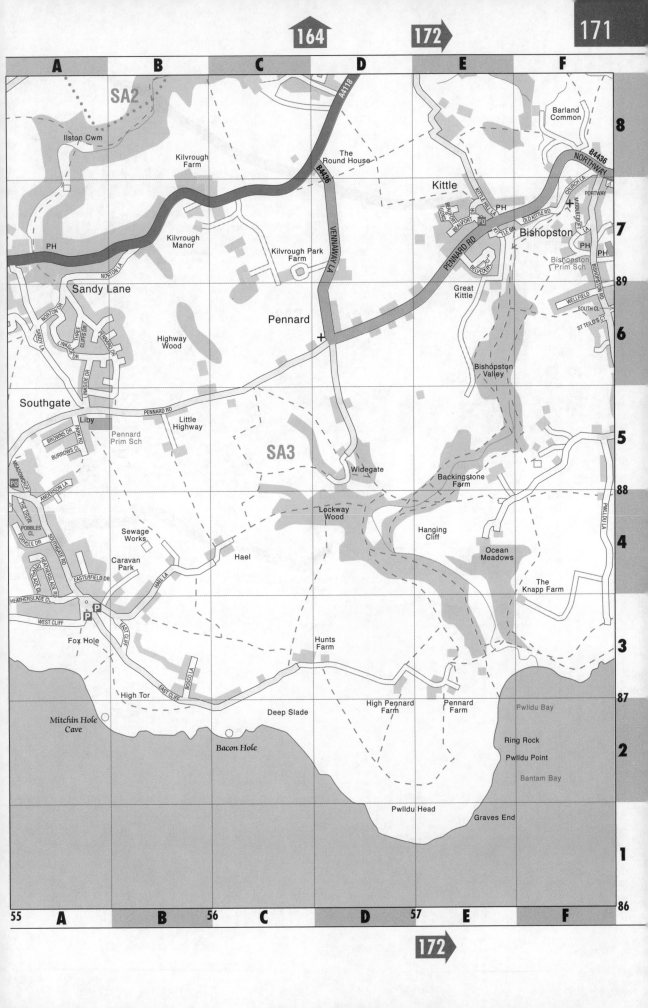

SA2

Ilston Cwm

Kilvrough Farm

Barland Common

The Round House

B4436

B4436 NORTHWAY

Kittle

Kilvrough Manor

PH

KITTLE HILL LA

Portway

Church la

PH

PO

OLD KITTLE RD

Bishopston

PH

Kilvrough Park Farm

BEAUFORT GDNS

BEAUFORT

PENNARD RD

KITTLE GN

MIDDLECROFT LA

VENNAWAY LA

BELVEDRE

Bishopston Prim Sch

PH

Norton La

PH

Sandy Lane

Pennard

Great Kittle

89

A4118

WELLFIELD

SOUTH CL

BISHOPSTON RD

ST TEILO'S CT

NORTON DR

THREE CLIFFS DR

LINKS DR

PENNARD DR

Highway Wood

Bishopston Valley

6

SANDY LA

LINKSIDE DR

Southgate

PENNARD RD

Little Highway

SA3

5

Liby

Pennard Prim Sch

Backingstone Farm

BROWNS DR

PARK RD

88

MEADOWCROFT

BURROWS CL

Lockway Wood

Hanging Cliff

PWLLDU LA

ANDERSON LA

PO

THE DRIVE

Sewage Works

Hael

Ocean Meadows

4

POBBLES CL

FOXHOLE DR

SOUTHGATE RD

Caravan Park

The Knapp Farm

HEATHERSLADE RD

HAEL LA

HEATHERSLADE CL

EASTERFIELD DR

P

P

Fox Hole

EAST CLIFF

Hunts Farm

WEST CLIFF

3

BOSCO LA

High Tor

EAST CLIFF

87

Deep Slade

High Pennard Farm

Pennard Farm

Pwlldu Bay

Mitchin Hole Cave

Bacon Hole

Ring Rock

2

Pwlldu Point

Bantam Bay

Pwlldu Head

Graves End

1

86

171
165

A B C D E F

8

B4436 MAYALS RD
GONHILL 1
NORTHERON 2
BETTSLAND 3
BROADPARKS 4
LEYSHAN WLK 5
CROSS ACRE 6
WHITE GR 7
YALTON 8

WHITESTONE
MAYALS GN 1
THE GLADE 2

FAIRWOOD RD

Sunnybank

Ryeground
Farm

Craig y nos
Sch

B4436
PORTWAY

NORTHWAY

Campion
Gardens

Clyne Common

7

The Glebe
Bishopston
Comp Sch

Murton
Green

Mansel
Green

Copley Cl

Bishopston
Prim Sch

PROVIDENCE LA

PH

Murton

Whitestone
Prim Sch

89

Manselfield

MANSELFIELD RD

REIGIT LA

SA3

6

South Cl

LONG ACRE
CT

LIME KILN LA

HILLAND
DR

MEAD CRES

MANSEL DR

MILES LA

YALONE

Oldway

Vensland

WITHY PK

RIDLEY WAY

GEORGE

PYLE CT

KILFIELD RD

HOLTS
FIELD

Lady Housty
Ho

Newton
Prim Sch

Colts Hill

Cemy

5

2 PO

BRANDY COVE RD

HEADLAND RD

WESTFIELD

CASWELL BAY RD

WHITESTONE RD

Pyle

Herberts Lodge
Farm

MURTON LA

Lady
Housty

SUMMERLAND LA

Newton

PO

1 DOUGLAS CT
2 PWLLDU LA

88

Sewage
Wks

Bishop's Wood
Nature Reserve

LONG SHEPHERD

CASWELL AVE

ST PETER'S RD

SOUTHWARD LA

B4593

4

Hareslade

CASWELL RD

CASWELL BAY
CT

P

B4593

CASWELL BAY

P

Bishop's Wood
Countryside Ctr

SUMMERCLIFFE
CHALET PK

VICTORIA CT

CASWELL RD

Langland

HIGHCLIFFE
CT

P

Brandy
Cove

LINKSIDE

WESTWINDS

CRAWSHAY

LINKS CT

CH

LANGLAND BAY RD

P

AEL-Y-DON   ST
LEONARDS

3

87

Newton Cliff

Snaple Point

Langland Bay

2

Whiteshell
Point

1

86

58 A B 59 C D 60 E F

171

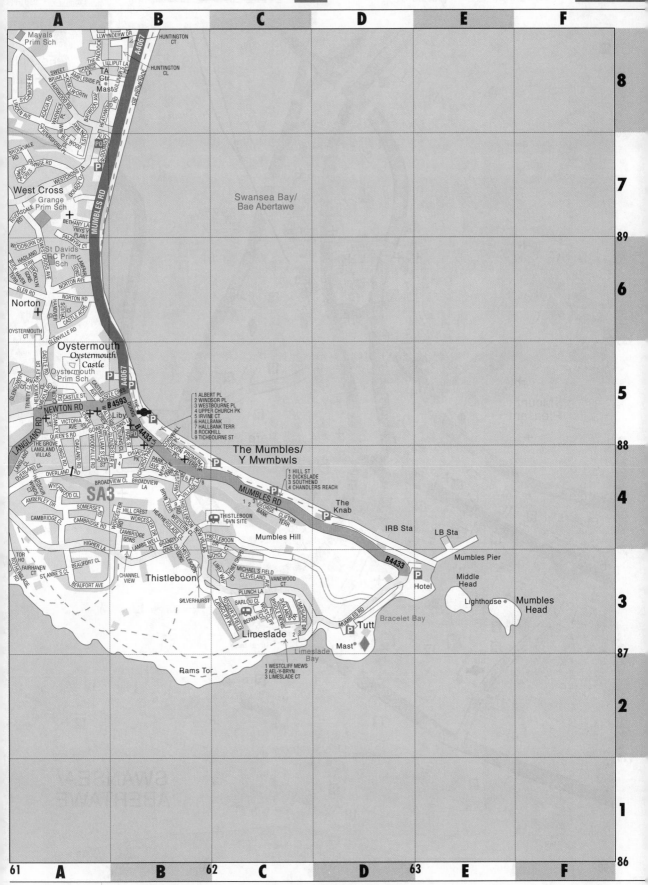

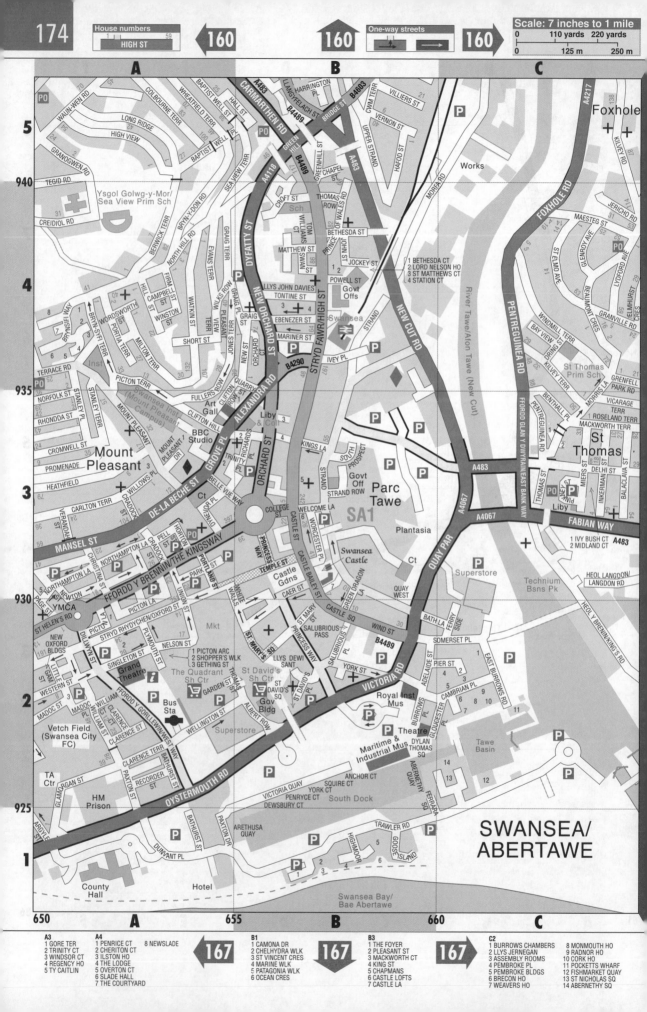

Index

Church Rd ⑥ Beckenham BR2..........**53** C6

Place name
May be abbreviated on the map

Location number
Present when a number indicates the place's position in a crowded area of mapping

Locality, town or village
Shown when more than one place has the same name

Postcode district
District for the indexed place

Page and grid square
Page number and grid reference for the standard mapping

Public and commercial buildings are highlighted in magenta   **Places of interest** are highlighted in blue with a star★

Abbreviations used in the index

Acad	Academy	Comm	Common	Gd	Ground	L	Leisure	Prom	Promenade
App	Approach	Cott	Cottage	Gdn	Garden	La	Lane	Rd	Road
Arc	Arcade	Cres	Crescent	Gn	Green	Liby	Library	Recn	Recreation
Ave	Avenue	Cswy	Causeway	Gr	Grove	Mdw	Meadow	Ret	Retail
Bglw	Bungalow	Ct	Court	H	Hall	Meml	Memorial	Sh	Shopping
Bldg	Building	Ctr	Centre	Ho	House	Mkt	Market	Sq	Square
Bsns, Bus	Business	Ctry	Country	Hospl	Hospital	Mus	Museum	St	Street
Bvd	Boulevard	Cty	County	HQ	Headquarters	Orch	Orchard	Sta	Station
Cath	Cathedral	Dr	Drive	Hts	Heights	Pal	Palace	Terr	Terrace
Cir	Circus	Dro	Drove	Ind	Industrial	Par	Parade	TH	Town Hall
Cl	Close	Ed	Education	Inst	Institute	Pas	Passage	Univ	University
Cnr	Corner	Emb	Embankment	Int	International	Pk	Park	Wk, Wlk	Walk
Coll	College	Est	Estate	Intc	Interchange	Pl	Place	Wr	Water
Com	Community	Ex	Exhibition	Junc	Junction	Prec	Precinct	Yd	Yard

Translations Welsh – English

Aber	Estuary, confluence	Cwrt	Court	Maes	Open area, field, square	Rhodfa	Avenue
Afon	River	Dinas	City	Môr	Sea	Sgwar	Square
Amgueddfa	Museum	Dôl	Meadow	Mynydd	Mountain	Stryd	Street
Bro	Area, district	Eglwys	Church	Oriel	Gallery	Swyddfa post	Post office
Bryn	Hill	Felin	Mill	Parc	Park	Tref, Tre	Town
Cae	Field	Fferm	Farm	Parc busnes	Business park	Tŷ	House
Caer	Fort	Ffordd	Road, way	Pen	Top, end	Uchaf	Upper
Canolfan	Centre	Gelli	Grove	Pentref	Village	Ysbyty	Hospital
Capel	Chapel	Gerddi	Gardens	Plas	Mansion, place	Ysgol	School
Castell	Castle	Heol	Road	Pont	Bridge	Ystad, stad	Estate
Cilgant	Crescent	Isaf	Lower	Prifysgol	University	Ystad ddiwydiannol	Industrial estate
Clòs	Close	Llan	Church, parish	Rhaeadr	Waterfall		
Coed	Wood	Llyn	Lake	Rhes	Terrace, row	Ystrad	Vale
Coleg	College	Lôn	Lane	Rhiw	Hill, incline		
Cwm	Valley						

Translations English – Welsh

Avenue	Rhodfa	Estuary	Aber	Lower	Isaf	Square	Sgwâr, maes
Bridge	Pont	Farm	Fferm	Mansion	Plas	Street	Stryd
Business Park	Parc busnes	Field	Cae	Meadow	Dôl	Terrace	Rhes
Castle	Castell	Fort	Caer	Mill	Felin	Top, end	Pen
Centre	Canolfan	Gallery	Oriel	Mountain	Mynydd	Town	Tref, tre
Chapel	Capel	Gardens	Gerddi	Museum	Amgueddfa	University	Prifysgol
Church	Eglwys	Grove	Gelli	Parish	Llan, plwyf, eglwys	Upper	Uchaf
City	Dinas	Hill	Bryn, rhiw	Park	Parc	Vale	Ystrad, glyn, dyffryn
Close	Clòs	Hospital	Ysbyty	Place	Plas, maes	Valley	Cwm
College	Coleg	House	Tŷ	Post office	Swyddfa post	Village	Pentref
Court	Cwrt, Llys	Industrial estate	Ystad ddiwydiannol	River	Afon	Waterfall	Rhaeadr
Crescent	Cilgant			Road	Heol	Way	Ffordd
District	Bro	Lake	Llyn	School	Ysgol	Wood	Coed
Estate	Ystad, stad	Lane	Lôn	Sea	Môr		

Index of localities, towns and villages

A

Aber Arad 119 F4
Aber-banc 18 F4
Abercastle 29 C6
Abercych 16 F3
Aberdaugleddau / Milford Haven 131 C1
Abereiddy 28 D4
Aber-Giâr 21 B4
Abergorlech 41 D4
Abergwaun / Fishguard 122 E2
Abergwesyn 9 A7
Abergwili 129 E7
Abernant 57 C2
Abertawe / Swansea 174 C1
Aberteifi / Cardigan 118 E3
Achddu 137 E3
Adpar 119 D6
Albert Town 124 E4
Allt 142 A1
Alltwalis 39 B2
Allt-wen 147 F3
Ambleston 51 F4
Ammanford / Rhydaman 98 A8
Amroth 90 D1
Angle 102 D6
Arberth / Narberth 70 D1
Ashfield 63 B7

B

Babel 45 D6
Backe 127 A3
Balaclava 155 B5
Bancffosfelen 95 F6
Bancycapel 76 A2
Bancyfelin 74 A4
Bancyffordd 38 E8
Bangor Teifi 19 A3
Begelly 134 B8
Bengal 31 A3
Berea 28 C2
Berry 117 B6
Bethesda 70 C4
Bethlehem 63 B4
Betws 98 C6
Betws Bledrws 4 E6
Bicton 85 B2
Bigyn 148 E4
Birchgrove 155 B2
Bishopston 171 F7
Black Pill 166 B2
Blaenffos 35 A8
Blaenwaun 55 E6
Blaen-y-coed 57 E6
Bletherston 69 F8
Blue Anchor 157 A3
Bolahaul 129 B1
Boncath 16 B1
Bon-y-maen 161 C3
Bosherston 111 E3
Boulston 87 C7
Box 148 F6
Brechfa 40 D1
Bridell 15 E5
Bridgend 118 D3
Brimaston 50 E4
Broadfield 134 E1
Broad Haven 85 C8
Broadlay 94 A4
Broadmoor 106 C8
Broad Oak 61 D1
Broadway Laugharne Township 92 E4
Broadway St Ishmael 94 B3
Broadway The Havens 85 E8
Brongest 18 A8
Brongwyn 17 D6
Bronwydd Arms 58 E2
Brook 92 B4
Broom 89 D3
Bryn Crofty 163 B7
Bryn Llanelli 149 F6
Brynamman 99 E8
Brynamman Quarter Bach 80 D1
Brynberian 33 C6
Bryngwyn Beulah 17 E8
Bryngwyn Brawdy 49 B3
Bryn-henllan 12 F4
Brynhyfryd 160 C4
Bryn Iwan 37 A2
Brynmill 166 E5
Brynteg 20 F6
Burry Green 115 A2
Burry Port / Porth Tywyn 137 D4
Burton 132 F6
Burton Ferry 132 F6
Bwlch-newydd 57 F3
Bwlchygroes 35 F6
Bynea 149 F3

C

Cadle 159 D7
Cae-mawr 153 E1
Caer-eithin 159 F5
Caerfarchell 48 C6
Caerfyrddin / Carmarthen 128 E7
Caio 24 A2
Camrose 67 E7
Capel 148 F7
Capel Dewi Llanarthney 76 E7
Capel Dewi Llandysul 20 C5
Capel Gwynfe 63 F1
Capel Hendre 97 E6
Capel Isaac 61 D6
Capel Iwan 36 D7
Capel Newydd / Newchapel 16 D2
Capel Seion 96 C8
Capel Tygwydd 17 C6
Cardigan / Aberteifi 118 E3
Carew 105 D6
Carew Cheriton 105 D5
Carew Newton 105 D7
Carmarthen / Caerfyrddin 128 E7
Carmel 78 D3
Carnglas 166 B8
Carnhedryn 48 C6
Carway 95 D1
Cas-Mael / Puncheston 51 F8
Castell Newydd Emlyn / Newcastle Emlyn 119 B4
Castlebythe 52 A7
Castlemartin 110 F7
Castlemorris 30 B2
Caswell 172 B4
Cefn-bryn-brain 100 B8
Cefncaeau 149 C4
Cefneithin 97 A8
Cefn-gorwydd 27 F8
Cefn Hengoed 161 C3
Cefn Parc 162 E6
Cefn-y-Garth 155 A6
Cefn-y-pant 55 A4
Cellan 4 F4
Cenarth 17 B4
Chapelhill 104 A1
Cheriton or Stackpole Elidor 112 A6
Churchton 134 E5
Cilau 11 B4
Cilgerran 16 A5
Cilgwyn Myddfai 64 B8
Cilgwyn Nevern 33 A7
Cilrhedyn 36 C5
Cilsan 61 E1
Cilycwm 25 C3
Cippyn 2 D3
Clarbeston 69 D8
Clarbeston Road 69 B7
Clase 160 D8
Cloigyn 76 A1
Clunderwen 70 F6
Clun-Du 153 F1
Clydach 154 D7
Clydau 36 A6
Cnap-Llwyd 160 D5
Coalbrook 151 B5
Cockett 159 E2
Coed Cae 149 A5
Coed-y-bryn 18 E8
Cold Blow 89 F7
Cold Inn 106 D8
Colston 51 D6
Cosheston 104 F6
Court Henry 61 A1
Craig-cefn-parc 146 A2
Craig Glyn-meirch 147 D4
Craig Trebanos 147 C3
Craig-y-duke 147 C2
Cresselly 88 F1
Cresswell Quay 88 E1
Crinow 70 F1
Croes-goch 29 A3
Croes-lan 19 B7
Croesyceilog 75 D3
Croes-y-Llan 3 D1
Crofty 156 B3
Crosshands 55 A1
Cross Hands 97 A7
Cross Hands Jeffreyston 89 A6
Crosswell / Ffynnoncroes 33 F7
Crugybar 42 F8
Crundale 68 C5
Crwbin 95 D8
Crymych 34 E4
Cuffern 67 A8
Cuttybridge 67 F6
Cwmann 120 E3
Cwmbach 56 A5
Cwmbwrla 160 C2
Cwm Capel 137 F5
Cwmcarnhywel 149 D5
Cwmcerdinen 98 C2
Cwm-cou 119 A7
Cwmcych 36 C7
Cwmdu 160 A2
Cwmdu Talley / Talyllychau 42 C1
Cwmduad 38 A2
Cwm Dulais 144 B4
Cwmdwr 43 E3
Cwmdwyfran 58 D3
Cwmfelin Boeth 126 B8
Cwm-felin-Fâch 154 A3
Cwmfelin Mynach 55 D3
Cwmffrwd 75 F4
Cwmgiedd 138 F3
Cwmgors 99 D5
Cwmgwili 97 C6
Cwm Gwyn 166 E8
Cwmhiraeth 37 D8
Cwmifor 62 E4
Cwm Irfon 9 A4
Cwmisfael 77 A2
Cwmllynfell 100 B7
Cwm-mawr 96 E7
Cwm-miles 54 C1
Cwmorgan 36 E5
Cwmpengraig 37 D7
Cwmrhydyceirw 153 E3
Cwm-twrch Isaf 138 B1
Cwm-twrch Uchaf 100 C6
Cwmwdig Water 28 D3
Cwm-y-glo 97 A8
Cwrt-y-cadno 24 B7
Cydweli / Kidwelly 136 D4
Cynghordy 26 C2
Cynheidre 95 F2
Cynwyl Elfed 58 A6

D

Dafen 149 B7
Dale 101 E4
Dan-y-graig 168 A7
Deerland 87 D5
Derwydd 79 B4
Dinas 36 C1
Dinas Cross 12 F3
Dinbych-y-pysgod / Tenby 135 C4
Doc Penfro / Pembroke Dock 132 B4
Dolgran 39 A5
Dreenhill 124 A2
Drefach Gorslas 96 D8
Drefach Llangeler 18 E1
Drefach Meidrim 73 E8
Dre-fach Dyffryn Cennen 79 E3
Dre-fach Llanwenog 21 B8
Drefelin 37 F8
Druidston 66 D3
Dryslwyn 78 A7
Dunvant 165 B8
Dyffryn 122 A4
Dyffryn Ceidrych 63 D4

E

East Trewent 112 C6
East Williamston 106 D8
Edwinsford 42 B5
Efailwen 54 A4
Eglwyswen 34 C7
Eglwyswrw 15 A1
Esgair 58 A7

F

Faedre 154 D8
Fagwr-isaf 146 B2
Fairwood 164 D7
Felindre Llangadog 63 D6
Felindre Llangathen 78 A8
Felindre Llangeler 18 E1
Felindre Llansadwrn 43 B1
Felindre Pontarddulais 144 F2
Felindre Farchog 14 D1
Felinfoel 141 A1
Felingwmisaf 60 B2
Felingwmuchaf 60 B3
Felin Newydd 23 F1
Ferryside 93 F5
Ffairfach 130 D4
Ffaldybrenin 23 C7
Ffarmers 23 E7
Fforest 143 A6
Fforest-fach 159 C4
Ffynnoncroes / Crosswell 33 F7
Ffynnon-ddrain 128 D8
Fishguard / Abergwaun 122 E2
Five Roads 140 A7
Foelgastell 77 F1
Folly 67 D7
Ford 51 A5
Four Roads 95 C4
Foxhole 174 C5
Freshwater East 105 B1
Freystrop 87 B6
Furnace 148 C7
Furnace Pembrey & Bury Port Town 137 C3

G

Garnant 99 B7
Garnswllt 98 B4
Gelli 70 B6
Gellygron 147 C6
Gellywen 56 D2
Gendros 159 F3
Gignog 49 F3
Glais 155 B6
Glanaman 99 A8
Glanaman Cwmamman 80 A1
Glan-Duar 21 E6
Glandŵr / Landore 160 D4
Glandwr 54 F7
Glandy Cross 54 B5
Glanrhyd 15 B5
Glan-rhyd 139 F7
Glan-y-mÙr 92 F6
Glenowen 104 A8
Glogue 35 C3
Glyntawe 82 F3
Godreír-graig 100 B1
Golden Grove 78 D6
Golden Hill Pembroke / Penfro 133 C6
Golden Hill Spittal 51 C3
Goodwick / Wdig 122 B6
Gorof 138 E1
Gorseinon 151 C3
Gorseinon Garden Village 158 D8
Gorslas 97 C8
Gowerton / Tre-gwyr 158 B4
Graig 137 E4
Graig Fawr 143 E6
Graigfelen 154 C8
Graig Trewyddfa 160 F7
Granston 30 A5
Green 133 C5
Grove 133 C3
Grovesend 151 C6
Guilford 87 D4
Gumfreston 106 D4
Gurnos 139 D7
Gwastad 52 D3
Gwaun-Cae-Gurwen 99 E6
Gwaun-Leision 99 D7
Gwbert 3 A6
Gwernogle 40 E5
Gwyddgrug 39 D6

H

Hafod 160 E2
Hakin 131 B2
Halfpenny Furze 92 B8
Halfway 42 D1
Half Way 149 B6
Halfway Farm 45 D3
Hanover Square 161 B3
Harbour Village 122 B7
Harddfan 150 A6
Haroldston West 66 D2
Hasguard 85 C4
Haverfordwest / Hwlffordd 124 D5
Haycastle Cross 50 B4
Hayscastle 50 A4
Haysford 67 D8
Hebron Cilymaenllwyd 54 F6
Hebron Llanfihangel-ar-Arth 38 E6
Hendy 143 A5
Hendy-Gwyn / Whitland 126 D3
Henllan 18 E3
Henllan Amgoed 71 F6
Henry's Moat 52 D6
Heol-ddu 109 C6
Heol-las 154 F2
Herbrandston 85 D2
Hermon Crymych 35 B2
Hermon Cynwyl Elfed 37 F1
High Street 71 F2
Hillend Burrows 114 B1
Hill Mountain 87 D3
Hiraeth 71 D8
Hodgeston 105 B2
Hook 87 D6
Hopkinstown 98 C7
Horeb Llandysul 19 C5
Horeb Llanegwad 60 C7
Horeb Llanelli Rural 140 B8
Horton 117 B4
Houghton 87 D2
Hubberston 131 B3
Hundleton 104 B3
Hwlffordd / Haverfordwest 124 D5

I

Idole 75 F2
Iet-y-bwlch 54 C7
Ilston 164 B2

J

Jameston 105 E2
Jeffreyston 89 C1
Jersey Marine 162 C1
Johnston 86 E5
Johnstown 128 C3
Jordanston 30 D3

K

Keeston 67 B6
Kete 101 D3
Kidwelly / Cydweli 136 D4
Kilgetty 134 D8
Killay 165 E7
Kittle 171 E7
Knelston 117 A7

L

Lambston 67 B4
Lampeter / Llanbedr Pont Steffan 120 E6
Lampeter Velfrey 71 C1
Lamphey 105 A3
Landimore 115 A4
Landore / Glandŵr 160 D4
Landshipping 88 A6
Langland 172 F4
Laugharne 92 E6
Lawrenny 88 A2
Lawrenny Quay 88 A1
Leason 115 C3
Leonardston 103 F8
Letterston 50 F8
Leweston 50 F1
Liddeston 131 B4
Limeslade 173 C3
Lisbon 160 C5
Little Haven 85 C8
Little Honeyborough 86 F1
Little Milford 87 B6
Little Newcastle 51 D7
Little Reynoldston 117 D8
Llanarthne 77 E7
Llanbedr Pont Steffan / Lampeter 120 E6
Llanboidy 55 D2
Llandarcy 162 D3
Llandawke 92 D6
Llanddarog 77 B3
Llanddeusant 64 E3
Llanddewi 117 A8
Llanddewi Velfrey 71 B3
Llanddowror 73 A1
Llandeilo 130 E5
Llandeilo'r-Fan 46 E5
Llandeloy 49 D5
Llandilo 53 D6
Llandissilio 70 F8
Llandovery / Llanymddyfri 121 B5
Llandre 24 A4
Llandruidion 48 B3
Llandudoch / St Dogmaels 118 A4
Llandybie 79 B2
Llandyfaelog 94 F6
Llandyfan 79 D4
Llandyfriog 18 C4
Llandygwydd 16 F6
Llandyry 109 A8
Llandysul 19 D3
Llanedi 97 D2
Llanegwad 77 D8
Llanelli 149 B5
Llanerch 148 E7
Llanfair Clydogau 5 B6
Llanfair-Nant-Gwyn 34 D8
Llanfallteg 71 C6
Llanfallteg West 71 B6
Llanfihangel-ar-arth 20 C2
Llanfihangel-uwch-Gwili 59 F1
Llanfynydd 61 B6
Llanfyrnach 35 D2

Llangadog
  Kidwelly / Cydweli 136 D5
Llangadog 63 E7
Llangain 75 B2
Llangathen 61 D1
Llangeler 19 A2
Llangennech 142 A1
Llangennith 114 C2
Llangloffan 30 B3
Llanglydwen 54 F5
Llangoedmor 3 D1
Llangolman 53 F6
Llangunnor 129 C5
Llangwm 87 D4
Llangybi 4 F8
Llangyfelach 153 A2
Llangyndeyrn 76 D1
Llangynin 73 A6
Llangynog 74 D3
Llanhowel 48 E6
Llanion 132 D3
Llanllawddog 59 C8
Llanllwch 128 A2
Llanllwni 21 A2
Llanmadoc 114 C4
Llan-mill 71 B1
Llanmiloe 92 A4
Llanmorlais 156 C2
Llannon 96 E3
Llanon 29 A4
Llanpumsaint 58 F8
Llanreath 132 A2
Llanrhian 28 E4
Llanrhidian 115 D2
Llansadurnen 92 C5
Llansadwrn 43 C2
Llansaint 94 B3
Llansamlet 161 D8
Llansawel 42 A7
Llansteffan 93 D5
Llanteg 90 E5
Llanteglos 90 E4
Llanwenog 21 A8
Llanwinio 56 B5
Llanwnda 11 A4
Llanwrda 43 E2
Llanwrtyd 9 B2
Llanwrtyd Wells 9 C2
Llanybri 93 C7
Llanybydder 21 D7
Llanycefn 53 C2
Llanychaer 31 D6
Llanymddyfri /
  Llandovery 121 B5
Llawhaden 69 F4
Llechryd 16 C7
Llidiad-Nenog 40 F8
Llwynbrwydrau 162 A7
Llwyndrain 36 B5
Llwynhendy 149 D4
Llwyn-rhyd-Owen 20 C7
Llwyn-y-brain 72 A1
Llys-y-frân 52 D3
Llywel 46 C1
Login 54 D2
Longstone 90 B4
Lon–Las 162 B7
Loughor 150 E2
Loveston 89 B3
Lower Brynamman 99 D8
Lower Fishguard 122 E4
Lower Freystrop 87 B7
Lower Sketty 166 B3
Lower Solva 48 E3
Lower Town 122 E3
Ludchurch 90 B5
Lunnon 170 F8
Lydstep 106 B1

M

Maenclochog 53 B6
Maerdy 130 D1
Maes llyn 18 F7
Maesybont 78 B3
Maesycrugiau 20 E4
Maesymeillion 19 E8
Maiden Wells 104 B2
Manorbier 113 C6
Manorbier Newton 105 D3
Manordeilo 63 A5
Manorowen 11 B1
Mansfield 172 C6
Manselton 160 B3
Marble Hall 148 E5
Marloes 84 C3
Marros 91 B4
Martletwy 88 C5
Mascle Bridge 104 A8
Mathry 29 E4
Mayals 165 F1
Mayeston 105 A6
Mayhill 160 A1
Meidrim 73 D8
Meinciau 95 C5
Merlin's Bridge 124 E2
Merlin's Cross 133 D3
Merrion 111 C6
Merthyr 74 E7
Mesur-y-dorth 29 A3
Middle Mill 48 E4
Middleton 116 C6
Milford Haven /
  Aberdaugleddau 131 C1
Millin Cross 87 E8
Milo 78 E4
Milton 105 C6

Minwear 88 C8
Monington 15 A6
Monkton 133 A5
Moore Town 162 E8
Morfa
  Ammanford / Rhydaman . . .97 C7
Morfa Llanelli 148 F2
Morfa Bach 93 F8
Morriston / Treforys 153 E1
Mount Pleasant
  Cosheston 105 A8
Mount Pleasant Llanelli . . .148 D7
Mount Pleasant
  Swansea / Abertawe 174 A3
Moylgrove / Trewyddel 14 E7
Murton 172 B6
Musselwick 84 F1
Myddfai 44 E1
Mynachlog-ddu 34 B1
Mynydd-Bâch 160 B8
Mynydd-bach-y-glo 159 A4
Mynydd-Garn-Lwyd 160 D7
Mynyddygarreg 136 F7

N

Nanhyfer / Nevern 14 B3
Nantgaredig 77 A8
Nant-y-Bai 25 E7
Nantycaws 76 D5
Nant-y-ffin 41 A3
Narberth / Arberth 70 D1
Narberth Bridge 70 D1
Neuadd 80 C8
Nevern / Nanhyfer 14 B3
Newcastle Emlyn / Castell
  Newydd Emlyn 119 B4
Newchapel /
  Capel Newydd 16 D2
Newchurch 58 B3
Newgale 49 C1
New Hedges 107 A5
New Inn Llanfihangel-ar-Arth 39 E7
New Inn
  Puncheston / Cas-Mael . . .32 E1
New Moat 52 E4
New Park 88 B6
Newport / Trefdraeth 13 F4
Newton 172 E5
Newton Cross 50 A6
Neyland 132 B5
Nicholaston 117 F7
Nine Wells 48 B3
Nolton 66 D5
Nolton Haven 66 D5

O

Oaklands 75 F3
Olchfa 166 A7
Oldwalls 115 C2
Oldway 172 B6
Overton 117 A4
Oxwich 117 D5
Oxwich Green 117 D5
Oystermouth 173 A5

P

Panteg 30 D5
Pantgwyn 61 A6
Pant-y-Caws 54 C5
Pantyffynnon 98 B5
Parc Melin Mynach 151 D2
ParcTawe 174 B3
Parc-y-Rhôs 120 C1
Parkmill 170 F7
Parrog 13 D4
Pelcomb 67 D5
Pelcomb Bridge 124 C8
Pelcomb Cross 67 D5
Pemberton 149 B5
Pembrey / Pen-bre 137 A3
Pembroke Dock /
  Doc Penfro 132 B4
Pembroke Ferry 132 E5
Pembroke / Penfro 133 F5
Penallt 148 F6
Penally / Penalun 135 C2
Penalun / Penally 135 C2
Penboyr 37 E7
Pen-bre / Pembrey 137 A3
Pencader 39 B6
Penceiliogi 149 C6
Pen-clawdd 156 E3
Pendine / Pentywyn 91 D3
Penffordd 53 B1
Penfilia 160 C5
Penfro / Pembroke 133 F5
Peniel 59 A3
Peniel Green 161 F8
Pen-lan 160 A5
Pen-lan-mabws 29 E2
Penllergaer 152 A2
Penmaen 170 B6
Pennar 132 A1
Pennard 171 C6
Pennar Park 103 F5
Penparc 3 F3
Penplas 74 E4
Penrherber 119 A2
Pen-Rhiw-fawr 100 B5
Penrhiwgoch 78 A5
Penrhiw-llan 19 A4
Penrhiw-pâl 18 D8

Penrice 117 D6
Pensarn 128 F3
Pentlepoir 134 B6
Pentre 160 D2
Pentre-bâch 4 A2
Pentrebach Myddfai 45 C4
Pentrebach Pontarddulais . .143 E7
Pentrecagal 18 C3
Pentre-Chwyth 161 A2
Pentre-cwrt 19 B1
Pentrefelin Llanfair Clydogau 5 A3
Pentrefelin Llangathen 61 E2
Pentreffynnon 162 F6
Pentre Galar 34 F1
Pentre-Gwenlais 79 A3
Pentrellwyn 19 E5
Pentre-Poeth 148 D8
Pentre-ty-gwyn 45 C6
Pentywyn / Pendine 91 D3
Penybanc 98 A6
Pen-y-banc Abergwili 129 C8
Pen-y-banc
  Manordeilo & Salem 62 A3
Penybedd 108 C5
Pen-y-bont 56 F6
Pen-y-Bryn 15 F5
Penycwm 49 B2
Penydre 146 F1
Pen-y-Fan 148 F3
Penyfeidr 49 E5
Pen-y-garn 41 C2
Penygroes 34 C6
Pen-y-groes 97 B3
Penyraber 122 C5
Penyrheol Gorseinon 151 B4
Penyrheol
  Swansea / Abertawe 166 B7
Pen-yr-Heol 162 F6
Pibwrlwyd 128 F1
Pill 131 E2
Pilton Green 116 E6
Pinged 108 F6
Pitton 116 C6
Plashett 92 C4
Plasmarl 160 E5
Pontanen / Pontamman . . .98 C7
Pontamman / Pontaman . . .98 C7
Pontantwn 95 B8
Pontardawe 147 D4
Pontarddulais 143 E5
Pont-ar-gothi 77 B8
Pont-ar-llechau 63 F3
Pontarsais 59 B7
Pont Creuddyn 4 A7
Pontfaen 32 B4
Pont-Henri 95 F4
Ponthirwaun 17 B8
Pontiago 11 A3
Pont-iets / Pontyates 95 D3
Pontlliw 152 A7
Pont-newydd 95 B2
Pontyates / Pont-iets 95 D3
Pontyberem 96 A6
Pont-y-Fenni 72 E4
Pontyglasier 34 B7
Pont-yr-hafod 50 B5
Pope Hill 86 F7
Port-Eynon 117 A4
Portfield Gate 67 C2
Portheiddy 28 E4
Porthgain 28 E5
Port Tywyn /
  Burry Port 137 D4
Porthyrhyd Llanddarog 77 C2
Porthyrhyd Llanwrda 43 D3
Port Lion 87 D3
Port Mead 159 D6
Port Tennant 168 C8
Poundffald 157 D2
Poyston 68 B6
Poyston Cross 68 C6
Prendergast 125 C7
Pren-gwyn 19 F7
Priory 131 C5
Pumsaint 23 E3
Puncheston / Cas-Mael . . .51 F8
Pwll 109 F4
Pwllcrochan 103 D5
Pwll-trap 127 C5
Pyle 172 A5

R

Rallt 163 A8
Ram 120 E2
Redberth 106 A7
Red Roses 91 B6
Reynalton 89 B3
Reynoldston 115 B1
Rhandirmwyn 25 E6
Rhodiad-y-Brenin 123 F8
Rhos 38 B6
Rhosaman 81 A1
Rhoscrowther 103 B4
Rhosfach 53 E7
Rhos-Hill 15 F3
Rhosmaen 130 F8
Rhossili 116 B7
Rhosson 47 B4
Rhosycaerau 10 F2
Rhydaman / Ammanford . . .98 A8
Rhydargaeau 59 B5
Rhydcymerau 22 C1
Rhydowen Crymych 55 A7
Rhydowen Llandysul 20 A8
Rhydyfelin 36 D8
Rhyd-y-fro 147 D8

Rhydygele 49 C3
Rhyd-y-gwin 146 A4
Rhyd-y-Pandy 145 F1
Rhydywrach 71 D6
Ridgeway 134 D4
Rinaston 51 D4
Robeston Back 70 A2
Robeston Wathen 70 B2
Robeston West 85 E4
Roch 66 E8
Rosebush 53 A8
Rosemarket 87 A3
Rosepool 85 D6
Rose Valley Farm 133 E3
Rudbaxton 68 A7

S

Sageston 105 E6
St Brides 84 C5
St Clears / Sanclêr 127 E4
St David's / Tyddewi 123 B5
St Dogmaels /
  Llandudoch 118 A4
St Florence 106 B4
St Ishmael 93 F3
St Ishmael's 85 A1
St Justinian 47 A4
St Nicholas 30 A6
St Petrox 111 E6
St Thomas 174 C3
St Twynnells 111 C6
Salem 62 B5
Sanclêr / St Clears 127 E4
Sandy 148 B6
Sandy Haven 85 B2
Sandy Lane 171 A6
Sardis 134 F7
Sarnau 74 D6
Saron 97 E7
Saron Llangeler 19 A1
Saundersfoot 134 F3
Sciwen / Skewen 162 D7
Scleddau 30 F4
Scurlage 117 A6
Seaside 148 C3
Shipping 89 E3
Silian 4 C6
Siloh 44 B8
Simpson Cross 67 A6
Skerryford 124 B3
Sketty 166 D6
Skewen / Sciwen 162 D7
Slade 117 C4
Slade Haverfordwest /
  Hwlffordd 124 E7
Slebech 69 B2
Soar 62 A7
Solva 48 D3
Southgate 171 A5
Spittal 51 D2
Square and Compass 29 C4
Stackpole 112 A5
Star 35 F6
Stepaside 90 A3
Steynton 131 E5
Summerhill 90 C2
Sutton 67 C2
Swansea / Abertawe 174 C1
Swiss Valley 141 B2
Sylen 96 B1

T

Tafarnspite / Tavernspite . .90 F7
Tafarn-y-bwlch 33 A4
Tairgwaith 99 F7
Tai'r-ysgol 161 E8
Talbenny 85 B6
Talley / Talyllychau 42 D3
Talog 57 B4
Talsarn 64 E5
Talyllychau / Talley 42 D3
Tanerdy 129 B6
Tangiers 68 A5
Tanglwst 37 A4
Tavernspite / Tafarnspite . .90 F7
Tegryn 35 E4
Temple Bar 78 E4
Templeton 89 E6
Tenby /
  Dinbych-y-pysgod 135 C4
The Mumbles /
  Y Mwmbwls 173 C4
The Rhos 68 F1
The Valley 134 B4
Thistleboon 173 B3
Thomas Chapel 89 D3
Thornton 131 C6
Three Crosses 157 E1
Tiers Cross 86 B5
Tirabad 27 C4
Tircanol 154 B2
Tircoed 152 C5
Tirdeunaw 160 B7
Tir-Nest 161 B3
Tirydail 154 A1
Townhill 167 A8
Trallwn 161 F6
Trapp 79 D5
Travellers' Rest 75 A6
Trebannws / Trebanos 147 B2
Trebanos / Trebannws 147 B2
Tre-boeth 160 B6
Trecwn 31 C3

Trefasser 10 D2
Trefdraeth / Newport 13 F4
Treffgarne 51 A2
Treffynnon 29 B1
Trefgarn Owen 49 D4
Trefin 29 E5
Treforys / Morriston 153 E1
Treginnis 47 C3
Treglemais 28 F1
Tre-glog 41 F6
Tregroes 19 E7
Tre-gwyr / Gowerton 158 B4
Tregyddulan 10 D1
Tre-gynwr 129 A3
Trelech 36 D1
Trelech-a'r-Bettws 56 F5
Treleddyd-fawr 47 E6
Trelerw 48 A3
Tresinwen 10 E5
Tretio 28 B1
Trevaughan
  Carmarthen / Caerfyrddin . .128 D7
Trevaughan Whitland /
  Hendy-Gwyn 126 D1
Trewyddel / Moylgrove 14 E7
Trewyddfa Fach 160 E7
Triffleton 51 C3
Trimsaran 109 C8
Troedyraur 18 B8
Trooper's Inn 87 B5
Tufton 52 C7
Tumble / Tymbl 96 F7
Tutt 173 D3
Twynllanan 64 C3
Twynmynydd 79 F1
Ty-coch 166 C8
Tycroes 97 F5
Tyddewi / St David's 123 B5
Ty-Draw 161 C2
Ty-hên 56 E3
Ty-Isaf 148 E3
Ty Mawr 21 E5
Tymbl / Tumble 96 F7
Tyn-y-cwm 144 D2
Tyrfran 148 E7

U

Uplands 166 F6
Upper Brynamman 80 F1
Upper Forge 154 D8
Upper Killay 165 A5
Upper Nash 105 B5
Upper Solva 48 C3
Uzmaston 125 E2

V

Vachelich 48 A4

W

Wallis 52 A4
Walton East 52 B2
Walton West 85 D7
Walwyn's Castle 85 E6
Warren 111 A6
Waterloo 132 E4
Waterston 103 F8
Waunarlwydd 158 E4
Waun Beddau 28 A2
Waungilwen 18 D2
Waungron 143 C1
Waun-Gron 160 D6
Waun y Clyn 109 B7
Wdig / Goodwick 122 B6
Welsh Hook 50 E6
Wern 148 D4
Wernbwll 157 A2
Wernffrwd 115 F5
Wern-olau 157 D4
West Cross 173 A7
Weston 88 C5
West Williamston 105 C8
Whitchurch 48 D4
Whitehill 105 E7
White Mill 76 D8
Whitland / Hendy-Gwyn . . .126 D3
Winch-wen 161 C5
Wiseman's Bridge 90 B1
Wiston 69 A5
Withybush 125 D8
Wolf's Castle 51 A5
Wolfsdale 67 E8
Wood 66 C8
Wooden 134 A4
Woodstock 52 B4

Y

Yerbeston 88 F3
Y Ferwig 3 C5
Y Mwmbwls /
  The Mumbles 173 C4
Ynysforgan 154 C4
Ynystawe 154 C6
Yspitty 150 B2
Ystalyfera 139 A6
Ystradffin 7 F1
Ystradowen 100 C7

3rd St SA73 ....103 E8
4th St SA73 ....103 E8
5th St SA73 ....103 E8
6th St SA73 ....103 E7
7th St SA73 ....103 E8
8th St SA73 ....103 E7
9th St SA73 ....103 E7
10th St SA73 ....103 E7
11th St SA73 ....103 E7
12th St SA73 ....103 D8
13th St SA73 ....103 D8

A

Abbey Mead SA31 ......129 B6
Abbey St SA17 ....136 C4
Abbey Terr SA19 ....130 D5
Abbots Cl SA61 ....125 A4
Aberbanc Cty Prim Sch
  SA44 ....18 E4
Abercedy SA4 ....157 A4
Aberclydach Pl SA6 ....154 D7
Aber Ct SA6 ....161 B7
Aberdyberthi St SA1 ...160 D2
Aberelddy Rd SA62 .....28 F3
Abergelly Rd SA5 ......159 C5
Aberglasney Gdns ★
  SA32 ....61 D1
Abergwili Rd SA31 .....129 D7
Aberlash Rd SA18 ......98 B8
Aber Llwchwr SA14 .....150 B7
Abernant CP Sch SA33 ..57 D2
Abernant Rd SA18 ......99 D5
Abernethy Quay SA1 ....174 B2
Abernethy Sq **14** SA1 ..174 C2
Aberystwyth SA43 ......118 E5
Acacia Rd SA3 ....173 A8
Acorn Ct SA6 ....154 B1
Adams Dr **3** SA67 .....70 D1
Adams Rd SA71 ....104 C4
Adam St SA43 ....16 D6
Addison Cl SA61 ....125 B4
Addlegutter La SA71 ...111 B4
Adelaide St
  Llandovery / Llanymddyfri
  SA20 ....121 D5
  Swansea / Abertawe SA1 ..174 B2
Admirals Wlk SA2 ......166 C6
Admiralty Way SA72 ....132 B3
Adulam Row SA14 ....140 F1
Aelybryn SA15 ....109 E4
Ael-y-Bryn
  Pen-clawdd SA4 ....156 F4
  The Mumbles / Y Mwmbwls
  SA3 ....173 C3
Aelybryn Cl SA15 ......148 E8
Aelybryn Dr SA15 ......148 E8
Ael-y-Bryn Rd SA5 .....159 E3
Ael-y-don SA3 ....172 F3
Ael-y-Felin SA62 ......29 B4
Ael-y-Fro SA8 ....147 D7
Aeron Pl SA1 ....161 B2
Afon-Llan Gdns SA5 ....159 D6
Afon Rd / Heol Afon
  SA14 ....150 C8
Alamein Rd SA1 ....160 E3
Alan Rd SA19 ....130 E6
Alban Cres SA73 ....103 E8
Alban Rd SA15 ....148 E6
Albany Cl SA5 ....160 C4
Albany Sq SA72 ....132 C1
Albany Terr SA61 ......125 A4
Alberto Rd SA6 ....161 A6
Albert Pl SA3 ....173 A5
Albert Row SA1 ....174 B2
Albert St SA15 ....148 C4
Albion Sq SA72 ....132 C2
Albion Sq CP Sch SA72 .132 C2
Albion St SA73 ....131 C3
Alden Dr SA2 ....159 D1
Alderbrook Ct SA5 .....159 F6
Alder Ave SA9 ....139 D7
Alder Way
  Gowerton / Tre-gwyr SA4 .158 C6
  The Mumbles / Y Mwmbwls
  SA3 ....172 F7
Alderwood Rd SA3 .....173 A7
Aldwyn Rd SA5 ....159 D2
Alexandra Rd
  Gorseinon SA4 ....151 A2
  Swansea / Abertawe SA1 ..174 B3
Alexandra Terr SA2 ....166 F6
Alfred St SA6 ....160 E6
Alice St SA5 ....160 A2
Allaway Ct **1** SA1 ....160 C2
Allendale Dr SA62 .....85 A2
Alloy Court Est SA8 ...147 F5
Alltacham Dr SA8 .....147 E5
Alltfach SA43 ....118 A3
Allt-Iago Rd SA4 .....143 D4
Allt Ioan SA31 ....128 A4
Allt Rhyd Y Groes National
  Nature Reserve ★ SA20 ..7 D3
Alltwalis Prim Sch / Ysgol
  Gynradd Alltwalis SA32 .39 B2
Alltwen Hill SA8 .....147 D7
Alltwen Prim Sch SA8 .147 F4
Allt Y Carne
  Fishguard & Goodwick SA64 .11 B2
  4 Goodwick / Wdig SA64 .122 A4
Alltycnap Rd
  Carmarthen / Caerfyrddin
  SA31 ....128 C3

Alltycnap Rd continued
  Llangain SA33 ....75 A5
Allt Y Gog SA31 ....128 B5
Allt-y-Graban Rd SA4 ..151 D8
Allt Y Grug SA10 ......162 C1
Alltygrug Farm Rd SA9 .139 B7
Alltygrug Rd SA9 .....139 B7
Allt-y-Waun SA8 ......147 D7
Alltywerin SA8 ....147 D6
Als St SA15 ....148 C4
Alstred St SA17 ......136 B4
Alun Rd SA1 ....160 B1
Amanwy SA14 ....149 D5
Amberley Dr SA1 ......173 A4
Ambleside Pl SA3 .....173 A8
Ammanford Inf Sch SA18 .98 C7
Ammanford Jun Sch
  SA18 ....98 C7
Ammanford Rd SA18 ....79 B1
Ammanford Rd / Heol
  Rhydaman SA18 ....97 F6
Ammanford Sta SA18 ...98 B7
Amman Rd / Heol Amman
  Brynamman SA18 ....99 E8
  Glanaman SA18 ....98 F8
Amman Valley Comp Sch
  SA18 ....98 C7
Amman Valley Hospl
  SA18 ....99 A8
Amos St SA15 ....148 C4
Amphion Ct SA72 ......133 A8
Amroth Rd SA67 ....90 D4
Anchor Ct SA1 ....174 B2
Anchor Down **9** SA62 ..48 D3
Anderson La SA3 ......171 A5
Andrew Cres SA6 ......154 B4
Andrew St SA15 ....148 E6
Aneurin Cl SA2 ....166 A6
Aneurin Way SA2 ......166 A6
Angle Rd SA71 ....104 C4
Angle VC Sch SA71 ....102 D6
Annesley St SA15 .....148 C5
Ann St SA15 ....148 A4
Anson Way SA70 ....105 D6
Anthony Way SA31 ....128 B3
Anthorn **2** SA65 .....122 D3
Apley Terr SA72 ......132 C3
Appledore Pl SA3 .....172 E6
Applegrove SA3 ......115 B1
Approach Rd SA5 .....160 C2
Aran St SA6 ....160 F7
Arcade **1** SA15 ......148 D5
Arcade Terr / Teras Yr Arced
  11 SA18 ....99 B8
Arcade The **20** SA18 ..98 B7
Ardent Cl SA3 ....131 F5
Ardwyn Rd **7** SA18 ...80 E1
Arennig Rd SA5 ......160 B5
Arethuea Quay SA1 ...174 B1
Arethusa Ct SA2 .....165 C6
Arethusa Quay SA1 ...174 B1
Arfryn SA18 ....80 E1
Arfryn Ave SA15 .....148 E7
Arfryn Prim Sch SA5 .160 B5
Arfryn Rd SA2 ....166 E8
Argoed Cres SA17 ....109 B8
Argoed Rd / Heol Argoed
  SA18 ....98 C5
Argyle St
  Pembroke Dock / Doc Penfro
  SA72 ....132 D2
  Swansea / Abertawe SA1 ..167 B6
Argyll Ave SA4 ......151 B2
Arlan Gwilli SA4 ....143 A4
Ar-lan-Morlais SA17 .109 B8
Armine Rd SA5 ....159 E3
Arnold Ct SA9 ....139 B6
Arnolds Hill SA61 ...125 E5
Arthur Morris Dr SA62 .132 C1
Arthur St Llanelli SA15 .148 D5
  Pembroke Dock / Doc Penfro
  SA72 ....132 D3
Arthur St / Stryd Arthur
  SA18 ....98 B8
Arthur Terr SA8 .....147 E5
Arwelfa SA1 ....153 C1
Ar-y-Bryn SA16 ......137 A4
Ashburnham Dr SA62 ..165 E2
Ashburnham Rd SA16 ..137 D2
Ashdale La Burton SA73 .87 C3
  Pembroke / Penfro SA71 ..133 C5
Ashes The SA17 ......95 D5
Ash Gr
  Ammanford / Rhydaman
  SA18 ....98 D7
  Carmarthen / Caerfyrddin
  SA31 ....128 C5
  Gorseinon SA4 ....151 A3
  Killay SA2 ....165 D7
  Milford Haven / Aberdaugleddau
  SA73 ....131 E3
  Waunarlwydd SA5 .....158 D4
Ashgrove **7** SA15 ..96 B6
Ash La SA34 ....90 E7
Ashleigh Cl SA3 .....166 C3
Ashleigh Rd SA2 .....166 C3
Ashleigh Terr SA10 ..169 C8
Ashmount Bsns Parc
  SA6 ....154 B1
Ash Pk SA68 ....134 C8
Ash St SA6 ....161 A7
Ashtree Cl SA73 .....87 C3
Asquith Ct SA1 ......167 A6
Assembly Rooms **3**
  SA1 ....174 C2
Athrofa Abertawe / Swansea
  Inst (Townhill Campus)
  SA1 ....166 F8

Atlantic Cl SA7 ......161 A5
Atlantic Dr SA62 ....85 D8
Atlantic Haven SA3 ..114 C2
Augustine Way SA1 ...125 A3
Augustus Pl **7** SA70 .135 E5
Avenue Cilfig The SA15 .148 D6
Avenue F SA73 ....103 E8
Avenue H SA73 ....103 E7
Avenue K-K SA73 .....103 E8
Avenue M SA73 ....103 E7
Avenue N SA73 ....103 E7
Avenue P SA73 ....103 E8
Avenue Q SA73 ....103 E7
Avenue The
  Carmarthen / Caerfyrddin
  SA31 ....129 A5
  Llanelli, Cwmcarnhywel
  SA14 ....149 C5
  Llanelli SA15 ....148 E2
  Slebech SA62 ....87 F8
Averil Vivian Gr SA2 ..166 E6
Avis Terr SA15 ......148 E5
Avondale Glass ★ SA68 .134 C8
Awel Tywi SA31 ......129 B4
Axton Hill SA71 .....103 E1
Aylesbury Rd SA2 ....166 F5

B

Back Dr SA10 ....162 B7
Back La
  Goodwick / Wdig SA64 ..122 A6
  Haverfordwest / Hwlffordd
  SA61 ....125 B6
  Laugharne Township SA33 .92 F5
  Llawhaden SA67 ......70 C1
Back Terr SA71 ......133 A4
Badminton Gdns SA5 ..159 E5
Baglan St SA1 ......168 A7
Bailey St SA17 .....136 B4
Balaclava Rd SA7 ...155 B5
Balaclava St SA1 ...174 C3
Baldwin's Cres SA1 ..168 E7
Ballards Ct SA10 ...162 F8
Banc Bach SA4 .....156 E4
Banc Pen-dre SA17 ..136 B3
Banc-y-cwm SA4 ....157 E5
Banc Y Ddraenen SA18 .97 C6
Bancyfelin CP Sch SA33 .74 B5
Banc Y Gors SA14 ...96 B7
Banc-yr-eithin SA14 .151 A3
Banfield Terr SA4 ..150 D5
Bank Bldgs SA19 ...130 D6
Bank La **7** SA70 ..135 E4
Bank Rd SA14 ......150 C8
Bank Terr SA19 ....130 D5
Banwell Ct SA6 ....160 F8
Banwell St SA6 ....160 F8
Banwen La SA8 .....147 F4
Banwen Pl / Y Bannen
  SA18 ....99 D8
Banwy Rd SA6 ......153 D1
Baptist La / Lon Y Bedydd **18**
  SA18 ....98 B7
Baptist Well Pl SA1 ..174 A5
Baptist Well St SA1 ..160 C1
Baran Rd Pontardawe SA8 .99 D1
  Rhyd-y-fro SA8 .....147 B8
Bardsey Ave SA5 ...159 E7
Barham Rd SA62 ....31 C3
Baring Gould Way SA61 .124 E3
Barley Mow SA48 ..120 C4
Barlow St SA73 ....131 C2
Barnabas Cl SA5 ...158 F3
Barn Ct **1** SA61 ..124 F4
Barn Rd SA31 ......128 C5
Barnsfield Terr **1** SA31 .128 C5
Barn St SA61 ......124 F4
Barry Rd / Heol Barri
  SA18 ....99 D7
Bartletts Well Rd SA70 .105 E6
Bartley Terr SA6 ...160 E6
Bassett Terr SA15 ..109 F3
Bath Ave SA5 ......153 F1
Bath House Rd **8** SA43 .118 C4
Bath La SA1 ....174 B2
Bath Rd SA6 ......160 F8
Bathurst St
  Swansea / Abertawe SA1 .174 A1
  Swansea / Abertawe SA1 .174 A2
Bath Villas SA1 ...160 F8
Battery Rd SA70 ...135 E4
Bay St SA1 ....168 A7
Bayswater Ct SA3 ..166 C3
Bayswater Rd SA2 ..166 C8
Bay Tree Ave SA2 ..166 B6
Bay View SA1 .....174 C4
Bay View Cl SA10 ..162 F5
Bay View Cres SA4 .167 A6
Bay View Dr SA73 ..102 F8
Bay View Gdns SA10 .162 E5
Bay View Rd SA14 ..149 A6
Bay View Terr SA1 ..167 A6
Baywood Ave SA3 ..173 A8
Beachfields **1** SA62 ..85 D8
Beach Hill SA3 ....131 E2
Beach Rd Llanelli SA15 .148 A6
  Pembroke Dock / Doc Penfro
  SA72 ....132 A2
  Pen-clawdd SA4 ....156 E4
Beaconing Rd SA73 ..86 F1
Beaconsfield Ct SA3 ..166 B7
Beaconsfield Way SA2 .166 B7
Beacons View Rd SA6 .153 D1
Beattie St SA5 ....160 B2

Beaufort Ave SA3 ...173 A3
Beaufort Cl SA3 ....173 A3
Beaufort Ct
  Swansea / Abertawe, Caer-eithin
  SA5 ....159 C5
  Swansea / Abertawe SA6 .160 F6
Beaufort Dr SA3 ....171 E7
Beaufort Gdns SA3 ..171 E7
Beaufort Rd
  Pembroke / Penfro SA71 .133 C5
  Swansea / Abertawe SA6 .160 F6
Beaumont Cres SA1 ..174 C4
Beck Ho SA2 ......166 F6
Bedford Ho **3** SA6 ..160 F8
Bedford St SA6 ....161 A8
Beech Cres SA4 ...151 A4
Beeches Cl The SA2 .166 A8
Beeches The SA44 ..19 E4
Beech Gr SA15 ....109 E4
Beechlands Pk SA61 .124 E3
Beech Rd SA31 ....128 D5
Beechtree Cl SA6 ..153 D1
Beech Tree La SA6 ..166 C5
Beechwood Ind Est
  SA19 ....130 E7
Beechwood Pl SA67 ..70 D2
Beechwood Rd SA2 ..166 F6
Begelly Pk Gdns ★ SA68 .134 C8
Beidr Non SA4 ....96 E3
Beili Glas SA4 ....150 E1
Belgrave Cl SA4 ...151 A1
Belgrave Gdns **2** SA1 .167 A6
Belgrave La SA1 ...167 A6
Belgrave Rd SA1 ..151 A1
Belle Vue SA4 ....156 F4
Bellevue Rd Llanelli SA14 .149 E3
  The Mumbles / Y Mwmbwls
  SA3 ....172 F6
Belle Vue St SA73 ..132 B6
Bellevue Terr SA72 ..132 B1
Belle Vue Way SA1 ..174 A3
Belmore Gdns **4** SA67 .70 D1
Belvedere Ave SA31 ..129 A6
Belvedere Cl SA3 ..171 E7
Belvedere Rd SA15 ..148 C6
Benallt Fawr SA14 ..143 A6
Benbow Cl SA2 ....166 C6
Bendrick Dr SA3 ...170 F4
Bennett St SA1 ....160 D3
Benson Rd SA4 ....156 F4
Benson St SA4 ....156 F4
Benson Terr SA4 ..156 F4
Benson Way / Parc Landwr
  SA6 ....161 A6
Benthall Pl SA1 ...174 C3
Benthel Villas **5** SA67 ..70 E1
Benton Castle ★ SA71 ..87 F1
Berkeley Cl SA7 ...155 A2
Berllan SA14 ......140 F1
Berllan Deg SA15 ..149 A6
Berma Cl SA3 .....173 C3
Bernard St SA2 ...166 F6
Berrington Villas / Filas
  Berrington SA9 .....100 C7
Berthllwyd **3** LD5 ....9 D1
Berwick Rd SA14 ..149 F3
Berwick Terr SA1 ..174 A4
Berw Rd SA1 .....167 B8
Berwyn Pl SA5 ....160 A4
Beryl Rd SA6 .....154 F8
Bethania Rd Clydach SA6 .154 D7
  Cross Hands SA14 ....97 A7
  Llannon SA14 ....96 F6
Bethania Terr SA15 ..148 E2
Bethany La SA3 ....173 A4
Bethany Rd SA61 ..124 D3
Bethel Ct SA5 ....160 C3
Bethel La SA4 ....156 E4
Bethel Rd
  Pembroke Dock / Doc Penfro
  SA72 ....133 A8
  Swansea / Abertawe SA7 .161 E7
  Ystradgynlais SA9 ...139 C8
Bethesda Ct SA1 ..174 B4
Bethesda Rd SA14 ..96 E6
Bethesda St SA1 ..174 B4
Bethlehem Rd
  Dyffryn Cennen SA19 ...130 E4
  Neath / Castell-Nedd SA10 .162 F7
  St Clears / Sanclêr
  SA33 ....127 B5
Bettisland SA3 ...172 F4
Bettws Rd SA5 ....160 A4
Betws Cty Prim Sch
  SA18 ....98 C6
Betws Ind Pk / Parc
  Ddiwydiannol Betws
  SA18 ....98 C7
Betws Rd / Fforrdd-y-Betws
  SA18 ....98 C6
Beulah Hill SA62 ..51 D7
Beulah Rd Beulah SA38 ..17 E8
  Llanwrtyd Wells LD5 ...9 D1
Bevans Row SA1 ..168 B7
Bevans Terr SA7 ..161 E5
Bevan Way SA5 ...158 E3
Bevelin Hall SA69 ..134 E2
Bevelyn La SA69 ..134 E2
Beverley Cl SA5 ..159 E4
Beverley Gdns SA5 ..159 E4
Bible Coll of Wales The
  SA2 ....166 B3
Bicton Rd SA62 ...85 B3
Biddulph SA15 ....148 E2

Bigny Cross SA66 ...53 C2
Bigyn La SA15 .....148 D4
Bigyn Park Ct SA15 ..148 E4
Bigyn Park Terr / Teras Parc
  Bigyn SA15 ....148 E4
Bigyn Prim Sch SA15 ..148 E4
Bigyn Rd SA15 ....148 E4
Birches The SA6 ...154 F8
Birchfield Rd
  Pontardawe SA8 ...147 F6
  The Mumbles / Y Mwmbwls
  SA3 ....172 F8
Birch Gr SA5 ......158 D4
Birchgrove Comp Sch
  SA7 ....155 B2
Birchgrove Jun & Inf Schs
  SA7 ....155 A1
Birchgrove Rd Glais SA7 .155 A4
  Swansea / Abertawe SA7 .162 A8
Birch Mead SA73 ..131 E3
Birch Tree Cl SA2 ..166 C6
Bird's La SA70 ....105 E6
Birkdale Cl SA3 ...160 F6
Birmingham Mount SA6 .160 F6
Bishop Gore Sch / Ysgol
  Esgob Gore SA2 ....166 C6
Bishop Rd **17** SA18 ..99 B8
Bishop Rd / Fforrdd Bishop
  SA18 ....98 B6
Bishop's Gr SA2 ..166 B5
Bishops La SA71 ..133 E3
Bishops Pk SA71 ..133 E3
Bishop's Rd SA67 ..71 B1
Bishopston Comp Sch
  SA3 ....172 A7
Bishopston Prim Sch
  SA3 ....171 F7
Bishopston Rd SA3 ..171 F6
Bishop's Wlk SA6 ..153 F2
Bishop's Wood Countryside
  Ctr ★ SA3 ....172 D4
Bishop's Wood Nature
  Reserve ★ SA3 ....172 C4
Bishop Vaughan RC Sch
  SA6 ....160 E8
Bishwell Rd SA4 ..158 D4
Blackberry La SA71 ..105 B5
Blackbridge Cres SA73 .131 F3
Blackbridge Dr SA73 .131 F2
Blackhill Rd SA4 ..151 A3
Blackhills La
  Fairwood SA2 ......164 C3
  Upper Killay SA2 ..165 B2
Black Lion Rd / Heol y Llew
  Du SA14 ....97 C7
Blackthorn Pl SA2 ..159 B1
Blaenau Rd
  Ammanford / Rhydaman
  SA18 ....98 A8
  Llandybie SA18 ....79 A1
Blaencedi SA4 ....156 F3
Blaencoed Rd SA7 ..161 F7
Blaencwm Rd SA7 ..162 A7
Blaen Emlyn SA14 ..97 D8
Blaenmorfa SA4 ..143 C3
Blaen Treweryll SA37 ..34 F7
Blaenwern SA38 ..119 D5
Blaen-y-Maes Dr SA5 .159 E6
Blaenymaes Prim Sch
  SA5 ....159 E7
Blaen-y-Morfa SA15 ..148 F2
Blean Nant SA14 ..141 B2
Blende Rd SA19 ..130 E6
Blenheim Dr SA73 ..132 C8
Blockett La SA62 ..85 C2
Blodwen Terr SA4 ..156 F4
Bloomfield Gdns SA67 ..70 C2
Blue Anchor Rd SA4 ..156 F3
Blue Anchor Way SA62 .101 C3
Bluebell Cl SA73 ..132 B7
Bluebell Way SA5 ..160 A5
Blue St SA31 .....128 F4
BMI Werndale Hospl
  SA33 ....74 B4
Boarlands The SA3 ..117 A4
Bog Rd SA7, SA10 ..161 B4
Bohun St SA5 ....160 C3
Bolgoed Rd SA4 ..143 E2
Bond Ave SA15 ...148 E4
Bond St SA1 .....167 B5
Bonllwyn SA18 ...98 B8
Bonvilles Cl SA69 ..134 D4
Bonville Terr SA4 ..167 A6
Bon-y-Maen Rd SA1 ..161 A3
Borough Rd SA4 ..150 F2
Bosco La SA3 ....171 B3
Bosworth Rd SA10 ..162 F7
Bowen Cl SA1 ....160 D2
Bowen Terr SA15 ..148 F3
Bowett La SA71 ..104 B2
Box Rd SA4 .....151 B7
Box Terr **3** SA15 ..148 E6
Bradford St **1** SA15 .148 F6
Bramble Hill SA62 ..49 E1
Bramley Dr SA3 ..172 F6
Bran Cl SA7 .....161 C7
Brandon Cres SA1 ..161 B3
Brandy Cove Cl SA3 ..173 B4
Brandy Cove Rd SA3 .172 A5
Brandyway SA15 ..96 A4
Brangwyn Cl SA6 ..153 E2
Branwen Gdns SA1 ..160 B3
Brawdy Bsns Pk SA62 .49 B3
Brawdy Cres SA62 ..49 B3
Brayley Rd SA6 ..153 F2
Brecon Ho **6** SA1 ..174 C2

Brecon Rd
Llandovery / Llanymddyfri
SA20 121 F4
Pontardawe SA8 147 F6
Ystradgynlais SA9 138 F1
Brenig Rd SA5 160 A4
Bres Rd SA15 148 D5
Brettenham St SA15 148 C6
Brewery Rd 3 SA31 128 E6
Brewery St SA72 132 C2
Briar Dene SA2 166 B6
Briar's Ct SA5 159 F6
Briarwood Gdns SA3 172 D5
Brickhurst Cl SA62 86 D6
Brickhurst Pk SA62 86 E6
Brickyard La SA31 128 E4
Brickyard Rd SA5 159 F3
Bridge End Sq 17 SA61 125 A5
Bridge La SA62 67 B6
Bridge Mdw La SA61 125 A6
Bridgend Terr SA71 133 B4
Bridge Rd SA5 158 E4
Bridge St
Burry Port SA16 137 E2
Cardigan / Aberteifi SA43 118 D3
2 Carmarthen / Caerfyrddin
SA31 128 F4
Clydach SA6 154 D7
Cwm Gwaun SA65 31 D6
Cwm-twrch Isaf SA9 138 B1
3 Fishguard & Goodwick
SA65 122 E4
Glais SA7 155 A6
Haverfordwest / Hwlffordd
SA61 125 A5
Kidwelly / Cydweli SA17 136 B4
Lampeter / Llanbedr Pont Steffan
SA48 120 C5
Llandeilo SA19 130 D5
Llandovery / Llanymddyfri
SA20 121 E4
Llanelli SA15 148 D6
Llangennech SA14 150 C8
Llanybyther SA40 21 D7
Milford Haven / Aberdaugleddau
SA73 131 B2
Newcastle Emlyn / Castell
Newydd Emlyn SA38 119 D5
10 Newport / Trefdraeth
SA42 13 E4
Penygroes SA14 97 D8
St Clears / Sanclêr
SA33 127 E2
Swansea / Abertawe SA1 174 B5
Tenby / Dinbych-y-pysgod
SA70 135 F4
Bridle Mews SA3 173 C3
Brighton Rd SA4 151 C2
Britannia Dr SA72 132 C1
Britannia Rd
Pembroke Dock / Doc Penfro
SA72 132 C1
Swansea / Abertawe SA6 160 E5
Brithdir SA31 129 A3
Brithwen Rd SA5 158 D3
Broadacre SA2 165 C7
Broadfield Hill SA69 134 E1
Broad Haven CP Sch
SA62 85 D8
Broad La SA68 88 B2
Broadmead SA2 165 D7
Broadmead Cres SA3 172 B6
Broadoak Ct SA4 150 E1
Broadparks SA3 172 F8
Broad St SA20 121 C3
Broadview Cl SA3 173 B4
Broadview La SA3 173 B4
Broadway SA2 166 D7
Broadway Ct SA2 166 D7
Broadwell Hayes SA70 135 D6
Bro Annedd 2 SA39 39 B6
Brockfield La SA71 133 D2
Bro Dauddwr 3 SA32 59 A2
Brodawel
Ammanford / Rhydaman
SA18 98 C6
5 Burry Port SA16 137 D2
Llannon SA14 96 E3
Bro Dawel Dunvant SA2 165 D7
Solva SA62 48 C3
Swansea / Abertawe SA6 153 C2
Bro Dedwydd SA2 165 D8
Bro Deri SA16 137 D3
Bro Dirion SA2 165 D8
Brodog La SA65 122 D4
Brodog Terr SA65 122 C4
Brodorion Dr SA6 153 E3
Bro Dulais 2 SA19 43 E2
Bro Einon SA40 21 D6
Bro Gwen 1 SA39 39 B6
Bro Gwynfaen SA44 19 B7
Bro Hedydd SA31 128 F6
Bro Helyg 1 SA32 59 B6
Bro Hyfryd 1 SA32 59 A2
Brokesby Cl SA1 161 A3
Brokesby Rd SA1 161 A3
Bromeddyg 6 SA42 13 E4
Bro Meigan Gdns★ SA41 15 E1
Bromeillion SA48 4 F3
Bromeini SA36 35 B2
Bron Afon SA4 152 B5
Bron Afon Uchaf SA4 152 B5
Bronallt Rd / Heol Bronallt
SA4 143 A5
Bro Nant Fer SA18 99 D7
Bro Nantlais SA39 39 D6
Brondeg SA5 160 B3
Brondeg Cres SA5 160 B3
Brondeg La SA8 147 F3
Brongwyn Ct SA43 3 F4
Bronhaul SA20 26 B3
Bronllan SA1 161 D5
Bronwydd SA7 162 C8
Bronwydd Arms Sta
SA33 58 E3
Bronwydd Rd SA31 129 B7
Bron-y-Bryn SA2 165 E8
Bron-y-Dre
Cardigan / Aberteifi SA43 118 D4
Carmarthen / Caerfyrddin
SA31 129 A3
Bron-y-Glyn SA33 58 E2
Bron Yr Allt SA9 139 A8
Bron Yr Aur SA31 128 C2
Bron-yr-Ynn 1 SA14 96 E8
Bronywawr SA8 147 E5
Brooke Ave SA73 131 D3
Brookfield Cl SA4 150 F3
Brookfield Pl SA5 159 E6
Brookland Pl SA69 134 E3
Brooklands Cl SA2 158 B1
Brooklands Pk SA61 124 E3
Brooklands Terr SA1 167 B7
Brooklyn Gdns SA3 173 A6
Brooklyns Cl SA63 69 A7
Brooklyn Terr SA3 172 F5
Brookside
Gowerton / Tre-gwyr SA4 158 D3
St Ishmael's SA62 85 A2
Brookside Ave SA62 86 E6
Brookside Cl SA62 86 E6
Brookside Villas SA67 90 D2
Brook St SA10 162 F7
Brook Terr SA18 99 E7
Brookvale Rd SA3 172 F7
Brookville Dr SA10 162 E7
Broom La SA68 89 D3
Bro-pedr SA17 94 E6
Bro'r Dderwen SA66 70 F5
Bro'r-hengil 4 SA32 59 A3
Bro'r Orsaf SA39 20 C2
Bro Ryan SA18 99 A8
Bro Stinian 2 SA65 30 F5
Bro Tawel SA48 4 B6
Bro Teifi SA43 118 E4
Broughton Ave SA5 159 E6
Bro-Wen SA14 149 C5
Brown Ave SA15 148 F2
Brownhills SA4 151 A3
Browns Dr SA3 171 A5
Bruce Rd SA5 159 B4
Brunant Rd SA4 151 B3
Brunel Ave SA73 132 B6
Brunel Ct 3 SA1 167 B7
Brunel Way SA1 160 F3
Brunner Dr SA6 146 E1
Brunswick St SA1 167 B6
Brychan 1 SA15 148 F4
Brynaeron SA2 158 C1
Bryn Aeron Ct SA2 158 C1
Brynafon Rd SA4 151 A3
Brynallt Terr SA15 148 F5
Brynamlwg Clydach SA6 146 F1
Llanelli SA15 148 F6
Brynamlwg Rd SA4 151 A2
Bryn-Amlwg Rd SA5 159 E3
Brynamman Cty Prim Sch
SA18 80 E1
Brynamman Rd / Heol
Brynamman SA18 99 D7
Brynau Dr SA3 165 F2
Bryn Ave 2 Brecon SA18 80 E1
Burry Port SA16 137 F2
Brynawel SA8 147 E5
Brynawel Cres SA5 160 D5
Brynawelon
Ammanford SA18 97 F7
Cefn-bryn-brain SA9 100 B8
Llanelli SA14 149 C6
Llanwenog SA40 21 A8
2 Llanwrtyd Wells LD5 9 D1
Brynawel Rd
Gorseinon SA4 151 A2
Ystradgynlais SA9 138 F1
Brynawel Terr
1 Llandeilo SA19 130 D5
Ystradowen SA9 100 C7
Bryn Bach SA4 152 C5
Bryn Bach Rd
Brynamman SA18 99 D8
Pontlliw SA4 144 B2
Bryn-Bach Rd SA4 152 A8
Bryn Bach Rd SA18 80 D1
Brynbedw SA43 16 C7
Brynbrain SA9 100 B8
Bryncaerau SA17 109 B8
Bryn Canol SA14 149 A6
Bryncaredig SA33 127 D4
Bryncelyn SA6 153 C1
Bryn Celyn
Pontardawe SA8 147 D5
Swansea / Abertawe SA7 162 A6
Bryncelyn Rd SA4 151 A2
Bryncerdin Rd SA3 172 E5
Bryncethin Rd SA18 99 C7
Brynceunant 8 SA18 80 E1
Bryn Cl Gorseinon SA4 151 B3
Gowerton / Tre-gwyr SA4 158 D4
Bryncoch SA14 149 C6
Brynconin CP Sch SA66 70 F8
Bryncwar Rd SA14 97 D8
Bryndedwyddfa SA14 97 D8
Brynderi Ammanford SA18 97 E8
Pontyates / Pont-iets SA15 95 D4
Bryn Deri Cl
Llandyfriog SA38 119 D6
Bryn Deri Cl *continued*
Penllergaer SA4 152 B2
Brynderwen SA31 129 C7
Bryn Derwen
Pontardawe SA8 147 D5
Swansea / Abertawe SA2 159 B1
Brynderwen Rd 2 SA18 98 B7
Bryn Derw Gdns SA6 153 E2
Bryndolau SA2 165 B8
Bryndulais 1 SA19 43 E2
Bryndulais Ave SA14 148 F7
Bryn-edda SA17 94 B3
Bryn Eglur Rd SA6 160 D7
Bryneinon Rd SA4 151 A3
Bryneithin SA16 137 C2
Bryn Eithin SA4 158 B5
Bryneithin Rd SA4 151 A2
Bryneithin Terr SA6 153 F1
Bryneithyn SA9 138 C1
Bryn Elfed SA65 122 C5
Bryn Elli SA14 149 A7
Bryn Euraidd SA18 98 A6
Brynfa Terr SA4 156 E4
Brynffordd SA1 159 E2
Brynffynnon Rd SA4 151 A3
Brynfield Ct SA3 172 F4
Brynfield Rd SA3 172 E4
Bryn-Gaer SA14 149 A7
Bryngelli Dr SA5 160 C7
Bryngelli Pk SA5 160 C7
Bryngelli Rd SA5 160 C7
Bryn Gerran 3 SA43 16 A5
Brynglas
Cross Hand SA14 96 D8
Penygroes SA14 97 D7
Bryn Glas SA6 153 C2
Brynglas Cres SA31 129 C4
Bryn-Glas Rd SA5 159 E3
Bryngolau Gorseinon SA4 151 A2
Llanelli SA14 149 A7
Bryn Golau
Brawdy SA62 49 D4
Pontardawe SA8 147 F4
Bryn Goleu Rd SA5 159 F3
Bryngoleu Terr SA2 166 D7
Bryn Gomer SA65 122 D5
Bryn Gorof SA9 139 D8
Bryn Gorwel SA31 128 E6
Bryngwastad Rd SA4 151 A2
Bryn Gwdig SA65 109 C4
Bryngwenllan SA34 126 E3
Bryngwili Rd SA4 142 F3
Bryngwyn
Cardigan / Aberteifi SA43 118 B2
Neath / Castell-Nedd
SA10 162 C6
Bryngwyn Ave SA4 158 D8
Bryngwyn Bach SA14 149 A7
Bryngwyn Comp Sch
SA14 149 A8
Bryngwyn Rd SA14 149 B7
Brynhafod SA18 97 F5
Bryn Hafod SA43 118 E4
Bryn Hawddgar SA6 154 E8
Bryn Hebog SA48 120 A5
Brynhedydd SA62 29 F4
Bryn Hedydd SA6 153 C1
Bryn Helyg SA1 161 D5
Brynheulog SA14 148 F8
Bryn Hir SA4 157 A2
Brynhyfryd
Burry Port SA16 137 E3
Llangennech SA14 150 B6
Llangunnor SA31 129 A3
Tircoed SA4 152 C5
Bryn Hyfryd SA32 77 B3
Brynhyfryd Inf Sch SA5 160 D4
Brynhyfryd Jun Sch
SA5 160 D4
Brynhyfryd Rd
Gorseinon SA4 151 A3
Llanelli SA15 148 D6
Brynhyfryd Sq 4 SA5 160 C4
Brynhyfryd St SA5 160 C4
Bryniago SA4 143 E4
Bryn Iago SA19 63 D7
Brynilltyd SA16 137 C2
Bryn Isaf SA14 149 D4
Bryn Llewellyn SA65 122 D2
Bryn Llewelyn SA8 147 F3
Bryn-Lloi Rd / Heol
Bryn-Lloi 5 SA18 99 A8
Brynlluan SA14 97 B8
Brynllwchwr Rd SA4 157 E8
Brynmawr Ave / Rhodfa
Bryn-Mawr 6 SA18 98 B7
Brynmawr La / Lon
Bryn-Mawr 9 SA18 98 B7
Brynmead SA14 149 E6
Brynmead Cl SA2 166 C8
Brynmead Ct SA2 166 C8
Brynmefys SA15 140 B1
Brynmelyn Ave SA15 148 E6
Bryn-Melyn St SA1 160 D2
Brynmeurig SA31 129 A3
Brynmill Ave SA2 166 F5
Brynmill Cres SA2 166 F5
Brynmill La SA2 166 E5
Brynmill Prim Sch SA2 166 F5
Brynmill Terr SA2 166 E5
Bryn Morfa SA1 161 D5
Bryn Morlais SA14 149 F6
Brynmor Rd SA15 148 C4
Bryn Myrddln SA31 129 F7
Brynnewydd Gdns SA2 166 C5
Bryn Onnen
Cardigan / Aberteifi SA43 118 C3
Pontardawe SA8 147 E5
Bryn Parc SA6 160 F7
Bryn Pen SA48 120 C6
Bryn Pl 6 SA15 148 C4
Bryn Prim Sch SA14 149 E6
Bryn Rd Clydach SA6 154 D8
Cwmllynfell SA9 100 B7
Fishguard / Abergwaun
SA65 122 D4
Lampeter / Llanbedr Pont Steffan
SA48 120 B5
Llanelli SA15 148 C4
Loughor SA4 150 F1
Penygroes SA14 97 D8
Pontarddulais SA4 143 B4
Pontlliw SA4 152 A8
Quarter Bach SA18 80 E1
St David's / Tyddewi SA62 123 C4
Swansea / Abertawe, Brynmill
SA2 166 F5
Swansea / Abertawe SA5 159 E3
Waunarlwydd SA5 158 E3
Bryn Rhos Llanelli SA14 149 C6
Llannon SA14 96 E4
Bryn Rhos Cres SA4 152 B2
Bryn Rhosog SA4 157 E8
Bryn Rhosyn SA6 153 C2
Brynsaron Prim Sch / Ysgol
Gynradd Brynsaron
SA44 38 B7
Brynseilo SA17 95 D1
Bryn Seion SA62 48 D3
Brynsierfel SA14 149 C5
Brynsifi Way SA1 174 A4
Bryn-sion Hill SA67 71 B1
Brynsiriol
Fishguard / Abergwaun
SA65 122 D3
Gwaun-Cae-Gurwen SA18 99 D7
Llanelli SA14 148 F7
Bryn Siriol SA5 159 E3
Bryn St SA5 160 C4
Bryn Steffan SA48 120 B6
Bryn-Syfi Terr SA1 174 A4
Bryntawe Hall Cl SA6 154 C5
Bryntawe Rd SA6 154 B5
Brynteg Capel Hendre SA18 97 E6
Carmarthen / Caerfyrddin
SA31 128 B6
Clydach SA6 154 D7
St David's / Tyddewi SA62 123 C4
Bryn Teg SA7 162 A7
Brynteg Rd SA4 151 B3
Bryn-Teg Terr / Teras
Brynteg 13 SA18 98 B7
Bryn Terr Gorseinon SA4 151 D1
1 Llanelli SA15 148 C3
Llanelli, Seaside SA15 148 C4
Swansea / Abertawe SA1 160 D3
The Mumbles / Y Mwmbwls
SA3 173 B4
Bryn The SA2 166 C5
Bryn Tirion Clydach SA6 154 E8
1 Pontyberem SA15 96 B6
Bryntirion Hospl SA15 148 E6
Bryntirion Rd
Pontarddulais SA4 143 F1
Pontlliw SA4 152 A8
Bryntirion Terr SA15 148 F6
Bryntywi SA31 129 A3
Bryn-tywod SA4 153 A3
Bryn Vernel SA4 150 E1
Bryn View Cl SA3 117 C8
Bryn Y Ael SA31 129 B7
Bryn-y-Don Rd SA1 174 A4
Bryn Y Felin SA14 141 A1
Bryn Y Gors SA6 153 B2
Brynygroes Cotts SA9 138 F2
Bryn-y-Grug SA9 139 A7
Brynymor SA16 137 C2
Bryn Y Mor SA15 109 F7
Bryn-y-Mor SA4 157 D1
Bryn-y-mor Cres SA2 167 A6
Brynymor Rd
Loughor SA4 150 E2
Swansea / Abertawe SA1 167 A6
Bryn-y-Mor Rd
Gowerton SA4 157 F6
Gowerton / Tre-gwyr SA4 158 A5
Bryn Yr Eglwys SA48 120 C5
Bryn-y-Wawr SA33 58 E8
Buckingham Rd SA1 161 A2
Bude Haven Terr SA3 173 A6
Bufferland Terr SA72 132 B1
Bulford Cl SA62 86 D5
Bulford Rd SA62 86 D5
Bullin's La SA1 167 A7
Bunkers Hill SA73 131 E4
Bunker's Hill SA3 116 C6
Burgage Gn Cl SA62 85 A2
Burgley Ct SA5 159 E5
Burman St SA1 167 B7
Burnham Dr SA3 172 E6
Burrows Chambers 1
SA1 174 C2
Burrows Cl SA3 171 A5
Burrows La SA3 114 C3
Burrows Pl SA1 174 B2
Burrows Rd
Neath / Castell-Nedd,
Pentreffynnon SA10 162 E6
Swansea / Abertawe SA1 167 B5
Burrows Terr SA16 137 F2
Burry Pl SA4 156 F4
Burry Port Inf Sch SA16 137 D3
Burry Rd
Burry Port SA16 137 C3
Llanelli SA15 148 E1
Burry St SA15 148 C3
Burton Rd SA73 132 F8
Bushes La SA67 70 E1
Bush Hill SA71 133 B6
Bush Rd SA6 154 A1
Bush St SA72 132 C2
Buttercup Ct SA3 172 E6
Butterhill SA73 87 D3
Buttermilk Cl SA72 133 B6
Buttermilk La SA72 133 B7
Butterslade Gr SA6 154 A4
Butts La SA70 105 D6
Butts The 2 SA33 92 E5
Bwlch La SA31 129 E6
Bwlch Rd SA4 150 E2
Bwlch Y Gwyn SA5 144 E2
Bwllfa Rd SA6 154 C5
Bwrw Rd SA4 157 D8
Bynea Prim Sch / Ysgol
Gynradd Bynea SA14 149 F3
Bynea Sta SA14 149 F3
Byng Morris Cl SA2 166 B5
Byng St SA1 160 D4
Byron Rd SA61 125 A3
Byron Way SA2 165 F8

C

Caban Isaac Rd SA4 156 F3
Cadfan Rd SA1 167 A8
Cadle Cl SA5 159 E6
Cadle Cres SA5 159 D5
Cadle Dell Pl SA5 159 E6
Cadle Mill SA5 159 C7
Cadle Pl SA5 159 E6
Cadle Prim Sch SA5 159 D5
Cadle-Wood Rd SA5 159 E6
Cadnant Rd SA5 160 A5
Cadogan Cl SA62 86 E6
Cadrawd Rd SA1 160 B1
Cadwaladr Cir 4 SA1 167 B8
Cadwgan Rd SA6 146 B2
Cae Banc SA2 166 D7
Cae-Bricks Rd SA5 160 B2
Cae-Bryn Ave SA2 166 C5
Cae Bryn Drain SA31 128 E6
Cae Castell SA4 157 D8
Cae Celyn SA31 128 E6
Caecerrig Rd SA4 143 D4
Caecoed SA18 79 A1
Caeconna Rd SA5 159 E5
Cae Cotton SA14 148 F6
Cae Crug
Carmarthen / Caerfyrddin
SA31 128 E6
Swansea / Abertawe SA6 153 B1
Cae Crwn SA2 165 E8
Cae Dash SA48 120 C4
Caedegar Rd SA9 138 F2
Cae Delyn Cl SA15 148 B7
Caedolau SA16 137 E3
Cae-Du-Bach 1 SA15 148 E6
Caedu Rd SA9 100 B7
Cae Eithin
Carmarthen / Caerfyrddin
SA31 128 E6
Swansea / Abertawe SA6 153 B2
Cae Ffynnon SA17 136 B5
Caeffynnon Rd SA18 79 B2
Cae Folland SA4 156 E4
Cae Gar SA14 149 E5
Caeglas Cross Hands SA14 97 B7
Llanelli SA14 148 F8
Cae Glas SA4 151 C2
Caeglas Cl SA19 130 D3
Cae Grawn SA4 158 B5
Cae-Gwyn Rd SA4 143 D4
Cae-is-Maen SA8 147 C3
Cae Lynch SA10 162 F6
Caemansel La SA4 158 A3
Cae Mansel Rd
Gowerton / Tre-gwyr SA4 158 A4
Three Crosses SA4 157 F3
Caemawr SA18 98 C6
Caemawr Rd SA6 160 E8
Cae Melyn SA6 153 C1
Caemorgan Rd SA43 3 D3
Cae-Nan SA6 154 B3
Caenant Terr SA10 162 F7
Cae Penpant SA6 153 B2
Cae Person SA32 77 B3
Caepistyll St SA1 160 D1
Caepontbren SA15 95 E3
Cae-Pys Rd SA5 160 C5
Cae Ram SA48 120 F2
Cae'r-Bryn Rd SA14, SA18 97 E8
Cae'r-Bryn Terr SA18 97 E8
Cae'r Felin Sch / Ysgol Cae'r
Felin SA39 39 B7
Cae'rffynnon SA48 4 F8
Caer Groes SA18 79 A1
Caer-Gynydd Rd SA5 158 F3
Caernarvon Way SA1 161 B4
Cae Rowland St SA5 160 B3
Caerphilly Ave SA1 161 C4
Caersalem Terr / Teras
Caersalem 2 SA15 148 D3
Caer St SA1 174 B3
Caerwenog SA33 36 D1
Cae Terr SA15 148 F5
Caio CP Sch SA19 24 A2
Caldey Island Mus★
SA70 107 J2
Caldey Pl SA5 159 E7
Caldicot Cl SA1 161 C4

Caldicot Rd SA1 . . . . .161 C4
Caldy Way SA73 . . . . .131 E5
Caledfwlch SA19 . . . . .62 E4
Calland St SA6 . . . . .160 E5
Callans Dr SA71 . . . . .133 E4
Calvert Terr 2 SA1 . . . . . .167 B7
Camarthen Rd SA5 . . . . . . .159 E4
Cambrian Ct SA6 . . . . .161 A7
Cambrian Mill Heritage Ctr★
LD5 .9 D2
Cambrian Pl
10 Carmarthen / Caerfyrddin
SA31 . . . . .128 E5
Cwm-twrch Uchaf SA9 . . .100 C6
2 Haverfordwest / Hwlffordd
SA61 . . . . .125 B5
5 Llanelli SA15 . . . . .148 C4
Pontardulais SA4 . . . . . . .143 C4
Swansea / Abertawe SA1 . .174 C2
Cambrian Rd
1 Lampeter / Llanbedr
Pont Steffan SA48 . . . . . .120 C5
Neyland SA73 . . . . .132 C6
Cambrian St SA15 . . . . . . .148 C4
Cambridge Cl SA3 . . . . . . .173 A4
Cambridge Gdns SA3 . . . . .173 B4
Cambridge Rd SA3 . . . . . . .173 A4
Cambridge St SA2 . . . . . . .166 F7
Camellia Dr SA6 . . . . .153 F3
Cameron Pl SA4 . . . . .151 A2
Camffrwd Way SA6 . . . . . .154 C1
Camona Dr 1 SA1 . . . . . . .174 B1
Campbell Rd 3 SA18 . . . . . .79 A2
Campbell St
Llanelli SA15 . . . . .148 E2
Swansea / Abertawe SA1 . .174 A4
Camrose Dr SA5 . . . . .158 E3
Camuset Cl SA73 . . . . .131 A3
Canal St SA9 . . . . .139 B6
Canaston Ct SA5 . . . . .159 F7
Candleston Pl SA1 . . . . . . .161 C3
Cannisland Pk SA3 . . . . . . .164 D1
Cannon St / Stryd Cannon
SA18 . . . . .99 D8
Canterbury Rd
Pembroke Dock / Doc Penfro
SA72 . . . . .132 D3
Swansea / Abertawe SA2 . .166 C5
Cantref Ct SA5 . . . . .159 E5
Can-Yr-Aderyn SA6 . . . . . .153 D2
Can-Yr-Eos SA6 . . . . .153 E2
Capel Bldgs SA6 . . . . .154 E7
Capel Colman Rd SA37 . . . .16 C1
Capel Evan Rd 4 SA31 . . . .129 A6
Capel Hendre Ind Est
SA18 . . . . .97 E5
Capel Isaf Rd SA15 . . . . .149 A6
Capel Newydd / Cross Rd
SA15 . . . . .148 D6
Capel-Newydd La SA15 . . .148 D6
Capel Rd Clydach SA6 . . . .154 F8
Llanelli SA14 . . . . .149 A6
Capel Road Workshops
SA6 . . . . .154 F8
Capel Seion Rd SA15 . . . . . .96 C7
Capel Sion Rd SA14 . . . . . . .96 D8
Capel Teilo Rd SA17 . . . . . .95 A2
Capel Terr SA15 . . . . .148 F6
Capital Bldgs SA9 . . . . . . .139 C7
Caradoc Pl 2 SA61 . . . . . .124 E4
Caradog Pl SA1 . . . . .167 A8
Caradog's Well Rd SA61 . . .124 E2
Cardifor St 3 SA31 . . . . . .128 E5
**Cardigan Castle (remains
of)**★ SA43 . . . . .118 D3
Cardigan Cres SA1 . . . . . .161 C5
**Cardigan & District Meml
Hosp** SA43 . . . . .118 E3
Cardigan Her Ctr★
SA43 . . . . .118 D3
**Cardigan Island Nature
Reserve**★ SA43 . . . . .3 A7
Cardigan Prim Sch
SA43 . . . . .118 E4
Cardigan Rd SA15 . . . . . . .125 B7
Cardigan Sec Sch SA43 . .118 D3
**Cardigan Swimming Pool &
Leisure Ctr** SA43 . . . . . . .118 E4
Cardonnel Rd SA10 . . . . . .162 F6
Cardonnel Villas SA10 . . . .162 F6
Carew Castle & Tidal Mill★
SA70 . . . . .105 D6
Carew La SA70 . . . . .105 E7
Carew Pl SA1 . . . . .161 C5
Carig Cres SA1 . . . . .160 B1
Carig Gdns SA1 . . . . .160 A1
Carlton Rd SA6 . . . . .146 E1
Carlton Terr SA1 . . . . .174 A3
**Carmarthen District Leisure
Ctr** SA31 . . . . .128 D2
Carmarthen Rd
Cross Hands SA14 . . . . . . .97 A8
Ferryside SA17 . . . . .93 F5
Fforest SA4 . . . . .142 F6
Llandeilo SA19 . . . . .130 C6
Swansea / Abertawe SA1 . .174 B5
**Carmarthenshire Coll of Tech
& Art**
Ammanford / Rhydaman
SA18 . . . . .98 B7
Llangunnor SA31 . . . . . . .128 F1
Carmarthenshire Cty Mus★
SA31 . . . . .129 F6
Carmarthen St SA19 . . . . .130 D5
Carmarthen Sta SA31 . . . .128 F4

Carmel Rd Pontlliw SA4 . .151 F7
Swansea / Abertawe SA1 . .161 D5
Carnglas Ave SA2 . . . . . . .166 C7
Carnglas Rd SA2 . . . . .166 C7
Carnhywel SA14 . . . . .149 C6
Carno Pl SA6 . . . . .160 D8
Caroline St 3 SA15 . . . . . .148 C3
Carregamman 19 SA18 . . . . .98 B7
Carregamman Isaf SA18 . . . .98 B6
**Carreg Cennen Castle
(remains of)**★ SA19 . . . . .79 F6
Carreg Cennen Gdns
SA1 . . . . .161 B4
Carreg Coetan 9 SA42 . . . .13 E4
Carreg Onnen SA65 . . . . . .122 C3
Carreg Yr Afon SA9 . . . . . .100 C2
Carrick Ave SA15 . . . . .148 D7
Carrier's La 1 SA43 . . . . . .118 D3
Carrog Rd SA5 . . . . .160 B5
Carr Terr SA72 . . . . .104 B5
Cartersford Pl SA3 . . . . . . .173 A8
Cartlett SA61 . . . . .125 B5
Cartlett Rd 4 SA61 . . . . . .125 B5
Cartref SA10 . . . . .162 F7
Carway Cty Prim Sch
SA17 . . . . .95 C1
Carway St SA16 . . . . .137 D2
Caryl Terr SA6 . . . . .160 E6
Cashfield Way SA61 . . . . . .125 A7
Casllwchwr Prim Sch
SA4 . . . . .150 D1
Castell Cl SA7 . . . . .161 C7
Castell Corwg SA43 . . . . . . .16 A5
Castell Ddu Rd SA4 . . . . . .143 B1
**Castell Henllys Iron Age
Fort**★ SA41 . . . . .14 E2
Castell Hywel SA31 . . . . . .128 C8
Castell Pigyn Rd SA31 . . . .129 E8
Castle Acre SA3 . . . . .173 A6
Castle Ave SA3 . . . . .173 A5
Castle Back 18 SA61 . . . . . .125 A5
Castle Bailey St SA1 . . . . . .174 B3
Castle Cl
Llangadog SA19 . . . . .63 D7
Nolton & Roch SA62 . . . . . .66 E8
Castle Cres SA3 . . . . .173 A5
Castle Ct Loughor SA4 . . . .157 D8
Swansea / Abertawe SA7 . .161 B6
Castle Graig SA5 . . . . .160 D5
Castle Graig Rd SA6 . . . . . .160 D5
Castle Hall Dr SA73 . . . . . .131 F2
Castle Hall Rd SA73 . . . . . .131 F2
Castle High SA61 . . . . .124 F5
Castle La Carew SA70 . . .105 D6
7 Swansea / Abertawe
SA1 . . . . .174 B3
Castle Lofts 6 SA1 . . . . . .174 B3
Castle Pill Cres SA73 . . . . .131 F6
Castle Pill Rd SA73 . . . . . .131 F4
Castle Rd
Kidwelly / Cydweli SA17 . .136 B5
Llanfihangel-ar-Arth SA39 . .39 B7
St Ishmael's SA62 . . . . . . .85 A2
The Mumbles / Y Mwmbwls
SA3 . . . . .173 A6
Castle Rise SA62 . . . . .51 C2
Castle Sports Gd SA20 . . .121 D4
Castle Sq
Swansea / Abertawe SA1 . .174 B2
Tenby / Dinbych-y-pysgod
SA70 . . . . .135 F5
The Mumbles / Y Mwmbwls
SA3 . . . . .173 A4
Castle St
Cardigan / Aberteifi SA43 . .118 D3
9 Haverfordwest / Hwlffordd
SA61 . . . . .125 A5
Kidwelly / Cydweli SA17 . .136 B4
Llandovery / Llanymddyfri
SA20 . . . . .121 D4
Loughor SA4 . . . . .150 D1
Narberth / Arberth SA67 . . .70 D1
Neath / Castell-Nedd SA10 .162 F7
Newcastle Emlyn / Castell
Newydd Emlyn SA38 . . . .119 D5
2 Newport / Trefdraeth
SA42 . . . . .13 E3
Pembroke Dock / Doc Penfro
SA72 . . . . .104 B5
Swansea / Abertawe SA1 . .174 B3
The Mumbles / Y Mwmbwls
SA3 . . . . .173 A5
Castle Terr
Milford Haven / Aberdaugleddau
SA73 . . . . .131 D3
8 Narberth / Arberth SA67 . .70 E1
Newcastle Emlyn / Castell
Newydd Emlyn SA38 . . . .119 D5
Castle View
Camrose SA62 . . . . .67 A4
Haverfordwest / Hwlffordd
SA61 . . . . .125 A6
Pembroke / Penfro SA71 . .133 B5
Saundersfoot SA69 . . . . . .134 E4
Castle Way SA62 . . . . .101 D4
Caswell Ave SA3 . . . . .172 E4
Caswell Bay Ct SA3 . . . . . .172 C4
Caswell Bay Rd SA3 . . . . . .172 A5
Caswell Dr SA3 . . . . .172 D4
Caswell Rd
Bishopston SA3 . . . . .172 B4
The Mumbles / Y Mwmbwls
SA3 . . . . .172 E4
Caswell St Llanelli SA15 . . .148 E3
Swansea / Abertawe SA1 . .167 B6
Cathan Cl SA5 . . . . .159 E6
Cathan Cres SA5 . . . . .159 E6
Catherines Gate SA61 . . . .125 A1

Catherine St
Llanelli SA15 . . . . .148 C3
St David's / Tyddewi SA62 . .123 B4
Causeway St SA17 . . . . . . .136 B4
Causeway The SA2 . . . . . . .166 E7
Causway The SA62 . . . . . . .50 B1
Cave St SA5 . . . . .160 A2
Cawdor Cl SA61 . . . . .124 E3
Cawdor Pl SA61 . . . . .148 D6
Cawdor Terr SA38 . . . . . . .119 D5
Cecil Rd Gorseinon SA4 . . .151 C2
Gowerton / Tre-gwyr SA4 . .158 C4
Cecil St SA1 . . . . .160 C3
Cedar Ave SA4 . . . . .151 A4
Cedar Cl SA4 . . . . .158 D4
Cedar Cres SA3 . . . . .172 F8
Cedric Cl SA2 . . . . .166 B5
Cedric St SA15 . . . . .148 E5
Cefn Brith SA14 . . . . .149 B6
Cefn Celyn SA2 . . . . .158 B1
Cefn Coed SA65 . . . . .30 F5
Cefn Coed Cres SA2 . . . . . .159 D1
Cefn Coed Hosp SA2 . . . . .159 C1
Cefncrug SA18 . . . . .97 E7
Cefn-Draw SA4 . . . . .157 D1
Cefneithin Prim Sch
SA14 . . . . .97 A8
Cefneithin Rd SA14 . . . . . . .97 B8
Cefn Gallod 2 SA62 . . . . . .29 B5
Cefn Glas
Swansea / Abertawe SA2 . .166 B8
Ynysforgan SA6 . . . . .154 A3
Cefn Helyg SA2 . . . . .159 B1
Cefn Hengoed Com Sch
SA1 . . . . .161 C4
Cefn Hengoed Rd SA1 . . . .161 D4
Cefnllan Rd SA8 . . . . .147 D6
Cefn Llwyn SA1 . . . . .161 C5
Cefn-Parc SA10 . . . . .162 E6
Cefn Rd Glais SA7 . . . . . . .154 F6
Gwaun-Cae-Gurwen SA18 . .99 D6
Swansea / Abertawe SA1 . .161 C3
Cefnsaeson Rd SA7 . . . . . .162 A8
Cefn Stylle Rd SA4 . . . . . . .157 D4
Cefn-y-Maes SA5 . . . . .159 E6
Ceidrim Rd SA18 . . . . .99 B8
Ceiriog Rd SA1 . . . . .167 A8
Cellan Rd SA48 . . . . .120 E4
Cellar Hill SA73 . . . . .131 E2
Cemaes St SA43 . . . . .16 A5
Cemetery Rd
Gwaun-Cae-Gurwen SA18 . .99 D6
Swansea / Abertawe SA5 . .160 D6
Cenarth Cl SA72 . . . . .132 D4
**Central Bsns Pk / Parc
Busnes Canolog** SA7 . . . .154 C2
Central Ct SA73 . . . . .131 D3
Century Cl 1 SA61 . . . . . .125 A7
Century Pk SA6 . . . . .161 A6
Ceri Rd SA4 . . . . .159 F1
Chaddesley Terr 1 SA1 . . .167 B7
Challacombe Pl SA3 . . . . . .172 E6
Chancery La 1 SA43 . . . . . .118 D4
Chandlers Reach SA3 . . . . .173 C4
Channel View
Swansea / Abertawe SA2 . .166 B5
The Mumbles / Y Mwmbwls
SA3 . . . . .173 B3
Chantry Ct SA5 . . . . .159 E5
Chapelfield Gdns 7
SA67 . . . . .70 D1
Chapel Hill La SA67 . . . . .89 F7
Chapel La
8 Haverfordwest / Hwlffordd
SA61 . . . . .125 A5
Lamphey SA71 . . . . .105 B1
Chapel Rd Crofty SA4 . . . . .156 B2
Crundale SA62 . . . . .68 C5
Pembroke Dock / Doc Penfro
SA72 . . . . .132 A2
Scleddau SA65 . . . . .30 F5
Three Crosses SA4 . . . . . .157 E1
Chapel Row 7 SA62 . . . . . .87 E4
Chapel St 6 Brecon SA18 . .80 E1
Carmarthen / Caerfyrddin
SA31 . . . . .128 F5
Gorseinon SA4 . . . . .151 D2
Milford Haven / Aberdaugleddau
SA73 . . . . .131 B2
Swansea / Abertawe SA1 . .174 B5
Templeton SA67 . . . . .89 E6
The Mumbles / Y Mwmbwls
SA3 . . . . .173 A5
Chapmans 5 SA1 . . . . .174 B3
**Chapman St / Stryd
Chapman** SA15 . . . . .148 C6
Charles Ct SA4 . . . . .151 A1
Charles Rd SA71 . . . . .133 D4
Charles St
10 Llandyssul SA44 . . . . . .19 E3
Llanelli SA15 . . . . .148 F5
Milford Haven / Aberdaugleddau
SA73 . . . . .131 C2
Neath / Castell-Nedd,
Skewen / Sciwen SA10 . . .162 E7
Neyland SA73 . . . . .132 B7
Charles Terr SA15 . . . . . . .148 C4
Charles Thomas Ave
SA72 . . . . .132 D3
Charlotte Ct SA1 . . . . .159 E2
Charlton Pl SA72 . . . . .132 B2
Charnwood Ct SA1 . . . . . . .161 D6
Chelhydra Wlk 2 SA1 . . . .174 B1
Chemical Rd
Morriston / Treforris SA6 . .154 A2
Swansea / Abertawe SA6 . .153 F2

Chemical Row SA9 . . . . . . .139 A4
Chepstow Pl SA1 . . . . .161 C4
Cheriton Cres SA1 . . . . . . .159 F5
Cheriton Ct 2 SA1 . . . . . .174 A4
Cheriton Rd SA72 . . . . . . .104 B5
Cherry Gr
Haverfordwest / Hwlffordd
SA61 . . . . .125 B5
Swansea / Abertawe SA2 . .166 B4
Cherry Tree Cl SA73 . . . . . .131 E3
Chesshyre St SA2 . . . . .166 E5
Chestnut Ave
Gorseinon SA4 . . . . .151 A4
The Mumbles / Y Mwmbwls
SA3 . . . . .172 E8
Chestnut Tree Dr SA62 . . . .86 E6
Chestnut Way SA73 . . . . . .131 E3
Cheviot Cl SA5 . . . . .159 E3
Childrens Orthopaedic Hospl
SA1 . . . . .167 B6
Chiltern Cl SA5 . . . . .159 E3
Chirk Gdns SA1 . . . . .161 C4
Christ Church Prim Sch
SA1 . . . . .167 B5
Christina St SA1 . . . . .174 A3
Christopher Ct SA6 . . . . . .161 A6
Christopher Rd
Neath / Castell-Nedd
SA10 . . . . .162 E7
Ynysforgan SA6 . . . . .154 B4
Christopher Rise SA4 . . . . .152 A5
Christopher St SA15 . . . . . .148 E4
Church Bank SA20 . . . . . . .121 C4
Church Bank Ind Est
SA20 . . . . .121 C4
Church Cl
Kilgetty / Begelly SA68 . . .134 B8
1 Marloes & St Brides
SA62 . . . . .84 C3
Swansea / Abertawe SA7 . .161 D8
Church Cotts SA5 . . . . .153 B2
Church Gdns SA2 . . . . .159 E2
Church Hill La SA62 . . . . . .125 F3
Churchill Cl SA70 . . . . . . .135 C5
Church Lake Terr SA73 . . . .132 A6
Church Mdw SA3 . . . . .115 B1
Church Park La SA3 . . . . . .173 B4
Church Pk
Tenby / Dinbych-y-pysgod
SA70 . . . . .135 E4
The Mumbles / Y Mwmbwls
SA3 . . . . .173 B4
Church Rd
Burry Port SA16 . . . . .137 F2
Burton SA73 . . . . .132 F6
Gorslas SA14 . . . . .78 B1
Llanedi SA4 . . . . .97 D1
Llangain SA33 . . . . .75 B2
Llanstadwell SA73 . . . . . .103 F7
Llansteffan SA33 . . . . .93 E5
Milford Haven / Aberdaugleddau
SA73 . . . . .131 A3
Neyland SA73 . . . . .132 A6
Nolton & Roch SA62 . . . . . .66 D7
Rosemarket SA62 . . . . .86 E4
Swansea / Abertawe SA7 . .161 D8
Ynysmeudwy SA8 . . . . . . .147 F7
Ystalyfera SA9 . . . . .147 D5
Church Rd / Heol Yr Eglwys
SA14 . . . . .97 B8
Church Rd Ind Est SA14 . . . .78 B1
Church Row 8 SA18 . . . . . . .99 D8
Church St
Cardigan / Aberteifi SA43 . .118 E4
2 Carmarthen / Caerfyrddin
SA31 . . . . .129 A5
Cilgerran SA43 . . . . .15 F5
Cynwyl Gaeo SA19 . . . . . . .24 A2
Gowerton / Tre-gwyr SA4 . .158 B5
7 Haverfordwest / Hwlffordd
SA61 . . . . .125 A5
2 Lampeter / Llanbedr
Pont Steffan SA48 . . . . . .120 C5
Laugharne Township SA33 . .92 E6
Llandeilo SA19 . . . . .130 D5
4 Llandybie SA18 . . . . . . .79 A2
2 Llandyssul SA44 . . . . . .19 E3
Llanelli SA15 . . . . .148 D5
Llangadog SA19 . . . . .63 D7
10 Narberth / Arberth
SA67 . . . . .70 D1
Pembroke Dock / Doc Penfro
SA72 . . . . .132 C2
Pontardawe SA8 . . . . .147 E5
St Dogmaels / Llandudoch
SA43 . . . . .118 A3
5 Tenby / Dinbych-y-pysgod
SA70 . . . . .135 E4
Church St / Stryd-yr-Eglwys
8 SA14 . . . . .98 B2
Church Terr
Pembroke / Penfro SA71 . .133 A4
Saundersfoot SA69 . . . . . .134 E4
Church View SA67 . . . . .90 B2

Church Way SA73 . . . . .132 A6
Cila Prim Sch SA2 . . . . . . .165 D5
Cilfrow Ct SA1 . . . . .160 C2
Cilgerran Castle (NT)★
SA43 . . . . .16 A6
Cilgerran C in W VC Sch
SA43 . . . . .16 A6
Cilgerran Pl SA1 . . . . .161 C5
Cillefwr Ind Est SA31 . . . . .128 C3
Cillefwr Rd E SA31 . . . . . . .128 B3
Cillefwr Rd W SA31 . . . . . .128 B3
Cilmaengwyn SA8 . . . . .100 B1
Cilonen Rd SA4 . . . . .157 D1
Cilsaig Rd SA14 . . . . .149 B8
Cil-y-Coed SA5 . . . . .159 A3
Cilycwm Rd SA20 . . . . .121 D5
Cilycwm VC Prim Sch
SA20 . . . . .25 C2
Cil Yr Onnen SA14 . . . . . . .150 B8
Cilyrychen Ind Est SA18 . . . .79 A2
Cinema Bldgs 3 SA15 . . . .148 D3
City Rd SA61 . . . . .124 F5
Clarbeston Rd Sta SA63 . . . .69 A8
Clare Ct SA4 . . . . .150 E1
Clarence Ct SA1 . . . . .174 A2
Clarence Rd SA19 . . . . . . .130 E6
Clarence St
Pembroke Dock / Doc Penfro
SA72 . . . . .132 B2
Swansea / Abertawe SA1 . .174 A2
Clarence Terr SA1 . . . . . . .174 A2
Clarendon Rd
1 Llandeilo SA19 . . . . . . .130 E6
Swansea / Abertawe SA2 . .166 D7
Clare Rd SA9 . . . . .139 B7
Clare St SA5 . . . . .160 C3
Clareston Cl 4 SA61 . . . . . .124 F5
Clareston Rd 6 SA70 . . . . .135 E5
Clare Wlk SA71 . . . . .133 C6
Clarion Cl
Llansamlet SA6 . . . . .154 B1
Swansea / Abertawe SA6 . .161 C8
Clarion Ct SA6 . . . . .161 C8
Clarke Way SA1 . . . . .161 D6
Clasemont Rd
Swansea / Abertawe,
Morriston / Treforys SA6 . .153 F2
Swansea / Abertawe SA6 . .153 D2
Clase Prim Sch SA6 . . . . . .160 D8
Clase Rd
Morriston / Treforris SA6 . .154 A1
Swansea / Abertawe SA6 . .161 B8
Clas-y-Bedw SA5 . . . . .158 F3
Clas-y-Deri SA5 . . . . .159 A3
Clas-yr-Onnen SA5 . . . . . . .159 A3
Claybogs La SA62 . . . . .50 E1
Clayford Rd SA69 . . . . .134 A4
Clay La Hundleton SA71 . .104 A2
Merlin's Bridge SA61 . . . . .125 B2
Milford Haven / Aberdaugleddau
SA73 . . . . .85 F1
Clayton Rd SA4 . . . . .143 A4
Clayton St SA1 . . . . .160 D4
Cleddau Ave
Haverfordwest / Hwlffordd
SA61 . . . . .125 B4
Neyland SA73 . . . . .132 B4
Cleddau Bridge Bsns Pk
SA72 . . . . .132 E5
Cleddau Cl SA73 . . . . .87 C3
Clees La SA9 . . . . .139 A5
Cleggars Pk SA71 . . . . .105 A3
Clement Rd SA64 . . . . .122 A6
Clement Terr SA70 . . . . . . .135 C6
Clerkenhill Adventure Farm★
SA67 . . . . .69 D2
Clevedon Ct SA2 . . . . .166 F7
Cleveland Ave SA3 . . . . . . .173 C3
Cleviston Pk SA14 . . . . . . .150 A6
Clickett La SA70 . . . . .135 C7
Clicketts Ct SA70 . . . . . . .135 B5
Clicketts The SA70 . . . . . . .135 B5
Clifflands Cl SA3 . . . . . . .172 F4
Cliff Rd Amroth SA67 . . . . . .90 C2
Laugharne Township SA33 . .92 F5
Pembroke Dock / Doc Penfro
SA72 . . . . .103 F5
Cliff Terr SA16 . . . . .137 C2
Clifton Ct SA5 . . . . .160 C6
Clifton Hill SA1 . . . . .174 A3
Clifton Row SA1 . . . . .174 A3
Clifton St SA33 . . . . .92 F6
Clifton Terr
2 Llanelli SA15 . . . . .148 E5
The Mumbles / Y Mwmbwls
SA3 . . . . .173 C4
Clive Rd SA65 . . . . .122 C4
Cloisters The SA1 . . . . . . .167 A6
Clordir Rd SA4 . . . . .152 A7
Clos Aderyn Du SA5 . . . . . .159 F3
Clos Affallon SA18 . . . . .99 D6
Clos Afon Llan SA4 . . . . . . .158 A4
Clos Alaw SA7 . . . . .161 E6
Clos Allt-y-Gog SA4 . . . . . .143 C3
Clos Andreas 3 SA15 . . . . .148 E6
Clos Aneira SA5 . . . . .159 D3
Clos Ar Ddafen SA14 . . . . .149 C5
Clos Banc Y Berllan
SA4 . . . . .143 D3
Clos Bevan SA4 . . . . .158 A5
Clos Blean Crymlyn SA7 . . .161 E6
Clos Brynafon SA4 . . . . . . .150 F3
Clos Bryncarn SA18 . . . . . . .99 C3
Clos Bryn Dafydd SA4 . . . . .152 C2
Clos Bryngwyn SA4 . . . . . .158 B8
Clos Bryn Isaf SA14 . . . . . .149 D4
Clos Burlais SA5 . . . . .160 A2

Clos Cadno
Llansamlet SA7 . . . . . .154 D1
Swansea / Abertawe SA6 . .153 F5
Clos Cae Dafydd SA4 . . . .158 A5
Clos Cae Fainc SA14 . . . .150 B7
Clos Caer Elms SA15 . . . .148 B6
Clos Caersalem SA6 . . . .160 C7
Clos Calfaria SA5 . . . . . .159 E3
Clos Camlas 10 SA6 . . . .161 A8
Clos Cefn-y-Maes SA14 . .149 C5
Clos Celyn SA7 . . . . . . .161 D6
Clos Cenawon SA6 . . . . .154 A3
Clos Cerdinen SA4 . . . . .152 C4
Clos Ceri SA6 . . . . .154 E8
Clos Cilfwnwr SA4 . . . . .152 B3
Clos Cilsaig SA14 . . . . . .149 C8
Clos Crucywel SA6 . . . . .154 A4
Clos Cwnin SA31 . . . . . .129 B7
Clos Cwningen SA7 . . . . .155 B1
Clos Cwrt Y Carne SA4 . .151 A4
Clos Cynan SA2 . . . . . . .165 F8
Clos Dan Y Lan SA14 . . .140 F2
Clos Ddu SA5 . . . . .160 B7
Clos Delyth SA4 . . . . . .151 C2
Clos Derwen SA7 . . . . . .162 A6
Clos Dewi Medi SA15 . . .148 E2
Clos Dyffrynlliw / Lliw Valley
Cl SA4 . . . . .158 C6
Clos Ebol SA6 . . . . .153 F4
Clos Eileen Chilcott
SA7 . . . . .161 E6
Clos Emily SA14 . . . . . .97 C7
Close The Gorseinon SA4 .151 A1
Hook SA62 . . . . .87 D6
Johnston SA62 . . . . . . .86 E5
Llanrhidian SA4 . . . . . .115 F4
Spittal SA62 . . . . .51 C1
Swansea / Abertawe SA5 .153 C2
Clos Felen 3 SA18 . . . . .99 B8
Clos Gathen SA15 . . . . . .148 D4
Clos George Morgan
SA6 . . . . .153 E4
Clos Ger-y-Bryn SA4 . . . .152 C5
Clos Ger-y-Maes SA4 . . . .152 C5
Clos Glanlliw SA4 . . . . . .152 A6
Clos Glanmor SA15 . . . . .148 C4
Clos Glan-y-Wern SA7 . . .161 E6
Clos Glyndwr SA4 . . . . . .142 F5
Clos Gors Fawr SA4 . . . . .151 C6
Clos Granby SA15 . . . . . .148 E2
Clos Gwernen SA4 . . . . .158 C6
Clos Healy SA4 . . . . . . .158 B6
Clos Helyg SA4 . . . . . . .158 B5
Clos Hendra SA6 . . . . . .146 B2
Clos Hermon SA16 . . . . .137 B3
Clos Islwyn SA2 . . . . . . .165 E8
Clos Leighton Davies
SA4 . . . . .158 B6
Clos Llandyfan SA4 . . . . .158 D8
Clos Llanfihangel SA14 . .149 B6
Clos Llwyn Cwm SA6 . . . .161 A6
Clos Llwyn Ty Gwyn
SA34 . . . . .126 E3
Clos Llyg SA7 . . . . .162 B8
Clos Madlen SA4 . . . . . .159 D4
Clos Maes Isaf SA14 . . . .150 C7
Clos Maes Yr Ysgol
SA4 . . . . .143 D3
Clos Marina SA4 . . . . . .158 B6
Clos Melin Mynach SA4 . .158 C8
Clos Min Yr Afon SA4 . . .150 F2
Clos Morgan 1 SA31 . . . .128 E5
Clos Morgannwg SA1 . . . .167 A8
Clos Morgan Owen SA4 . .158 A5
Clos Nant Bran SA7 . . . .155 A2
Clos Nant-y-Ci SA4 . . . . .97 F7
Clos Nantydd SA14 . . . . .149 C4
Clos Penbwl SA4 . . . . . .152 C2
Clos Pendderi SA14 . . . . .149 F5
Clos Penderri SA4 . . . . .152 C2
Clos Pengelli SA4 . . . . . .151 C7
Clos Penllwyngwyn
SA14 . . . . .149 E6
Clos Pen Pant SA4 . . . . .143 D4
Clos Pentyle SA8 . . . . . .147 B2
Clos Pen y Banc SA6 . . . .160 C8
Clos Penyfai SA15 . . . . . .148 B7
Clos Pen Y Waun SA4 . . .97 C7
Clos Plas Isaf SA14 . . . . .150 C7
Clos Pluguen SA20 . . . . .121 C3
Clos Rebecca SA14 . . . . .96 F3
Clos Rhandir SA4 . . . . . .157 E8
Clos Rhedyn SA6 . . . . . .154 A4
Clos Rhymni SA6 . . . . . .154 A4
Clos Sant Paul SA15 . . . .148 D4
Clos Sant Pedr 5 SA15 . .148 D4
Clos Sant Teilo SA5 . . . . .153 B1
Clos Saron SA5 . . . . . . .159 F3
Clos St Cenydd SA3 . . . .114 C2
Clos Sticle SA31 . . . . . . .129 A3
Clos Tawel SA48 . . . . . . .4 B6
Clos Tirffordd SA4 . . . . . .152 C2
Clos Trafle SA4 . . . . .158 C6
Clos Tygwyn Clydach SA6 .154 E8
Gowerton / Tre-gwyr SA4 .158 B6
Clos Ty-Gwyn SA4 . . . . .142 F4
Clos Ty Mawr SA4 . . . . . .152 B2
Clos Ty Tafol SA15 . . . . .148 D3
Clos Vernon Watkins
SA4 . . . . .151 A4
Clos Waun Wen SA6 . . . .153 B1
Clos Y Banc-yr-Eithin
SA4 . . . . .151 A3
Clos-y-Berllan SA14 . . . . .149 F5
Clos-y-bigney SA65 . . . . .122 C3
Clos Y Binwydd / Pine Tree
Cl SA16 . . . . .137 F3

Clos Y Bont Faen
Cwmrhydyceirw SA6 . . . .154 A5
Swansea / Abertawe SA6 . .153 F4
Clos Y Coedwr SA14 . . . .154 D7
Clos-Y-Cwm SA14 . . . . . .97 D7
Clos Y Dderwen SA16 . . .137 B3
Clos Y Dderwen / Oak Tree
Cl SA18 . . . . .98 D7
Clos Y Ddraenen SA14 . . .141 B3
Clos Y Deri SA31 . . . . . .129 A5
Clos-y-Deri SA4 . . . . . . .97 D2
Clos-Y-Deri
Llanegwad SA32 . . . . . .77 A8
Llanelli SA14 . . . . .149 B8
Clos-y-Derwen / Oaklands Cl
SA14 . . . . .97 B8
Clos-y-Felin SA18 . . . . . .98 D7
Clos Y Faran SA7 . . . . . .155 A6
Clos Y Fynwent SA4 . . . .143 D3
Clos Y Gafel 2 SA41 . . . .34 C4
Clos-y-gerddi SA37 . . . . .34 E8
Clos-y-Gweydd SA4 . . . . .158 A5
Clos-y-Maerdy SA41 . . . .158 C8
Clos Y Meini SA41 . . . . . .34 C4
Clos Y Morfa SA4 . . . . . .150 F3
Clos Y Mynydd SA4 . . . . .150 F2
Clos Y Nant SA4 . . . . . . .150 F2
Clos Yr Ael SA1 . . . . . . .159 F2
Clos Yr Allt SA1 . . . . . . .159 F2
Clos Yr Eglwys SA1 . . . . .159 F2
Clos Yr Hesg SA7 . . . . . .154 D1
Clos Yr Onnen
Abergwili SA31 . . . . . . .129 E7
Kidwelly / Cydweli SA17 . .136 D3
Llansamlet SA7 . . . . . . .154 D1
Clos Yr Orsaf 9 SA6 . . . .161 A8
Clos Yr Ysgol SA7 . . . . . .162 A7
Clos Ysgallen SA7 . . . . . .161 D6
Clos Ysgol Gymraeg
SA5 . . . . .160 B2
Clos Y Waun SA14 . . . . . .97 B7
Clovelly Pl SA3 . . . . .172 E6
Clover Pk SA14 . . . . .125 C5
CIUs Griffith Jones
SA33 . . . . .127 E6
Club La SA9 . . . . .138 F1
Clunderwen Sta SA66 . . . .70 E6
Clwyd Com Prim Sch
SA5 . . . . .160 A4
Clwyd Rd
Gwaun-Cae-Gurwen SA18 . .99 D6
Swansea / Abertawe SA5 . .160 B4
Clwyd -Wen SA4 . . . . . . .158 A5
Clydach Hospl SA6 . . . . .154 D7
Clydach Infl Sch SA6 . . . .154 D7
Clydach Jun Sch SA6 . . . .154 D8
Clydach Rd
Craig-cefn-parc SA6 . . . .146 B2
Ynysforgan SA6 . . . . . . .154 A2
Ynystawe SA6 . . . . .154 C5
Clyndu St SA6 . . . . .160 F8
Clyne Cl SA3 . . . . .165 F1
Clyne Cres SA3 . . . . .165 F1
Clyne Ct SA2 . . . . .166 B7
Clyne Dr SA2 . . . . .166 B1
Clyne Farm Activties Ctr★
SA3 . . . . .166 A4
Clyne Valley Cotts SA2 . . .165 E5
Clyne Valley Ctry Pk★
SA2 . . . . .166 A4
Clyne Valley La SA2 . . . . .166 B2
Clyne Valley Rd SA2 . . . . .165 E5
Clyne View SA2 . . . . .165 E6
Clyngwyn Rd SA9 . . . . . .139 B7
Clynmaes Pl SA5 . . . . . . .159 E6
Clyro Ct SA1 . . . . .161 C4
Cnap Llwyd Rd SA6 . . . . .160 D6
Cnwc Y Dintir SA43 . . . . .118 C5
Coalbrook Rd
Grovesend SA4 . . . . . . .151 C5
Pontyberem SA15 . . . . . .96 B6
Coal La SA70 . . . . .105 E3
Cobblers Ct 1 SA15 . . . .148 D6
Cobham Cl SA4 . . . . .151 A3
Cob La Manorbier SA70 . .105 E1
1 Tenby / Dinbych-y-pysgod
SA70 . . . . .135 F4
Coch-y-Cwm Rd SA1 . . . .161 C2
Cockett Rd SA2 . . . . .159 D2
Coedbach Rd SA4 . . . . . .143 C3
Coedcae SA8 . . . . .147 F6
Coedcae Comp Sch
SA15 . . . . .148 F5
Coed Cae Rd
Llanelli SA15 . . . . .148 F5
Llanelli SA15 . . . . .149 A5
Coed Cae Uchaf SA15 . . .148 F5
Coed Ceirios SA7 . . . . . .154 D1
Coed Celyn Rd SA2 . . . . .166 B4
Coedfan SA2 . . . . .166 A6
Coedffaldau SA9 . . . . . . .100 B6
Coedffranc Inf Sch
SA10 . . . . .162 F7
Coedffranc Jun Sch
SA10 . . . . .162 F7
Coedlan SA9 . . . . .139 D8
Coed Lan SA4 . . . . .157 D1
Coedmawr SA15 . . . . . . .95 F4
Coed Mor SA2 . . . . .166 B5
Coedmor Ave SA33 . . . . .75 B2
Coedmore La SA38 . . . . .119 D6
Coedmor National Nature
Reserve★ SA43 . . . . . .16 A4
Coed Nant Ho SA1 . . . . .160 D2
Coedrath Pk SA69 . . . . . .134 E4
Coed-Saeson Cres SA2 . . .166 D7
Coedwig Pl SA5 . . . . .160 A3

Coed Y Bronallt SA4 . . . .143 A5
Coedybryn Cty Prim Sch
SA44 . . . . .18 E7
Coed-y-Bwlch SA14 . . . . .150 A2
Coed y Cadno SA14 . . . . .97 C5
Coed Y Clun SA17 . . . . . .109 B7
Coed-y-crwys SA41 . . . . .157 E1
Coed-y-Felin SA31 . . . . . .129 E7
Coed Y Pin / Pinewood
SA18 . . . . .98 D7
Coed Y Plas SA41 . . . . . .128 C2
Colbourne Terr SA1 . . . . .174 A5
Colbren Sq SA18 . . . . . . .99 D6
Colby Rd SA16 . . . . .137 E3
Colby Woodland Gdn (NT)★
SA67 . . . . .90 C3
Coldstream St SA15 . . . . .148 C6
Coldwell Terr SA71 . . . . . .133 C5

Coleg = college

Coleg Abertawe / Swansea
Coll (Tycoch Campus)
SA2 . . . . .166 D7
Coleg Celf Dyfed / Dyfed Coll
of Art SA15 . . . . .128 C5
Coleg Llanymddyfri /
Llandovery Coll SA20 . .121 C5
Coleg Sir Benfro /
Pembrokeshire Coll
SA61 . . . . .124 E3
Coleg y Drindod / Trinity
Coll SA31 . . . . .128 C5
Coleridge Cres SA2 . . . . .165 F8
Coleshill Terr SA15 . . . . .148 C5
College Hill SA15 . . . . . .148 E5
College Pk SA73 . . . . . . .132 B6
College Rd SA31 . . . . . . .128 C5
College Row
Cardigan / Aberteifi SA43 .118 D4
Ystradgynlais SA9 . . . . .139 F8
College Sq SA15 . . . . . . .148 E5
College St
Lampeter / Llanbedr Pont Steffan
SA48 . . . . .120 C5
Newcastle Emlyn / Castell
Newydd Emlyn SA38 . . .119 D5
Swansea / Abertawe SA1 .174 B3
College St / Stryd-y-Coleg
SA18 . . . . .98 B7
College View SA20 . . . . . .121 C4
Colley Ct SA71 . . . . .104 C4
Colonel Rd /
Fforddd-y-Cyrnol SA18 . .98 C6
Colonel Road SA18 . . . . . .98 C6
Coltshill Dr SA3 . . . . .172 F5
Columbia Row 12 SA15 . .148 D5
Colwyn Ave SA1 . . . . . . .161 C5
Commercial Rd SA8 . . . . .147 C8
Commercial Row SA72 . . .132 B2
Commercial St
Ystalyfera SA9 . . . . . . .139 B6
Ystradgynlais SA9 . . . . .138 F1
Common Rd SA71 . . . . . .133 B4
Compass Row SA8 . . . . . .147 D5
Compass St SA1 . . . . . . .160 C3
Compton Ave SA10 . . . . .162 F7
Conduit La SA73 . . . . . . .131 A2
Coniston Wlk SA2 . . . . . .166 D7
Conkland Hill SA62 . . . . . .69 A4
Connacht Way SA72 . . . . .132 D4
Connaught Pl SA72 . . . . .132 D4
Constitution Hill SA1 . . . .167 B7
Convent St SA1 . . . . .160 D1
Conway Ct SA5 . . . . .160 A4
Conway Dr SA73 . . . . . . .131 F6
Conway Rd SA5 . . . . .160 A4
Cooks Cl SA71 . . . . .133 E4
Cooksyeat View SA68 . . . .134 E8
Coombes Rd SA10 . . . . . .162 E7
Coombe-Tennant Ave
SA10 . . . . .162 D7
Coombs Dr SA73 . . . . . . .131 E3
Coombs Rd SA73 . . . . . . .131 E3
Coopers Est SA18 . . . . . .97 E5
Coopers Rd / Heol Cwper
SA18 . . . . .97 E5
Copley Cl SA3 . . . . .172 B7
Copley Lodge SA3 . . . . . .172 B7
Copperworks Inf Sch
SA15 . . . . .148 D4
Copperworks Rd / Heol
Copperworks SA15 . . . .148 D3
Coracle Way SA31 . . . . . .128 F4
Coram Dr SA73 . . . . .132 C2
Cork Ho 10 SA1 . . . . . . .174 C2
Cormorant Cl SA15 . . . . .148 B6
Cormorant Way SA3 . . . . .172 E6
Cormoront Cl SA62 . . . . .124 F7
Cornish Pl SA15 . . . . . . .148 E2
Cornwall Pl SA3 . . . . . . .173 B5
Coronation Ave
Haverfordwest / Hwlffordd
SA61 . . . . .125 B6
6 Llangwm SA62 . . . . . .87 A1
Coronation Dr SA43 . . . . .118 B8
Coronation Rd
1 Brecon SA18 . . . . . . .80 E1
Carmarthen / Caerfyrddin
SA31 . . . . .128 E6
2 Fishguard / Abergwaun
SA65 . . . . .122 D4
Coronation Rd / Heol Y
Coroni 16 SA18 . . . . . .99 B8
Coronation Terr SA18 . . . .98 D6
Coronet Way SA4 . . . . . .161 A7
Corporation Ave SA15 . . . .148 E7

Corporation Cl SA15 . . . .148 E6
Corporation Rd
Loughor SA4 . . . . .150 E1
Swansea / Abertawe SA5 .159 C4
Corrymore Mans SA2 . . . .166 F6
Cors Goch; Llanllwch
National Nature Reserve★
SA33 . . . . .74 F5
Cory St SA2 . . . . .166 D6
Cots La SA62 . . . . .69 A5
Cotswold Cl SA5 . . . . . . .159 E3
Cotswold Gdns SA68 . . . .134 C8
Cott La SA67 . . . . .88 E7
Cotts Rd SA62 . . . . .85 C5
Courtenay Rd SA15 . . . . .148 C6
Courtenay St SA15 . . . . . .160 C2
Courtfield Dr SA62 . . . . . .67 A6
Court La SA67 . . . . .147 E5
Courtlands SA5 . . . . .159 E5
Courtlands Way SA5 . . . . .159 E5
Court Rd SA61 . . . . .124 D5
Court Rise SA73 . . . . . . .131 A3
Court Terr SA71 . . . . .133 B5
Courtyard The 7 SA1 . . . .174 A4
Courtyard Units SA10 . . . .162 D5
Cowell Prec 8 SA15 . . . . .148 D5
Cowell Rd / Heol Cowell
SA18 . . . . .99 C7
Cowell St SA15 . . . . .148 D5
Cowpark La SA70 . . . . . .105 D2
Cowper Cl SA2 . . . . .165 F7
Cox Hill SA67 . . . . .70 C2
Crackwell Cl SA70 . . . . . .135 A1
Crackwell St SA70 . . . . . .135 E4
Cradock St Llanelli SA15 . .148 D4
Swansea / Abertawe SA1 .174 A3
Craig-cefn-parc Prim Sch
SA6 . . . . .146 B4
Craig-las SA62 . . . . .50 F8
Craigwen SA14 . . . . .149 E4
Craig-y-Bwldan SA2 . . . . .165 E8
Craig y nos Sch SA3 . . . . .172 C7
Cranfield Ct SA5 . . . . . . .159 E5
Cranham Pk 3 SA62 . . . . .86 E5
Cranmer Ct SA5 . . . . . . .159 E5
Cranog Cl SA62 . . . . .29 B5
Crawshay Ct SA3 . . . . . . .172 F3
Crayland Parc SA17 . . . . .136 A5
Creamston Rd SA61 . . . . .125 E4
Creidiol Rd SA1 . . . . .174 A4
Crescent Rd
Gwaun-Cae-Gurwen SA18 . .99 D6
Llandeilo SA19 . . . . . . .130 E6
Crescent The
Burry Port SA16 . . . . . .137 E3
Gorslas SA14 . . . . .97 C8
1 Narberth / Arberth SA67 .70 E1
Swansea / Abertawe SA5 .159 F5
Cresswell Rd SA62 . . . . . .67 B6
Cresswell St SA70 . . . . . .135 E4
Crest Acre Cl SA3 . . . . . .172 E5
Creswell Rd SA62 . . . . . .160 D8
Cribin La SA14 . . . . .141 A2
Cribyn Clos SA14 . . . . . . .141 A3
Criccieth Pl SA1 . . . . . . .161 C5
Cricket Gr SA71 . . . . . . .104 A3
Crickhowell Pl SA1 . . . . . .161 C5
Crickmarren Cl SA71 . . . .133 F3
Criney Hill SA65 . . . . . . .31 C6
Crispin Ave SA31 . . . . . . .128 D5
Criterion Way SA72 . . . . .132 C4
Croesffyrdd SA14 . . . . . . .97 D7
Croesgoch CP Sch SA62 . .28 F3
Croeso Rd 4 SA71 . . . . . .133 D4
Croes-Y-ceiliog SA14 . . . .96 C4
Croft Ave SA73 . . . . .85 F1
Croftfield Cres SA3 . . . . . .172 F5
Croft La SA70 . . . . .105 D2
Croft Rd 5 SA62 . . . . . . .85 C8
Croft St SA1 . . . . .174 A4
Croft Terr
Pembroke Dock / Doc Penfro
SA72 . . . . .132 B2
2 Swansea / Abertawe
SA5 . . . . .160 C4
Croft The Loughor SA4 . . .150 D1
Tenby / Dinbych-y-pysgod
SA70 . . . . .135 E4
Croft Villas 4 SA67 . . . . .70 E1
Crofty Cl SA62 . . . . .28 F3
Crofty Ind Est SA4 . . . . . .156 B3
Crole St SA1 . . . . .167 B7
Cromie Ave SA61 . . . . . . .124 F4
Cromwell Ct 2 SA71 . . . . .133 D4
Cromwell Drive SA70 . . . .106 B7
Cromwell Rd SA73 . . . . . .131 C5
Cromwell St
Pembroke Dock / Doc Penfro
SA72 . . . . .132 D2
Swansea / Abertawe SA1 .167 B7
Cross Acre SA3 . . . . .172 E4
Cross Hands Bsns Pk
SA14 . . . . .97 B7
Cross Hands Prim Sch
SA14 . . . . .97 A8
Cross Hands Rd / Heol Cross
Hands SA14 . . . . .97 B8
Cross Inn Bldgs 16 SA18 . .98 B7
Cross La SA62 . . . . .68 C5
Crosslands Rd SA67 . . . . .90 E6
Cross Pk
Pembroke Dock / Doc Penfro
SA72 . . . . .132 B1
St Mary out Liberty SA70 . .107 A4
Cross Rd / Capel Newydd
SA15 . . . . .148 D6
Cross Sq SA62 . . . . .123 C4

Cross St
Goodwick / Wdig SA64 . . .122 A5
Gorseinon SA4 . . . . . . .151 C2
Pontarddulais SA4 . . . . .143 C4
Swansea / Abertawe SA5 .160 C4
Whitland / Hendy-Gwyn
SA34 . . . . .126 C3
Cross The
Cosheston SA72 . . . . . .104 F6
Llanrhidian SA3 . . . . . .115 D2
Crossways SA73 . . . . .87 A1
Crow Hill SA62 . . . . .125 A8
Crowhill Rd SA61 . . . . . . .125 A6
Crown Cotts SA9 . . . . . . .138 C2
Crown Prec 13 SA15 . . . .148 D5
Crown St
Swansea / Abertawe SA6 .160 F8
Swansea / Abertawe SA6 .161 A8
Crud-yr-Awel SA4 . . . . . .158 B8
Crug Yr Efydd SA41 . . . . .34 F4
Crwys Prim Sch / Ysgol
Gynradd y Crwys SA4 . . .157 E1
Crwys Terr SA4 . . . . .160 B6
Crychiau SA31 . . . . .129 E8
Crymlun Bog Nature
Reserve★ SA1, SA7 . . . .161 E2
Crymlyn Bog Visitor Ctr★
SA1 . . . . .161 D1
Crymlyn Parc SA10 . . . . .162 C6
Crymlyn Prim Sch / Ysgol
Gynradd Crymlyn
SA10 . . . . .162 C1
Crymlyn Rd SA7, SA10 . . .162 B6
Crymlyn St SA1 . . . . .168 B7
Crymlyn Terr SA1 . . . . . . .161 C2
Cuckoo La SA62 . . . . . . .124 B6
Cuffern Cl 1 SA61 . . . . . .124 C5
Cuffern Rd SA62 . . . . . . .67 A6
Cuffern View SA62 . . . . . .67 A6
Culfor Rd SA4 . . . . .157 E8
Culla Rd SA17 . . . . .109 C8
Culver Pk SA70 . . . . .135 C4
Cumby Terr SA71 . . . . . . .132 B2
Cunningham Cl SA2 . . . . .166 C6
Curlew Cl
2 Haverfordwest / Hwlffordd
SA61 . . . . .124 E5
The Mumbles / Y Mwmbwls
SA3 . . . . .165 E1
Curry Cl SA2 . . . . .165 E8
Cutty Sark Dr SA73 . . . . .131 E5
Cwmamman Rd SA18 . . . .98 F3
Cwm Arian SA6 . . . . .154 A2
Cwmbach Rd
Llanelli Rural SA15 . . . . .109 F4
Llanelli SA15 . . . . .109 A8
Swansea / Abertawe SA5 .159 C3
Cwm Bath Rd SA6 . . . . .153 F1
Cwmbwrla Prim Sch
SA5 . . . . .160 B2
Cwm Cadle SA5 . . . . . . .159 E6
Cwm Catti SA32 . . . . . . .77 C2
Cwm Chapel Rd SA1 . . . .161 B4
Cwm Clyd SA5 . . . . .159 A3
Cwm Clydach Nature
Reserve★ SA6 . . . . . . .146 B3
Cwmdegwel SA43 . . . . . .118 A2
Cwm Deri Vineyard★
SA67 . . . . .88 C5
Cwmdonkin Dr SA2 . . . . .167 A7
Cwmdonkin Terr SA2 . . . .166 F7
Cwm Du Cl SA5 . . . . . . .159 F3
Cwmdu Ind Est SA5 . . . . .159 F2
Cwmdu Rd SA8 . . . . .100 B1
Cwmerchon Nature Pk★
SA19 . . . . .43 C5
Cwmfelin Rd SA14 . . . . . .149 F3
Cwmfelin Way SA1 . . . . . .160 C2
Cwmfferws Rd / Heol
Cwmfferws SA18 . . . . . .97 F6
Cwm-ffrwd Rd 2 SA18 . . .80 A1
Cwmgarw Rd
Brecon SA18 . . . . .80 F1
Cefn-bryn-brain SA18 . . .100 A8
Cwmgelli Cl SA6 . . . . . . .160 D6
Cwmgelli Dr SA6 . . . . . . .160 C6
Cwmgelli Rd SA6 . . . . . . .160 C7
Cwmglas Prim Sch SA1 . . .161 C4
Cwmgors Workshops /
Gweithdau-cwm-gors
SA18 . . . . .99 D6
Cwm Gwennol SA69 . . . . .134 E3
Cwmgwili Prim Sch
SA14 . . . . .97 C5
Cwmifor CP Sch SA19 . . . .62 F4
Cwm Ivor Rd SA16 . . . . . .137 F3
Cwmlan Terr SA1 . . . . . . .160 D4
Cwm Level Rd SA6 . . . . . .160 D5
Cwm-Mwyn SA14 . . . . . . .97 B8
Cwmnanthir Terr SA18 . . .99 E7
Cwmphil Rd SA9 . . . . . . .138 C1
Cwm Prim Sch SA1 . . . . .161 B4
Cwm Rd SA1 . . . . .160 D1
Cwmrhydyceirw Prim Sch
SA6 . . . . .153 F3
Cwmrhydyceirw Rd SA6 . .153 F2
Cwmtawe Bsns Pk SA8 . . .147 F3
Cwmtawe Coll SA8 . . . . .147 E6
Cwmtawe Comp Sch / Ysgol
Gyfun Cwmtawe SA8 . . .147 F6
Cwm Terr
2 Llanelli SA15 . . . . . .148 C7
Swansea / Abertawe SA1 .174 B5
Cwm The SA16 . . . . .137 C3

Cwm-yr-Wch SA2 ....165 B8
Cwm-ystrad Parc SA31 ..128 C2
Cwndonkin Cl SA2 ....167 A7
Cwrt Cilmeri SA6 ....154 A2
Cwrt Coed Saeson SA7 ..162 B8
Cwrt Elusendy **4** SA15 ..148 E5
Cwrt Emily SA14 ....154 F1
Cwrt Henri Cty Prim Sch
 SA32 ....61 A2
Cwrt Hocys SA7 ....161 D6
Cwrt Hydd SA6 ....153 F5
Cwrt Isaf SA7 ....155 B1
Cwrt Ivor Sims SA6 .....154 A2
Cwrt Lafant SA7 ....161 E6
Cwrt Llwyn Fedwen
 SA6 ....154 A1
Cwrt Llwynog SA6 ....153 F4
Cwrt Melin SA33 ....74 B5
Cwrt Merlyn SA6 ....153 F5
Cwrt Neville **2** SA13 ...148 D4
Cwrt Olwyn Ddwr SA7 ..155 A1
Cwrt Rhian SA4 ....151 C2
Cwrt Rhosyn SA7 ....161 D6
Cwrt Stanllyd SA18 .....98 B6
Cwrt Tomos SA18 ....99 C8
Cwrt Waddl **3** SA15 ....148 D4
Cwrt Wooford SA33 ......92 E5
Cwrt Y Cadno SA7 ....162 B8
Cwrt Y Castell SA4 .....156 E4
Cwrt-y-Clafdy SA10 .....162 F8
Cwrt-y-Clafdy Rd SA10 .162 F8
Cwrt-y-Fedw SA7 ....155 B1
Cwrt Y Fedwen SA7 .....154 D1
Cwrt Y Gloch **2** SA32 ..59 A3
Cwrt-y-glyn SA14 ....78 D2
Cwrt Yr Aeron SA6 ......154 A4
Cwrt Y Waun SA8 ....147 D7
Cwt-y-barcud La SA67 ..71 C1
Cyfyng Rd SA9 ....139 A5
Cygnet Cl SA2 ....165 E6
Cyncoed Cl SA2 ....165 C8
Cynghordy Sta SA20 .....26 B3
Cynon Cl SA6 ....161 A7
Cynwal Terr SA9 ....100 C5
Cypress Ave SA3 ....172 F8
Cyril Evans Way SA6 ....153 E4
Cysgod-y-Fro SA8 ....147 D7
Cysgod-y-graig SA16 ....137 D3
Cysgod Y Llan SA15 .....148 D6

D

Dafen Inn Row SA14 ....149 C7
Dafen Rd
 Llanelli, Dafen SA14 ...149 B7
 Llanelli SA14 ....149 A8
Dafen Row SA15 ....148 E2
Daffodil Dr **2** SA61 ....125 A4
Dairy Pk SA73 ....131 B3
Dale Cl SA5 ....159 B4
Dale Cty Prim Sch SA62 ..84 D1
Dale Fort Field Ctr★
 SA62 ....101 F4
Dale Rd SA61 ....124 D3
Dana Dr SA2 ....166 C6
Dan Danino Way SA6 ...153 E4
Dandorlan Rd SA16 .....137 E4
Daniel James Com Sch
 SA5 ....160 C7
Danlan Pk SA16 ....137 A3
Danlan Rd SA16 ....137 A3
Dan Lan Rd SA16 ....108 F4
Dantwyn Rd SA4 ....143 F5
Dan-y-banc **4** SA31 ...129 A5
Danybanc Rd SA15 .....95 C2
Danybryn SA33 ....39 B2
Dan Y Bryn SA65 ....122 E3
Dan-y-bryn SA16 ....108 F4
Danybryn Rd SA4 ......151 A1
Dan-y-Coed Rd SA7 ....162 A8
Danycoed Sta SA33 .....58 B5
Danycwm SA14 ....148 F8
Dan Y Dderwen **2** SA32 ..59 B6
Danygraig Clydach SA6 ..154 C8
 Cwm-twrch Isaf SA9 ....138 A2
Danygraig Prim Sch
 SA8 ....168 A7
Danygraig Rd SA1 ......168 B7
Dan Y Graig Rd SA4 ....147 C2
Dan Y Lan SA14 ....140 F2
Dan-y-Parc SA6 ....153 C1
Danyrallt SA14 ....148 F8
Dan Yr Allt SA4 ....158 A5
Danyrhelyg SA38 ....119 B3
Dan-yr-ogof The National
 Showcaves Ctr for Wales★
 SA9 ....82 E3
D'arcy Bsns Ctr SA10 ..162 D5
Dark Gate **4** SA31 .....128 F5
Dark St SA61 ....125 A5
Darran Cl SA10 ....155 F1
Darran Pk SA10 ....155 F1
Darren-las **3** SA14 ....96 A6
Darren Rd SA9 ....139 B6
Darren Terr SA8 ....147 B3
Dartford Dr SA1 ....161 A3
Dartford Pl SA1 ....161 A3
Dartford Rd SA1 ....161 A3
Dartmouth Gdns SA73 ..131 C3
Dartmouth St SA73 .....131 C3
David Issac Cl SA1 .....160 D3

David St
 St Dogmaels / Llandudoch
 SA43 ....118 B3
 Swansea / Abertawe SA5 ..160 B2
David's Way / Ffordd Dafydd
 SA14 ....97 D7
David Williams Terr
 SA1 ....168 C7
Davies Rd SA8 ....147 F6
Davies Row SA5 ....160 D5
Davies Sq **3** SA15 .....148 E5
Davies's St SA39 ....39 B6
Davies St **2** SA6 ......161 A8
Davis St SA6 ....160 E5
Dawlish Cl SA3 ....172 A6
Dderi Rd SA9 ....100 B5
Ddol Rd SA2 ....165 B7
Dean's Cl **2** SA61 .....125 A3
De-Breos St SA2 ....166 F5
Deeley Rd SA9 ....139 B6
Deepford La SA63 ......69 D7
Dee Pl SA6 ....154 A4
Deepslade Cl SA3 ......171 A4
Deerland Rd SA62 ......87 D5
Deer Pk Cl SA62 ....86 B5
Deer Pk La SA21 ....105 B4
Deer Pk View SA71 .....112 A5
De-La-Beche Rd SA2 ...166 D6
De-La-Beche St SA1 ....174 A1
Delabeche St / Ffordd
 Delabeche **12** SA15 ...148 D4
De La Beche Terr SA6 ..153 F1
Delapoer Dr SA61 ......124 E4
Delfan
 Swansea / Abertawe, Llangyfelach
 SA6 ....153 C2
 Swansea / Abertawe, Trallwn
 SA7 ....161 F5
Delfryn Capel Hendre SA18 ..97 D6
 Llanelli SA14 ....149 D6
Delhi St SA1 ....174 C3
Dell The Llanelli SA15 ...148 C8
 Pontlliw SA4 ....151 F6
 Swansea / Abertawe SA2 ..165 E6
Denant Hill SA62 ....86 C7
Denbigh Cres SA6 ......154 B5
Denham Ave SA15 ......148 A7
Denver Rd SA5 ....159 B5
Derby La SA3 ....119 D5
Deri Rd / Heol Y Deri
 SA18 ....98 F8
Derlin Pk / Parc Derlin
 SA18 ....97 F5
Derlwyn SA2 ....165 D8
Derlwyn Cl SA14 ....77 F1
Derwen Cl SA5 ....158 D4
Derwendeg SA32 ....77 D3
Derwen Deg SA8 ....147 D6
Derwen Fawr SA18 .....79 B1
Derwen Fawr Rd SA2 ...166 B4
Derwen Fechan SA31 ...128 D6
Derwen Gdns SA38 ....119 D6
Derwenlas SA34 ....71 D6
Derwen Rd
 Llannon SA4 ....96 D7
 Pontardawe SA8 ....147 D2
 Ystradgynlais SA9 .....138 F1
Derwent Ave SA73 .....131 F6
Derwent St SA15 ....148 C6
Derwlas SA4 ....152 B5
Derw Rd SA8 ....147 D3
Derwydd Ave SA18 .....99 D6
Devereaux Dr SA31 ....128 E6
Devon Dr SA71 ....133 C6
Devon Pl SA3 ....173 B4
Devonshire Dr
 East Williamston SA69 ..134 A1
 St Florence SA70 ......106 C5
Devonshire Rd SA72 ...132 D4
Devon Terr SA1 ....167 A7
Devon View SA2 ....166 B7
Dewing Ave SA70 ......113 D6
Dewi Terr SA1 ....160 A1
Dewsbury Ct SA1 ......174 B2
Dewsland St SA73 .....131 C3
Dew St SA61 ....125 A4
Diana Rd SA19 ....130 D6
Dickslade SA3 ....173 C4
Dillwyn Ct Pontlliw SA4 ..151 F6
 Swansea / Abertawe SA2 ..165 E6
Dillwyn Rd SA2 ....166 C6
Dillwyn St Llanelli SA15 ..148 D4
 Swansea / Abertawe SA1 ..174 A2
Dilwyn Cl SA4 ....151 F2
Dilwyn Rd SA4 ....151 F2
Dimond St SA72 ....132 C3
Dimpath Terr SA15 .....148 E7
Dinam Rd SA1 ....161 D1
Dinas Cty Prim Sch SA42 ..12 F3
Dinas Nature Reserve★
 SA20 ....7 F1
Dinas St SA6 ....160 C7
Dinefwr Pk (NT)★ SA19 ..130 B5
Dingat Cl SA20 ....121 C4
Dingat View SA20 ......121 C4
Dingle La SA62 ....68 C4
Dock St SA4 ....157 C8
Dolafon SA14 ....149 E3
Dolau Bran SA20 ......121 E4
Dolaucothi Goldmines (NT)★
 SA19 ....23 F3
Dolau Ct SA15 ....148 E2
Dolau Fach SA15 ......148 E3
Dolau Fan Rd SA16 ....137 F4
Dolau Fawr SA15 ......148 E3
Dolau Rd SA15 ....148 E3
Dolau Tywi SA19 ......63 A5
Dolawel SA9 ....100 C7

Dolecoed Rd LD5 ......9 C1
Dolgoy Cl SA3 ....173 A7
Dolgwili Rd
 Abergwili SA33 ....59 A1
 Carmarthen / Caerfyrddin
 SA31 ....129 C7
Dolphin St SA73 ....132 C5
Dolwar Fach SA14 .....149 C5
Dolwerdd Llanelli SA14 ..148 F8
 Llangeler SA38 ....18 C3
 Y Ferwig SA43 ....3 C1
Dol Y Brenin / Kings Mead
 SA48 ....120 C4
Dol-y-Coed SA2 ....165 B8
Dolycoed Ave SA16 ....137 E3
Dol-y-dderwen SA33 ...75 B2
Dol Yr Onnen SA31 ....128 D4
Donovan Reed Gdns
 SA72 ....132 D3
Douglas Ct SA3 ....172 A5
Douglas James Cl SA14 ..124 D5
Douglas James Way
 SA61 ....124 D5
Dove Rd SA5 ....159 E7
Downing St SA15 ......148 C4
Down Leaze SA2 ......159 D1
Downs Cl SA5 ....159 E3
Down St SA6 ....154 E7
Downs The SA3 ....117 C8
Dragon Auto Ctr SA1 ..161 B7
Dredgman Hill SA61 ...124 E2
Drefach Rd SA33 ......73 E8
Dreflan SA9 ....138 F4
Dreonen **5** SA15 .....96 B6
Dring St SA1 ....174 C4
Drive The
 Pontardawe SA8 ....147 C3
 Southgate SA3 ....171 A4
Drovers Rd SA48 ......120 C4
Druce St SA15 ....148 C3
Druids Cl SA3 ....173 A6
Druidstone Way SA4 ...152 B2
Drumau Cl SA10 ......162 F8
Drumau Pk SA10 ......162 F8
Drumau Rd
 Birchgrove SA7 ....155 B1
 Neath / Castell-Nedd SA7,
 SA10 ....162 D8
Druslyn Cl SA3 ....172 F7
Dryslwyn Cl SA4 ......152 B2
Duffryn Rd SA4 ....151 B1
Dukefield SA4 ....164 E8
Duke St SA1 ....167 B6
Dulais Gr SA2 ....166 A5
Dulais Rd SA4 ....143 C4
Dumbarton House Ct **4**
 SA1 ....167 A6
Dumfries Pl SA9 ......139 E7
Duncan St SA33 ......92 F5
Dunns Cl SA3 ....173 B5
Dunns La SA3 ....173 B5
Dunns The SA3 ....173 B5
Dunraven Cl SA4 .....156 E4
Dunraven Rd SA2 .....166 B7
Dunsany Pk SA61 .....125 B5
Dunster Cl SA3 ....172 E6
Dunston La SA62 .....67 B5
Dunvant Jun & Inf Sch
 SA2 ....165 E8
Dunvant Pl SA1 ....174 A1
Dunvant Rd Dunvant SA2 ..165 D8
 Three Crosses SA2, SA4 ..158 A1
Dunvant Sq SA2 ......165 C8
Dupre Rd SA1 ....167 F8
Dwyfor SA14 ....149 D5
Dwynant
 Burry Port SA16 ......137 C3
 Llangyndeyrn SA15 ....95 D3
Dyfatty St SA1 ....174 B4
Dyfed Ave SA1 ....167 A8
Dyfed Cl
 2 Carmarthen / Caerfyrddin
 SA31 ....128 C2
 Swansea / Abertawe SA1 ..166 F5
Dyfed Coll of Art / Coleg Celf
 Dyfed SA31 ....128 C3
Dyfed Pembrey Ski Slope
 SA16 ....108 C3
Dyfed Shires & Leisure
 Farm★ SA41 ....34 A8
Dyffryn SA16 ....137 F3
Dyffryn-Aur Rd SA7 ...161 E6
Dyffryn Cl SA1 ....161 A8
Dyffryn Rd
 Pontardawe SA8 ......147 F4
 Saron SA18 ....97 F7
Dyffryn Rd / Hoel Y Dyffryn
 SA18 ....98 A7
Dylan SA14 ....149 D5
Dylan Cl SA3 ....165 F7
Dylan Rd SA2 ....165 F7
Dylan's Wlk SA33 ....92 F5
Dylan Thomas Com Sch
 SA2 ....159 D2
Dylan Thomas Sq SA1 ..174 B2
Dylan Thomas Theatre★
 SA1 ....174 B2
Dynevor Ave **3** SA19 ..130 D6
Dynevor Cl SA10 .....162 F8
Dynevor Pl
 Neath / Castell-Nedd
 SA10 ....162 D7
 Swansea / Abertawe SA1 ..174 A3
Dynevor Rd SA10 .....162 F8
Dynevor Rd / Heol Dinefwr
 SA18 ....99 B7
Dynevor Terr SA8 .....147 E5

Dyrus Rd SA6 ....160 E5
Dysgwylfa SA2 ....166 C6
Dyson Cl SA6 ....146 C1
Dythel Pk SA15 ....109 D6

E

Eagles Pl SA5 ....159 E6
Earl St SA1 ....160 D1
East Back SA71 ....133 C4
East Bank Way / Ffordd Glan
 Y Dwyrain SA1 ....174 C3
Eastbourne Gr SA2 ...166 C7
East Burrows Rd SA1 ..174 C2
East Cliff SA3 ....171 B3
East Crossways SA8 ...147 A4
Easterfield Dr SA3 ....171 A4
Eastern Ave SA72 ....132 E3
Eastern La SA70 ......106 A3
Eastfield Cl SA1 ......159 E2
East La SA72 ....104 F3
Eastland Ct SA3 ......172 E7
Eastlands Pk SA3 ....172 A4
Eastleigh Dr SA73 ....131 D3
Eastmoor Park Cres
 SA3 ....172 E7
East Perimeter Rd SA73 ..103 E7
East St SA42 ....13 C4
Eaton Cres SA1 ....167 A6
Eaton Cl SA5 ....159 C6
Eaton Rd SA6 ....160 C3
Ebenezer St
 Newcastle Emlyn / Castell
 Newydd Emlyn SA38 ..119 D4
 Swansea / Abertawe SA1 ..174 B4
Ebens La **5** SA43 ....118 D4
Ebenzer Row SA61 ...125 A5
Eden Ave SA2 ....166 F7
Edgar Morgan Way
 SA72 ....132 A3
Edge Gr SA62 ....28 F3
Edgemoor Cl SA2 ....165 B5
Edgemoor Dr SA2 ....165 B6
Edgeware Rd SA2 ....166 E7
Edison Cres SA6 .....146 D1
Edward St
 Milford Haven / Aberdaugleddau
 SA73 ....131 C3
 9 Tenby / Dinbych-y-pysgod
 SA70 ....135 E4
Eglwys Ger Yr SA33 ..93 E5
Eglwyswrw CP Sch / Ysgol
 Gymunedol Eglwyswrw
 SA41 ....15 B1
Egypt Ctr Mus★ SA2 ..166 E5
Eiddil SA14 ....149 D6
Eiddwen Rd SA5 ......160 B4
Eigen Cres SA1 ......167 B8
Eighth Ave SA6 ......153 D1
Eileen Rd SA7 ....161 F7
Einon Ct SA4 ....151 D2
Elan Ave SA6 ....153 D1
Elba Cres SA1 ....169 A2
Elba St SA4 ....158 C6
Elder Gr SA31 ......129 B3
Elfed Rd SA1 ....167 B8
Elgin Rd SA15 ......109 E4
Elgin St SA5 ....160 B3
Elim Rd SA3 ....128 D7
Eliot Cl SA2 ....165 F8
Elizabeth Cl SA6 ....154 B4
Elizabeth Ct SA72 ...132 C1
Elizabeth St SA15 ...148 D5
Elkington Pk SA16 ...137 D3
Elkington Rd SA16 ...137 E3
Ellen's Rd SA10 .....162 D7
Elm Cl SA5 ....158 D4
Elm Cres SA4 ....152 C2
Elm Ct SA4 ....158 D4
Elm Gr Gorseinon SA4 ..151 A3
 Neyland SA73 ....132 B8
 Pembroke / Penfro SA71 ..133 C5
Elmgrove Rd SA3 ....172 F8
Elm Gr Rd SA17 .....136 C4
Elmhurst Cres SA2 ...174 C4
Elm La SA73 ....131 E4
Elm Pk SA62 ....68 B5
Elphin Cres SA1 .....159 E1
Elphin Gdns SA1 ....160 A1
Elphin Rd SA1 ......160 F1
Elwy Cres SA2 ......159 F1
Elwy Gdns SA2 .....159 F1
Embankment Rd SA15 ..148 E2
Emlyn Gdns SA1 ....160 B1
Emlyn Rd SA1 ......160 B1
Emlyn Sq **2** SA38 ..119 D4
Emlyn Terr SA6 .....160 B1
Emmanuel Gdns SA2 ..166 B3
Emma St / Stryd Emma **13**
 SA15 ....148 D4
Enfield Cl SA6 ......153 E4
Enid Rd SA6 ....154 F8
Eppynt Rd SA5 ......160 A4
Ermigate La SA71 ...111 A4
Ernald Pl SA2 ......166 F6
Erw Haf **1** LD5 ....9 D1
Erw Hydref SA9 ....139 D8
Erwlas SA14 ....149 D3
Erw Las
 Fishguard & Goodwick
 SA65 ....122 C4
 Llannon SA14 ....96 F3
Erw Lon SA62 ....49 B2
Erw Non SA14 ......96 E2
Erw Rd SA15 ....148 C5
Erw Terr SA16 ......137 E4

Erw-wen SA37 ......34 F7
Espalone SA3 ....172 C6
Esplanade
 Carmarthen / Caerfyrddin
 SA31 ....129 A5
 Tenby / Dinbych-y-pysgod
 SA70 ....135 E4
Essex Rd SA72 ......132 D4
Essex Terr SA6 ......160 E6
E St SA71 ....103 C6
Esther's La **1** SA62 ..87 E4
Estuary Pk SA14 ....150 C7
Evans Terr SA1 .....174 A4
Evans' Terr SA15 ...148 F6
Eva Terr SA17 ......93 F5
Evelyn Rd SA10 ....162 E7
Eversley Rd SA2 ....166 D6
Ewart Pl SA5 ....160 C4
Ewenny Pl SA6 .....160 D8
Exchange Row SA14 ..149 C7
Exeter Rd SA73 ....131 F5
Eynon St SA4 ......151 D2

F

Fabian Way SA1, SA10 ..168 C7
Factory Rd Clydach SA6 ..154 D7
 Pembrey & Bury Port Town
 SA16 ....108 E3
Fagwr Isaf SA6 .....146 B2
Fagwr Pl SA6 ......154 A1
Fagwr Rd SA6 .....146 B2
Fairbush Cl SA62 ...68 C5
Fairfield Terr SA1 ..167 B7
Fairhaven Ct SA3 ..173 A3
Fair La SA31 ......128 F5
Fairmeadow Cl SA73 ..85 E2
Fairoak SA18 .....98 D7
Fair Oakes SA61 ...124 C2
Fairsea Cl SA73 ...102 F8
Fair View SA62 ...86 E5
Fair View Cl SA7 ..161 F6
Fairview Rd SA5 ..153 C2
Fairway SA72 ....132 B1
Fairway Dr SA8 ...147 D6
Fairwood Hospl / Ysbyty
 Fairwood SA2 ......165 A6
Fairwood La SA2 ..165 B5
Fairwood Rd
 Dunvant SA2 ....165 C8
 The Mumbles / Y Mwmbwls
 SA3 ....173 A8
Fairwood Terr SA4 ..158 C6
Fairy Gr SA2 ......165 E7
Falcon Chambers **4**
 SA15 ....148 D6
Falcondale Dr SA48 ..120 A6
Falcon Pl SA5 .....159 E7
Falcon Rd SA61 ...124 E5
Fan Rd The SA69 ...134 C5
Faraday Rd SA6 ...146 E1
Farmers Row SA14 ..140 F1
Farm Rd SA8 .....147 B1
Faull St SA6 ......153 E1
Feidr Bentick SA42 ..13 E4
Feidr Brenin SA42 ..13 D4
Feidr Castell SA65 ..122 C3
Feidr Castell Bsns Pk
 SA65 ....122 C2
Feidr Cefn SA65 ...12 E3
Feidr Chwech-erw
 SA62 ....123 B6
Feidr Dwyll SA62 ..123 C5
Feidr Dylan SA65 ..122 C5
Feidr Fach **2** SA42 ..13 A4
Feidr Fain SA62 ...51 D6
Feidrfair SA43 ....118 D4
Feidr Fawr
 Dinas Cross SA42 ...13 A4
 St Dogmaels / Llandudoch
 SA43 ....118 A4
Feidr Felin **1** SA42 ..13 E3
Feidr Fraich SA65 ..122 C2
Feidr Ganol SA42 ..13 D4
Feidr Gongol **4** SA65 ..122 D3
Feidr Henfordd SA43 ..118 F5
Feidr-ist SA65 ....53 A1
Feidr Las SA62 ...48 B5
Feidr Pant-y-bryn
 SA62 ....123 D4
Feidr Pen-y-bont SA42 ..13 F4
Feidr Pont Eglwys SA64 ..11 D2
Feidr Treginnis SA62 ..123 A4
Feidr Y Foel **1** SA41 ..34 E4
Felin-fach SA9 ....100 C6
Felinfoel Jun Sch SA14 ..149 A8
Felinfoel Rd SA15 ..148 E7
Felin Fran SA7 ....154 E2
Fendrod Bsns Pk SA6 ..161 A6
Fendrod Way SA7 ..161 C2
Fenton CP Sch SA61 ..124 F4
Fenton Trad Est SA61 ..124 F4
Fermoy Ct SA5 ...159 F6
Fern Ct SA5 ......160 A5
Ferndale Dr SA4 ..157 D8
Fernhill Cl SA2 ...166 B1
Fern Hill Rd SA61 ..125 A2
Fern Rise SA73 ...132 B7
Fern St SA5 ......160 B2
Ferrara Sq SA1 ...174 B1
Ferrar St SA31 ...128 E5
Ferryboat Cl SA6 ..161 A7
Ferry La SA72 ...133 A8
Ferry Rd
 Kidwelly / Cydweli SA17 ..136 B5
 Loughor SA4 ......150 C1

Ferry Rd *continued*
Pembroke Dock / Doc Penfro
  SA72 . . . . .132 B1
Ferry Side SA1 . . . . . . .174 C2
Ferryside Sta SA17 . . . . .93 F5
Ferryside VCP Sch SA17 . .93 F5
Ferry Terr SA72 . . . . . . .132 E3
Ferry Way SA61 . . . . . .125 A1
Ffairfach Sta SA19 . . . . . .23 D7
Fferws Rd SA18 . . . . .97 F6
Ffinant Sq 3 SA38 . . . . .119 D4

Fford = road, way

Ffordd Abercastell SA62 . .29 B5
Ffordd Abiah SA6 . . . . . .154 E8
Ffordd Afon 4 SA29 . . . .29 B5
Ffordd Alltwen SA4 . . . . .158 A5
Ffordd Aneurin SA15 . . . .96 A6
Ffordd Aneurin Bevan
  SA2 . . . . .166 C8
Ffordd Beck SA4 . . . . . .158 B6
Ffordd Bedd Morris
  Cwm Gwaun SA65 . . . . .32 C6
  Newport / Trefdraeth SA42 . .13 D2
Ffordd Bishop / Bishop Rd
  SA18 . . . . .98 B6
Ffordd Briallu SA7 . . . . .161 D6
Ffordd Bryngwyn SA4 . . .158 B8
Ffordd Brynheulog SA8 . .147 D5
Ffordd Butler SA4 . . . . . .158 B6
Ffordd Cae Duke SA4 . . .158 A8
Ffordd Caerfai SA42 . . . .123 D4
Ffordd Cilgwyn SA42 . . . .13 F3
Ffordd Cumbrian Way 4
  SA31 . . . . .128 F4
Ffordd Cwmaman /
  Cwmamman Rd SA18 . .99 B8
Ffordd Cwm Tawe
  Swansea / Abertawe SA6 .160 F6
  Ynysforgan SA6, SA7 . . . .154 C5
Ffordd Cynghordy SA7 . . .161 D7
Ffordd Cynore SA5 . . . . .159 C6
Ffordd Dafydd / David's Way
  SA14 . . . . .97 D7
Ffordd Dawel SA7 . . . . .161 E6
Ffordd Delabeche /
  Delabeche St 12 SA15 . .148 D4
Ffordd Dewi SA6 . . . . . .153 B1
Ffordd Dillwyn-Llewellyn
  SA4 . . . . .152 C2
Ffordd Draenen Ddu
  SA3 . . . . .172 E6
Ffordd Dryden SA2 . . . . .165 E8
Ffordd Eira SA4 . . . . . . .151 C4
Ffordd Ellen SA6 . . . . . .146 B2
Ffordd Emlyn SA9 . . . . . .139 B5
Ffordd Florence / Florence
  Rd 1 SA18 . . . . .98 B7
Ffordd Ger-y-Llwyn
  SA4 . . . . .152 C4
Ffordd Glandwr SA9 . . . .139 B6
Ffordd Glan y Dwyrain / East
  Bank Way SA1 . . . . . .174 C3
Ffordd Gwyn SA7 . . . . . .161 D7
Ffordd Is-Cennen / Iscennen
  Rd 14 SA18 . . . . .98 B7
Ffordd Kilby SA4 . . . . . .158 A8
Ffordd Llundain SA7 . . . .161 D7
Ffordd Llyffant SA7 . . . . .162 B8
Ffordd Maescwarrau /
  Maesquarre Rd SA18 . .98 D6
Ffordd Melyn Mair SA7 . .161 D6
Ffordd Parc Ynysderw
  SA8 . . . . .147 E4
Ffordd Pen Twyn / Pentwyn
  Rd SA18 . . . . .98 C7
Ffordd Porth Clais
  SA62 . . . . .123 A3
Ffordd Scott
  Birchgrove SA7 . . . . . . .154 F1
  Swansea / Abertawe SA7 . .162 A8
Ffordd Silkin SA8 . . . . . .147 E5
Ffordd Stewart / Stewart Dr
  12 SA18 . . . . .98 B7
Ffordd Talbot / Talbot Rd 10
  SA18 . . . . .98 B7
Ffordd Talfan SA4 . . . . . .158 D8
Ffordd Taliesin SA2 . . . . .165 F8
Ffordd Tollborth SA7 . . . .161 D7
Ffordd Tyn-y-Coed
  SA6 . . . . .155 A8
Ffordd Villers / Villers Rd
  SA18 . . . . .98 B6
Ffordd Walter / Walter Rd 9
  SA18 . . . . .98 C7
Ffordd Waun Gron / Waun
  Gron Rd SA18 . . . . . . .98 D6
Ffordd Wern-Ddu /
  Wern-Ddu Rd SA18 . . .98 D8
Ffordd-y-Betws / Betws Rd
  SA18 . . . . .98 C6
Ffordd Y Blodau SA18 . . . .79 B1
Ffordd-y-blodau SA43 . . . .3 E3
Ffordd Y Brain SA5 . . . . .159 E5
Ffordd Y Brennin / Kingsway
  The SA1 . . . . .174 A3
Ffordd-y-Bryn
  Birchgrove SA7 . . . . . . .155 B1
  Swansea / Abertawe SA7 . .162 A8
Ffordd Y Cwm SA43 . . . .118 A3
Ffordd-y-Cyrnol / Colonel
  Rd SA18 . . . . .98 C6
Ffordd Y Faenor / Manor Rd
  15 SA18 . . . . .98 B7
Ffordd Y Felin / Mill Terr
  SA18 . . . . .98 A5

Ffordd Y Gamlas SA4 . . . .158 B6
Ffordd Y Glowr SA4 . . . . .143 D2
Ffordd Y Goedwig SA4 . . .152 D6
Ffordd Y Gorllewin / West
  Way SA1 . . . . .174 A2
Ffordd Y Morfa SA4 . . . . . .97 C7
Ffordd-y-Mynydd
  Birchgrove SA7 . . . . . . .155 B1
  Swansea / Abertawe SA7 . .162 B8
Ffordd-y-Parc SA6 . . . . . .153 B1
Ffordd-yr-Afon 3 SA62 . .29 B5
Ffordd Y Rhyd SA18 . . . . .98 B6
Ffordd Yr Afon 3 SA62 . . . .29 B5
Ffordd Yr Odyn SA4 . . . . .143 D2
Ffordd-yr-Orsaf / Station Rd
  5 SA18 . . . . .98 B7
Ffordd Y Wagen / Railway Pl
  8 SA15 . . . . .148 C4
Ffordd Y Wiwer SA7 . . . . .154 D1
Fford Y Felin 1 SA62 . . . .29 A5
Fforestfach Ret Pk SA5 . .159 C6
Fforest Rd / Heol Fforest
  SA4 . . . . .143 B5
Ffos Felen SA4 . . . . .158 B5
Ffoss Rd 2 LD5 . . . . .9 C1
Ffos Y Mynach SA62 . . . .123 F8
Ffos-yr-Efail Terr SA4 . . .143 C4
Ffrwd-y-Felin SA18 . . . . . .98 B8
Ffwrdwen SA12 . . . . .75 F3
Ffynnonbedr Prim Sch
  SA48 . . . . .120 B5
Ffynnongain La SA33 . . . .127 B8
Ffynnon Llys SA31 . . . . . .128 E6
Ffynnon Samlet SA7 . . . .161 D7
Ffynnon Wen
  Clydach SA6 . . . . .154 C7
  St David's / Tyddewi SA62 . .123 B4
Ffynon Bedr SA48 . . . . . .120 B5
Ffynone CI SA1 . . . . .167 A7
Ffynone Dr SA1 . . . . .167 A7
Ffynone Rd SA1 . . . . .167 A7
Ffynonn Las SA18 . . . . . . .98 B6
Field CI SA6 . . . . .154 A2
Field St SA1 . . . . .160 D3
Fifth Ave SA6 . . . . .153 D1
Fifth La SA71 . . . . .133 F4
Filas Berrington / Berrington
  Villas SA9 . . . . .100 C7
Finch CI
  2 Haverfordwest / Hwlffordd
  SA62 . . . . .125 C2
  Pembroke Dock / Doc Penfro
  SA72 . . . . .132 C1
Finch's Sq 1 SA43 . . . . .118 E4
Finch St SA43 . . . . .118 A4
Finsbury Terr SA2 . . . . . .166 F5
Fir Gr SA68 . . . . .89 E3
Firm St SA1 . . . . .174 A4
First Ave SA6 . . . . .160 C8
First La SA71 . . . . .133 E4
First St SA71 . . . . .103 C6
Firth Rd SA15 . . . . .148 E4
Fishgaurd Rd SA62 . . . . . .68 A5
Fishguard CP Inf Sch
  SA65 . . . . .122 A4
Fishguard Harbour Sta
  SA65 . . . . .122 C7
Fishguard High Sch / Ysgol
  Bro Gwaun SA65 . . . . .122 C4
Fishguard JMCP Sch
  SA65 . . . . .122 A4
Fishguard RC Sch SA65 . .122 C4
Fishguard Rd SA65 . . . . .125 B7
Fishguard Rd Ind Est
  SA62 . . . . .68 A4
Fishguard Sports Ctr
  SA65 . . . . .122 B4
Fishmarket Quay 12
  SA1 . . . . .174 C2
Flatholm Pl SA5 . . . . . . .159 E7
Fleet St
  Pembroke Dock / Doc Penfro
  SA72 . . . . .104 B3
  Swansea / Abertawe SA1 . .167 B5
Fleming Cres SA61 . . . . .124 E5
Fleming Way SA73 . . . . .132 B7
Flemish CI SA70 . . . . . . .106 B4
Flemish Ct SA71 . . . . . . .105 A4
Flimstone La SA67 . . . . . .70 C2
Florence Rd / Ffordd
  Florence 1 SA18 . . . . .98 B7
Florence St SA15 . . . . . .148 E3
Foel Rd SA18 . . . . .80 C2
Foley Way SA61 . . . . . . .124 E5
Folkestone Hill SA62 . . . . .66 E6
Folkestone Rd SA62 . . . . .66 E6
Folland Ct SA2 . . . . .166 B1
Folland Rd / Heol Folland
  SA18 . . . . .99 B8
Folly Farm Adventure Pk★
  SA68 . . . . .89 E3
Forbes St SA6 . . . . .160 E5
Ford La SA68 . . . . .89 E2
Forest Rd SA48 . . . . .120 C6
Forge Fach SA6 . . . . . . .154 C7
Forge Rd SA4 . . . . .156 B2
Fort Rd
  Pembroke Dock / Doc Penfro
  SA72 . . . . .132 A3
  Solva SA62 . . . . .48 C3
Fort Rise SA73 . . . . .131 A2
Foss Way SA72 . . . . .104 F6
Foundry Rd SA6 . . . . . . .154 A1
Foundry Rd /
  Heol-y-Ffowndri 5
  SA18 . . . . .98 C7

Foundry Row
  3 Ammanford / Rhydaman
  SA18 . . . . .98 C7
  Neath / Castell-Nedd
  SA10 . . . . .162 E8
Fountain Hall Terr SA31 . .128 E5
Fountain Rd SA14 . . . . . . .96 F3
Fountain Row 2 SA61 . . .124 F4
Fourth Ave SA6 . . . . .153 D1
Fourth St SA71 . . . . .103 C6
Fourwinds La SA70 . . . . .135 B3
Fox Gr SA45 . . . . .159 A4
Foxgrove SA4 . . . . .158 B8
Foxhole Dr SA3 . . . . .171 A4
Foxhole Rd SA1 . . . . . . .174 C4
Foyer The 1 SA1 . . . . . .174 B3
Frampton Ct SA4 . . . . . .150 F2
Frampton Rd SA4 . . . . . .151 A3
Frances St SA69 . . . . . . .134 F4
Francis Rd SA6 . . . . .153 E1
Francis St
  Milford Haven / Aberdaugleddau
  SA73 . . . . .131 D2
  Neath / Castell-Nedd SA10 .162 F7
  Pontardawe SA8 . . . . . .147 E4
  Swansea / Abertawe SA1 . .167 A5
Francis Terr SA31 . . . . . .128 F5
Fransham St 2 SA15 . . . .148 E6
Frederick Pl SA7 . . . . . . .161 F7
Frederick St
  2 Llanelli SA15 . . . . . .148 D5
  Neyland SA73 . . . . .132 B6
  Swansea / Abertawe SA5 . .160 C3
Freeman St SA5 . . . . . . .160 C3
Freemans Way SA61 . . . .125 A3
Freemans Wlk SA71 . . . .133 D4
French Wlk SA65 . . . . . .122 C5
Freshwater E Rd SA71 . . .105 A2
Friars Pk SA31 . . . . .128 E4
Friars The 10 SA61 . . . . .125 A5
Froglane SA3 . . . . .114 E4
Frogmore Ave SA2 . . . . .166 D6
Frogmore Gdns SA33 . . . .92 F5
Frondeg Terr SA15 . . . . .148 F6
Fronhaul SA14 . . . . .141 B3
Fron Hill SA34 . . . . .71 D4
Fron Terr SA15 . . . . .148 E3
Front St
  Pembroke Dock / Doc Penfro
  SA72 . . . . .132 B3
  Rosemarket SA73 . . . . . .87 A3
F St SA71 . . . . .103 C6
Fulke St SA73 . . . . .131 D2
Fullers Row SA1 . . . . . . .174 A3
Fuller St SA8 . . . . .147 E5
Fulmar CI SA3 . . . . .172 E7
Furnace Bank SA31 . . . . .129 B6
Furnace Prim Sch SA15 . .148 B7
Furnace Rd
  Burry Port SA16 . . . . . .137 C2
  Carmarthen / Caerfyrddin
  SA31 . . . . .128 F5
Furnace Terr 3 SA15 . . . .96 B6
Furze Cres SA4 . . . . .153 D2
Furzeland Dr SA2 . . . . . .166 B6
Furzy Bank SA72 . . . . . .132 C1
Furzy Pk SA61 . . . . .124 D4
Fynnon Caeconna SA5 . . .159 E6

G

Gabalfa Rd SA2 . . . . . . .166 B5
Gables The SA4 . . . . . . .164 E8
Gaddarn Reach SA73 . . . .132 C6
Gail Rise SA62 . . . . .87 D4
Gail The SA62 . . . . .87 D4
Gainer Way SA70 . . . . . .105 E1
Gainsborough CI SA2 . . .166 E6
Gardde SA14 . . . . .149 E4
Gardd Fotaneg Genedlaethol
  Cymru / The National
  Botanic Gdn of Wales★
  SA32 . . . . .77 D5
Garden Cres SA4 . . . . . .158 D8
Garden La SA20 . . . . . . .121 D4
Garden St SA14 . . . . . . .174 A2
Gardens The SA9 . . . . . .139 B6
Garfield Gdns SA67 . . . . .70 D1
Garn Fawr SA65 . . . . . . .122 D3
Garnfoel SA14 . . . . .97 D7
Garngoch Hospl SA4 . . . .158 F7
Garngoch Ind Est SA4 . . .151 E1
Garngoch Terr SA4 . . . . .158 B8
Garn Ingli SA65 . . . . . . .122 D3
Garnlwyd CI SA6 . . . . . .160 C7
Garnon's Mill Rd SA43 . . .16 B5
Garnswllt Rd SA4 . . . . . . .97 F1
Garn Wnda 5 SA65 . . . . .122 D3
Garode Fields SA33 . . . . .127 D4
Garreg Hollt SA14 . . . . . .97 A8
Garreglwyd SA16 . . . . . .108 F4
Garrod Ave SA2 . . . . . . .158 C2
Garth Rd Glais SA7 . . . . .154 F6
  Gwaun-Cae-Gurwen SA18 . .99 E6
  Ynystawe SA6 . . . . .154 D4
Garth The SA72 . . . . . . .104 F6
Garth View SA6 . . . . . . .154 B4
Gas La SA70 . . . . .135 E6
Gateholm Ave SA73 . . . . .131 E4
Gate Rd
  Llanfihangel Aberbythych
  SA14 . . . . .78 C1
  Penygroes SA14 . . . . . . .97 D8
Gathen Terr 11 SA15 . . . .148 D4
Gay La SA62 . . . . .84 C3

Gay's La SA72 . . . . .132 B1
Geiriol Gdns SA1 . . . . . .159 E1
Geiriol Rd SA1 . . . . .159 F1
Gelert St SA5 . . . . .160 C5
Gelli Aur SA33 . . . . .58 E3
Gelli Aur / Golden Gr
  SA5 . . . . .160 D6
Gellideg SA8 . . . . .147 D6
Gelli Deg
  Llandovery / Llanymddyfri
  SA20 . . . . .121 E4
  Llanelli SA14 . . . . .149 A6
Gelliderw SA8 . . . . .147 D6
Gellifach Cres SA6 . . . . .160 D7
Gellifawr Rd SA6 . . . . . .160 D7
Gelli Gdns SA7 . . . . .162 B8
Gelliglas Rd SA6 . . . . . .160 D7
Gelligron Rd SA8 . . . . . .147 D6
Gelligwyn Rd SA6 . . . . . .160 D7
Gelli-Gynore SA4 . . . . . .151 F2
Gelli Hill SA66 . . . . .70 A6
Gellihyll Rd SA4 . . . . . . .151 F2
Gelli La SA18 . . . . .98 A5
Gellionen Rd
  Clydach SA6, SA8 . . . . . .146 F2
  Pontardawe SA8 . . . . . .147 B5
Gelli-Onn SA15 . . . . .148 D6
Gellionnen CI SA6 . . . . . .154 E8
Gelli Rd SA14 . . . . .149 D6
Gelli St SA1 . . . . .168 B7
Gelliswick Rd SA73 . . . . .131 A3
Gelliwen SA43 . . . . .16 C7
Gelliwriddon SA18 . . . . . .98 A6
Gellyceiros Trad Est
  SA32 . . . . .75 F3
Gelly Rd SA18 . . . . .79 A1
Gendros Ave E SA5 . . . . .160 A3
Gendros Ave W SA5 . . . .159 F4
Gendros CI SA5 . . . . . . .160 A3
Gendros Cres SA5 . . . . . .160 A3
Gendros Dr SA5 . . . . . . .160 A3
Gendros Prim Sch SA5 . . .159 F3
Genwen Rd SA14 . . . . . .149 F4
George Bank SA3 . . . . . .173 C4
George Hill 3 SA19 . . . . .130 D5
George Manning Way
  SA4 . . . . .158 B4
George St
  Llandeilo SA19 . . . . . . .130 D5
  Llanelli SA15 . . . . .148 D3
  Milford Haven / Aberdaugleddau
  SA73 . . . . .131 C3
  Neyland SA73 . . . . .132 B7
  Pontardawe SA8 . . . . . .147 E5
  Swansea / Abertawe SA1 . .167 B6
Geotre Bellaf Rd SA2 . . .165 C2
Gerald Rd SA61 . . . . . . .124 E5
Gerald St SA1 . . . . .160 D2
Gerddi Alexander SA5 . . .160 B3
Gerddi Brenhinol SA14 . . .149 B6
Gerddi Mair SA33 . . . . . .127 D3
Gerretts CI SA3 . . . . . . .172 A5
Ger-y-Capel SA33 . . . . . .75 B3
Ger-y-Castell SA17 . . . . .136 C4
Ger Y Coed SA15 . . . . . .109 E4
Ger Y Coed SA15 . . . . . . .95 F2
Ger Y Duad SA33 . . . . . . .58 A6
Ger-y-Ffrwd SA7 . . . . . .161 E5
Ger-y-Gwendraeth
  SA17 . . . . .136 C4
Ger Y Llan SA43 . . . . . . .16 A6
Ger-y-Llan SA42 . . . . . . .77 E7
Ger Y Llan Llanelli SA15 . .148 D4
  Manordeilo & Salem SA19 . .62 E4
Ger-y-Maes SA14 . . . . . .149 A7
Gerymanwydd 4 SA18 . . .98 C7
Ger Y Marbell 1 SA33 . . .93 C7
Ger Y Mor SA15 . . . . . . .148 C3
Ger Y Nant
  Carmarthen / Caerfyrddin
  SA31 . . . . .129 B4
  Llangennech SA14 . . . . .150 B8
Ger-y-Nant SA33 . . . . . . .73 E8
Ger-Y -Parc SA6 . . . . . . .153 E1
Ger-yr-Afon SA9 . . . . . . .138 A1
Ger-yr-Afon SA18 . . . . . . .99 A8
Ger-yr-Afon SA18 . . . . . . .99 D6
Ger-yr-Eglwys SA4 . . . . .143 B4
Gethin CI SA5 . . . . .160 A3
Gething St SA1 . . . . .174 A2
Gibbas Way SA71 . . . . . .133 E4
Gilbert Cres SA15 . . . . . .148 B6
Gilbert Rd SA15 . . . . . . .148 B6
Gilbertscliffe SA3 . . . . . .172 F4
Gilfach SA4 . . . . .152 A2
Gilfach Hill SA67 . . . . . . .71 C1
Gilfach Rd
  Cwm-twrch Uchaf SA9 . . .100 C6
  Lampeter Velfrey SA67 . . .71 C1
Gilgal Terr SA72 . . . . . . .104 C5
Gilsea Bsns Pk SA6 . . . . .161 A5
Giltar Terr SA70 . . . . . . .135 B2
Giltar Way SA70 . . . . . . .135 A1
Gilton La SA62 . . . . .85 E8
Glade The SA3 . . . . .172 F8
Glais Prim Sch SA7 . . . . .155 A6
Glais Rd SA7 . . . . .147 D1
Glamorgan St SA1 . . . . .174 A2
Glan Aber SA16 . . . . . . .137 B2
Glanamman Cty Prim Sch
  SA18 . . . . .99 C8
Glanamman Workshops 1
  SA18 . . . . .99 A8
Glanarberth SA43 . . . . . .16 D6
Glanbran Rd SA1 . . . . . .162 A8
Glanbrydan Ave SA2 . . . .166 F6
Glan Cleddau Sch SA61 . .124 F3

Glandafen Rd SA15 . . . . .148 F2
Glan Dulais SA2 . . . . . . .165 C7
Glandulas Terr SA48 . . . .120 D5
Glandwr Cres SA1 . . . . . .160 D4
Glanffrwd Rd SA4 . . . . . .143 D6
Glan-ffynnon SA31 . . . . .129 B3
Glangleddau SA62 . . . . . .51 A5
Glanhafan SA22 . . . . .48 C3
Glan Hafan 4 SA62 . . . . .87 E4
Glan Llwyd SA4 . . . . . . .143 C6
Glanllyn Rd SA7 . . . . . . .155 A5
Glanmor Cres SA2 . . . . .166 F7
Glanmor CI SA2 . . . . . . .166 F7
Glanmorfa SA4 . . . . .158 B5
Glan Morfa SA17 . . . . . . .94 A5
Glanmor La SA2 . . . . . . .166 F7
Glanmor Mews SA2 . . . . .166 F7
Glanmor Park Rd SA2 . . .166 F7
Glanmor Pl 3 SA15 . . . . .148 C4
Glanmor Rd Llanelli SA15 .148 C3
  Swansea / Abertawe SA2 . .166 E7
Glanmor Terr
  2 Llanelli SA15 . . . . . .148 C4
  Pen-clawdd SA4 . . . . . .156 E4
Glan Nant SA43 . . . . .16 C7
Glannant Rd
  Carmarthen / Caerfyrddin
  SA31 . . . . .128 C5
  Pontarddulais SA4 . . . . .143 E5
Glannant Terr SA31 . . . . .139 E7
Glanrhyd Prim Sch SA9 . .139 D6
Glan-Rhyd Rd
  Pontardawe SA8 . . . . . .147 D5
  Ystradgynlais SA9 . . . . .139 E7
Glanrhyd Terr SA4 . . . . . .158 C8
Glan Tawelan SA31 . . . . .128 C4
Glantawe Pk SA9 . . . . . .139 D7
Glantawe Row SA9 . . . . .139 F8
Glantawe St
  2 Morriston / Treforris
  SA6 . . . . .154 A1
  Swansea / Abertawe SA6 . .161 A8
Glantowy SA31 . . . . .129 B7
Glantwrch SA9 . . . . .139 C7
Glan Tywi SA17 . . . . .94 A5
Glanwern SA16 . . . . .137 E3
Glan-y-Gors SA14 . . . . . .97 D8
Glan Y Lli SA42 . . . . .157 A4
Glan-y-Mor SA33 . . . . . . .93 E5
Glan-y-Mor Comp Sch
  SA16 . . . . .137 D3
Glanymor La SA4 . . . . . .150 E1
Glanymor Park Dr SA4 . . .150 D1
Glanymor Rd
  Goodwick / Wdig SA64 . . .122 A5
  Loughor SA4 . . . . .150 E1
Glan-y-Mor Terr SA16 . . .137 E2
Glan yr Afon
  Ammanford / Rhydaman
  SA18 . . . . .98 D8
  Llanelli SA15 . . . . .148 F8
Glanyrafon CI SA4 . . . . . .152 B2
Glan-yr-Afon Gdns SA2 . .166 C6
Glanyrafon Rd SA4 . . . . .143 D4
Glan Yr Afon Rd SA2 . . . .166 C7
Glan Yr Avon
  Pantyffynnon SA9 . . . . .139 A5
  Ystalyfera SA9 . . . . . . .139 C5
Glan-yr-Ysgol SA9 . . . . .139 B6
Glan-y-Ystrad
  Carmarthen / Caerfyrddin
  SA31 . . . . .128 C2
  Ferryside SA17 . . . . . . .94 A5
Glan-y-Wern Rd SA7 . . . .161 E7
Glasbrook Pl SA5 . . . . . .159 E5
Glasbury Rd SA6 . . . . . .160 D7
Glascoed SA15 . . . . .109 E4
Glasdir SA43 . . . . .3 F3
Glasfryn Llanelli SA14 . . .149 A7
  St Clears / Sanclêr
  SA33 . . . . .127 E6
Glasfryn CI SA2 . . . . . . .159 E2
Glasfryn Rd
  Pontarddulais SA4 . . . . .143 C3
  St David's & the Cathedral Close
  SA62 . . . . .123 D4
Glasfryn Terr SA15 . . . . .148 E7
Glaslyn Pl SA1 . . . . .153 D1
Glasplant Terr SA38 . . . .119 F4
Glebe La SA62 . . . . .84 C3
Glebelands
  5 Johnston SA62 . . . . . .86 E5
  Milford Haven / Aberdaugleddau
  SA73 . . . . .131 A3
Glebe Rd SA4 . . . . .150 F1
Glebe The
  Bishopston SA3 . . . . . . .172 A7
  Tenby / Dinbych-y-pysgod
  SA70 . . . . .135 D6
Glenalla Rd SA15 . . . . . .148 E5
Glenfield CI SA2 . . . . . . .166 A4
Glenfield Pk SA3 . . . . . . .132 F6
Glenfields Rd SA61 . . . . .124 E2
Glengower CI SA3 . . . . . .173 A5
Glenover Pk SA61 . . . . . .124 D3
Glen Owen Hill SA73 . . . .87 A1
Glen Rd
  Laugharne Township SA33 . .92 F6
  The Mumbles / Mwmbwls
  SA3 . . . . .172 F6
Glenroy Ave SA1 . . . . . . .174 C4
Glenside Rd SA5 . . . . . . .159 E6
Glen The SA69 . . . . .134 F2

Glen View
Haverfordwest / Hwlffordd
SA61 ....124 E2
Tenby / Dinbych-y-pysgod
SA70 ....135 C6
Glenview Ave SA72 ....132 D3
Glenville Rd SA3 ......173 A6
Glevering St SA15 .....148 E5
Glien Rd SA31 ....128 B3
Globe Row SA14 ....149 B8
Globe St **1** SA6 ......161 A8
Gloster Row **2** SA43 ...118 D3
Gloucester Pl
Swansea / Abertawe SA1 ..174 C2
The Mumbles / Y Mwmbls
SA3 ....173 B4
Gloucester Way SA72 ..132 D3
Glyn-coch Studios★
SA33 ....73 A4
Glyncoed Terr SA15 ....149 A5
Glyncollen Cres SA6 ...154 A3
Glyncollen Dr SA6 .....154 B3
Glyncollen Prim Sch
SA6 ....154 A4
Glyn Cres SA3 ....166 C2
Glyncynwal Rd SA9 .....100 C6
Glynderi SA31 ....129 B7
Glyn Deri SA18 ....98 F8
Glynderwen Cl SA2 .....166 B3
Glynderwen Cres SA2 ..166 B3
Glynderwen Rd SA14 ...149 D4
Glyndwr Pl SA1 ....167 A8
Glyn Hirnant SA6 ......154 A3
Glynhir Rd
Llandybie SA18 ....79 C1
Pontarddulais SA4 .....143 D5
Glyn-Llwchwr Rd SA4 ..143 C4
Glyn-Meirch Rd SA8 ...147 C3
Glyn Moch Cotts SA18 .98 F8
Glynn Vivian Art Gall
SA1 ....174 A3
Glyn Rd / Heol Glyn
SA18 ....99 D8
Glyn Rhosyn SA4 ......151 B1
Glyn St SA1 ....160 D2
Glynteg Rd SA4 ....143 D5
Glyn-y-Mel Rd SA65 ...122 E4
Glyn Y Swistir SA14 ...140 F3
Gnoll Rd SA9 ....100 C1
Goat St
Haverfordwest / Hwlffordd
SA61 ....125 A5
3 Newport / Trefdraeth
SA42 ....13 E3
St David's / Tyddewi SA62 ..123 C4
Godre Coed SA6 ....153 D2
Godre'r Fro SA8 ....147 D7
Goldborough Rd SA71 ..103 D4
Goldcrest Ave
Haverfordwest / Hwlffordd
SA61 ....124 D5
RAF Brawdy SA62 ......49 B2
Golden Cl SA3 ....172 F7
Golden Gr / Gelli Aur
SA5 ....160 D6
Golden Hill Rd SA71 ...133 C5
Golden La SA71 ....133 C5
Golden Manor CP Sch
SA71 ....133 D5
Gollop Prep Sch The
SA20 ....121 C5
Golwgfor SA16 ....108 F4
Golwg Hafren SA2 .....166 C4
Golwg Tywi SA31 ......129 B3
Golwg-y-Castell SA43 ..118 D3
Golwg-y-Cwm SA18 ....99 D5
Golwg-y-Gan SA19 .....62 B5
Golwg Y Garn SA41 ....34 F4
Golwg Y Mor SA4 ......156 F4
Golwg Y Mor / Ocean View
SA10 ....169 C8
Golwg Y Mynydd
Craig-cefn-parc SA6 ...146 B1
Godrergraig SA9 ......139 A3
Golwg-y-Mynydd SA19 .63 D7
Golwg Y Preseli **6** SA43 ..16 A5
Golwg-y-Afon SA14 ....150 B7
Golwg Yr Eglwys SA66 .70 E6
Golwg Y Twr
Llanarthney SA32 ......77 C2
Pontarddulais SA4 .....143 D3
Golwg-y-Tywyn SA16 ..137 D3
Golwyg Yr Allt SA19 ...42 C3
Golygfor SA15 ....148 F4
Gomer Gdns SA1 ....160 A1
Gomer Rd SA1 ....159 F1
Gonhill SA3 ....172 E8
Good Hook La SA62 ....68 D3
Goodmoors La SA72 ...105 A6
Goodwick Cty Prim Sch
Fishguard & Goodwick SA64 ..11 B3
Goodwick / Wdig SA64 ..122 A6
Goodwick Hill
Fishguard & Goodwick SA64 ..11 B3
Goodwick / Wdig SA64 ..122 A6
Goodwick Ind Est SA64 ..122 A6
Goole Rd SA5 ....159 D5
Goose Island SA1 ......174 B1
Goose's La SA71 ....133 C4
Goppa Rd SA4 ....143 E3

Gordon Parry Cl SA73 ..132 A7
Gordon Rd SA14 ....149 B7
Gordon Rowley Way
SA6 ....153 E4
Gordon St SA72 ....132 C3
Gordon Thomas Cl **4**
SA1 ....160 C2
Gore Terr **1** SA1 .....174 A3
Goring Rd / Heol Goring
SA15 ....148 D6
Gorof Rd SA9 ....139 D8
Goronwy Rd SA2 ......159 E1
Gors Ave SA1 ....160 B1
Gorsddu Rd SA14 .....97 D8
Gorsddu Terr SA14 ....97 C8
Gorsedd SA15 ....148 F4
Gorseinon Bsns Pk SA4 ..151 C1
Gorseinon Coll
Gorseinon SA4 ....151 A1
Loughor SA4 ....150 F1
Gorseinon Cty Jun Sch
SA4 ....151 B2
Gorseinon Inf Sch SA4 ..151 C2
Gorseinon Rd SA4 .....151 L1
Gorse La SA1 ....167 A5
Gorse La / Heol Y Gors
SA19 ....62 B5
Gorsewood Dr SA73 ...131 A1
Gors-Fach SA14 ......149 C6
Gors Fach SA3 ....127 B5
Gors Goch Rd / Heol Gors
Goch SA18 ....99 D8
Gors La SA18 ....99 D6
Gorslwyn Terr SA18 ...99 D5
Gors Prim Sch SA1 ....159 E1
Gors Rd
Burry Port SA16 ....137 D2
Cross Hand SA14 ......96 F6
Penllergaer SA4 ....152 A3
Gorsto Rd
Gwaun-Cae-Gurwen SA18 ..99 D7
Pen-Rhiw-fawr SA9 ....100 B3
Gorwydd Rd SA4 ......158 C4
Goshawk Rd SA61 .....124 E5
Goshen Pk SA10 ......162 F8
Gospel La SA62 ....123 C4
Gosport St SA33 ......92 E5
Gothic Rd SA73 ....132 A6
Gough Ave SA9 ....139 D7
Gough Rd SA9 ....139 B6
Gower Heritage Ctr★
SA3 ....170 E7
Gower Holiday Village
SA3 ....117 A6
Gower Pl SA3 ....173 A5
Gower Rd Killay SA2 ..165 D5
Swansea / Abertawe SA2 ..166 C7
Gower Rise SA4 ....158 C4
Gower Terr SA4 ....156 F4
Gowerton Rd
Pen-clawdd SA4 ......157 A4
Three Crosses SA4 ....157 E1
Gowerton Sch SA4 ....158 C4
Gowerton Sta SA4 ....158 C5
Gower View SA4 ......148 E8
Gower View Rd SA4 ...151 A4
Grafog St SA1 ....168 B7
Graham Berry Ct SA5 ..160 A5
Graham St SA1 ....160 D2
Graham Terr SA10 ....162 E7
Graigfelen Prim Sch
SA6 ....154 C8
Graig Inf Sch SA6 .....160 F8
Graiglwyd Rd SA2 .....166 E8
Graiglwyd Sq SA2 .....166 F8
Graig Newydd SA9 ....100 C2
Graig Pl SA1 ....174 B4
Graig Rd Glais SA7 ....155 A6
Glanaman SA18 ....99 C7
Godrergraig SA9 ......100 C2
Llandysul SA44 ....19 E1
Neath / Castell-Nedd
SA10 ....162 D7
Swansea / Abertawe SA6 ..160 F7
Trebanos / Trebannws
SA8 ....147 C3
Graig St SA1 ....174 B4
Graig Terr Glais SA7 ...155 A6
Swansea / Abertawe SA1 ..174 A4
Graig Twrch SA9 ......138 D5
Graig-y-Coed SA4 .....156 D4
Graig Y Darren SA9 ...139 A3
Graig-y-Dderi SA9 .....155 A6
Graigymerched SA9 ...139 A3
Graig Y Pal SA7 ....155 A5
Grampian Way SA5 ...159 E3
Grandison St **2** SA1 ...160 D1
Grand Theatre★ SA1 ..174 A2
Grange Cres SA3 ......173 A7
Grange La SA3 ....173 A8
Grange Prim Sch SA3 ..173 A7
Grange Rd SA3 ....173 A7
Granogwen Rd SA1 ...174 A5
Grant St SA15 ....148 E4
Granville Rd SA1 ......174 C4
Granville Terr SA14 ...149 C6
Grassholm Cl SA3 .....131 E4
Grassholme Pl SA2 ....85 E8
Grassholm Gdns SA5 ..159 E7
Gravel La SA72 ....132 C3
Gray Ave SA7 ....113 D6
Great Eastern Terr
SA73 ....132 B5
Great House Ct SA3 ...117 B5
Great N Rd SA73 ......131 D2

Great Western Cres
SA15 ....148 D3
Great Western Terr **1**
SA15 ....148 D3
Greenacre Dr SA7 .....155 A5
Greenacres SA4 ....156 D4
Green Bank Rd SA3 ...172 F7
Green Bridge of Wales The★
SA71 ....111 A3
Green Cl
Milford Haven / Aberdaugleddau
SA73 ....131 F6
The Mumbles / Y Mwmbls
SA2 ....166 A1
Green Cres **2** SA70 ...135 E5
Green Dragon La SA1 ..174 B2
Greenfield Cl
Haverfordwest / Hwlffordd
SA61 ....125 B7
Swansea / Abertawe SA7 ..161 F7
Greenfield Cres SA7 ..161 F7
Greenfield Pl
2 Llandeilo SA19 ....130 D6
Loughor SA4 ....157 F8
Greenfield Rd / Heol
Maesglas **6** SA18 ....99 B8
Greenfield Row SA43 ..118 D4
Greenfields SA4 ....142 F4
Greenfields Cl **7** SA67 ..89 E6
Greenfield Sq SA43 ...118 D4
Greenfields Terr SA2 ..166 C7
Greenfield Terr
Lampeter / Llanbedr Pont Steffan
SA48 ....120 B4
Pontyberem SA15 .....96 B6
Swansea / Abertawe,
Landore / Glandwr SA1 ..160 D4
Swansea / Abertawe, Llansamlet
SA7 ....161 D8
Greenhall Pk **4** SA62 ..86 E5
Green Hayes SA70 ....106 B4
Green Hill SA1 ....174 B5
Greenhill Ave SA70 ...135 E5
Greenhill Cl **4** SA31 ..128 F6
Greenhill Cres SA61 ..125 A1
Greenhill Pk Dr SA61 ..125 A1
Greenhill Rd
Pembroke Dock / Doc Penfro
SA72 ....104 B5
Tenby / Dinbych-y-pysgod
SA70 ....135 E5
Greenhill Sch The SA70 ..135 D5
Greenhill St SA1 ......174 B5
Green La Neyland SA73 ..132 C5
Oil Refinery SA73 .....103 E8
Greenland Cl SA62 ....67 A6
Greenland Mdws SA43 ..118 E5
Green Mdw Ave SA71 ..133 B5
Green Mdw Cl
East Williamston SA70 ..106 C7
3 Marloes & St Brides
SA62 ....84 C3
Green Pk SA69 ....134 B5
Green St SA6 ....161 A8
Green The
Manorbier SA70 ....106 B1
Pembroke / Penfro SA71 ..133 B5
Greenway SA62 ......87 C6
Greenway Cl SA62 ....87 C6
Greenways SA3 ......158 D3
Greenway The SA10 ..162 C3
Greenwell Cl SA62 ....68 C4
Greenwood Cl SA2 ...166 C6
Greenwood Pl SA5 ...159 D6
Grenfell Ave SA4 .....151 A3
Grenfell Park Rd SA1 ..167 F7
Grenfell Town SA1 ...160 F3
Grenig Rd / Heol Grenig
SA18 ....98 F8
Greville Rd SA73 .....131 D3
Greyfriars Sh Ctr SA31 ..128 E4
Grey St SA1 ....160 D3
Greys Terr SA7 ....155 B1
Griffith John St SA1 ..160 D1
Griffith Jones Prim Sch /
Ysgol Gruffydd Jones
SA33 ....127 F5
Grist The SA33 ....92 F5
Groesffordd **4** SA18 ..80 E1
Groesffordd Fach 3
SA31 ....129 A6
Gron Rd SA18 ....99 D6
Grosvenor Rd SA2 ....166 D7
Grove CP Sch SA71 ...133 C4
Grove Cn SA70 ....106 B4
Grove Dr SA71 ....133 C3
Grove Farm Rd SA4 ...151 C4
Grove Hill SA71 ......133 D3
Grove Hill Pk / Parc
Bryngelli SA14 ....97 C8
Grove La SA10 ....162 E7
Groveland Leisure Pk★
SA33 ....73 A4
Grove Pk SA43 ....118 E6
Grove Pl
Swansea / Abertawe SA1 ..174 A3
The Havens SA62 .....85 D7
Grove Rd Clydach SA6 ..146 D1
Pontardawe SA8 .....147 F5
St Ishmael's SA62 ....85 A2
Groves Ave SA3 ......172 F4
Grove St Gorseinon SA4 ..151 B3
Pembroke Dock / Doc Penfro
SA72 ....104 B4
Grove The
Carmarthen / Caerfyrddin
SA31 ....128 D5

Grove The continued
Hook SA62 ....87 D6
Kilgetty / Begelly SA68 ..134 B7
The Mumbles / Y Mwmbls
SA3 ....173 A5
Grove Way SA71 ......133 C2
Grugos Ave **2** SA15 ...96 B6
Guildford Row SA73 ...87 A7
Guildhall Rd N SA1 ...167 A5
Guildhall Rd S SA1 ...167 A5
Guillemot Ave SA61 ...125 A7
Gulliver's Cl SA3 ......173 B8
Gurnos CP Jun Sch
SA9 ....139 D8
Gurnos Rd
Gowerton / Tre-gwyr SA4 ..158 B5
Ystradgynlais SA9 ....139 C7
Gwalia Cl SA4 ....151 D2
Gwalia Cres SA4 .....151 D2
Gwalia Ct Clydach SA6 ..154 D7
Swansea / Abertawe SA1 ..167 B5
Gwalia Terr SA14 .....151 D2
Gwaun Henllan SA18 ..98 B8
Gwaun View SA65 ....122 E3
Gwbert Rd SA43 .....118 D7
Gweithdau-cwm-gors /
Cwmgors Workshops
SA18 ....99 D6
Gwelfor
3 Burry Port SA16 ...137 D2
Dunvant SA2 ....165 E8
Fishguard / Abergwaun
SA65 ....122 D3
Llanelli SA14 ....149 E4
Gwel-y-creuddyn SA48 ..120 B6
Gwendraeth Pl SA1 ...160 D4
Gwendraeth Rd SA14 ..96 E7
Gwenlais Rd SA4 .....151 E7
Gwent Gdns SA1 .....159 F1
Gwent Gr SA2 ....166 A6
Gwent Rd SA1 ....160 A1
Gwern Einon Rd SA2 ..166 B3
Gwern Fadog Rd SA6 ..154 A3
Gwernllwynchwyth Rd
Birchgrove SA7 ......154 F1
Swansea / Abertawe SA7 ..161 F8
Gwernos SA4 ....154 A2
Gwili Ave SA14 ....97 C6
Gwili Pottery★ SA33 ..57 B4
Gwili Rd SA73 ....131 B2
Gwili Steam Rly★ SA33 ..58 E4
Gwili Terr SA1 ....160 B1
Gwilliam Ct SA71 ....104 C4
Gwilym Rd SA9 ....100 B8
Gwlad-y-Gan SA6 ....153 D1
Gwscwm Pk SA16 ....137 C3
Gwscwm Rd / Heol Gwscwm
SA16 ....137 C3
Gwydr Cres SA2 ......166 F6
Gwydr Mews SA2 .....166 F6
Gwydr Pl SA4 ....150 D1
Gwydr Sq SA2 ....166 F6
Gwylfa SA14 ....149 D6
Gwylfa Rd SA1 ....159 F1
Gwylym St SA5 ......160 A2
Gwyn CP Sch SA15 ...95 D4
Gwyndy Rd SA1 ......161 A2
Gwynedd Ave SA1 ....159 F1
Gwynedd Gdns SA1 ..160 A1
Gwynfan SA32 ....76 C5
Gwynfe Rd
Dyffryn Cennen SA19 ..130 F6
Loughor SA4 ....150 E3
Gwynfi St SA5 ....160 C5
Gwynfor Rd SA2 .....159 E1
Gwynfryn Rd SA4 ....143 C3
Gwynne Terr SA1 ....168 A8
Gwyn's Pl SA8 ....147 F3
Gwyn St SA8 ....147 E3
Gwyrddgoed SA8 ....147 E6
Gwyrosydd Jun & Inf Sch
SA5 ....160 C5
Gwysfa Rd SA4 ......154 B5
Gwysfryn SA9 ....100 C6
Gwyther St SA72 ....132 C2
Gyfre Gdns SA31 .....129 E7
Gynol Rd SA9 ....100 B7
Gyrnosfa SA9 ....139 D8

H

Hadland Terr SA3 .....173 A6
Hael La SA3 ....171 B4
Hafan **4** SA15 ......148 D4
Hafan Glyd SA6 ......154 E8
Hafan Y Don SA2 .....165 E8
Hafan-y-morfa SA15 ..148 F2
Hafnant SA1 ....161 D5
Hafod Bryan SA14 ....149 C4
Hafod Cwnin SA31 ...129 B7
Hafod Elfed SA31 ....128 E6
Hafod Pl SA1 ....160 D2
Hafod Prim Sch SA1 ..160 D2
Hafod Rd SA18 ......97 F6
Hafod St SA1 ....174 B5
Haig Pl SA5 ....159 F4
Hakin CP Sch SA73 ..131 A2
Hakin Infants Sch SA73 ..131 A2
Halfway Prim Sch SA14 ..149 A6
Halkon Cres **6** SA67 ..70 E1

Hallbank SA3 ....173 B4
Hallbank Terr SA3 ....173 B4
Hall La SA4 ....156 D4
Hall's Nook SA3 .....87 A3
Hall St
8 Ammanford / Rhydaman
SA18 ....98 C7
Brynamman SA18 ....99 E8
Llanelli SA15 ....148 D6
Swansea / Abertawe SA1 ..174 A5
Hamilton Cl SA72 ....132 B1
Hamilton Ct SA72 ....133 A8
Hamilton St
6 Fishguard / Abergwaun
SA65 ....122 D3
Swansea / Abertawe SA1 ..160 D4
Hamilton Terr SA73 ..131 C2
Hammond Ave SA61 ..125 A4
Hampshire Dr SA72 ..132 D4
Hangman's Cross SA3 ..117 C5
Hanover Cl SA3 ......173 A6
Hanover Ct SA2 .....166 D7
Hanover La SA1 .....167 A7
Hanover St SA1 ......167 B7
Harbour Cl SA73 .....132 B6
Harbour View Rd SA1 ..168 A8
Harbour Village SA64 ..122 B7
Harbour Way
Milford Haven / Aberdaugleddau
SA73 ....131 A2
Pembroke Dock / Doc Penfro
SA72 ....132 C3
Harbour Winds Ct SA3 ..173 B4
Harcourt St SA1 .....167 B7
Harddfan SA14 ......149 F6
Harding Cl SA4 ......158 A8
Hardingsdown La SA3 ..114 E2
Harding St SA70 .....135 E5
Harebell Cl SA6 .....154 B4
Harford Cl SA2 ......166 C5
Harford Sq **4** SA48 ..120 C5
Harlech Cl SA1 ......166 B7
Harlech Cres SA2 ....166 B7
Harlech St SA18 .....99 E7
Harleyford Rd SA4 ...143 A4
Harlington Rd SA5 ...160 A2
Haroldston Cl SA61 ..125 A2
Haroldston Hill SA62 ..66 C3
Harold St / Stryd Harold 4
SA18 ....98 B7
Harrier Rd SA61 .....124 E5
Harries Ave SA15 ....148 C6
Harries La SA15 .....148 C6
Harries St
Swansea / Abertawe SA1 ..167 B8
Tenby / Dinbych-y-pysgod
SA70 ....135 E4
Harrington Pl SA1 ...174 B5
Harrington Rd SA1 ...160 D1
Harris Rd SA9 ....100 B7
Harris St SA6 ....160 F8
Harry St SA6 ....153 E1
Hartfield Cl SA2 .....166 A7
Hasguard Cross SA62 ..85 C5
Hatfield Ct SA3 ......159 E5
Hatherleigh Dr SA3 ..172 E5
Haulfryn Bryn SA14 ..149 E6
Haulwen Rd
Carmarthen / Caerfyrddin
SA31 ....129 A3
Pontardawe SA8 .....147 E5
Haul Fryn SA7 ....155 A2
Haulwen Rd SA2 .....159 D1
Haul-y-Bryn SA62 ...51 A5
Havard Cl SA62 ......87 C6
Havard Rd SA14 .....149 A6
Havelock St SA15 ....148 E2
Haven Ct SA71 .....104 C4
Haven Dr
Milford Haven / Aberdaugleddau
SA73 ....102 F3
Pembroke Dock / Doc Penfro
SA72 ....103 F5
Haven Pk Ave SA61 ..124 D4
Haven Pk Cl SA61 ...124 D4
Haven Pk Cres SA61 ..124 C4
Haven Pk Dr SA61 ...124 D4
Haven Rd SA61 ......124 B4
Haven's Head Bsns Pk
SA73 ....131 B3
Haven's Pk SA73 ....85 E2
Havenway Day Hospl
SA72 ....132 A3
Haverfordwest Castle (Ruin)
& Town Mus★ SA61 ..125 A5
Haverfordwest Rd SA62 ..50 D4
Haverfordwest Sta
SA61 ....125 C5
Haverfordwest Swimming
Pool SA61 ....125 A5
Haverfordwest VC Sch
SA61 ....124 F5
Haverfordwest (Withybush)
Airfield SA62 ....68 A6
Havergal Cl SA3 .....172 D4
Hawkstone Cl SA3 ...172 F5
Hawkstone Rd SA72 ..132 D2
Hawthorn Ave SA4 ...151 A2
Hawthorne Ave SA2 ..166 F7
Hawthorn Rise SA61 ..124 D5
Hawthorn Villas SA9 ..138 F1
Hayguard La SA61 ...125 A5
Haylands La SA70 ....105 C4
Haylett Grange Sch SA62 ..86 F8
Hayston Ave SA73 ...131 B2
Hayston Rd SA62 ....86 D4
Haytor Gdns SA70 ...135 D6
Hazel Bank Hill SA73 ..103 F8

Hazelbeach Rd SA73 ....103 E8
Hazel Ct SA2 ....166 B6
Hazel Gr SA73 ....103 F8
Hazelmere Rd SA2 ....166 D7
Hazel Rd SA2 ....166 E7
Hazeltree Copse SA4 ....156 B2
Headland Cl SA3 ....172 A5
Headland Rd
Bishopston SA3 ....172 A5
Swansea / Abertawe SA1 ..167 F8
Hean Cl SA69 ....134 E4
Heaselands Pl SA2 ....165 D7
Heath Cl Johnston SA62 ....86 E6
The Mumbles / Y Mwmbwls
SA3 ....172 F6
Heath Ct SA3 ....172 F6
Heather Cres SA2 ....166 B6
Heatherslade Cl
Southgate SA3 ....171 A3
The Mumbles / Y Mwmbwls
SA3 ....173 B4
Heatherslade Rd SA3 ....171 A4
Heatherton Sports Pk*
SA70 ....106 C5
Heathfield
Gorseinon SA4 ....151 A1
Swansea / Abertawe SA1 ..174 A3
Heathfield Ind Pk SA14 ..97 C6
Heathfield Rd SA8 ....147 F6
Heathwood Rd SA3 ....173 A8
Hebron Cl SA6 ....154 D7
Hebron Rd SA6 ....154 D7
Hedley Terr SA15 ....148 D6
Helwick Cl SA3 ....173 A5
Hendre SA2 ....165 D8
Hendre Cl SA14 ....150 A7
Hendre Cres SA14 ....150 B7
Hendrefoilan Ave SA2 ..166 B7
Hendrefoilan Cl SA2 ..166 A7
Hendrefoilan Ct SA2 ..166 B8
Hendrefoilan Dr SA2 ..166 A7
Hendrefoilan Prim Sch
SA2 ....165 F7
Hendre-Foilan Rd SA2 ..166 B8
Hendrefoilan Student Village
SA2 ....166 A8
Hendre Isaf SA14 ....149 D4
Hendremawr Cl SA2 ..166 C8
Hendre Owain SA2 ....166 C8
Hendre Pk SA14 ....150 A7
Hendre Rd
Llangennech SA14 ....150 B7
Tycroes SA18 ....97 F6
Hendre Rd / Heol Hendre
4 Glanaman SA18 ....99 B8
Llanelli SA14 ....149 D4
Hendy Cl SA2 ....166 B4
Hendy Cty Prim Mixed Sch
SA4 ....143 A4
Hendy Ind Est SA4 ....143 A4
Hendy Rd SA4 ....156 F4
Heneage Dr SA2 ....166 B1
Hen Felin SA9 ....139 C7
Hen Heol Llangynnwr
SA31 ....129 A4
Henllan Amgoed CP Sch
SA34 ....71 E6
Henllan Ind Est SA44 ....18 E3
Henllan Sta SA44 ....18 E3
Hen Parc Ave SA2 ....165 B5
Hen Parc La SA2 ....165 C4
Henrietta St SA1 ....167 B6
Henton La SA63 ....69 D7
Heol Aaron SA9 ....139 D8
Heol Abram SA9 ....139 D8
Heol Afallon SA14 ....96 D7
Heol Afon / Afon Rd
SA14 ....150 C8
Heol Amman SA18 ....79 F1
Heol Amman / Amman Rd
Brynamman SA18 ....99 E8
Glanaman SA18 ....98 F8
Heol-aneddfa 4 SA15 ....96 B6
Heol Arfryn SA31 ....128 B6
Heol Argoed / Argoed Rd
SA18 ....98 C5
Heol Aur Llanelli SA14 ....141 C1
Llanelli SA14 ....149 C8
Heol Awstin SA5 ....159 E5
Heol Bancyroffis SA15 ....95 D3
Heol Barcud SA7 ....162 B8
Heol Barri / Barry Rd
SA18 ....99 D7
Heol Beca SA31 ....128 C4
Heol Bedw SA43 ....118 F5
Heol Bedwas SA7 ....155 A1
Heol Beili Glas SA14 ....141 A2
Heol Beili-glas SA20 ....44 E2
Heol Bethel SA15 ....96 C2
Heol Blaengwastod
SA31 ....129 A3
Heol Blaenhirwaun SA14 .96 E8
Heol Bolahaul
Llandyfaelog SA31 ....75 F4
Llangunnor SA31 ....129 A1
Heol Briallu SA6 ....153 F2
Heol Brithdir SA7 ....162 B8
Heol Broch SA7 ....162 B8
Heol Bronallt / Bronallt Rd
SA4 ....143 A5
Heol Brown SA18 ....98 A5
Heol Brynamman /
Brynamman Rd SA18 ....99 D7
Heol Brynbrain SA9 ....100 B8
Heol Bryncelyn SA14 ....149 C8
Heol Bryncyn SA7 ....155 A1
Heol Brynglas SA4 ....158 B8
Heol Bryngwili SA14 ....97 A7
Heol Brynhaul SA15 ....95 D3
Heol Bryn-Lloi / Bryn-Lloi
Rd 5 SA18 ....99 A8
Heol Brython SA2 ....165 B8
Heol Buckley SA15 ....148 E8
Heol Cadifor SA5 ....160 B6
Heol Cadnawes SA6 ....153 F4
Heol Cae Copyn SA4 ....150 E1
Heol Cae-du SA20 ....44 E2
Heol Cae-ffynnon SA31 ..129 F7
Heol Cae-Glas SA7 ....161 F6
Heol-cae-globe SA4 ....157 F8
Heol-Cae-Gurwen SA18 ..99 D6
Heol Caegwyn SA14 ....96 D8
Heol Cae Rhosyn SA7 ....155 A1
Heol Caerllion SA6 ....154 B5
Heol Cae Tynewydd
SA4 ....150 F1
Heol Calfin SA5 ....159 E4
Heol Callwen SA9 ....82 F3
Heol Camlan SA7 ....155 A1
Heol Capel Dewi SA31 ..129 C4
Heol Capel Ifan SA15 ....96 A5
Heol Capel Sion SA14 ....96 C8
Heol Caradog SA65 ....122 E3
Heol Cefni SA6 ....160 E8
Heol Ceirios SA18 ....79 B1
Heol Cennen SA19 ....130 D4
Heol Ceri SA5 ....158 D3
Heol Cerwyn SA65 ....122 D3
Heol Cleddau
3 Fishguard / Abergwaun
SA65 ....122 D3
Waunarlwydd SA5 ....158 D3
Heol Cledwyn SA7 ....155 A1
Heol Copperworks /
Copperworks Rd SA15 .148 D3
Heol Cowell / Cowell Rd
SA18 ....99 C7
Heol Cropin SA14 ....149 C8
Heol Cross Hands / Cross
Hands Rd SA14 ....97 B8
Heol Crwys
Fishguard / Abergwaun
SA65 ....122 C5
Gorseinon SA4 ....151 B4
Llanrhian SA62 ....29 A5
Heol Crych-gwyn SA19 ..64 E4
Heol Cwmbach SA14 ....96 D7
Heol Cwmfferws /
Cwmfferws Rd SA18 ....97 F6
Heol Cwmmawr SA14 ....96 D8
Heol Cwper / Coopers Rd
SA18 ....97 E5
Heol Cynan
Fishguard / Abergwaun
SA65 ....122 C4
Gorseinon SA4 ....151 B4
Heol Dalycopa SA7 ....161 E6
Heol Daniel
Cwmllynfell SA9 ....100 B7
Llanelli SA14, SA15 ....148 F8
Heol Dderwen SA15 ....148 F4
Heol Ddu
Ammanford / Rhydaman
SA18 ....98 D8
Cross Hand SA14 ....96 D8
Llandybie SA18 ....79 E1
Swansea / Abertawe SA5 ..160 B7
Trimsaran SA15 ....109 C6
Tycroes SA18 ....97 F5
Heol Ddwr SA4 ....143 E6
Heol Derw
Cardigan / Aberteifi SA43 ..118 F5
Cynwyl Elfed SA33 ....58 A5
Heol Derwen
Cross Hands SA14 ....97 C7
Haverfordwest / Hwlffordd
SA61 ....125 A2
Heol Dewi
Fishguard / Abergwaun
SA65 ....122 C5
St David's / Tyddewi SA62 ..123 D5
Heol Dewi Sant SA4 ....152 A2
Heol Dinbych SA15 ....148 F4
Heol Dinefwr / Dynevor Rd
SA18 ....99 B7
Heol Disgwylfa 1 SA31 ..128 E6
Heol Dolfain SA6 ....154 A4
Heol Drindod SA31 ....128 C2
Heol Dulais SA7 ....155 A1
Heol Dwr SA18 ....98 E7
Heol Dyddgen SA17 ....95 E8
Heol Dyfan SA6 ....153 F3
Heol Dyfatty SA16 ....137 F2
Heol Dyfed
Fishguard / Abergwaun
SA65 ....122 C4
Gorseinon SA4 ....151 B4
Heol Dyfnallt SA31 ....128 C4
Heol Dylan SA4 ....151 B4
Heol Dynys SA5 ....159 E5
Heol Dywyll SA6 ....154 C7
Heol Eglwys SA9 ....138 F1
Heol Eifion SA4 ....151 C2
Heol Eifion Wyn SA7 ....161 E6
Heol Eirlys SA6 ....153 F2
Heol Eithrim SA6 ....154 D8
Heol Elfed
Burry Port SA16 ....137 D2
Gorseinon SA4 ....151 B4
Llanelli SA14 ....149 C5
Swansea / Abertawe SA7 ..161 E6
Heol Elisabeth SA16 ....137 E3
Heol Elli SA15 ....148 F5
Heol Emrys
Fishguard / Abergwaun
SA65 ....122 D5
Heol Emrys *continued*
Swansea / Abertawe SA5 ..160 A5
Heol Fach
Ammanford SA18 ....97 E8
Swansea / Abertawe, Llangyfelach
SA5 ....153 B3
Swansea / Abertawe, Waun-Gron
SA5 ....160 C6
Heol Fedw SA6 ....153 F3
Heol Felen
Cwmamman SA18 ....80 B1
Glanaman SA18 ....99 B8
Heol Felin Newydd / New
Mill Rd SA43 ....118 F6
Heol Ffion SA4 ....151 C2
Heol Fforest / Fforest Rd
SA4 ....143 B5
Heol Ffranc SA10 ....162 C6
Heol Ffynnon
Llanelli SA15 ....148 F4
Loughor SA4 ....150 E1
Heol Ffynnonau 2 SA32 ..59 A2
Heol Ficeroi / Vicarage Rd 7
SA18 ....99 B8
Heol Folland / Folland Rd
SA18 ....99 B8
Heol Frank SA5 ....160 B5
Heol Gelli SA38 ....17 B4
Heol Gelli-ddu SA19 ....64 E3
Heol Gelli Fawr SA15 ....109 F7
Heol Gelligron SA44 ....20 B8
Heol Gelynen
3 Brecon SA18 ....80 E1
Brynamman SA18 ....99 D8
Heol Gerrig SA5 ....160 C6
Heol Giedd
Cwmgiedd SA9 ....138 F3
Ystradgynlais SA9 ....138 F2
Heol Glan-gwendraeth
SA15 ....95 D3
Heol Glanllechau SA8 ..147 E3
Heol Glan-Nant SA6 ....154 A4
Heol Glasfryn 5 SA32 ..59 A2
Heol Glasnant SA2 ....165 F7
Heol Gleien SA9 ....138 A2
Heol Glyndernwen SA8 ..147 E3
Heol Glyndwr
Fishguard / Abergwaun
SA65 ....122 D3
Llangyndeyrn SA15 ....95 D4
Heol Glyn-Dyfal SA5 ....144 F4
Heol Glyn / Glyn Rd
SA18 ....99 D8
Heol Godfrey SA18 ....99 D8
Heol Goffa SA15 ....148 E7
Heol Gollen SA43 ....118 F5
Heol Goring / Goring Rd
SA15 ....148 D6
Heol Gors Goch / Gors Goch
Rd SA18 ....99 D8
Heol Graig-Felen SA6 ..154 D8
Heol Grenig / Grenig Rd
SA18 ....99 B6
Heol Gron SA9 ....139 D8
Heol Gruffydd SA5 ....159 F5
Heol Grug SA6 ....153 E2
Heol Gwalia SA14 ....149 C5
Heol Gwanwyn SA7 ....161 F7
Heol Gwell SA5 ....160 D5
Heol Gwenallt SA4 ....151 B4
Heol Gwendraeth 2
SA16 ....137 D2
Heol Gwermont SA17 ....94 B2
Heol Gwernen
Cwmrhydyceirw SA6 ....154 A3
Swansea / Abertawe SA6 ..153 F3
Heol Gwernfelen
Llandovery / Llanymddyfri
SA20 ....121 F4
Llandovery / Llanymddyfri
SA20 ....44 F5
Myddfai SA20 ....45 A4
Heol Gwili Gorseinon SA4 .151 B4
Llanelli SA14 ....149 D5
Swansea / Abertawe SA7 ..161 E6
Heol Gwilym SA18 ....79 A2
Heol Gwscwm / Gwscwm Rd
SA16 ....137 C3
Heol Gwyr SA15 ....148 F4
Heol Gwyrosydd SA5 ....160 B5
Heol Gwys SA9 ....100 C6
Heol Hafdy SA7 ....161 F7
Heol Hafod SA43 ....118 E4
Heol Hathren SA48 ....120 E3
Heol Haydn SA18 ....98 B7
Heol Helyg SA43 ....118 F5
Heol Hen
Llanelli Rural SA15 ....109 F8
Llanelli SA14 ....149 C4
Heol Hendre / Hendre Rd
4 Glanaman SA18 ....99 B8
Llanelli SA14 ....149 D4
Heol Hermas SA5 ....160 B6
Heol Hir SA18 ....99 E6
Heol Hirwaun Olau SA14 .96 E7
Heol Horeb SA15 ....140 A7
Heol Innes SA15 ....148 E8
Heol Iscoed / Iscoed Rd
SA4 ....143 A4
Heol Islwyn SA4 ....151 B4
Heol Langdon / Langdon Rd
Swansea / Abertawe SA1 ..167 F7
Swansea / Abertawe SA1 ..168 A6
Heol-Las
Ammanford / Rhydaman
SA18 ....98 B6
Birchgrove SA7 ....154 F2
Heol Las SA14 ....97 B8
Heol-Las Cl SA7 ....154 F1
Heol Llandeilo / Llandeilo Rd
SA14 ....78 C1
Heol Llanelli
Pontyates / Pont-iets SA15 ..95 E3
Trimsaran SA17 ....109 C7
Heol Llangynnwr SA31 ..129 B4
Heol Llansaint SA17 ....94 B3
Heol Llwyd SA18 ....98 B8
Heol Llwyn Bedw SA4 ..142 F4
Heol Llwyncelyn /
Llwyncelyn Rd SA18 ....98 F8
Heol Llwynhendy /
Llwynhendy Rd SA14 ..149 D4
Heol Login SA31 ....129 C3
Heol Lotwen / Lotwen Rd
SA18 ....97 D6
Heol Lucy / Lucy Rd
SA10 ....162 D7
Heol Maesbryn SA4 ....150 F1
Heol Maes Eglwys SA6 ..153 E4
Heol Maesglas / Greenfield
Rd 6 SA18 ....99 B8
Heol Maes / Maes Rd
SA14 ....150 C8
Heol Maesoderwen /
Oakfield Rd 5 SA18 ....99 B8
Heol Maespica SA9 ....138 B2
Heol Maesuchel / Highfield
Rd SA18 ....99 C8
Heol Maes Y Cerrig
SA4 ....150 E1
Heol Maes-y-Dre SA9 ..138 F1
Heol Maes-y-Gelynen
SA6 ....153 F2
Heol Mafon SA39 ....20 B2
Heol Mair SA31 ....128 B6
Heol Mansant SA15 ....95 D4
Heol Mansel / Mansel St 15
SA15 ....148 D4
Heol Marlais
Ammanford / Rhydaman
SA18 ....98 B8
Llandybie SA18 ....79 A1
Heol Meurig SA9 ....139 D8
Heol Miaren SA6 ....153 F2
Heol Morfa SA15 ....148 F3
Heol Morfa Brenin
SA31 ....128 C2
Heol Morlais Hendy SA4 ..142 F3
Llannon SA14 ....96 E2
Trimsaran SA17 ....109 B8
Heol Morlais / Morlais Rd
SA14 ....150 B7
Heol Mwrwg SA14 ....150 B8
Heol Myddfai SA5 ....144 F2
Heol Myrddin SA19 ....130 D3
Heol Nant Llanelli SA14 ..141 A2
Llannon SA14 ....96 F3
Heol Nant Bran SA7 ....155 A2
Heol Nant Gelli SA5 ....160 D5
Heol Nant Gwinau / Nant
Gwineu Rd SA18 ....99 C8
Heol Nant-y-Felin SA15 .148 E7
Heol Nantyglasdwr SA31 ..75 F4
Heol Nant Y Glyn / Nantyglyn
Rd SA18 ....98 F8
Heol Nazareth SA15 ....95 D3
Heol Newydd SA5 ....159 F5
Heol Newydd / New Rd
Neath / Castell-Nedd
SA10 ....162 C1
Ystradowen SA9 ....100 C7
Heol Norman / Norman Rd
3 SA18 ....98 B7
Heol Onnen SA43 ....118 F6
Heol Palleg / Palleg Rd
SA9 ....138 C2
Heol Panteg SA16 ....137 C3
Heol Pantycelyn 1
SA16 ....137 D2
Heol Pant Y Dwr SA4 ....150 F2
Heol Pantyffynnon /
Pantyffynnon Rd SA18 ..98 B6
Heol Pant-y-Lliw SA4 ..152 A6
Heol Parc Mawr SA14 ....97 C7
Heol Penar SA5 ....160 B6
Heol Pendref SA19 ....63 D7
Heol Penfelyn SA6 ....153 F5
Heol Penlan SA64 ....11 B3
Heol Penlanffos SA31 ....129 B7
Heol Pen-nant
Llanelli SA14 ....141 B3
Ynysforgan SA6 ....154 A4
Heol Penprys SA14 ....149 E6
Heol Pen Storom SA19 ..130 D1
Heol Pen-Tir-Garw SA5 .159 F6
Heol Pentre Bach SA4 ..150 F2
Heol Pentre Felen SA6 ..153 C1
Heol Pentregwenlais
SA18 ....78 F3
Heol Pentwyn SA10 ....162 C6
Heol Pentyla SA7 ....161 F6
Heol Pen-y-Beili SA4 ..150 E1
Heol Pen Y Cae SA4 ....150 F2
Heol Penygarn / Penygarn
Rd SA18 ....97 F5
Heol Penygroes / Penygroes
Rd
Ammanford SA18 ....97 F8
Gorslas SA14 ....97 C8
Heol Pen-y-Scallen
SA4 ....150 E1
Heol Philip SA9 ....138 D1
Heol Phillip SA8 ....147 E3
Heol Plas Isaf SA14 ....150 B7
Heol Pluguffan SA20 ....121 C4
Heol Preseli SA65 ....122 D3
Heol Rehoboth / Rehoboth
Rd SA15 ....109 E7
Heol Rhian SA62 ....28 E4
Heol Rhos SA20 ....121 A6
Heol-Rhosybonwen
Cefneithin SA14 ....97 A8
Gorslas SA14 ....96 F8
Heol Rhosyn SA6 ....153 F2
Heol Rhuddos SA7 ....162 A7
Heol Rhyd SA6 ....146 B3
Heol Rhydaman /
Ammanford Rd SA18 ....97 F6
Heol Rhyd-Ddu-Fach
SA9 ....100 B8
Heol Roberts / Roberts Rd
SA1 ....167 F5
Heol Rudd SA31 ....128 E6
Heol Saffrwm SA6 ....153 F2
Heol Salem SA31 ....128 C3
Heol Santes Ann 3 SA32 ..75 F3
Heol Saron / Saron Rd
Ammanford SA18 ....97 F8
Capel Hendre SA18 ....97 E6
Heol Seion SA14 ....150 B7
Heol Siloh SA15 ....148 C4
Heol Smyrna SA33 ....75 B3
Heol Spurrell SA31 ....128 E6
Heol Stanllyd SA14 ....97 B7
Heol Tabernacle /
Tabernacle Rd SA18 ....98 F8
Heol Tabernacl / Tabernacle
Rd 2 SA18 ....99 A8
Heol Tircoed SA4 ....152 B5
Heol Tir Du
Cwmrhydyceirw SA6 ....154 A3
Swansea / Abertawe SA6 ..153 F3
Heol Tir Y Coed / Tirycoed
Rd 3 SA18 ....99 A8
Heol Tir Y Coed / Woodland
Rd SA9 ....100 C7
Heol Tir-y-Parc / Parklands
Rd SA18 ....98 A7
Heol Tredeg SA9 ....100 C6
Heol Treffynnon SA6 ....154 B5
Heol Trefin SA65 ....122 D5
Heol Trefor SA5 ....160 B6
Heol Trefrhiw / Trefrhiw Rd
SA18 ....98 A6
Heol Tregoning SA15 ....148 F2
Heol Tregwyr SA17 ....94 B3
Heol-Treventy SA14 ....97 A8
Heol Troeon Bach SA4 ....97 D2
Heol Trosserch / Troserch
Rd / SA14 ....142 B2
Heol Trubshaw SA15 ....148 E8
Heol Twrch SA9 ....138 B1
Heol Tycroes / Tycroes Rd
Ammanford / Rhydaman
SA18 ....98 A5
Tycroes SA18 ....97 F5
Heol Tylluan SA7 ....162 B8
Heol Ty Newydd 7 SA43 ..16 A5
Heol Uchaf Yr Orsaf / Upper
Station Rd 9 SA18 ....99 B8
Heol Valentine SA6 ....154 D8
Heol Vaughan SA16 ....137 C2
Heol Wallasey SA18 ....98 C7
Heol Waterloo / Waterloo Rd
SA14, SA18 ....97 D7
Heol Waun Dwfn SA18 ....98 D6
Heol Waunllystir SA20 ....44 F2
Heol Waun-wen SA16 ....137 C3
Heol Waun Wen SA6 ....153 B1
Heol Waunyclun SA17 ....137 F8
Heol Wepner SA15 ....95 D3
Heol Westfa SA14 ....148 F8
Heol Will George SA5 ....158 E3
Heol Wyllt SA4 ....143 E4
Heol Y Banc SA15 ....95 F7
Heol Y Barna SA4 ....144 A3
Heol Y Bedw SA44 ....18 E3
Heol y Brenin / King's Rd
SA1 ....174 C2
Heol-y-Bryn SA14 ....96 F6
Heol Y Bryn SA15 ....96 B6
Heol-y-Bwlch SA14 ....150 A2
Heol-y-Cae Clydach SA6 .154 D7
Pontarddulais SA4 ....143 E5
Heol Y Capel SA14 ....78 D3
Heol Y Celyn SA7 ....154 D1
Heol Y Cnap SA5 ....160 D5
Heol-y-Coed SA4 ....143 E5
Heol-y-Coedcae SA9 ....100 B7
Heol Y Coroni / Coronation
Rd 16 SA18 ....99 B8
Heol Y Cwmdu SA5 ....159 F2
Heol Y Cwrt SA19 ....79 E4
Heol Y Cyw SA7 ....162 B8
Heol Y Dderi SA40 ....21 D6
Heol Y Dderwen SA44 ....19 D2
Heol-y-Delyn SA31 ....128 F7
Heol-y-Deri
Cwmgwili SA14 ....97 C5
Cwmrhydyceirw SA6 ....154 A3
Swansea / Abertawe SA6 ..153 F3
Heol Y Deri / Deri Rd
SA18 ....98 F8
Heol-y-Dre SA14 ....97 A8
Heol Y Drudwen SA6 ....153 F5
Heol-y-Fagwr SA6 ....146 F1
Heol-y-Felin
Ammanford / Rhydaman
SA18 ....98 C6
Burry Port SA16 ....137 E3
Heol Y Felin SA4 ....142 F5

Heol-y-Felin SA4 ......152 B2
Heol Y Felin SA15 ......96 A6
Heol-y-Felin SA43 ......3 F4
Heolyffin SA8 ......147 B1
Heol Y Ffinant SA38 ......119 D4
Heol-y-Ffowndri / Foundry Rd 5 SA18 ......98 C7
Heol Y Fran SA6 ......153 F5
Heol-y-Gaer
  Clynderwen SA66 ......70 F6
  Llanybyther SA40 ......21 D6
Heol Y Garn SA18 ......98 B4
Heol-y-Garreg-Las SA19 ......130 E6
Heol Y Garreg Wen SA3 ......172 E6
Heol-y-Geifr SA3 ......153 B2
Heol Y Gelli
  Llangadog SA19 ......81 B4
  Llansadwrn SA19 ......43 C2
Heol-y-Gelli SA15 ......151 F2
Heol-y-Gilfach SA44 ......19 E3
Heol-y-Goedlan SA9 ......100 B6
Heol Y Gof SA38 ......119 D4
Heol-y-Gog SA4 ......158 B5
Heol-y-Gors
  Gwaun-Cae-Gurwen SA18 ......99 D5
  Swansea / Abertawe SA1, SA5 ......160 A2
Heol Y Gors / Gorse La SA19 ......62 B5
Heol-y-Graig SA6 ......154 D7
Heol Y Graig SA14 ......149 E4
Heol-y-Lan SA32 ......75 F2
Heol-y-Llan
  Burry Port SA16 ......137 D2
  Llandissilio West SA66 ......70 F8
  Loughor SA4 ......157 E8
Heol y Llew Du / Black Lion Rd SA14 ......97 C7
Heol Y Llidiart-coch SA19 ......80 E8
Heol Y Lloetrach SA16 ...137 A2
Heol-y-Llwynan SA8 ......147 B1
Heol-y-Maes SA40 ......21 E8
Heol-y-Maes SA4 ......143 D4
Heol Y Meinciau SA15 ......95 D4
Heol Y Merwydd SA44 ......19 B5
Heol Y Mynydd SA18 ......98 B3
Heol Y Mynydd SA14 ......149 F6
Heol Y Mynydd SA4 ......151 D3
Heol Y Mynydd / Mountain Rd SA16 ......137 A3
Heol Y Nant SA6 ......154 E8
Heol Y Nant SA4 ......150 F3
Heol Y Nantlais SA4 ......151 B4
Heol-Y-neuadd SA14 ......96 E7
Heol-Y-Neuadd 6 SA44 ...19 E3
Heol-Y-Parc SA14 ......97 A8
Heol Y Parc Hendy SA4 ...142 F4
  Llangennech SA14 ......150 C7
  Pontardawe SA8 ......147 F3
Heol-y-Parc SA4 ......152 A7
Heol Y Parc SA15 ......96 B6
Heol Y Pentre
  Pont Henri SA15 ......95 E4
  Pontybrenin SA4 ......96 B5
Heol Y Pistyll SA19 ......23 C7
Heol-y-Plas Fforest SA4 ...142 F6
  Llannon SA14 ......96 E3
Heol Yr Eglwys / Church Rd SA14 ......97 B8
Heol Yr Eithen SA6 ......154 A3
Heol-yr-Eos SA4 ......151 F2
Heol Yr Eryr
  Cwmrhydyceirw SA6 ......154 A5
  Swansea / Abertawe SA6 ...153 F5
Heol-y-Rhedyn SA6 ......153 E2
Heol Y Rhosfa / Rhosfa Rd SA18 ......80 F1
Heol Yr Wylan SA6 ......153 F5
Heol-yr-Ysgol
  Cefneithin SA14 ......97 A8
  Gorslas SA14 ......78 A1
Heol Yr Ysgol / School Rd
  Brynamman SA18 ......99 D8
  Cefn-bryn-brain SA9 ......100 B8
  Neath / Castell-Nedd SA10 ......162 C1
Heol Ysgawen SA2 ......166 C8
Heol Ysgol Newydd / New School Rd 15 SA18 ...99 B8
Heol Ysgyfarnog SA7 ......162 B8
Heol-y-Twyn SA4 ......151 F7
Heol-y-Waun SA4 ......143 D5
Heol Y Waun SA4 ......151 F7
Heol Y Waunfach SA14 ...149 C8
Heol Y Wawr SA31 ......128 B6
Heol-y-Wern
  Cardigan / Aberteifi SA43 ...118 F6
  Loughor SA4 ......157 E4
Heol-y-Wyrddol SA18 ......98 B8
Herberdeg Rd SA15 ......95 E2
Herbert St SA8 ......147 E4
Herbrandston Cty Prim Sch SA73 ......85 E3
Heritage Gate SA61 ......125 C7
Heritage Pk SA61 ......125 C8
Hermitage Gr SA61 ......125 C8
Hermon CP Sch SA36 ...35 B3
Hermons Hill SA61 ......125 A4
Heron Ave SA15 ......96 B5
Heron's Brook Leisure Pk* SA67 ......89 D8
Heron Way SA6 ......161 B8
Hewlett Rd SA15 ......96 B5

Hewson St SA1 ......167 B8
Heywood Ct SA70 ......135 C5
Heywood La SA70 ......135 D5
Hick St SA15 ......148 D4
Highbury Cl SA5 ......160 B2
Highcliffe Ct SA3 ......172 F4
Highfield SA4 ......158 A8
Highfield Pk 1 SA67 ......70 D1
Highfield Rd / Heol Maesuchel SA18 ......99 C8
Highfields Holiday Pk SA3 ......117 A4
Highfield Terr SA15 ......148 E4
Highgate La SA71 ......104 B3
Highgrove SA70 ......106 F6
Highland Cl SA10 ......162 F8
Highlands Ave SA61 ......124 F5
Highlands The SA10 ......162 F8
Highland Terr SA4 ......143 E3
Highmead Ave
  Llanelli SA15 ......148 E8
  The Mumbles / Y Mwmbwls SA3 ......172 E6
Highmead Cl SA3 ......172 E5
Highmead Terr SA40 ......21 C7
Highmoor SA1 ......174 B1
Highpool Cl SA3 ......172 E5
Highpool La SA3 ......172 E5
High St Abergwili SA31 ...129 E7
  Allt-wen SA8 ......147 E5
  Cardigan / Aberteifi SA43 ...118 D4
  Cilgerran SA43 ......16 A5
  Clydach SA6 ......154 E7
  Cross Hand SA14 ......96 F6
  Ffairfach / Abergwaun SA65 ......122 C3
  Gorseinon SA4 ......151 C2
  Grovesend SA4 ......151 C6
  Haverfordwest / Hwlffordd SA61 ......125 A5
  Lampeter / Llanbedr Pont Steffan SA48 ......120 C5
  Lampeter Velfrey SA34 ......71 F2
  Llandovery / Llanymddyfri SA20 ......121 D4
  2 Llandybie SA18 ......79 A2
  4 Llandyssul SA44 ......19 E3
  Llangadog SA19 ......63 D7
  Llansteffan SA33 ......93 D5
  Narberth / Arberth SA67 ...70 D1
  Neath / Castell-Nedd, Pentrefffynnon SA10 ......162 F7
  Newcastle Emlyn / Castell Newydd Emlyn SA38 ......119 E4
  Neyland SA73 ......132 B6
  Pontardawe SA8 ......147 E5
  Pontarddulais SA4 ......143 C5
  Saundersfoot SA69 ......134 F3
  Solva SA62 ......48 D3
  St Clears / Sanclêr SA33 ......127 D4
  St David's / Tyddewi SA62 ...123 C4
  St Dogmaels / Llandudoch SA43 ......118 A3
  Tenby / Dinbych-y-pysgod SA70 ......135 E5
High St SE 3 SA12 ......132 C1
High St / Prif Ffordd SA15 ......148 C4
High St / Stryd Fawr
  4 Glanaman SA18 ......99 A8
  Swansea / Abertawe SA1 ...174 B4
High View SA1 ......174 A1
High View Gdns SA2 ......166 B2
Hilland Dr SA3 ......172 B6
Hillbrook Cl SA5 ......158 D3
Hill Cres SA73 ......87 B9
Hill Crest SA3 ......173 B4
Hillcroft SA62 ......86 E5
Hillfield Villas SA17 ......136 A4
Hillgrove SA3 ......172 E4
Hill House Hospl SA2 ......166 D8
Hill La Camrose SA62 ......67 A4
  Haverfordwest / Hwlffordd SA61 ......125 A5
  Jeffreyston SA68 ......89 B1
Hill Pk SA70 ......135 D6
Hill Rd SA62 ......31 C3
Hill Rise SA69 ......134 C6
Hillrise Pk SA6 ......154 C7
Hillside Llanelli SA15 ......148 C7
  Loughor SA4 ......150 E1
Hillside Cl SA64 ......122 A4
Hillside Cres
  3 Goodwick / Wdig SA64 ...122 A4
  Swansea / Abertawe SA2 ...167 A7
Hillside Terr 4 SA67 ......89 C9
Hill St
  Goodwick / Wdig SA64 ...122 A6
  Gowerton / Tre-gwyr SA4 ...158 B5
  Haverfordwest / Hwlffordd SA61 ......125 A5
  Milford Haven / Aberdaugleddau SA73 ......131 D2
  Pembroke Dock / Doc Penfro SA72 ......132 B1
  Swansea / Abertawe SA1 ...174 A4
  The Mumbles / Y Mwmbwls SA3 ......173 C4
Hill Terr
  4 Ffairfach / Abergwaun SA65 ......122 A4
  Neyland SA73 ......132 C6
Hilltop / Penrhiw SA14 ...141 A2
Hill Top Rd SA71 ......103 B6
Hill View SA10 ......169 B8
Hill View Cres SA6 ......160 D8
Hilton Ave SA73 ......131 E4

Hilton Ct Gdns* SA62 ...66 F6
Hodgson's Rd SA9 ......139 A4
Hoel Llwchwr SA18 ......98 B6
Hoel Y Dyffryn / Dyffryn Rd SA18 ......98 A7
Hoel-y-Felin
  Goodwick / Wdig SA64 ...122 A4
  Scleddau SA65 ......11 B1
Holbrook Rd 4 SA62 ......85 D8
Hole in the Wall 13 SA61 ......125 A5
Hollett Rd SA5 ......160 C4
Holloway SA61 ......125 A5
Holloway Ct SA70 ......135 B3
Holloway Rd SA70 ......135 A3
Holloway Hill SA70 ......135 A3
Holloway Rd SA33 ......92 F5
Hollybush Dr SA2 ......166 B8
Holly La SA73 ......87 D3
Holly St SA8 ......147 E5
Holts Field SA3 ......172 C5
Holyland Dr SA71 ......133 E5
Holyland Rd SA71 ......133 D4
Home Farm Way SA4 ......152 C2
Honddu Pl SA1 ......153 D1
Honeyborough SA73 ......132 A7
Honeyborough Gr SA73 ...132 B7
Honeyborough Ind Est SA73 ......132 B8
Honeyborough Rd SA73 ...132 B7
Honeysuckle Dr SA6 ......153 D2
Hook CP Sch SA62 ......87 C6
Hoo St SA1 ......168 B7
Hop Gdn Rd SA70 ......105 E6
Hopkin St
  Pontardawe SA8 ......147 E5
  Swansea / Abertawe SA5 ...160 C4
Hopshill La SA69 ......134 C3
Horeb Rd
  Kidwelly / Cydweli SA17 ...136 F7
  Swansea / Abertawe SA6 ...153 F1
Horizon Pk SA6 ......161 A6
Horn's La SA61 ......125 A4
Horsepool Rd SA33 ......92 E6
Horton St SA1 ......174 A3
Hosea Row SA1 ......160 D4
Hospital Rd
  Gorseinon SA4 ......158 F8
  Penllergaer SA4 ......151 E1
Hottipass St SA65 ......122 D3
Hounsell Ave SA70 ......113 D6
Howard's Cres SA62 ......68 C5
Howards Way SA4 ......151 C3
Howarth Cl SA73 ......131 C4
Howells Ave 1 SA61 ......125 A4
Howells Cl SA71 ......104 C4
Howells Rd SA2 ......165 C8
Hoyles Cl SA70 ......135 B3
Hubberston VC Prim Sch SA73 ......131 A2
Humphrey St SA1 ......167 B7
Hunters Pk SA70 ......107 A5
Huntingdon Way SA2 ......166 B8
Huntington Cl SA3 ......173 B8
Huntington Ct SA3 ......173 B8
Huntsmans Cove SA3 ......172 E7
Hurelgy Pk SA68 ......134 D8
Hydfron Cl SA33 ......73 A1
Hywel Dda Gdns* SA34 ......126 D3
Hywel Rd SA61 ......124 D5
Hywel Way SA71 ......133 D3

I

Ian's Wlk SA6 ......154 B4
Idris Terr SA6 ......160 E6
Idwal Pl SA5 ......160 B5
Ilston Ho 3 SA1 ......174 A4
Ilston Way SA3 ......173 A7
Imble Cl SA72 ......132 D1
Imble La SA72 ......132 D1
Imble St SA72 ......132 B1
Imogen Pl SA73 ......131 D3
Imperial Ctr SA7 ......161 B7
Incline The SA69 ......134 D4
Incline Way SA69 ......134 D4
India Row SA71 ......104 C4
Inkerman St
  Llanelli SA15 ......148 D5
  Swansea / Abertawe SA1 ...174 C3
Iorwerth St SA5 ......160 C2
Irfon Cres LD5 ......9 C1
Irfon Terr 4 LD5 ......9 D1
Irvine Ct SA3 ......173 B4
Iscennen Rd / Ffordd Is-Cennen 14 SA18 ......98 B7
Iscoed SA15 ......148 B6
Iscoed Rd / Heol Iscoed SA4 ......143 A4
Isfryn Burry Port SA16 ...137 E4
  Llangynog SA33 ......74 C3
Isgraig SA16 ......137 E4
Island Pl SA1 ......148 D5
Islwyn SA14 ......149 E5
Islwyn Rd SA1 ......167 B8
Ismyrddin SA31 ......129 E6
Is Y Bryn SA31 ......128 B8
Is-y-Bryniau SA9 ......100 B8
Is-y-Llyn SA14 ......78 A1
Ivey Pl SA1 ......174 B4
Ivy Bush Ct SA1 ......174 C3
Ivy Chy La SA69 ......134 E7

J

Jackson Dr SA73 ......132 C8
Jackson's Way
  Fishguard & Goodwick SA64 ...11 B2
  Goodwick / Wdig SA64 ...122 A5
James Ct SA1 ......161 D6
James Griffiths Ct SA18 ...98 D7
James John Cl 2 SA67 ...70 E1
James Pk SA68 ......134 C8
James St Gorof SA9 ......139 F8
  Llanelli SA15 ......148 E4
  Milford Haven / Aberdaugleddau SA73 ......131 B3
  Neyland SA73 ......132 B7
Jasmine Cl SA2 ......166 B7
Jason Rd SA71 ......105 B1
Jeffreys Ct SA5 ......160 B5
Jenkins' Cl SA61 ......125 A2
Jericho Rd SA1 ......174 C4
Jersey Rd SA1 ......161 B4
Jersey St SA1 ......160 D1
Jersey Terr SA67 ......70 E1
Jesse Rd SA67 ......70 E1
Jessop Ct SA6 ......153 E4
Jim Harvard Ct 5 SA6 ...161 A8
Job's Well Rd SA31 ......128 C5
Jockey Fields SA61 ......125 B6
Jockey St SA1 ......174 B4
Jogram Ave SA71 ......133 C4
John Lewis St SA73 ......85 F1
John Morgan Cl 7 SA67 ...70 E1
John Penry Cres SA5 ......160 B6
John St
  Carmarthen / Caerfyrddin SA31 ......128 F5
  Llanelli SA15 ......148 D5
  Neyland SA73 ......132 B6
  Swansea / Abertawe, Cockett SA2 ......159 D2
  Swansea / Abertawe SA1 ...174 B4
  The Mumbles / Y Mwmbwls SA3 ......173 A4
Johnston Cty Prim Sch SA62 ......86 E5
Johnston Sta SA62 ......86 D5
Johnstown Cty Prim Sch SA31 ......128 C4
Joiners Rd SA4 ......157 D1
Jolly Rd SA18 ......99 C8
Jones St SA8 ......147 E5
Jones Terr SA1 ......174 A4
Jones' Terr / Teras Jones SA18 ......98 F8
Jordan's Cl SA73 ......131 F6
Jordanston Hill SA65 ......30 D4
Joseph Davies' Cl 6 SA1 ......160 C2
Jubilee Cl 1 SA2 ......50 F8
Jubilee Cres SA10 ......162 F8
Jubilee Ct SA5 ......159 C4
Jubilee Gdns 2 SA67 ......89 E6
Jubilee La SA1 ......158 A8
Juniper Cl SA2 ......166 B8
Jury La SA61 ......124 F5

K

Kavanagh Ct SA72 ......133 A8
Keats Gr
  Haverfordwest / Hwlffordd SA61 ......125 B3
  Swansea / Abertawe SA2 ...165 F7
Keepers Cl SA4 ......152 C2
Keep Hill End SA62 ......66 F6
Keeston Hill SA62 ......67 A6
Keeston La SA62 ......67 C6
Kelvin Rd SA6 ......146 D1
Kemble St SA1 ......166 F5
Kemys Way SA6 ......161 B7
Kendle Dr SA2 ......166 C8
Kenfig Pl SA1 ......161 A2
Kenilworth Pl SA3 ......173 A8
Kennington Cl SA2 ......165 D6
Kensington Cl 2 SA67 ...89 E6
Kensington Rd SA3 ......132 B7
Kensington St 7 SA65 ...122 D3
Kenystyle SA70 ......135 B3
Kerr's Way SA68 ......89 F2
Kesteven St SA70 ......105 D6
Kestrel Rd SA61 ......124 E5
Kew Gdns SA14 ......96 F6
Kidwelly Castle* SA17 ...136 B5
Kidwelly Ind Mus* SA17 ......136 E6
Kidwelly Sta SA17 ......136 A4
Kildare St SA5 ......160 C3
Kilfield Rd SA3 ......172 B5
Kilgetty La SA67 ......90 A3
Kilgetty Sports Club SA68 ......134 B8
Kilgetty Sta SA68 ......134 D8
Killan Rd SA2 ......165 B8
Kiln House La SA70 ......105 E2
Kiln Pk Rd SA67 ......70 E1
Kiln Rd
  Haverfordwest / Hwlffordd SA61 ......125 A5
  Johnston SA62 ......86 E6
Kilns The SA62 ......87 D4
Kilvey Rd SA1 ......174 C5
Kilvey Terr SA1 ......174 C4
Kimberley Cl SA2 ......166 D7
Kimberley Rd SA2 ......166 D7

King Edward Rd SA18 ...99 F6
King Edward's Rd SA1 ...167 A6
King Edward St SA34 ...126 C2
Kingfisher Ct SA15 ......149 A5
King George Ave SA15 ...148 E5
King George Ct SA2 ......166 B3
Kingrosia Pk SA6 ......155 A8
Kingsbridge Bsns Pk SA4 ......158 C8
Kingsbridge Dr SA71 ......133 D4
Kings Ct 8 SA67 ......70 D1
Kings Gdns SA72 ......132 B1
King's Head Rd SA5 ......159 F3
Kings La SA1 ......174 B3
Kings Mead / Dol Y Brenin SA48 ......120 C4
Kingsmere Cl SA62 ......125 C8
Kingsmoor Cl SA69 ......134 D7
Kings Rd Llandybie SA18 ...79 B2
  The Mumbles / Y Mwmbwls SA3 ......173 A4
King's Rd SA20 ......121 D4
King's Road / Heol Y Brenin SA1 ......174 C2
King St
  Carmarthen / Caerfyrddin SA31 ......128 F5
  Laugharne SA33 ......92 F5
  Llandeilo SA19 ......130 D5
  Llandyssul SA44 ......19 E3
  Pembroke Dock / Doc Penfro SA72 ......132 B3
  4 Swansea / Abertawe SA1 ......174 B3
Kingston Rd SA2 ......166 D7
Kingsway SA5 ......159 C4
Kingsway The / Ffordd Y Brennin SA1 ......174 A3
King William St SA72 ...132 D3
Kinley St SA1 ......167 F7
Kitchener Cl SA72 ......132 B2
Kittle Gn SA3 ......171 E7
Kittle Hill La SA3 ......171 E7
Knelston Pl SA5 ......159 F7
Knelston Prim Sch SA3 ...117 A8
Knightston Cl SA70 ......135 D8
Knoll Ave SA2 ......166 E6
Knowling Mead SA70 ...135 B5
Knoyle Dr SA5 ......160 C7
Knoyle St SA5 ......160 C7
Kyfts La SA3 ......114 C3

L

Laburnham Pl SA2 ......166 B6
Laburnum Gr SA61 ......124 E3
Lacques The SA33 ......92 E5
Lady Housty Ave SA3 ...172 E5
Lady Margaret Villas SA2 ......166 E7
Lady's Cross SA62 ......50 D2
Lady St SA17 ......136 B4
Lake Dr SA70 ......106 F5
Lakefield Cl 1 SA15 ......148 D4
Lakefield Pl 1 SA15 ......148 C4
Lakefield Prim Sch SA15 ......148 C4
Lakefield Rd SA15 ......148 C4
Lakeside Tech Pk SA7 ...161 B6
Lake View Cl SA15 ......148 C7
Lakeview Terr SA15 ......148 C7
Lamack Vale SA70 ......135 C6
Lamb La SA2 ......166 E7
Lamborough Cres SA63 ...69 A7
Lamborough La SA62 ......69 C7
Lambourne Dr SA3 ......172 E6
Lambston Hill SA62 ......67 B3
Lambs Well Cl SA3 ......173 B4
Lammas St SA31 ......128 E5
Lampeter Comp Sch / Ysgol Gyfun Llanbedr Pont Steffan SA48 ......120 B4
Lampeter Leisure Ctr SA48 ......120 B4
Lamphey Cty Prim Sch SA71 ......105 A3
Lamphey Sta SA71 ......105 A3
Lampit Way SA65 ......122 D4
Lan Ave 1 SA6 ......160 F8
Lancaster Ct SA5 ......159 D5
Lan Coed SA1 ......161 D5
Landeg St SA6 ......160 E5
Lan Deri SA1 ......161 C5
Landor Ave SA2 ......165 F7
Lando Rd SA16 ......108 E4
Landor Dr SA4 ......150 D1
Landsdowne Ct SA5 ......159 C3
Langcliff Pk SA3 ......173 C3
Langdon Rd / Heol Langdon
  Swansea / Abertawe SA1 ...167 F7
  Swansea / Abertawe SA1 ...168 A6
Langer Way SA6 ......146 E1
Langford Rd SA62 ......86 E5
Langland Bay Rd SA3 ...172 F3
Langland Cl SA3 ......173 A4
Langland Court Rd SA3 ...172 F4
Langland Mews SA15 ...148 E3
Langland Rd
  Llanelli SA15 ......148 C3
  The Mumbles / Y Mwmbwls SA3 ......173 A4
Langland Terr SA3 ......166 E5
Langland Villas SA3 ......173 A4
Lan Manor SA6 ......160 E8
Lansdown SA3 ......172 F4
Lan St SA6 ......153 F1

Lapwing Rd SA15 ......148 B5
Larch Cres SA14 ......141 A2
Larch Rd SA73 ......131 E4
Lark Pl SA5 ......159 E7
Larkspur Cl 6 SA67 ...89 E6
Larkspur Dr SA3 ......172 E2
Latimer Ct SA5 ......159 E5
Latimer Rd SA19 ......130 E5
Lauderdale Rd 1 SA73 ...99 E7
Laugharne Castle★ SA33 .92 F5
Laugharne Cl SA71 .....133 C6
Laugharne Ct SA4 ......166 A6
Laugharne VC Prim Sch
  SA33 ......92 A4
Laurel Dr
  Ammanford / Rhydaman
  SA18 ......98 D7
  Haverfordwest / Hwlffordd
  SA61 ......124 E3
  Waunarlwydd SA5 ......158 D4
Laurel Pl SA2 ......166 B6
Lavinia Dr SA72 ......132 C1
Lawrence Terr 2 SA15 ...148 E5
Lawrenny St SA73 ......132 C6
Laws St SA72 ......132 C2
Layton Cl 5 LD5 ......9 D1
Leach Way SA70 ......135 D5
Le-Breos SA3 ......165 F1
Le-Breos Ave SA2 ......166 E6
Lee St SA1 ......167 F7
Leonardston Rd SA73 ...104 A8
Leonardston View SA73 ..132 A7
Letterston VC Sch SA62 ..50 E8
Leven Cl SA62 ......87 D6
Lewis Ave SA9 ......100 B8
Lewis Cres SA14 ......149 D5
Lewis St
  Llanfihangel-ar-Arth SA44 ..19 E3
  Pembroke Dock / Doc Penfro
  SA72 ......132 C2
  Swansea / Abertawe, Sketty
  SA2 ......166 C6
  Swansea / Abertawe, St Thomas
  SA1 ......167 F7
Leyshan Wlk SA3 ......172 E8
Leyshon Rd
  Gwaun-Cae-Gurwen SA18 ...99 D7
  Ynysmeudwy SA8 ......147 F6
Leys La SA3 ......66 E3
Libanus Rd SA4 ......151 C1
Libby Rd SA3 ......173 C3
Libby Way SA3 ......173 C3
Liddeston Cl SA73 ......131 A4
Liddeston Valley SA73 ...131 A4
Lighthouse Dr SA73 ......103 F7
Lilac Cl
  Milford Haven / Aberdaugleddau
  SA73 ......131 E4
  The Mumbles / Y Mwmbwls
  SA3 ......172 F8
Lilliput La SA3 ......173 B8
Lime Gr Killay SA2 ......165 D7
  2 Lampeter Velfrey SA34 ..109 F7
Lime Gr Ave SA31 ......128 D6
Lime Kiln La SA3 ......172 B6
Limekiln Rd SA3 ......173 A5
Limeslade Ct SA3 ......173 C3
Limeslade Dr SA3 ......173 C3
Lime St SA4 ......151 C2
Lime Tree Gr 6 SA6 ...161 A8
Lincoln St 5 SA44 ......19 E3
Linden Ave SA3 ......173 A8
Lindsway Pk SA61 ......125 C7
Links Ct SA3 ......172 E3
Linkside SA3 ......172 E4
Linkside Dr SA3 ......171 E4
Links The SA16 ......137 B2
Link The SA2 ......166 A5
Linney Way SA73 ......131 E5
Lion St SA1 ......160 C2
Lion Way SA7 ......161 B7
Little Bridge St 1 SA31 ..128 F4
Little Castle Gr SA73 ....85 D2
Little Gam St SA1 ......174 A2
Little Wr St SA31 ......128 F5
Llain Delyn 4 SA31 .....93 C7
Llanbed Ind Est SA48 ...120 C7
Llandafen Rd SA14 ......149 B5
Llanddowror VC Sch
  SA33 ......73 A1
Llandeilo Prim Sch / Ysgol
  Gynradd Llandeilo
  SA19 ......130 D6
Llandeilo Rd
  Cross Hands SA14 ......97 B8
  Cwmamman SA18 ......80 A1
  Glanaman SA18 ......99 C8
  Llandovery / Llanymddyfri
  SA20 ......121 B4
  1 Llandybie SA18 ......79 A2
Llandeilo Rd / Heol Llandeilo
  SA14 ......78 C1
Llandeilo Rd Ind Est
  SA18 ......79 B3
Llandeilo Sta SA19 ......130 E6
Llandovery Castle (remains
  of)★ SA20 ......121 D4
Llandovery Coll / Coleg
  Llanymddyfri SA20 ...121 C5
Llandovery Hospl / Ysbyty
  Llanymddyfri SA20 ...121 D5
Llandovery Sta SA20 ...121 C5
Llandovery Theatre
  SA20 ......121 D5
Llandybie Cty Prim Sch
  SA18 ......79 A2
Llandybie Rd SA18 ......98 B8

Llandybie Sta SA18 .....79 B2
Llandyry SA14 ......141 A2
Llandysul CP Sch SA44 ..19 E3
Llandysul Swimming Pool
  SA44 ......19 E3
Lloyd's Terr SA14 ......129 E7
Llanedi Rd Llanedi SA4 ...97 D1
  Pontarddulais SA4 ......143 A7
Llanelli Ent Workshops
  SA15 ......148 B3
Llanelli Sta SA15 ......148 D3
Llanelli Workshops
  SA14 ......149 A3
Llanerch Cotts SA15 ....148 E7
Llanerch Cres SA4 ......151 B3
Llanerch Rd
  Dunvant SA2 ......165 D8
  Swansea / Abertawe SA1 ..161 B3
Llanerch Terr SA15 ......148 E7
Llanfaes SA9 ......139 F8
Llanfair Gdns SA3 ......173 A6
Llanfair Rd
  Lampeter / Llanbedr Pont Steffan
  SA48 ......120 E5
  Llandovery / Llanymddyfri
  SA20 ......121 D5
Llanfynydd VAP Sch
  SA32 ......61 A6
Llangadog Rd CP Sch SA19 .63 E7
Llangadog Sta SA19 ....136 E6
Llangain CP Sch SA33 ...75 D7
Llangan Rd SA34 ......126 C3
Llangennech Jun & Inf Schs
  SA14 ......142 C1
Llangennech Sta SA14 ..150 C7
Llangiwg Prim Sch SA8 ..147 F6
Llangloffan Farmhouse
  Cheese Ctr★ SA62 .....30 B3
Llangorse Rd SA5 ......160 B5
Llangunnor CP Sch
  SA31 ......129 A3
Llangwm SA5 ......159 F6
Llangwm CP Sch SA62 ....87 E4
Llangyfelach Prim Sch
  SA5 ......153 D8
Llangyfelach Rd SA5 ....160 C5
Llangyfelach St SA1 ....160 D1
Llangyndeyrn CP Sch
  SA17 ......76 C1
Llangynin CP Sch SA33 ...73 A7
Llangynog CP Sch SA33 ..74 C3
Llanion Cotts SA72 ......133 A8
Llanllienwen Cl
  Swansea / Abertawe SA6 ..153 F4
  Ynysforgan SA6 ......154 A4
Llanllienwen Rd
  Swansea / Abertawe SA6 ..153 F3
  Ynysforgan SA6 ......154 A3
Llanmiloe Cty Prim Sch
  SA33 ......92 A4
Llanmorlais Prim Sch
  SA4 ......156 B1
Llannant Rd SA4 ......150 F5
Llannion Pk Ind Est
  SA72 ......132 D4
Llannon Rd
  Cross Hand SA14 ......96 F6
  Llanelli Rural SA14 ......141 A4
  Pontyberem SA15 ......96 B5
Llanrhian Rd SA62 ......28 E4
Llanrhidian Cvn Pk SA3 ..115 F3
Llanrhidian Prim Sch
  SA3 ......115 D2
Llanrwtyd Sta LD5 ......9 D1
Llansadwrn Cty Prim Sch
  SA19 ......43 C2
Llansaint CP Sch SA17 ...94 B3
Llansamlet Ind Est
  Swansea / Abertawe SA6 ..160 F5
  Swansea / Abertawe SA7 ..161 B4
Llansamlet Sta SA7 ......161 F8
Llansteffan Rd SA31 ....128 C1
Llanstephan Castle★
  SA33 ......93 E5
Llanwnen Rd SA48 ......120 A4
Llanwrda Prim Sch / Ysgol
  Gynradd Llanwrda SA19 .43 D2
Llanwrda Sta SA19 ......43 E2
Llanybydder Cty Prim Sch
  SA40 ......21 D6
Llanychllwydog CP Sch
  SA65 ......32 C4
Llancrwys CP Sch SA19 ..23 D7
Llan-Y-newydd SA4 .....156 F3
Llarwydden Cl SA4 ......152 C2
Llechyfedach SA14 ......96 F7
Llechyfedach CP Sch / Ysgol
  Gynradd Llechyfedach
  SA14 ......96 F7
Llethri Rd SA14 ......141 A1
Llety Rd SA14 ......96 F6
Llewellyn Dr SA71 ......133 B3
Llewellyn Rd SA4 ......151 F2
Llewellyn St / Stryd
  Llewellyn 14 SA15 ....148 D4
Llewelyn Circ SA1 ......167 B8
Llewelyn Park Dr SA6 ...160 E7
Llewelyn St SA2 ......166 C6
Llewitna Terr SA5 ......159 B6
Lliedi Cres SA15 ......148 E6
Lliw Cotts SA4 ......151 D6
Lliw Valley Cl / Clos
  Dyffrynlliw SA4 ......158 C6
Llon Cardi Bach 2 SA43 ..16 A5
Lloyd George La SA71 ..133 B3
Lloyd Rd SA5 ......160 C5

Lloyd St
  17 Ammanford / Rhydaman
  SA18 ......98 B7
  Pontardawe SA8 ......147 B2
Lloyd St / Stryd Lloyd
  SA15 ......148 C5
Lloyd Terr SA38 ......119 D6
Lluest-yr-bryn 1 SA31 ..128 F6
Llundain Fach SA14 ....140 E1
Llwyfan Cerrig Sta SA33 ..58 D5
Llwyn Afanc SA6 ......153 F5
Llwyn Arosfa SA2 ......166 C7
Llwyn Bedw SA5 ......159 D4
Llwyn Brwydrau SA7 ...162 A6
Llwyn Carw SA6 ......153 F5
Llwyncelyn
  Capel Hendre SA18 ......97 D6
  Llanelli SA15 ......148 E4
  Mathry SA62 ......30 B2
Llwyn Celyn SA5 ......159 D4
Llwyncelyn Ave SA4 ....143 D4
Llwyncelyn Rd SA18 ....99 E6
Llwyncelyn Rd / Heol
  Llwyncelyn SA18 ......98 F8
Llwyncethin Rd SA5 ....160 A3
Llwyn Cl SA15 ......148 F5
Llwyncrwn SA15 ......95 E3
Llwyn-Crwn Rd SA7 ....161 D7
Llwyncyfarthwch SA15 ..149 A5
Llwynderw
  Gorseinon SA4 ......151 B1
  Three Crosses SA4 ......157 E1
Llwyn Derw
  Pontardawe SA8 ......147 E4
  Swansea / Abertawe SA5 ..159 D4
Llwynderw Cl SA2 ......166 B1
Llwynderw Dr SA3 ......173 B8
Llwyn Eithin SA5 ......159 D4
Llwyneryr Unit Hospl
  SA6 ......153 E2
Llwyn Helyg SA5 ......159 D5
Llwynhendy Jun Sch
  SA14 ......149 D5
Llwynhendy Rd / Heol
  Llwynhendy SA14 ......149 D4
Llwyn Hen Rd SA18 ......99 D5
Llwynifan SA14 ......142 B2
Llwyn Mawr Cl SA2 .....166 B8
Llwynmawr La SA4 ......157 C5
Llwyn Mawr La SA2 .....159 B1
Llwyn Mawr Rd
  Swansea / Abertawe SA2 ..159 B1
  SA2 ......166 C8
Llwyn Meredydd SA31 ..129 A7
Llwyn-Nant SA18 ......99 D4
Llwynon SA6 ......146 E1
Llwyn On SA5 ......159 D4
Llwyn Rd SA18 ......99 D5
Llwyn Rhedyn SA2 ......166 B8
Llwynwhilwg Terr 3
  SA14 ......148 F4
Llwyn Y Bioden SA6 ....153 F5
Llwyn-y-Bryn
  Ammanford / Rhydaman
  SA18 ......98 B8
  Neath / Castell-Nedd
  SA10 ......162 C6
Llwyn Y Gog
  Cwmrhydyceirw SA6 ....154 A5
  Swansea / Abertawe SA6 ..153 F5
Llwyn Y Golomen SA6 ..154 A5
Llwyn Y Graig SA4 ......151 F1
Llwyn-Y-Mor SA3 ......172 E4
Llwyn Yr Eos SA14 ......149 B6
Llwyn-Yr-Eos SA4 ......153 E2
Llwyn Yr Hebog SA6 ....154 A5
Llwyn Yr Iar SA4 ......154 A5
Llwyn Yr Ynys SA14 ....149 C4
Llygad-yr-Haul
  Burry Port SA16 ......137 B3
  Carmarthen / Caerfyrddin
  SA31 ......129 B3
Llynfa Rd SA4 ......157 A4
Llyn Llech Owain Ctry Pk★
  SA14 ......78 B2
Llyn Tircoed SA4 ......152 C5
Llyn Y Fran SA44 ......19 E3

Llys = court

Llys Aaron SA4 ......143 C4
Llys Afallon SA17 ......136 A5
Llys Alys SA15 ......148 E5
Llys Andrew SA10 ......162 F6
Llys Aneirin SA4 ......158 D8
Llys Baldwin SA4 ......158 B6
Llys Bethel SA14 ......149 C5
Llys Brynteg SA4 ......151 B3
Llys Caermedi SA31 ....129 B6
Llys Caradog SA14 ......149 D5
Llys Cennech SA14 ......142 C1
Llys Cilsanws SA14 ......149 B8
Llys-Coed SA7 ......155 B1
Llys Dewi SA38 ......119 B6
Llys Dewi Sant
  Gorseinon SA4 ......151 C2
  Swansea / Abertawe SA4 ..174 A3
Llys Dol SA6 ......154 A2
Llys Dur SA6 ......154 A2
Llys Dwrgi SA6 ......162 B8
Llys Eithin SA14 ......97 C8
Llys Elba SA4 ......158 B6
Llys Felin Newydd SA7 ..161 C6
Llys Fran SA15 ......148 E7

Llys Fredrick Jones
  SA9 ......139 C7
Llys Ger Y Llan SA4 ....143 D3
Llys Glanrafon SA8 ....147 E4
Llys Glan Y Mor 2
  SA15 ......148 C3
Llys Gwalia SA4 ......151 D2
Llys Gwenci SA7 ......162 B8
Llys Gwenllian SA17 ...136 B5
Llys Gwernen
  Cwmrhydyceirw SA6 ....154 A2
  Swansea / Abertawe SA6 ..153 F2
Llysgwyn SA6 ......153 C2
Llys Gwynfaen SA4 .....150 F2
Llysgwyn Terr SA4 ......143 D5
Llys Hebog SA7 ......162 B8
Llys Hendre SA14 ......150 B7
Llys Holcwm SA17 ......93 F4
Llys Iwan 10 SA18 ......98 C7
Llys Jernegan 2 SA1 ...174 C2
Llys John Davies SA1 ...174 B4
Llys-Le-Breos SA3 ......165 F1
Llys Llanfair SA20 ......121 D6
Llys Llwyfen SA7 ......154 D1
Llys Lotwen SA18 ......97 E6
Llys Mair SA6 ......137 F2
Llys Moreia SA5 ......160 C6
Llysmorfa SA31 ......129 A4
Llys Nant Fer SA18 ......99 D7
Llysnewydd 4 SA15 ....148 C3
Llysonen Rd SA31 ......128 A3
Llys Onnen 2 SA64 .....122 A4
Llys Owen SA43 ......118 D4
Llys Pat Chown / Pat Chown
  Ct SA4 ......148 E4
Llys Penallt 4 SA15 ....148 F6
Llys Pencrug SA19 ......130 E6
Llys Pendderi SA14 .....149 F5
Llys Penpant SA6 ......153 C2
Llys Pentre SA5 ......160 D4
Llys Perl SA6 ......154 F3
Llys Sant Teilo SA5 .....153 B2
Llys Seion SA14 ......96 C8
Llys Tawel SA9 ......138 F1
Llys-Teg SA2 ......165 D8
Llys-uchaf
  Birchgrove SA7 ......155 B1
  Swansea / Abertawe SA7 ..162 B8
Llys Warner SA15 ......148 E7
Llys Y Brenin SA4 ......158 B8
Llys-y-Bryn SA7 ......162 B8
Llys-y-Coed
  Burry Port SA16 ......137 A3
  Loughor SA4 ......150 D1
Llys Y Dderwen
  Llangennech SA14 ......150 B7
  Pont Henri SA15 ......95 F4
Llys-y-Deri SA18 ......98 D7
Llys Y Drindod SA15 ...148 E3
Llys Y Felin
  Llangennech SA14 ......142 B1
  St Clears / Sanclêr
  SA33 ......74 B4
Llys-y-Felin SA5 ......160 C3
Llys-y-Ferin SA4 ......77 B8
Llys-y-Frân Ctry
  Pk★ SA63 ......52 C4
Llys-y-Frân Visitor
  Ctr★ SA63 ......52 C3
Llys Y Gof SA15 ......148 C4
Llys-y-graig SA10 ......162 F8
Llys-y-Llyfrgell 6
  SA16 ......137 D2
Llys Y Morwr SA15 .....148 D4
Llys Y Nant 2 SA31 ....128 F6
Llys Ynyscedwyn SA9 ..139 D8
Llys Y Pobydd SA15 ....148 C3
Llys Yr Ardd
  Morriston / Treforris SA6 ..154 A2
  Swansea / Abertawe SA6 ..153 F2
Llys Yr Onnen SA14 ....149 A8
Llys Yr Orsaf 7 SA15 ...148 C4
Llys Yr Ysgol SA18 ......97 E6
Llys-y-Waun SA7 ......155 B1
Llythrid Ave SA2 ......166 E6
Lochturffin Cross SA62 ..29 C2
Lodge Cl The SA4 ......166 A7
Lodge The 4 SA1 ......174 A4
Login Rd SA4 ......159 A3
Lon Aber SA15 ......148 F4
Lon Alfa SA7 ......165 F8
Lon Bedwen SA2 ......166 D8
Lon Beili Glas SA18 .....99 D6
Lon Bele SA44 ......19 F7
Lon Brydwen SA4 ......151 B1
Lon Brynawel SA7 ......161 F6
Lon Bryngwyn SA2 .....166 E8
Lon Bryn-Mawr / Brynmawr
  La 9 SA18 ......98 B7
Lon Bronneuadd SA18 ..99 D7
Lon Cadog SA2 ......166 E7
Lon Cae Banc SA4 ......150 D7
Lon Cae Ffynnon 4
  SA19 ......130 D6
Lon Camlad SA6 ......160 E8
Lon Caron SA4 ......166 E7
Lon Carreg Bica SA7 ...162 B8
Lon Cedwyn SA2 ......166 E7
Lon Ceiriog SA14 ......149 D5
Lon Cendy SA33 ......57 C2
Lon Channing 7 SA44 ...19 E3
Lon Clychavr Gog SA31 ..129 E7
Lon Coed Bran SA2 .....166 E8
Lon Coed Parc SA2 .....166 E8
Lon Cothi SA2 ......159 E1
Lon Cwmgwyn SA2 .....166 E6
Lon Cynfor SA2 ......166 E7

Lon Cynlais SA2 ......166 D7
Lon-cywyn SA33 ......74 B5
Lon Dan-y-Coed SA2 ...166 E6
Lon Ddewi SA33 ......73 E7
Londeg SA8 ......147 D6
Lon Derw SA2 ......166 D8
London Rd SA72 ......132 D3
London Rd Ind Est SA72 .132 F3
London Rd Mall The
  SA72 ......133 B8
Lon Draenen SA2 ......166 C7
Lon Draenog SA6 ......153 F5
Lon Drewen SA38 ......119 A7
Lon Einon SA4 ......151 F2
Lon Eithrym SA6 ......154 D8
Lon Enfys SA7 ......161 D6
Lone Rd SA6 ......146 D1
Lon Fair SA33 ......127 D3
Lon Fedwen 8 SA44 .....19 E3
Lon Ffos - Las SA17 ....109 B8
Long Acre SA3 ......172 B6
Long Acre Ct SA3 ......172 B6
Long Acre Gdns SA3 ...165 F1
Long Acre Rd SA31 ....128 F6
Lon Gaer SA4 ......151 F2
Longdown St SA43 ......118 B2
Lon Ger-y-Coed
  Ammanford / Rhydaman
  SA18 ......98 D7
  Swansea / Abertawe SA2 ..166 E8
Longfellow Cl 1 SA61 ...125 B3
Longfield
  Manorbier SA70 ......106 A1
  Tenby / Dinbych-y-pysgod
  SA70 ......135 A3
Longford Cres SA1 ......168 A7
Longhouse Gdns SA62 ...69 B5
Long La
  The Havens SA62 ......66 E1
  Walwyn's Castle SA62 ....85 C5
Long Mains SA71 ......104 C4
Long Oaks Ave SA2 ....166 E6
Long Oaks Ct SA2 ......166 E7
Long Oaks Mews SA2 ..166 E7
Long Ridge SA1 ......174 A5
Longridge Rd SA66 .....53 A1
Long Row Llanelli SA14 ..140 F1
  Llanelli SA15 ......148 E6
Long Shepherds Dr
  SA3 ......172 E4
Long St SA42 ......13 E4
Longstone SA70 ......106 A3
Longstone La SA71 ......111 B3
Long View Rd SA6 ......153 D1
Lon Gwendraeth SA6 ...160 E8
Lon Gwesyn SA7 ......155 A1
Lon Gwynfryn SA2 ......166 E7
Lon Hafren
  St Clears / Sanclêr
  SA33 ......127 C4
  Swansea / Abertawe SA6 ..160 E8
Lon Heddwch
  Craig-cefn-parc SA6 ....146 B2
  Swansea / Abertawe SA7 ..161 E6
Lon Hir
  Carmarthen / Caerfyrddin
  SA31 ......128 E6
  Pontardawe SA8 ......147 F4
Lon Hywel SA34 ......126 C4
Lon Illtyd SA2 ......166 E7
Lon Iorwg SA2 ......166 C7
Lon Irfon SA2 ......159 E1
Lon Ithon SA2 ......160 E8
Lon Killan SA2 ......165 C8
Lon Lash SA2 ......162 C2
Lonlas Bsns Pk SA10 ...162 D7
Lonlas Village Workshops
  SA10 ......162 D8
Lonlas Villas SA10 ......162 C7
Lon Letty 3 SA44 ......19 E3
Lon Llwyd 1 SA18 ......99 B8
Lon Llysalaw SA33 ......127 B5
Lon Llys Havard SA18 ...98 C6
Lon Mafon SA2 ......166 C6
Lon Masarn SA2 ......166 C8
Lon Mefus SA2 ......166 D8
Lon Menai SA7 ......155 A1
Lon Nedd SA6 ......160 E8
Lon Ogwen SA2 ......155 A1
Lon Olchfa SA2 ......166 A6
Lon Penfro SA6 ......154 A4
Lon Penpound / Penpound
  La SA18 ......98 F8
Lon Pen-y-Coed SA2 ...159 D1
Lon Pen Y-coed SA2 ...166 E8
Lon Rhys SA19 ......130 C2
Lon Rhys Pritchard
  SA20 ......121 C4
Lon Sawdde SA6 ......160 E8
Lon Sutcliffe La SA4 ...158 B5
Lon Tanyrallt SA8 ......147 E3
Lon Teify SA2 ......159 E1
Lon Tir-y-Dail / Tir-y-Dail
  La 11 SA18 ......98 B7
Lon Towy SA2 ......159 D1
Lon Tyr Haul SA2 ......161 F6
Lon Wesley 9 SA44 .....19 E3
Lon Y Bedydd / Baptist La 18
  SA18 ......98 B7
Lon-y-Coed SA8 ......147 D6
Lon Y Derwen
  Llanelli Rural SA15 ......140 E1
  Llanelli SA15 ......148 E8
Lon Y Deri SA33 ......93 D7
Lon Y Derwydd SA18 ...99 C8

Lon-y-Felin SA18 ....98 B5
Lon-y-Gruglas SA18 .....98 A6
Lon Y Maes SA14 ....149 B6
Lon Y Parc / Park La
  SA18 ....99 D8
Lon Y Plas SA31 ....128 C2
Lon-y-Prior SA33 ....127 E3
Lon Yr Eglwys SA14 ....141 A2
Lon Yr Ysgol SA32 ......75 F2
Lon Yr Ysgol SA14 .....149 A7
Lon Yr Ysgol SA14 .....150 C7
Lon-y-Wern SA8 ....147 F3
Lord Nelson Ho SA1 ....174 B4
Lords Mdw View SA71 ..133 D4
Lota Pk Rd SA65 ....122 C3
Lotwen Rd / Heol Lotwen
  SA18 ....97 D6
Loughor Castle ★ SA4 ..157 D8
Loughor Comm SA4 .....151 B2
Loughor Rd SA4 ....158 B8
Loveston Cty Prim Sch
  SA68 ....89 A4
Lower Banwell St 6
  SA6 ....160 F8
Lower Colbren Rd SA18 ..99 D6
Lower Cross Rd SA15 ...148 F5
Lower Dell The 1 SA15 .148 C7
Lower Frog SA14 ....135 E4
Lower La SA68 ....105 C8
Lower Lamphey Rd
  SA71 ....133 D3
Lower Mwldan 3 SA43 .118 C3
Lower New Hos SA9 ....138 A1
Lower Pantteg SA9 .....139 A4
Lower Pk Rd SA70 .....135 D5
Lower Quay Rd SA62 ....87 D6
Lower Rd SA20 ....121 C3
Lower Row SA71 ....133 C6
Lower Station Rd 10
  SA18 ....99 B8
Lower St Mary's St 8
  SA42 ....13 E4
Lower Thornton SA7 ....131 C7
Lower Trostre Rd SA15 .148 F5
Lower Wern Rd SA9 ....139 B6
Lowless SA71 ....133 C2
Lucas Rd SA7 ....155 A5
Lucy Rd / Heol Lucy
  SA10 ....162 D7
Lucy Walters Cl SA73 ...87 A3
Lundy Cl SA73 ....131 E5
Lundy Dr SA3 ....172 F7
Lundy View SA71 ......105 A1
Lunnon Cl SA3 ....170 F8
Luton Terr 4 SA15 ....148 C7
Lydbrook Ct 2 SA1 ....160 C2
Lydford Ave SA1 ......174 C4
Lynden SA9 ....138 D1
Lyndhurst Ave SA68 ...106 C8
Lynne Brianne Visitor Ctr★
  SA20 ....8 A3
Lynn St SA5 ....160 B2
Lynsdale Rd SA5 ......160 C4
Lynton Bungalow SA16 .137 F5
Lynton Ct SA3 ....172 E6
Lyric Ct SA8 ....147 E4
Lyserry La SA71 ....111 D4

M

Mabon Cl SA4 ....150 F3
Machynys Rd SA15 ....148 E1
Mackworth Ct 3 SA1 ..174 B3
Mackworth Terr SA1 ...174 C3
McRitchie Pl SA5 .....159 F3
Madoc Pl SA1 ....174 A2
Madoc St SA1 ....174 A2
Maen-dedwydd Rd SA62 .51 C6
Maengwyn SA8 ....100 B1
Maengwynne SA15 ....140 B1
Maenol Glasfryn SA14 .150 B7
Maenor Helyg
  Burry Port SA16 ......137 A3
  Pembrey & Bury Port Town
  SA16 ....108 F3
Maerdy Rd SA18 ....98 B5
Maes-Ar-Ddafen Rd
  SA14 ....149 C4
Maes Awel 1 SA65 .....30 F5
Maes Awelon SA32 .....61 A2
Maes Briallu SA7 ......161 F7
Maes Brynglas 6 SA33 ..59 A3
Maes Cader SA39 ......39 B6
Maescanner Rd SA14 ..149 B7
Maescelyn SA19 ....42 C3
Maes Collen SA6 ......153 F3
Maes Conwy SA14 .....149 B6
Maescynog SA9 ....138 F1
Maes Dafydd SA4 .....158 B8
Maesderi Hendy SA4 ..142 F4
Maes 4 Llandyfaelog SA32 75 F3
Maes-Deri SA1 ....161 D5
Maes Derwen SA14 ....97 C7
Maes Derwenydda SA39 .39 B7
Maes Dewi
  Carmarthen / Caerfyrddin
  SA31 ....128 B5
  St David's / Tyddewi SA62 .123 D5
Maesdolau SA32 ....75 F2
Maesdyfed SA62 ......123 D4
Maesegryn SA35 ....35 E3
Maes Elfryn 1 SA19 ...130 D6
Maes Elwyn John SA68 .89 C3
Maes Ernin SA62 ......29 F5

Maes Ewan SA62 ....48 C3
Maes Gareth Edwards
  SA18 ....99 D7
Maesglas
  Cardigan / Aberteifi SA43 .118 E5
  Llandovery / Llanymddyfri
  SA20 ....121 D5
  Penygroes SA14 ....97 D7
  Pontyates / Pont-iets SA15 .95 D4
Maes Glas SA4 ....151 B1
Maes Glasnant
  Llandyfaelog SA31 .....75 F4
  Llangunnor SA31 ......76 A4
Maesglas Rd SA5 ....160 B3
Maes Golau SA15 .....148 F8
Maesgriffith SA33 .....93 E5
Maesgrug SA4 ....11 B3
Maesgwyn SA15 ....95 D4
Maesgwyn Dr SA4 ....143 C4
Maesgwynne Rd SA65 .122 C3
Maesgwyn Rd SA4 ....143 C4
Maes Hafren SA15 .....15 B1
Maes-henffordd SA43 .118 E5
Maeshyfryd SA43 .....118 A4
Maes Ingli 3 SA42 ....13 E4
Maes-Lan SA7 ....161 F6
Maesllan SA48 ....120 B5
Maesllawddog 1 SA43 .16 A5
Maes-llewelyn 2 SA31 .129 A6
Maes Llewelyn SA18 ...98 F8
Maes Lliedi SA15 .....148 F8
Maesllwyn SA18 ......98 B8
Maes Maddock SA4 ...151 B1
Maes Margam / Margam Pl
  SA15 ....148 E4
Maes Marlog SA38 ....119 E4
Maes Meigan SA41 ....34 F5
Maes Meillion SA7 ....161 F7
Maesmynach SA43 ....118 B3
Maesolbri 2 SA33 .....93 C7
Maes Penrhyn SA14 ...149 B6
Maespiode SA18 ....79 A2
Maesquarre Rd / Ffordd
  Maescwarrau SA18 ....98 D6
Maes Rd / Heol Maes
  SA14 ....150 C8
Maes Sant Teilo SA5 ..153 B2
Maes St SA1 ....167 F7
Maes Teg SA4 ....143 D5
Maesteg St SA1 ......174 C4
Maestir SA15 ....148 F7
Maestir Rd SA48 ......120 B3
Maes Tomos SA17 ....109 B8
Maestref SA15 ....148 F8
Maes Ty Cwrdd / Meadow Ct
  SA14 ....149 D4
Maes Ty Gwyn SA14 ..142 C1
Maeswerdd SA15 .....148 F8
Maesybedol SA18 .....99 B8
Maes-y-berllan
  Ammanford / Rhydaman
  SA18 ....98 C6
  Llangyndeyrn SA17 ....95 C8
Maesybont SA18 ......98 F8
Maesybont CP Sch SA14 .78 B3
Maesybryn SA66 ......70 F8
Maes Y Bryn SA33 ....127 E7
Maes-y-Bryn SA6 ....153 F2
Maes-y-Capel SA16 ...137 B3
Maes Y Celyn SA4 ....157 D1
Maes-y-Cnwce 1 SA42 .13 E4
Maesycoed
  Ammanford / Rhydaman
  SA18 ....98 D7
  Cardigan / Aberteifi SA43 .118 E6
Maes-y-Coed
  Gorseinon SA4 ....158 B8
  Llanelli SA15 ....148 B6
  Swansea / Abertawe SA6 .153 F2
Maesycoed Rd
  Godregraig SA8 ....100 B1
  Lampeter / Llanbedr Pont Steffan
  SA48 ....120 C6
Maes-y-Coleg SA20 ..121 C5
Maesycwm SA9 ......138 F1
Maes-y-Dail SA18 .....98 A4
Maes-y-darren SA9 ...139 C6
Maesydderwen
  Beulah SA38 ....17 B4
  Llangennech SA14 ....142 D1
  Ystradgynlais SA9 ....139 E7
Maes-y-Dderwen
  Bronwydd SA33 ......58 E3
  Carmarthen / Caerfyrddin
  SA31 ....128 D4
  Swansea / Abertawe, Llangyfelach
  SA6 ....153 B2
  Swansea / Abertawe,
  Llwynbrwydrau SA7 ..162 A6
Maesydderwen Comp Sch
  SA9 ....139 E7
Maes Y Dderwen Gdns
  SA9 ....139 E7
Maesyderi SA15 ....96 B6
Maes Y Deri SA18 .....99 E8
Maes-y-Deri
  Gowerton / Tre-gwyr SA4 .158 A6
  Lampeter / Llanbedr Pont Steffan
  SA48 ....120 B6
Maes Y Deri SA7 .....154 D1
Maes-y-Dre SA20 .....121 D4
Maesydre Ind Est LD5 ..9 D1
Maes Y Farchnad 2
  SA19 ....130 E6
Maes Y Fedwen SA6 ..153 F3

Maesyfelin
  Lampeter / Llanbedr Pont Steffan
  SA48 ....120 C6
  Pontyberem SA15 .....96 A6
Maes Y Felin SA5 .....159 D5
Maesyffynnon
  Dinas Cross SA42 .....13 A3
  Ferryside SA17 ....93 F5
  Trimsaran SA17 ......109 B7
Maes Y Ffynnon SA14 ..96 F5
Maes Y Forwen SA2 ..48 C3
Maes Y Frenni SA41 ..34 F4
Maes Y Fron 18 SA18 ..99 B8
Maesyglyn SA18 ......98 F8
Maes Y Gollen SA2 ...166 B6
Maesygors SA14 ......97 C8
Maes Y Gors SA15 ...148 D4
Maes Y Gruffydd Rd
  SA2 ....166 C8
Maes Y Gwernen Cl
  SA6 ....153 D1
Maes Y Gwernen Dr
  SA6 ....153 D1
Maes-y-Gwernen Rd
  SA6 ....153 D4
Maes-y-Hedydd SA62 .123 D4
Maes Y Mynach SA62 .123 E4
Maes Y Neuadd 5 SA43 .16 A3
Maes Y Parc
  Kidwelly / Cydweli SA17 .136 B3
  Swansea / Abertawe SA6 .159 D5
Maes-yr-Awel SA16 ...108 E4
Maes Yr Awel SA7 ....161 F7
Maes-yr-Efail
  Dunvant SA2 ....165 D8
  Gorseinon SA4 ....151 B1
Maes Yr Efail SA14 ...150 B7
Maes Yr Eglwys SA2 ..48 C3
Maes-yr-Eglwys SA17 ..94 B3
Maes-yr-Eithin SA7 ...155 B1
Maesyrhaf
  Cardigan / Aberteifi SA43 .118 A4
  Cross Hands SA14 .....97 B7
  Llanelli Rural SA15 ...109 E4
  Llanelli SA15 ....148 F7
Maes-yr-Haf SA18 .....98 A7
Maes-yr-Haf SA4 .....156 E4
Maes-yr-Haf SA7 .....161 F6
Maes-yr-Helyg SA18 ...79 B1
Maesyrhendre SA18 ...99 B8
Maesyrodyn SA44 .....20 B8
Maes-yr-Onnen SA6 ..154 A3
Maes Yr Orsaf 4 SA43 .16 A5
Maes Yr Ysgol
  3 Abergwili SA32 .....59 A3
  1 Templeton SA67 ....89 E7
Maes Y Wennol SA31 .128 B5
Maesywerin SA18 ......99 D7
Maes-y-Wern SA17 ....95 D1
Magdalen St SA1 .....174 A2
Maidens Gr SA18 .....79 A2
Main Rd SA73 ....103 E8
Main St
  Fishguard / Abergwaun
  SA65 ....122 D4
  Llangwm SA62 ....87 D4
  Pembroke / Penfro SA71 .133 C4
  Solva SA62 ....48 A3
Mainwaring Terr SA1 .160 D2
Major St SA5 ....160 C2
Maliphant St SA1 .....160 E1
Malt Hall SA3 ....115 D3
Malvern Terr SA2 ....166 F5
Manchester Sq SA73 .131 C3
Mandinam Pk SA2 ...166 A4
Mannesmann Cl SA7 .161 C7
Manorbier Castle ★
  SA70 ....113 C6
Manorbier Sta SA70 .105 F2
Manorbier Voluntary CP Sch
  SA70 ....105 F2
Manor Cres
  Carmarthen / Caerfyrddin
  SA31 ....128 A3
  Manorbier SA70 ......105 F1
Manor Ct SA5 ....160 C3
Manor Daf Gdns SA33 .127 E2
Manordeifi C in W VC Sch
  SA37 ....16 E2
Manor House Wildlife Pk★
  SA70 ....106 B5
Manorowen Walled Gdn★
  SA65 ....11 B1
Manor Par SA64 ......122 A5
Manor Rd SA5 ....158 B5
Manor Rd / Ffordd Y Faenor
  15 SA73 ....98 B7
Manor Way
  Carmarthen / Caerfyrddin
  SA31 ....128 A3
  Goodwick / Wdig SA64 .122 A5
Mansel Ct SA4 ....158 B5
Mansel Dr SA3 ......172 C6
Manselfield Rd SA3 ...172 C6
Mansel Rd SA1 ......161 B4
Mansel St
  Burry Port SA16 .....137 D3
  5 Carmarthen / Caerfyrddin
  SA31 ....128 F5
  Gowerton / Tre-gwyr SA4 .158 B5
  Pembroke / Penfro SA71 .133 B4
  Swansea / Abertawe SA1 .174 A3
Mansel St / Heol Mansel 16
  SA15 ....148 D4

Manselton Prim Sch
  SA5 ....160 C3
Manselton Rd SA5 ...160 B3
Mansfield SA73 ....131 D2
Maple Ave SA61 .....124 E3
Maple Cl SA4 ....151 A3
Maple Cres
  Carmarthen / Caerfyrddin
  SA31 ....128 C5
  Swansea / Abertawe SA2 .166 E4
Maple Dr SA5 ....158 D4
Maple Gr SA2 ....166 E6
Mapletree Cl SA6 ....153 D1
Marble Hall Cl SA73 ..131 D4
Marblehall Rd SA15 ..148 E5
Marble Hall Rd SA73 .131 D3
Marchgate Paddock 1
  SA65 ....122 D4
Mardy Trad Est SA4 .158 C8
Margam Ave SA6 ....161 A8
Margam Pl / Maes Margam
  SA15 ....148 E4
Margaret Rd 5 SA18 ..79 A1
Margaret St / Stryd Marged
  6 SA18 ....98 C7
Margarets Way SA71 .133 D4
Margaret Terr SA1 ...168 A7
Marged St SA15 .....148 D3
Marine Dr SA71 .....103 C6
Marine Rd SA2 ....85 C8
Mariners Sq 3 SA61 .125 A5
Mariner St SA1 ......174 B4
Mariners The SA15 ..148 C3
Mariners Way SA73 .131 F5
Marine St SA15 ......148 C3
Marine Wlk 4 SA1 ...174 B1
Maritime Ind Pk SA72 .132 C4
Market La
  Cardigan / Aberteifi SA43 .118 C4
  Laugharne SA33 ......92 F5
Market Mews 4 SA6 .160 F8
Market Pl
  Llanwenog SA40 ......21 C6
  Newcastle Emlyn / Castell
  Newydd Emlyn SA38 .119 D5
  Wiston SA63 ....69 A7
Market Sq
  Llandovery / Llanymddyfri
  SA20 ....121 D4
  Newcastle Emlyn / Castell
  Newydd Emlyn SA38 .119 D5
Market St
  Haverfordwest / Hwlffordd
  SA61 ....125 A5
  3 Lampeter / Llanbedr
  Pont Steffan SA48 ...120 C5
  Laugharne SA33 ......92 F5
  2 Llanelli SA19 ......130 D5
  Llanelli SA15 ....148 D5
  13 Narberth / Arberth
  SA67 ....70 D1
  4 Newport / Trefdraeth
  SA42 ....13 E4
  8 Swansea / Abertawe
  SA1 ....161 A8
  Whitland / Hendy-Gwyn
  SA34 ....126 D3
Marlais Pk SA14 ......78 D4
Marlborough Rd
  Gorseinon SA4 ....158 B8
  Swansea / Abertawe SA2 .166 F6
Marloes Ct SA5 ......159 F6
Marsden St 5 SA6 ...160 C2
Marshal Rd SA71 ....133 A5
Marshlands SA9 ......39 B6
Marsh Rd
  Pendine / Pentywyn SA33 .91 E3
  Tenby / Dinbych-y-pysgod
  SA70 ....135 C5
Marsh St SA15 ......148 D4
Martell St SA5 ....159 E3
Martin Rd SA15 .....148 E4
Martin St Clydach SA6 .154 D7
  Swansea / Abertawe SA4 .160 F8
Martletwy Cross SA67 .88 D6
Mary Immaculate RC Sch
  SA61 ....124 F3
Mary St SA14 ....96 D8
Mary Twill La SA3 ...172 E4
Masefield Dr SA61 ...125 B4
Masefield Way SA2 ..166 E6
Mathry Hill SA62 .....29 F4
Mathry Voluntary Controlled
  Sch SA62 ....29 F3
Matthew St SA1 .....174 B4
Maxime Ct SA2 ......166 D6
Mayals Ave SA2 .....166 A1
Mayals Gn
  The Mumbles / Y Mwmbwls
  SA3 ....165 F1
  The Mumbles / Y Mwmbwls
  SA3 ....172 F8
Mayals Prim Sch SA3 .173 A8
Mayals Rd
  The Mumbles / Y Mwmbwls
  SA2 ....166 A1
  The Mumbles / Y Mwmbwls
  SA3 ....172 F8
Mayfield Dr SA70 ....135 D6
Mayfield Rd SA73 ...132 B7
Mayfield Terr SA5 ...160 B3
Mayflower Cl SA2 ...166 B6
Mayford La SA17 .....95 C1
Mayhill Gdns SA1 ...160 B1
Mayhill Rd SA1 ......160 B1
Maytree Ave SA3 ....172 F7

Maytree Cl Loughor SA4 .150 F2
  Swansea / Abertawe SA6 .158 F2
Meadow Bank SA71 ..111 C6
Meadowcroft SA3 ....171 A5
Meadow Croft Cl SA5 .158 E4
Meadow Ct / Maes Ty Cwrdd
  SA14 ....149 D4
Meadow Dr SA4 .....150 F2
Meadow Pk SA73 ....132 F6
Meadow Rd SA70 ...105 E2
Meadow Rise
  Swansea / Abertawe, Cockett
  SA1 ....159 E2
  Swansea / Abertawe,
  Lower Sketty SA2 ....166 C4
Meadows Rd
  Cross Hands SA14 ....97 B7
  Cross Hands SA14 ....97 C6
Meadow St SA1 .....159 F2
Meadows The
  East Williamston SA69 .134 B6
  Fishguard & Goodwick SA64 .11 B2
Meadows The / Y Waun
  SA10 ....162 E7
Meadow View
  Dunvant SA2 ....165 C8
  Haverfordwest / Hwlffordd
  SA61 ....125 A6
  Swansea / Abertawe SA7 .162 A6
Meadow Wlk 1 SA61 .125 C7
Meads Ct SA73 ......131 C4
Meads Inf Sch The
  SA73 ....131 D3
Meads Sports & Leisure Ctr
  The SA73 ....131 C4
Meads The SA62 .....87 D6
Mead The SA3 ....165 D8
Medway Workshops
  SA4 ....151 F1
Megan Cl SA4 ....151 C2
Megan St SA5 ....160 A2
Meidrim CP Sch SA33 .73 E7
Meidrim Rd SA33 ....127 F7
Meinciau Rd SA17 ...136 C4
Melcorn Dr SA3 .....172 E5
Melin-y-Coed SA43 .118 E6
Melin Y Dre SA43 ...118 C3
Melrose Cl SA6 ......161 B7
Melville St SA72 .....132 B2
Melville Terr SA72 ...132 A2
Memorial Sq SA16 ..137 E2
Mendip Cl SA5 ......159 D3
Merchant's Pk SA71 .133 B4
Merlin Cres SA41 ....166 F6
Merlins Ave SA61 ...124 F2
Merlins Ct SA70 .....135 E5
Merlins Gdns 1 SA70 .135 E5
Merlin's Hill SA61 ...124 F2
Merlin's Hill Ctr★ SA32 .76 C8
Merlin St SA31 ......128 E5
Merrion Cross SA71 .111 B5
Methodist La SA62 ...68 C5
Mewslade Ave SA5 .159 E6
Meyler Cres SA73 ...131 D4
Meyrick Owen Way
  SA72 ....132 B3
Meyrick St SA72 .....132 C2
Michael's Field SA3 .173 C3
Middlecroft La SA3 ..171 F7
Middlekilns Rd SA73 ..85 D2
Middle Mwldan SA43 .118 C4
Middle Rd SA5 ......159 F4
Middle Row 3 SA71 .133 C6
Middle St SA73 ......87 A3
Middleton St SA1 ...167 F7
Middle Walls La SA70 .135 E4
Midland Ct SA1 .....174 C3
Midland La SA62 .....50 E8
Midland Pl SA7 .....161 D7
Midland Rd SA7 ....161 D7
Midland Terr SA9 ...139 D8
Miers St SA1 ....174 C4
Milborough Ct SA9 .139 B7
Milborough Rd SA9 .139 B7
Mile End Cl SA5 .....159 F3
Miles La SA3 ....172 C6
Miles Rd SA5 ....160 C4
Miles St SA15 ....148 C7
Milford Com Coll SA73 .131 B2
Milford Haven Jun Sch
  SA73 ....131 D3
Milford Haven Mus★
  SA73 ....131 C2
Milford Haven Sec Sch
  SA73 ....131 B1
Milford Haven Sta SA73 .131 B3
Milford Rd
  Haverfordwest / Hwlffordd
  SA61 ....124 F4
  Tiers Cross SA62 .....86 C4
Milford St SA69 .....134 F3
Milford Way SA5 ....159 F6
Military Rd SA73 ....132 A6
Millands Cl SA3 .....172 D5
Millard Pk SA62 ....123 D4
Mill Back SA71 ......104 B4
Mill Bank SA61 .....125 B5
Millbank Rd SA31 ...128 B3
Millbrook Cres 4 SA31 .128 E5
Millbrook St SA6 ....160 D5
Millennium Coastal Park★
  SA14, SA15 ....149 B1
Millennium Coastal Pk★
  SA14 ....149 B1
Millennium Coast Pk Visitor
  Ctr★ SA15 ....148 B4
Miller's Ct SA5 ......159 F5

Millfield Cl
Pentlepoir SA69 . . . . .134 A5
Swansea / Abertawe SA2 . .166 B5
Millfield Rd SA14 . . . . . .140 F1
Mill Hill SA67 . . . . .88 A6
Mill La
Haverfordwest / Hwlffordd
SA61 . . . . .124 F2
Llanelli SA15 . . . . .148 D6
Llanrhidian SA3 . . . . .115 D3
Narberth / Arberth SA67 . .70 D1
Newport / Trefdraeth SA42 . .13 E3
The Mumbles / Y Mwmbwls
SA3 . . . . .166 B2
Millmoor Way SA62 . . . . .66 D1
Mill Pill SA33 . . . . .92 E3
Mill Pond Rd SA67 . . . . . .70 D1
Mill Rd SA61 . . . . .125 B5
Mill Row SA8 . . . . .147 F4
Mills Dr SA73 . . . . .132 B8
Mill St
Carmarthen / Caerfyrddin
SA31 . . . . .128 E4
Gorseinon SA4 . . . . .151 C2
Gowerton / Tre-gwyr SA4 . .158 B5
Lampeter / Llanbedr Pont Steffan
SA48 . . . . .120 C5
Llangwm SA62 . . . . .87 D4
Newcastle Emlyn / Castell
Newydd Emlyn SA38 . . . .119 F4
Pen-clawdd SA4 . . . . . . .156 F4
St Dogmaels / Llandudoch
SA43 . . . . .118 B3
Mill Terr / Ffordd Y Felin
SA18 . . . . .98 A5
Millway La SA68 . . . . . . .88 E1
Millwood Ct **3** SA1 . . . .160 C2
Millwood St SA1 . . . . . . .160 C3
Milton Cl SA61 . . . . .125 B4
Milton Cres SA73 . . . . . .131 E2
Milton Mdws SA70 . . . . .105 C6
Milton Terr
Pembroke Dock / Doc Penfro
SA72 . . . . .132 C2
Swansea / Abertawe SA1 . .174 A4
Milward Cl **5** SA61 . . . .124 F5
Mincing La SA15 . . . . . .148 D5
Minster Cl SA6 . . . . .161 B7
Minster Ct SA6 . . . . .161 B7
Min Y Dre **1** SA38 . . . .119 D4
Minyffordd SA9 . . . . .139 B6
Min-y-Graig SA15 . . . . . . .96 B7
Min-y-Llan SA62 . . . . .50 E8
Min Y Mor SA15 . . . . . . .148 C5
Minyrafon SA9 . . . . .139 B5
Minyrafon Rd SA6 . . . . . .146 D1
Mirador Cres SA2 . . . . . .167 A6
Misty Hills Cl SA4 . . . . . .157 C1
Mitre La SA62 . . . . .123 C4
Mixen Cl SA3 . . . . .172 F5
Model C in W Sch SA31 . .128 D5
Molleston Cross SA67 . . . .89 C7
Mona Cl SA6 . . . . .161 A6
Monger St **1** SA1 . . . .160 D1
Monksford St SA17 . . . . .136 C4
Monksland Rd SA3 . . . . .117 A6
Monkton SA71 . . . . .133 A4
Monkton Priory CP Sch
SA71 . . . . .133 A5
Monmouth Ho **8** SA1 . .174 C2
Monmouth Pl SA6 . . . . . .154 A4
Monnow Cl SA73 . . . . . . .86 D2
Montana Pl SA1 . . . . . . .160 D3
Monterey St SA5 . . . . . . .160 C3
Montgomery Cl SA71 . . . .133 A4
Monton Terr SA1 . . . . . . .168 A7
Montpellier Terr SA1 . . . .167 B7
Monument Hill SA31 . . . .128 C4
Moorfield Ave SA3 . . . . . .69 A7
Moorfield Rd **5** SA67 . . .70 D1
Moorings The SA43 . . . . .118 A5
Moor La SA4 . . . . .114 C2
Moorland Ave SA3 . . . . .172 E6
Moorland Rd SA2 . . . . . . .87 A6
Moorside Rd SA3 . . . . . .172 E6
Moorview Cl SA5 . . . . . .159 F4
Moorview Rd SA5 . . . . . .159 F4
Morawel SA1 . . . . .161 D5
Mor-Awel Llanelli SA14 . .149 C5
Llanrhian SA62 . . . . .28 F3
Morfa CP Jun Mix Sch
SA15 . . . . .148 F3
Morfa Inf Sch SA15 . . . . .148 E2
Morfa La
Carmarthen / Caerfyrddin
SA31 . . . . .128 E5
Kidwelly / Cydweli SA17 . .136 B4
Morfa Las SA65 . . . . . . .122 D3
Morfa Maen SA17 . . . . . .136 B3
Morfa Rd SA1 . . . . .174 B4
Morfydd St SA6 . . . . . . .160 F8
Morgan Cl SA4 . . . . .151 F2
Morgan St
3 Cardigan / Aberteifi
SA43 . . . . .118 C4
Carmarthen / Caerfyrddin
SA31 . . . . .128 E5
Pontardawe SA8 . . . . . . .147 C2
Swansea / Abertawe SA6 . .160 D2
Morgans Way **2** SA67 . .90 C2
Moriah Rd SA5 . . . . .160 C6
Morlais Rd SA5 . . . . .160 B5
Morlais Rd / Heol Morlais
SA14 . . . . .150 B7
Morlan Terr SA16 . . . . . .137 F2
Morley St SA31 . . . . .128 C5
Morris La SA1 . . . . .174 C3
Morris St **7** SA6 . . . . .161 A8

Morris Terr SA5 . . . . . . .159 B6
Morriston Comp Sch
SA6 . . . . .153 F4
Morriston Hospl SA6 . . . .153 E5
Morriston North Ind Est
Llansamlet SA6 . . . . .154 B1
Swansea / Abertawe SA6 . .161 C8
Morriston Pl SA18 . . . . . .99 E6
Morriston Prim Sch / Ysgol
Gynradd Treforys SA6 . . .161 A8
Morriston South Ind Est
SA6 . . . . .161 A7
Mostyn Ave SA31 . . . . . .129 C7
Mountain La SA67 . . . . . .89 C8
Mountain Rd
Craig-cefn-parc SA6 . . . .146 C1
Cwmamman SA18 . . . . . .80 A1
Llandybie SA18 . . . . .79 D1
Quarter Bach SA18 . . . . .80 E1
Mountain Rd / Heol Y
Mynydd SA16 . . . . .137 A3
Mount Airey Cty Prim Sch
SA61 . . . . .125 A3
Mountbatten Ct SA5 . . . .159 F5
Mount Cres
Penllergaer SA4 . . . . . . .151 F2
Swansea / Abertawe SA6 . .153 D2
Mount Hill Rise SA31 . . . .129 A3
Mount La SA62 . . . . .67 C3
Mounton View SA67 . . . . .89 A7
Mount Pleasant
Gowerton / Tre-gwyr SA4 . .158 B4
Swansea / Abertawe SA1 . .174 A3
Mount Pleasant Bldgs **2**
SA15 . . . . .148 D6
Mount Pleasant Ct
SA10 . . . . .162 E4
Mount Pleasant Dr SA1 . .174 A3
Mount Pleasant Way
SA73 . . . . .131 E4
Mount Sch The SA73 . . . .131 F3
Mount Sion La SA71 . . . .110 F5
Mount St
Gowerton / Tre-gwyr SA4 . .158 B5
Swansea / Abertawe SA6 . .153 E4
Mount The
7 Carmarthen / Caerfyrddin
SA31 . . . . .128 F5
Gowerton / Tre-gwyr SA4 . .158 B5
Mount Wlk SA48 . . . . . . .120 B5
Moylgrove Cty Prim Sch
SA43 . . . . .14 E7
Muirfield Dr SA3 . . . . . . .165 F1
Mulberry Ave SA3 . . . . . .172 F8
Mulgrave Way SA2 . . . . .166 A1
Mumbles Bay Ct SA2 . . . .166 B1
Mumbles Head Pk SA16 . .137 B4
Mumbles Pier★ SA3 . . . .173 E3
Mumbles Rd
Swansea / Abertawe SA2 . .166 D3
The Mumbles / Y Mwmbwls
SA3 . . . . .173 C4
West Cross SA3 . . . . . . .173 A4
Munro Ct SA72 . . . . .133 A8
Murrayfield Cl SA5 . . . . .159 D3
Murray Rd SA73 . . . . . . .131 E2
Murray St SA15 . . . . . . .148 D5
Murton La SA3 . . . . .172 D5
Museum of Speed★
SA33 . . . . .91 E3
Musselwick Rd SA62 . . . . .84 F1
Mwtshwr SA43 . . . . .118 B3
Mydam La SA4 . . . . .151 A2
Myddynfych SA18 . . . . . . .98 B8
Mylett's Hill SA71 . . . . . .133 D7
Mynyddbach SA18 . . . . . .97 F5
Mynydd Garnllwyd Rd
SA6 . . . . .160 D8
Mynydd Gelli Wastad Rd
Clydach SA6 . . . . .154 B6
Swansea / Abertawe SA6 . .153 E5
Mynydd Mawr Woodland
Pk★ SA14 . . . . .96 F7
Mynydd-Newydd Rd
SA5 . . . . .160 A7
Myrddin CP Sch SA31 . . . .128 E6
Myrddin Cres SA31 . . . . .128 F6
Myrddin Gdns SA1 . . . . . .161 B3
Myrddin Rd SA1 . . . . . . .161 B3
Myrtle Gr SA2 . . . . .166 E7
Myrtle Hill
Carmarthen / Caerfyrddin
SA31 . . . . .128 F2
Llanelli Rural SA15 . . . . .109 F3
Pen-clawdd SA4 . . . . . . .156 E3
Pontardulais SA4 . . . . . . .143 C5
Pont Henri SA15 . . . . . . .95 F4
Myrtle Hill Ret Area
SA31 . . . . .128 E2
Myrtle Rd SA4 . . . . .158 D8
Myrtle Terr Llanelli SA15 . .148 C5
The Mumbles / Y Mwmbwls
SA3 . . . . .173 B4
Mysydd Rd SA1 . . . . . . .160 D4
Mysydd Terr SA1 . . . . . .160 D3

N

Nant Arw SA18 . . . . .97 D6
Nant Cadle SA5 . . . . . . .159 E6
Nant-fach SA14 . . . . . . .141 B2
Nant Fach SA66 . . . . .53 C2
Nant Glas SA4 . . . . .152 C5
Nant Gwineu Rd SA18 . . . .80 C1
Nant Gwineu Rd / Heol Nant
Gwiniau SA18 . . . . .99 C8

Nantlais
Ammanford / Rhydaman
SA18 . . . . .98 B8
Cefn-bryn-brain SA9 . . . .100 B8
Nantong Way SA1 . . . . . .160 F4
Nantucket Ave **3** SA73 . .131 C3
Nantwen SA14 . . . . .149 F4
Nantybryn SA14 . . . . . . .149 F4
Nant Y Berllan SA43 . . . .118 A5
Nant-y-Ci Rd SA18 . . . . . .97 F7
Nant-y-Coy Mill★ SA62 . .51 A4
Nant-y-Cwm Steiner Sch /
Ysgol Rudolf Steiner
Nant-y-Cwm SA66 . . . . . .53 D3
Nant-y-Dderwen SA18 . . . .97 F7
Nant Y Dderwen SA14 . . . .96 D8
Nantydd Terr SA14 . . . . .149 C5
Nantyffin SA32 . . . . .77 D2
Nantyffin N SA7 . . . . . . .161 D7
Nantyffin Rd
Pontardulais SA4 . . . . . . .143 D3
Swansea / Abertawe SA7 . .161 C7
Nantyffin S SA7 . . . . . . .161 C6
Nantyglyn SA18 . . . . .79 F1
Nantyglyn Rd / Heol Nant Y
Glyn SA18 . . . . .98 F8
Nant-y-Gro Llanelli SA14 . .149 C6
Llangennech SA14 . . . . . .142 B1
Nantygroes CP Sch SA18 . .78 E4
Nant-yr-Arian SA31 . . . . .128 C5
Nant Yr Eglwys SA62 . . . . .51 F4
Nant-yr-Ynys SA33 . . . . . .58 E3
Napier Gdns SA43 . . . . . .118 E4
Napier St SA43 . . . . .118 D4
Narberth CP Sch SA67 . . . .70 D1
Narberth Mus Bookshop★
SA67 . . . . .70 E1
Narberth Rd
Tenby / Dinbych-y-pysgod
SA70 . . . . .135 C7
Uzmaston & Boulston
SA61 . . . . .125 D5
Narberth Sta SA67 . . . . . .70 F1
Nash Ave SA31 . . . . .129 B7
Nathan St SA15 . . . . . . .148 C3
National Botanic Gdn of
Wales The / Gardd Fotaneg
Genedlaethol Cymru★
SA32 . . . . .77 D5
National Coracle Ctr★
SA38 . . . . .17 B4
National Wetlands Centre
Wales★ SA14 . . . . .149 C2
National Woollen Mus★
SA44 . . . . .18 E2
Neath Rd
Morriston / Treforris SA6 . .154 A2
Swansea / Abertawe, Plasmarl
SA1, SA6 . . . . .160 E5
Swansea / Abertawe, Tircanol
SA6 . . . . .154 A2
Ystradgynlais SA9 . . . . . .139 F6
Nell's La SA42 . . . . .14 C5
Nelson Ave SA73 . . . . . .131 B2
Nelson St
Pembroke Dock / Doc Penfro
SA72 . . . . .104 B5
Swansea / Abertawe SA1 . .174 A2
Nelson Terr SA15 . . . . . .148 C4
Netherwood Sch SA69 . . .134 E5
Netpool Rd SA43 . . . . . .118 C4
Neuadd Rd SA18 . . . . . . .99 C8
Nevills Cl SA4 . . . . .154 C6
Nevill St SA15 . . . . .148 C4
Newbridge Rd SA33 . . . . .92 F5
Newcastle Emlyn Castle
(rems of)★ SA38 . . . . . .119 E5
Newcastle Emlyn Ind Est
SA38 . . . . .119 E5
New Ceidrim Rd **14** SA18 . .99 B8
New Cross Bldgs **1**
SA6 . . . . .154 A1
New Cut Rd SA1 . . . . . . .174 B4
New Dock Rd SA15 . . . . .148 D3
New Dock St SA15 . . . . . .148 D2
Newell Hill SA70 . . . . . . .135 D5
Newell Rd SA10 . . . . .162 E8
Newgale Cl SA5 . . . . . . .159 F7
Newgale Hill SA62 . . . . . .49 B1
New Hill SA64 . . . . .122 B6
New Inn Prim Sch / Ysgol
Gynradd New Inn SA39 . . . .39 E8
New Mill Rd SA2 . . . . . . .166 A6
New Mill Rd / Heol Felin
Newydd SA43 . . . . .118 F6
Newnham Cres SA2 . . . . .166 E7
New Orchard St SA1 . . . .174 B4
New Oxford Bldgs SA1 . . .174 A2
New Park Holiday Pk
SA3 . . . . .117 A4
Newport Bsns Pk SA42 . . . .13 E4
Newport Castle★ SA42 . . .13 E3
Newport Rd **2** SA65 . . .122 E4
New Quarr Rd SA5 . . . . .160 C5
New Rd
Ammanford / Rhydaman
SA18 . . . . .98 B6
Birchgrove SA7 . . . . .154 F1
Brecon SA18 . . . . .80 E1
Crofty SA4 . . . . .156 B3
Freystrop SA62 . . . . .87 B6
Goodwick / Wdig SA64 . . .122 A5
Grovesend SA4 . . . . .151 C6
Gwaun-Cae-Gurwen SA18 . .99 F3
Haverfordwest / Hwlffordd
SA61 . . . . .125 B4
Kilgetty / Begelly SA68 . . .134 B8

New Rd continued
Llandeilo SA19 . . . . .130 D5
Llandovery / Llanymddyfri
SA20 . . . . .121 C5
1 Llandysul SA44 . . . . . .19 E3
Llanelli, Mount Pleasant
SA15 . . . . .148 C6
Llanelli, Penceiliogi SA14 . .149 B6
Neath / Castell-Nedd SA10 . .162 F7
Newcastle Emlyn / Castell
Newydd Emlyn SA38 . . . .119 C5
Pontarddulais SA4 . . . . . .143 B4
Pontyberem SA15 . . . . . . .96 B5
Swansea / Abertawe SA2 . .159 D1
Swansea / Abertawe, Tre-boeth
SA5 . . . . .160 C6
Trebanos / Trebannws
SA8 . . . . .147 D5
New Rd / Heol Newydd
Neath / Castell-Nedd
SA10 . . . . .162 C1
Ystradowen SA9 . . . . . . .100 C7
New School Rd / Heol Ysgol
Newydd **15** SA18 . . . . .99 B8
Newslade **8** SA1 . . . . .174 A4
New St Burry Port SA16 . . .137 F2
Kidwelly / Cydweli SA17 . .136 B4
Lampeter / Llanbedr Pont Steffan
SA48 . . . . .120 C4
Llanelli SA15 . . . . .148 E2
Solva SA62 . . . . .48 D3
St David's / Tyddewi SA62 . .123 D5
Swansea / Abertawe SA1 . .174 B4
Ystalyfera SA9 . . . . .139 A4
Newton La SA8 . . . . .88 C2
Newton Prim Sch SA3 . . .172 F5
Newton Rd Clydach SA6 . .146 D1
Llanstadwell SA73 . . . . . .103 F3
Oystermouth SA3 . . . . . .172 F5
The Mumbles / Y Mwmbwls
SA3 . . . . .173 A5
Newton St SA1 . . . . .174 A2
Newton Terr SA68 . . . . . .89 F2
Newtown SA18 . . . . .98 A7
Newtown Cl SA18 . . . . . .98 A7
Newtown Rd
Ammanford / Rhydaman
SA18 . . . . .98 A7
Hook SA62 . . . . .87 C5
New Villas SA3 . . . . .173 B4
New Way SA71 . . . . .133 C5
New Well La SA3 . . . . . . .172 F5
New Wells Rd SA73 . . . . . .87 D3
New Zealand St SA15 . . . .148 C6
Neyland Athletic Club
SA73 . . . . .132 B7
Neyland CP Sch SA73 . . . .132 B7
Neyland Dr SA5 . . . . .159 F7
Neyland Hill SA73 . . . . . .132 B6
Neyland Hts SA73 . . . . . .132 B7
Neyland Inf Sch SA73 . . . .132 B6
Neyland Rd SA73 . . . . . .131 F6
Neyland Terr SA73 . . . . . .132 B5
Neyland Vale SA73 . . . . . .132 A7
Nicander Par SA1 . . . . . .167 B8
Nicander Pl SA1 . . . . . . .167 B8
Nicholas Cl SA4 . . . . .151 C3
Nicholas Rd SA7 . . . . . . .155 A6
Nicholl Ct SA3 . . . . .173 C3
Nicholls Rd SA71 . . . . . . .133 E3
Nicholl St SA1 . . . . .167 B6
Nightingale La SA15 . . . . .149 A5
Ninth Ave SA6 . . . . .153 D2
Nixon Terr SA6 . . . . .154 A1
Noddfa Dewi SA62 . . . . . .123 D5
Nolton Ct SA5 . . . . .159 F6
Norfolk St SA1 . . . . .167 B7
Norgans Hill SA71 . . . . . .133 A5
Norgan's Terr SA73 . . . . .133 B4
Normandy Rd SA1 . . . . . .160 E3
Norman Rd / Heol Norman
3 SA18 . . . . .98 B7
Northampton La SA1 . . . .174 A3
North Bank SA19 . . . . . .130 D5
North Cl SA69 . . . . .134 D4
North Cottage Dr SA4 . . .151 B1
North Cres SA61 . . . . . . .125 A6
North Ct SA61 . . . . .125 C6
North Dock Bsns Workshops
SA15 . . . . .148 B4
North End SA62 . . . . .29 A5
Northeron SA3 . . . . .172 F8
Northfield Rd SA67 . . . . . .70 D1
Northgate SA71 . . . . .133 B6
North Hall Est SA62 . . . . .85 A2
North Hill Rd SA1 . . . . . .174 A4
North Hills La SA3 . . . . . .170 C6
North La
Castlemartin SA71 . . . . . .111 B6
Marloes & St Brides SA62 . .84 C3
Northlands Pk SA3 . . . . . .172 A1
North Par SA31 . . . . .129 A5
North Rd
Cardigan / Aberteifi SA43 . .118 D4
Lampeter / Llanbedr Pont Steffan
SA48 . . . . .120 C6
Loughor SA4 . . . . .150 F1
Whitland / Hendy-Gwyn
SA34 . . . . .126 C4
North St
Haverfordwest / Hwlffordd
SA61 . . . . .125 A5
Pembroke Dock / Doc Penfro
SA72 . . . . .132 B1
North Terr SA14 . . . . . . .149 B7
Northway SA3 . . . . .172 B7
Northway Ct SA3 . . . . . . .172 A7

Norton SA70 . . . . .135 E5
Norton Ave SA3 . . . . .173 A6
Norton Dr SA3 . . . . .171 A6
Norton La SA3 . . . . .171 B7
Norton Rd
Penygroes SA14 . . . . . . .97 D8
The Mumbles / Y Mwmbwls
SA3 . . . . .173 A6
Norwood Gdns★ SA39 . . .21 A3
Nottage Mews SA3 . . . . .172 E4
Nottage Rd SA3 . . . . . . .172 E4
Notts Gdns SA2 . . . . . . .166 F7
Nubian Ave SA1 . . . . . . .124 D4
Nubian Cres SA73 . . . . . .131 B2
Nun St SA62 . . . . .123 C5
Nurseries The SA15 . . . . .109 F3
Nursery Cl **3** SA34 . . . . .90 F4
Nurses Cnr SA4 . . . . . . .156 F4
Nythfa SA4 . . . . .152 C5

O

Oakdene SA2 . . . . .165 D7
Oak Dr SA5 . . . . .158 D4
Oakfield Dr SA68 . . . . . . .134 D8
Oakfield Rd SA4 . . . . . . .147 E5
Oakfield Rd / Heol
Maesoderwen **5** SA18 . .99 B8
Oakfield St SA4 . . . . .143 C4
Oakfield Terr **7** SA18 . . . .98 C7
Oakford Pl SA5 . . . . .159 D6
Oak Hill Pk SA10 . . . . . . .162 B8
Oakland Cl SA7 . . . . .155 A5
Oakland Rd SA3 . . . . . . .173 A4
Oaklands Llanelli SA14 . . .141 A2
The Mumbles / Y Mwmbwls
SA3 . . . . .172 F6
Oaklands Cl / Clos-y-derwen
SA14 . . . . .97 B3
Oaklands Ct SA2 . . . . . . .166 A1
Oaklands Rd SA4 . . . . . .152 A6
Oaklands Terr
Swansea / Abertawe SA1 . .167 B7
Wiston SA62 . . . . .69 B4
Oakleigh House Sch
SA2 . . . . .166 F7
Oakleigh Rd SA4 . . . . . . .150 F2
Oak Rd SA72 . . . . .132 B1
Oak Ridge SA2 . . . . .166 A6
Oakridge Acres SA70 . . . .135 B5
Oak St SA4 . . . . .158 D8
Oak Tree Ave SA2 . . . . . .166 C6
Oak Tree Cl SA3 . . . . . . .172 E6
Oak Tree Cl / Clos Y
Dderwen SA18 . . . . .98 D7
Oak Way SA4 . . . . .152 C2
Oakwood Ave SA6 . . . . . .153 D1
Oakwood Cl SA8 . . . . . . .147 A1
Oakwood Dr Clydach SA8 . .147 A1
Gowerton / Tre-gwyr SA4 . .158 D4
Oakwood Gr SA4 . . . . . . .125 A6
Oakwood Leisure Pk★
SA67 . . . . .88 F7
Oakwood Rd SA2 . . . . . .166 F6
Oakwood Rise SA8 . . . . . .147 A1
Oberon Gr SA73 . . . . . . .131 F5
Observatory Ave SA73 . . .131 A2
Ocean Cres **6** SA1 . . . .174 B1
Ocean View Cl SA2 . . . . .166 B3
Ocean View / Golwg Y Mor
SA10 . . . . .169 C8
Ocean Way SA72 . . . . . .103 F5
Ochr-y-Waun Rd SA9 . . . .100 B7
Oddfellows' St SA9 . . . . .138 F2
Odo St SA1 . . . . .160 D2
Ogmore Rd SA1 . . . . . . .161 A2
Olchfa Cl SA2 . . . . .166 A6
Olchfa La SA2 . . . . .166 A7
Olchfa Sch SA2 . . . . .166 A6
Old Amroth Rd SA67 . . . . .90 C4
Old Bridge SA61 . . . . . . .125 C3
Old Castle Rd
Cardigan / Aberteifi SA43 . .118 B4
Llanelli SA15 . . . . .148 C5
Old Conduit The SA71 . . .133 A4
Old Farm Ct SA7 . . . . . . .161 F6
Old Graig St SA38 . . . . . .119 C5
Old Hakin Rd SA61 . . . . .124 E4
Old Keg Yd The **9** SA67 . .70 D1
Old Kittle Rd SA3 . . . . . .171 F7
Old Llangyfelach Rd
SA4 . . . . .152 B3
Old Llansteffan Rd
SA31 . . . . .128 D3
Old Lodge SA15 . . . . . . .148 D4
Old Newport Rd **1**
SA65 . . . . .122 E4
Old Oak La SA31 . . . . . . .129 A6
Old Priory Rd SA31 . . . . .129 A5
Old Rd
Ammanford / Rhydaman
SA18 . . . . .98 B8
Llanelli SA15 . . . . .148 D6
Llansteffan SA33 . . . . . . .93 D5
Neath / Castell-Nedd SA10 . .162 F7
Old Road Prim Sch
SA15 . . . . .148 D6
Old Sch Rd SA33 . . . . . . .93 C6
Old Sta Rd **5** SA31 . . . .129 A5
Old Tenby Rd SA33 . . . . .127 C3
Old Tramway SA16 . . . . .137 E2
Oldway SA3 . . . . .172 A6
Old Wern Rd SA9 . . . . . .139 B6
Olive Rd SA3 . . . . .172 F8

Olive St SA15 . . . . .148 F3
Orange Way SA71 . . . . .133 B4
Orchard Bldgs **3** SA71 . . .133 D4
Orchard Cl
  Burry Port SA16 . . . . .137 C3
  Porteynon SA3 . . . . .117 A4
Orchard Ct SA1 . . . . .174 B4
Orchard Dr SA4 . . . . .157 D1
Orchard Gr SA4 . . . . .152 A2
Orchard Pk SA33 . . . . .92 E5
Orchard Row **2** SA62 . . . . .87 E4
Orchard St
  2 Carmarthen / Caerfyrddin
  SA31 . . . . .128 F5
  Llandovery / Llanymddyfri
  SA20 . . . . .121 D4
  Pontardawe SA8 . . . . .147 E5
  Swansea / Abertawe SA1 . .174 B3
Orchard Terr SA4 . . . . .115 F4
Orchard The SA3 . . . . .172 F5
Orchid Ct SA3 . . . . .172 E6
Orielton CP Sch SA71 . . . . .104 A3
Orielton Field Ctr★
  SA71 . . . . .104 A2
Orielton Terr SA72 . . . . .104 A6
Ormes Rd SA10 . . . . .162 E8
Ormsby Terr SA1 . . . . .168 A7
Orpheus Rd SA6 . . . . .154 B4
Orton La SA63 . . . . .69 A7
Osborn Cl SA73 . . . . .132 C7
Osborne Pl SA4 . . . . .156 B2
Osborne Terr SA2 . . . . .166 F5
Osborn Pk SA73 . . . . .132 C6
Osprey Cl SA3 . . . . .172 E7
Osprey Dr **5** SA61 . . . . . . .124 E5
Osterley St SA1 . . . . .168 A7
Ostrey Bank SA33 . . . . .127 D4
Overdale Sch SA61 . . . . . . .124 E3
Overland Cl SA3 . . . . .173 A4
Overland Rd SA3 . . . . .173 A4
Overton Ct **5** SA1 . . . . . . .174 A4
Owenffordd SA62 . . . . .123 C4
Owen's La SA9 . . . . .100 C2
Owen St SA71 . . . . .133 B4
Owls Lodge La SA3 . . . . . . .165 F1
Oxford Street / Stryd
  Rhydychen SA1 . . . . .174 A2
Oxwich Castle★ SA3 . . . . .117 D5
Oxwich Cl SA6 . . . . .161 A7
Oxwich Leisure Pk SA3 . . .117 D5
Oxwich Nature Reserve★
  SA3 . . . . .117 E5
Oystermouth Castle★
  SA3 . . . . .173 A5
Oystermouth Ct SA3 . . . . . .173 A6
Oystermouth Prim Sch
  SA3 . . . . .173 A5
Oystermouth Rd SA1 . . . . . .174 A1
Ozanam Ct SA5 . . . . .159 F6

P

Paddock La SA70 . . . . .105 D5
Paddock St SA15 . . . . .148 D4
Paddock The
  Tenby / Dinbych-y-pysgod
  SA70 . . . . .135 B3
  The Mumbles / Y Mwmbls
  SA3 . . . . .173 A8
Page La SA1 . . . . .167 B6
Page St SA1 . . . . .167 B7
Palace Ave SA15 . . . . .148 E5
Pale Rd SA10 . . . . .162 F6
Palleg Rd / Heol Palleg
  SA9 . . . . .138 C2
Palmerston Rd SA61 . . . . . .124 D3
Palmyra Ct SA3 . . . . .173 A6
Pant Bryn Isaf SA14 . . . . . .149 D5
Panteg Rd SA62 . . . . .48 D3
Pantglas
  Carmarthen / Caerfyrddin
  SA31 . . . . .129 C8
  Gorseinon SA4 . . . . .151 B1
Pantgwyn SA2 . . . . .166 C6
Pantiago Rd SA4 . . . . .143 D4
Pant St SA1 . . . . .168 B7
Pant-Teg SA9 . . . . .139 A4
Pant-Teg SA15 . . . . .148 F8
Pant-y-Blawd Rd
  Llansamlet SA14 . . . . .154 B1
  Swansea / Abertawe, Llansamlet
  SA7 . . . . .161 D8
  Swansea / Abertawe SA7 . .161 A8
Pant-y-Blodau SA6 . . . . . . .153 B2
Pantyblodau Rd SA18 . . . . . .97 F8
Pant Y Brwyn SA9 . . . . .100 C7
Pantycelyn SA4 . . . . .151 B1
Pant Y Celyn SA14 . . . . .149 C5
Pant-y-Celyn Rd SA1 . . . . . .166 F8
Pant-y-dwr SA4 . . . . .157 D1
Pant Y Fedwen
  1 Abergwili SA32 . . . . .59 A3
  Gwaun-Cae-Gurwen SA18 . . .99 D6
Pant-y-Felin Rd SA4 . . . . . .143 D2
Pantyffynnon Rd / Heol
  Pantyffynnon SA18 . . . . . . .98 B6
Pantyffynnon Sta SA18 . . . .98 B5
Pantyffynnon Terr SA9 . . . .139 A4
Pantyffynon Rd SA9 . . . . . .139 F8
Pantygwydr Rd SA2 . . . . . . .166 F6
Pant-y-Pistyll SA8 . . . . .147 C3
Pant Yr Helys SA5 . . . . .159 B6

Pant-yr-Odyn SA2 . . . . .159 C1
Pant-y-Ychain SA64 . . . . . . .122 A6
Pant-y-Sais SA10 . . . . .162 C1
Parade Rd **3** SA31 . . . . . . .129 A5
Parade The
  Carmarthen / Caerfyrddin
  SA31 . . . . .129 A5
  Pembroke / Penfro SA71 . . .133 B4
Paradise Cotts SA14 . . . . . .149 D4
Paradise Row SA1 . . . . .133 B5
Paradise View SA1 . . . . .167 A8
Paragon **2** SA70 . . . . .135 E4
Parc Andrew SA10 . . . . .162 F6
Parc Ave
  Swansea / Abertawe SA6 . .160 F6
  Swansea / Abertawe SA6 . .160 F7
Parc Bagnall SA14 . . . . .128 E6
Parc Berwig SA14 . . . . .149 F2
Parc Bryn SA10 . . . . .162 E5
Parc Bryngelli / Grove Hill
  Pk SA14 . . . . .97 C8
Parc Brynmawr
  Llanelli SA15 . . . . .140 E1
  Llanelli SA15 . . . . .148 E1
Parc Bryn Rhos SA18 . . . . . .99 A8
Parc Busnes Canolog /
  Central Bsns Pk SA7 . . . . .154 C2
Parc Busnes Glan yr Afon /
  Riverside Bsns Pk SA6 . . .154 B1
Parc Bwtrimawr SA18 . . . . . .98 C6
Parc Cawdor SA19 . . . . .130 D3
Parc Cilddewi SA31 . . . . . . .128 B3
Parc Ddiwydiannol Betws /
  Betws Ind Pk SA18 . . . . . . .98 C7
Parc Derlin / Derlin Pk
  SA18 . . . . .97 F5
Parc Frenni SA37 . . . . .34 F7
Parc Gitto SA14 . . . . .149 D4
Parc Glanffrwd **12** SA18 . . .99 B8
Parc Glan Yr Afon **2**
  SA18 . . . . .99 B8
Parc Glas SA10 . . . . .162 F6
Parcgweydd Hill SA43 . . . . .16 F6
Parc-gwyn SA31 . . . . .128 C8
Parc Hendy Cres SA4 . . . . .156 F3
Parc-Henry La SA18 . . . . . . .98 B8
Parc Heol Ddu SA15 . . . . . .109 D6
Parc Howard Ave SA15 . . . .148 D7
Parc Howard Mus★
  SA15 . . . . .148 D7
Parc Landwr / Benson Way
  SA6 . . . . .161 A6
Parc Le Breos Burial
  Chamber★ SA3 . . . . .170 D8
Parcmaen St SA31 . . . . .128 E5
Parc Mansant SA15 . . . . .95 D4
Parc Mawr SA4 . . . . .152 B2
Parc Menter SA14 . . . . .97 C7
Parc Morlais SA14 . . . . .142 C1
Parc Newydd SA14 . . . . .77 F1
Parc Noi SA43 . . . . .118 A4
Parc Onen SA10 . . . . .162 E6
Parc Pant Glas SA19 . . . . . .130 E7
Parc Pendre SA17 . . . . .136 B3
Parc Penrhiw SA18 . . . . .98 C5
Parc Pensarn Ret Pk
  SA31 . . . . .128 F2
Parc Rd SA6 . . . . .160 F6
Parc Richard SA14 . . . . .149 E4
Parc Roberts **2** SA67 . . . . .70 C1
Parc Sandringham /
  Sandringham Pk SA6,
  SA7 . . . . .154 C1
Parc Teifi SA43 . . . . .118 F4
Parc Teifi Bsns Pk SA43 . . .118 F4
Parc Terr SA6 . . . . .160 F7
Parc Thomas SA31 . . . . .128 F6
Parc Tyisha SA16 . . . . .137 F3
Parc Wern SA10 . . . . .162 F6
Parc Wern Rd SA2 . . . . .166 E7
Parc Y Delyn
  Carmarthen / Caerfyrddin
  SA31 . . . . .128 F6
  3 Llansteffan SA33 . . . . . .93 C7
Parc-y-Delyn SA10 . . . . .153 B1
Parc-y-Deri SA10 . . . . .162 E6
Parc-y-DucTerr SA6 . . . . . . .160 F7
Parc Y Felin SA48 . . . . .120 D6
Parc Y Ffordd SA31 . . . . . . .128 A4
Parc-y-Gwenyn SA17 . . . . . .94 B3
Parc Y Llan SA18 . . . . .79 A2
Parc-y-Minos SA18 . . . . . . .137 E2
Parcymynach **6** SA15 . . . . .96 B6
Parc Yr Efail SA41 . . . . .14 C2
Parc Yr Eglwys **1** SA42 . . .13 A4
Parc Yr Eos SA36 . . . . .35 B2
Parc-yr-Helig Rd
  Birchgrove SA7 . . . . .155 B1
  Swansea / Abertawe SA7 . .162 B8
Parcyrhun SA18 . . . . .98 B6
Parc Yr Odyn SA31 . . . . .128 A3
Parc Yr Onen SA31 . . . . .129 A6
Parc-yr-Ynn SA44 . . . . .19 E4
Parc-y-Saint SA17 . . . . .94 B3
Parc Y Shwt **8** SA65 . . . . . .122 D3
Park Ave
  Capel Hendre SA18 . . . . . . .97 D6
  Cardigan / Aberteifi SA43 . .118 E5
  Kilgetty / Begelly SA68 . . . .134 D8
  Neath / Castell-Nedd
  SA10 . . . . .162 C4
  The Mumbles / Y Mwmbls
  SA3 . . . . .173 A8
Park Cl Gorseinon SA4 . . . .151 B2
  Pontardulais SA4 . . . . .143 C2
  Swansea / Abertawe, Bon-y-maen
  SA1 . . . . .161 B3

Park Cl continued
  Swansea / Abertawe, Cae-mawr
  SA6 . . . . .153 E1
Park Cnr Rd SA61 . . . . .124 B4
Park Cres Llanelli SA15 . . . .148 C5
  Neath / Castell-Nedd
  SA10 . . . . .162 C7
Park Dr
  Neath / Castell-Nedd
  SA10 . . . . .162 C7
  Swansea / Abertawe SA2 . .166 F7
Parkes St SA16 . . . . .137 E2
Park Eynon **6** SA15 . . . . . .148 D5
Park Hall SA31 . . . . .129 A6
Parkhill Rd SA5 . . . . .160 C5
Parkhill Terr SA5 . . . . .160 C5
Park Howard Rd SA18 . . . . . .99 D6
Park La
  Dyffryn Cennen SA18 . . . . . .78 F6
  Llangennech SA14 . . . . . . .150 C8
  Pembroke Dock / Doc Penfro
  SA72 . . . . .132 C2
Park La / Lon Y Parc
  SA18 . . . . .99 D8
Parkland Prim Sch SA2 . . .166 B6
Parklands SA70 . . . . .106 A4
Parklands Ct
  Ammanford / Rhydaman
  SA18 . . . . .98 A6
  Swansea / Abertawe SA2 . .166 B6
Parklands Rd / Heol
  Tir-y-Parc SA18 . . . . .98 A7
Parklands View SA2 . . . . . .166 B5
Park Mill Rd SA18 . . . . .98 A7
Park Pl
  Swansea / Abertawe SA2 . .166 F5
  Tenby / Dinbych-y-pysgod
  SA70 . . . . .135 D4
Park Rd Clydach SA6 . . . . . .154 E8
  Gorseinon SA4 . . . . .151 B2
  Gowerton / Tre-gwyr SA4 . .158 C4
  Haverfordwest / Hwlffordd
  SA61 . . . . .125 B6
  Pen-clawdd SA4 . . . . .156 E4
  Southgate SA3 . . . . .171 A5
  Tenby / Dinbych-y-pysgod
  SA70 . . . . .135 D4
  Ynystawe SA6 . . . . .154 C4
Park St
  Fishguard / Abergwaun
  SA65 . . . . .122 D3
  Llanelli SA15 . . . . .148 D5
  Pembroke Dock / Doc Penfro
  SA72 . . . . .132 C2
  Swansea / Abertawe SA1 . .174 A3
  The Mumbles / Y Mwmbls
  SA3 . . . . .173 B5
  Whitland / Hendy-Gwyn
  SA34 . . . . .126 C3
Park St / Stryd Y Parc
  Brynamman SA18 . . . . .99 D8
  Ammanford / Rhydaman
  SA18 . . . . .98 C6
ParkTerr
  Burry Port SA16 . . . . .137 D3
  Pontarddulais SA4 . . . . . . .143 D4
  Swansea / Abertawe SA1 . .160 C1
  10 Tenby / Dinbych-y-pysgod
  SA70 . . . . .135 E4
ParkThe SA2 . . . . .166 A7
ParkView
  Lamphey SA71 . . . . .105 A3
  Llanelli SA14 . . . . .140 F1
  Loughor SA4 . . . . .157 D8
Park View Cres SA72 . . . . . .132 C2
Park View Dr SA17 . . . . .136 A4
Park View Terr SA2 . . . . . . .166 D6
Parkview Terr / Trem Y Parc
  SA15 . . . . .148 C5
Park Way SA2 . . . . .166 B6
Parkway Cl SA62 . . . . .68 B4
Parkwood SA4 . . . . .158 C4
Parrog Rd SA42 . . . . .13 E4
ParrogThe SA64 . . . . .122 B5
Parry Rd SA6 . . . . .153 E1
Parsonage La SA68 . . . . . . .134 A8
Parsons Gn SA70 . . . . .106 B4
Paskeston Rd SA70 . . . . . . .105 C6
Pastoral Way SA2 . . . . .166 B8
Patagonia Wlk **5** SA1 . . . .174 B1
Pat Chown Ct / Llys Pat
  Chown SA8 . . . . .147 E4
Paterchurch SA72 . . . . .133 B8
Paviland Pl SA5 . . . . .159 F5
Paxton Dr SA1 . . . . .174 A1
Paxton St SA1 . . . . .174 A2
Paxton's Twr (NT)★
  SA15 . . . . .77 F6
Paynter St SA71 . . . . .133 C4
Pearl St SA6 . . . . .154 F8
PebblesThe SA62 . . . . .123 C4
Pedrog Terr SA1 . . . . .160 B1
Peggys La **4** SA61 . . . . . . .124 C5
Pegler St SA5 . . . . .160 C3
Pelcomb Hill SA62 . . . . .124 C8
Pelcomb Villas SA62 . . . . . . .67 D5
Pelican St SA9 . . . . .138 F2
Pell St SA1 . . . . .174 A3
Pemberton Ave **4**
  SA16 . . . . .137 D2
Pemberton Pk SA14 . . . . . .149 C6
Pemberton Rd SA14 . . . . . .149 C5
Pemberton's Chocolate
  Farm★ SA34 . . . . .55 C4
Pemberton St SA15 . . . . . . .148 D4
Pembrey & Burry Port Sta
  SA16 . . . . .137 E2

Pembrey Ctry Pk★
  SA16 . . . . .108 D3
Pembrey Properties Ind Est
  SA16 . . . . .108 E3
Pembrey Rd
  Kidwelly / Cydweli SA17 . . .136 B2
  Llanelli SA15 . . . . .148 C6
Pembrey Village CP Sch
  SA16 . . . . .137 A2
Pembroke Bldgs **5**
  SA1 . . . . .174 C2
Pembroke Castle (remains
  of)★ SA71 . . . . .133 B5
Pembroke Dock Com Sch
  SA72 . . . . .132 D2
Pembroke Dock Sta
  SA72 . . . . .132 D3
Pembroke Leisure Ctr
  SA72 . . . . .133 A7
Pembroke Pl **4** SA1 . . . . .174 C2
Pembroke Rd
  Freystrop SA62 . . . . .87 A6
  Haverfordwest / Hwlffordd
  SA61 . . . . .124 F2
  Pembroke Dock / Doc Penfro
  SA72 . . . . .132 C1
  Pembroke / Penfro SA72 . . .133 A7
  Pembroke Sch SA72 . . . . . .133 A7
Pembrokeshire Candle Ctr★
  SA42 . . . . .33 A7
Pembrokeshire Coll / Coleg
  Sir Benfro SA61 . . . . .124 E3
Pembrokeshire Cty
  Showground★ SA62 . . . . . .68 A5
Pembrokeshire Motor Mus★
  SA62 . . . . .67 A6
Pembroke St
  Pembroke Dock / Doc Penfro
  SA72 . . . . .132 B2
  Swansea / Abertawe SA5 . .160 B3
Pembroke Sta SA71 . . . . . . .133 D4
Penallt SA2 . . . . .165 E8
Penallt Rd SA15 . . . . .148 F6
Penallt Terr SA15 . . . . .148 F6
Penally Hts SA70 . . . . .135 A2
Penally Pottery★ SA70 . . . .135 B2
Penally Rd SA70 . . . . .135 E4
Penally Sta SA70 . . . . .135 E4
Penally VC Sch SA70 . . . . . .135 B3
Penbanc SA65 . . . . .122 C3
Penblewin SA67 . . . . .70 E3
Penbryn SA48 . . . . .120 C6
Penbryn Ave SA31 . . . . .128 D5
Penbryn Rd SA10 . . . . .162 F7
Penbryn Terr SA2 . . . . .166 F7
Pen-Cae-Crwn Rd SA4 . . . .151 A3
Pencaerfenni Ct SA4 . . . . . .156 B3
Pencaerfenni La SA4 . . . . . .156 B3
Pencaerfenni Pk SA4 . . . . . .156 B3
Pencae Terr SA15 . . . . .148 F5
Pen-Cefn-Arda Rd SA4 . . . .151 B4
Penclawdd Prim Sch
  SA4 . . . . .156 E4
Penclawdd Rd SA4 . . . . .157 C5
Pencoed SA2 . . . . .165 E8
Pen Coed Isaf Rd SA4 . . . . .150 B4
Pencoed Rd SA16 . . . . .137 E3
Pencwmdu SA8 . . . . .100 A1
Pendarren SA8 . . . . .100 B1
Pendderi Rd Bynea SA14 . . .150 A4
  Llanelli SA14 . . . . .149 F5
Penderry Rd SA5 . . . . .160 B4
Pendine Hill SA33 . . . . .91 D3
Pendre SA43 . . . . .118 D4
Pendre SA43 . . . . .118 D4
Penffordd CP Sch SA63 . . . .53 A1
Penfilia Rd SA5 . . . . .160 C4
Penfilia Terr **3** SA5 . . . . . .160 C4
Pengelli Prim Sch SA4 . . . .151 C6
Pengorof Ct SA9 . . . . .138 E1
Pengors Rd SA5 . . . . .153 B2
Pengry Rd SA4 . . . . .150 F1
Pengwern Rd SA6 . . . . .160 C8
Peniel Green Rd SA7 . . . . . .162 A8
Peniel Rd SA5 . . . . .160 D5
Pen Isa Coed SA1 . . . . .167 F7
Penlan SA1 . . . . .150 A6
Penlan / Castell-Nedd
  SA10 . . . . .162 D8
  Swansea / Abertawe SA5 . .160 C6
PenlanTerr
  Newcastle Emlyn / Castell
  Newydd Emlyn SA38 . . . . .119 D4
  Swansea / Abertawe SA5 . .160 C6
Penlan-uchaf Farm Gdns★
  SA65 . . . . .32 D6
Penlan Village SA38 . . . . . . .17 A3
Penllech SA15 . . . . .109 E4
Penllergaer Bsns Pk
  SA4 . . . . .152 D3
Penllergaer Forest Walks★
  SA4 . . . . .152 A2
Penllergaer Prim Sch
  SA4 . . . . .152 A2
Penllwyngwyn Farm Dr
  SA14 . . . . .149 F6
Penllwyngwyn Rd SA14 . . .150 A6
Pen-Llwyn-March Rd
  SA5 . . . . .160 A3

Penllwynrhodyn Rd
  SA14 . . . . .149 E4
Penmachno SA6 . . . . .153 D1
Penmaen Burrows Burial
  Chamber★ SA3 . . . . .170 C5
Penmaen Terr SA1 . . . . .167 B7
Penmynydd SA4 . . . . .151 B1
Penmynydd Rd SA5 . . . . . . .160 B5
Pen-nant SA14 . . . . .141 D6
Pennar CP Schools
  SA72 . . . . .132 A1
Pennard Dr SA3 . . . . .171 A6
Pennard Prim Sch SA3 . . . .171 A5
Pennard Rd
  Bishopston SA3 . . . . .171 E7
  Southgate SA3 . . . . .171 B5
Pennard St SA5 . . . . .160 C3
Pennine Cl SA5 . . . . .159 E3
Penn's Cl SA61 . . . . .124 D3
Pen Parc SA14 . . . . .96 E6
Penplas Rd
  Swansea / Abertawe, Cadle
  SA5 . . . . .159 C7
  Swansea / Abertawe SA5 . .159 F8
Penpound La / Lon
  Penpound SA18 . . . . .98 F8
Penprys Rd
  Llanelli, Bryn SA14 . . . . . . .149 E7
  Llanelli Rural SA14 . . . . . . .141 E1
  Llanelli SA14 . . . . .149 E8
Pen Rhiw SA62 . . . . .123 B6
Penrhiw / Hilltop SA14 . . . .141 A2
Penrhiwiau SA8 . . . . .147 E3
Penrhiw Rd SA6 . . . . .153 D2
Penrhos SA4 . . . . .151 A1
Penrhos Cottage★ SA66 . . .53 D4
Penrhos Pl SA5 . . . . .159 F4
Penrhyn Ave SA5 . . . . .160 B4
Penrhyn Ct SA6 . . . . .154 A3
Penrice Ct
  Swansea / Abertawe,
  Graig Trewyddfa SA6 . . . . .161 A6
  1 Swansea / Abertawe,
  Mount Pleasant SA1 . . . . . .174 A4
Penrice Forest Wlks★
  SA3 . . . . .117 C7
Penrice St SA6 . . . . .153 F1
Penryce Ct SA1 . . . . .174 B2
Penry Pl SA15 . . . . .148 E5
Penry Point SA73 . . . . .87 C3
Pensalem Rd SA5 . . . . .160 B5
Penshannel
  Neath Abbey SA10 . . . . . . .155 F1
  Neath / Castell-Nedd SA10 .162 F8
Penslade SA65 . . . . .122 D4
Pentewan Cl SA6 . . . . .154 A4
Pentip Church in Wales Prim
  Sch SA15 . . . . .148 C6
Pentland Cl SA5 . . . . .159 D4
Pentle Dr SA69 . . . . .134 B6
Pentlepoir CP Sch SA69 . . .134 B6
Pentood Ind Est SA43 . . . . .118 E3
Pentre Banadl SA2 . . . . .165 E4
Pentrechwyth Prim Sch
  SA1 . . . . .161 A3
Pentrechwyth Rd SA1 . . . . .160 F2
Pentre-Chwyth Rd SA1 . . . .161 A3
Pentre-Dwr Rd SA7 . . . . . . .161 E5
Pentrefelin St SA31 . . . . . . .128 E5
Pentregethin Rd SA5 . . . . . .159 E5
Pentreguinea Rd SA1 . . . . . .174 C4
Pentrehafod Comp Sch
  SA1 . . . . .160 D3
Pentre Hedyn SA38 . . . . . . .119 D6
Pentremalwed Rd SA6 . . . . .160 F7
Pentre Mawr Rd SA1 . . . . . .160 D2
Pentremeurig Rd SA31 . . . .128 A6
Pentrepoeth Jun & Inf Schs
  SA6 . . . . .154 A1
Pentrepoeth Rd
  Llanelli SA15 . . . . .148 D8
  Swansea / Abertawe SA6 . .153 F2
Pentrepoeth School Rd
  Morriston / Treforris SA6 . .154 A1
  Swansea / Abertawe SA6 . .153 F1
Pentre Rd
  Pontarddulais SA4 . . . . . . .143 C2
  St Clears / Sanclêr
  SA33 . . . . .127 E4
Pentre-Treharne Hill
  SA1 . . . . .160 D4
Pentre-Treharne Rd
  SA1 . . . . .160 D3
Pentwyn SA4 . . . . .157 A3
Pentwyn Rd SA9 . . . . .139 B7
Pentwyn Rd / Ffordd Pen
  Twyn SA18 . . . . .98 C7
Pentyla SA10 . . . . .162 F7
Pentyla Rd SA2 . . . . .166 E8
Penuel Cl SA4 . . . . .151 A1
Penuel St SA31 . . . . .129 A5
Pen Wallis SA65 . . . . .122 D2
Penybanc
  Carmarthen / Caerfyrddin
  SA31 . . . . .129 B7
  Llangunnor SA31 . . . . .128 C3
Penybanc La SA4 . . . . .151 A4
Penybanc Rd SA18 . . . . .98 A6
Penybedd Rd SA16 . . . . . . .108 D2
Pen-y-Bigyn SA15 . . . . .148 E4
Penybryn Llanelli SA14 . . . .141 B3
  Llanelli SA14 . . . . .149 E6
  Pontyberem SA15 . . . . .95 F3
Pen-y-Bryn
  Cwmllynfell SA9 . . . . .100 D3
  Fishguard / Abergwaun
  SA65 . . . . .122 C3

Pen-y-Bryn *continued*
Neath / Castell-Nedd, Pen-yr-Heol
SA10 . . . . .162 E6
Penybryn Ave SA16 . . . .137 E3
Pen-y-Bryn Cl SA4 . . . .151 B2
Pen-y-bryn Cvn Site
SA14 . . . . .149 E2
Penybryn Rd SA4 . . . . .151 E2
Penybryn Senior Specl Sch
SA6 . . . . .160 D7
Pen Y Cae SA31 . . . . . .128 A3
Pen-y-Cae La SA4 . . . .150 E2
Pen Y Cwm SA2 . . . . . .159 D2
Pen-y-Dre SA4 . . . . . . .158 B4
Penydre Rd SA6 . . . . . .146 F1
Penyfai La SA15 . . . . . .148 B8
Pen-y-Fai La SA15 . . . .140 B1
Pen-y-Fan SA7 . . . . . . .161 F6
Penyfan Rd SA15 . . . . .148 F4
Pen-y-Fforrd SA33 . . . .127 D4
Pen-y-Fon St SA15 . . . .148 E3
Pen-y-Fro SA2 . . . . . . .158 B1
Pen-y-Fro Cl SA2 . . . . .158 B1
Pen Y fro Prim Sch SA2 . .165 B8
Penygaer Prim Sch
SA14 . . . . .148 F7
Penygaer Rd SA14, SA15 .148 F6
Pen-y-Garn
St David's & the Cathedral Close
SA2 . . . . .123 C4
Swansea / Abertawe SA1 .161 A3
Penygarn Rd / Heol
Penygarn SA18 . . . . . . .97 F5
Penygraig Dr ⑪ SA67 . . .89 E6
Penygraig Rd SA14 . . . .149 E4
Pen-y-Graig Rd
Pontardawe SA8 . . . . . . .147 F3
Swansea / Abertawe SA1 .167 B8
Ystradowen SA9 . . . . . . .100 C7
Penygroes Prim Sch
SA14 . . . . .97 D8
Penygroes Rd / Heol
Penygroes
Ammanford SA18 . . . . . . .97 C5
Gorslas SA14 . . . . .97 C6
Pen-y-Heol SA10 . . . . . .162 D4
Pen Y Lan SA4 . . . . . . .156 F3
Pen Y Maes SA4 . . . . . .153 C2
Penymorfa SA31 . . . . . .129 A3
Pen-y-Morfa SA15 . . . . .148 E3
Pen Y Morfa SA4 . . . . .157 A4
Penymorfa La SA31 . . . .129 A3
Pen-y-Mor Rd SA5 . . . .160 C5
Pen Y Pwll SA4 . . . . . . .143 D3
Penyrber SA62 . . . . .48 D3
Pen-yr-Alley Ave SA10 . .162 E6
Penyrallt SA9 . . . . .99 C7
Pen-yr-Allt SA9 . . . . . . .139 B8
Pen-yr-Grug SA9 . . . . . .139 A8
Pen-yr-Heol SA10 . . . . .162 E5
Penyrheol Com Sch
SA4 . . . . .151 B3
Penyrheol Dr SA15 . . . . .148 E8
Pen-yr-Heol Dr SA2 . . . .166 B7
Penyrheol Prim Sch
SA4 . . . . .151 B3
Penyrheol Rd SA4 . . . . .151 A4
Pen-y-Rhiw
Cardigan / Aberteifi SA43 . . .2 F2
Pen-Rhiw-fawr SA9 . . . . .100 B5
St Dogmaels / Llandudoch
SA43 . . . . .118 A4
Pen-Yr-Yrfa SA6 . . . . . .153 D1
Penywarc SA15 . . . . . . .148 F5
Ystalyfera SA9 . . . . .139 A7
Penywern Rd SA9 . . . . .139 A6
Pen-y-Wern Rd SA6 . . . .154 E8
Pen-y-Wern Terr SA1 . . .160 D4
Peregrine Cl ⑪ SA61 . . .124 E5
Peris Rd SA5 . . . . .160 A5
Perrot Ave ② SA61 . . . .125 A5
Perrots Rd SA61 . . . . . .125 A5
Peter Cash Ho SA1 . . . .167 A5
Peter's Finger La SA67 . .89 D7
Peter's La SA62 . . . . . .123 C4
Peter St SA1 . . . . .160 C1
Peter Terr SA1 . . . . . . .160 C1
Peterwell Terr SA48 . . . .120 B5
Pheasant Rd SA8 . . . . . .147 B2
Phoenix Pk Rugby & Soccer
Gd SA64 . . . . .122 B5
Philadelphia Ct ④ SA6 . .161 A8
Philadelphia La SA1 . . . .160 D2
Phillips Ave SA73 . . . . . .131 D4
Phillips La SA72 . . . . . . .132 B1
Phillip's La SA71 . . . . . .104 F5
Phillips Par SA1 . . . . . . .167 B6
Phillip St SA5 . . . . .160 A2
Phoenix Bowl & Seal Hospl★
SA73 . . . . .131 B2
Phoenix Bsns Pk SA7 . . .161 B7
Phoenix Ctr SA7 . . . . . .161 C7
Phoenix Way
Penllergaer SA4 . . . . . . .151 F1
Swansea / Abertawe SA7 .161 B8
Phyllis St SA5 . . . . .160 A2
Pibwrlwyd La SA31 . . . . .128 F1
Picket Mead Rd SA3 . . . .172 E5
Picton Arc SA1 . . . . . . .174 A2
Picton Castle★ SA62 . . . .88 A8
Picton Castle Gdns★
SA62 . . . . .87 F8
Picton Cl
Milford Haven / Aberdaugleddau
SA73 . . . . .131 A2
③ Templeton SA67 . . . . . .89 E6

Picton Ct SA31 . . . . . . .128 D5
Picton La
Lampeter / Llanbedr Pont Steffan
SA48 . . . . .120 C4
Swansea / Abertawe SA1 .174 A2
Picton Pl
Carmarthen / Caerfyrddin
SA31 . . . . .128 D5
① Haverfordwest / Hwlffordd
SA61 . . . . .125 B5
⑫ Narberth / Arberth
SA67 . . . . .70 D1
Picton Rd
Milford Haven / Aberdaugleddau
SA73 . . . . .131 A2
Neath / Castell-Nedd SA10 .162 F7
Neyland SA73 . . . . .132 B5
Tenby / Dinbych-y-pysgod
SA70 . . . . .135 E4
Picton Terr
Carmarthen / Caerfyrddin
SA31 . . . . .128 D4
Swansea / Abertawe SA1 .174 A4
Tenby / Dinbych-y-pysgod
SA70 . . . . .135 E4
Pier Hill SA70 . . . . .135 F5
Pier Rd
Milford Haven / Aberdaugleddau
SA73 . . . . .131 D2
Pembroke Dock / Doc Penfro
SA72 . . . . .132 C3
Pier St SA1 . . . . .174 C2
Pigsfoot La SA62 . . . . . .123 C4
Pilgrim's Way SA62 . . . . .66 E8
Pill La SA73 . . . . .131 D2
Pill Parks Way ⑤ SA62 . .87 E4
Pill Rd Hook SA62 . . . . . .87 D6
Milford Haven / Aberdaugleddau
SA73 . . . . .131 E3
Pilot St SA43 . . . . .118 A4
Pineacre Cl SA2 . . . . . . .166 C5
Pine Cres SA6 . . . . .153 E2
Pine Tree Cl / Clos Y
Binwydd SA16 . . . . .137 F3
Pinetree Ct SA2 . . . . . . .166 C6
Pineway SA5 . . . . .160 C6
Pinewood Cl SA6 . . . . . .153 D1
Pinewood / Coed Y Pin
SA18 . . . . .98 D8
Pinewood Ct SA14 . . . . .149 D6
Pinewood Rd SA2 . . . . . .166 E6
Pinkney St SA1 . . . . . . .174 C3
Pitch La SA67 . . . . .89 D7
Pit St SA2 . . . . .123 B4
Pittsburgh Ct SA5 . . . . .159 F7
Plantasia★ SA1 . . . . . . .174 B3
Plas Cadwgan SA4 . . . . .152 C2
Plas-Cadwgan Rd SA6 . .154 C5
Plas Croeso SA4 . . . . . . .151 B1
Plas Gwernfadog Dr
SA6 . . . . .154 A5
Plasgwyn SA4 . . . . .143 D4
Plas-Gwyn Rd SA14 . . . . .97 D8
Plas Hos SA4 . . . . .151 C6
Plas Ioan SA31 . . . . .128 C2
Plasmarl Ind Est SA6 . . .160 F6
Plasmarl Prim Sch SA6 . . .160 E5
Plasmarl Terr SA6 . . . . .160 E5
Plas Melyn SA5 . . . . . . .159 F6
Plas Newydd
Dunvant SA2 . . . . .165 B8
Grovesend SA4 . . . . .151 C6
Plas Penwern SA31 . . . .128 D2
Plas Rd SA4 . . . . .151 C6
Plascycoed SA4 . . . . . . .138 F2
Plas Y Coed Ave SA6 . . .160 F8
Plas Y Coed Rd SA6 . . . .160 F8
Plas Y Ddol SA4 . . . . . . .128 C2
Plas-y-Fforest
Fforest SA4 . . . . .142 F4
Penllergaer SA4 . . . . . . .152 C2
Plas-y-Fron SA65 . . . . . .122 E3
Plas-y-Gamil Rd SA64 . .122 A6
Players Ave SA6 . . . . . .154 D8
Pleasant Cl SA4 . . . . . . .150 F3
Pleasant Rd SA4 . . . . . .151 D2
Pleasant Row
⑤ Llanelli SA15 . . . . . . .148 E5
Swansea / Abertawe SA5 .160 C4
Pleasant St
Swansea / Abertawe, Clun-Du
SA6 . . . . .153 F1
② Swansea / Abertawe,
Mount Pleasant SA1 . . . .174 B3
Pleasant View
Hundleton SA71 . . . . . . .103 B5
Llanelli SA15 . . . . .148 F8
Trimsaran SA17 . . . . .109 C7
Pleasant View Terr
Swansea / Abertawe,
Mount Pleasant SA1 . . . .174 A4
① Swansea / Abertawe, Penfilia
SA5 . . . . .160 C4
Plough Rd SA1 . . . . .160 D3
Plover Cl SA62 . . . . .160 C7
Plum Tree Dr SA62 . . . . . .67 D7
Plunch La SA3 . . . . .173 C3
Plymouth St SA1 . . . . . .174 A2
Pobbles Cl SA3 . . . . . . .171 A4
Pocketts Wharf ⑪ SA1 . .174 C2
Pointfields Cresent
SA73 . . . . .131 B1
Point La SA72 . . . . .104 E6
Point Rd SA62 . . . . .85 C7
Point St SA73 . . . . .131 B2

Pond Mdw SA73 . . . . . . .131 F5
Pondside SA1 . . . . .128 C4
Pond St ② SA31 . . . . . .128 E5
Pontamman Rd SA18 . . . .98 D7
Pontardawe Ind Est
SA8 . . . . .147 F5
Pontardawe Rd
Clydach SA6 . . . . .155 A8
Pontardawe SA8 . . . . .99 D3
Pontarddulais Prim Sch
SA4 . . . . .143 D3
Pontardulais Comp Sch
SA4 . . . . .143 D5
Pontardulais Ind Est
SA4 . . . . .143 C6
Pontardulais Junction
SA4 . . . . .143 B5
Pontardulais Rd
Cross Hands SA14 . . . . . . .97 B6
Gorseinon SA4 . . . . .151 C3
Llangennech SA14 . . . . . .142 C2
Swansea / Abertawe SA5 .159 C6
Tycroes SA18 . . . . .97 E5
Pontardulais Workshops
SA4 . . . . .143 C6
Pont Aur SA9 . . . . .139 E7
Pont-ceri SA38 . . . . .119 B7
Pontfaen SA32 . . . . .77 C3
Pontfaen Rd
Cwm Gwaun SA65 . . . . . . .32 B4
Lampeter / Llanbedr Pont Steffan
SA48 . . . . .120 B5
Pontgarreg SA31 . . . . . .128 B4
Ponthenry Ind Est SA15 . .95 E4
Pontiets CP Sch SA15 . . .95 E3
Pontlliw Prim Sch SA4 . .152 A4
Pontyberem CP Sch
SA15 . . . . .96 A6
Pontybrenin Prim Sch /
Ysgol Gynradd Y Sir
Pontybrenin SA4 . . . . . .151 B1
Pont-y-Cleifion SA43 . . .118 E4
Pont-y-Cob Rd
Gowerton SA4 . . . . .157 F6
Gowerton / Tre-gwyr SA4 .158 A6
Pont-y-Glasdwr ④ SA1 . .160 D1
Pont-y-Shoot SA1 . . . . .160 D5
Poplar Cl
Cross Hands SA14 . . . . . . .97 B7
Swansea / Abertawe SA2 .166 B8
Poplar St SA14 . . . . .97 B7
Poppy Dr SA73 . . . . .132 B7
Popton Rd SA71 . . . . . . .103 B5
Portfield SA61 . . . . .124 E4
Portfield Ave SA61 . . . . .124 F4
Portfield Specl Sch
SA61 . . . . .124 E4
Porth St SA38 . . . . .119 D4
Porth Y Plas SA31 . . . . .128 C3
Porth Y Waun SA4 . . . . .158 A6
Portia Terr SA1 . . . . . . .174 A4
Portland Sq SA62 . . . . . . .48 D3
Portmead Ave SA5 . . . . .159 E7
Portmead Pl SA5 . . . . . .159 E7
Portmead Prim Sch
SA5 . . . . .159 F6
Port Talbot Pl SA5 . . . . .159 C6
Port Tennant Rd SA1 . . .168 A7
Portway SA3 . . . . .172 A7
Port Way SA17 . . . . .93 F5
Post-gwyn SA35 . . . . . . .36 C3
Pothouse Rd SA73 . . . . .128 E4
Pottery Pl SA15 . . . . . . .148 D5
Pottery St / Stryd Y
Crochendy ⑦ SA15 . . . .148 D5
Pound The SA72 . . . . . . .104 F6
Powell Cl SA71 . . . . .133 C5
Powell St SA1 . . . . .174 B4
Powys Ave SA1 . . . . . . .167 A8
Powys Gdns SA1 . . . . . .166 F8
Poyer's Ave SA71 . . . . . .133 D4
Poyers Gr SA71 . . . . .89 E6
Poyston Cl ③ SA61 . . . . .124 F5
Precelly Cres SA64 . . . . .122 A6
Prendergast
Haverfordwest / Hwlffordd
SA61 . . . . .125 B6
Solva SA62 . . . . .48 D4
Prendergast Cty Prim Jun
Sch SA61 . . . . .125 B6
Prendergast Infants Sch /
Ysgol Fabanod Prendergast
SA61 . . . . .125 C6
Prendergast St SA15 . . . .148 E4
Prescelli Rd SA5 . . . . . . .160 A5
Prescelly Pl ⑪ SA61 . . . .125 B7
Prescelly Pl SA73 . . . . . .131 C3
Prescelly Rd ⑦ SA61 . . . .124 F5
Preseli Mohair Ctr★
SA66 . . . . .34 C1
Preseli Venture Activity Ctr★
SA62 . . . . .29 F6
Preseli View SA43 . . . . . .16 C7
Presely View SA72 . . . . .132 B2
Presswylfa Ho SA15 . . . .148 D3
Preswylfa Row ⑤ SA15 . .148 D3
Prettyman Dr SA10 . . . . .162 D3
Prif Fordd / High St
SA15 . . . . .148 C4
Prifysgol Cymru Abertawe /
Univ of Wales Swansea
SA2 . . . . .166 D4
Prifysgol Cymru Llanbedr
Pont Steffan / Univ of
Wales Lampeter SA48 . . .120 D5
Prifysgol Cymru / Univ of
Wales SA31 . . . . .75 E4

Primrose Cl SA73 . . . . . .132 B7
Primrose Ct SA5 . . . . . . .160 A5
Primrose Dr SA62 . . . . . .125 A7
Primrose Hill
Carmarthen / Caerfyrddin
SA31 . . . . .129 A3
Swansea / Abertawe SA1 .167 B7
Primrose La SA8 . . . . . . .147 D5
Primrose Row SA8 . . . . .147 D5
Primrose St SA1 . . . . . . .167 B7
Prince of Wales Cl SA73 . .87 C2
Prince Of Wales Rd
SA1 . . . . .174 B4
Prince Philip Hospl The
SA14 . . . . .149 E7
Princess Ct SA15 . . . . . .148 C5
Princess of Wales Ct
SA1 . . . . .161 C5
Princess Royal Way
SA61 . . . . .125 A4
Princess St
Gorseinon SA4 . . . . .151 B2
Llanelli SA15 . . . . .148 C5
Princess Way SA1 . . . . .174 B2
Princes St SA72 . . . . . . .132 B2
Priors Cres SA2 . . . . . . .165 B8
Priors Town SA3 . . . . . . .114 C2
Priors Way SA2 . . . . . . .165 B8
Priory Ave SA61 . . . . . . .125 A3
Priory Cl SA31 . . . . .129 B6
Priory Day Hospl SA31 . .129 C7
Priory Lodge Dr SA73 . . .131 C3
Priory Lodge Est SA73 . .131 C3
Priory Rd SA73 . . . . .131 C3
Priory St
⑦ Cardigan / Aberteifi
SA43 . . . . .118 C4
Carmarthen / Caerfyrddin
SA31 . . . . .129 A5
Kidwelly / Cydweli SA17 . .136 C4
Milford Haven / Aberdaugleddau
SA73 . . . . .131 C2
Priory St / Stryd Y Prior
SA17 . . . . .136 C5
Prioryville SA73 . . . . . . .131 D3
Promenade SA1 . . . . . . .174 A3
Promenade Cl SA73 . . . .132 B6
Promenade Dr SA73 . . . .132 A6
Promenade Terr SA3 . . . .173 B4
Promenade The
Llanstadwell SA73 . . . . . .132 A5
Pen-clawdd SA4 . . . . . . .156 C4
Swansea / Abertawe SA2 .166 E4
The Mumbles / Y Mwmbwls
SA3 . . . . .173 B8
Prospect Pl
Cwmllynfell SA9 . . . . .100 B7
Llanelli SA15 . . . . .148 D6
Pembroke Dock / Doc Penfro
SA72 . . . . .132 C2
Swansea / Abertawe SA2 .166 C7
Ystalyfera SA9 . . . . .139 B6
Prospect Terr SA3 . . . . .172 B6
Prosser Cl SA31 . . . . . . .129 A6
Providence La SA3 . . . . .172 A7
Pryce St SA15 . . . . .148 C6
Pryderi Foopath SA1 . . .167 B8
Prydwen Rd SA5 . . . . . . .159 B4
Puffin Way ③ SA62 . . . . .85 D8
Pumporth SA43 . . . . .16 A4
Puncheston Cty Prim Sch
SA62 . . . . .51 F8
Pwll CP Sch SA15 . . . . . .109 E4
Pwlldu La SA3 . . . . .171 F4
Pwllhai SA43 . . . . .118 C4
Pwll Melyn SA62 . . . . . . .48 C3
Pwll Rd Burry Port SA16 . .137 F3
Pembrey & Bury Port Town
SA16 . . . . .109 E4
Pwll St
Castlemartin SA71 . . . . . .103 C1
Swansea / Abertawe SA1 .160 D4
Pwll-y-Domen Rd SA5 . . .160 B3
Pwll-yr-Hwyaid SA5 . . . .159 E6
Pyle Ct SA3 . . . . .172 A5
Pyle Rd SA3 . . . . .172 A5
Pyntws Terr ② SA15 . . . .148 E4
Pyst Gwynion SA35 . . . . .36 A4

Quay St *continued*
Llandeilo SA19 . . . . .130 D5
Quay St / Stryd Y Cei ② . . .
. . . . .98 C7
Quay The SA31 . . . . .128 F4
Quay W SA1 . . . . .174 A3
Queen Elizabeth Ave
SA73 . . . . .132 B6
Queen Elizabeth Cambria
Comp Sch SA31 . . . . . . .128 D2
Queen Elizabeth Maridunum
Comp Sch SA31 . . . . . . .128 D2
Queen Mary's Wlk / Rhodfa'r
Frenhines Mary SA15 . . .148 E4
Queen's Ave SA4 . . . . . .151 B1
Queen's Ct ⑥ SA67 . . . . .70 D1
Queens Ditch ⑥ SA61 . . .124 F5
Queens Par SA70 . . . . . .135 D4
Queens Rd SA2 . . . . .166 D6
Queen's Rd
Neath / Castell-Nedd SA10 .162 F7
The Mumbles / Y Mwmbwls
SA3 . . . . .173 A5
Queen's Sq ⑭ SA61 . . . .125 A5
Queen St
⑥ Carmarthen / Caerfyrddin
SA31 . . . . .128 F5
Llandovery / Llanymddyfri
SA20 . . . . .121 D4
Pembroke Dock / Doc Penfro
SA72 . . . . .132 C3
Queen's Terr ⑥ SA43 . . .118 D4
Queensway
Haverfordwest / Hwlffordd
SA61 . . . . .125 B5
Llandovery / Llanymddyfri
SA20 . . . . .121 C4
Swansea / Abertawe SA1 .159 D4
Queen Victoria Rd SA15 . .148 C4
Quickwell Hill SA62 . . . . .123 C5

R

Raby St / Stryd Raby
SA15 . . . . .148 C6
Rackhill Ct ② SA61 . . . . .124 F5
Radford La SA70 . . . . . . .105 C6
Radnor Dr SA6 . . . . .154 D4
Radnor Ho ⑨ SA1 . . . . . .174 C2
Radyr Ave SA4 . . . . .165 F2
Ragged Staff SA69 . . . . .134 E2
Raglan Rd SA2 . . . . .166 C2
Railway Cotts SA6 . . . . . .153 F3
Railway Pl SA14 . . . . .96 E6
Railway Pl / Ffordd Y Wagen
⑧ SA15 . . . . .148 C4
Railway Terr
Cwmllynfell SA9 . . . . .100 B7
Ffairfach SA19 . . . . .130 D4
Gorseinon SA4 . . . . .151 C1
Neyland SA73 . . . . .132 C6
Swansea / Abertawe SA5 .159 E3
Railway Terr / Rhes Yr Orsaf
⑨ SA15 . . . . .148 C4
Rainbow Bsns Ctr SA7 . . .161 B6
Raleigh Ct SA2 . . . . .166 C6
Ralph St SA15 . . . . .148 D5
Ralph Terr SA15 . . . . . . .148 C4
Ramsay Gdns SA62 . . . . .123 A4
Ramsay Rd SA6 . . . . . . .146 E1
Ramsden Ct SA71 . . . . . .104 C4
Ramsden Rd SA6 . . . . . .154 C7
Ramsey Dr
Milford Haven / Aberdaugleddau
SA73 . . . . .131 D4
Swansea / Abertawe SA6 .153 D1
Ramsey Pl SA5 . . . . .159 F2
Randell Sq SA16 . . . . . . .137 A3
Rath The SA73 . . . . .131 D2
Ravenhill Rd SA5 . . . . . .159 F4
Raven Ind Est SA18 . . . . .99 B8
Ravensfield SA4 . . . . . . .158 D3
Ravens Wlk SA3 . . . . . . .172 F6
Rawlings Rd SA18 . . . . . .79 A2
Recorder St SA1 . . . . . . .174 A2
Rectory Ave SA73 . . . . . .131 A3
Rectory Cl
Letterston SA62 . . . . .50 E8
③ Llangwm SA62 . . . . . . .87 E4
Loughor SA4 . . . . .150 F1
Rectory Ct ③ SA70 . . . . .135 E5
Rectory Rd
Llangwm SA62 . . . . .87 E4
Trecwn SA62 . . . . .31 F4
Redford Hill SA71 . . . . . .103 F2
Redhill Pk SA61 . . . . . . .125 A7
Redstone Cross SA67 . . . .70 F4
Redstone Rd SA67 . . . . . .70 E2
Redwood Cl SA5 . . . . . . .160 A5
Redwood Rd SA3 . . . . . .172 F7
Refinery Rd SA71 . . . . . .103 B5
Regalia Terr SA15 . . . . . .148 E5
Regency Ho ④ SA1 . . . . .174 A3
Reginald Cl SA71 . . . . . .104 C3
Reginald St SA1 . . . . . . .168 A7
Rehoboth Rd / Heol
Rehoboth SA15 . . . . . . .109 E2
Reigit La SA3 . . . . .172 C6
Rembrandt Ct SA2 . . . . .166 E6
Reservoir Rd
Carmarthen / Caerfyrddin
SA31 . . . . .129 B7
Rhoscrowther SA71 . . . . .103 C5
Retreat Rd SA70 . . . . . . .135 B3

Rhandir SA14 ....149 E4
Rhandirfelin SA15 ......140 E1
Rhandir Terr SA14 ......142 B1
Rhandir Wen **3** SA39 ....39 B6
Rheidol Ave SA6 ....160 C8
Rheidol Ct SA6 ....160 C8
Rhes Gwaith Tyn SA15 ..148 F2
Rhestr Fawr SA9 ....138 F2
Rhes Yr Orsaf / Railway Terr
  9 SA15 ....148 C4
Rhianfa Gdns SA1 ......167 A6
Rhianfa La SA1 ....167 A7
Rhiw Babell SA31 ....128 F3
Rhiwderyn
  Birchgrove SA6 ....155 B1
  Swansea / Abertawe SA7 .162 B8
Rhiw-dol-Badau **8** SA43 .16 A5
Rhiwfawr Rd SA8 ....138 A1
Rhiw Felen SA41 ....33 E8
Rhiwlas SA2 ....165 E8
Rhiw Peter SA42 ....33 A7
Rhiw'r Cyrph SA19 ....24 A2
Rhiw Rd SA9 ....100 C5
Rhiw Rhydings SA20 ....121 F2
Rhiw Ydw SA20 ....44 C1
Rhodfa Bryn-Mawr /
  Brynmawr Ave **6** SA18 .98 B7
Rhodfa Bryn Rhos SA18 ..99 A8
Rhodfa Deg SA43 ....15 E5
Rhodfa Fadog
  Cwmrhydyceirw SA6 ...154 A4
  Swansea / Abertawe SA6 .153 F4
Rhodfa Frank SA18 ......98 B7
Rhodfa Llwyneithin
  SA15 ....148 D7
Rhodfa'r Brain SA15 ....159 E5
Rhodfar Capel SA16 .....137 B3
Rhodfa'r Dryw
  Cwmrhydyceirw SA6 ...154 A5
  Swansea / Abertawe SA6 .153 F5
Rhodfa'r Eos
  Cwmrhydyceirw SA6 ...154 A5
  Swansea / Abertawe SA6 .153 F6
Rhodfa'r Frenhines Mary /
  Queen Mary's Wlk
  SA15 ....148 E4
Rhodfar Gwendraeth
  SA17 ....136 D5
Rhodfa'r Wennol SA6 ...154 A5
Rhodfa'r Wiwer / Squirrel
  Wlk SA4 ....143 A5
Rhondda St SA1 ....166 B7
Rhoose Ferry Rd SA73 ...87 E1
Rhos Cotts SA10 ....139 F3
Rhosdeg SA19 ....130 F8
Rhosfa Rd SA18 ....80 F1
Rhosfa Rd / Heol Y Rhosfa
  SA18 ....80 F1
Rhoslan **1** SA14 ......96 F6
Rhos Las SA31 ....129 A3
Rhosmaen St SA19 .....130 E6
Rhos Rd SA5 ....159 F4
Rhossili Visitor Ctr★
  SA3 ....116 B6
Rhos-y-Dre SA43 ....118 E4
Rhyddings Park Rd SA2 .166 F6
Rhyddings Terr SA2 .....166 F6
Rhyddwen Pl SA6 ......146 B1
Rhyddwen Rd
  Craig-cefn-parc SA6 ...146 B1
  Swansea / Abertawe SA6 .145 F1
Rhydlanfair SA48 ....4 F7
Rhydwen SA9 ....139 E6
Rhyd Wen SA18 ....100 A8
Rhyd-y-Coed SA7 ....162 A8
Rhyd-y-Defaid Dr SA2 ..166 B5
Rhyd-y-Felin SA7 ....161 F5
Rhyd Y Fenni SA4 ......156 B3
Rhydyffynnon SA15 ......95 E3
Rhyd Y Fro SA19 ....63 D7
Rhyd-y-fro Prim Sch
  SA8 ....147 D8
Rhyd-y-Glyn SA7 ....161 F6
Rhyd-y-Gors SA33 ......127 C3
Rhyd-y-Pandy Rd SA6 ..153 E7
Rhyd Y Polan SA4 ......151 B1
Rhydyrafon SA15 ....148 F7
Rhyd-yr-Helyg SA2 .....166 C5
Rhys Prichard Sch / Ysgol
  Rhys Prichard SA20 ...121 D5
Rice St SA15 ....148 E4
Rice Street SA18 ....98 C6
Rice St / Stryd Rice
  SA18 ....98 C6
Richard John Rd SA73 ..131 D3
Richardson Rd SA1 .....167 B6
Richardson St
  Pontardawe SA8 ......147 C3
  Swansea / Abertawe SA1 .168 B6
Richard's Pl SA1 ....174 B3
Richard St
  10 Llanelli SA15 ....148 D5
  Swansea / Abertawe SA5 .160 C2
Richmond Cres SA61 ...124 F4
Richmond Ct SA1 ....167 A7
Richmond Mews **1**
  SA1 ....167 A6
Richmond Pk SA4 ......150 F1
Richmond Pk CP Sch / Ysgol
  Gynradd Parc Waundew
  SA31 ....129 A6
Richmond Rd
  Loughor SA4 ....150 F1
  Pembroke Dock / Doc Penfro
  SA72 ....132 C4

Richmond Rd continued
  Swansea / Abertawe SA2 .167 A7
Richmond Terr
  Carmarthen / Caerfyrddin
  SA31 ....129 A6
  Llanelli SA15 ....148 C4
  Swansea / Abertawe SA2 .166 F7
Richmond Villas SA1 ...167 A7
Richmond Way SA5 .....159 E5
Ridge Acre SA2 ....166 C4
Ridge The SA2 ....166 C4
Ridgeway
  Cardigan / Aberteifi SA43 .118 D2
  Killay SA2 ....165 D6
  Llanelli SA14 ....141 A2
Ridgeway La SA72 ......104 F7
Ridgeway The
  Cardigan / Aberteifi SA43 .118 D2
  Lamphey SA70 ....105 D3
  Penally SA70 ....135 A3
  Saundersfoot SA69 ...134 D4
  St Florence SA70 .....106 B4
Ridgewood Pk SA15 ....149 A5
Ridley Way SA3 ....172 A6
Rifleman's Row SA1 ....160 F2
Riga Ave SA73 ....132 B6
Rise The SA61 ....125 B5
Ritec Row SA73 ....135 B3
River Hill SA43 ....118 A4
Riversdale Rd SA3 .....172 F6
Riverside SA4 ....156 B2
Riverside Arc **11** SA61 .125 A5
Riverside Ave SA73 ....132 B6
Riverside Bsns Pk / Parc
  Busnes Glan yr Afon
  SA6 ....154 B1
Riverside Cvn Pk SA6 ..154 B3
Riverside Ind Pk SA14 ..150 C8
Riverside Quay Sh Ctr
  SA61 ....125 A6
Riverside View SA62 ...125 E3
River Terr SA4 ....143 A4
Riverview SA4 ....143 A5
River View
  Hundleton SA71 ......104 B3
  Llangwm SA62 ....87 E3
Robert Davies Ct SA4 ..143 C4
Robert Owen Gdns SA1 .168 B8
Roberts Rd / Heol Roberts
  SA1 ....167 F5
Robert St
  Milford Haven / Aberdaugleddau
  SA73 ....131 D2
  Swansea / Abertawe SA5 .160 C3
Robeston Cross SA73 ....85 F4
Robin Rd SA5 ....159 E7
Robins La SA3 ....115 C1
Robinson St SA15 .....148 D5
Roch Com Prim Sch
  SA62 ....66 E4
Roche Castle (rems of)★
  SA33 ....92 E5
Roch Hill SA62 ....49 E1
Rock Chwyth Rd SA8 ..147 F3
Rockhill SA3 ....173 B4
Rock La SA3 ....117 B4
Rockland Terr SA1 .....160 C1
Rock Mill Woollen & Water
  Mill★ SA44 ....20 B5
Rock St SA19 ....24 A2
Rock Terr
  Pembroke / Penfro SA71 .133 C4
  Swansea / Abertawe SA6 .153 F1
Rocky Pk SA71 ....133 B5
Rodfa Glyndwr SA31 ..129 A7
Rodney St SA1 ....167 B5
Roebuck Cl SA73 ......131 F5
Roger Beck Way SA2 ..166 E6
Roger St SA5 ....160 B7
Roland Ave SA15 ......148 C7
Roman Bridge Cl SA3 ..166 B2
Roman Ct SA3 ....166 B2
Roman Rd SA31 ....129 A3
Romilly Cres SA73 .....131 B3
Romney Way SA73 .....131 A3
Roperwright Cl SA4 ...158 B5
Ropewalk SA65 ....122 C4
Ropewalk Rd SA15 ....148 F2
Ropewalk Terr SA71 ...133 D4
Rope Wlk The SA73 ....131 B2
Ropeyard Cl SA65 .....122 C3
Rose Ave SA61 ....125 A2
Roseberry Terr SA6 ....160 E5
Rose Cotts SA4 ....115 F5
Rose Hill SA1 ....167 A7
Rosehill Terr SA1 ......167 B7
Roseland Rd SA5 .....158 F4
Roseland Terr SA1 .....167 F7
Rosemary Cl SA2 .....159 B1
Rosemary Ct SA6 .....153 F1
Rosemary La
  Amroth SA67 ....90 B4
  Carew SA68 ....105 C8
  Haverfordwest /
  SA61 ....125 A4
Rosemoor Nature Reserve★
  SA62 ....85 E6
Rosemount Gdns SA70 .135 D5
Rosewarne Cl SA5 ....158 F3
Rosewood Way SA5 ...159 F5
Ross Ave SA31 ....129 A6
Rosser's Field SA3 ....173 C3
Rotary Way SA16 ......108 E3
Rotherslade Rd SA3 ...172 F4
Rowan Ave SA2 ....166 B8
Rowan Cl Gorseinon SA4 .151 A4
  Killay SA2 ....165 D5
Rowland's Way SA71 ..133 C3
Royal Oak Rd SA2 .....166 B3

Rufus Lewis Ave SA4 ..151 A3
Ruggles Terr SA4 ......153 D1
Rumsey Dr SA73 ....132 B7
Runnymede SA2 ....166 E7
Rural Way SA2 ....166 B8
Rushacre La SA67 ......70 D2
Rushwind Cl SA3 ......172 C6
Rushwind Mews SA3 ..172 C6
Russell St Llanelli SA15 .148 D3
  Swansea / Abertawe SA1 .167 B6
Russell Terr SA31 .....128 D6
Rustic Cl SA2 ....166 B8
Ruther Pk SA61 ....124 C4
Ryelands La SA48 .....134 D8
Ryelands Way SA68 ....89 F2
Ryw Blodyn SA7 ......161 D6

S

Saddler St SA1 ....160 D4
Sageston CP Sch SA70 .105 E6
St Aidans VA Sch SA62 ..69 B5
St Aiden Dr SA3 ....165 D6
St Alban's Rd SA1 .....166 F5
St Andrews Cl SA3 ....165 E1
St Andrews Rd **3** SA31 .128 F5
St Andrew's Rd SA72 ..132 D2
St Anne's Ave **2** SA32 ..75 F3
St Anne's Cl SA3 ......173 A3
St Anne's Dr
  Milford Haven / Aberdaugleddau
  SA73 ....131 B2
  St Mary out Liberty SA70 .106 F6
St Anne's Pl SA73 .....131 B2
St Anne's Rd SA73 ....131 B2
St Ann's Cres SA71 ...133 B5
St Anthony's Way SA61 .124 F3
St Brides Cl SA43 .....143 D4
St Bride's La SA69 ....134 F2
St Brides Rd SA62 .....85 C7
St Brides View SA62 ...48 C2
St Bride's View SA62 ...66 E8
St Brides Way SA73 ...131 D5
St Catherines Cl SA67 ..90 A7
St Catherine St SA31 ..128 E5
St Catwg Wlk SA2 .....166 A2
St Cenydd Rd SA2 .....159 F6
St Christopher Dr SA2 .165 D6
St Clears Bsns Pk SA33 .127 D4
St Clears Leisure Ctr
  SA33 ....127 E5
St Clears Pl SA5 ......160 B7
St Clears Rd SA31 ....128 B4
St Clements Pk SA62 ...87 A6
St Clement's Rd SA73 .132 B5
St Daniel's Dr SA71 ...133 C3
St Daniel's Hill SA71 ..133 B3
St David Dr SA2 ......165 D6
St David's Ave
  Carmarthen / Caerfyrddin
  SA31 ....128 E5
  Whitland / Hendy-Gwyn
  SA34 ....126 C3
St David's Cath SA62 ..123 C4
St Davids Cl SA4 .....152 B2
St David's Cl Hendy SA4 .143 B4
  Llanelli SA15 ....148 C3
  Loughor SA4 ....150 F1
  Tenby / Dinbych-y-pysgod
  SA70 ....135 C5
St David's Cty Sec Sch /
  Ysgol Dewi Sant SA62 .123 E5
St David's Est SA6 ....161 B8
St Davids Hospl SA31 .128 C5
St David's Pl
  Goodwick / Wdig SA64 .122 A5
  2 Swansea / Abertawe
  SA1 ....174 B2
St Davids RC Prim Sch
  SA3 ....173 A6
St Davids Rd SA18 .....99 E7
St David's Rd
  Camrose SA62 ....124 D6
  Letterston SA62 ......30 D1
  Milford Haven / Aberdaugleddau
  SA73 ....131 C3
  Pembroke / Penfro SA71 .133 E4
  Swansea / Abertawe SA6 .161 B8
  Ystalyfera SA9 ......139 C6
St David's Sh Ctr SA1 .174 B2
St David's Sq SA1 .....174 B2
St David's St SA31 ....128 E5
St Degmans SA71 .....103 B5
St Dogmaels Rd SA43 .118 C3
St Donat's Ave SA2 ...166 B7
St Elli Sh Ctr SA15 ....148 D5
St Elmo Ave SA71 .....174 C4
St Faith's SA71 ....105 A3
St Florence Cheese & Maze★
  SA70 ....106 B4
St Florence Par **1**
  SA70 ....135 E4
St Florence VC Sch
  SA70 ....106 A4
St Francis RC Prim Sch
  SA73 ....131 D4
St George SA15 ....149 A4
St George's Ave SA34 .126 C1
St George's St **4** SA70 .135 C1
St George's Terr SA1 ..115 C1
St Giles Ct SA62 ....50 E8
St Govans Pl SA5 .....159 E5
St Govans Sh Ctr SA72 .132 C3
St Helen's Ave SA1 ....167 A5
St Helen's Cres SA1 ...167 A5
St Helens Prim Sch SA1 .167 B6

St Helen's Rd SA1 .....167 B6
St Helens Rugby & Cricket
  Gd 166 F5
St Hilary Dr SA2 ......165 D7
St Illtyd Rise SA16 ....137 B3
St Illtyd's Cres SA1 ...168 A7
St Illtyd's RC Prim Sch
  SA1 ....161 A3
St Ishmaels CP Sch
  SA62 ....85 A2
St Issell's Ave SA61 ...125 A2
St James Ct **3** SA1 ...167 A6
St James Gdns SA1 ...167 A7
St James's Cres SA1 ..167 A6
St James St SA67 ......70 E1
St John Lloyd RC Comp Sch /
  Ysgol Gyfun Gatholig Sant
  Ioan Llwyd SA14 ....149 B6
St Johns Ct SA6 ....154 B1
St John's Hill SA70 ....135 D5
St John's Rd Clydach SA6 .154 E7
  Pembroke Dock / Doc Penfro
  SA72 ....132 D2
  Swansea / Abertawe SA5 .160 B3
St John's St SA34 .....126 C3
St Joseph's Ct SA15 ..148 E5
St Joseph's RC Inf Sch
  SA1 ....160 D1
St Joseph's RC Jun Sch
  SA1 ....160 D1
St Joseph's RC Prim Sch
  SA6 ....155 A7
St Judes Cl SA5 ......160 C7
St Julian's St SA70 ...135 E4
St Katherines Ct SA1 ..161 D6
St Lawrence Ave SA73 .131 B3
St Lawrence Cl SA73 ..131 B3
St Lawrence Ct SA5 ...160 B7
St Lawrence Hill SA73 .131 B3
St Leger Cres SA1 ....167 F7
St Leonards St SA3 ...172 F3
St Leonards Ave SA62 ..68 C5
St Leonard's Pk SA73 ..87 A3
St Lukes Ct SA1 ......161 D6
St Margaret's Ave SA10 .169 C8
St Margaret's Cl SA61 .125 A2
St Margaret's Dr SA15 .148 B7
St Margaret's Way SA73 .85 E2
St Marks C in W Sch
  SA61 ....125 A2
St Marks Cl SA61 .....125 A2
St Martin's Pk SA61 ...125 A6
St Martin's Rd SA71 ..133 A4
St Marys Cath Prim Sch
  SA72 ....132 C1
St Mary's Pl SA68 ....134 D8
St Mary's RC Prim Sch
  SA14 ....149 B6
St Mary's RC Sch SA31 .128 D5
St Mary's Rd SA72 ...132 D2
St Mary's Rise SA16 ..137 F2
St Mary's Sq SA1 .....174 B2
St Mary's St
  5 Haverfordwest / Hwlffordd
  SA61 ....125 A5
  3 Tenby / Dinbych-y-pysgod
  SA70 ....135 E4
  Whitland / Hendy-Gwyn
  SA34 ....126 C2
St Mary St
  Cardigan / Aberteifi SA43 .118 D3
  Swansea / Abertawe SA1 .174 B2
St Matthews Ct SA1 ...174 B4
St Michael's Ave SA4 .143 B4
St Michael's Rd SA71 .133 E4
St Michael's Sch SA14 .149 E6
St Nicholas Cl SA5 ....158 E3
St Nicholas Ct
  Pembroke / Penfro SA71 .133 B5
  Tenby / Dinbych-y-pysgod
  SA70 ....135 B3
St Nicholas Ct SA2 ...165 F6
St Nicholas La **8** SA70 .135 E4
St Nicholas Sq **13** SA1 .174 C2
St Non's Ave SA31 ....128 D5
St Non's Cl SA62 .....123 C4
St Oswalds VA Sch SA68 ..88 F1
St Patrick's Rd SA72 ..132 D2
St Paul's Terr SA4 ....158 D8
St Peter's Ave SA5 ...159 D3
St Peter's Ct SA31 ....129 A5
St Peters Rd **6** SA62 ..86 E5
St Peter's Rd
  Milford Haven / Aberdaugleddau
  SA73 ....131 C3
  Pembroke Dock / Doc Penfro
  SA72 ....132 D2
  The Mumbles / Y Mwmbwls
  SA3 ....172 E5
St Peter's St **8** SA31 ..128 F5
St Peters Terr **1** SA15 .148 C4
St Peter's Terr SA2 ...159 E2
St Petrox Cl **3** SA71 .133 C3
St Rhidian Dr SA2 .....165 D7
St Rhidian Rd SA5 ....159 F6
St Teilo's Ct SA3 .....171 F6
St Teilo RC Prim Sch
  SA70 ....135 E6
St Teilo's Rd SA72 ....132 D2
St Teilo St SA4 ....143 C4
St Thomas Ave SA61 ..125 A2
St Thomas Gn SA61 ..125 A4
St Thomas Prim Sch
  SA1 ....174 C4
St Thomas St **5** SA48 .120 C5
St Twynnell's Cl **2**
  SA71 ....133 C3

St Tygwydd's Sch SA43 ..16 E6
St Vincent Cres **3** SA1 .174 B1
Salem Rd Llanelli SA15 .148 F8
St Clears / Sanclêr
  SA33 ....127 E8
  Swansea / Abertawe SA6 .160 D5
Salisbury Cl SA3 ......117 A6
Saltern Ind Est SA70 ..135 D4
Salthouse Cl SA4 .....156 A3
Salubrious Pass SA1 ..174 B2
Salubrious Pl SA1 .....174 B2
Samlet Rd SA7 ....161 C8
Samlet Sh Ctr SA7 ...161 C8
Samuel Cres SA5 .....160 A3
Samuels Rd SA9 ......100 B7
Sanderling Cl **3** SA61 .124 E5
Sandfield Rd SA16 ....137 E2
Sandhurst Rd SA73 ...131 D2
Sandpiper Rd SA15 ...148 B6
Sandringham Cl SA4 ..158 B8
Sandringham Pk SA7 ..154 C1
Sandringham Pk / Parc
  Sandringham SA6, SA7 .154 C1
Sandy Hill Rd SA69 ...134 D2
Sandyke Rd SA62 ......85 D8
Sandy La SA3 ....171 A6
Sandy Rd Llanelli SA15 .109 F3
  Llanelli SA15 ....148 A6
Sardis Cl SA5 ....158 E3
Sarlou Cl SA3 ....173 C3
Sarlou Ct SA2 ....166 F6
Sarn Helen SA19 ....23 E6
Saron Cl SA4 ....150 F3
Saron Rd Bynea SA14 ..149 F4
  Llangeler SA44 ....19 B1
Saron Rd / Heol Saron
  Ammanford SA18 ......97 F8
  Capel Hendre SA18 ...97 E6
Saundersfoot CP Sch
  SA69 ....134 C4
Saundersfoot Sta SA69 .134 C6
Saunders Rd SA70 ....105 C6
Saunders Way SA2 ...166 B5
Sawdern Rd SA71 .....103 B6
Sawel Ct SA4 ....143 A4
Sawel Terr SA4 ....143 A4
Scandinavia Hts SA69 .134 E2
Scarrowscant La SA61 .124 E3
School Gdns SA72 ....132 B1
School La
  Llandovery / Llanymddyfri
  SA20 ....121 D5
  Penally SA70 ....135 B3
  Pontardawe SA8 .....147 E5
  Tycroes SA18 ....97 F5
School Rd Glais SA7 ..155 A5
  Llanelli SA15 ....109 C4
  Llanelli SA15 ....148 F2
  Ystalyfera SA9 ......139 B6
  Ystradgynlais SA9 ..139 D8
School Rd / Heol Yr Ysgol
  Brynamman SA18 .....99 D8
  Cefn-bryn-brain SA9 ..100 B8
  Neath / Castell-Nedd
  SA10 ....162 C1
Scolton Manor Ctry Pk★
  SA62 ....68 D8
Scotchwell La SA61 ...125 C6
Scotchwell View SA61 .125 B6
Scotchwlk **3** SA61 ..125 B5
Scotsborough View
  SA70 ....135 C6
Scoveston Rd SA73 ....86 E2
Scurlock Dr SA73 .....132 B8
Sealands Dr SA3 .....173 C3
Seascape SA70 ....135 D6
Seaside Cres **4** SA15 .148 C4
Sea View SA4 ....156 A4
Sea View Com Prim Sch /
  Ysgol Golwg-y-Mor
  SA1 ....174 A4
Seaview Cres SA64 ...122 A5
Seaview Terr SA1 .....161 C2
Sea View Terr SA1 ....174 A4
Sebastopol St SA1 ....167 F1
Second Ave SA6 ......160 C8
Second St SA71 ......103 B5
Seion Hill SA44 ....19 E3
Senny Pl SA6 ....154 A5
Sentence Gdns **5** SA67 ..89 C4
Serecold Ave SA10 ...162 D6
Serpentine Rd SA70 ..135 C5
Settlands Hill SA62 ....85 C8
Severn Rd SA6 ....160 D8
Shakespeare Ave SA73 .131 D3
Shakespeare Cl SA61 .125 A3
Shands Rd SA18 ......98 B8
Sharpsburgh Pl SA1 ..160 D3
Shaw St SA4 ....158 B5
Shearwater Cl SA3 ...172 F6
Sheepwalk Rd SA66 ...70 A8
Sheffield Dr SA73 ....131 F5
Shelley Rd SA61 .....125 A3
Sheltery Hill SA62 .....67 E6
Shepherd's Rd SA6 ...160 E6
Shepherd's Terr SA4 ..151 A3
Sherborne Wlk SA21 .166 A1
Sherringham Dr SA3 ..172 F5
Shingrig SA43 ....118 B3
Shipman's La SA61 ...125 A4
Shirburn Cl SA71 .....102 D5
Shire Horse Ctr★ SA9 ..82 E3
Shoals Hook La SA61 .125 B7
Shopper's Wlk SA1 ...174 A2
Short St Clydach SA6 ..146 D1
  Swansea / Abertawe SA1 .174 A4
Shoulder of Mutton **2**
  SA71 ....133 C5

Shropshire Rd SA72 . . . . .132 D4
Shute La SA67 . . . . .89 F8
Siding Terr SA10 . . . . .162 D7
Sidney Webb Cl SA73 . . . .132 B6
Siemens Way SA7 . . . . . . .161 A5
Signal View SA61 . . . . . . .124 F7
Silent World Aquarium★
  SA70 . . . . .135 E6
Siloh Cres SA14 . . . . .160 D4
Siloh Rd SA1 . . . . .160 D4
Silver Cl SA3 . . . . .172 F7
Silverhurst SA73 . . . . .173 B3
Silverstream SA73 . . . . . .131 A4
Silverstream Cres SA73 . .131 A3
Silverstream Dr SA73 . . . .131 A3
Silver Terr SA16 . . . . .137 E2
Singleton Botanical Gdns★
  SA2 . . . . .166 D6
Singleton Hospl SA2 . . . . .166 D4
Singleton St SA1 . . . . .174 A2
Sir Thomas Picton Sch
  SA61 . . . . .125 B5
Siskin Cl SA61 . . . . .124 E5
Six Pit Junction Sta★
  SA7 . . . . .161 C6
Sixth La SA71 . . . . .104 F4
Sketty Ave SA2 . . . . .166 D7
Sketty Ct SA2 . . . . .166 D6
Sketty La SA2 . . . . .166 D6
Sketty Park Cl SA2 . . . . . .166 C6
Sketty Park Dr SA2 . . . . . .166 B6
Sketty Park Rd SA2 . . . . . .166 C6
Sketty Prim Sch SA2 . . . . .166 C7
Sketty Rd SA2 . . . . .166 E6
Skewen Sta SA10 . . . . . . .162 E7
Skinners La 15 SA61 . . . . .125 A5
Skinner St SA1 . . . . .160 C1
Skomer Dr SA73 . . . . .131 D4
Skomer Marine Nature
  Reserve★ SA62 . . . . .83 D5
Skomer Pl SA5 . . . . .159 D7
Slade SA65 . . . . .122 D4
Slade Gdns SA3 . . . . .172 F6
Slade Hall 6 SA1 . . . . . . .174 A4
Slade La SA62 . . . . .124 E7
Slade Pk SA61 . . . . .125 A6
Slade Rd SA3 . . . . .172 F5
Sladeway SA65 . . . . .122 D4
Slate St
  Swansea / Abertawe SA6 .160 F8
  Swansea / Abertawe SA6 .161 A8
Slaughter House La 2
  SA73 . . . . .131 C3
Slip Hill SA73 . . . . .131 D1
Slippery Back SA70 . . . . . .135 D8
Smithfield SA8 . . . . .147 E5
Smyrna St SA6 . . . . .160 E5
Smyth St SA65 . . . . .122 D4
Snady Hill Pk SA69 . . . . . .134 D2
Snowdon Dr SA3 . . . . . . .159 D3
Snowdon Rd SA16 . . . . . .137 E2
Snowdrop Cl 3 SA14 . . . .124 E4
Snowdrop La SA61 . . . . . .124 E4
Snow Terr SA9 . . . . .139 E6
Soar Cl SA4 . . . . .150 F1
Soar Rd SA14 . . . . .149 E4
Soar Terr SA6 . . . . .154 A1
Solva Cty Prim Sch SA62 . .48 C3
Solva Rd SA6 . . . . .160 C8
Solva Woollen Mill★
  SA62 . . . . .48 D4
Somerset Pl SA1 . . . . .174 C2
Somerset Rd SA4 . . . . . . .173 A4
Somerville Ct SA2 . . . . . . .166 E7
Southall Ave SA10 . . . . . .162 E6
Southampton Row
  SA72 . . . . .132 A2
South Cl SA3 . . . . .172 A6
South Cliff St SA70 . . . . . .135 E4
South Ct SA61 . . . . .124 D5
Southdown Cl SA71 . . . . . .133 C4
Southend SA3 . . . . .173 C4
Southerndown Ave SA3 . .165 F1
Southgate Pk SA62 . . . . . . .51 C1
Southgate Rd SA3 . . . . . . .171 A4
South Hook Rd SA73 . . . . .102 F8
Southlands
  Pembroke / Penfro SA71 . .133 C3
  Tenby / Dinbych-y-pysgod
  SA70 . . . . .135 D6
Southlands Dr SA3 . . . . . .172 F6
South Mdws SA71 . . . . . . .133 B4
South Mews SA71 . . . . . . .133 B4
South Par SA72 . . . . .132 A2
South Pembrokeshire Hospl
  SA72 . . . . .132 A2
South Prospect SA1 . . . . .174 B3
South Rd SA71 . . . . .133 C4
South Row SA68 . . . . .88 F1
South St SA62 . . . . .101 C4
South Terr SA71 . . . . .133 A4
South View SA4 . . . . .151 D2
Southward La SA3 . . . . . . .172 F4
Spencer Cl SA70 . . . . .105 C1
Spencer St SA5 . . . . .160 C4
Spencer Terr SA9 . . . . . . .139 D8
Spenser Way SA61 . . . . . .125 B4
Sperricomb La SA70 . . . . .135 D7
Spien Rd SA14 . . . . .97 D7
Spike's La SA73 . . . . .131 B2
Spilman St SA31 . . . . .128 F5
Spinney The SA2 . . . . .166 A6
Spionkop Rd SA6 . . . . . . .154 C6
Spittal VC Sch SA62 . . . . . .51 C3
Sportsway SA73 . . . . .132 B6
Spowart Ave SA15 . . . . . .148 C6
Springbourne Cl SA4 . . . .158 D3

Springburn Cl 1 SA67 . . .90 A2
Springfield SA3 . . . . .117 B4
Springfield Ave
  Neyland SA73 . . . . .132 B7
  Upper Killay SA2 . . . . . . .165 B5
Springfield Cl
  Gowerton / Tre-gwyr SA4 .158 B5
  2 Haverfordwest / Hwlffordd
  SA61 . . . . .125 B7
  Neyland SA73 . . . . .132 B7
Springfield Pk SA67 . . . . . .70 E2
Springfield Rd
  Carmarthen / Caerfyrddin
  SA31 . . . . .128 F6
  Neath / Castell-Nedd SA10 .162 F7
  Pembroke Dock / Doc Penfro
  SA72 . . . . .132 D1
Springfields SA15 . . . . . . .148 F2
Springfield St SA6 . . . . . . .153 F1
Springfield Terr SA16 . . . .137 E2
Spring Gdns
  Gorseinon SA4 . . . . .151 D1
  Letterston SA62 . . . . .50 F8
  Narberth / Arberth SA67 . .70 D1
  Whitland / Hendy-Gwyn
  SA34 . . . . .126 D3
Spring Gdns Ind Est
  SA34 . . . . .126 F3
Spring Gdns La 1 SA61 . .125 A5
Spring Gdns N SA10 . . . . .162 F7
Spring Gdns S SA10 . . . . .162 F7
Spring Terr SA1 . . . . .167 B6
Sprinkle La SA62 . . . . .87 D5
Spruce Way SA4 . . . . .152 C2
Square The SA65 . . . . .122 D3
Squire Ct SA1 . . . . .174 B2
Squirrel Wlk / Rhodfa'r
  Wiwer SA4 . . . . .143 F5
Stackpole Rd SA71 . . . . . .112 C6
Stackpole VC Sch SA71 . .112 A5
Stadwen Rd SA7 . . . . .161 E7
Stafford Comm SA4 . . . . .158 D7
Stafford St SA15 . . . . .148 D3
Stambridge La SA70 . . . . .105 C5
Stammers Gdn★ SA69 . . .134 E3
Stammers La SA69 . . . . . .134 E2
Stammers Rd SA69 . . . . . .134 E3
Stanley Pl SA1 . . . . .174 A3
Stanley Rd
  4 Llanelli SA15 . . . . .148 D3
  Neath / Castell-Nedd SA10 .162 F7
Stanley St
  Gwaun-Cae-Gurwen SA18 . .99 D6
  Llanelli SA15 . . . . .148 D2
  The Mumbles / Y Mwmbwls
  SA3 . . . . .173 A6
Stanley Terr SA1 . . . . .174 A3
Stapleton Pl 2 SA6 . . . . .160 F8
Starbuck Rd SA73 . . . . . . .131 C3
Station App
  Carmarthen / Caerfyrddin
  SA31 . . . . .128 F4
  Narberth / Arberth SA67 . .70 E1
Station Ct SA1 . . . . .174 B4
Station Hill
  Goodwick / Wdig SA64 . . .122 B6
  St Clears / Sanclêr
  SA33 . . . . .127 E7
Station Rd Brecon SA18 . . .80 E1
  Brynamman SA18 . . . . .99 E8
  Burry Port SA16 . . . . .137 E2
  Bynea SA14 . . . . .150 A3
  Cardigan / Aberteifi SA43 . .118 D3
  Crymych SA41 . . . . .34 F4
  Glais SA7 . . . . .155 A6
  Glanaman SA18 . . . . .99 A8
  Glan-rhyd SA9 . . . . .139 F8
  Gowerton / Tre-gwyr SA4 .158 C5
  Grovesend SA4 . . . . .151 D6
  Kidwelly / Cydweli SA17 . .136 A3
  Kilgetty / Begelly SA68 . . .134 D8
  Letterston SA62 . . . . .50 F8
  Llandeilo SA19 . . . . .130 E6
  Llandyssul SA44 . . . . .19 E3
  Llanelli SA15 . . . . .148 D4
  Llanfihangel-ar-Arth SA39 . .39 B7
  Llangadog SA19 . . . . .63 D7
  Llangennech SA14 . . . . . .150 C8
  Llanmorlais SA4 . . . . .156 C2
  Llanwrtyd Wells LD5 . . . . . .9 D1
  Loughor SA4 . . . . .157 C8
  Narberth / Arberth SA67 . .70 E8
  Neath / Castell-Nedd
  SA10 . . . . .162 E7
  Newcastle Emlyn / Castell
  Newydd Emlyn SA38 . . . .119 E4
  Neyland SA73 . . . . .132 C6
  Pembroke / Penfro SA71 . .133 C4
  Pen-clawdd SA4 . . . . .156 F4
  Pentlepoir SA69 . . . . .134 C7
  Pontarddulais SA4 . . . . . .143 B5
  Pontyberem SA15 . . . . . . .96 B6
  St Clears / Sanclêr
  SA33 . . . . .127 E5
  Swansea / Abertawe, Cockett
  SA5 . . . . .159 E3
  Swansea / Abertawe,
  Landore / Glandwr SA1 . . .160 D4
  Swansea / Abertawe, Trallwn
  SA7 . . . . .161 C2
  Tenby / Dinbych-y-pysgod
  SA70 . . . . .135 D4
  Whitland / Hendy-Gwyn
  SA34 . . . . .126 F2
  Ystradgynlais SA9 . . . . . . .138 F1
Station Rd / Ffordd-yr-Orsaf
  5 SA18 . . . . .98 B7

Station Terr
  Lampeter / Llanbedr Pont Steffan
  SA48 . . . . .120 C5
  Newcastle Emlyn / Castell
  Newydd Emlyn SA38 . . . .119 E4
  Pen-clawdd SA4 . . . . .156 F4
Stebonheath Prim Sch /
  Ysgol Gynradd Stebonheath
  SA15 . . . . .148 F5
Stebonheath Terr SA15 . . .148 F5
Steele Ave SA31 . . . . .128 D5
Stembridge Ave SA5 . . . . .159 E5
Stepaside CP Sch SA68 . . .134 D8
Stepaside Craft Village★
  SA67 . . . . .90 A2
Stephen's Gn La SA70 . . . .105 C4
Stephen's La SA62 . . . . . . .123 C4
Stephenson Rd SA2 . . . . . .165 F6
Stephen St 1 SA73 . . . . . .131 C3
Stephens Way SA31 . . . . . .128 F3
Stephens Way Ret Pk
  SA31 . . . . .128 F4
Stepney La SA2 . . . . .159 D1
Stepney Pl SA15 . . . . .148 D5
Stepney Prec 4 SA15 . . . .148 D5
Stepney Rd
  Burry Port SA16 . . . . .137 E3
  Glanaman SA18 . . . . .99 C8
  Llandeilo SA19 . . . . .130 E6
  Llanelli SA15 . . . . .109 F3
  Waunarlwydd SA5 . . . . . . .158 E3
Stepney St
  3 Llanelli SA15 . . . . .148 D5
  Swansea / Abertawe SA5 . .160 B2
Steps Rd SA70 . . . . .105 C6
Sterry Rd SA4 . . . . .158 B5
Stewart Dr / Ffordd Stewart
  12 SA18 . . . . .98 B7
Stewart Hall SA2 . . . . .166 D6
Stewart St SA15 . . . . .148 C6
Steynton Rd SA73 . . . . . . .131 D3
Stockwell Rd SA72 . . . . . .132 C4
Stokes Ave SA61 . . . . .125 B6
Stone Ct SA73 . . . . .131 D3
Stone St SA20 . . . . .121 D5
Stoneway Rd SA33 . . . . . . .92 E5
Stradey Ct 3 SA15 . . . . . .148 C7
Stradey Hill SA15 . . . . . . .109 F4
Stradey Park Ave SA15 . . .148 C6
Stradey Rd SA15 . . . . .148 C7
Strand
  Cardigan / Aberteifi SA43 . .118 C3
  Swansea / Abertawe SA1 . .174 B4
Strand Row SA1 . . . . .174 B3
Strand The
  Laugharne Township SA33 . .92 F5
  Saundersfoot SA69 . . . . . .134 E4
Stranraer Ave SA72 . . . . . .132 A1
Stranraer La SA72 . . . . . . .132 A1
Stranraer Rd SA72 . . . . . . .132 A1
Stratford Rd SA73 . . . . . . .131 C3
Strawberry Gdns SA70 . . .135 D4
Strawberry Hill SA62 . . . . .85 C7
Strawberry La SA70 . . . . . .135 B2
Strawberry Pl SA6 . . . . . . .153 F1
Strongbow Wlk SA71 . . . .133 B6
Stryd Arthur / Arthur St
  SA18 . . . . .98 B7
Stryd Cannon / Cannon St
  SA18 . . . . .99 D8
Stryd Chapman / Chapman
  St SA15 . . . . .148 C5
Stryd Emma / Emma St 13
  SA15 . . . . .148 D4
Stryd Fawr / High St
  4 Glanaman SA18 . . . . .99 A8
  Swansea / Abertawe SA1 . .174 B4
Stryd Fawr / High Street
  SA18 . . . . .98 C7
Stryd Harold / Harold St 4
  SA18 . . . . .98 B7
Stryd Llewellyn / Llewellyn
  St 14 SA15 . . . . .148 D4
Stryd Lloyd / Lloyd St
  SA15 . . . . .148 D4
Stryd Marged / Margaret St
  6 SA18 . . . . .98 C7
Stryd Raby / Raby St
  SA15 . . . . .148 D4
Stryd Rhydychen / Oxford St
  SA1 . . . . .174 A2
Stryd Rice / Rice St
  SA18 . . . . .98 C6
Stryd Y Cei / Quay St 2
  SA18 . . . . .98 C7
Stryd-y-Coleg / College St
  SA18 . . . . .98 B7
Stryd Y Crochendy / Pottery
  St 7 SA15 . . . . .148 D5
Stryd-y-Gwynt / Wind St
  SA18 . . . . .98 B7
Stryd Y Parc / Park St
  Brynamman SA18 . . . . .99 D8
  Ammanford / Rhydaman
  SA18 . . . . .98 C6
Stryd Y Prior / Priory St
  SA17 . . . . .136 C5
Stryd-yr-Eglwys / Church St
  8 SA18 . . . . .98 B7
Studio Pottery★ SA62 . . . .48 C6
Style Pk SA61 . . . . .125 C5
Sugar Loaf Sta LD5 . . . . . . .26 F6
Summercliffe Chalet Pk
  SA3 . . . . .172 D4
Summer Hill 2 SA62 . . . . .50 F8
Summerhill Cl SA62 . . . . . .66 F6

Summerhill La SA70 . . . . .105 D3
Summerhill Pk 7 SA67 . . . .90 C2
Summerland La SA3 . . . . . .172 E5
Summerland Pk SA2 . . . . .165 B5
Summerdale Ave SA3 . . . .165 F1
Summer Pl SA7 . . . . .161 F7
Summers Villas SA70 . . . . .105 C6
Sunderland Ave SA72 . . . .132 B2
Sunningdale Ave SA3 . . . .165 F1
Sunningdale SA4 . . . . .151 B4
Sunninghill Terr SA15 . . . .148 E6
Sunnybank Cl SA3 . . . . . . .172 F8
Sunny Hill SA15 . . . . .148 D6
Sunnyland Cres SA10 . . . .162 F8
Sunnymead Cl SA1 . . . . . .159 E2
Sunny Rd SA15 . . . . .148 D6
Sunny View SA19 . . . . .63 C7
Sussex Rd SA16 . . . . .137 E3
Sutton St SA70 . . . . .135 E4
Swallow Dale SA69 . . . . . .134 E2
Swan Ct SA2 . . . . .165 E6
Swanfield St SA9 . . . . .139 C7
Swanfield Pl 3 SA15 . . . . .148 D6
Swan La SA9 . . . . .139 C7
Swansea Castle★ SA1 . . . .174 B3
Swansea Coll / Coleg
  Abertawe (Tycoch Campus)
  SA2 . . . . .166 D7
Swansea Coll of Art
  SA1 . . . . .174 B3
Swansea Ent Pk SA7 . . . . .161 B7
Swansea Inst / Athrofa
  Abertawe (Townhill
  Campus) SA1 . . . . .166 F8
Swansea Inst (Mount
  Pleasant Campus) SA1 . . .174 A3
Swansea Maritime &
  Industrial Mus★ SA1 . . . .174 B2
Swansea Mus★ SA1 . . . . .174 B2
Swansea Rd
  Gorseinon SA4 . . . . .158 C5
  Llanelli, Box SA15 . . . . . .148 F6
  Llanelli, Marble Hall SA15 .148 E6
  Penllergaer SA4 . . . . .152 B2
  Pontardawe SA8 . . . . .147 C2
  Pontlliw SA4 . . . . .152 A4
  Swansea / Abertawe, Cadle
  SA5 . . . . .159 C7
  Swansea / Abertawe, Llangyfelach
  SA5 . . . . .153 B2
  Waunarlwydd SA5 . . . . . . .158 E4
Swansea Sta SA1 . . . . .174 A4
Swansea Vale Rly★
  SA7 . . . . .161 B5
Swansea West Ind Pk
  SA5 . . . . .159 C4
Swansquare 16 SA61 . . . .125 A5
Swan St SA1 . . . . .174 B4
Swan Wlk SA15 . . . . .148 B5
Sway Rd SA6 . . . . .154 A1
Sweet Briar La SA43 . . . . .173 A8
Swiss Valley SA14 . . . . . . .141 A2
Swiss Valley Prim Sch
  SA14 . . . . .141 A2
Swn-y-gwent Day Hosp
  SA18 . . . . .98 B7
Swn-y-Nant SA9 . . . . .138 B2
Swn Yr Afon SA34 . . . . . . .126 B8
Swn yr Eos SA9 . . . . .139 E7
Sybil St SA6 . . . . .154 E7
Sycamore Cl
  Milford Haven / Aberdaugleddau
  SA73 . . . . .131 E4
  Swansea / Abertawe SA2 . .166 A7
Sycamore Rd SA3 . . . . . . .173 A8
Sycamore Way
  Newcastle Emlyn / Castell
  Newydd Emlyn SA38 . . . .119 D5
  Pembroke Dock / Doc Penfro
  SA72 . . . . .132 B1
Sydney Rees Way SA61 . . .125 B6
Sydney St SA5 . . . . .160 C4
Sylen Rd SA15 . . . . .96 B5
Sylvan Way SA2 . . . . .166 C7
Sylvia Terr SA5 . . . . .160 C4
Symmons St SA1 . . . . .160 C1

T

Tabernacle La 3 SA67 . . . .70 E1
Tabernacle Rd / Heol
  Tabernacl 2 SA18 . . . . . . .99 A8
Tabernacle Rd / Heol
  Tabernacle SA18 . . . . .98 B7
Tabernacle St
  Neath / Castell-Nedd SA10 .162 F7
  Swansea / Abertawe SA1 . .160 D3
Tabernacle Terr 3
  SA31 . . . . .128 F6
Tabor Terr SA14 . . . . .149 E6
Tai Gwalia SA18 . . . . .100 C5
Tair Ffynnon 1 SA34 . . . . .90 E7
Tairgwaith Prim Sch
  SA18 . . . . .99 E6
Talbot Gn SA4 . . . . .158 C5
Talbot Rd SA10 . . . . .162 F6
Talbot Rd / Fflordd Talbot 10
  SA18 . . . . .98 B7
Talbot St
  Gowerton / Tre-gwyr SA4 . .158 B5
  Llanelli SA15 . . . . .148 D4
Talfan Rd SA1 . . . . .161 B3
Taliesin Ct SA48 . . . . .120 C4
Taliesin Pl SA4 . . . . .150 E1
Taliesyn Rd SA1 . . . . .167 A8
Talley CP Sch SA19 . . . . . . .42 D3
Talley Rd SA5 . . . . .160 B5

Tall Trees Cl 2 SA62 . . . . . .86 E5
Tal-y-bont Hill SA67 . . . . . .70 B4
Talyclun SA14 . . . . .142 E2
Tal Y Coed SA14 . . . . .142 F3
Talycopa Prim Sch SA7 . . .161 F7
Talywern SA14 . . . . .150 B7
Tan Bank SA61 . . . . .125 B6
Tanerdy SA31 . . . . .129 B6
Tank Farm Rd SA10 . . . . . .162 C3
Tanner's La
  Lampeter Velfrey SA67 . . . .90 A6
  Templeton SA67 . . . . .89 E6
Tanyard La SA38 . . . . .119 D4
Tan-y-Bryn SA16 . . . . .137 C2
Tan Y Bryn SA14 . . . . .19 C2
Tan-y-bryn Terr SA4 . . . . .156 F4
Tanycoed Rd SA6 . . . . . . .146 F1
Tanydarren SA8 . . . . .100 B1
Tan y fan SA18 . . . . .97 E6
Tan-y-Farteg SA9 . . . . . . .139 C7
Tan-y-Gelli SA18 . . . . .99 B8
Tanygraig Rd SA14 . . . . . .149 E4
Tan Y Lan SA18 . . . . .79 B1
Tan-y-Lan Terr SA6 . . . . . .160 F8
Tan-y-Lon SA18 . . . . .146 D1
Tan Y Marian Rd SA1 . . . .167 B8
Tanyrallt SA14 . . . . .146 D1
Tan-y-Rhiw SA43 . . . . .118 A3
Tanyrhodyn SA15 . . . . . . .140 F1
Tanywern La SA9 . . . . .139 E3
Taplow Terr SA1 . . . . .160 F2
Targate Rd SA62 . . . . .87 A5
Tasker Milward Sch / Ysgol
  Tasker Milward SA61 . . . .124 E4
Taskers La SA62 . . . . .66 E1
Tavernspite CP Sch SA34 . .90 F7
Tavistock Cl SA2 . . . . .166 E7
Tavistock Rd SA2 . . . . .166 D7
Tawe Ave SA1 . . . . .160 F4
Tawe Bsns Village SA6 . . .161 B5
Tawelan SA2 . . . . .77 B8
Tawelfan Tircoed SA4 . . . .152 C5
  Ystradgynlais SA9 . . . . . . .138 F4
Tawel Fan SA14 . . . . .149 A6
Tawe Pk SA9 . . . . .139 F7
Tawe Pl SA6 . . . . .154 E7
Tawe Rd SA7 . . . . .161 E8
Tawe St SA6 . . . . .161 A8
Tawe Terr SA8 . . . . .147 E4
Tawe View Cres SA6 . . . . .153 F1
Technium Bsns Pk SA1 . . .174 C3
Tegfan
  Swansea / Abertawe SA7 . .161 F5
  Tircoed SA4 . . . . .152 C5
Teg Fan SA10 . . . . .162 E6
Tegfynydd SA14 . . . . .141 A2
Tegid Rd SA1 . . . . .174 A5
Teglan Pk SA18 . . . . .97 F5
Teglyn Rd SA18 . . . . .70 C2
Teifi Marshes Nature
  Reserve★ SA43 . . . . .118 F3
Teifi Terr SA48 . . . . .120 C4
Teifi Valley Bsns Pk
  SA38 . . . . .119 F4
Teilo Cres SA1 . . . . .167 B8
Telyn Aur SA6 . . . . .153 E2
Temperance La SA9 . . . . . .138 F1
Templebar Rd SA68 . . . . . .134 A6
Temple St Llanelli SA15 . . .148 E5
  Swansea / Abertawe SA1 . .174 B3
Temple Terr SA48 . . . . . . .120 B5
Templeton Cty Prim Sch
  SA67 . . . . .89 F7
Templeton Way SA5 . . . . .159 F7
Tenby Cottage Hospl
  SA70 . . . . .135 E4
Tenby CP Sch SA70 . . . . . .135 C5
Tenby Ct SA71 . . . . .104 C4
Tenby Leisure Ctr SA70 . . .135 B5
Tenby Mus & Art Gall★
  SA70 . . . . .135 F5
Tenby Rd
  Cardigan / Aberteifi SA43 . .118 E2
  St Clears / Sanclêr
  SA33 . . . . .127 D4
Tenby Sta SA70 . . . . .135 D5
Tenby VC Inf Sch / Ysgol
  Wirfoddol Babanod
  SA70 . . . . .135 D5
Tennyson Way SA2 . . . . . .165 F6
Tenth Ave SA6 . . . . .153 D2
Teras Brynteg / Bryn-Teg
  Terr 13 SA18 . . . . .98 B7
Teras Caersalem /
  Caersalem Terr 2
  SA15 . . . . .148 D3
Teras Jones / Jones' Terr
  SA18 . . . . .98 F8
Teras Parc Bigyn / Bigyn
  Park Terr SA15 . . . . .148 E4
Teras Tyisha / Tyisha Terr
  SA15 . . . . .148 E8
Teras Waterloo / Waterloo
  Terr SA18 . . . . .97 D6
Teras Yr Arced / Arcade Terr
  11 SA18 . . . . .99 B8
Terrace Rd SA1 . . . . .167 B7
Terrace Road Prim Sch
  SA1 . . . . .167 B7
Theatre Mwldan SA43 . . . .118 D4
Third Ave SA6 . . . . .153 D1
Third La SA71 . . . . .133 C4
Third St SA71 . . . . .103 C5
Thistleboon Cvn Site
  SA3 . . . . .173 C4

Thistleboon Dr SA3 . . . .**173** C4
Thistleboon Gdns SA3 . .**173** B3
Thistleboon Rd SA3 . . .**173** B4
Thomas Ave SA15 . . . .**95** E4
Thomas Evans Ho SA1 . .**159** F1
Thomas Parry Way
SA61 . . . .**124** F6
Thomas Row SA1 . . . . . .**174** B4
Thomas St
Llandeilo SA19 . . . .**130** E6
Llanelli SA15 . . . .**148** D6
Pembroke / Penfro SA71 .**133** B4
Pontardawe SA8 . . . .**147** E5
Swansea / Abertawe SA6 .**174** C3
Thomas Terr
Llandeilo SA19 . . . .**130** E6
Swansea / Abertawe SA6 .**160** E6
Thompson Ct SA4 . . . . . .**158** D8
Thornberry Gdns SA67 . . .**90** A5
Thornhill Rd SA14 . . . .**97** C6
Thornton Bsns Pk SA73 .**131** D5
Thornton Ind Trading Est
SA73 . . . .**131** D6
Thornton Rd SA73 . . . . .**131** D6
Three Cliffs Dr SA3 . . . .**171** A6
Three Ships Ct SA3 . . . .**173** C3
Thurston La
Burton SA73 . . . .**132** E8
Rosemarket SA73 . . . .**87** B3
Tichbourne St SA3 . . . . .**173** B4
Tirbach Rd SA9 . . . .**139** C7
Tir Becca SA14 . . . .**96** E6
Tir Capel SA14 . . . .**149** A6
Tir Dafydd SA15 . . . .**95** D4
Tirdeunaw Cl SA14 . . . . .**160** C7
Tir Einon SA14 . . . .**149** C4
Tirforgan SA14 . . . .**149** A7
Tirgof SA14 . . . .**150** B8
Tir John North Rd SA1 . .**168** C8
Tir Llan SA32 . . . .**77** E7
Tirmynydd SA4 . . . .**151** B1
Tirmynydd Rd SA2, SA4 .**164** D8
Tir Newydd SA14 . . . . . .**149** D4
Tir-owen SA33 . . . .**127** E5
Tirpenry St SA6 . . . .**154** A1
Tirprys SA18 . . . .**98** A5
Tir Treharn **2** SA42 . . . . . .**13** E4
Tirwaun
Burry Port SA16 . . . .**137** C2
Cross Hands SA14 . . . .**97** B7
**Tirycoed Rd / Heol Tir Y
Coed 3** SA14 . . . .**99** A8
Tir-y-Dail La / Lon
Tir-y-Dail **11** SA18 . . . . . .**98** B7
Tirynys SA15 . . . .**148** E8
Tir Yr Hen Ysgol SA14 . .**149** F3
Tir Ysgawen SA31 . . . . .**129** B3
Tir Ysgol SA15 . . . .**148** D6
Tlysfan **1** SA65 . . . .**122** D3
Toft Pl SA15 . . . .**148** E6
Tom Williams Ct SA1 . . .**174** B4
Tontine St SA1 . . . .**174** B4
Tor Ho SA3 . . . .**173** A3
Tori-gwddwg Hill SA62 . . .**68** D5
Tor La **2** SA70 . . . .**135** F4
Torrington Rd SA5 . . . . .**160** A3
Tor View SA3 . . . .**170** B5
Tower Ct
Swansea / Abertawe, Llansamlet
SA6 . . . .**161** B8
Swansea / Abertawe SA4 .**166** F8
Tower Gdns SA1 . . . .**159** F1
Tower Hill
Fishguard / Abergwaun
SA65 . . . .**122** E4
4 Haverfordwest / Hwlffordd
SA61 . . . .**125** A5
Tower View **2** SA62 . . . . .**84** C3
Town Hall La SA62 . . . . .**123** D5
Townhill Com Prim Sch
SA1 . . . .**167** A8
Townhill Gdns SA2 . . . . .**166** F8
Townhill Rd SA2 . . . .**167** A8
Towy Ave SA20 . . . .**121** C5
Towy Cl **1** SA31 . . . .**128** C2
Towy-side **3** SA31 . . . . .**128** F4
Traeth Ffordd
Llanelli SA15 . . . .**148** B4
Llanelli SA15 . . . .**148** C4
Trafalgar Rd SA2 . . . . . .**166** F5
Trafalgar Rd
Haverfordwest / Hwlffordd
SA61 . . . .**124** E5
Milford Haven / Aberdaugleddau
SA73 . . . .**131** C3
6 Tenby / Dinbych-y-pysgod
SA70 . . . .**135** E4
Trafalgar Terr
Neyland SA73 . . . .**132** B5
The Havens SA62 . . . .**85** D8
Trallwm SA14 . . . .**149** D5
Trallwn Pl SA7 . . . .**161** E6
**Trallwn Prim Sch / Ysgol
Gynradd Trallwn** SA7 . .**161** E7
Trallwn Rd SA7 . . . .**161** E6
Trawler Rd SA1 . . . .**174** B1
Trawsffordd SA9 . . . . . .**139** E8
Trebuan SA15 . . . .**140** E1
Tre Cynon SA48 . . . .**4** F3
Tredafydd VC Sch SA65 . .**30** E4
Tredegar Rd SA4 . . . . . .**151** C1
Tree-tops SA14 . . . .**141** A2
Trefasser Cross SA64 . . .**10** D2
Trefloyne La SA70 . . . . .**135** A4
Treforis SA18 . . . .**98** C6

Trefrhiw Rd / Heol Trefrhiw
SA18 . . . .**98** A6
Tregarne Cl SA6 . . . .**153** F4
Tregelles Ct
Cwmrhydyceirw SA6 . . . .**154** A4
Swansea / Abertawe SA6 .**153** F3
Tre-gendeg Rd SA16 . . . . .**53** B1
**Tregeyb Wood Nature
Reserve ★** SA19 . . . .**79** D8
**Tregroes Cty Prim Sch /
Ysgol Gynradd Tregroes**
SA44 . . . .**19** D7
Tregwyr Inf Sch SA4 . . .**158** B5
Tregwyr Jun Sch SA4 . .**158** B5
Treharne Rd SA6 . . . . . .**153** F1
Treherbert St SA42 . . . . .**120** E3
Tremeyrick St SA72 . . . .**132** D3
**Tremoilet VCP Sch / Ysgol
Gynradd Wr Tremoilet**
SA33 . . . .**91** D4
Trem-y-Bedol **1** SA38 . .**129** A6
Trem Y Ddol SA38 . . . . .**119** B6
Trem-y-Dref **2** SA31 . . .**128** E6
Trem Y Mor
Fishguard & Goodwick
SA65 . . . .**122** C4
Llanmorlais SA4 . . . .**156** B2
Trem-y-Mynydd SA16 . . .**137** D3
Trem Y Parc / Parkview Terr
SA15 . . . .**148** C6
Trem Y Teifi SA44 . . . .**19** E3
Tre-nel SA14 . . . .**108** E4
Treowen Rd SA72 . . . . . .**132** B1
Tre Uchaf Prim Sch
SA4 . . . .**150** F1
Trevaughan Cl SA61 . . . .**125** D4
Trevaughan Gdns SA34 . .**126** C2
Trevaughan Lodge Rd
SA34 . . . .**126** C1
Trevaughan Rd SA31 . . .**128** D7
Trewarren Cl SA62 . . . . . .**85** A2
Trewarren Dr SA62 . . . . . .**85** A2
Trewarren Rd SA62 . . . . . .**85** A2
Trewen Rd
Birchgrove SA7 . . . .**155** A1
Swansea / Abertawe SA7 .**162** A8
Trewent Hill SA62 . . . . . .**105** A1
Trewyddfa Comm SA6 . . .**160** F6
Trewyddfa Gdns SA6 . . .**160** F6
Trewyddfa Rd SA6 . . . . .**160** E6
Trewyddfa Terr SA6 . . . .**160** E6
Trilwm SA17 . . . .**109** C4
Trimsaran CP Sch SA17 . .**109** C7
Trimsaran Rd SA15 . . . . .**109** E6
Trinity Cl
Pontarddulais SA4 . . . . .**143** C3
The Mumbles / Y Mwmbwls
SA3 . . . .**173** A5
**Trinity Coll / Coleg Y
Drindod** SA31 . . . .**128** C5
Trinity Ct **2** SA1 . . . . . .**174** A3
Trinity La SA4 . . . .**156** D4
Trinity Pl Neyland SA73 .**132** B6
Pontarddulais SA4 . . . . .**143** C3
Swansea / Abertawe SA4 .**174** B3
Trinity Rd Llanelli SA15 . .**148** E3
Pembroke Dock / Doc Penfro
SA72 . . . .**132** D2
Trinity St SA4 . . . .**151** C1
Trinity Terr Llanelli SA15 .**148** D3
Neyland SA73 . . . .**132** B4
Trippis Rd SA73 . . . .**70** B1
Troed Y Bryn SA14 . . . . . .**96** F4
Troed-y-Bryn SA40 . . . . . .**21** E6
Troed Y Rhiw
1 Goodwick / Wdig SA64 .**122** A4
Pencaer SA64 . . . .**11** B2
Troed-y-Rhiw SA7 . . . . .**161** E6
Troed-y-Rhiw Rd SA34 . . .**71** E2
Troedyrynys SA33 . . . . . .**58** F3
**Troserch Rd / Heol
Trosserch** SA14 . . . . . .**142** B2
Tros- Maen SA14 . . . . . .**148** F8
Trostre Ind Pk SA14 . . . .**149** A3
Trostre Rd
Llanelli SA14, SA15 . . . .**148** F3
Llanelli SA15 . . . .**148** F4
Tro Tircoed SA4 . . . .**152** C4
Tudno Pl SA5 . . . .**160** A5
Tudor Cl SA71 . . . .**133** C3
Tudor Ct Bishopston SA3 .**172** A6
Llanedi SA4 . . . .**97** D1
Tudor Gdns SA61 . . . . .**125** A1
**Tudor Merchants House (NT)
The★** SA70 . . . .**135** F4
Tudor Pl SA62 . . . .**86** B5
Tudor Rd SA5 . . . .**160** C5
Tudor St SA9 . . . .**139** E7
Tudor Way
Bishopston SA3 . . . .**172** B7
Haverfordwest / Hwlffordd
SA61 . . . .**124** D4
Tenby / Dinbych-y-pysgod
SA70 . . . .**135** C5
Tunnel Rd SA15 . . . .**148** E5
Twll La SA67 . . . .**70** C1
Twopenny Hay Cl **1**
SA71 . . . .**133** D4
Twyn Bedw Rd SA6 . . . .**154** D7
Twyniago SA4 . . . .**143** D4
Twyni Teg SA2 . . . .**165** E8
Twynrefail Pl SA18 . . . . . .**99** D6
Twyn-yr-Ysgol SA9 . . . . .**139** B7

Ty = house

Ty Beddoe SA1 . . . .**168** B7
Ty Caitlin **5** SA1 . . . . . .**174** A3

**Ty Canol National Nature
Reserve★** SA41 . . . .**33** C8
Ty-coch Maisonettes
SA2 . . . .**166** D7
Tycoch Rd SA2 . . . .**166** D7
Tycroes Rd / Heol Tycroes
Ammanford / Rhydaman
SA18 . . . .**98** A5
Tycroes SA18 . . . .**97** F5
Ty Cydwel **10** SA15 . . . .**148** D4
Ty Dewi Sant SA15 . . . . .**159** E3
Ty-Draw Cres SA1 . . . . .**161** B2
Ty-Draw Pl SA1 . . . .**161** B2
Ty-Draw Rd SA1 . . . .**161** C2
Ty Elizabeth **6** SA15 . . .**148** D4
Ty Fforest **3** SA6 . . . . .**154** A1
Ty Florence Asher SA6 . .**146** E1
Ty Gwyn SA4 . . . .**158** C5
Ty Horeb SA6 . . . .**153** F1
Ty Howard **7** SA15 . . . .**148** D4
Tyisha Rd Llanelli SA15 . .**148** E4
Llannon SA14 . . . .**96** E6
Tyisha Terr / Teras Tyisha
SA15 . . . .**148** E8
Tyle Catherine SA15 . . . .**109** E3
Tyle Glas SA18 . . . .**99** C7
Tyle Teg
Burry Port SA16 . . . .**137** F3
Clydach SA6 . . . .**154** C7
Ty-mawr SA14 . . . .**147** E4
Tymawr St SA1 . . . .**168** B7
Ty Meriel **8** SA15 . . . . .**148** D4
Ty-myrtwydd SA4 . . . . . .**157** E8
Tynewydd Terr SA14 . . . . .**97** B8
Ty'n-y-Bonau Rd SA4 . . .**143** C5
Tyn-y-Cae SA4 . . . .**147** F3
Tyn-y-Cae Rd SA7 . . . . .**161** D7
Ty'n-y-Pant Rd SA8 . . . .**147** C5
Tyn-y-Waun Rd SA7 . . . .**161** E6
Ty'r Felin SA7 . . . .**159** F6
Ty'r Fran SA7 . . . .**155** A2
Ty'rfran Ave SA15 . . . . .**148** E7
Ty Rhiannon SA2 . . . . . .**166** E5
Tyrisha Ave SA4 . . . .**151** C6
Tyrisha Ct SA4 . . . .**151** C6
Tyrisha Rd SA4 . . . .**151** C6
Ty'r Maes SA15 . . . .**159** F6
Tyrwaun SA15 . . . .**109** D4
Ty Sivertsen SA1 . . . . . .**167** B6
Ty Stafford **9** SA15 . . . .**148** D4
Tywi Ave SA20 . . . .**121** C5

U

Ullswater Cres SA6 . . . . .**160** E7
Underhill La SA3 . . . .**117** B4
Under Par Rd SA1 . . . . . .**129** A5
Under the Hills SA61 . . . .**124** E2
Union Bldgs SA15 . . . . .**148** D7
Union Hill SA61 . . . .**125** B4
Union St
1 Ammanford / Rhydaman
SA18 . . . .**98** C7
Swansea / Abertawe SA1 .**174** A2
**United Counties
Showground★** SA31 . . . . .**75** A5
**University of Wales Lampeter
/ Prifysgol Cymru Llanbedr
Pont Steffan** SA48 . . . . .**120** D5
**University of Wales /
Prifysgol Cymru** SA31 . . .**75** E4
**Univ of Wales Swansea /
Prifysgol Cymru Abertawe**
SA2 . . . .**166** D4
Uplands
Gowerton / Tre-gwyr SA4 .**158** B5
Gwaun-Cae-Gurwen SA18 . .**99** D5
Uplands Cres SA2 . . . . . .**166** F6
Uplands Rd SA8 . . . .**147** D4
Uplands Terr
Swansea / Abertawe,
Graig Trewyddfa SA6 . . .**160** F8
Swansea / Abertawe, Uplands
SA2 . . . .**166** F6
Upper Banks Sta★ SA1 . .**161** A4
Upper Church Pk SA3 . . .**173** B4
Upper Colbren Rd SA18 . . .**99** D6
Upper Cross Rd SA15 . . .**148** F5
Upper Fforest Way
Llansamlet SA6 . . . .**154** B1
Swansea / Abertawe SA6 .**161** B8
Upper Frog St SA70 . . . .**135** E5
Upper Gendros Cres
SA5 . . . .**160** A3
Upper Heathfield Rd
SA8 . . . .**147** E6
Upper Hill St SA73 . . . . .**131** B2
Upper Inkerman St **9**
SA15 . . . .**148** D5
Upper King's Head Rd
SA5 . . . .**159** F4
Upper La SA68 . . . .**105** D7
Upper Lamphey Rd
SA71 . . . .**133** C4
Upper Mill SA15 . . . .**148** E6
Upper Mill Rd SA4 . . . . .**143** D4
Upper Mkt St SA61 . . . . .**125** A4
Upper Mwldan **4** SA43 . .**118** D4
Upper Park St **5** SA15 . .**148** D4
Upper Pk Rd SA70 . . . . .**135** E4
Upper Robinson St 11
SA15 . . . .**148** D5
Upper Row SA71 . . . .**133** C4
**Upper Station Rd / Heol
Uchaf Yr Orsaf 9** SA18 . . .**99** B8

Upper St Mary's St 5
SA42 . . . .**13** E4
Upper Strand SA1 . . . . . .**174** B5
Upper Terr SA62 . . . .**50** F8
Upper Thornton SA73 . . .**131** C7
Upper William St 1
SA15 . . . .**148** E5
Upper W St SA42 . . . .**13** E4
Upton Castle★ SA72 . . . .**105** B7
Upton Castle Gdns★
SA72 . . . .**105** A7
Upton Terr SA1 . . . .**168** A7
Usk Pl SA6 . . . .**154** A5
Uwch Gwendraeth **3**
SA14 . . . .**96** E8
Uzmaston Rd SA61 . . . . .**125** C4

V

Vale Ct SA1 . . . .**160** D7
Valence Wlk **1** SA71 . . .**133** C6
Vale Of Wern Terr SA1 . .**168** B7
Vale Rd Burton SA73 . . . . .**87** D2
Llanstadwell SA73 . . . . .**132** A6
Valley Cl SA69 . . . .**134** A4
Valley Rd
Llawhaden SA67 . . . .**70** C1
Pentlepoir SA69 . . . .**134** C4
Valley View SA2 . . . .**166** B5
Valley Way SA6 . . . .**161** A6
Vanderhoot Way SA69 . . .**134** E4
Vanewood Cl SA3 . . . . . .**173** C3
Vardre Rd SA6 . . . .**154** E8
Varteg Rd SA9 . . . .**139** B5
Vaughan Pl SA1 . . . .**150** E1
Vaughan St SA15 . . . . . .**148** D5
Vauxhall St SA15 . . . . . .**148** D5
Vawers Cl SA61 . . . .**124** F5
Vaynor Rd SA73 . . . .**131** D3
Velfrey Rd SA34 . . . .**126** B1
Venables Cl SA5 . . . .**159** D2
Vennaway La SA3 . . . . . .**171** D7
Venns Cl SA61 . . . .**125** A1
Vensland SA3 . . . .**172** A6
Verandah St SA1 . . . . . .**174** A3
Vera Rd SA6 . . . .**154** E8
Vergam Terr SA65 . . . . . .**122** C4
Verig St SA5 . . . .**160** C3
Vernon Cl SA4 . . . .**152** A5
Vernon St SA1 . . . .**160** D1
Veron St SA1 . . . .**174** B5
Versil Terr SA4 . . . .**157** F8
Vetch Cl SA71 . . . .**133** C4
**Vetch Field (Swansea City
Fball Gd)** SA1 . . . .**174** A2
Vicarage Cl SA17 . . . .**93** F5
Vicarage Dr SA8 . . . .**147** F6
Vicarage Field SA71 . . . .**133** D4
Vicarage Fields SA70 . . .**105** F1
Vicarage La
Kidwelly / Cydweli SA17 . .**136** B3
Swansea / Abertawe SA5 .**160** D2
Vicarage Rd
Llangadog SA19 . . . .**63** D7
Swansea / Abertawe SA6 .**153** F1
Vicarage Rd / Heol Ficeroi 7
SA18 . . . .**99** B8
Vicarage Terr SA1 . . . . . .**174** C3
Vicary Cres SA73 . . . . . .**131** E2
Vicary St SA73 . . . .**131** E2
Victoria Ave
Fishguard / Abergwaun
SA65 . . . .**122** C4
Swansea / Abertawe SA1 .**167** A5
The Mumbles / Y Mwmbwls
SA3 . . . .**173** A5
Victoria Cres SA20 . . . . .**121** D5
Victoria Ct SA3 . . . .**172** C4
Victoria Pl SA61 . . . .**125** A5
Victoria Quay SA1 . . . . .**174** B2
Victoria Rd
Gowerton / Tre-gwyr SA4 .**158** B7
Llanwrtyd Wells LD5 . . . . . .**9** C1
Milford Haven / Aberdaugleddau
SA73 . . . .**131** C3
Pembroke Dock / Doc Penfro
SA72 . . . .**132** A2
Pen-clawdd SA4 . . . .**156** E3
Pont Henri SA15 . . . .**95** E4
Swansea / Abertawe SA1 .**174** B2
Waunarlwydd SA5 . . . . . .**158** E3
Victoria Row SA4 . . . . . .**156** E4
Victoria St
Laugharne SA33 . . . .**92** E4
Llandovery / Llanymddyfri
SA20 . . . .**121** D5
Swansea / Abertawe SA2 .**166** F7
Tenby / Dinbych-y-pysgod
SA70 . . . .**135** D4
Victoria Terr
Lampeter / Llanbedr Pont Steffan
SA48 . . . .**120** C4
Swansea / Abertawe SA1 .**167** A5
View Rd SA4 . . . .**154** D7
Viking Way SA1 . . . .**161** D6
Village La SA3 . . . .**173** B4
Villas Eynon SA67 . . . . . .**90** B5
Villa Terr SA2 . . . .**160** C5
Villers Rd / Fford Villers
SA18 . . . .**98** B6
Villers St SA1 . . . .**174** B5
Villiers St SA1 . . . .**160** D1
Vincent St SA1 . . . .**167** B6
Vine Rd SA62 . . . .**86** E5
Vine Row SA9 . . . .**139** A6
Vineyard Vale SA69 . . . . .**134** B4

Vivian Ct SA2 . . . .**166** D7
Vivian Dr SA73 . . . .**131** B2
Vivian Ho SA3 . . . .**166** B2
Vivian Mans SA2 . . . . . .**166** D7
Vivian Rd SA2 . . . .**166** D7
Vivians Row SA6 . . . .**153** D4
Vivian St SA1 . . . .**160** D2
Voylart Cl SA2 . . . .**165** C8
Voylart Rd SA2 . . . .**165** C8

W

Wade Ave SA9 . . . .**139** B6
Waldhof Ct SA5 . . . .**159** E7
Wallace Rd SA1 . . . .**167** F7
Wallaston Cross SA71 . . .**103** B4
Wallis St SA65 . . . .**122** D3
Wallsfield La **4** SA70 . . .**135** E5
Walnut Cl SA3 . . . .**172** E2
Walter Rd SA1 . . . .**167** B6
Walter Rd / Fford Walter 9
SA18 . . . .**98** C7
Walter's Ave SA61 . . . . .**125** A2
Walters Cres SA3 . . . . . .**173** A5
Walters La SA3 . . . .**114** C2
Walters Rd
Cwmllynfell SA9 . . . .**100** B7
Llangadog SA19 . . . .**63** D7
Llansamlet SA7 . . . .**154** E1
Swansea / Abertawe SA7 .**161** D8
Walter's Rd SA15 . . . . . .**148** E4
Walters Row SA2 . . . . . .**165** C8
Walters St SA5 . . . .**160** C3
Waltham Cl SA6 . . . .**160** D7
Walton Hill SA62 . . . .**85** C7
Walton Rd SA62 . . . .**85** D8
Warborough Cl SA15 . . .**148** C6
Warborough Rd SA15 . . .**148** C7
Warlow's Mdw SA70 . . . .**105** F1
Warner Pl SA15 . . . .**148** D4
Warren St SA70 . . . .**135** E5
Warrior Way
Milford Haven / Aberdaugleddau
SA73 . . . .**131** E6
Pembroke Dock / Doc Penfro
SA72 . . . .**132** E3
Warwick Pl SA3 . . . .**173** A8
Warwick Rd
Milford Haven / Aberdaugleddau
SA73 . . . .**131** D2
Swansea / Abertawe SA2 .**166** B4
Washington St SA1 . . . . .**160** D3
Water La
Llanstadwell SA73 . . . . . .**87** A4
Llansteffan SA33 . . . .**93** E5
Swansea / Abertawe SA6 .**161** A5
Waterloo Ind Est SA72 . .**132** E3
Waterloo Pl SA2 . . . . . .**166** F5
Waterloo Rd
Milford Haven / Aberdaugleddau
SA73 . . . .**131** A5
Pembroke Dock / Doc Penfro
SA72 . . . .**132** D4
Waterloo Rd / Heol Waterloo
SA14, SA18 . . . .**97** D7
Waterloo St
Llandovery / Llanymddyfri
SA20 . . . .**121** D4
Llanelli SA15 . . . .**148** D4
Waterloo Terr SA31 . . . .**128** F5
**Waterloo Terr / Teras
Waterloo** SA18 . . . .**97** D6
Water St
Carmarthen / Caerfyrddin
SA31 . . . .**128** E5
Ferryside SA17 . . . .**93** F5
Gwaun-Cae-Gurwen SA18 . .**99** D5
Kidwelly / Cydweli SA17 . .**136** B5
1 Laugharne SA33 . . . . .**92** E4
Llandovery / Llanymddyfri
SA20 . . . .**121** D4
Llanelli SA15 . . . .**148** D6
11 Narberth / Arberth
SA67 . . . .**70** D1
Newcastle Emlyn / Castell
Newydd Emlyn SA38 . . . .**119** D4
Neyland SA73 . . . .**132** B7
Pontarddulais SA4 . . . . .**143** B4
Pontarddulais SA4 . . . . .**143** C4
Waterston Rd SA73 . . . . .**103** F8
Waterwynch La SA70 . . .**135** E7
Watery La SA71 . . . .**133** A3
Watkin St SA1 . . . .**174** A4
Waunarlwydd Prim Sch
SA5 . . . .**158** D3
Waunarlwydd Rd SA2,
SA5 . . . .**159** B2
Waun Burgess SA31 . . . .**128** C5
Waun Cl SA4 . . . .**157** F8
Waun Deri SA16 . . . .**137** B3
Wauneos Rd SA15 . . . . .**109** F4
Waunfarlais Rd
Ammanford / Rhydaman
SA18 . . . .**98** A3
Llandybie SA18 . . . .**79** B1
Waunfawr SA18 . . . .**98** A7
Waun Giach SA43 . . . . . .**16** B7
Waun Gron SA8 . . . .**147** D6
Waun-Gron Cl SA6 . . . . .**160** C6
Waun-Gron Rd SA6 . . . .**160** C6
Waun Gron Rd / Fford
Waun Gron SA18 . . . .**98** D6
Waunhafog Rd SA18 . . . .**98** A8
Waunhwyad La **1** SA18 . .**80** A1
Waun Isaf SA42 . . . .**123** B4
Waunlanyrafon SA15 . . .**148** C5

Waun Las SA65 ....30 F5
Waunleision SA18 ....99 D7
Waun Penlan SA8 ....147 D7
Waun Rd Llanelli SA15 ...148 E7
  Loughor SA4 ....157 F8
  Morriston / Treforris SA6 ..154 A2
  Swansea / Abertawe SA6 ..153 F2
Waun Sidan SA16 ....108 F4
Waun Sterw SA8 ....147 D7
Waun Wen Prim Sch
  SA1 ....160 C2
Waun-Wen Rd SA1 ....174 A5
Waun-Wen Terr SA1 ......160 C1
Waun Y Felin SA4 ....157 A4
Waun-y-Pistyll SA5 ......160 C5
Wavell Cres SA72 ....133 A8
Waverley Dr SA3 ....173 A5
Waverley St SA6 ....154 D7
Waverly Cl SA6 ....154 F8
Waverly Pk SA6 ....154 F8
Wda Ind Est SA16 ....137 F2
Weavers Ho **7** SA1 ......174 C2
Weavers Mill SA1 ....160 C4
Webbons Way SA1 ....159 F2
Weig Fach La SA5 ....159 D3
Weig Gdns SA5 ....160 A4
Weig La SA5 ....159 F3
Weig Rd SA5 ....159 F3
Welcome La SA1 ....174 B3
Wellfield SA3 ....171 F6
Well Field SA2 ....165 E8
Wellfield Cl SA4 ....151 B1
Wellfield Rd SA31 ....128 F6
Wellhead La SA62 ....87 E4
Well Hill SA71 ....133 C4
Wellington Gdns SA73 ....131 B2
Wellington Rd SA73 ......131 B2
Wellington St
  Pembroke Dock / Doc Penfro
  SA72 ....132 B2
  Swansea / Abertawe SA1 ..174 A2
Well La SA61 ....125 B7
Wellpark SA3 ....114 C2
Well Rd SA73 ....103 E8
Well St SA44 ....19 E4
Welsh Bird of Prey Ctr★
  SA43 ....16 D5
Welsh Mus of Public Road
  Transport★ SA1 ....161 A4
Welsh Rd SA62 ....66 C6
Welsh Wildlife Ctr The★
  SA43 ....118 F2
Wembley Gdns SA73 .....127 E4
Wembley Rd SA9 ....139 A6
Wentworth Cres SA3 .....165 E1
Weobley Castle★ SA3 ...115 B3
Weobley Ct SA5 ....162 E5
Wern Cres SA10 ....162 E6
Wern-ddu Rd SA18 ....79 D1
Wern-Ddu Rd / Ffordd
  Wern-Ddu SA18 ....98 D8
Wern Fawr Rd SA1 ......168 C2
Wernoleu Rd SA18 ....98 D7
Wern Rd Glanaman SA18 ...99 B8
  Goodwick / Wdig SA64 ..122 A5
  Llanelli SA15 ....148 E5
  Llanmorlais SA4 ....156 C1
  Neath / Castell-Nedd
  SA10 ....162 E7
  Swansea / Abertawe SA1 ..160 D4
  Ystalyfera SA9 ....139 B6
Wern Terr
  Ammanford / Rhydaman
  SA18 ....98 D6
  Swansea / Abertawe SA1 ..168 C7
Wernwood Rd SA9 ....139 B6
Wesley Cl **1** SA67 ......90 B2
Wesley Ct SA72 ....133 A8
Wesley Pl SA62 ....31 B3
Wesley Rd SA62 ....85 C7
Westaway Dr SA73 ......131 A2
Westaway Pk SA73 ....87 A3
Westbourne Gr SA2 ......166 C7
Westbourne Pl SA3 ......173 B4
Westbourne Rd SA2 .....166 C7
Westbury Bglws SA15 ...148 E2
Westbury La SA1 ....167 A6
Westbury St
  Llanelli SA15 ....148 E3
  Swansea / Abertawe SA1 ..167 A6
Westcliff SA3 ....173 C3
West Cliff SA3 ....171 A3
Westcliff Mews SA3 .....173 C3
Westcross Ave SA3 ......173 A6
Westcross La SA3 ....172 F7
West Crossways SA8 ....147 D6
West Ct SA6 ....124 D5
West End Llanelli SA15 ...148 C6
  Pen-clawdd SA4 ....156 D4
Western Cl SA3 ....173 B4
Western La SA3 ....173 B4
Western Rd Clydach SA6 ..154 C6
  Pontardawe SA8 ....147 D4
Western St SA1 ....167 B6
Western Terr SA1 ....160 D3
Western Way SA2 ....132 C3
Westerton Ct SA67 ....90 B5
Westfa SA14 ....141 A1
Westfa Rd SA2 ....166 F7
Westfield Ct SA70 ....105 E6
Westfield Dr
  Milford Haven / Aberdaugleddau
  SA73 ....131 E4
  Neyland SA73 ....132 B8
Westfield Pill Nature
  Reserve★ SA73 ....87 B1
Westfield Rd

Westfield Rd continued
  Waunarlwydd SA5 ....158 D4
Westgate Hill SA71 ......133 B5
West Gr La SA71 ....104 A4
Westgrove Ct SA4 ....151 B4
Westhaven SA72 ....104 F6
West Hill SA71 ....105 A3
Westhill Ave SA73 ....131 D4
West Hill Cres SA17 .....136 A4
West Hook Rd SA62 ......87 C6
West La Camrose SA62 ....67 A6
  Castlemartin SA71 ......111 A6
  Cosheston SA72 ....133 F8
  Llanstadwell SA73 ....86 F1
  Neyland SA73 ....132 A7
  Nolton & Roch SA62 ......66 D5
  Templeton SA67 ....89 C7
West La Cl SA62 ....67 B6
Westland Ave SA3 ....172 E7
Westland Cl SA4 ....150 E1
Weston La SA67 ....88 B5
West Perimeter Rd
  SA73 ....103 D8
Westport Ave SA2 ....166 A2
West St
  Fishguard / Abergwaun
  SA65 ....122 D4
  Gorseinon SA4 ....151 B1
  Newport / Trefdraeth SA42 ..13 D3
  Pembroke / Penfro SA71 ..133 B4
  Rosemarket SA73 ....87 A3
  Whitland / Hendy-Gwyn
  SA34 ....126 C3
West Wales Arts Ctr★
  SA65 ....122 D4
West Wales Bsns Pk
  SA67 ....70 E2
West Wales Eco Ctr★
  SA42 ....13 D2
West Wales General Hospl
  SA31 ....129 D7
Westward Cl SA2 ....166 A1
West Way / Fforddy Y
  Gorllewin SA1 ....174 A2
Westwinds SA3 ....172 A5
Westwinds Cl SA3 ....158 E3
Wheatfield Terr SA1 .....174 A5
Wheatsheaf Dr SA6 .....154 A4
Wheeler's Way
  Manorbier SA70 ....113 D6
  4 Pembroke / Penfro
  SA71 ....133 C3
White City Rd SA5 ......159 D4
Whiteford Bay L Pk
  SA3 ....114 C4
Whiteford Rd SA5 ....159 F6
Whitegates SA2 ....166 A1
White Gr SA3 ....172 E7
Whitehall Ave SA71 .....133 B6
Whitehall Dr SA72 ......133 B6
White Lion St **8** SA70 ...135 E5
Whites Farm Way SA72 ..132 A3
Whiteshell Dr SA3 ......172 E4
White St SA1 ....167 B7
Whitestone Ave SA3 .....172 A5
Whitestone Cl SA3 ......172 F8
Whitestone La SA3 ......172 E5
Whitestone Prim Sch
  SA3 ....172 E7
Whitestone Rd SA3 ......172 A5
Whitethorn Ct SA5 ......159 F5
Whitethorn Pl SA2 ......166 B6
White Walls SA1 ....174 B2
Whitland Abbey★ SA34 ..126 E6
Whitland Cl SA5 ....159 F6
Whitley Rd SA4 ....150 F1
Whitlow SA69 ....134 E4
Whittington Terr SA4 ...151 D2
Wilks Row SA1 ....174 A4
William Bowen Cl SA4 ...158 A5
William Ct SA1 ....174 A2
William Dennis Ave
  SA4 ....158 A8
William Morris Gdns
  SA1 ....168 B7
Williams Ct SA67 ....70 E2
Williamson St SA1 ......133 B4
Williams Row **2** SA43 ..118 D4
Williams St SA4 ....143 C4
William St
  Cardigan / Aberteifi SA43 ..118 D4
  Pontardawe SA8 ....147 B1
  Swansea / Abertawe SA1 ..174 A2
  The Mumbles / Y Mwmbwls
  SA3 ....173 A5
  Ystradgynlais SA9 ......139 E7
Williams Terr **2** SA43 ...118 E4
Williams'Terr SA16 .....137 E3
Williamston Cl **1** SA61 ..124 E4
Willow Bank SA4 ....158 D3
Willowbrook Gdns SA3 ..165 F1
Willows Pl SA1 ....174 A3
Willows The SA15 ....148 C7
Wilson Mdw **2** SA62 ....85 D8
Wimble Wood Cl SA3 ....173 A7
Wimmerfield Ave SA2 ...165 E7
Wimmerfield Cl SA2 .....165 E7
Wimmerfield Cres SA2 ..165 E7
Wimmerfield Dr SA2 ....165 E7
Winch Cres SA61 ....125 A4
Winch La SA61 ....125 A4
Winch Wen Ind Est SA1 ..161 C6
Windermere Rd SA6 .....160 E2
Windmill La SA1 ....103 E1
Windmill Terr SA1 ......174 C4

Wind Rd SA9 ....139 D7
Windsor Ct **3** SA1 .....174 A3
Windsor Pl SA3 ....173 B5
Windsor Rd
  Pembroke / Penfro SA71 ..133 C5
  Stackpole SA71 ....111 E3
Windsor St SA2 ....166 F7
Windsor Terr SA4 ....151 D2
Windsor Way SA1 ....125 B4
Wind St
  Llanfihangel-ar-Arth SA44 ..19 E3
  Swansea / Abertawe SA1 ..174 B2
Wind St / Stryd-y-Gwynt
  SA18 ....98 B7
Windyhall SA65 ....122 C5
Windy Ridge SA70 ......106 A1
Winifred Rd SA10 ....162 E7
Winston St SA1 ....174 A4
Wiston St SA71 ....133 C6
Withybush General Hospl
  SA61 ....125 B7
Withybush Rd
  Haverfordwest / Hwlffordd
  SA62 ....125 B8
  Withybush SA62 ....68 B5
Withybush Trad Est SA62 ..68 A5
Withy Pk SA3 ....172 A6
Wogan Rd **1** SA71 .....133 C5
Wogan St SA33 ....92 F5
Wogan Terr SA69 ....134 F3
Wolfscastle CP Sch SA62 ..51 A5
Wolfscastle Pottery★
  SA62 ....51 A5
Woodbine Cl SA73 ......133 C5
Woodbine Terr SA71 ....133 B5
Woodbine Way SA73 .....85 F1
Woodbrook Terr SA16 ...137 F2
Woodburn Dr SA3 ......173 A6
Woodcote SA2 ....165 D6
Woodcote Gn SA4 ....151 C7
Woodend Rd SA15 ......148 E6
Woodfield Ave
  Kilgetty / Begelly SA68 ...89 F2
  Llandybie SA18 ....79 A2
  Pontlliw SA4 ....152 A5
Woodfield Gr SA72 ......104 F7
Woodfield Rd SA18 ......79 A1
Woodfield St SA6 ....160 F8
Woodfield Terr SA18 .....98 D7
Woodford La SA67 ....70 B2
Woodford Rd SA5 ....159 E7
Wood Hill SA62 ....66 C8
Woodholm Cl SA62 ......68 B4
Wood La SA73 ....132 B8
Woodland Ave SA3 ......172 F7
Woodland Cl
  Llanddowror SA33 ......92 A3
  Neath / Castell-Nedd
  SA10 ....162 E8
Woodland Cres SA73 ....131 E3
Woodland Ct SA2 ....166 A6
Woodland Dr SA73 ......131 E3
Woodland Pk
  Llanstadwell SA73 ......132 A6
  Ynystawe SA6 ....154 B5
Woodland Rd SA10 ......162 E8
Woodland Rd / Heol Tir Y
  Coed SA9 ....100 C7
Woodlands SA4 ....158 C5
Woodlands Ave SA6 .....154 F8
Woodlands Bsns Pk
  SA9 ....139 D7
Woodlands Pk
  Ammanford / Rhydaman
  SA18 ....98 C6
  Haverfordwest / Hwlffordd
  SA61 ....124 F2
  Nolton & Roch SA62 .....67 A8
Woodlands Rd SA4 ......150 F1
Woodland St SA8 ....147 F5
Woodlands Terr
  Cross Hands SA14 ....97 B7
  Swansea / Abertawe SA1 ..167 B7
Woodlands View **1** SA62 ..86 E5
Woodmans Terr SA9 ....139 B6
Woodridge Ct SA3 ......172 F4
Woodside Ave
  Pembroke / Penfro SA71 ..133 B5
  Swansea / Abertawe SA2 ..165 E6
Woodside Cl
  Bishopston SA3 ....172 A5
  Swansea / Abertawe SA2 ..165 E6
Woodside Cres SA6 .....154 C8
Wood's Row SA31 ......128 F5
Woodview SA4 ....158 D4
Woodview Pl SA5 ....159 E6
Woodville Rd SA3 ....173 A4
Woodville St SA4 ....143 C5
Woollacott Dr SA3 ......172 D5
Woollacott Mews SA3 ...172 D5
Worcester Ct SA7 ......161 C7
Worcester Dr SA3 ......173 B4
Worcester Pl SA3 ......174 B1
Worcester Rd SA3 ......173 B4
Wordsworth Ave SA61 ..125 B3
Wordsworth St SA1 .....174 A4
Works Rd SA8 ....147 E4
Wrench Cl **1** SA71 .....133 C3
Wychtree St SA6 ....161 A7
Wychwood Cl SA3 ......173 A4
Wye Cl SA1 ....161 B3
Wyndham Cl SA4 ....143 C4
Wyndham Ct SA6 ....161 C8
Wyndham St SA1 ....167 B6
Wyngarth SA1 ....161 D5
Wynter Ct SA5 ....160 C6

Y

Yalton SA3 ....172 F7
Y Bannen / Banwen Pl
  SA18 ....99 D8
Y Berllan Dunvant SA2 ..165 D7
  Swansea / Abertawe SA6 ..153 C2
Y Bwthyn Llanelli SA15 ..148 E4
  Maenclochog SA66 ......53 A8
Y Clos Cwmllynfell SA9 ..100 B7
  Llanelli SA15 ....149 A5
Y Crofft SA17 ....94 B3
Y Cyswllt SA4 ....152 C5
Y Dderwen Maes SA42 ...12 F3
Y Ddwyberth SA16 ......137 E3
Y Derwydd SA16 ....137 D2
Ydgol Gruffydd Jones /
  Griffith Jones Prim Sch
  SA33 ....127 F5
Y Dolau SA6 ....153 C2
Y Drim SA15 ....95 F3
Yewtree Cl SA3 ....172 F8
Y-fan SA14 ....149 C5
Y Felin Mill★ SA43 .....118 B3
Y Fron Cefneithin SA14 ...97 A8
  Llanelli SA15 ....140 F1
Y-Gaer SA14 ....149 A8
Y Garn SA4 ....152 A2
Y Garreg Llwyd SA4 .....97 D2
Y Gefnen SA7 ....161 F6
Y Gerddi Gdn Suburbs
  SA17 ....109 C7
Y Gilfach SA9 ....139 B7
Y Gilwern SA9 ....139 B6
Y Glyn Cefneithin SA14 ...97 A8
  Dunvant SA2 ....165 D7
Y Goedlan SA9 ....100 C6
Y Gorlan SA9 ....165 D7
Y Gorsedd **7** SA18 .....98 B7
Y Gribin SA62 ....48 D3
Y Gwernydd SA7 ....154 F6
Y Llan SA14 ....141 A2
Y Llanerch SA4 ....152 A7
Y Llwyn SA15 ....149 A5
Y Llwyni SA6 ....153 C2
Yniscedwyn Rd SA9 ....139 E8
Ynisderw Rd SA8 ......147 E4
Ynysallan Rd SA6, SA7 ..154 D3
Ynyscedwyn Ind Est
  SA9 ....139 E8
Ynys-Cedwyn Lodge
  SA9 ....139 D7
Ynys Ct SA6 ....161 B7
Ynys Dawel SA62 ....48 C3
Ynysderw Ho SA8 ......147 D4
Ynys-Las SA14 ....149 C5
Ynys Newydd Rd SA2 ...166 B4
Ynys-Penllwch Rd SA6,
  SA7 ....154 F7
Ynystawe Prim Sch SA6 ..154 C5
Ynyswen SA14 ....149 A8
Ynyswerdd SA4 ....152 B2
Ynys Y Cwm Rd SA15 ..148 C7
Ynys-y-gwial SA9 .....138 F5
Ynys-y-Mond Rd
  Glais SA7 ....155 B7
  Pontardawe SA8 ....147 B2
Ynys Y Plant SA3 ......173 A7
York Ct SA1 ....174 B2
Yorke Cl SA73 ....131 E2
Yorke St SA73 ....131 D2
York St SA1 ....174 B2
Yr Allt SA14 ....142 B1
Yr Aran SA2 ....158 D1
Yr Elain SA2 ....165 D8
Yr Hafod Llanelli SA15 ..148 E7
  Swansea / Abertawe SA6 ..153 C2
Y Rhodfa SA16 ....137 F3
Y-rhos SA43 ....118 F5
Y Rhos SA15 ....148 F7
Yr Rhos SA42 ....13 A3

Ysbyty = hospital

Ysbyty Fairwood / Fairwood
  Hospl SA2 ....165 A6
Ysbyty Gymuned
  Ystradgynlais SA9 ......139 E7
Ysbyty Llanymddyfri /
  Llandovery Hospl
  SA20 ....121 D5
Ysbyty Mynydd Mawr
  SA14 ....96 F5

Ysgol = school

Ysgol Bancffosfelen
  SA15 ....95 F7
Ysgol Beca SA4 ....54 A4
Ysgol Brechfa SA32 .....40 D1
Ysgol Bro Dewi SA62 ...123 C5
Ysgol Bro Gwaun / Fishguard
  High Sch SA65 ....122 C4
Ysgol Cae'r Felin / Cae'r
  Felin Sch SA39 ....39 B7
Ysgol Capel Dewi SA44 ...20 C5
Ysgol Capel Iwan SA38 ...36 D7
Ysgol Carreg Hirfaen
  SA48 ....120 E1
Ysgol Cefnbrynbrain
  SA9 ....100 B8
Ysgol Cenarth SA38 .....17 B4
Ysgol Clydau SA35 ......35 E3
Ysgol Crug Glas SA1 ...174 B4
Ysgol Crymych SA41 ....34 F4

Wau – Ysg | **195**

Ysgol Cwmbach SA34 ....56 A4
Ysgol Cynlais Prim Sch
  SA9 ....138 F2
Ysgol Cynwyl Elfed SA33 ..58 A6
Ysgol Dewi Sant / St David's
  Cty Sec Sch SA62 ......123 E5
Ysgol Dolafon LD5 ....9 C1
Ysgol Drefach SA14 .....96 E8
Ysgol Dyffryn Taf SA34 ..126 C3
Ysgol Esgob Gore / Bishop
  Gore Sch SA2 ....166 C6
Ysgol Fabanod Prendergast /
  Prendergast Infants Sch
  SA61 ....125 C6
Ysgol Glandwr SA34 .....55 A7
Ysgol Golwg-y-Mor / Sea
  View Com Prim Sch
  SA1 ....174 A4
Ysgol Grynradd Parcyrhun
  SA18 ....98 B6
Ysgol Gyfun Bryn Tawe
  SA5 ....160 A6
Ysgol Gyfun Cwmtawe /
  Cwmtawe Comp Sch
  SA8 ....147 E3
Ysgol Gyfun Dyffryn Teifi
  SA44 ....19 D3
Ysgol Gyfun Emlyn
  SA38 ....119 D4
Ysgol Gyfun Gatholig Sant
  Ioan Llwyd / St John Lloyd
  RC Comp Sch SA14 ....149 B6
Ysgol Gyfun Gwyr SA4 ..158 C5
Ysgol Gyfun Llanbedr Pont
  Steffan / Lampeter Comp
  Sch SA48 ....120 B4
Ysgol Gyfun Maes Yr Yrfa
  SA14 ....97 A8
Ysgol Gyfun Pantycelyn
  SA20 ....121 C5
Ysgol Gyfun Tre-gib
  SA19 ....130 E4
Ysgol Gyfun Ystalyfera
  SA9 ....139 D7
Ysgol Gyfun Y Strade
  SA15 ....148 A6
Ysgol Gymraeg Brynsierfel
  SA14 ....149 D5
Ysgol Gymraeg Cwmtwrch
  SA9 ....138 B1
Ysgol Gymraeg Dewi Sant
  SA14 ....148 F7
Ysgol Gymraeg Gwenllian
  SA17 ....136 B4
Ysgol Gymraeg Pontybrenin
  SA4 ....158 B8
Ysgol Gymraeg Teilo Sant
  SA19 ....130 E6
Ysgol Gymraeg Ynysgedwyn
  SA9 ....139 F8
Ysgol Gymraeg Y Wern
  SA9 ....139 D5
Ysgol Gymunedol Eglwyswrw
  / Eglwyswrw CP Sch
  SA41 ....15 B1
Ysgol Gynradd Alltwalis /
  Alltwalis Prim Sch SA32 ..39 B2
Ysgol Gynradd Bethlehem
  SA19 ....63 B4
Ysgol Gynradd Blaenau
  SA18 ....97 F8
Ysgol Gynradd Brynsaron /
  Brynsaron Prim Sch
  SA44 ....38 B7
Ysgol Gynradd Bynea /
  Bynea Prim Sch SA14 ..149 F3
Ysgol Gynradd Crymlyn /
  Crymlyn Prim Sch
  SA10 ....162 C1
Ysgol Gynradd Ffairfach
  SA19 ....130 E4
Ysgol Gynradd Gorslas
  SA14 ....97 B8
Ysgol Gynradd Gymraeg
  Bryniago SA4 ....143 D4
Ysgol Gynradd Gymraeg
  Bryn-y-mor SA2 ....166 F5
Ysgol Gynradd Gymraeg
  Draddodiadol Rhiwfawr
  SA9 ....100 B5
Ysgol Gynradd Gymraeg
  Draddodiadol Trebannws
  SA8 ....147 C2
Ysgol Gynradd Gymraeg
  Draddodianol Cwmllynfell
  SA9 ....100 B7
Ysgol Gynradd Gymraeg
  Draddodiaol Cwmgors
  SA18 ....99 D5
Ysgol Gynradd Gymraeg
  Draddodiol Glyn SA18 ...99 D8
Ysgol Gynradd Gymraeg
  Felindre SA5 ....144 F2
Ysgol Gynradd Gymraeg
  Garnswllt SA18 ....98 B3
Ysgol Gynradd Gymraeg
  Gellionnen SA6 ....154 E8
Ysgol Gynradd Gymraeg
  Gwaun Cae Gurwen
  SA18 ....99 D7
Ysgol Gynradd Gymraeg
  Llwynderw SA2 ....166 D6
Ysgol Gynradd Gymraeg
  Lonlas SA7 ....161 D8

Ysgol Gynradd Gymraeg
  Pontardawe SA8 ...... **147** E6
Ysgol Gynradd Gymraeg Y
  Login Fach SA5 .... **158** F3
Ysgol Gynradd Llandeilo /
  Llandeilo Prim Sch
  SA19 .... **130** D6
Ysgol Gynradd Llanedi
  SA4 .... **97** D2
Ysgol Gynradd Llanwrda /
  Llanwrda Prim Sch
  SA19 .... **43** D2
Ysgol Gynradd Llechryd
  SA43 .... **16** C6
Ysgol Gynradd Llechyfedach
  / Llechyfedach CP Sch
  SA14 .... **96** F7
Ysgol Gynradd
  Mynyddygarreg SA17 ..**136** F7
Ysgol Gynradd New Inn /
  New Inn Prim Sch SA39 ..**39** E8
Ysgol Gynradd Parc
  Waundew / Richmond Pk
  CP Sch SA31 ....**129** A6

Ysgol Gynradd Saron
  SA18 .... **97** E6
Ysgol Gynradd Stebonheath
  / Stebonheath Prim Sch
  SA15 .... **148** F5
Ysgol Gynradd Trallwn /
  Trallwn Prim Sch SA7 ..**161** E7
Ysgol Gynradd Treforys /
  Morriston Prim Sch
  SA6 .... **161** A8
Ysgol Gynradd Tregroes /
  Tregroes Cty Prim Sch
  SA44 .... **19** D7
Ysgol Gynradd Trewen
  SA38 .... **119** A8
Ysgol Gynradd Tycroes
  SA18 .... **97** F5
Ysgol Gynradd Wr Tremoilet
  / Tremoilet VCP Sch
  SA33 .... **91** D4
Ysgol Gynradd y Crwys /
  Crwys Prim Sch SA4 ...**157** E1
Ysgol Gynradd Y Sir
  Pontybrenin / Pontybrenin
  Prim Sch SA4 ....**151** B1
Ysgol Gynradd Ystradowen
  SA9 .... **100** C7

Ysgol Gynrad Llandudoch
  SA43 ....**118** B4
Ysgol Hafodwenog SA33 ..**36** C1
Ysgol Hayscastle SA62 ...**50** B5
Ysgol Heol Goffa SA15 ..**148** E7
Ysgol Llanarthne SA32 ...**77** D7
Ysgol Llanboidy SA34 ...**55** C2
Ysgol Llanddarog SA32 ...**77** B3
Ysgol Llanfihangel-ar-arth
  SA39 .... **20** C2
Ysgol Llanllwni SA39 ....**20** F2
Ysgol Llanonl SA14 ......**96** F3
Ysgol Llanpumsaint SA33 ..**58** F8
Ysgol Llansawel SA19 ...**42** B7
Ysgol Llansteffan SA33 ...**93** E5
Ysgol Llanwenog SA40 ...**21** A8
Ysgol Maenclochog
  SA66 .... **53** B6
Ysgol Myddfai SA20 .....**44** D1
Ysgol Mynyddcerrig
  SA15 .... **96** B8
Ysgol Nantgaredig SA32 ..**77** A8
Ysgol Penboyr SA44 .....**18** E1
Ysgol Peniel SA32 ....**59** A3
Ysgol Ponthenri SA15 ...**95** E4
Ysgol Pum Heol SA15 ...**109** F8

Ysgol Rhydcymerau
  SA19 .... **22** C2
Ysgol Rhydgors SA31 ..**128** C1
Ysgol Rhys Prichard / Rhys
  Prichard Sch SA20 ...**121** D5
Ysgol Rudolf Steiner
  Nant-y-cwm / Nant-y-cwm
  Steiner Sch SA66 ...... **53** D3
Ysgol St SA1 ....**168** B7
Ysgol Tasker Milward /
  Tasker Milward Sch
  SA61 ....**124** E4
Ysgol Trapp SA19 ....**79** E5
Ysgol Tymbl SA14 ....**96** E7
Ysgol Wirfoddol Abergwili
  SA31 ....**129** F7
Ysgol Wirfoddol Babanod /
  Tenby VC Inf Sch
  SA70 ....**135** D5
Ysgol Y Babanod SA14 ..**149** A8
Ysgol Y Dderwen SA31 ..**128** E6
Ysgol Y Ddwylan SA38 ..**119** D5
Ysgol Y Ferwig SA43 ...... **3** C5
Ysgol Y Gwendraeth
  SA14 .... **96** E7
Ysgol Y Preseli SA41 .....**34** F4
Ysgol Yr Ynys SA14 .....**149** C4

Ysgubor Fach St SA1 ....**160** C2
Yspitty Rd SA14 ....**150** B1
Ystrad Cl 🖪 SA31 ......**128** C2
Ystrad Dr SA31 ....**128** D2
Ystrad Einon SA4 ......**151** B1
Ystradgynlais Workshops
  SA9 ....**139** E8
Ystrad Rd SA5 ....**159** B4
Ystwyth Pl SA6 ....**153** D1
Y Talar SA31 ....**129** A3
Y Waun SA14 ....**149** C6
Y Waun Fach SA6 ......**153** B2
Y Waun / Meadows The
  SA10 ....**162** E7
Y-Wern SA6 ....**153** B2

Z

Zammit Cres SA15 .....**149** A5
Zion Row SA15 ....**148** E6
Zion St 🖪 LD5 .... **9** C1
Zoar Rd SA9 ....**139** B6
Zouch St SA5 ....**160** C3

NG	NH	NJ	NK
NM	NN	NO	NP
NR	NS	NT	NU
NX	NY	NZ	
SC	SD	SE	TA
SH	SJ	SK	TF	TG
SM	SN	SO	SP	TL	TM
SR	SS	ST	SU	TQ	TR
SW	SX	SY	SZ	TV

Any feature in this atlas can be given a unique reference to help you find the same feature on other Ordnance Survey maps of the area, or to help someone else locate you if they do not have a Street Atlas.

The grid squares in this atlas match the Ordnance Survey National Grid and are at 500 metre intervals. The small figures at the bottom and sides of every other grid line are the National Grid kilometre values (**00** to **99** km) and are repeated across the country every 100 km (see left).

To give a unique National Grid reference you need to locate where in the country you are. The country is divided into 100 km squares with each square given a unique two-letter reference. Use the administrative map to determine in which 100 km square a particular page of this atlas falls.

The bold letters and numbers between each grid line (**A** to **F**, **1** to **8**) are for use within a specific Street Atlas only, and when used with the page number, are a convenient way of referencing these grid squares.

Example   *The railway bridge over DARLEY GREEN RD in grid square B1*

Step 1: Identify the two-letter reference, in this example the page is in **SP**

Step 2: Identify the 1 km square in which the railway bridge falls. Use the figures in the southwest corner of this square: Eastings **17**, Northings **74**. This gives a unique reference: **SP 17 74**, accurate to 1 km.

Step 3: To give a more precise reference accurate to 100 m you need to estimate how many tenths along and how many tenths up this 1 km square the feature is (to help with this the 1 km square is divided into four 500 m squares). This makes the bridge about **8** tenths along and about **1** tenth up from the southwest corner.

This gives a unique reference: **SP 178 741**, accurate to 100 m.

Eastings (read from left to right along the bottom) come before Northings (read from bottom to top). If you have trouble remembering say to yourself "Along the hall, THEN up the stairs"!

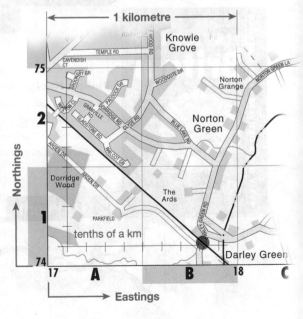

PHILIP'S MAPS

the Gold Standard for drivers

◆ **Philip's street atlases cover every county in England, Wales, Northern Ireland and much of Scotland**

- ◆ Every named street is shown, including alleys, lanes and walkways
- ◆ Thousands of additional features marked: stations, public buildings, car parks, places of interest
- ◆ Route-planning maps to get you close to your destination
- ◆ Postcodes on the maps and in the index
- ◆ Widely used by the emergency services, transport companies and local authorities

For national mapping, choose
Philip's Navigator Britain
the most detailed road atlas available of
England, Wales and Scotland. Hailed by
Auto Express as 'the ultimate road atlas',
the atlas shows every road and lane in
Britain.

Street atlases currently available

England
Bedfordshire
Berkshire
Birmingham and West Midlands
Bristol and Bath
Buckinghamshire
Cambridgeshire
Cheshire
Cornwall
Cumbria
Derbyshire
Devon
Dorset
County Durham and Teesside
Essex
North Essex
South Essex
Gloucestershire
Hampshire
North Hampshire
South Hampshire
Herefordshire Monmouthshire
Hertfordshire
Isle of Wight
Kent
East Kent
West Kent
Lancashire
Leicestershire and Rutland
Lincolnshire
London
Greater Manchester
Merseyside
Norfolk
Northamptonshire
Northumberland
Nottinghamshire
Oxfordshire
Shropshire
Somerset
Staffordshire
Suffolk
Surrey

East Sussex
West Sussex
Tyne and Wear
Warwickshire
Birmingham and West Midlands
Wiltshire and Swindon
Worcestershire
East Yorkshire Northern Lincolnshire
North Yorkshire
South Yorkshire
West Yorkshire

Wales
Anglesey, Conwy and Gwynedd
Cardiff, Swansea and The Valleys
Carmarthenshire, Pembrokeshire and Swansea
Ceredigion and South Gwynedd
Denbighshire, Flintshire, Wrexham
Herefordshire Monmouthshire
Powys

Scotland
Aberdeenshire
Ayrshire
Dumfries and Galloway
Edinburgh and East Central Scotland
Fife and Tayside
Glasgow and West Central Scotland
Inverness and Moray
Lanarkshire
Scottish Borders

Northern Ireland
County Antrim and County Londonderry
County Armagh and County Down
Belfast
County Tyrone and County Fermanagh

How to order Philip's maps and atlases are available from bookshops, motorway services and petrol stations. You can order direct from the publisher by phoning **01903 828503** or online at **www.philips-maps.co.uk** For bulk orders only, e-mail philips@philips-maps.co.uk